PEACE
PROCESS

REVISED EDITION

PEACE
PROCESS

AMERICAN DIPLOMACY AND
THE ARAB-ISRAELI CONFLICT
SINCE 1967

William B. Quandt

BROOKINGS INSTITUTION PRESS
Washington, D.C.

UNIVERSITY OF CALIFORNIA PRESS
Berkeley and Los Angeles

Copyright © 2001
THE BROOKINGS INSTITUTION
1775 Massachusetts Avenue, N.W., Washington, DC 20036
www.brookings.edu
and
UNIVERSITY OF CALIFORNIA PRESS
2120 Berkeley Way, Berkeley, CA 94720

Library of Congress Cataloging-in-Publication data

Quandt, William B.
   Peace process : American diplomacy and the Arab-Israeli conflict since 1967 / William B. Quandt. — Rev. ed.
      p.   cm.
   Includes bibliographical references and index.
   ISBN 0-520-22374-8 (cloth : alk. paper) —
   ISBN 0-520-22515-5 (pbk. : alk. paper)
   1. Arab-Israeli conflict—1967–1973. 2. Arab-Israeli conflict—1973–1993. 3. Arab-Israeli conflict—1993—Peace. 4. Middle East—Foreign relations—United States. 5. United States—Foreign relations—Middle East. 6. United States—Foreign relations—20th century. I. Title.
   DS119.7 .Q69 2001   00-012148
   327.73056—dc21   CIP

9 8 7 6 5 4 3 2 1

The paper used in this publication meets minimum requirements of the American National Standard for Information Sciences—Permanence of Paper for Printed Library Materials: ANSI Z39.48-1992.

Typeset in Sabon

Composition by Cynthia Stock
Silver Spring, Maryland

Printed by R. R. Donnelley and Sons
Harrisonburg, Virginia

To my mother—
who encouraged me to learn about the world

Foreword

Every president since World War II has become embroiled in the complex diplomacy surrounding the Arab-Israeli conflict. This book focuses on the period since the 1967 Six-Day War, a major turning point in Middle East history. It concentrates on how American policy is made in the special circumstances surrounding this conflict. Domestic politics and grand strategy set certain limits on the choices available to any president, but the author does not believe that policy is entirely determined by such factors. He instead places special emphasis on the mind of the president, on how that powerful individual and his closest advisers see the issues at stake and their priority in the larger scheme of things, and on how delicate trade-offs between complex interests are evaluated. Initial predispositions are assessed, as is each president's learning curve.

This is, of course, an unfinished story. As the manuscript goes to press the outlook for Israeli-Palestinian peace looks bleak. But we should not forget that significant accomplishments have been registered by American diplomacy over the past several decades. Peace between Egypt and Israel was achieved in 1979, and between Jordan and Israel in 1994. Israel and Syria came close to agreement on several occasions, but have still not bridged the crucial gap on territorial issues. Israeli troops have been withdrawn from Lebanon, and it is widely assumed that peace on that front could be achieved in tandem with progress toward Israeli-Syrian peace.

The recent spate of violence between Israelis and Palestinians has obscured the fact that even here the parties have made some headway, including mutual recognition and preliminary discussion of most of the truly difficult issues that will eventually have to be resolved if there is to be peace in the Holy Land.

William B. Quandt is Edward R. Stettinius, Jr., Professor of Government and Foreign Affairs at the University of Virginia and a nonresident senior fellow in the Foreign Policy Studies program at the Brookings Institution. He participated twice in the policymaking process, as a member of the National Security Council staff in both the Nixon and the Carter administrations. He brings his direct experience to bear on the analysis of how decisions are made on a particularly sensitive foreign-policy issue.

This volume is the second edition of *Peace Process*. Originally published in 1993, the book now carries the narrative through the two terms of the Clinton presidency. The author has also revised earlier chapters in light of new information, particularly for the Bush period. In assessing the Clinton presidency, the author has been helped by Helena Cobban, Edward Djerejian, Richard Haass, Martin Indyk, Daniel Kurtzer, Samuel Lewis, Robert Malley, Aaron Miller, Robert Pelletreau, Christopher Ross, Dennis Ross, Shibley Telhami, and Edward Walker. He was assisted in his research by Katherine Carroll, Agnieszka Paczynska, and especially Oliver Wilcox. Deborah Styles edited the manuscript, fact checking was done by Todd DeLelle and Susan Jackson, Tanjam Jacobson and Carlotta Ribar proofread the pages, and the index was prepared by Sherry L. Smith.

The views expressed in this book are solely those of the author and should not be ascribed to any persons or institutions acknowledged above or to the trustees, officers, or other staff members of the Brookings Institution.

MICHAEL H. ARMACOST
President

November 2000
Washington, D.C.

Author's Note

IN MY RECENT incarnation as a professor, I am aware that books on contemporary issues are less and less used in the classroom as they become out of date. Over the years, *Peace Process* has been widely adopted in classes on the international politics of the Middle East. Much has happened in the past eight years, however, and I think a new edition is warranted.

Bill Clinton began his presidency with an ongoing Arab-Israeli peace process, but no one in 1993 could have foreseen the specific turn of events over the succeeding years. The first and biggest surprise was the Oslo agreement, negotiated behind the backs of the Americans. It resulted in mutual recognition between long-time enemies, Israel and the Palestine Liberation Organization. Ironically, Clinton's presidency came to an end with the Israelis and Palestinians once again locked in a bitter and violent conflict. In the years between, optimists had concluded that peace was inevitable; pessimists countered that it was impossible. Clinton and his team waxed and waned in their enthusiasms for promoting peace between Israel and its Arab neighbors, sometimes signaling that it was up to the parties to set the pace, at other times pushing them forward even when there seemed little enthusiasm for serious negotiating among the parties themselves.

Inevitably, the account of these past eight years will be revised as we learn more about the inner workings of the Clinton administration. Memoirs will be written, secrets will be leaked, and we will eventually have a fuller understanding of the confusing Clinton era and the way this talented and flawed president tackled the problems of the Middle East. I have written a first draft of that history, knowing that it will have to be rewritten in due course.

The earlier parts of the book have already gone through several versions. The present edition condenses the chapters dealing with presidents Johnson, Nixon, Ford, and Carter. Where new material has become available, I have incorporated it, but the general picture has not changed. In the case of the Johnson administration, it has become possible to put to rest a rumor of American complicity with Israel in the Six-Day War. In the first edition, I noted the rumor, stating that I thought it unlikely to be true, and I can now affirm that it is not. The other background factor that deserves more attention than in the first edition is the reality of Israel's nuclear capability. We now know much more than we did a decade ago, although it is still difficult to judge the precise significance of this asset for the diplomacy studied here.

In the interests of keeping the book to a reasonable length, the appendixes have all been placed on a website. It is still important for students to have ready access to these documents, but it is simply not an efficient use of the printed page to put them in the book.

A final point. As I conclude this note, the prospects for peace between Israel and the Palestinians, to say nothing of Israel and Syria, seem bleak. It is tempting to see this, in part, as a failure of American diplomacy. There is something to that argument, although the parties to the conflict bear much of the responsibility as well. With the perspective of more than thirty years, the period covered in this book, I am discouraged by the return to violence and hatred in the Arab-Israeli arena, but I also feel that this is not the last chapter in the search for peace in the region.

Since no party to the conflict can hope to impose its will on the other side, and no one is happy with the status quo, at some point negotiations will resume. The United States, because of its interests, will almost certainly remain involved in the peace process. I only hope that in the next round, whenever that comes, we can be helpful in forging the substantive compromises on which peace will have to be built. What those will have to be are not much of a mystery. The peace talks of the past ten years have come close to defining eventual areas of agreement. In the next phase, the task will be to bridge remaining gaps, to restore confidence, to provide a vision of peace as the key to regional development and improved governance, and to promote a concept of security that does not rest exclusively on the gun. This may sound like an impossible dream in late 2000, as this book goes to press. But it is a worthy goal of American diplomacy, no matter who is president.

W.B.Q.

Contents

The Arab-Israeli Arena

MEDITERRANEAN SEA

Beirut

LEBANON

•Damascus

SYRIA

Tyre

GOLAN
HEIGHTS

Haifa• Nazareth

ISRAEL

WEST
BANK

Irbid

Jerusalem•

•Amman

GAZA
STRIP
•Gaza

Hebron•

Dead Sea

Port Said

Rafah•

Al-Arish•

•Beersheba

JORDAN

Alexandria•

Suez Canal

Great Bitter
Lake

E   G   Y   P   T

Cairo•

Suez•

S I N A I

Elat
Taba• •Aqaba

Litani River

Nile River

Gulf of Suez

Gulf of Aqaba

**S A U D I
A R A B I A**

▲Mt. Sinai

Sharm
al-Sheikh•

Red Sea

1 *Introduction*

Sometime in the mid-1970s the term *peace process* began to be widely used to describe the American-led efforts to bring about a negotiated peace between Israel and its Arab neighbors. The phrase stuck, and ever since it has been synonymous with the gradual, step-by-step approach to resolving one of the world's most difficult conflicts.

In the years since 1967 the emphasis in Washington has shifted from the spelling out of the ingredients of "peace" to the "process" of getting there. This procedural bias, which frequently seems to characterize American diplomacy, reflects a practical, even legalistic side of American political culture. Procedures are also less controversial than substance, more susceptible to compromise, and thus easier for politicians to deal with. Much of U.S. constitutional theory focuses on how issues should be resolved—the process—rather than on substance—what should be done.

Yet whenever progress has been made toward Arab-Israeli peace through American mediation, there has always been a joining of substance and procedure. The United States has provided both a sense of direction and a mechanism. That, at its best, is what the "peace process" has been about. At worst, it has been little more than a slogan used to mask the marking of time.

The Pre-1967 Stalemate

The stage was set for the contemporary Arab-Israeli peace process by the 1967 Six-Day War. Until then, the conflict between Israel and the Arabs had seemed almost frozen, moving neither toward resolution nor toward war. The ostensible issues in dispute were still those left unresolved by the armistice agreements of 1949. At that time, it had been widely expected that those agreements would simply be a step toward final peace talks. But the issues in dispute were too complex for the many mediation efforts of the early 1950s, and by the mid-1950s the cold war rivalry between Moscow and Washington had left the Arab-Israeli conflict suspended somewhere between war and peace. For better or worse, the armistice agreements had provided a semblance of stability from 1949 to 1967.

During this long truce the Israelis had been preoccupied with questions of an existential nature. Would the Arabs ever accept the idea of a Jewish state in their midst? Would recognition be accompanied by security arrangements that could be relied on? Would the Arabs insist on the return of the hundreds of thousands of Palestinian refugees who had fled their homes in 1948–49, thereby threatening the Jewishness of the new state? And would the Arabs accept the 1949 armistice lines as recognized borders, or would they insist on an Israeli withdrawal to the indefensible lines of the 1947 United Nations partition agreement? As for tactics, would Israel be able to negotiate separately with each Arab regime, or would the Arabs insist on a comprehensive approach to peacemaking? Most Israelis felt certain that the Arabs would not provide reassuring answers to these questions and therefore saw little prospect for successful negotiations, whether with the conservative monarchs or with the new brand of nationalistic army officers.

From the Arab perspective, the conflict also seemed intractable, but the interests of existing regimes and the interests of the Palestinians, who had lost most from the creation of Israel, were by no means identical. The regimes struck the pose of defending the rights of the Palestinians to return to their homes or to be compensated for their losses. They withheld recognition from the Jewish state, periodically engaging in furious propaganda attacks against the "Zionist entity." The more militant Arabs sometimes coupled their harsh rhetoric with support for guerrilla attacks on Israel. But others, such as Jordan and Lebanon, were fairly content with the armistice arrangements and even maintained under-the-table contacts with the Israelis. "No war, no peace" suited them well.

The Palestinians, not surprisingly, used all their moral and political capital to prevent any Arab regime from recognizing the Jewish state, and by the mid-1950s they had found a champion for their cause in Egypt's president Gamal Abdel Nasser. From that point on, Arab nationalism and the demand for the restoration of Palestinian rights were Nasser's most potent weapons as he sought to unify the ranks of the Arab world. But Nasser also sought to steer a course between war and peace, at least until the momentous days of May 1967. Then, as tensions rose, Palestinian radicals, who had hoped to draw the Arab states into conflict with Israel on their behalf, rallied to Nasser's banner and helped to cut off any chance that he might retreat from the brink to which he had so quickly advanced.

The 1967 Watershed

The 1967 war transformed the frozen landscape of the Arab-Israeli conflict in dramatic ways. Israel revealed itself to be a military power able to outmatch all its neighbors. By the end of the brief war, Israel was in control of the Sinai desert; the West Bank of the Jordan River, including all of East Jerusalem; Gaza, with its teeming refugee camps; and the strategically important Golan Heights. More than a million Palestinians came under the control of the Israeli military, creating an acute dilemma for Israel. None of the post-1921 British mandate of Palestine was now free of Israeli control. If Israel kept the newly conquered land and granted the people full political rights, Israel would become a binational state, which few Israelis wanted. If it kept the land but did not grant political rights to the Palestinians, it would come to resemble other colonial powers, with predictable results. Finally, if Israel relinquished the land, it would retain its Jewish character, but could it live in peace and security? These were the alternatives debated within the fractious, often boisterous Israeli democracy.

Given the magnitude of their victory in the 1967 war, some Israelis seemed to expect right afterward that the Arabs would have no option but to sue for peace. But that did not happen. So, confident of its military superiority and assured of American support, Israel decided to wait for the Arabs to change their position. But what would happen to the occupied territories while Israel waited? Would they be held in trust, to be traded for peace and security at some future date? Or would they gradually and selectively be incorporated into Israel, as the nationalists on the right demanded? East Jerusalem, at least, would not be returned, and almost immediately Israel announced the unilateral expansion of the municipal boundaries and the annexation of the Arab-inhabited parts of the city. Palestinians living in Jerusalem would have the right to become Israeli citizens, but few took up the offer. Israel signaled its willingness to return most of the occupied territories, apart from Jerusalem, although the passage of time and changing circumstances gradually eroded that position.

The 1967 war was a shock to Arabs who had believed Nasser could end their sense of weakness and humiliation at the hands of the West. Indeed, although Nasser lived on for another three years after the war, his prestige was shattered. Arab nationalism of the sort he preached would never again be such a powerful force. Instead, regimes came to look more and more after their own narrow interests, and the Palestinians followed suit by organizing their own political movement, free of control by any Arab government. One of the few dynamic developments in the Arab world after the 1967 war was the emergence of a new generation of Palestinians leading the fight for their rights.

The Palestine Liberation Organization (PLO), originally supported by Arab regimes to keep the Palestinians under control, quickly became an independent actor in the region. It symbolized the hopes of many Palestinians and caused much concern among established Arab regimes, which were not used to seeing the Palestinians take matters into their own hands.

In theory, these changes in the Arab world might have opened the way for an easing of the Arab-Israeli conflict. A certain amount of self-criticism took place in Arab intellectual circles. Political realism began to challenge ideological sloganeering. But no one made any serious peace effort immediately after the 1967 war, and by September of that year the Arab parties had all agreed there would be no negotiations with Israel, no peace, and no recognition. Once again, "neither war nor peace" seemed to be a tolerable prospect for both Arabs and Israelis.

The Need for a Mediator

With the parties to the conflict locked into mutually unacceptable positions, the chance for diplomatic movement seemed to depend on others, especially the United States. Because of the close U.S.-Israeli relationship, many Arabs looked to Washington to press Israel for concessions. The example of President Dwight D. Eisenhower, who had pressed Israel to relinquish its gains from the Suez war of 1956, was still a living memory. The two main areas of Arab concern were the return of territories seized in the 1967 war and some measure of justice for the Palestinians. In return, it was implied, something short of peace would be offered to Israel, perhaps an end to belligerency or strengthened armistice arrangements.

The Arab regimes were still reluctant to promise full peace and recognition for Israel unless and until the Palestinians were satisfied, and that would require more than Israeli withdrawal from occupied territories. As time went by, and the PLO gained in prestige, it became more and more difficult for the Arab states to pursue their narrowly defined interests with no regard for Palestinian claims. And the Arabs were reluctant to deal directly with Israel. If a deal were to be struck, it would be through the efforts of the two superpowers—the United States and the Soviet Union—and the United Nations.

By contrast, Israel was adamant that territory would not be returned for less than peace, recognition, and security. And the means for getting to a settlement would have to include direct negotiations with Israel by each Arab party. For most Israelis, the claims of the Palestinians were impossible to deal with. At best, Jordan could act as a stand-in for the Palestinians, who would have to be satisfied with some form of internationally supported rehabilitation and compensation scheme. Above all, Palestinians would not be allowed to return to their homes, except in very special circumstances of family reunions and in very small numbers.

American Ambivalence: Positions and Policies

Confronted with these almost contradictory positions, the United States was reluctant to get deeply involved in Arab-Israeli diplomacy. The Vietnam War was still raging in 1967, and the needs of the Middle East seemed less compelling than the daily demands of a continuing war in Southeast Asia. Still, from the outset the United States staked out a position somewhere in between the views of Israelis and Arabs. Israel, it was believed, was entitled to more than a return to the old armistice arrangements. Some form of contractually binding end to the state of war should be achieved, and Israeli security concerns would have to be met. At the same time, if the Arabs were prepared to meet those conditions, they should recover most, if not all, of the territory lost in 1967. These views were spelled out by President Lyndon Johnson soon after the war, and they became the basis for UN Resolution 242 of November 22, 1967, which thereafter provided the main reference point, with all its ambiguities, for peacemaking.[1]

The basic American position adopted in 1967 has remained remarkably consistent. For example, each American president since 1967 has formally subscribed to the following points:

—Israel should not be required to relinquish territories captured in 1967 without a quid pro quo from the Arab parties involving peace, security, and recognition. This position, summarized in the formula "land for peace" and embodied in UN Resolution 242, applies to each front of the conflict.

—East Jerusalem is legally considered to be occupied territory whose status should eventually be settled in peace negotiations. Whatever its final political status, Jerusalem should not be physically redivided. Reflecting the legal American position on the city, the American embassy has remained in Tel Aviv, despite promises by many presidential candidates to move the embassy to Jerusalem.

—Israeli settlements beyond the 1967 armistice lines—the "green line"—are obstacles to peace. Until 1981 they were considered illegal under international law, but the administration of Ronald Reagan reversed position and declared they were not illegal. But Reagan, and especially George Bush, continued to oppose the creation of settlements. No American funds are to be used by Israel beyond the green line.

—However Palestinian rights may eventually be defined, they do not include the right of unrestricted return to homes within the 1967 lines, nor do they entail the automatic right of independence. All administrations have opposed the creation of a fully independent Palestinian state, preferring, at least until the mid-1990s, some form of association of the West Bank and Gaza with Jordan. Over time, however, the Jordan option—the idea that Jordan should speak for the Palestinians—has faded, and since 1988 the United States has agreed to deal directly with Palestinian representatives.

—Israel's military superiority, its technological edge against any plausible coalition of Arab parties, has been maintained through American military assistance. Each U.S. administration has tacitly accepted the existence of Israeli nuclear weapons, with the understanding that they will not be brandished and can be regarded only as an ultimate deterrent, not as a battlefield weapon. American conventional military aid is provided, in part, to ensure that Israel will not have to rely on its nuclear capability for anything other than deterrence.

With minor adjustments, every president from Lyndon Johnson to Bill Clinton has subscribed to each of these positions. They have been so fundamental that they are rarely even discussed. To change any one of these positions would entail costs, both domestic and international. These positions represent continuity and predictability. But they do not always determine policy. Policy, unlike these positions, is heavily influenced by tactical considerations, and here presidents and their advisers differ with one another, and sometimes with themselves, from one moment to the next.

Policies involve judgments about what will work. How can a country best be influenced? What levers exist to influence a situation? Should aid be offered or withheld? Will reassurance or pressure—or both—be most effective? When is the optimal time to launch an initiative? Should it be done in public or private? How much prior consultation should take place, and with whom? On these matters, there is no accepted wisdom. Each president and his top advisers must evaluate the realities of the Middle East, of the international environment, of the domestic front, and of human psychology before reaching a subjective judgment. While positions tend to be predictable, policies are not. They are the realm where leadership makes all the difference. And part of leadership is knowing when a policy has failed and should be replaced with another.

How Policy Is Made: Alternative Models

More than any other regional conflict, the Arab-Israeli dispute has consistently competed for top priority on the American foreign-policy agenda. This study tries to account for the prominence of the Arab-Israeli peace process in American policy circles since 1967. It seeks to analyze the way in which perceived national interests have interacted with domestic political considerations to ensure that Arab-Israeli peacemaking has become the province of the president and his closest advisers.

Because presidents and secretaries of state—not faceless bureaucrats— usually set the guidelines for policy on the Arab-Israeli dispute, it is important to try to understand how they come to adopt the views that guide them through the labyrinthine complexities of Arab-Israeli diplomacy. Here several models compete for attention.

One model would have us believe that policies flow from a cool deliberation of national interest. This *strategic* model assumes that decisions are made by rational decisionmakers. Such a perspective implies that it does not much matter who occupies the Oval Office. The high degree of continuity in several aspects of the American stance toward the conflict since 1967 would serve as evidence that broad interests and rational policy processes provide the best explanation for policy.

But anyone who has spent time in government will testify that policymaking is anything but orderly and rational. As described by the *bureaucratic politics* model, different agencies compete with one another, fixed organizational procedures are hard to change, and reliable information is difficult to come by. This perspective places a premium on bureaucratic rivalries and the "game" of policymaking. Policy outcomes are much less predictable from this perspective. Instead, one needs to look at who is influencing whom. Microlevel analysis is needed, in contrast to the broad systemic approach favored by the strategic model. Much of the gossip of

Washington is based on the premise that the insiders' political game is what counts in setting policy. Foreign embassies try desperately to convince their governments back home that seemingly sinister policy outcomes are often simply the result of the normal give and take of everyday bureaucratic struggles, the compromises, the foul-ups, the trading of favors that are part of the Washington scene. If conspiracy theorists thrive on the strategic model—there must be a logical explanation for each action taken by the government—political cynics and comics have a field day with the bureaucratic politics model.[2]

A third model, one emphasizing the importance of *domestic politics*, is also injected into the study of American policy toward the Arab-Israeli conflict. Without a doubt Arab-Israeli policymaking in Washington does get tangled up in internal politics. Congress, where support for Israel is usually high, and where pro-Israeli lobbies tend to concentrate their efforts, can frequently exert influence over foreign policy, largely through its control over the budget.[3] While some senators and representatives no doubt do consider the national interest, for many others positions taken on the Arab-Israeli conflict are little more than part of their domestic re-election strategy. Some analysts have maintained that American Middle East policy is primarily an expression of either the pro-Israeli lobby or the oil lobby. Little evidence will be found here for such an extreme view, even though in some circumstances the lobbies can be influential.

Besides considering the role of Congress, one must also take into account the effect of the workings of the American political system, especially the four-year cycle of presidential elections. This cycle imposes some regular patterns on the policymaking process that have little to do with the world outside but a great deal to do with the way power is pursued and won through elections.[4] One should hardly be surprised to find that every four years the issue of moving the American embassy to Jerusalem reemerges, arms sales to Arab countries are deferred, and presidential contenders emphasize those parts of their programs that are most congenial to the supporters of Israel. Nor should one be surprised to find that once the election is over, policy returns to a more evenhanded course.

The Mind of the President

As much as each of these approaches—strategic-rational analysis, bureaucratic politics, and domestic politics—can illuminate aspects of how the United States has engaged in the Arab-Israeli peace process,[5] the most important factor, as this book argues, is the view of the conflict—the definition of the situation—held by the president and his closest advisers, usually including the secretary of state. The president is more than just the first among equals in a bureaucratic struggle or in domestic political debates. And he is certainly not a purely rational, strategic thinker.

More than anything else, an analyst studying American policy toward the Arab-Israeli conflict should want to know how the president—and the few key individuals to whom he listens—makes sense of the many arguments, the mountain of "facts," the competing claims he hears whenever his attention turns to the Arab-Israeli conflict. To a large degree he must impose order where none seems to exist; he must make sense out of something he may hardly understand; he must simplify when complexity becomes overwhelming; and he must decide to authorize others to act in his name if he is not interested enough, or competent enough, to formulate the main lines of policy.

What, then, do the president and his top advisers rely on if not generalized views that they bring with them into office? No senior policymaker in American history has ever come to power with a well-developed understanding of the nuances of the Arab-Israeli dispute, the intricacies of its history, or even much knowledge of the protagonists. At best policymakers have general ideas, notions, inclinations, biases, predispositions, fragments of knowledge. To some extent "ideology" plays a part, although there has never really been a neat liberal versus conservative, Democrat versus Republican divide over the Arab-Israeli conflict.

Any account of policymaking would, however, be incomplete if it did nothing more than map the initial predispositions of key decisionmakers. As important as these are in setting the broad policy guidelines for an administration, they are not enough. Policy is not static, set once and forever after unchanged. Nor is policy reassessed every day. But over time views do change, learning takes place, and policies are adjusted. As a result, a process of convergence seems to take place, whereby the views of senior policymakers toward the Arab-Israeli conflict differ most from those of their predecessors when they first take office and tend to resemble them by the end of their terms. Gerald Ford and Jimmy Carter disagreed on Middle East policy in 1976–77 but were later to coauthor articles on what should be done to resolve the Arab-Israeli conflict. Even Ronald Reagan in his later years seemed closer to his predecessor's outlook than to his own initial approach to Arab-Israeli diplomacy.

It is this process of adjustment, modification, and adaptation to the realities of the Middle East and to the realities of Washington that allows each administration to deal with uncertainty and change. Without this on-the-job learning, American foreign policy would be at best a rigid, brittle affair.

What triggers a change in attitudes? Is the process of learning incremental, or do changes occur suddenly because of crises or the failure of previous policies? When change takes place, are core values called into account, or are tactics merely revised? The evidence presented here suggests that change rarely affects deeply held views. Presidents and their advisers seem reluctant to abandon central beliefs. Basic positions are adhered to with remarkable tenacity, accounting for the stability in the stated positions of the United States on the issues in dispute in the Arab-Israeli conflict. They represent a deep consensus. But politicians and diplomats have no trouble making small adjustments in their understanding of the Arab-Israeli conflict, and that is often enough to produce a substantial change in policy, if not in basic positions or in overall strategy. One simple change in judgment—that President Anwar Sadat of Egypt should be taken seriously—was enough to lead to a major reassessment of American policy in the midst of the October 1973 war.

Since most of the American-led peace process has been geared toward procedures, not substance, the ability of top decisionmakers to experiment with various approaches as they learn more about the conflict has imparted an almost experimental quality to American foreign policy in the Middle East. Almost every conceivable tactic is eventually considered, some are tried, and some even work. And if one administration does not get it right, within a matter of years another team will be in place, willing to try other approaches. Although American foreign policy is sometimes maddening in its lack of consistency and short attention span, this ability to abandon failed policies and move on has often been the hallmark of success.

Foreign-policymaking seems to involve an interplay among the initial predispositions of top policymakers, information about the specific issues being considered, the pull of bureaucratic groupings, the weight of domestic political considerations, the management of transitions from one presidency to the next, and the impact of events in the region of concern. It is often in the midst of crises that new policies are devised, that the shortcomings of one approach are clearly seen, and that a new definition of the situation is imposed. And it is in the midst of crises that presidential powers are at their greatest.

Only rarely are crises anticipated and new polices adopted to ward them off. As a result, American policy often seems to run on automatic pilot until jolted out of its inertial course by an event beyond its control. Critics who find this pattern alarming need to appreciate how complex it is to balance the competing perspectives that vie for support in the Oval Office and how difficult it is to set a course that seems well designed to protect the multiple interests of a global power like the United States—and to do all this without risking one's political life.

National Interests

To get a sense of the difficulty, consider the nature of American interests in the Middle East, as seen from the perspective of the White House. An assessment of these interests almost always takes place at the outset of a new administration, or just after a crisis, in the belief, usually unjustified, that light will be shed on what should be done to advance the prospects of Arab-Israeli peace at the least risk to American interests.

Politicians and some analysts like to invoke the national interest because it seems to encompass tangible, hard-headed concerns as opposed to sentimental, emotional considerations. There is something imposing about cloaking a decision in the garb of national security interests, as if no further debate were needed.

In the real world of policymaking, interests are indeed discussed, but most officials understand that any definition of a national interest contains a strong subjective element. Except for limited areas of foreign affairs, such as trade policy, objective yardsticks do not exist to determine the national interest.

In discussions of the Arab-Israeli conflict, several distinct national interests often compete, confounding the problems of policymaking. For example, most analysts until about 1990 would have said that a major American interest in the Middle East, and therefore related to the handling of Arab-Israeli diplomacy, was the *containment of Soviet influence* in the region. This interest derived from a broader strategy of containment that had been developed initially for Europe but was gradually universalized during the cold war.

In Europe the strategy of containment had led to creation of the Marshall Plan and the North Atlantic Treaty Organization (NATO). But the attempt to replicate these mechanisms of containment in the Middle East had failed, in part because of the unresolved Arab-Israeli conflict. So, however much American policymakers might worry about the growth of Soviet influence in the region, they rarely knew what should be done about it. In the brief period of a few months in 1956–57, the United States opposed the Israeli-French-British attack on Egypt (the Suez war), announced the Eisenhower Doctrine of support to anticommunist regimes in the area, forced the Israelis to withdraw from Sinai, and criticized Nasser's Egypt for its intervention in the affairs of other Arab countries. How all that contributed coherently to the agreed-on goal of limiting Soviet influence was never quite clear.

Over the years many policies toward the Arab-Israeli conflict have been justified, at least in part, by this concern about the Soviet Union. Arms sales have been made and denied in pursuit of this interest; and the Soviets have been excluded from, and included in, discussions on the region, all as part of the goal of trying to manage Soviet influence in the region.

One might think that a strategy of challenging the Soviets in the region would have led the United States to adopt belligerent, interventionist policies, as it did in Southeast Asia. But in the Middle East the concern about overt Soviet military intervention was high, especially from the mid-1960s on, and therefore any American intervention, it was felt, might face a comparable move by the Soviets. Indeed, on several occasions, in the June 1967 war, in 1970 in Jordan, during the October 1973 war, and to a lesser degree in 1982 in Lebanon, the United States feared a possible military confrontation with the Soviet Union. Thus, however ardently American officials might want to check Soviet advances, they wanted to do so without much risk of direct military confrontation with Moscow. In brief, the Soviet angle was never far from the minds of policymakers, but it did little to help clarify choices. With the collapse of the Soviet Union in 1990–91, this interest suddenly disappeared, leaving oil and Israel as the two main American concerns in the Middle East.

Oil has always been a major reason for the United States to pay special attention to the Middle East, but its connection to the Arab-Israeli conflict has not always been apparent. American companies were active in developing the oil resources of the area, especially in Saudi Arabia; the industrialized West was heavily dependent on Middle East oil; and American import needs began to grow from the early 1970s on.[6]

The basic facts about oil in the region were easy to understand. Saudi Arabia, Iraq, and Iran, along with the small states of the Persian Gulf littoral, sit atop about two-thirds of the known reserves of oil in the world—reserves with remarkably low production costs. Thus Middle East stability seemed to go hand in hand with access to relatively inexpensive supplies of oil.

Throughout most of the 1950s and 1960s Middle East oil was readily available for the reconstruction of Europe and Japan. American companies made good profits, and threatened disruptions of supply had little effect. A conscious effort to keep Persian Gulf affairs separate from the Arab-Israeli conflict seemed to work quite well.

But by the late 1960s the British had decided to withdraw their military presence from east of Suez. How, if at all, would that affect the security of Gulf oil supplies? Should the United States try to fill the vacuum with forces of its own, or should it try to build up regional powers, such as Iran and Saudi Arabia? If arms were sold to Saudi Arabia to help ensure access to oil supplies, how would the Israelis and the other Arab countries react? What would the Soviets do? In short, how could an interest, which everyone agreed was important, be translated into concrete policies?

American calculations about oil were further complicated by the fact that the United States is both a large producer and a large importer of oil. For those concerned with enhancing domestic supplies, the low production costs of Middle East oil are always a potential threat. Texas oil producers argue for quotas to protect them from "cheap" foreign oil. But consumers want cheap oil and will therefore resist gasoline taxes, tariffs, or quotas designed to prop up the domestic oil industry. No American president would know how to answer the question of the proper price of Middle East oil. If forced to give an answer, he would have to mumble something like "not too high and not too low." In practice, the stability and predictability of oil supplies have been seen as more important than a specific price. This perception has reinforced the view that the main American interest is in reliable access to Middle East oil, and therefore in regional stability. Still, price cannot be ignored. In 2000 the annual American import bill for oil from the Middle East exceeded $20 billion, out of a total oil import bill of more than $60 billion. Each one-dollar increase in the price of oil added more than $1 billion to the oil import bill.

The other main interest that has dominated discussion of the Arab-Israeli conflict is the *special American commitment to Israel*. The United States was an early and enthusiastic supporter of the idea of a Jewish state in part of Palestine. That support was clearly rooted in a sense of moral commitment to the survivors of the holocaust, as well as in the intense attachment of American Jews to Israel. During the 1980s a "strategic" rationale was added to the traditional list of reasons for supporting Israel, although this view was never universally accepted.

Support for Israel was always tempered by a desire to maintain some interests in surrounding Arab countries, because of either oil or competition with the Soviet Union. As a result, through most of the years from 1949 until the mid-1960s, the United States provided few arms and only modest amounts of aid. As Eisenhower demonstrated in 1956, support for Israel did not mean offering a blank check.

Managing the relationship with the Soviet Union in the Middle East, access to inexpensive oil, and support for Israel were American interests readily accepted by successive administrations. Yet what the implications for policy were of any one, to say nothing of all three, of these interests was not clear. To take the most difficult case, what should be done when one set of interests seemed to be at variance with another? Which should get more weight, the economic interest of oil, the strategic interest of checking Soviet advances, or the moral interest of supporting Israel?

Without a common yardstick, the interests were literally incommensurate. How could arms for the Saudis or Jordanians be squared with support for Israel? How could Soviet inroads in a country like Egypt be checked? Was it better to oppose Nasser to teach him a lesson about the costs of relying on the Soviets, or should an effort be made to win him away from dependence on Moscow? And what would either of these approaches mean for relations with Israel and Saudi Arabia?

In brief, U.S. national interests were clearly involved in the Middle East and would be affected by every step of the Arab-Israeli peace process. But there was almost no agreement on what these interests meant in terms of concrete policies. Advocates of different perspectives, as will be seen, were equally adept at invoking national interests to support their preferred courses of action. Often policy preferences seemed to come first, and then the interests were found to justify the policy. Precisely because of these dilemmas, policymaking could not be left to bureaucrats. The stakes were too high, the judgments too political. Thus Arab-Israeli policy, with remarkable frequency, landed in the lap of the president or his secretary of state. More than for most issues of foreign policy, presidential leadership became crucial to the Arab-Israeli peace process.

Insofar as presidents and their advisers saw a way to resolve the potential conflict among American interests in the Middle East, it was by promoting the Arab-Israeli peace process. This policy is the closest equivalent to that of containment toward the Soviet Union—a policy with broad bipartisan support that promises to protect a range of important American interests. If Arab-Israeli peace could be achieved, it was thought, Soviet influence in the region would decline, Israeli security would be enhanced, and American relations with key Arab countries would improve. Regional stability would therefore be more easily achieved, and oil supplies would be less threatened. Obviously, other sources of trouble would still exist in the region, but few disagreed on the desirability of Arab-Israeli peace or the need for American leadership to achieve it. The differences, and they were many, came over the feasibility of a peace settlement and over appropriate tactics. In making these judgments, presidents made their most important contribution to the formulation of policy.

Presidential Leadership and Policymaking

In U.S. politics, there is a strong presumption that who is president matters. Huge sums are spent on electoral campaigns to select the president. The office receives immense respect and deference, and most writers of American political history assume that the man occupying the White House can shape events. Does this perspective merely reflect an individualism rooted in American culture, or does it contain a profound truth?

One can easily imagine situations in which it would be meaningless to explain a policy by looking at the individuals responsible for making the decisions. If no real margin for choice exists, individuals do not count for much. Other factors take precedence. For example, to predict the voting behavior of senators from New York on aid to Israel, one normally need not consider their identity. It is enough to know something about the constituency, the overwhelming support for Israel among New Yorkers, and the absence of countervailing pressures to be virtually certain about the policy choice of an individual senator.

If context can account for behavior, so can the nature of perceived interests or objectives. If we were studying Japan's policies toward the Arab-Israeli conflict, we would not be especially concerned with who was prime minister at any given moment. It would make more sense to look at the dependence of Japan on Arab oil and the lack of any significant cultural or economic ties to Israel to predict that Japan would adopt a generally pro-Arab policy. When interests easily converge on a single policy, individual choice can be relegated to the background.

Finally, if a nation has no capability to act in foreign policy, we will not be particularly interested in the views of its leaders. To ask why a small European country does not assume a more active role in promoting an Arab-Israeli settlement does not require us to examine who is in charge of policy. Instead, the absence of significant means to affect the behavior of Arabs and Israelis is about all we need to know. A country without important economic, military, or diplomatic assets has virtually no choices to make in foreign policy. Obviously none of these conditions holds for the United States in its approach to the Arab-Israeli conflict. Capabilities for action do exist. The nature of American interests, as generally understood by policymakers, does not predetermine a single course of action. And, despite the obvious constraints imposed by the structure of the international system and domestic politics, choices do exist on most issues, even though at times the margin of choice may be narrow.

Confronting Complexity and Uncertainty

Most political leaders, with no noteworthy alteration in personality or psychodynamics, are likely at some point to change positions on policy issues. Often such changes will be portrayed as opportunism or waffling. But they could instead be a reaction to a complicated situation, suggesting that people can learn as new information is acquired. Particularly when dealing with complex events and ambiguous choices, people may shift their positions quite suddenly, without altering the fundamental aspects of their approaches to policy. As Raymond Bauer said, "Policy problems are sufficiently complex that for the vast majority of individuals or organizations it is conceivable—given the objective features of the situation—to imagine them ending up on any side of the issue."[7]

Policymakers often find it difficult to recognize the difference between a good proposal and a bad proposal. In normal circumstances, bargaining and compromise may be rational courses for a politician to follow, but adopting either of these courses of action assumes that issues have been defined according to some understood criteria. When such criteria are not obvious, what should one do?

On most issues of importance, policymakers operate in an environment in which uncertainty and complexity are dominant. Addressing an unknowable future with imperfect information about the past and present, policymakers must use guidelines and simplifications drawn from their own experience, the "lessons of history," or the consensus of their colleagues. The result is often a cautious style of decisionmaking that strives merely to make incremental changes in existing policies.[8] At times, however, very sudden shifts in policy may also take place. How can one account for both these outcomes?

Leadership is only rarely the task of selecting between good and bad policies. Instead, the anguish and challenge of leadership is to choose between equally plausible arguments about how best to achieve one's goals. For example, most presidents and their advisers have placed a very high value on achieving peace in the Middle East. But values do not easily translate into policy. Instead, several reasonable alternatives, such as the following, are likely to compete for presidential attention:

—If Israel is to feel secure enough to make the territorial concessions necessary to gain Arab acceptance of the terms of a peace agreement, it must continue to receive large quantities of American military and economic aid.

—If Israel feels too strong and self-confident, it will not see the need for any change in the status quo. U.S. aid must therefore be used as a form of pressure.

Presidents Nixon, Ford, Carter, and Bush subscribed to both the foregoing views at different times.

Similarly, consider the following propositions, which were widely entertained by U.S. presidents until the breakup of the USSR:

—The Soviet Union has no interest in peace in the Middle East, because it would lose influence unless it could exploit tensions in the area. Hence the United States cannot expect cooperation from the Soviet Union in the search for a settlement.

—The Soviets, like ourselves, have mixed interests in the Middle East. They fear a confrontation and are therefore prepared to reach a settlement, provided they are allowed to participate in the diplomatic process. By leaving the Soviet Union out, the United States provides it with an incentive to sabotage the peacemaking effort. Therefore, U.S.-Soviet agreement will be essential to reaching peace in the Middle East.

Concerning the Arabs, one may also hear diverse opinions:

—Only when the Arabs have regained their self-respect and feel strong will they be prepared to make peace with Israel.

—When the Arabs feel that time is on their side, they increase their demands and become more extreme. Only a decisive military defeat will convince them that Israel is here to stay and that they must use political means to regain their territory.

Each of these propositions has been seriously entertained by recent American presidents and secretaries of state. One could almost say that all of them have been believed at various times by some individuals. The key element in selecting among these plausible interpretations of reality is not merely whether one is pro-Israeli or pro-Arab, or hard line or not so hard line on relations with Moscow. A more complex process is at work.

Lessons of History

In choosing among plausible, but imperfectly understood, courses of action, policymakers inevitably resort to simplifications.[9] Categorical inferences are thus made; confusing events are placed in comprehensible structures; reality is given a definition that allows purposive action to take place. Recent experience is a particularly potent source of guidance for the future. If a policy has worked in one setting, policymakers will want to try it in another context as well. Secretary of State Henry A. Kissinger, for example, apparently relied on his experiences in negotiating with the Chinese, Russians, and Vietnamese when he approached negotiations with the Arabs and Israelis in 1974–75. Step-by-step diplomacy was the result.

More general historical "lessons" may loom large in the thinking of policymakers as they confront new problems.[10] President Harry Truman was especially inclined to invoke historical analogies. He well understood that the essence of presidential leadership was the ability to make decisions in the face of uncertainty and to live with their consequences. By relying on history, he was able to reassure himself that his decisions were well founded.[11]

Several historical analogies have been notably effective in structuring American views of reality. The lessons of Munich, for example, have been pointed to repeatedly over the years, principally that the appeasement of dictators serves only to whet their appetite for further conquest. Hence a firm, resolute opposition to aggression is required. The "domino theory" is a direct descendant of this perspective, as was the policy of containment.

A second set of guidelines for policy stems from President Woodrow Wilson's fourteen points after World War I, especially the emphasis on self-determination and opposition to spheres of influence. As embodied in the Atlantic Charter in 1941, these principles strongly influenced American policy during the Second World War.[12] Since the failure of U.S. policy in Southeast Asia, new "lessons" have been drawn, which warn against overinvolvement, commitments in marginal areas, excessive reliance on force, and risks of playing the role of world policeman. Whether these will prove as durable as the examples of Munich and Wilsonian idealism remains to be seen, but American policy continues to be discussed in terms of these historical analyses.

When recent experience and historical analogies fail to resolve dilemmas of choice, certain psychological mechanisms may come to the rescue. Wishful thinking is a particularly potent way to resolve uncertainty. When in doubt, choose the course that seems least painful, that fits best with one's hopes and expectations; perhaps it will turn out all right after all. In any event, one can almost always rationalize a choice after making it. Good reasons can be found even for bad policies, and often the ability to come up with a convincing rationale will help to overcome uncertainties.

Apart from such well-known but poorly understood aspects of individual psychology, the social dynamics of a situation often help to resolve uncertainty. If through discussion a group can reach consensus on the proper course of action, individuals are likely to suppress their private doubts. Above all, when a president participates in a group decision, a strong tendency toward consensus is likely. As some scholars have emphasized, presidents must go to considerable lengths to protect themselves from the stultifying effects of group conformity in their presence and the tendency to suppress divergent views.[13] Neither President Johnson's practice of inviting a large number of advisers to consult with him nor President Nixon's effort to use the National Security Council to channel alternatives to him are guarantees against the distortions of group consensus, in part because presidents value consensus as a way to resolve doubts.

At any given moment presidents and their key advisers tend to share fairly similar and stable definitions of reality. However such definitions emerge, whether through reference to experience or to history, through wishful thinking and rationalization, or through group consensus, they will provide guidelines for action in the face of uncertainty. Complexity will be simplified by reference to a few key criteria. In the Arab-Israeli setting, these will usually have to do with the saliency of issues, their amenability to solution, the role of the Soviet Union (up until late 1990), and the value of economic and military assistance to various parties.

Crises and the Redefining of Issues

Crises play an extremely important role in the development of these guidelines. By definition, crises involve surprise, threat, and increased uncertainty. Previous policies may well be exposed as flawed or bankrupt. Reality no longer accords with previous expectations. In such a situation a new structure of perceptions is likely to emerge, one that will reflect presidential perspectives to the degree that the president becomes involved in handling the crisis. If the crisis is satisfactorily resolved, a new and often quite durable set of assumptions will guide policy for some time.

Often crises can produce significant policy changes without causing a sweeping reassessment of a decisionmaker's views. It may be only a greater sense of urgency that brings into play a new policy. Or it may be a slight shift in assumptions about the Soviet role, for example, or the advantages of pursuing a more conciliatory policy toward Egypt. Small adjustments in a person's perceptions, in the weight accorded to one issue as opposed to another, can lead to substantial shifts of emphasis, of nuance, and therefore of action. Again, policymakers do not change from being pro-Israeli to being pro-Arab overnight, but crises may bring into focus new relations among issues or raise the importance of one interest, thus leading to changes in policy. Basic values will remain intact, but perceptions and understanding of relationships may quickly change.

In the case studies that follow, I explore the important role of crises in defining issues for presidents and their advisers. And I try to account for their views, to understand their reasoning, and to see situations from their standpoint. Between crises, as is noted, it is difficult to bring about changes in policies that were forged in crisis and have the stamp of presidential approval.

Admittedly, this approach shortchanges the role of Congress, public opinion, interest groups, the media, and the bureaucracy. All these are worthy subjects of study and undoubtedly have influenced American diplomacy toward the Arab-Israeli conflict. Nor do I discuss in this book why Arabs and Israelis made the decisions that they did. Only in passing do I deal with the protagonists in the conflict, describing their views but not subjecting them to the kind of analysis reserved for American policy.

Starting, then, with the key role of the president and his advisers in shaping policy, particularly in moments of crisis, when domestic and organizational constraints are least confining, the book examines how politics and bureaucratic habits affect both the formulation and implementation of policies in normal times. But at the center of the study are those rare moments when policymakers try to make sense out of the confusing flow of events, when they strive to relate action to purposes, for it is then that the promises and limitations of leadership are most apparent.

PART ONE

THE JOHNSON
PRESIDENCY

2

Yellow Light: Johnson and the Crisis of May–June 1967

LYNDON BAINES JOHNSON brought to the presidency a remarkable array of political talents. An activist and a man of strong passions, Johnson seemed to enjoy exerting his power. As majority leader in the Senate, he had used the art of persuasion as few other leaders had; building consensus through artfully constructed compromises had been one of his strong suits. His political experience did not, however, extend to foreign-policymaking, an area that demanded his attention, especially as American involvement in Vietnam grew in late 1964 and early 1965.

Fortunately for the new president, one part of the world that seemed comparatively quiet in the early 1960s was the Middle East. Long-standing disputes still simmered, but compared with the turbulent 1950s, the situation appeared to be manageable. The U.S.-Israeli relationship had been strengthened by President Kennedy, and Johnson obviously was prepared to continue on this line, particularly with increases in military assistance. His personal sentiments toward Israel were warm and admiring. To all appearances he genuinely liked the Israelis he had dealt with, many of his closest advisers were well-known friends of Israel, and his own contacts with the American Jewish community had been close throughout his political career.[1]

Johnson's demonstrated fondness for Israel did not mean he was particularly hostile to Arabs, but it is fair to say that Johnson showed little sympathy for the radical brand of Arab nationalism expounded by Egypt's president Gamal Abdel Nasser. And he was sensitive to signs that the Soviet Union was exploiting Arab nationalism to weaken the influence of the West in the Middle East. Like other American policymakers before him, Johnson seemed to waver between a desire to try to come to terms with Nasser and a belief that Nasser's prestige and regional ambitions had to be trimmed. More important for policy than these predispositions, however, was the fact that Johnson, overwhelmingly preoccupied by Vietnam, treated Middle East issues as deserving only secondary priority.

U.S.-Egyptian relations had deteriorated steadily between 1964 and early 1967, in part because of the conflict in Yemen, in part because of quarrels over aid. By 1967, with Vietnam becoming a divisive domestic issue for Johnson, problems of the Middle East were left largely to the State Department. There the anxiety about increased tension between Israel and the surrounding Arab states was growing after the Israeli raid on the Jordanian town of Al-Samu' in November 1966, and especially after an April 1967 Israeli-Syrian air battle that resulted in the downing of six Syrian MiGs. Under Secretary of State Eugene Rostow was particularly concerned about the drift of events, suspecting that the Soviets were seeking to take advantage in the Middle East of Washington's preoccupation with Vietnam.[2]

If the tensions on the Syrian-Israeli border provided the fuel for the early stages of the 1967 crisis, the spark that ignited the fuel came in the form of erroneous Soviet reports to Egypt on May 13 that Israel had mobilized some ten to thirteen brigades on the Syrian border. Against the backdrop of Israeli threats to take action to stop the guerrilla raids from Syria,[3] this disinformation apparently helped to convince Nasser the time had come for Egypt to take some action to deter any Israeli moves against Syria and to restore his own somewhat tarnished image in the Arab world.[4] The Soviets, he seemed to calculate, would provide firm backing for his position.

On May 14 Nasser made the first of his fateful moves. Egyptian troops were ostentatiously sent into Sinai, posing an unmistakable challenge to Israel, if not yet a serious military threat. President Johnson and his key advisers were quick to sense the danger in the new situation. Because of his well-known sympathy for Israel and his forceful personality, Johnson might have been expected to take a strong and unambiguous stand in support of Israel at the outset of the crisis, especially as such a stand might have helped to prevent Arab miscalculations. Moreover, reassurances to Israel would lessen the pressure on Prime Minister Levi Eshkol to resort to preemptive military action. Finally, a strong stand in the Middle East would signal the Soviet Union that it could not exploit tensions there without confronting the United States.

The reality of U. S. policy as the Middle East crisis unfolded in May was, however, quite different. American behavior was cautious, at times ambiguous, and ultimately unable to prevent a war that was clearly in the offing. Why was that the case? This is the central puzzle to solve in examining Johnson's reaction to the events leading up to the June 1967 war. Also, one must ask how hard Johnson really tried to restrain Israel. Some have alleged that, in fact, Johnson gave Israel a green light to attack, or in some way colluded with Israel to draw Nasser into a trap.[5] These charges need to be carefully assessed. And what role did domestic political considerations play in Johnson's thinking? Did the many pro-Israeli figures in Johnson's entourage influence his views?

Initial Reactions to the Crisis

Nasser's initial moves were interpreted in Washington primarily in political terms. Under attack by the conservative monarchies of Jordan and Saudi Arabia for being soft on Israel, Nasser was seen as attempting to regain prestige by appearing as the defender of the embattled and threatened radical regime in Syria. Middle East watchers in the State Department thought they recognized a familiar pattern. In February 1960 Nasser had sent troops into Sinai, postured for a while, claimed victory by deterring alleged Israeli aggressive designs, and then backed down.[6] All in all, a rather cheap victory, and not one that presented much of a danger to anyone. Consequently the initial American reaction to Nasser's dispatch of troops was restrained. Even the Israelis did not seem to be particularly alarmed.

On May 16, however, the crisis took on a more serious aspect as the Egyptians made their initial request for the removal of the United Nations Emergency Force (UNEF).[7] This prompted President Johnson to sound out the Israelis about their intentions and to consult with the British and the French. On May 17 Johnson sent Eshkol the first of several letters exchanged during the crisis, in which he urged restraint and specifically asked to be informed before Israel took any action. "I am sure you will understand that I cannot accept any responsibilities on behalf of the United States for situations which arise as the result of actions on which we are not consulted."[8]

From the outset, then, Johnson seemed to want to avoid war, to restrain the Israelis, and to gain allied support for any action that might be taken. Two possible alternative courses of action seem not to have been seriously considered at this point. One might have been to stand aside and let the Israelis act as they saw fit, even to the extent of going to war.[9] The danger, of course, was that Israel might get into trouble and turn to the United States for help. Johnson seemed to fear this possibility throughout the crisis, despite all the intelligence predictions that Israel would easily win a war against Egypt alone or against all the surrounding Arab countries.

The second alternative not considered at this point was bold unilateral American action opposing Nasser's effort to change the status quo. Here the problems were twofold. A quarrel with Egypt might inflame the situation and weaken American influence throughout the Arab world. The Suez precedent, and what it had done to British and French positions in the region, was very much in the minds of key American officials. Nasser was not noted for backing down when challenged. Moreover, U.S. military assets were deeply committed in Vietnam, so that a full-scale military confrontation with Egypt was ruled out. But even if American forces had been available, Congress was in no mood to countenance unilateral military action, even in support of Israel. Therefore, the initial United States effort was directed toward restraining Israel and building a multilateral context for any American action, whether diplomatic or military.

Eshkol's reply to Johnson's letter reached Washington the following day, May 18. The Israeli prime minister blamed Syria for the increase in tension and stated that Egypt must remove its troops from Sinai. Then, appealing directly to Johnson, Eshkol requested that the United States reaffirm its commitment to Israeli security and inform the Soviet Union in particular of this commitment. Johnson wrote to Premier Aleksei Kosygin the following day, affirming the American position of support for Israel as requested, but suggesting in addition a "joint initiative of the two powers to prevent the dispute between Israel and the UAR [United Arab Republic, or Egypt] and Syria from drifting into war."[10]

After Egypt's initial request for the withdrawal of the UNEF on May 16, there was danger that Nasser might overplay his hand by also closing the Strait of Tiran to the Israelis. The opening of the strait to Israeli shipping was the one tangible gain made by Israel in the 1956 war. American commitments concerning the international status of the strait were explicit. It was seen as an international waterway, open for the free passage of ships of all nations, including Israel. The Israelis had been promised that they could count on U.S. support to keep the strait open.[11]

The UNEF had stationed troops at Sharm al-Shaykh since 1957, and shipping had not been impeded. If the UNEF withdrew, however, Nasser would be under great pressure to return the situation to its pre-1956 status. Israel had long declared that such action would be considered a casus belli.

In light of these dangers, one might have expected some action by the United States after May 16 aimed at preventing the complete removal of the UNEF. But the record shows no sign of an urgent approach to UN secretary general U Thant on this matter, and by the evening of May 18 U Thant had responded positively to the formal Egyptian government request that all UNEF troops leave Egyptian territory.

The strait still remained open, however, and a strong warning by Israel or the United States about the consequences of its closure might conceivably have influenced Nasser's next move. From May 19 until midday on May 22, Nasser took no action to close the strait, nor did he make any threat to do so. Presumably he was waiting to see how Israel and the United States, among others, would react to withdrawal of the UNEF. The United States made no direct approach to Nasser until May 22, the day Nasser finally announced the closure of the strait. It issued no public statements reaffirming the American view that the strait was an international waterway, nor did the reputedly pro-Israeli president respond to Eshkol's request for a public declaration of America's commitment to Israel's security.[12]

On May 22 Johnson finally sent a letter to the Egyptian leader. The thrust of the message was to assure Nasser of the friendship of the United States while urging him to avoid any step that might lead to war. In addition, Johnson offered to send Vice President Hubert Humphrey to Cairo. Johnson ended the letter with words he had personally added: "I look forward to our working out a program that will be acceptable and constructive for our respective peoples." The message was not delivered by ambassador-designate Richard Nolte until the following day, by which time the strait had already been declared closed to Israeli shipping and strategic cargoes bound for Israel.[13]

Johnson informed Eshkol the same day that he was writing to the Egyptian and Syrian leaders warning them not to take actions that might lead to hostilities.[14] In addition, another message from Johnson to Kosygin was also sent on May 22. Reiterating his suggestion of joint action to calm the situation, Johnson went on to state, "The increasing harassment of Israel by elements based in Syria, with attendant reactions within Israel and within the Arab world, has brought the area close to major violence. Your and our ties to nations of the area could bring us into difficulties which I am confident neither of us seeks. It would appear a time for each of us to use our influence to the full in the course of moderation, including our influence over action by the United Nations."[15]

These messages, which might have helped to calm the situation earlier, were rendered meaningless by the next major escalation of the crisis.[16] The well-intentioned American initiative of May 21–22 was too little and too late. Shortly after midnight May 22–23, Nasser's speech announcing the closure of the strait was broadcast.

The Crisis over the Strait

If Johnson had feared that Israel might resort to force unilaterally before May 23, the danger now became acutely real. Therefore he requested that Israel not make any military move for at least forty-eight hours.[17] During the day of May 23 arrangements were made for Foreign Minister Abba Eban to visit Washington for talks prior to any unilateral action. Johnson also decided to accede to an Israeli request for military assistance worth about $70 million, but he rejected an Israeli request for a U.S. destroyer to visit the port of Eilat.[18]

American diplomacy went into high gear. Johnson issued a forceful public statement outlining the U.S. position: "The United States considers the gulf to be an international waterway and feels that a blockade of Israeli shipping is illegal and potentially disastrous to the cause of peace. The right of free, innocent passage of the international waterway is a vital interest of the international community."[19]

In Tel Aviv, U.S. ambassador Walworth Barbour repeated the request for a forty-eight-hour delay before any unilateral Israeli action and raised the possibility of pursuing a British idea of a multinational naval force to protect maritime rights in the event that UN action failed to resolve the crisis. Eban's trip to Washington was designed in part to explore the feasibility of this idea.

In Washington, Israeli ambassador Avraham Harman and minister Ephraim Evron met with Under Secretary Eugene Rostow and were told that "the United States had decided in favor of an appeal to the Security Council. . . . The object is to call for restoring the status quo as it was before . . . the blockade announcement. Rostow explained that the congressional reaction compels a president to take this course."[20] Rostow reportedly referred to the realities created by the Vietnam War in describing Johnson's approach to the blockade.[21]

The basic elements of Johnson's approach to the crisis as of May 23 were:

—Try to prevent war by restraining Israel and warning the Egyptians and Soviets.

—Build public and congressional support for the idea of an international effort to reopen the Strait of Tiran. (Unilateral U.S. action was ruled out without much consideration.)

—Make an effort through the UN Security Council to open the strait. If that failed, as was anticipated, a multilateral declaration in support of free shipping would be drawn up. This would be followed, as the British suggested, by a multinational naval force transiting the strait.

Noteworthy was the continuing reluctance either to consider unilateral American action or to "unleash Israel," as a second option came to be known. These alternatives had been ruled out virtually from the beginning, and even the closure of the strait did not lead to a reevaluation of the initial policy. Instead, the two key elements of policy dating from May 17 were merely embellished as conditions changed.

A complex multilateral plan was discussed with the British that would surely be supported by Congress and public opinion, but could it produce results rapidly enough to ensure the other element in the U.S. approach— restraint of Israel? A dilemma clearly existed. To keep Israel from acting on its own, as even the United States acknowledged it had a right to do in order to reopen the strait, an acceptable alternative had to be presented. The stronger the stand of the United States and the firmer its commitment to action, the more likely it was that Israel could be restrained; by the same token, the less likely it was that Nasser would probe further. Yet a strong American stand was incompatible with the desire for multilateral action, which had to be tried, in Johnson's view, to ensure congressional and public support. Such support was essential at a time of controversy over the U.S. role in Vietnam.

Johnson was mindful of the furor over his handling of the Gulf of Tonkin incident in 1964. Then he had seized on a small incident to broaden his power, with full congressional approval, to act in Vietnam. Subsequently, however, he had been charged with duplicity, with misleading Congress concerning the event, and with abusing the authority he had received. In mid-1967 Johnson was not about to lead the United States into another venture that might entail the use of force unless he had full congressional and public backing. Consequently he insisted on trying the United Nations first, and only then seeking a multilateral maritime declaration and sending ships through the strait. By moving slowly, cautiously, and with full support at home, Johnson would minimize the domestic political risks to his position.

The goals of restraining Israel and pursuing a multilateral solution were not necessarily incompatible, if sufficient time was available. For time to be available, perhaps as much as two to three weeks, the situation on the ground could not be allowed to change radically, nor could the balance of forces within Israel shift toward those who favored war. At a minimum, then, Nasser had to sit tight, the Soviet Union had to remain on the sidelines, and Eshkol had to be given something with which to restrain his hawks. If any of these conditions could not be met, the assumptions of U.S. policy would be undermined, and war would probably ensue.[22]

Eban's Visit to Washington

The impending visit of Israel's foreign minister served as a catalyst for the further definition of an American plan of action for dealing with the closure of the Strait of Tiran. If Israel was to refrain from forceful action, it needed to be given a credible alternative to war. But the process of moving from general principles—restrain Israel, act within a multilateral context—to a more detailed proposal revealed inherent contradictions and ambiguities, as well as bureaucratically rooted differences of opinion. What had initially been a fairly widespread consensus among Johnson's top advisers on how to deal with the crisis began to fragment as the crisis grew more acute. When Johnson felt most in need of broad support for his cautious, restrained approach, the viability of that position came under question.

The key to Johnson's policy on the eve of Eban's visit was the idea of a multinational naval force. On May 24 Eugene Rostow met with the British minister of state for foreign affairs, George Thomson, and an admiral of the Royal Navy to discuss the British proposal. They agreed to try for a public declaration on freedom of shipping through the Strait of Tiran, to be signed by as many countries as possible. A multinational naval force would then be set up, composed of ships from as many maritime countries as were prepared to act, and a flotilla, soon to be known as the Red Sea Regatta, would then pass through the strait.[23] Rostow talked to Johnson later in the day about the plan and found the president receptive toward it.

The Pentagon was charged with coming up with a concrete plan for forming a naval force. At this point, consensus began to erode.[24] Although some Pentagon analysts reported that the United States was capable of managing a crisis involving possible military intervention in the Middle East as well as Vietnam, most believed that Israel could deal with the Arab threat perfectly well on its own and that there was no need for a costly American commitment of forces. In any event, it would take time to get the necessary forces in place to challenge Nasser's blockade.

The idea of a token display of U.S. force to reopen the strait did not have many fans in the Pentagon. What would happen if the Egyptians fired on an American ship? Would the United States respond with force? Would Egyptian airfields be attacked? Would ground troops be required? If so, how many? Furthermore, what could the Navy do about the growing numbers of Egyptian ground troops deployed along Israel's borders?

On balance, the military was not in favor of the use of U.S. force. Bureaucratic self-interest and a professional attitude that dictated the use of force only when success was assured and when superior power was available lay at the root of the opposition. The multinational fleet was a military man's nightmare. It was not the way the military would plan such an operation. It was too political. Deeming it undesirable, the military did little to make it feasible.

The State Department, at least at the top levels, was, by contrast, enthusiastic about the idea. Secretary of State Dean Rusk endorsed it, and Under Secretary Rostow became its chief advocate. From their point of view, the fact that it was a flawed military concept was less important than its politically attractive features. First, it would associate other nations with the United States in defense of an important principle—freedom of navigation—and in the upholding of a commitment to Israel. Second, it would deflate Nasser's prestige, which was once again on the rise, without putting him in an impossible position. If Nasser wanted to back down from confrontation with Israel, the fleet would provide him with an honorable excuse to do so. The State Department therefore set out to find cosigners to the maritime declaration and donors of ships for the fleet. This essentially political task was what State was best at performing; the planning of the fleet was the province of Defense. Unfortunately, little coordination went on between the two.

Foreign Minister Eban arrived in Washington on the afternoon of May 25. His first talks were held at the State Department at 5:00 p.m. The result was to sow confusion among U.S. policymakers, who had just adjusted to the crisis and thought they saw a way out of it. Eban, who had left Israel with instructions to discuss American plans to reopen the Strait of Tiran, arrived in the United States to find new instructions awaiting him.[25] No longer was he to emphasize the issue of the strait. A more urgent danger, that of imminent Egyptian attack, had overshadowed the blockade. Eban was instructed to inform the highest authorities of this new threat to peace and to request an official statement from the United States that an attack on Israel would be viewed as an attack on the United States.[26] Despite his own skepticism, Eban followed his instructions in his first meeting with Secretary Rusk, Under Secretary Rostow, and Assistant Secretary Lucius Battle.

Rusk quickly ended the meeting so that he could confer with Johnson about the new situation. The meeting with Eban resumed at 6:00 p.m. for a working dinner. The Israelis were told that U.S. sources could not confirm an Egyptian plan to attack.[27]

After the talks ended, Israeli ambassador Harman returned to the State Department at about midnight to reemphasize Israel's need for a concrete and precise statement of U.S. intentions.[28] He also warned that Israel could not accept any plan in which the strait might be opened to all ships except those of Israel.

American intelligence experts spent the night of May 25–26 analyzing the Israeli claim that an Egyptian attack was imminent. Several specific items had been presented by the Israelis in making their case, and by the morning of May 26 the intelligence community had analyzed each of these charges and concluded that an attack was not pending.[29] The Israelis suffered a loss of credibility at an important moment, and Johnson seems to have become suspicious that he was being pressured to make commitments that he either could not make, such as a statement that he would view an attack on Israel as an attack on the United States, or did not want to make yet, such as a precise plan on the multinational fleet. According to those who worked with him during this period, Johnson did not want to be crowded, he disliked ultimatums and deadlines, and he resented the mounting pressure on him to adopt Israel's definition of the situation. After all, as president he had to worry about the Soviet Union, about Congress and public opinion, and even about U.S.-Arab relations; he did not want to be stampeded, to use the imagery of his native Texas.[30]

Johnson was obviously reluctant to see Eban on Friday, May 26. He knew it would be an important, perhaps crucial meeting. The Israeli cabinet was to meet on Sunday, and what Johnson told Eban might make the difference between war and peace. The Israelis were pressing for a specific commitment, for a detailed plan, for promises to act, and for understanding in the event Israel took matters into its own hands. Faced with these pressures, Johnson tried to stall. Rusk called Harman early in the morning to find out whether Eban could stay in Washington through Saturday. This would allow Johnson to learn the results of U Thant's mission to Cairo. Eban, stressing the importance of the Sunday cabinet meeting, said he had to leave Friday evening for Israel.[31]

Meanwhile Secretary Rusk and Under Secretary Eugene Rostow had prepared a policy memorandum for the president. Rusk's memo to the president began with a review of his talk with Eban the previous evening, including the Israeli information that an Egyptian and Syrian attack was imminent and the request for a public statement of American support for Israel against such aggression. Eban, it was stated, would not press this point with Johnson, and the president's talk could concentrate on the British proposal for a multinational fleet. Rusk then outlined two basic options:

—"to let the Israelis decide how best to protect their own national interests, in the light of the advice we have given them: i.e., to 'unleash' them"; or

—"to take a positive position, but not a final commitment, on the British proposal."

Rusk recommended strongly against the first option. Noting that the British cabinet would meet on the plan for the multinational fleet the following day, Rusk endorsed the second option, which he then reviewed in some detail. Included in his outline was the idea that a UN force should take a position along both sides of the Israeli-Egyptian frontier. If Egypt refused, Israel might accept.

Eban's need for a strong commitment from Johnson was made clear in the Rusk memorandum. Congressional views were reviewed, and the option of unilateral U.S. action was referred to with caution. A draft joint resolution of the Congress was being prepared to support international action on the strait. In closing, Rusk referred to the possibility of offering Israel economic and military aid to help offset the strains of continuing mobilization.[32]

On May 26, shortly after noon, President Johnson convened at the White House the most important full-scale meeting of his advisers held during the crisis. One by one, each of Johnson's advisers expressed his views to the president. Discussion turned to the idea of a multinational fleet, with Secretary of Defense Robert McNamara stating his disapproval of the idea on military grounds.[33] Rusk then reported on U Thant's talks in Cairo, which had elicited from Nasser a promise not to take preemptive action and had led to some discussion of how the blockade might be modified. He then introduced a phrase that was to be repeated to the Israelis frequently in the coming two weeks: "Israel will not be alone unless it decides to go alone."[34] To Rusk, it clearly mattered who opened fire first.[35] Johnson, who seemed to be reassured by the judgment that the military situation would not deteriorate suddenly, spoke of the maritime effort approvingly, terming it his "hole card" for his talk with Eban. But he realized this might not be enough for Eban. He asked his advisers if they thought Eban would misinterpret this as a "cold shoulder." Johnson expressed his feeling that he could not make a clear commitment to use force because of congressional sentiment.

Supreme Court Justice Abe Fortas, a close friend of Johnson who was invited especially for this NSC meeting, joined the discussion, stating that the problem was to keep Israel from making a first strike. This required an American commitment that an Israeli ship would get through the strait. Fortas recommended that Johnson promise to use whatever force was necessary. Johnson said he was in no position to make such a promise. Eban was not going to get everything he wanted. Congress, he said, was unanimously against taking a stronger stand. He wondered out loud if he would regret on Monday not having given Eban more today. Then he left the meeting. The others talked on for a few minutes, with both McNamara and Rusk taking the strong stand that Israel would be on its own if it decided to strike first. Fortas countered by saying that Johnson could not credibly say to Israel that it would be alone. The president did not have a choice of standing on the sidelines.[36]

Thus were the two main schools of thought among Johnson's advisers presented. The president seemed to be taking his cues from McNamara and Rusk, but no doubt he was also attentive to what Fortas was saying. The drama of the next few days in American policy circles involved the gradual shift on Johnson's part from supporting Rusk's "red light" views to siding with Fortas, who began to argue that Israel should be allowed to act on its own if the United States was unwilling or unable to use force to reopen the strait—the "yellow light" view.

By late afternoon the Israelis were becoming anxious to set a definite time for Eban's meeting with the president.[37] Minister Evron called National Security Adviser Walt Rostow and was invited to come to the White House to talk. Johnson, he was told, did not want any leaks to the press from the meeting, and several details of the visit had to be discussed. While Evron was in his office, Rostow contacted Johnson, who, on learning of Evron's presence, asked him in for an informal talk. Johnson knew and liked Evron, and presumably felt that it would be useful to convey his position through Evron before the more formal meeting with Eban. Johnson began by stressing that any American action would require congressional support of the president. He repeated this point several times. Talks in the UN, though not expected to produce anything, were an important part of the process of building support. On a more positive note, Johnson mentioned the multinational-fleet effort. He acknowledged that Israel, as a sovereign state, had the right to act alone, but if it did, the United States would feel no obligation for any consequences that might ensue.[38] He stated that he did not believe Israel would carry out such unilateral action. In closing, Johnson stressed that he was not a coward, that he did not renege on his promises, but that he would not be rushed into a course of action that might endanger the United States simply because Israel had set Sunday as a deadline.[39]

Eban arrived at the White House unannounced while Evron was with the president. After some confusion, their meeting began shortly after 7:00 p.m. In response to Eban's appeal that the United States live up to its explicit commitments, Johnson emphasized that he had termed the blockade illegal and that he was working on a plan to reopen the strait. He noted that he did not have the authority to say that an attack on Israel would be considered an attack on the United States. He again stressed the two basic premises of American policy: any action must have congressional support, and it must be multilateral. He told Eban he was fully aware of what three past presidents had said, but their statements were "not worth five cents" if the people and Congress did not support the president.

Twice Johnson repeated the phrase that Rusk had coined: "Israel will not be alone unless it decides to go alone." He said he could not imagine Israel's making a precipitate decision. In case Eban doubted his personal courage, Johnson stressed that he was "not a feeble mouse or a coward." Twice Eban asked the president if he could tell the cabinet that Johnson would do everything in his power to get the Gulf of Aqaba open to all shipping, including that of Israel. Johnson replied "yes."[40] Eban was given an aide-mémoire spelling out U.S. policy along the lines that the president had just laid out.[41]

As Eban left the White House, Johnson turned to his advisers and stated: "I've failed. They'll go."[42]

Prelude to the June 1967 War

Johnson obviously was aware of the awkwardness of the policy he was pursuing. The multinational-fleet effort would take time, and even then might fall through for any number of reasons. The alternative of unilateral American action was not seriously considered. Congress was obviously a major concern, and behind Congress lay the realities of the Vietnam conflict. Johnson understood that Israel was subject to a different set of pressures and might be forced to go to war. But if so, the United States, he had said, would not be committed to act. He apparently still wanted the

Israelis to hold off on military action, but as time went by he seems to have become resigned to letting the Israelis take whatever action they felt was necessary. Above all, he was not prepared to give Israel the one thing that might have kept it from acting on its own—a firm guarantee to use force if necessary to reopen the strait. Eban had almost extracted such a promise, but in Johnson's mind it was clearly hedged by references to United States constitutional processes and "every means within my power."

What Johnson had asked for was time—time for the fleet idea to be explored, for passions to cool, for compromises to be explored. He had tried to pin the Israelis down with a commitment to give him two weeks, beginning about May 27. On that day the Soviets had told Johnson they had information that Israel was planning to attack. The president replied to Kosygin and sent a message to Eshkol, which reached him on May 28, repeating the information from Moscow and warning Israel against starting hostilities.[43] Meanwhile, the president decided to initiate further contacts with Nasser.

Rusk followed up Johnson's message to Eshkol with one of his own to Ambassador Barbour, for transmittal to the Israelis: "With the assurance of international determination to make every effort to keep the strait open to the flags of all nations, unilateral action on the part of Israel would be irresponsible and catastrophic."[44] Rusk also paralleled Johnson's message to Kosygin, which had called for a U.S.-USSR effort to find a prompt solution to the Strait of Tiran issue, with a message to Foreign Minister Andrei Gromyko calling for a two-week moratorium on the Egyptian closure of the strait. The message to Eshkol had its intended effect. At its Sunday, May 28, meeting, the cabinet seemed evenly split on the issue of whether to go to war. Eshkol, reflecting on Johnson's letter and Eban's report of his talks, decided to accede to the president's request.

From this point on, many Washington officials began to act as if they had at least two weeks in which to work toward a solution. The critical period, it was felt, would begin after Sunday, June 11. Although there was reason to believe that the Israelis would stay their hand until that date, as Johnson had requested, clearly such a pledge would lose validity if the situation on the ground or within Israel changed substantially. And in the ensuing days, changes did indeed occur.

Informal Lines of Communication

During this period, Justice Abe Fortas, presumably with Johnson's blessing, spoke frequently with Israel's respected ambassador, Avraham

Harman.[45] Fortas and Harman were close personal friends who met on a regular basis during late May and the first days of June. And with considerable regularity, Fortas talked to the president by telephone. The Israelis had every reason to assume they were dealing with one of Johnson's true confidants, although Harman reportedly did not view his talks with Fortas as constituting an alternative channel for dealing with the U.S. government. He and Evron, who also talked to Fortas, did know, of course, that they were dealing with someone who was close to Johnson and whose views deserved careful attention. They were also dealing with a man who was deeply committed to Israel and who seems to have been suspicious of the State Department, and Dean Rusk in particular.[46] What they heard from Fortas would be one more piece of evidence they could use in trying to fathom Johnson's thinking.

Eban's report of Johnson's views was not universally credited in Israel. Some thought he had misunderstood the import of the phrase "Israel will not be alone unless its decides to go alone." It was not an absolute prohibition. In fact, Johnson had acknowledged that Israel had the right to act on its own. But he had urged them not to do so, at least not right away. And he had made it clear that he could not do much to help if they got into trouble. Over the next several days the Israelis mounted a major effort to check on exactly where Johnson stood and to signal that time was working against Israeli interests. Central to this effort was a visit by Meir Amit, the head of Israel's intelligence service (the Mossad), who traveled to Washington under an assumed name on May 31.[47]

Just before Amit's arrival in Washington, an extremely important change took place in the Middle East situation. Jordan's King Hussein, under great pressure to join the Arab nationalist mainstream, had flown to Cairo and signed a mutual-defense pact with Nasser. He returned to Jordan with an Egyptian general in tow who would head the joint military command. Walt Rostow saw this as a major turning point, and he underscored the military danger represented by the dispatch of Egyptian commandos to Jordan. From this point on, he believed, Arab actions were making war virtually inevitable. Unless the Arabs backed down, or unless enough time was available for American power to make itself felt, Israel was bound to take matters into its own hands.[48]

Eshkol replied to Johnson's letter of May 28 on May 30, noting that American assurances to take "any and all measures to open the straits" had played a role in Israel's decisions not to go to war and to agree to wait for "a week or two."[49] Within that time frame, Eshkol urged, a naval escort must move through the strait. Apprised of this message on May 31,

Johnson became angry, claiming he had not promised Israel that he would use "any and all measures," but rather had stressed that he would make every effort within his constitutional authority.

From Cairo, the president's special envoy, Charles Yost, reported on May 30 his impression that Nasser "cannot and will not retreat," that "he would probably welcome, but not seek, military showdown with Israel," and that any American effort to force the strait would "undermine, if not destroy, US position throughout Arab world."[50] The following day, another presidential envoy, Robert Anderson, met with Nasser and discussed the possibility that Egyptian vice president Zakariyya Muhieddin would visit Washington on June 7.[51]

Rumors began to circulate in Washington on May 31 that the United States was looking for possible compromises to end the crisis.[52] In fact, some consideration was being given in the State Department to such steps, and Rusk's consultations with Congress to this effect rapidly reached Israeli ears and caused alarm.[53] That same day the Israelis picked up a report that Rusk had told a journalist, "I don't think it is our business to restrain anyone," when asked if the United States was trying to restrain Israel.[54]

This was the atmosphere that Amit found when he filed his first report on his soundings in Washington. His advice was to wait a few more days, but he observed that the mood was beginning to change. In his opinion the fleet idea was increasingly seen as bankrupt. If Israel were to act on its own, and win decisively, no one in Washington would be upset. The source for these impressions, it is worth noting, was not the State Department or the president. Amit's talks on June 1 and the morning of June 2 were focused on the Pentagon, where he saw McNamara, and on the CIA, where he talked with Director Richard Helms and James Angleton.[55] On June 1 the simmering political crisis in Israel broke. Late in the day Moshe Dayan, hero of the 1956 Suez campaign, was brought into the cabinet as minister of defense. War now seemed likely in the near future. Some leaders in the Israeli military were eager to strike quickly. Eban, however, was mindful of the Suez experience, when Israel had gone to war without the blessing of the United States. He wanted Johnson's support, or at least acquiescence, if Israel took military action. And based on what he had heard on May 26 in the Oval Office, reinforced by Rusk's stern message of May 28, that support could not be taken for granted if Israel acted preemptively.

Then on June 1 Eban received a message that contributed to his change of position. It was an account of a meeting that Minister Evron had had with Fortas. Fortas reportedly said that "Eshkol and Eban did great service to Israel by giving the U.S. a chance to explore options other than

Israeli force. If they had not done so, it would have been difficult to secure the President's sympathy."[56] Eban concluded that this was as near a green light as a president could safely give, and he then called on Generals Yitzhak Rabin and Aharon Yariv to tell them that he no longer saw any diplomatic necessity for further military restraint.[57]

June 2 was the last occasion for serious diplomatic efforts before Israel's decision to fight. The Israeli ambassador was scheduled to leave for Israel later that day, and another "fateful" cabinet meeting would be held on June 4. At about 11:00 a.m. on June 2, Minister Evron, without instructions from Jerusalem, called on Walt Rostow at the White House. He wanted to make sure Johnson understood that time was very short and that Israel might have to go to war. He was seeking further confirmation of Amit's impression that the United States would not object too strenuously if Israel acted on its own. Evron stressed that he was not conveying an official communication from his government, but his points were taken seriously. First he emphasized that time was working against Israel and that the military cost of war with Egypt was rising every day. He then asked what the American response would be if an Israeli ship tried to break the blockade, drawing Egyptian fire, and then Israel responded with an attack on Sharm al-Shaykh. Would the United States see this as a case of Israel's asserting its legitimate right of self-defense? What if the Soviet Union intervened?

Rostow said this scenario was very different from the one discussed with Eban, but was an alternative that might be considered. He would seek Johnson's views. He then asked Evron how much time remained, in reply to which Evron referred to June 11, although he stressed that there was nothing ironclad about that date.[58] Evron noted, and Rostow confirmed, that intelligence reports indicated Nasser would probably not fire on a U.S.-escorted probe of the strait.[59] Therefore, the issue of Israeli access to the Gulf of Aqaba might be left hanging indefinitely.

Evron then mentioned the 1957 commitment given by Eisenhower to the Israelis, emphasizing that it had two parts: an American commitment to assert the right of free passage in the strait, and acknowledgment of Israel's right to act with force if the strait was closed. It was this second track he was now exploring, the former having been discussed with Eban. Among other things, he noted, it would be better for U.S.-Arab and U.S.-Soviet relations if Israel acted alone rather than relying on the United States to use force to open the strait.[60] This was a point that several American ambassadors in Arab countries had also made, and it was not lost on Rostow, who urged Johnson to "urgently consider" Evron's suggestion.

Johnson's reaction to Evron's ideas is unknown, although he reportedly discussed them with Rusk.[61] But the letter he sent to Eshkol the following day shows little hint of a new approach. Evron noted, however, that the letter did specifically refer to him and also contained the following sentence: "We have completely and fully exchanged views with General Amit."[62] Johnson, in fact, had inserted the sentence on Amit by himself after having received on June 2 a full memorandum from Helms of his talks with Amit, coupled with a warning that Israel was on the verge of striking.[63] Otherwise, the letter, a reply to Eshkol's message of May 30, largely repeated what Eban had already been told.[64]

Ambassador Harman had a last talk on June 2 with Secretary Rusk before departing for Israel. Rusk had little new to report. Efforts to gain adherents to the maritime declaration were continuing. The necessary multilateral context for action in the Gulf of Aqaba did not yet exist. The question of which side fired first would be extremely important, and Rusk cautioned Harman against Israeli action.[65]

That same caution, however, was not heard when Harman called on Fortas just before leaving for the airport. According to Fortas's law clerk, who overheard the comments, Fortas, who had spoken to the president earlier in the day, said to Harman: "Rusk will fiddle while Israel burns. If you are going to save yourselves, do it yourselves."[66]

The following day, June 3, it was announced in Cairo that Muhieddin would visit the United States for talks on June 7.[67] Rusk had informed Harman of the planned visit the day before. The Israelis were obviously irritated. Such a visit could only work to their disadvantage. In Israel, both Harman and Amit, who had returned together, reported to Eshkol that there was no chance of unilateral U.S. action or of successful multilateral action. The conclusion was inescapable: Israel was on its own. Amit judged that the United States could not object if Israel opened the blockade in its own way.[68] Sensing that time was running out, Rusk cabled ambassadors in the Arab world with the warning that Israel might act soon. He underscored the American commitment to the political independence and territorial integrity of all the nations of the area, reminded them of American commitments made to Israel in 1957 concerning the strait, and urged that they send in any ideas on how to avoid war.[69]

That same evening Johnson flew to New York for a Democratic party event that had apparently been much on his mind over the previous days. He referred to his "deep concern" about the situation in the Middle East but did not elaborate. While at dinner, Johnson was reportedly told that the Israelis had made the decision to go to war. Abe Feinberg, a prominent banker and fund-raiser for the Democratic party, leaned over and whispered in his ear: "Mr. President, it can't be held any longer. It's going to be within the next twenty-four hours."[70] Thus, it seems, the president learned war was imminent.

In the twenty-four hours, more or less, remaining before the Israeli attack, Johnson took no further action. He was not officially informed by the Israelis of their decision, but he had no reason to be surprised when he was awakened on the morning of June 5 with the news that war had begun. After all, he had taken steps to assure the Israelis that the "red light" of May 26 had turned yellow. Johnson, while far from instigating the Israelis to attack, seemed to feel he had nothing to offer them. The "yellow light," hinted at in his letter to Eshkol on June 3, and reiterated in remarks from Fortas and Goldberg, meant "be careful," and "don't count on the United States if you get into trouble." But, as for most motorists, the yellow light was tantamount to a green one.

War Breaks Out

The Middle East would never again be the same. A war that might have been avoided was soon to transform the politics and the map of the region. American policy toward the region was about to be radically overhauled. A conflict that Washington had tried to consign to the "icebox" for the past decade could no longer be so casually ignored.

The outbreak of war on June 5 created a profoundly changed situation for U.S. policymakers. The premises of the preceding three weeks were invalidated overnight, and new issues assumed priority. How would President Johnson cope with the urgent problems that now confronted him? Would he hold Israel responsible for preempting, or would he recognize there really was no alternative? Secretary of State Rusk had repeatedly told the Israelis that it would matter who opened fire, but Johnson had hinted that he did not share this view. What about the territorial integrity of all countries in the region, which the United States had pledged to uphold? Would that now apply to Arab countries that had lost land to Israel? Fundamentally, would U.S. policy aim for a return to something like the status quo ante, or would an effort be made to devise a different basis for Arab-Israeli relations in the future? In short, were the armistice agreements of 1949 now obsolete? And, if so, what would take their place?

Johnson never blamed the Israelis for starting the war, although he did express his "disappointment" that they had not taken his advice.[71] And in a meeting with his advisers on June 7, when Israeli success on the battlefield was clearly evident, Johnson expressed his pessimism about the war's solving deep-seated problems of the region.[72] His national security adviser, Walt Rostow, who talked to the president more frequently than did anyone else during the crisis, maintained years later that Johnson had firmly opposed the Israeli decision to go to war.[73]

If Johnson had genuinely had qualms about Israel's resort to force, why did he become such an ardent supporter of Israel once the fighting began? Was he responding to pressures from pro-Israeli opinion in the United States, or to his own sympathy for the Jewish state? Certainly his sympathies did play a part, as did the fact that he knew he had been unable to solve the crisis for the Israelis. Only an early American commitment to use force to reopen the Strait of Tiran could have stayed Israel's hand, and that was more than he had been prepared to contemplate. Perhaps his own bitter experience with Vietnam made him skeptical that military solutions could be found to complex political problems. Johnson had not quite given the Israelis a green light, but he had removed a veto on their actions. He had signaled that there would be no repeat of Suez. But what would there be? Would the United States underwrite Israel's occupation of sizable pieces of Arab land indefinitely? Would it seek an early political settlement? If so, on what terms? All these issues would soon have to be tackled. But once it had become clear that Israel had won an overwhelming victory, "there was a great sense of relief," because the United States would not have to get involved militarily.[74]

The United States quickly turned its attention to obtaining a cease-fire and ensuring that the Soviet Union would not intervene. The question of how the war had begun, which excited some interest in the early hours, was quickly overtaken by events.

Johnson was anxious to convey the impression that the United States was not involved in the fighting. This might help to minimize the danger to U.S. interests in the Arab world, reduce the likelihood of Soviet intervention, and facilitate a cease-fire. Here again the memory of the Suez crisis seemed to play a part. The United States did not want to be perceived in the Arab world as a co-conspirator with Israel, as Britain and France had been in 1956. Once hostilities were under way, the United States imposed an embargo on new arms agreements to all countries of the Middle East, including Israel. The embargo remained in force through the end of the year, despite urgent Israeli requests to lift it.

The first news of the fighting reached Johnson early on the morning of June 5. Three hours after the start of hostilities, Secretary Rusk, after consultations with the president, sent a message through normal channels to

Moscow expressing surprise at the outbreak of war and calling for an early end to the fighting.[75] At 7:47 a.m. Premier Kosygin replied over the "hot line"—the first use of this channel of communication in a crisis. He referred to the dangerous situation and the need for U.S.-Soviet cooperation in bringing about a cease-fire. Johnson's answer, sent by the hot line at 8:47 a.m., stated that both superpowers should stay out of the conflict and encourage a cease-fire. In all, twenty messages were exchanged over the hot line during the crisis.

The American position quickly became one of support for a cease-fire, but there was ambiguity about whether it would be linked to a provision for return to the prehostility borders. Restoration of the immediate status quo ante of June 4 was clearly ruled out, inasmuch as that would have kept the strait closed; but a withdrawal of Israeli forces in conjunction with a lifting of the blockade might have found support in Washington if the Soviets or the Arabs had pressed the issue on the first day.

By June 6, however, the United States had come out in favor of a simple cease-fire in place.[76] Kosygin had communicated with Johnson during the day on the need for a cease-fire coupled with Israeli withdrawal, but by the end of the day the Soviets had agreed to accept the American position. The Egyptians, however, rejected a cease-fire in place. By that time Johnson was not in a mood to help President Nasser, who that day had falsely accused the United States of directly participating in the air attacks against Egypt. The result of his charge was that six Arab states broke off diplomatic relations with Washington, all of which created considerable bitterness toward Nasser, even among the State Department Arabists.

Apart from denying Nasser's accusations and continuing to support a cease-fire, the United States did little on the next day of the war, June 7.[77] On the 8th, however, an American intelligence ship stationed off the Sinai coast, the USS *Liberty*, was attacked by unidentified aircraft and ships, which proved later to be Israeli. When news of the attack was flashed to Washington, Secretary of Defense McNamara and Johnson both feared that the Soviet Union might be responsible, and dark predictions of "World War III" were briefly heard in the White House situation room. The identity of the attackers was soon clarified, and Johnson informed Moscow by the hot line of the incident and the dispatch of aircraft from the Sixth Fleet to the scene of the attack.[78]

The incident shows the extraordinary degree to which Johnson was attuned to Soviet behavior once the war began. If during the May crisis he had been prepared to see the conflict primarily in terms of Arabs and Israelis, once hostilities were under way the main focus of his attention was the Soviet Union. With Israel secure from defeat by the Arabs, only Soviet behavior could trigger a direct American military response. The regional dispute paled in significance before the danger of superpower confrontation. The risk of Soviet intervention appeared once again before an effective cease-fire on all fronts went into effect on the sixth day, June 10. On the Syrian front, where fighting was particularly intense on June 9 and 10, the Israelis seemed capable of threatening Damascus. Although American officials were sure that Israel was on the verge of agreeing to a cease-fire once the Golan Heights had been secured, the Soviets were apparently less sanguine. At 8:48 a.m. on June 10, Washington time, Kosygin sent a hot-line message to Johnson warning that they would take necessary actions, "including military," if Israel did not stop its advance.[79] Johnson responded by assuring the Soviets that Israel was prepared to stop and by instructing McNamara to turn the Sixth Fleet toward the Syrian coast to make certain that the Soviet Union would not underestimate Johnson's determination to meet any Soviet military move with one of his own.[80]

By noon the crisis was nearly over, a cease-fire soon went into effect, and the Sixth Fleet stopped its eastward movement. The war was over. Once again, a new situation existed and new policies were called for.[81]

Postwar Diplomacy

Johnson and his advisers were mindful of how Eisenhower had dealt with the Israelis after the Suez War. They were determined not to adopt the same strategy of forcing Israel to withdraw from conquered territories in return for little in the way of Arab concessions.[82] This did not mean that the United States endorsed Israel's indefinite hold on the occupied territories, but rather that the territories should be exchanged for a genuine peace agreement, something that had been missing in the Middle East since Israel's creation. This would take time, obviously, but time seemed to be on Israel's side. And the Israelis had officially made it clear that they did not intend to enlarge their borders as a result of the war.[83] The need, as American officials saw it, was to establish such a framework for a peace settlement and then to allow time to pass until the Arabs were prepared to negotiate to recover their territories. Apart from helping to establish the diplomatic framework, the United States need only ensure that the military balance not shift against Israel. Such a change was not likely in the near future, however, because the Egyptian, Syrian, and Jordanian armed forces lay in ruins.

In brief, a major shift in U.S. policy took place in the days following the war. But there is no record that this change was accompanied by much debate or consideration of alternative courses of action. Instead, it was almost as if the president and his top aides just assumed that they could not go back to the old, failed policy. Quite possibly, the intensely pro-Israeli tone of public opinion, the views of Congress, the private lobbying of Johnson's many Jewish friends, and Nasser's unfounded accusations all played a part. Perhaps. But Johnson also had his own memories of Suez. He had opposed Eisenhower's policy of forcing Israel to withdraw from Suez without peace in return. He would not emulate Eisenhower now, not when Israel's moral and legal case seemed so much stronger than in 1956.

Johnson apparently did not believe the United States should launch a high-level, intensive peacemaking effort immediately. Either he considered that such a move could not succeed, given the minimal influence of the United States in Arab capitals, or he did not feel he could sustain such an effort at a time when Vietnam was demanding so much of his attention. In either event, the option seems never to have been seriously considered. Instead, Johnson suggested a general outline of a settlement in a major policy statement on June 19, on the eve of his meeting with Soviet premier Kosygin at Glassboro, New Jersey.[84]

In his June 19 statement, drafted in large measure by his special adviser McGeorge Bundy, Johnson clearly placed the major responsibility for the war on Egypt, terming the closure of the Strait of Tiran an "act of folly." He then stated that the United States would not press Israel to withdraw in the absence of peace. Five principles essential to such a peace were spelled out: the recognized right to national life, justice for the refugees, innocent maritime passage, limits on the arms race, and political independence and territorial integrity for all. In brief, Johnson contemplated a full settlement of all the issues stemming from 1947–49 and 1967.

In the course of the next five months, American diplomatic efforts were aimed at achieving a UN Security Council resolution that would incorporate Johnson's five points. The main areas of disagreement between Israel and the Arabs, as well as between the United States and the Soviet Union, rapidly emerged. The Arabs, on the one hand, insisted on full Israeli withdrawal from newly occupied territory prior to the end of belligerency. Israel, on the other hand, held out for direct negotiations and a "package settlement" in which withdrawal would occur only after the conclusion of a peace agreement. The Soviet Union generally backed the Arab position, whereas the United States agreed with Israel on the "package" approach, but was less insistent on direct negotiations.

As to the withdrawal of Israeli forces, the American position changed between June and November.[85] Initially the United States was prepared to support a Latin American draft resolution that called on Israel to "withdraw all its forces from all territories occupied by it as a result of the recent conflict." The resolution was defeated, as was a tentative joint U.S.-Soviet draft in mid-July that was never considered because of radical Arab objections to provisions calling for an end of war with Israel. In late August the Arab position hardened further at the Khartoum conference, where Nasser and King Hussein of Jordan, in return for subsidies from the oil-producing Arab countries, were obliged to subscribe to guidelines for a political settlement with Israel based on no recognition, no negotiations, no peace agreement, and no abandonment of Palestinian rights.[86]

When the UN debate resumed in late October, the United States position, in part because of Eban's persuasive efforts with Goldberg, had shifted to support for "withdrawal of armed forces from occupied territories." The ambiguity was intentional and represented the maximum that Israel was prepared to accept. Even with this change, however, the United States made it clear in an early October minute of understanding signed with the British that the text "referring to withdrawal must similarly be understood to mean withdrawal from occupied territories of the UAR, Jordan and Syria, the details to be worked out between the parties taking security into account."[87] Finally, on November 22, 1967, a British compromise, known as UN Resolution 242, was passed.[88] It incorporated all of Johnson's five points, along with a deliberately balanced call for "withdrawal of Israeli armed forces from territories occupied in the recent conflict" and "termination of all claims of belligerency and respect for and acknowledgement of the sovereignty, territorial integrity, and political independence of every state in the area and their right to live in peace within secure and recognized boundaries free from threats or acts of force." As a sop to the Arabs, the preambular language emphasized "the inadmissibility of the acquisition of territory by war." But in UN documents, preambular language has no binding effect, so Eban raised only perfunctory objections.

In brief, the resolution fell just short of calling on Israel to withdraw from all territories and on the Arabs to make "full peace" with Israel. Note that the Palestinians were nowhere referred to by name, an omission much remarked on in later years. But the United States did maintain from the outset that 242 did not mean that Israel should gain any significant amount of territory beyond the 1967 lines once peace was established.[89] Much of the diplomacy of the subsequent years revolved around efforts to make more precise and binding this deliberately vague wording. The resolution called for a UN-appointed representative to work with the parties to find a solution, a task that fell to Gunnar Jarring, Sweden's ambassador to Moscow, whose only Middle East experience was as a Turkic language specialist who had lived in Kashgar in the 1930s—a long way from the vicissitudes of the Arab-Israeli conflict.

During most of 1968 the Johnson administration assumed a comparatively low profile in Arab-Israeli diplomacy, leaving the main task to Jarring. In private, American officials consistently told the Israelis that a peace settlement would have to be based on virtually complete Israeli withdrawal, but in public nothing was said to modify the language of Resolution 242. Johnson was clearly preoccupied with Vietnam, especially after the Tet offensive in February, and in late March he announced his intention not to seek the presidency for another term, a decision that set off an intense political campaign within his own party and, after Hubert Humphrey's nomination, between the two parties. In this atmosphere major initiatives for peace in the Middle East could not be expected. Instead, Johnson acted to ensure that the post-1967 status quo would not be disrupted by Soviet arms shipments to Syria and Egypt. With a war on his hands in Vietnam, he was not anxious to see a resumption of fighting in the Middle East. In January 1968 he ended the American embargo on new arms shipments to the region.[90] Both Jordan and Israel were the beneficiaries, though on quite different scales.[91]

Johnson met with Prime Minister Eshkol in January 1968 to discuss Israeli arms requests. Topping the Israeli list was the high performance F-4 Phantom jet. Before 1967 the United States had not been a primary supplier of military equipment to Israel. The Israeli air force was of French origin, but France, because of Charles de Gaulle's Arab policy, was no longer a reliable arms supplier; hence the need for American arms.

Johnson reportedly assured Eshkol that Phantoms would be provided, but left unspecified the terms, timing, and possible conditions.[92] Within the bureaucracy many officials felt the United States should link the furnishing of F-4s to some concessions from Israel. Two possibilities were considered. First, to reverse Israel's growing appetite for territory, some felt that Israel should be asked to agree to the principle of full withdrawal in the context of peace in exchange for the jets. Others, fearful of Israeli nuclear development, argued that Israel should be required to sign the Nuclear Nonproliferation Treaty (NPT) before receiving U.S. arms.

The NPT issue was discussed at length with Israeli representatives. The most the Israelis would say was that they would not be the first ones to "introduce" nuclear weapons into the Middle East. In trying to clarify what this meant, U.S. officials discovered that Israeli ambassador Yitzhak Rabin understood it to mean that Israel would not be the first to "test" such weapons or to reveal their existence publicly.[93] Before the issue was ever resolved, Johnson ordered the bureaucracy to end the search for a quid pro quo on the F-4s. Pressure was mounting for an affirmative United States response to the Israeli request. Finally, on October 9 Johnson publicly announced that Israel would be allowed to purchase the Phantoms.[94] The two countries signed a deal for fifty F-4s in late December, providing for delivery of sixteen aircraft late in 1969 and the rest in 1970.

Perhaps in the hope of offsetting negative Arab reactions to the Phantom deal, Secretary of State Rusk, on his own initiative, informed the Egyptians on November 2 that the United States favored full Israeli withdrawal from Sinai as part of a peace settlement.[95] A year later, this position was publicly disclosed in the Rogers Plan, but in fact it had consistently been part of the American official consensus on the terms of an Israeli-Egyptian agreement. It did little, however, to win the confidence of the Israelis, and the last months of the Johnson administration were marked by a perceptible chill between the two countries.

In December, with the administration of Richard Nixon on the verge of taking office, the Soviet Union sent the United States a diplomatic note urging a more active search for an Arab-Israeli settlement. Britain and France were also pushing for a role in any Middle East peace talks. But time had run out on the Johnson presidency, and these issues would be passed on to Nixon, against a background of escalating violence and mounting guerrilla activity on the part of the Palestinian fedayeen.

Analyzing Johnson's Middle East Policy

The development of American policy before, during, and after the June 1967 Arab-Israeli war highlights the importance of a few key assumptions held by top decisionmakers, especially the president, at each stage of the crisis. The situation in the Middle East in May and June 1967 was extraordinarily complex. To make sense of the flow of events, decisionmakers needed some simplifying guidelines. They found them, not surprisingly, among the "lessons of the past" and the categorical inferences that had served well in other circumstances. An element of wishful thinking also existed. Together, several key principles provided a gyroscope of sorts for the decisionmaking process; order was perceived where it might have otherwise been missing. Little real discussion took place on these core assumptions:

—Prewar imperatives: do not commit American forces unilaterally, primarily because of Congress.

—Wartime policy: deter Soviet intervention; seek a cease-fire (but not a return to the status quo ante, which had been dangerous and unstable).

—Postwar policy: try for "full peace"; do not consider a Suez-like return to the status quo ante; insist that occupied territory will ultimately be traded for peace; keep Israel strong through arms shipments.

Several things about the decisionmaking process during the crisis are noteworthy. First is the obvious preeminence of the president. Crises, by their nature, bring the president to the center of the policymaking arena. His perceptions tend to define the situation for others; his needs tend to dominate the process. In May and June 1967 that meant a great sensitivity to congressional views, a desire not to become involved in another war, and a hope that time could be found to pursue the more cumbersome, but politically preferable, multilateral alternative. When this policy began to lose credibility, Johnson signaled his acquiescence to Israel's taking action on its own. When war began on June 5, it was primarily the president again who defined the stakes in the new game, as he did once more after the cease-fire went into effect on June 10.

Although Johnson's advisers did not completely agree on policy during the crisis, they nonetheless showed a remarkable degree of consensus. No one made a case for unilateral United States action; only a few voices were raised on behalf of "unleashing Israel"; little debate occurred over policy on a cease-fire in place as opposed to a cease-fire plus withdrawal; nor did anyone challenge the "package settlement" approach that emerged almost imperceptibly after the war. When divergent perceptions did appear, they seem to have been more deeply rooted in bureaucratic rivalries than in anything else.

Advisers did not split primarily along pro-Israeli or pro-Arab lines. In fact, it was hard to say what course of action might be most dangerous for American interests in the Arab world. Some American ambassadors in the Arab countries, sensing that war was inevitable, hoped that Israel would act quickly, but on a limited scale, to break the blockade without involving the United States. Such a view came close to being the "unleash Israel" option that the Israelis were seeking by late May. The State Department, however, normally thought to tilt toward the Arabs, did not favor this option, at least not at the policymaking level of Rusk and Rostow.

An important lesson of the crisis, and one often encountered in Middle Eastern policymaking, is that American policy choices rarely come to be seen in simple pro-Israeli or pro-Arab terms. Thus individuals, whatever their particular sympathies, may find themselves in support of policies that to the outside observer seem inconsistent with those sympathies. In a crisis, however, policy evolves in complex circumstances, is defined under presidential directive, and comes to be rationalized in terms of principles that are easily supported by high-level policymakers.

Outside the circle of the president's official advisers, however, there were people in his entourage who were very committed to Israel and very close to its leaders. Johnson spoke frequently with Justice Abe Fortas, quite possibly in the knowledge that Fortas could convey Johnson's real views to the Israelis.[96] The Israelis knew they had many friends around Johnson—U.S. Ambassador to the UN Arthur Goldberg, Fortas, Vice President Humphrey, Eugene and Walt Rostow, Arthur and Mathilde Krim, Abe Feinberg, and White House aides Joseph Califano, Harry McPherson, and John Roche, to mention just a few.[97]

What seems to have been missing from the policymaking process during the crisis was an explicit effort to relate policies to outcomes, as the rational decisionmaker is supposed to do. To a limited degree, of course, outcomes were discussed. But no one seems to have thought through the full implications of Israel's going to war, especially the problems this might cause in the long run. The future is indeed unknowable, but policymakers can be expected to consider consequences. They do so, however, in fairly simple ways. For example, Johnson gave serious consideration to the extremely low-probability event of Israel's being militarily defeated by the Arabs, to such an extent that it became one of the chief reasons for his effort to restrain Israel. He acknowledged the more likely outcome, predicted by the intelligence community, of rapid Israeli victory, but did not think through its consequences in detail. No one asked what Israel would do with Sinai, the West Bank, and the Golan Heights after the war was over. Would East Jerusalem ever be returned to Jordan once it had been conquered in war?[98] What would happen to the Palestinians on the West Bank? These were all important questions and came to be seen as such after 1967, but they paled in comparison with the overriding question of what would happen if Israel faced defeat.

Noteworthy by their unimportance during the crisis were the allegedly powerful pro-Israeli interest groups and the oil lobby. Johnson was sympathetic to Israel already and did not need to be reminded of the U.S. interest in supporting the Jewish state. He paid no attention to the formal pro-Israel lobby, but he was in constant touch with Americans who were friendly to Israel, some of whom were also key personalities in the Democratic party. His desire to keep the fund-raisers of the party in his camp, and not see them drift toward his nemesis, Robert Kennedy, may have had some impact on his thinking about the crisis.[99] During the crucial days of late May he spent many more hours in the close company of the Krims, for example, than he did with any of his top advisers. And we know from the official records that Mathilde Krim regularly passed messages, documents, and suggestions to him. To say the least, she had a strong pro-Israeli point of view.

More important, however, than the pro-Israeli personalities that surrounded him was Congress. This was the institution in which Johnson had spent most of his political life. And Congress did not want another open-ended unilateral commitment of American troops. More than any other single political fact, that seemed to weigh on Johnson and helped to turn this normally energetic and aggressive personality into a cautious, reluctant leader in this crisis.

Once the war had begun, and especially in its aftermath, the extremely pro-Israeli tone of American public opinion, coupled with Nasser's hostility, probably did make it easier for Johnson to adopt a policy of unquestioning support for Israel. Lobbying, however, was not a significant factor.

Oil was of only marginal significance to the formulation of policy. It was clear to some policymakers that any increase in Nasser's prestige would weaken the positions of the pro-Western oil-rich Arab countries, such as Saudi Arabia and Libya. Some officials also recognized that unilateral American use of force to open the strait could damage U.S. interests in the oil-producing Arab countries. And some feared that an oil embargo as part of an Arab-Israeli war might have dangerous consequences for NATO allies and Japan. But, on balance, oil was very much a secondary factor in presidential policy considerations in 1967.[100]

Finally, an important lesson of the policymaking process can be learned from the 1967 Arab-Israeli crisis: the initial definition of a situation tends to endure unless subjected to overwhelming evidence to the contrary from external sources. Between May 16 and the end of the month, Johnson and his key aides maintained essentially the same basic perceptions, adding details to a framework created in the initial stages of the crisis but not fundamentally altering policy. The president seems to have changed his views during his long weekend at the ranch at the end of May. At least the signals the Israelis began to receive started to change. But the evidence is not clear as to what, precisely, the president was thinking as the possibility of war became more and more real. The available record, however, is certainly consistent with the Israeli belief that the red light that had been switched on in mid-May had turned to yellow by early June.

When war did occur, a new definition was required and was quickly provided. Not surprisingly, the Soviet Union assumed a much greater salience once war had begun.[101] Then, with the cease-fire achieved, the third basic policy framework emerged, which emphasized the need to pursue a full peace agreement. This last policy was largely a reaction to the 1956–57 approach of pressing Israel for immediate withdrawal. The war of 1967 had shown that the Eisenhower decision had not brought peace; Johnson had opposed Eisenhower's pressure on Israel at the time, and now he had the chance to try an alternative approach. With little discussion and no apparent dissent, the United States found itself supporting Israel's hold on the newly conquered territories pending Arab willingness to make peace. Such is the power of the lessons of history that accumulate in the minds of presidents. "No repeat of Suez" may have seemed to President Johnson as plausible as "no more Munichs," but it would not be long before the dilemmas of the new policy became evident.

PART TWO

THE NIXON AND FORD PRESIDENCIES

3

Cross-Purposes: Nixon, Rogers, and Kissinger, 1969–72

RICHARD M. NIXON was, to say the least, an unusual president. By the time he resigned from office in disgrace on August 9, 1974, his domestic support had virtually disappeared. The Watergate scandal, exposed in exquisite detail by the press, Congress, and the tapes of the president's conversations, revealed a suspicious man in the White House who lied, who was vindictive, and who appeared to be strangely indecisive and incoherent when it came to dealing with important policy issues. Many Americans, as well as foreigners, had difficulty reconciling this image with that of the Richard Nixon who was overwhelmingly reelected in 1972 to a second term in office, a man whose achievements in the realm of foreign policy won him the grudging support of many former opponents.

These two faces of President Nixon were no doubt part of the same complex, unhappy personality, but it is Nixon as foreign-policy strategist who is of primary concern here. Nixon viewed his experience in international affairs as one of his strongest assets, and foreign relations as a particularly important arena for presidential action. As Eisenhower's vice president for eight years, Nixon had been on the margins of key foreign-policy decisions of the 1950s. He had earned a reputation as a tough-minded anticommunist and an advocate of a strong international role for the United States.

During his period of exile from elective politics, from 1961 through 1968, Nixon had traveled widely and had met many heads of state. By chance, he was in Morocco at the time of the June 1967 war. His cable to Secretary of State Dean Rusk gives a glimpse of his views, uncluttered by those of subsequent advisers, at that defining moment:

> I hope that with the outbreak of the Arab-Israel hostilities, our government will bring all possible influence to bear to have all major powers stand up to their responsibility for the maintenance of peace. Let us make it clear that the key to peace in the Middle East is now in Moscow and that peace efforts in the United Nations and multi-laterally up to this time have been blocked by the Soviet Union. I hope, too, that in considering our actions in this situation, we remember that while all Arabs have strong feelings on the subject of Israel, many are not in agreement with Nasser and his ambitions for the UAR [United Arab Republic] and leadership of the Arab world.
>
> My fear in the present circumstances is that unless we can demonstrate that our attachment to peace is impartial, we will have given the Soviet Union an unparalleled opportunity to extend its influence in the Arab world to the detriment of vastly important United States and free world interests.[1]

These trips to the Middle East must have made an impression on Nixon, for he spoke of them frequently in later years. In discussions of the region, he would refer to his talks with Israeli, Egyptian, and Saudi leaders, emphasizing his personal knowledge of key individuals and their countries. His experience in foreign affairs, such as it was, came largely through his own firsthand experience and discussions. He had little patience with academic studies or lengthy briefing materials. Nixon was very much a loner, rarely reaching out to others to discuss his views.

Unlike President Johnson, Nixon never betrayed a strong desire to immerse himself in the day-to-day flow of events and information. He prided himself instead on his detachment and his analytical ability to see problems in their broad strategic context. He admired strength and toughness and firmly believed that foreign policy should be formulated in secret, with only minimal contributions from Congress and public opinion. And Nixon boasted that he was not beholden to the pro-Israeli lobby, since relatively few Jews had voted for him.[2]

Nixon's Team

From the outset it was clear that President Nixon intended to make the basic decisions in foreign policy. To ensure his control of the vast foreign-policy bureaucracy—which he distrusted as being a bastion of the Democrats—he decided to reinvigorate the National Security Council system.[3] Nixon's NSC evolved substantially over the years, but at the beginning it was designed for two purposes: to provide the president with genuine policy alternatives, or options; and to educate the bureaucracy concerning the new themes in Nixon's foreign policy. Toward both these ends, Nixon requested an unprecedented number of policy studies in his first few months in office, mostly in the form of National Security Study Memoranda (NSSMs). These were to be discussed by a Senior Review Group (SRG),[4] then referred to the full NSC for decision, after which a National Security Decision Memorandum (NSDM) would be issued. Overseeing this elaborate system was a former Harvard professor, Henry A. Kissinger, Nixon's national security affairs adviser.

Kissinger was a well-known foreign-policy analyst. He first gained public recognition with the publication in 1957 of an influential book, *Nuclear Weapons and Foreign Policy*. Subsequently he became a consultant to both the Kennedy and Johnson administrations, but his closest ties were with his earliest patron, Nelson Rockefeller. Kissinger's acceptance of the national security affairs position was as unexpected as Nixon's offer. The two men seemed fundamentally different in temperament and character, but they quickly recognized in each other a remarkable intellectual compatibility. Nixon was instinctual and decisive; Kissinger was analytical and subtle. Nevertheless, they held similar views of the international role of the United States, of the need for strength wedded to diplomacy, of the intimate links between domestic and foreign policy, and of the danger of nuclear war.

Within a short time, the Nixon-Kissinger team was working smoothly, and Kissinger had ascended from the obscurity of the White House basement to a well-appointed office on the first floor of the west wing.[5] Nixon and Kissinger both had a keen sense for the symbols as well as the realities of power. Nonetheless, Nixon deliberately kept Kissinger from dominating Middle East policy during the first year and one-half, at least in part because of his Jewish origins.[6]

For the position of secretary of state, Nixon named a close personal friend, William P. Rogers, a lawyer by profession who had served as attorney general in Eisenhower's cabinet. He was not particularly experienced in foreign policy, nor was his a strong, assertive personality. He did, however, have an affable, reassuring style and a dignified bearing. Given the modest role that Nixon envisaged for him, these were perhaps enough. Nonetheless, Nixon decided to entrust Rogers with the Middle East dos-

sier, perhaps realizing that success there was unlikely and domestic controversy could be deflected toward the State Department rather than the
White House.[7]

The new assistant secretary of state for the Near East and South Asia
was a controversial figure. Joseph Sisco, formerly assistant secretary of
state for international organizations, was a Democrat and had never served
overseas in his long career in the State Department. His knowledge of the
Middle East came from his years in Washington. He was a consummate
bureaucratic politician; he knew the ins and the outs of the State Department; he was a man of drive, a skillful speaker, and a shrewd tactician.
Working closely with him was Alfred L. Atherton Jr., first as office director for Israel and Arab-Israeli affairs and later as deputy assistant secretary for the Near East. Atherton represented continuity, experience, and
professional expertise. He was cool when Sisco was hot. The two were a
formidable pair in Middle East policymaking circles.[8]

Nixon's Foreign Policy

President Nixon, with the assistance of Henry Kissinger and some parts of
the State Department, quickly established a set of priorities and guidelines
for American foreign policy. Some represented new departures; others reflected continuities and standard responses to long-standing problems.
Inevitably, Vietnam stood at the top of Nixon's agenda of foreign policy
issues. Domestic dissent over Vietnam had destroyed Lyndon Johnson's
chances for reelection and had produced a grave crisis of confidence and
of conscience within the United States. Nixon was no doubt less tempted
by the prospects of "victory" in Vietnam than Johnson had been, but at
the same time he was strongly opposed to a sudden withdrawal of American forces.[9]

Apart from Vietnam, Nixon and Kissinger were primarily concerned
with the other major powers, especially the Soviet Union. Both men were
preoccupied with the dangers of nuclear war; both were intrigued by the
possibility of establishing a new relationship with the Soviet Union that
would help to ensure global stability and to minimize the risks of confrontation; both were prepared to transcend the ideological rivalry of the cold
war and to establish ties with adversaries based on mutual interest.

Part of Nixon's strategy of restructuring the relations between the superpowers involved China. Little public notice was taken of China during
Nixon's first two years in office, but it is clear in retrospect that the president and Kissinger were already laying the groundwork for a dramatic

opening to Peking. Apart from the intrinsic benefits of restoring U.S.-Chinese relations after a generation of hostility, Nixon recognized that an American-Chinese connection could have a moderating effect on Soviet foreign policy. In addition, improved ties to Moscow and Peking might help bring about a Vietnam settlement and ensure that the post-Vietnam era in Asia would be comparatively free of conflict. Consequently, Vietnam, the Soviet Union, and China came to be linked as priority concerns to the Nixon administration. Significantly, each was managed almost exclusively from the White House, the president providing general guidance and Kissinger and his staff working on the details of the new policies and overseeing their implementation.

One priority area remained for the State Department to deal with: the Middle East. The Arab-Israeli conflict was generally seen as potentially dangerous, although hopelessly complex and perhaps less urgent than the other tasks facing the administration. Some momentum had already been established under Johnson, and around it a modified policy might be constructed. The State Department was anxious to play a leading role and was able to call on impressive expertise. Thus, with some skepticism about the likelihood of immediate results, Nixon authorized the State Department to develop and carry forward a new American policy toward the Arab-Israeli conflict. If it should succeed, there would be credit enough for everyone; if it were to fail, Nixon and Kissinger would be relatively free of blame.

Nixon's own views on the Middle East seemed to combine a strong inclination to confront the Soviets and an expressed belief that the United States could best compete with Moscow by being "impartial" in the Arab-Israeli conflict. The concern with the Soviets was similar to Kissinger's, but Nixon's "evenhandedness" was closer to the conventional State Department position. In short, Nixon embodied in his own mind the two competing paradigms for how best to tackle the Arab-Israeli conflict. What came to be seen as a great battle between Kissinger and Rogers was also, apparently, an unresolved debate within Nixon's own mind.[10]

By contrast, Kissinger had well-developed, if not well-informed, views on the Middle East. This was not a part of the world he knew well. His inclination was to look at issues in the Middle East in terms of the broader U.S.-Soviet rivalry. His views may have crystallized at the time of the Suez crisis, when he concluded that Eisenhower's policy of checking the British-French move against Nasser was misguided. One should not, he believed, weaken friends and help Soviet clients.[11] In terms of the realities of 1969, this led Kissinger to advocate strong backing for Israel until such time as the Arabs decided to break with Moscow.

A favorite Nixon-Kissinger concept was linkage. This meant that issues would not be negotiated with Moscow in isolation from one another. Rather, the United States in its talks with the Soviet Union would aim for a global settlement of issues. Progress should be made across the board on Vietnam, strategic-arms limitation, and the Middle East. Simultaneous negotiations in each of these areas would mean that trade-offs could be made, thus adding flexibility and nuance to the negotiations. A Soviet concession on Vietnam might be reciprocated by an American move in the Middle East. As an intellectual construct, it made sense; in practice, it rarely worked. Nevertheless, throughout 1969, linkage was one of the key concepts of the Nixon foreign policy.

"Negotiations" became another theme of the Nixon diplomacy. Nixon and Kissinger shared the view that force and diplomacy must go hand in hand, which meant that negotiation with adversaries was not incompatible with threats or the actual use of military might. Kissinger in particular was fascinated by the process of negotiations and proved to be an astonishingly successful negotiator in his own right. Soon after Nixon took office, negotiations on a wide range of issues—the Middle East, Vietnam, China, and strategic arms—were begun or accelerated.

The objective of the negotiations was to create, in the Nixon-Kissinger jargon, a "structure of peace," the main components of which would be U.S.-Soviet "détente," arms limitations, and eventually a normalization of U.S.-Chinese relations. All this was to be accomplished without detriment to traditional allies—the NATO partners and Japan—and without much regard for the third world, where détente would limit the dangers to global peace inherent in local conflicts.

To pursue such an ambitious foreign policy at a time of great popular disenchantment, President Nixon sought to meet the demand that America no longer play the role of world policeman, while at the same time avoiding the extreme of isolationism. This delicately balanced posture of restrained internationalism came to be known as the Nixon Doctrine, one manifestation of which was Vietnamization—the gradual disengagement of American combat troops from Vietnam coupled with high levels of aid to the Saigon regime and an active search for a political settlement.[12]

Nixon's great hope during his first term was that he would be able to recreate a domestic consensus on behalf of his foreign-policy goals. The style and timing of each major foreign-policy step were chosen with an eye toward domestic public opinion.

Nixon seemed to worry about the explosive potential of the Arab-Israeli conflict—he repeatedly used the pre–World War I Balkans analogy. Tempering Nixon's willingness to tackle the Arab-Israeli conflict, however, was the poisoned domestic political climate created by the Vietnam War. And Middle East diplomacy held little prospect of restoring the shattered domestic consensus. On the contrary, a serious effort to resolve the differences between Israel and its Arab neighbors was bound to be controversial. In addition, the president's key advisers were not in agreement on how to proceed. Public opinion was very pro-Israeli, still seeing the Jewish state as a heroic David facing a pro-Soviet, aggressive Arab Goliath. Nor was there a compelling strategic reason for tackling the Arab-Israeli conflict, since the oil issue was generally not seen as related, the Arabs were not believed to have a serious military option, and American interests therefore did not seem to be immediately at risk. With these perceptions in mind, it seems, Nixon was only prepared to allow the State Department to test the waters of Arab-Israeli diplomacy, and was reluctant to throw the full weight of his office behind an activist policy.

The Debate over Interests

Two sets of concerns dominated the thinking of policymakers in early 1969 as the administration undertook its first review of the situation in the Middle East. The president and Kissinger seemed to be chiefly worried by the global ramifications of the Arab-Israeli conflict. Nixon repeatedly used highly colored and explosive imagery in describing the area. Again and again the theme of confrontation between the superpowers was mentioned in discussions of the Middle East. This, it was said, was what made the Arab-Israeli conflict even more dangerous than Vietnam.[13]

The State Department professionals tended to agree that the situation in the Middle East was dangerous, but their perceptions were more affected by the prospective threats to American interests arising from trends within the area. At State, one heard of the "erosion" of American influence, the "deterioration" of the American position, the "radicalization" of the Arab world, and "polarization." The region was viewed in stark, sometimes simplistic terms: the United States, with Israel and the "moderate" Arabs, aligned against the Soviet Union and the "radical" Arabs.

The combination of these preoccupations led to several related policy guidelines that shaped the American approach to the Middle East from early 1969 until August 1970. Most important was the broad consensus, minus Kissinger, that the United States should adopt an active diplomatic role in promoting a political settlement based on the principles embodied in UN Resolution 242. The United States, in concert with the other major powers, and in particular the Soviet Union, should seek to engage the regional parties in a negotiating process, the first step of which would be a refinement of the principles of a settlement to be worked out in talks between the two superpowers. The hoped-for result would be considerably less than an imposed settlement, which the administration rejected, but would be something other than the directly negotiated peace agreement that the Israelis desired.[14]

The State Department had long advocated an "evenhanded" approach to the Arab-Israeli conflict. In essence, this meant adopting a posture that was neither overtly pro-Arab nor openly pro-Israeli. With respect to arms deliveries to Israel, the evenhanded approach urged restraint, and on territorial withdrawal it favored a clear statement opposing Israeli acquisition of territory from the 1967 war. As to the quality of the peace agreement, the standards to be applied to Arab commitments were not too rigorous. From the Israeli perspective, an "evenhanded" American policy was tantamount to being pro-Arab.

Fortunately for the Israelis, Kissinger was skeptical of the virtues of evenhandedness, and at an early date the Israelis began to bypass Rogers in favor of direct dealing with the White House. Kissinger, unlike Rogers and Sisco, believed a diplomatic stalemate in which Israel was kept strong would ultimately persuade the Arabs that it was pointless to rely on Soviet support. Then they would turn to the United States for assistance, the price for which would be a break with Moscow. The Arabs, in Kissinger's view, should not be given the impression they could count on both superpowers to pressure Israel to make concessions unless they were prepared to make far-reaching concessions of their own. Kissinger had little patience with the view that the Arabs would show more moderation if the United States took some distance from Israeli positions and acted with restraint on arms supplies to the Jewish state.[15]

The basic difference between State and Kissinger could be summed up fairly easily. State saw tensions in the Middle East as growing from regional conditions that the Soviets could exploit for their own advantage. To reduce Soviet options, State Department officials argued, the United States should try to resolve the underlying disputes. Kissinger was less sanguine about the prospects for resolving the regional conflicts, and in any case he believed it was Soviet involvement in the disputes that made them particularly dangerous. From his balance-of-power perspective, the first order of business was to reduce the Soviet role. Nixon, interestingly, seemed to agree with both schools of thought, depending on circumstances.

Policymaking

In January 1969 President Nixon expressed the view that the Middle East situation was potentially explosive. His thinking was best reflected in his answers to questions posed during a press conference on January 27, 1969, just one week after he took office:

> I believe we need new initiatives and new leadership on the part of the United States in order to cool off the situation in the Mideast. I consider it a powder keg, very explosive. It needs to be defused. I am open to any suggestions that may cool it off and reduce the possibility of another explosion, because the next explosion in the Mideast, I think, could involve very well a confrontation between the nuclear powers, which we want to avoid.[16]

On February 1 the National Security Council met for an exhaustive review of Middle East policy. Three alternatives, each discussed at length in NSSM 2, were considered:

—Leave the search for a settlement of the Arab-Israeli conflict to the parties and to Ambassador Jarring.

—Pursue a more active U.S. policy, involving U.S.-USSR talks.

—Assume that no settlement is possible and concentrate efforts on objectives short of a settlement.

The second alternative was decided on, the third remaining available as a fallback position in the event of failure. The NSC discussions identified several principles that should guide U.S. policy:

—The parties to the dispute must participate in the negotiations at some point in the process. Although the United States would not hesitate to move somewhat ahead of Israel, any final agreement would be reached only with Israel's participation and consent.

—The objective of a settlement would be a binding agreement, not necessarily in the form of a peace treaty, but involving some form of contractual commitments. The administration was concerned about the imbalance in the concessions to be sought from each side. The Israelis would give up territory; the Arabs would give promises to respect Israel's sovereignty.

—Withdrawal of Israeli forces should take place back to the international frontier between Israel and Egypt, with a special arrangement for Gaza. There should be Israeli evacuation of the West Bank of Jordan, with only minor border changes.

—Some critical areas should be demilitarized.

—Jordan should have a civilian and religious role within a unified city of Jerusalem.

—There should be a settlement of the refugee problem.

Issues of a guarantee to Israel and assurances of arms were also discussed. Then the NSC considered two possible diplomatic strategies. First, the United States could unilaterally present a peace plan. This was rejected. Second, the United States could follow a step-by-step approach whereby specific elements of a settlement would be gradually injected into the negotiations. It was recognized that withdrawal and the nature of the peace agreement would be the most critical issues. Primacy would be given to developing common ground in the U.S.-Soviet talks, with the aim of producing a joint document that could then be approved by the four powers—the United States, the Soviet Union, Britain, and France—and given to Ambassador Gunnar Jarring to present to the local parties.[17] For the rest of the year U.S. policy adhered closely to the guidelines laid down in February. The eventual result was the Rogers Plan.

Several simultaneous rounds of negotiations were soon under way. U.S.-Israeli meetings were frequent, as the administration tried to allay the apprehensions of the Israeli government, now headed by Prime Minister Golda Meir.[18] Once the U.S.-Soviet talks began in earnest, Israel was initially kept closely informed of the progress in the talks, although by the fall this pattern of consultations had weakened. Finally, the four-power talks proceeded simultaneously with the U.S.-Soviet ones.

The U.S.-Soviet talks, conducted primarily by Sisco and Soviet ambassador Anatoly Dobrynin, quickly took center stage. Between March 18 and April 22, they met nine times. The American objective in this round was to determine whether there was sufficient agreement on general principles to justify trying to reach a joint proposal. During this phase the United States spelled out its position on a settlement in a document presented to the participants in the four-power talks on March 24. The main points of this document were the following:

—Final borders would be agreed on by the parties. Minor adjustments in the 1967 lines were possible.

—There would be no imposed settlement.

—The four powers would work closely with and through Ambassador Jarring.

—A final agreement would take the form of a contract signed by all parties.

—Peace would be achieved as part of a package settlement.[19]

The last point, on the need for a package settlement, was of fundamental importance. It meant that there would be no Israeli withdrawal until all elements of a peace agreement on all fronts had been achieved. This stood in stark contrast to the insistence of the Soviets and the Arabs that Israel should withdraw first, after which an end to belligerency and other issues could be discussed.

During March and April the situation in the Middle East began to deteriorate significantly. Fighting broke out along the Suez Canal; fedayeen attacks mounted in severity, as did Israeli retaliation; and in early April Nasser announced the abrogation of the cease-fire, initiating what came to be known as the war of attrition.[20]

King Hussein met with Nixon and Rogers on April 8. The administration was sympathetic to Jordan but realized that the king was unable to move on a settlement without Nasser. To help Jordan, it would also be necessary to help Egypt. Hussein did bring with him a concession from Nasser that might smooth the path of U.S.-Egyptian relations. The king publicly declared that he was authorized to state that, as part of a settlement, there would be freedom of navigation in the Suez Canal for all nations.[21]

Several days later Nixon met with a top aide of Nasser, Mahmoud Fawzi, who confirmed this point and added privately that Egypt would not feel constrained by Syria's opposition to a political settlement. In short, Egypt and Jordan indicated they were prepared for a settlement, even if Syria was not. Kissinger, however, was not persuaded by Fawzi that Egypt was prepared for much real flexibility.[22]

A crucial debate within the American administration concerned the role of the Soviet Union. Some at State felt that the Soviet Union, for global-strategy reasons, would be prepared to cooperate with the United States in the Middle East, even if that might cause Moscow some strain in its relations with Nasser. In fact, it was privately hoped that the Soviets might weaken their position in Egypt by trying to force Nasser to accept the U.S.-Soviet proposals. Kissinger doubted that the Soviets would be prepared to sacrifice regional interests for the sake of improved U.S.-Soviet relations. He argued that the Soviet Union had worked hard to build a position of influence in the Middle East; to maintain that position, it depended chiefly on providing arms to key clients; and if peace was established, these arms would no longer be needed in large quantities. The Soviets therefore had an interest in preventing a real peace agreement, preferring instead a state of "controlled tension." From this perspective, the U.S.-Soviet talks had one purpose, as seen by Moscow and Cairo: to get the

United States to pressure Israel to withdraw from Arab territory in return for only minimal Arab concessions. Nixon appeared to be suspicious of the Soviets but felt they should be tested.

An early indication of Soviet intentions was provided by Soviet foreign minister Gromyko's trip to Cairo from June 10 to 13. The Soviets reported that they had persuaded Nasser to accept informal direct talks with the Israelis, patterned on the Rhodes armistice negotiations in 1949.

For the rest of the summer the positions of the superpowers remained essentially frozen,[23] but the situation in the Middle East did not. Fighting along the canal intensified; Israel informally approached the United States in July with a request for an additional 100 A-4 Skyhawks and 25 F-4 Phantoms to make up for the Mirages that France was refusing to sell.[24] Then, on September 1, one of the most conservative and pro-Western of the Arab governments, that of King Idris of Libya, was overthrown in a surprise coup d'état led by young Nasserist army officers. Coupled with the "radical" coup in Sudan the previous May, this seemed to confirm the fears of those who saw a trend toward extremism and violence in the Arab world in the absence of progress toward a peace agreement.

Early in September, the first F-4 Phantom jets (the furnishing of which President Johnson had agreed to in late 1968) reached Israel. They soon became a potent symbol to the Arabs of American support for Israel, and an intensive campaign began in the Arab world to prevent further such agreements.

Nixon met with Prime Minister Golda Meir on September 25. Meir treated Nixon as if he were a great friend of the Jewish people, and in return he indicated considerable sympathy for Israeli concerns. Meir requested additional arms—25 more F-4 Phantoms and 100 A-4 Skyhawks— as well as $200 million a year to help pay for them. Nixon's response was somewhat elliptical, suggesting that he would trade "hardware for software," which seemed to mean that arms supplies would be linked to political concessions.[25]

During Meir's visit Nixon also agreed that a direct channel of communications between the two leaders should be established, bypassing the State Department. Nixon was fond of using such back channels, and soon Henry Kissinger and Israel's ambassador, Yitzhak Rabin, were linked by a private phone line. Rabin used this improved access to the White House to argue forcefully that Israel should intensify its bombardments deep inside Egypt. Even if the State Department might be urging restraint, Rabin could argue that his sources were egging Israel on.[26]

Seemingly unaffected by Meir's visit, the State Department continued to press forward with its plan for reaching a common position on principles with the Soviet Union. Rogers asked for authority to reveal to the Soviets the fallback position on Israeli withdrawal to the international border. Nixon agreed, and on October 28 Sisco handed Dobrynin the final paragraph of a proposed joint document containing the U.S. fallback position on Israeli withdrawal. But, according to Kissinger, the president characteristically sought "to hedge his bets by asking John Mitchell and Leonard Garment—counselor to the President and adviser on Jewish affairs—to let Jewish community leaders know his doubts about State's diplomacy. Nixon implied strongly to them that he would see to it that nothing came of the very initiatives he was authorizing."[27]

The Rogers Plan and Its Reception

The Rogers Plan, as it came to be known, consisted of a short preamble calling for the conclusion of a "final and reciprocally binding accord" between Egypt and Israel, to be negotiated under the auspices of UN ambassador Jarring following procedures used at Rhodes in 1949, and to be based on ten points. The gist of the plan was:

—The state of war between Egypt and Israel would end, and a formal state of peace would be established.

—The agreement would include the establishment of demilitarized zones, the taking of effective measures in the Sharm al-Shaykh area to guarantee freedom of navigation in the Strait of Tiran, and arrangements for security and the final disposition of Gaza. Within this framework, "the former international boundary between Egypt and the mandated territory of Palestine would become the secure and recognized boundary between Israel and the UAR."

—In exercising sovereignty over the Suez Canal, Egypt would affirm the right of ships of all nations, including Israel, to pass freely through the canal without discrimination or interference.

—Egypt and Israel would agree to mutually respect and acknowledge each other's sovereignty, territorial integrity, and right to live in peace within secure and recognized borders.[28]

On November 10 both the United States and the Soviet Union presented the text of the plan to Egypt. Several days later, the Egyptian foreign minister sent a noncommittal reply to Rogers, noting some positive elements in the proposals, but holding off on a final commitment until an "integrated formula" for a comprehensive settlement was put forward. In brief, Egypt was not prepared to consider a bilateral deal with Israel even if it stood to recover all its territory.[29] After nearly a month with no further reply from Egypt and no official reaction from the Soviet Union, Secretary Rogers, on December 9, outlined the basic elements of the plan in a public speech.[30] The following day Israel rejected Rogers's proposals.

On December 18 the United States presented a parallel plan for a Jordan-Israel settlement to the four powers.[31] It was hoped that this would strengthen King Hussein at the Arab summit meeting that was to open in Rabat the following day. The plan contained many of the same points as the October 28 document, adding or modifying a few points to fit the special circumstances on the Jordanian front.[32] The permanent border, for example, would "approximate" the armistice demarcation line existing before the 1967 war but would allow for modifications based on "administrative or economic convenience." In addition, point four of the December 18 document stressed that Israel and Jordan would settle the problem of Jerusalem, recognizing that the city would be unified, with both countries sharing the civic and economic responsibilities of city government. Point eight provided guidelines for a settlement of the refugee problem that would allow for repatriation or resettlement with compensation. An annual quota of refugees to be repatriated would be agreed on between the parties.[33] King Hussein was reported to be pleased with the American proposal.

On December 22 the Israeli cabinet issued a statement saying that "Israel will not be sacrificed by any power or inter-power policy and will reject any attempt to impose a forced solution on her. . . . The proposal submitted by the USA cannot but be interpreted by the Arab rulers as an attempt to appease them at the expense of Israel."[34] As Rogers was deploring the Israeli use of the word "appease" the following day, the Soviets delivered an official note rejecting the Rogers proposals virtually in their entirety.[35]

The Israeli and Soviet rejections of the Rogers Plan, and Egypt's nonacceptance, put a sudden end to the first Middle East initiative of the Nixon administration. With it died the hope that "linkage" diplomacy would help provide the key to peace in that area. Not for the first time, a basic reassessment of policy toward the Arab-Israeli conflict was undertaken. And although the Rogers proposals remained the most explicit statement of a preferred American peace settlement, they ceased to be the operational basis for American policy toward the Arab-Israeli conflict.

Reassessment

The Rogers initiative of 1969 had clearly failed, at least for the time being. Apart from Jordan there were simply no takers, and the Israeli reaction in particular was extremely hostile. What had gone wrong? Most policymakers agreed in retrospect that it had been naive to assume that the United States would be able to separate the Soviet Union from Egypt during the process of negotiations. The justification for the two-power talks had been that the United States and the Soviet Union would find it easier to reach agreement on principles than would Israel and Egypt, and that they could both use their influence constructively to moderate the positions of their "clients." The concept fit nicely with Nixon's emphasis on "linkage," "détente," and "negotiations."

Even if the Soviets could have been persuaded to sign on to the Rogers Plan, it is not at all obvious that Israel could have been budged. Kissinger actively opposed the plan, and he had been signaling Rabin that Washington would welcome a more aggressive Israeli military campaign against Nasser. Unless Nixon had been prepared to back Rogers fully, and he apparently was not, the Israelis would not conceivably comply. The Rogers-Kissinger feud, and Nixon's own ambivalence, meant that the Rogers Plan never really had a chance of succeeding.

Domestic politics in the United States played a role. Kissinger and Nixon respected the strength of Israel's support in Congress and in public opinion generally. Kissinger also found it misguided and possibly dangerous for the United States to try to improve its relations with adversaries—the Soviet Union and Egypt—by pressuring its own friend, Israel. While such things might be done in the interest of achieving a genuine peace agreement, they should not become part of the standard American negotiating repertoire. The Soviets and Arabs should instead learn that U.S. influence with Israel was conditional on their restraint and moderation.

The lessons drawn from the failure of the Rogers Plan of 1969 were fairly obvious by early 1970. First, since it was impossible to separate the Soviet Union from Egypt, Washington would henceforth deal directly with Nasser when necessary, rather than through Moscow. Second, since American concessions had not been reciprocated, the next move would have to come from the Soviets or the Egyptians. No further unilateral U.S. concessions would be made. The United States and Israel could afford to sit tight until the "other side" had completed its own reassessment and concluded that a resumption of serious negotiations was needed. Third, any future American initiative would be less legalistic in tone, less public, and perhaps less ambitious. The package-settlement approach, though appealing in theory, was simply too complicated. Failure on one issue would prevent progress anywhere. More modest initiatives would henceforth be considered.

Two developments threatened this new consensus almost as rapidly as it emerged. First, the fighting in the Middle East escalated sharply during the spring of 1970, particularly with the introduction of Soviet SAM-3 surface-to-air missiles in Egypt, Israeli deep-penetration bombing attacks near Cairo, the dispatch of 10,000 or more Soviet advisers to Egypt, and the appearance of Soviet combat pilots flying air cover over the Egyptian heartland.[36] Second, the domestic pressures on the Nixon administration to abandon the Rogers Plan and to accede to an Israeli request for 100 A-4 and 25 F-4 jets mounted rapidly. With congressional elections on the horizon, members of both the House and the Senate became particularly vocal in support of Israel.

The administration now faced two urgent problems in the Arab-Israeli dispute. One was to take some type of political initiative to end the fighting and to begin talks on a settlement. The other was to respond to Israeli arms requests, especially as Soviet involvement in the conflict grew. A dilemma, however, was acutely perceived by State Department officials. To pursue a credible political initiative aimed at Nasser, the United States would have to appear to be evenhanded. This was particularly difficult at a time when American-made Phantom jets were bombing the outskirts of Cairo with impunity and the Israelis were virtually declaring that their goal was to topple the Nasser regime. At the same time the United States could not indefinitely stand by and watch Soviet arms and personnel flow into Egypt without some response. This need to respond had as much to do with global politics as with the Middle East. Kissinger was especially insistent on this latter point, and his influence with Nixon was on the rise. The somewhat schizophrenic nature of U.S. policy during the next seven months was rooted in this bureaucratic and conceptual dualism.

Resumption of Diplomacy and Arms for Israel

The first signs of a new tone in American Middle East policy after the abortive Rogers effort came in January 1970. President Nixon, in several public statements, tried to mend the U.S.-Israeli relationship and warn the Soviet Union about the consequences of its uncooperative policy in the area. In a press conference on January 30, Nixon surprised his staff and the Israelis by stating that he would announce his decision on Israel's pending arms requests within thirty days. The issue of arms to Israel had become particularly acute in the aftermath of the French decision to sell Libya more than 100 Mirage jets, some of which had originally been earmarked for Israel.

While Nixon was seeking to mend fences with the Israelis, President Nasser was seeking to accelerate the flow of arms and aid from the Soviet Union. Early in January the Israelis, finally taking the advice of their ambassador in Washington, had begun an intensified bombing campaign in Egypt's heartland, ostensibly designed to force Nasser to divert some of his forces from the sensitive canal area but also aimed at exposing his weakness to his own people.[37] In response, Nasser decided to make a secret visit to the Soviet capital. According to Egyptian sources, Nasser pleaded not only for an effective missile defense against the Israeli Phantoms but also for Soviet personnel and pilots to ensure that the system would operate effectively while Egyptians were being trained for the new equipment.[38] The Soviet reply was affirmative, and by March large quantities of arms and advisers were arriving in Egypt.

The stepped-up Soviet role in the conflict did not come as a total surprise in Washington. In a very frank letter to President Nixon dated January 31, Premier Kosygin had stated: "We would like to tell you in all frankness that if Israel continues its adventurism, to bomb the territory of the UAR and other Arab states, the Soviet Union will be forced to see to it that the Arab states have means at their disposal with the help of which due rebuff to the arrogant aggressor could be made."[39]

Kissinger forwarded Kosygin's letter to Nixon, with the notation that this was the first Soviet threat to the Nixon administration. Kissinger recommended a tough reply, which was forthcoming on February 4.[40] President Nixon rejected the Soviet effort to place the blame for the fighting on Israel alone and called for the prompt restoration of the cease-fire and an understanding on limitations of arms shipments into the area.

Faced with a tough Soviet stance, Nixon seemed to be leaning toward an early and positive decision on Israel's arms requests. The rest of the bureaucracy was generally opposed to the supply of more Phantom jets, arguing that Israeli military superiority was still unquestioned and that Soviet arms shipments were a response to Israel's reckless campaign of deep-penetration bombing using the Phantoms.[41]

In March, after several hints of moderation from the Soviets, Kissinger met with Rabin to signal the impending decision to hold in abeyance Israel's request for aircraft. At the same time he told Rabin that new supplies of aircraft would be forthcoming in due course, but that deliveries should not be accompanied by so much fanfare. Rabin then met with Nixon, who reiterated these points and left Rabin with the impression that Israel should consider attacking Egypt's newly deployed SAM-3 missiles.[42]

Finally, on March 23 Secretary Rogers announced that the president had decided to hold Israel's request for 100 A-4s and 25 F-4s in abeyance pending further developments in the area. As a consolation, economic credits of $100 million were offered.[43]

An Approach to Egypt

In an effort to build on the limited credibility with the Arabs generated by the decision on the Phantoms, the administration decided to send Joseph Sisco to Cairo for direct talks with Nasser. The Soviets had said that Nasser was prepared to make concessions; the Americans would try to find out for themselves. During his stay in Cairo from April 10 to 14, Sisco essentially invited Nasser to try dealing with the United States as an honest broker.[44] Although Nasser had little reason to hope for much from the United States, he was experiencing great losses in the continuing fighting with Israel, and his dependence on the Soviet Union was growing; perhaps a positive approach to the Americans would prevent new shipments of Phantoms to Israel. Nasser's reply to Sisco came in his May 1 speech, in which he invited the United States to take a new political initiative.[45]

The Sisco visit and the Nasser speech marked the turning point of one aspect of American diplomacy and led the State Department, during the following three months, to pursue an intensive effort to restore the cease-fire. A parallel, partly related, strand of policy involved both arms to Israel and the growing Soviet involvement in Egypt. The White House assumed control of this area. Nixon had denied that arms supply would be used as a form of leverage over Israel, but in the ensuing months that fiction was dropped.

The last half of April was a very important period in the Middle East and for American foreign policy generally. Within the region, riots in Jordan prevented Sisco from visiting Amman, and King Hussein requested the replacement of the American ambassador there. In Egypt, Soviet pilots were first noted flying combat patrols on April 18. Several days later President Nixon began planning for a bold, and very controversial, military move into Cambodia. The operation began on April 30; violence flared on university campuses; and several of Kissinger's closest aides resigned their positions. The atmosphere in Washington was extraordinarily tense. In the midst of it all, Nixon, long preoccupied by other issues, finally ordered a full investigation of the expanded Soviet role in Egypt.

On May 21 President Nixon met with Israeli foreign minister Abba Eban. The president assured Eban that the flow of military equipment to Israel would be quietly resumed, but he urged that no publicity be given to this. He gave no specific commitment on the A-4s and F-4s but made it clear that the jets that remained to be delivered from the December 1968 agreement would be delivered without conditions.[46] In return, Nixon asked for a public Israeli statement that would indicate a degree of flexibility on the terms of a settlement. This was forthcoming on May 26, when Prime Minister Meir formally announced that Israel continued to accept UN Resolution 242 as the basis for a settlement and would agree to something like the Rhodes formula for talks.[47]

The National Security Council met on June 10 and 18 to discuss the Middle East.[48] The president authorized Rogers in NSDM 62 to request the parties to agree to a cease-fire of at least three months' duration and renewed talks under Ambassador Jarring's auspices. This was done on June 19.[49] Rogers publicly revealed the initiative on June 25.

Israel's immediate reaction was to reject the appeal. Ambassador Rabin, however, refused to deliver the note of official rejection, and during the next month the White House devoted considerable energy to persuading the Israelis to accept the new initiatives.[50]

The first step in the campaign was to reassure the Israelis on continuing arms deliveries. This was done in a letter from Nixon to Golda Meir dated June 20. Next, Henry Kissinger was quoted on June 26 as saying: "We are trying to get a settlement in such a way that the moderate regimes are strengthened, and not the radical regimes. We are trying to expel the Soviet military presence, not so much the advisers, but the combat pilots and the combat personnel, before they become so firmly established."[51]

Although still holding back on new commitments on aircraft, the administration was now prepared to help Israel attack the SAMs with new, sophisticated equipment. On July 10 the president also ordered that the remaining A-4s and F-4s under the existing contract be shipped to Israel at an accelerated pace.[52]

President Nasser had left for Moscow on June 29, primarily for a health cure. While there, he discussed the American proposal with the Soviet leaders and reportedly informed them that he intended to accept it.[53] At a minimum, it would provide him a breathing space to complete the construction of the "missile wall." Accordingly, shortly after his return from Moscow, on July 22, Nasser accepted unconditionally the Rogers initiative of June 19.[54] On July 26 Jordan also accepted.[55]

The United States now had to bring about a positive Israeli response or risk the collapse of its Middle East diplomacy. President Nixon wrote to Prime Minister Meir on July 23, urging that Israel accept the proposal and making several important commitments. First, the United States would not insist that Israel agree to the Arab definition of UN Resolution 242. Second, Israel would not be forced to accept a refugee settlement that would fundamentally alter the Jewish character of the state or jeopardize its security. Third, and most important at the moment for the Israelis, Israel would not be asked to withdraw any of its troops from the occupied areas "until a binding contractual peace agreement satisfactory to you has been achieved." In addition, Nixon promised to continue the supply of arms to Israel.

In reply, Prime Minister Meir sought assurances that Israel would be allowed to purchase Shrike missiles and Phantom jets, that the Rogers Plan would be withdrawn, and that the United States would veto any anti-Israeli resolutions in the United Nations.[56] Israel received a commitment only on arms, but that was apparently enough for Meir to accept, with clear reservations, the American initiative on July 31.[57] The previous day Israeli pilots had downed four Soviet MiG-21s over Egypt.

On August 7 a three-month cease-fire, with a provision for a complete military standstill in a zone fifty kilometers wide on each side of the Suez Canal, went into effect. In the State Department the mood was one of elation. It was not to last for long.[58]

End of a Delicate Balance

Between January 1969 and August 1970 the Middle East policy of the Nixon administration passed through two stages. During the first year an apparent consensus existed that the State Department should take the lead in negotiating with the Soviet Union to produce a set of principles that would spell out in some detail the terms of an Arab-Israeli settlement. As part of this policy the administration adopted a restrained position on new arms agreements with Israel.

Two potentially divergent concepts underlay this policy. The first saw the Middle East as primarily an issue in global politics and was characteristic of Nixon and Kissinger. This view underscored the danger of superpower confrontation and the desirability of U.S.-Soviet talks. The second perspective stressed regional trends more than global "linkages." It emphasized that the American position in the Middle East was eroding and that radicalization of the area was inevitable in the absence of a peace agreement. As long as the Soviets seemed cooperative and the regional conflict remained within manageable limits, these two approaches were compatible with a single policy.

The second stage of policy toward the Middle East began with the failure of the Rogers Plan and the escalation of Soviet involvement in Egypt early in 1970. The shift in policy was the result of both developments in the Middle East and the growing influence on Middle East policy of Henry Kissinger, who all along had been critical of Rogers's handling of Middle East diplomacy.

The intensified fighting along the canal and the growing role of the Palestinian fedayeen in Jordan confirmed the worst fears of the State Department specialists. In their view the best way to reverse the trends was with a new diplomatic initiative, this time less ambitious in scope than the Rogers Plan and less dependent on Soviet cooperation. A simple "stop shooting, start talking" formulation was therefore proposed directly to each party on June 19.

The State and White House perspectives risked collision on one issue, namely, arms to Israel. New U.S.-Israeli arms agreements might lead Nasser to reject the American initiative and might provide the "radical" Arabs with strong arguments to use against the United States. Nixon recognized the danger and therefore dealt with the arms issue circumspectly.[59] Above all, he tried to ensure that arms for Israel would be coupled with Israeli acceptance of the new American initiative.

On August 7, as the cease-fire went into effect, it seemed as if both the State Department and the president could feel satisfied that their preferred policies had produced a successful outcome. Within days, however, the provisions of the cease-fire were being violated and a new crisis was in the making. The tenuous, delicate balance between the State Department and Kissinger, who opposed the cease-fire initiative, was also shattered.[60] By the time the next crisis was over, Kissinger had won Nixon to his side, and those in the State Department who had urged evenhandedness were virtually banished from center stage.

As the guns along the Suez Canal fell silent on August 7, 1970, a new phase of the Arab-Israeli conflict opened. The cease-fire, ironically, unleashed forces that quickly undermined the prospects for peace talks and instead led to a crisis of unprecedented danger for the Nixon administration.

During August and September Nixon and his national security adviser, Henry Kissinger, were increasingly preoccupied with the crisis in the Middle

East. They held a particularly stark view of Soviet intentions, and as they began to reshape American policy in the midst of the Jordanian civil war, the U.S.-Soviet perspective dominated their thinking. The result was a new definition of issues in the Middle East and a revised understanding of the political dynamics of the region, in which the U.S.-Israeli relationship came to be seen as the key to combating Soviet influence in the Arab world and attaining stability.

From the standpoint of the Nixon administration, the Jordan crisis was successfully handled: King Hussein remained in power; the militant fedayeen were crushed; U.S.-Israeli relations were strengthened; and the Soviet Union was forced to back down, reining in its Syrian clients under U.S.-Israeli pressure. Finally, Nasser's death, just as the crisis was ending, seemed to open the door to a more moderate Egyptian foreign policy. This image proved to be flawed in many respects, but for nearly three years it served as justification for an American policy aimed primarily at reducing Soviet influence in Egypt, mainly through a generous provision of U.S. arms to Israel.

The Hijackings

When Egypt, Jordan, and Israel agreed to a U.S.-sponsored cease-fire in late July 1970, a danger signal went out to the Palestinian fedayeen. From February 1970 on, the fedayeen had succeeded in undercutting King Hussein's authority to the point of virtually becoming a state within a state. Now their position was endangered, as President Nasser, their most prestigious backer, was apparently joining Hussein in a political settlement that could only be at their expense.

The fedayeen movement had reached a decisive crossroads in late August 1970, when it convened an emergency session of the National Council in Amman.[61] Some of the more radical groups called for the overthrow of the Hashemite monarchy, but Fatah, the mainstream movement, led by Yasir Arafat, continued to temporize. Before any consensus could emerge, however, the maverick Popular Front for the Liberation of Palestine (PFLP), led by George Habash, hijacked three commercial jetliners on September 6. On September 9 another plane was hijacked and flown to Dawson Field in the Jordanian desert.[62] Altogether, the PFLP held nearly five hundred hostages, many of whom were Americans.

The PFLP's announced objective was to force Israel to release fedayeen prisoners held in Israel. Beyond that, the PFLP sought to upstage other

Palestinian groups by appearing more militant than they were. Most dangerous of all, the PFLP sought to provoke a confrontation between Hussein and the fedayeen movement, with Iraq and Syria throwing their weight behind the Palestinians. Iraq had nearly twenty thousand troops in Jordan, and the Syrian army was just across the border, within an easy two-day march of Amman.

The United States had been concerned about Hussein's weakened position for some time. The situation in Lebanon was also worrisome. These two moderate Arab states might well be taken over by radicals, just as Nasser seemed ready to move toward a settlement with Israel. On June 17 a National Security Council meeting was held to discuss contingencies for U.S. military intervention if Lebanon or Jordan should be threatened. According to Kissinger, Nixon spoke to these possibilities: "Let us suppose late in the summer we get a request from Lebanon or Jordan for assistance. . . . There comes a time when the US is going to be tested as to its credibility in the area. The real question will be, will we act? Our action has to be considered in that light. We must be ready. . . . Is the question really a military one or is it our credibility as a power in that area?"[63]

Several days later the Washington Special Action Group (WSAG), a high-level committee of the National Security Council convened in times of crisis and chaired by Kissinger, met to plan for these Middle East contingencies. The conclusions were somber: without access to bases in the eastern Mediterranean, the United States would find it difficult to send a sizable ground force into the area. The Sixth Fleet could provide some air support if it was on station, but otherwise American military capabilities were not impressive. If a serious military option was required, Israel was far better placed to provide both ground forces and air cover, particularly on short notice, but that issue, of course, was politically sensitive.

No Arab regime would want to be rescued by Israel if there was any alternative. Hussein was a realist, however, and had gone so far as to query the United States early in August on the full range of available options, including Israeli intervention, if Iraqi troops were to move against him. At the end of the month, on August 31, the king informed the American embassy in Amman that he might soon have to take drastic measures against the fedayeen and hoped he could count on the United States.

When faced with the hijacking challenge, Hussein militarily played for time. His choices were not very attractive. If he did nothing, the Jordanian army might move on its own against the fedayeen, thus destroying his authority. If he acted, Syria or Iraq might intervene. Hussein knew his army could handle the fedayeen alone, but what about their friends? Hussein was therefore forced to look for possible support against outside intervention, and that meant the United States and Israel.

The initial American response to the hijackings was cautious. Rogers felt that nothing much could be done. Nixon, by contrast, wanted to use the crisis as a pretext to crush the fedayeen, and apparently went so far as to order that Palestinian strongholds be bombed. Secretary of Defense Melvin Laird reported that the weather was not suitable for such attacks, and Nixon did not raise the issue again. But at the outset of the crisis Nixon was much more prepared to use American force than to countenance Israeli intervention.[64] At a minimum, it might prove necessary to evacuate the several hundred Americans in Amman. Perhaps an opportunity to rescue the hostages—most were released in the early days of the crisis, but not all—would present itself. Looking a bit further ahead, Nixon could see the need for a strong show of American force in the eastern Mediterranean as a deterrent to Soviet, Syrian, or Iraqi moves.

Determined to take a tough stand, Nixon ordered a series of steadily escalating military moves as deliberate signals of intent and to provide a modest intervention capability if needed. On September 10 the 82d Airborne Division at Fort Bragg, North Carolina, was placed on semialert; six C-130 transport planes were also flown from Europe to Incirlik air base in Turkey, where they could be available for evacuation of Americans from Jordan. The following day units of the Sixth Fleet began to leave port as part of what the White House termed "routine precautions in such a situation for evacuation purposes." Four more C-130s, escorted by twenty-five F-4 jets, were flown to Turkey. That same day the fedayeen blew up the aircraft and moved the remaining fifty-four hostages in their hands, thirty-four of whom were Americans, to an undisclosed location.[65]

On September 15 King Hussein told the British, who then contacted the United States, that he was forming a military government with the intention of moving against the fedayeen. He indicated that he might need to call on the United States and others for help. When the news reached Washington, Kissinger quickly convened a meeting of the WSAG at 10:30 p.m. Further military moves were ordered. The aircraft carrier *Saratoga* would proceed to the eastern Mediterranean, where it would join the *Independence* off the Lebanese coast; airborne units in West Germany would be placed on semialert; additional C-130s would fly to Turkey. Despite these preparations, it was decided that the United States would not unilaterally try to rescue the hostages, but the administration was determined to try to keep King Hussein in power.[66]

Civil War in Jordan

With the outbreak of heavy fighting in Jordan between the army and the fedayeen on September 16 and 17, the United States suddenly faced a new set of dangers in the Middle East. At one extreme, the conflict in Jordan might ignite an Arab-Israeli war if Israel intervened directly. Egypt and the Soviet Union could then be drawn in, which might lead to a U.S.-Soviet confrontation, the fear that all along had haunted Nixon and Kissinger. Almost as dangerous would be Hussein's overthrow: a close friend of the United States would have been defeated by radical forces armed with Soviet weapons. Even if the Soviet Union was not directly involved, the symbolism of a fedayeen victory would work to Moscow's advantage.

Nixon clearly wanted Hussein to crush the fedayeen, but he also wanted the conflict contained within Jordan. The American role, as he and Kissinger saw it, was to encourage Hussein to act while restraining the Israelis from precipitate military moves. At the same time an American and Israeli show of force might help to deter the Syrians, Iraqis, and Soviets. The balance between restraint and belligerence would be difficult to establish; too much of either on the part of the United States or Israel could be counterproductive. Timing and a close monitoring of events on the ground were essential, and a high degree of coordination among Jordan, the United States, and Israel would be vital.

Nixon's first moves were to warn against outside intervention. At Kansas State University on September 16, he gave a tough law-and-order speech in which he denounced the fedayeen. He then flew to Chicago, where he met with Kissinger and Sisco for an update on the crisis. There were conflicting views in the intelligence community on the likelihood of Syrian or Iraqi intervention. On the whole, it was discounted as a possibility.

Nixon thought otherwise, however, and on September 17 he met twice with editors of Chicago newspapers to discuss the crisis in Jordan. The *Sun-Times* rushed to print that evening with a story summarizing Nixon's views. The United States was reportedly "prepared to intervene directly in the Jordanian war should Syria and Iraq enter the conflict and tip the military balance against Government forces loyal to Hussein."[67] Hussein's survival was judged by Nixon to be essential to the American peace-settlement effort. Israeli intervention against the fedayeen would be dangerous, and if Syria or Iraq were to enter the battle, the United States would have to intervene. Nixon reportedly also told the editors that it would not be such a bad thing if the Soviets believed he was capable of irrational or reckless action.[68] This was vintage Nixon—be tough; keep your opponents off balance; remain mysterious and unpredictable. With luck, no one would then test to see if you were bluffing.

Nixon and Meir met on September 18 for what the *New York Times* termed the most important talks between the United States and Israel in twenty-two years. Relations were judged to be at an "extraordinary low ebb" because of the quarrel over the cease-fire and restraint in providing arms.[69] The reality actually was less stark. Nixon's promise to give Israel's aid requests his "sympathetic attention" helped to set the stage for a remarkable improvement in the ties between the two countries during the next few days. In view of subsequent developments it seems odd that Nixon apparently did not discuss the possibility of intervention in the Jordan civil war with Meir. That was left to Rogers, Sisco, and Kissinger, for it still seemed a remote contingency. The king seemed to be gaining the upper hand in Jordan, and the Soviets were behaving themselves.

It was not until Saturday, September 19, that the first reports of a Syrian armored probe into Jordan reached Washington.[70] The Soviet Union was quick to warn against outside intervention in Jordan and joined President Nasser in a call for a cease-fire. The Soviet chargé in Washington, Yuli Vorontsov, informed the State Department that the Soviets were urging restraint on the Syrians and were themselves in no way involved in the attack. Kissinger relayed this news to Nixon at Camp David. Nixon was unimpressed and skeptical. Syria, a Soviet client, was sending tanks into Jordan. Could this really be done without the Soviets' at least giving their tacit blessing? More likely, Nixon believed, the Soviets were egging the Syrians on.[71] Whatever the truth, U.S. diplomatic and military moves would thenceforth be aimed at getting the Soviets to pressure the Syrians to withdraw their forces.

Crisis Management

Several military measures were ordered by Nixon in response to the Syrian intervention. In addition, U.S. diplomacy was engaged in two other vital tasks on September 20. First came King Hussein's urgent request for American help against the Syrians. The situation in Amman was under control, but in the north it was very threatening. Late in the evening in Jordan, King Hussein requested intervention by air and land from any quarter against the Syrian tanks.[72]

In Washington, the WSAG met at 7:00 p.m. to consider the king's extraordinary appeal. According to Kissinger, "A quick review of the pros and cons of American military intervention strengthened our conviction that our forces were best employed in holding the ring against Soviet interference with Israeli operations. To be effective unilaterally we would have to commit our entire strategic reserve; we would then be stretched to near the breaking point in two widely separated theaters and naked in the face of any new contingency. Our forces would have to go in without heavy equipment and with air support only from carriers."[73]

Nixon called Kissinger from the meeting at 7:50 p.m. and invited the other senior members of the WSAG to his office at 8:00 p.m. Shortly thereafter Kissinger's deputy, Alexander M. Haig Jr., received a call from the British ambassador with the news that the king was now requesting immediate air strikes. He also informed the WSAG that Irbid had fallen to Syrian troops.[74] Responding to these developments, the WSAG recommended placing the airborne brigade in Germany and the 82d Airborne on a higher-alert status and flying a reconnaissance plane from a carrier to Tel Aviv to pick up targeting information and to signal that American military action might be nearing.[75]

At about 9:30 p.m. Kissinger, joined by Sisco, went to see Nixon, who happened to be at the bowling alley in the Old Executive Office Building. Nixon approved the WSAG recommendations and agreed it was important to establish contact with Ambassador Rabin.

Golda Meir and Rabin were in New York at that moment at a fundraising dinner. At 10:00 p.m. Kissinger managed to reach Rabin by phone. He told Rabin that the king had asked for assistance, but the United States urgently needed intelligence on Syrian positions before it could respond. Could Israel fly reconnaissance as soon as the sun was up? Rabin asked if the U.S. favored an Israeli air strike. Kissinger said he first wanted to see the results of the reconnaissance. At this point, according to Kissinger, a new message arrived from King Hussein, and he broke off the conversation.[76]

The king's new message spoke of a rapidly deteriorating situation and an urgent need for air strikes. Ground troops might also be needed. Kissinger spoke with Rogers, and both decided to recommend to Nixon that the United States endorse an Israeli air strike. Sisco and Kissinger returned to the bowling alley to seek the president's approval, which was forthcoming. Kissinger again called Rabin, this time informing him that the United States would look favorably on an Israeli air attack if Israeli reconnaissance confirmed that Syria was in control of Irbid with large armored forces.[77] Before midnight Rabin called back with Golda Meir's response. Israel would fly reconnaissance at daybreak. Air operations might not be sufficient, but Israel would take no further action without consultations.

Early on September 21 Rabin contacted the White House to say that Israel did not believe air strikes alone would suffice. Ground action might also be needed. Kissinger called Nixon, and, after a short period of deliberation, Nixon dictated a message to Rabin. According to Kissinger, he said: "I have decided it. Don't ask anybody else. Tell him 'Go.'"[78] Kissinger then consulted with Rogers and Laird, who had reservations. Nixon reluctantly agreed to convene a full meeting of the NSC at 8:45 a.m. Present were Laird, Rogers, Packard, Thomas Moorer (chairman of the joint chiefs), and Kissinger. Moorer was opposed to U.S. ground intervention because the capability simply was not there. Hence if ground action was needed, Israel would have to act. Intelligence estimates from Israel claimed that 250 to 300 Syrian tanks were in the Irbid area.[79] Nixon finally decided that Sisco should tell Rabin that the United States agreed to Israeli ground action in principle, subject to determining the king's view and prior consultation.[80]

As events unfolded, the Israelis developed a plan for sending 200 Israeli tanks toward Irbid, combined with air strikes. Israel would guarantee that its forces would be withdrawn from Jordan once the military operation was over. Kissinger and Sisco relayed to Rabin the king's preference for Israeli ground action inside Syria, not Jordan. Such action was considerably more risky for the Israelis and might provoke an Egyptian military response along the canal, or even Soviet threats to intervene. Rabin therefore sought an American commitment to prevent Soviet intervention against Israel, as well as a promise of aid if Egypt attacked.

The next day, Tuesday, September 22, was decisive. Israel, with U.S. encouragement but no binding agreement, was poised to act. Hussein, with the assurance that Israel and the United States were behind him, finally ordered his own small air force to attack the Syrian tanks around Irbid, which it did with satisfactory results.[81] By afternoon Syrian tanks were beginning to withdraw from Jordan. The need for Israeli intervention was less urgent. The king, speaking in code, informed Ambassador Brown that Israeli intervention was all right "up high" but should be directed elsewhere "down below."[82] An Israeli air strike would still be welcome, but land intervention should be only against Syria. Israel did not wish to undertake ground action in Syria, and by the end of the day the prospects for Israeli or American intervention had virtually passed.[83]

By Wednesday the acute phase of the Jordan crisis had passed. Shortly after noon Nixon met with Rogers and Kissinger in the Oval Office. While discussing the crisis, they received the news that all Syrian tanks had left Jordan. A statement was soon released from the White House welcoming the Syrian withdrawal, and Sisco was asked to contact Rabin to obtain his assurance that Israel would make no military move.[84] The Jordanians had the situation under control and no longer wanted outside intervention. For the United States and Israel, the crisis was over. Nixon celebrated on Thursday by playing golf at Burning Tree Country Club with Rogers, Attorney General John N. Mitchell, and AFL-CIO president George Meany. The following day a cease-fire was announced in Jordan.

Meanwhile President Nasser of Egypt was trying to arrange a stable cease-fire and a new modus vivendi between Jordan and the PLO. Nasser had differed with the fedayeen in their opposition to the Rogers initiative and in their desire to bring down King Hussein, but he did not want to see the PLO crushed by Hussein's troops. He therefore summoned Hussein, Arafat, and other Arab leaders to Cairo to work out an agreement that would govern the PLO presence in Jordan and prevent further clashes. The agreement was signed on September 27. The following day, while seeing off his last guests at the airport, President Nasser fell ill. He returned home, where, several hours later, he died of a heart attack. With Nasser's death, an era in Arab politics came to an end. By chance, it coincided with the beginning of a new U.S.-Israeli strategic relationship.

The Aftermath

The outcome of the Jordan crisis was widely considered a successful result of American policy. Certainly Nixon and Kissinger portrayed it as such, and in terms of declared American objectives the claim seemed justified. King Hussein was securely in power. The fedayeen had been badly weakened, and the hostages had all been rescued. The Syrian military intervention had been turned back by Jordan without Israeli or American involvement. The Soviet Union had refrained from direct intervention once the United States made a strong show of force. And U.S.-Israeli relations were stronger than ever. The outcome of the crisis being consistent with U.S. goals, few bothered to consider the extent to which American or Israeli actions were responsible for these developments, nor were the premises of American policy closely examined. Apparently successful policies are spared the type of critical scrutiny reserved for failures.

U.S.-Israeli relations, which had reached a low point in mid-1970, were quickly brought to an unprecedentedly high level by the Jordan crisis. There had been a long-standing debate within the bureaucracy concerning policy toward Israel. The conventional wisdom, especially in the State Department, was that American support for Israel was an impediment to

U.S.-Arab relations. By granting economic and military aid to the enemy of the Arabs, the United States was providing the Soviet Union with an opportunity to extend its influence in the Middle East. Although few questioned that Israel's existence should be defended by the United States in an extreme case, many felt that an "evenhanded" policy, whereby the United States would not always align itself with Israel and would not become its primary arms supplier, was the best guarantee of U.S. interests in the region. In this view Israel was more of an embarrassment for U.S. policy than a strategic asset. Even if Israel was an impressive military power, that power could be used only to defend Israel, not to advance American interests elsewhere in the region.

Israelis have generally resented the idea that American support is rooted primarily in domestic politics or in some vaguely felt moral commitment. They reject the reasoning of the proponents of "evenhandedness," who regard Israel as a burden on U.S. diplomacy in the Middle East. Particularly after the spectacular military victory of June 1967, Israelis began to argue that a strong Israel was in America's strategic interest.

The aftermath of the Jordan crisis constituted a momentary period of comparative stability. The cease-fire remained in force on all fronts. King Hussein successfully reestablished his authority in Jordan, from which the remnants of the fedayeen were expelled in July 1971. U.S.-Jordanian relations flourished, resulting in substantial levels of economic and military aid. Jordan came to be treated as a regional partner of the United States. Jordan's special task on behalf of American interests, in King Hussein's view, would be to promote stability in the small oil-producing Arab states of the Persian Gulf after the British departure at the end of 1971.[85] Nixon and Kissinger gave the king some encouragement and boosted aid to Jordan accordingly. In true Nixon-doctrine style, Israel, Jordan, and Iran were emerging in official Washington's view as regional peacekeepers. Aid and arms to these U.S. partners would serve as a substitute for a costly American military presence in the region or unpopular military intervention.

Elsewhere in the Middle East, post–Jordan crisis trends also seemed favorable. In Syria the faction of the Baath party most closely associated with the intervention in Jordan was ousted by General Hafiz al-Asad in November 1970. Syria's new leaders were reportedly more moderate, or at least more cautious, than the former regime. Sadat was also viewed in Washington as a considerable improvement over Nasser. Sadat, at any rate, had less prestige in the Arab world than Nasser had possessed, and therefore less troublemaking potential. Perhaps he would turn to Egypt's domestic problems instead of promoting revolution elsewhere. This had long been the hope of American policymakers and had served as a major justification for aid programs to Egypt in the early 1960s.

Lessons Learned

The net effect of the regional developments growing out of the Jordan crisis was to breed a sense of complacency in Israel and the United States. The fears of radicalization, polarization, and confrontation that had haunted policymakers from 1967 to 1970 all but disappeared after September 1970. Now the region seemed to be relatively stable, and the key to this stability was a military balance that unquestionably favored Israel. The chief remaining threat came from the continuing Soviet military presence in Egypt and Syria. It thus became a prime objective of U.S.-Israeli policy to demonstrate to Sadat that the Soviet military presence in his country was an obstacle to his recovering Sinai. Soviet arms to Egypt would be matched by American arms to Israel, thus ruling out Sadat's military option. And as long as a Soviet military presence remained in Egypt, the United States would make only half-hearted diplomatic attempts to promote a settlement.

In retrospect, one can see that American policy became a captive of the perceived success in handling the Jordan crisis. The global dimension of the conflict was virtually all that Nixon and Kissinger seemed to care about. By ignoring regional trends, they misjudged the very forces that would within three years lead to a much more dangerous outbreak of war. During the interval the State Department launched several ineffectual diplomatic efforts, but Nixon and Kissinger, having taken charge of Middle East policy during the Jordan crisis, were reluctant to relinquish authority to Rogers and Sisco. The result was a series of half-hearted State Department initiatives, lacking White House support, that simply raised the level of Arab frustrations while reinforcing the sense of complacency felt in Israel and in Washington.

Several important opportunities to pursue a political settlement of the conflict may have been missed during this period. Caught in a perceptual trap largely of their own making, Nixon and Kissinger failed to notice them. The period of "standstill diplomacy" from 1970 to 1973 will not go down in the annals of American foreign policy as one of the more enlightened. In many ways the success in Jordan in 1970 resulted in a series of failures in the succeeding years, culminating in the October 1973 war.

Kissinger's Standstill Diplomacy

With the continuation of a cease-fire along the Suez Canal, the restoration of King Hussein's authority in Jordan, and the death of Egyptian president Nasser, the situation in the Middle East appeared to American policymakers to be less dangerous and more manageable than at any time since the 1967 war. The danger of U.S.-Soviet confrontation had passed. U.S. interests had survived intact through a difficult period, and less urgency was now attached to new American diplomatic initiatives.

Before the Jordan crisis the State Department had been primarily responsible for the formulation and conduct of policy toward the Arab-Israeli conflict. Thereafter Nixon and Kissinger were to play a more important role, chiefly through their emphasis on the Soviet dimension of the regional conflict and their desire for a close relationship with Israel. Over the next three years the White House refrained from day-to-day involvement in Middle East diplomacy but kept a careful eye on the State Department to ensure against excessive activism. Ultimately Nixon and Kissinger succeeded in undermining State Department initiatives and in establishing almost complete control over policy toward the Middle East.

To understand this uninspiring chapter in American diplomacy between the Jordan crisis and the October 1973 war, one must recall the administration's intense preoccupation with other parts of the world. It was with relief that policymakers turned away from the Middle East to areas of higher priority. The Vietnam War was still raging, but in May 1971 Kissinger began a series of secret talks with top-level North Vietnamese representatives to try to reach a negotiated settlement. In parallel to these important talks, Nixon and Kissinger were planning a momentous opening toward Peking, symbolized by Kissinger's secret trip to China in July 1971. Finally, serious negotiations with the Soviet Union on limiting strategic armaments were under way.

Each of those three areas was so handled that in 1972, the presidential election year, Nixon would be able to point to visible achievements—visits to Peking and Moscow, and, it was hoped, an end to the war in Vietnam. The same election-year imperatives dictated a very low profile in the Middle East.[86] In the absence of any chance for a negotiated agreement there, Nixon focused instead on maintaining the military balance in Israel's favor, thereby preventing an unwelcome outbreak of fighting and no doubt earning the gratitude of Israel's many supporters in the United States.

The Jarring Talks and U.S.-Israeli Relations

During the post–Jordan crisis policy reviews on the Middle East, American officials considered several alternative approaches, including one dealing more directly with the Palestinians, before deciding to resume the interrupted Rogers initiative of the preceding June.[87] This time, however, the U.S.-Israeli relationship would remain close. Kissinger, in particular, felt that if Israel was ever going to make concessions, it would be from a position of strength and self-confidence, not under American pressure.

The first step in the new American initiative was to bring Israel back into the Jarring talks and to extend the cease-fire beyond its expiration in early November. On October 15 Nixon approved an arms package of $90 million for Israel, consisting of antitank weapons, reconnaissance aircraft, and other minor items.[88] In addition, the administration decided to seek a $500 million supplemental appropriation for Israel in the current fiscal year to cover arms expenditures.[89] Israel was particularly anxious to receive a guarantee for the supply of high-performance aircraft in 1971 and had requested 54 F-4s and 120 A-4s. The Israelis were also beginning to press for long-term military agreements that would prevent the periodic supply disruptions and quarrels that had marked the previous two years.

Despite the American decision to send substantial quantities of arms to Israel, Egypt's new president, Anwar al-Sadat, agreed to a three-month extension of the cease-fire in early November. During this period he expected the Jarring talks to resume and to produce results. Egypt and the Soviet Union also began to show interest in outside guarantees as part of a peace settlement.

After a number of tense exchanges between Nixon and Meir, on December 28 Meir announced that Israel would also return to the Jarring talks. According to Meir, the United States had made commitments to preserve the balance of power in the Middle East. Israel would be allowed to negotiate freely, without fear that the United States would be a party to any UN effort to determine borders or the terms of a refugee settlement. The United States, she claimed, upheld the principle that Israel should have defensible borders, that Israel should be strong, that Israel should not be forced to withdraw to the June 4, 1967, lines, and that Israel would not be obliged to accept the Arab version of a refugee settlement. Furthermore, the conflict must be ended by a binding, contractual commitment to peace. Until that was achieved, not a single Israeli soldier would be expected to withdraw from the cease-fire lines. And finally, Jarring's terms of reference should not be altered.[90]

The Egyptian Reaction

While Nixon's exchanges with the Israelis were going on, Nixon and Rogers had been in contact with Sadat as well. Sadat had sent Nixon a letter dated November 23, which reached him on December 14, indicating Egypt's interest in the Jarring talks. Nixon had replied orally through Mahmoud Fawzi on December 22, and Sadat sent word two days later through Donald Bergus, the American minister in Cairo, that he was genuinely interested in peace. Sadat, who had originally been viewed as something of a lightweight by Washington officials, was beginning to be taken more seriously.[91]

Rogers had been in contact with the Egyptian foreign minister, Mahmoud Riad, earlier in the month. The Egyptians were clearly more interested in knowing what role the United States was prepared to play and what type of settlement it envisaged than they were in receiving Israeli proposals through Jarring. They had long believed that Israel was little more than an extension of the United States, so that if Washington favored full Israeli withdrawal, Israel would have to comply.

On January 27 Rogers sent Riad an oral message through Bergus. He appealed for an extension of the cease-fire, promising that Israel would submit new "substantive ideas" for a peace settlement immediately thereafter. Rogers confirmed that the views he had expressed in his December 9, 1969, speech were still valid and that the United States was prepared to make an "all out effort to help the parties reach a settlement this year."

With these assurances in hand, Sadat announced on February 4 that he would agree to a one-month extension of the cease-fire. Although he castigated the United States for its "full alignment with Israel," Sadat nonetheless presented a "new Egyptian initiative, compliance with which we shall consider as a true yardstick of the desire to implement the UN Security Council resolution." He went on to say:

> We demand that during the period when we refrain from opening fire that a partial withdrawal of the Israeli forces on the east bank of the Suez Canal be achieved as the first stage of a timetable which will be prepared later to implement the other provisions of the Security Council resolution. If this is achieved within this period, we shall be prepared to begin immediately to clear the Suez Canal and re-open it to international navigation to serve the world economy. We

believe that by this initiative, we shall be turning envoy Jarring's efforts from ambiguous words into definite measures.[92]

In fact, Sadat's initiative was soon to supersede Jarring's mission, but not before Jarring had made one last effort. On February 8 Jarring presented a memorandum to Egypt and Israel in which he asked both parties for "parallel and simultaneous commitments." Israel was asked to agree in principle to withdraw to the former international boundary between Egypt and the British mandate of Palestine, subject to practical security arrangements and freedom of navigation in the Suez Canal and the Strait of Tiran. Egypt was asked to enter into a peace agreement with Israel, including an end to belligerency, respect for Israel's independence and right to live in peace within secure and recognized boundaries, and noninterference in Israel's domestic affairs.

On February 15 Egypt replied, accepting all of Jarring's points and adding a number of others. Israel's reply was not forthcoming until February 26. Israel welcomed Egypt's unprecedented expression of readiness to enter into a peace agreement with Israel, but on the crucial issue of withdrawal the reply was blunt: "Israel will not withdraw to the pre–June 5, 1967, lines." Instead, Israel offered to negotiate without prior conditions. Egypt, however, viewed Israel's refusal to accept the principle of full withdrawal as an unacceptable prior condition. Under these circumstances the Jarring talks came to an abrupt end.[93]

The Interim Canal Agreement Initiative

As Jarring was making his last effort to get the parties to agree to the outlines of an overall settlement, an alternative approach based on a partial agreement involving the Suez Canal was gaining increasing attention. Thus the collapse of the Jarring talks did not leave the diplomatic field empty. In fact, the idea of an "interim agreement," which had been in the wings for some time, was now to move to center stage.

As soon as Sadat had announced his initiative, the Israelis were urged by Washington to take his proposal seriously. Egypt was pressing for a rapid reply. On February 9 Golda Meir stated that Israel was prepared to consider the idea of reopening the canal but that Israeli troops would not withdraw from the existing cease-fire lines until an overall settlement had been reached. Three days later Israel asked the United States to convey a message to Egypt reiterating Israel's interest in discussing the reopening of the canal. This message was sent on February 14.

After a secret two-day trip to Moscow on March 1 and 2, Sadat sent Nixon a long letter on March 5. In it he set forward his reasons for not renewing the cease-fire on its expiration two days later. More important, he appealed to Nixon to launch an initiative to bring about an interim agreement along the lines of his February 4 speech. Nixon took Sadat's bid seriously, and the State Department was instructed to begin work on the interim canal settlement idea.

As the American initiative began to get under way, the Israelis complained that arms agreements were being delayed as a form of pressure.[94] Reacting to questions about Israel's peace map, Prime Minister Meir publicly stated on March 13 that Israel must retain Sharm al-Shaykh and an access road to it, that Sinai must be demilitarized, that the border around Eilat must be changed, that the Egyptians must not return to Gaza, that the Golan Heights would remain under Israeli control, that Jerusalem must remain united, and that border changes on the West Bank would be necessary.[95]

As these exchanges suggest, it was difficult to keep the diplomacy focused on a limited, partial agreement involving the Suez Canal and a thinning out of forces. Both sides wanted to know the other's position on broader issues, and when those were disclosed, the gap was enormous, especially on the issue of territory.

In an effort to get the talks back to the issue of the Suez Canal and a partial agreement, the United States encouraged the Israelis to set forth their position in writing. As an inducement, it was announced on April 19 that twelve more F-4s would be sent to Israel.[96] That same day Israel offered a proposal containing the following terms:

—After the reopening of the canal, Israeli ships and cargoes should be allowed through.

—A cease-fire of unlimited duration should be part of any future agreement.

—Israel would retain control of the Bar Lev line along the canal.

—Egypt would thin out its forces to the west of the canal.

—The line of withdrawal established in the interim agreement would not be considered a final border.

In addition, Israel asked for full U.S. support for its position and a reaffirmation of the assurances contained in Nixon's letters of July 23, 1970, and December 3, 1970. Two days later Nixon conveyed the desired assurances but declined to offer full support. The Egyptians were told that an Israeli proposal had been received, but its content was not immediately disclosed.

Reacting to press reports of the Israeli proposal, Sadat met with Bergus and Michael Sterner, the Egyptian-desk officer from the State Department, on April 23. Egyptian forces, he said, must be allowed to cross the canal; Egypt must control the strategically important Mitla and Giddi passes; demilitarized zones could be established; and Israel could retain Sharm al-Shaykh in the first stage, but within six months a full settlement must be reached. If Israel was not prepared to give up the passes, said Sadat, the United States should end its initiative.

Sadat's statement, if taken literally, would have brought the American effort to a halt. Israel was obviously not prepared to accept these terms. The White House drew the conclusion that there was little chance of agreement, but State was not prepared to give up so easily. Instead, hoping that Sadat would moderate his position, Rogers decided to travel to the Middle East, the first secretary of state since 1953 to visit Egypt and Israel.

By the time Rogers reached Cairo on May 4, Sadat's domestic political situation was clearly somewhat shaky. Two days earlier he had dismissed the powerful secretary general of the Arab Socialist Union, Ali Sabri. Since Sabri had a reputation for being pro-Soviet, his removal was welcomed by the Americans, and in this atmosphere the talks with Sadat went well. Sadat was polite, charming, and apparently willing to be flexible.

Rogers encountered more difficulty in Israel. The Israelis were cool to Rogers personally and suspected him of being pro-Arab. Nonetheless, the discussions were detailed and quickly hit on the key issues. How would an interim agreement be linked to an overall peace settlement? Israel wanted no linkage, whereas Sadat wanted a timetable for full Israeli withdrawal, of which the interim agreement would merely be the first step. How long would the cease-fire last? Israel wanted an indefinite extension, whereas Egypt preferred a short renewal. How far would Israel withdraw from the canal? A few kilometers, or halfway or more across Sinai? How would the agreement be supervised? Would Egyptian troops be allowed across the canal? Would Israel's ships be allowed to use the canal after its opening? On each of these points the parties were far apart. Defense Minister Moshe Dayan sensed the danger of deadlock, and in talks with Sisco he outlined some modifications of the Israeli position. Israel would be prepared to accept Egyptian civilians and technicians on the east bank of the canal, but no military forces. Once the canal was reopened, Israel would agree to talk about the withdrawal of its forces.[97] Sisco was authorized to return to Egypt to discuss these ideas with Sadat and to report on the talks in Israel.

In Cairo, Sisco offered a number of ideas that he hoped might bridge the gap between the two parties.[98] Sadat indicated a willingness to con-

sider only a limited Egyptian force on the canal's east bank and promised
to send his trusted aide, Mahmoud Fawzi, to Washington with a reply to
Sisco's other suggestions. A few days later, having just deposed some of his
key ministers for plotting against him,[99] Sadat asked for clarification of
the points raised by Sisco. Was it correct to assume that the Israelis might
consider a line of withdrawal east of the passes? Sisco replied on May 18
that such a line was not precluded, that there was some flexibility in the
Israeli position.

Rogers and Sisco must have realized they were in a very delicate position. With the Egyptians, they were trying to present Israeli proposals as
more forthcoming than they actually were. With the Israelis, the Egyptian
statements were recast in the best possible light. But instead of succeeding
in convincing either party of the other's good intentions, Rogers and Sisco
seemed instead to lose credibility, especially with the Israelis. With the
Egyptians it took a bit longer, but ultimately the sense of deception was
equally great. At the White House, meanwhile, support for Rogers and
Sisco was quickly fading.[100] Before long, Sadat seemed to realize that he
could not count on Nixon and he soon abandoned his own initiative.

Kissinger Takes Charge

The failure of the interim canal settlement effectively ended the predominance of Rogers and Sisco as Middle East policymakers. If there were to
be any new American initiatives, Nixon and Kissinger would be in charge.[101]

Kissinger was critical of the way the State Department had handled the
Middle East from the beginning. He had little admiration for Secretary
Rogers and was unenthusiastic about the plan that bore his name. His
attitude toward Sisco was more complex. He genuinely admired the assistant secretary's energy and intelligence but felt he was too much of an
activist, a tactician more than a strategist, and more interested in procedure than in substance. Perhaps Sisco's worst fault, however, was that he
did not defer sufficiently to Kissinger's authority.

With respect to the interim-settlement effort, Kissinger drew a number
of lessons that later guided his own diplomacy after the October 1973
war. The United States, he thought, had become involved too quickly in
the substance of the negotiations. Once that happened, the role of impartial negotiator was in jeopardy. Only when the parties were near agreement was it appropriate for the United States to make substantive
recommendations.

Kissinger strongly believed negotiations, to be successful, had to be carried out in secret. To do so was always difficult with both the Arabs and the Israelis, but Rogers and Sisco had deliberately conducted too much of the negotiations in the glare of publicity. And when secrecy was maintained, as during Rogers's talks in Cairo, it was the White House that was kept in the dark![102]

The idea of an interim agreement unlinked to the final terms of settlement very much appealed to Kissinger. He was particularly anxious for such an accord if it would ensure the departure of the Soviet military advisers from Egypt. In practice, however, the interim-agreement approach had quickly drifted back to the package-settlement concept, with the canal pullback as only the initial stage of a comprehensive accord. Therefore Kissinger's initial interest in the approach had begun to fade by April, and by summer he was prepared to see it die an ignominious death, even at some risk to U.S.-Egyptian relations.

Kissinger also disagreed with the State Department's contention that Israel could be persuaded to moderate its negotiating stance if arms were withheld. Kissinger argued that to do so would simply make the Israelis feel more insecure and therefore intransigent. It would raise the hopes of the Arabs, particularly since Soviet arms were being delivered to Egypt and Syria in large quantities. Only if Israel felt strong would it be reasonable in negotiations, and only if the Arabs saw that Soviet arms did not hold the promise of a military solution would they turn to diplomacy in a serious way. Finally, Kissinger felt that the Israelis were on firm ground in refusing to make concessions to Egypt while the Soviet military presence there remained so large. Let Sadat expel the Soviets; then peace talks could begin.[103]

Kissinger's hope that the Soviet position in the Middle East might be undercut had been strengthened since the Jordanian civil war. First, Sadat had moved against his allegedly pro-Soviet advisers in May; then Jordan had eliminated the remnants of the PLO remaining in the country. Even more important, a communist coup d'état in Sudan in July had been reversed by the combined intervention of Egypt and Libya.

Sadat soon realized it was not worth dealing with Rogers and Sisco any longer. After the talks between Rogers and Riad in September 1971, Sadat communicated with Kissinger or Nixon through intermediaries, including his adviser on national security, Hafiz Ismail.[104] This link, which bypassed the State Department by relying on each country's intelligence channels, was rarely used in the following months, but it was available when needed.

U.S.-Israeli relations, meanwhile, were stronger than ever. Throughout 1972 Nixon was able to portray his administration as a firm supporter of Israel. Arms agreements helped to ease tensions. All the old disputes seemed forgotten, and Ambassador Rabin came very close to endorsing Nixon's bid for the presidency against the Democratic contender.

During late 1971 and 1972 U.S. Middle East policy consisted of little more than open support for Israel. The White House explicitly told the State Department not to consider any new initiatives until after the elections. Meanwhile Nixon set out to reap the rewards of Kissinger's negotiations with the Chinese and the Soviets. A successful foreign policy was clearly going to be a major theme in his reelection campaign.

Summitry

Toward the end of February 1972 President Nixon traveled to Peking for talks with Chairman Mao Tse-tung and Prime Minister Chou En-lai. The occasion was not only historic for U.S.-Chinese relations but also carried broader significance. Nixon and Kissinger were attempting to alter relations among the major powers in the interests of stability and the avoidance of nuclear war. They assumed the Soviet Union would remain the principal adversary of the United States and the greatest threat to U.S. interests. To help induce restraint on the part of the Soviet Union, the United States was prepared to develop ties with Moscow's main rival, the leadership in Peking. This was a classic stroke of balance-of-power politics, and if successful it would lend substance to the policy of détente that Nixon and Kissinger had widely promoted. Peking was thus an important waystation on the road to Moscow, where Nixon was expected in May.

Between the Peking and Moscow summits, developments in Vietnam took an alarming turn for the worse. The North Vietnamese sent troops across the demilitarized zone on March 30, and for several weeks the communist forces made impressive gains. The United States responded with intensified bombing and with a major concession to the North Vietnamese during Kissinger's talks in Moscow in late April.[105] On May 8 Nixon made a controversial decision to resume the heavy bombing of North Vietnam and to mine the harbor of Haiphong, hoping by those actions to cut the flow of arms to Hanoi. He realized this might bring the United States into open conflict with both the Soviet Union and China. Many of his advisers were sure that Brezhnev would feel compelled to cancel the upcoming summit conference. Nixon held firm, however, and the Soviets swallowed their pride and received Nixon in Moscow on May 22.

One of the great hopes of the Nixon-Kissinger foreign policy had been that détente between the superpowers would have benefits for American policy elsewhere. The summits seemed to confirm their belief that neither the Chinese nor the Soviets would allow developments in Vietnam to stand in the way of their interests in dealing with the United States. Perhaps Moscow could also be persuaded to subordinate its Middle East policies to the requirements of détente. In any event, Nixon and Kissinger were prepared to explore the possibility as one means of reducing the chances of superpower confrontation in the Middle East and, they hoped, of undercutting Soviet influence in Egypt.

In essence, this was a return to the linkage concept that had guided the Rogers-Sisco initiative of 1969, but now there was more to build on in the U.S.-Soviet relationship, particularly with the achievement of a treaty limiting strategic nuclear arms. Equally important, from Kissinger's point of view, was the fact that he, not Rogers or Sisco, would handle the talks with the Russians on the Middle East.

Kissinger's ostensible goal was to reach agreement with the Soviet leadership on a set of principles that could serve as a framework for an Arab-Israeli peace settlement. Next he would enlist their support for beginning a step-by-step negotiating process based on those principles, but leaving key issues such as final borders to be negotiated by the parties themselves.[106]

In the joint communiqué issued on May 29, the United States and the Soviet Union reaffirmed their support of UN Resolution 242 and of the Jarring mission. A settlement of the Arab-Israeli conflict "would open prospects for the normalization of the Middle East situation and would permit, in particular, consideration of further steps to bring about a military relaxation in that area."[107]

Read in Cairo, the basic principles and the joint communiqué seemed to confirm Sadat's worst fears. Both the United States and the Soviet Union had agreed to freeze the Middle East situation for fear of damaging their own relations. Under the guise of détente, the United States had persuaded the Soviets to reduce their support for the Arabs. This would explain the Soviet reluctance to provide advanced weaponry and the delays in deliveries that had been irritating Sadat for months.

Sadat was well aware that the Americans viewed the Soviet presence in Egypt as an obstacle to a peace settlement. Rogers had raised the issue in May. Now, with the results of the summit meeting available, it seemed clear to Sadat that the Soviets were not prepared to press his case with the Americans. In June Saudi Arabia's minister of defense, Prince Sultan, reported on his conversations with Nixon and Kissinger. Until the Soviet presence in Egypt was eliminated, the Americans would not press Israel for concessions.[108]

Which of these factors was most compelling to Sadat is unknown, but in early July he decided to act. On July 8 Sadat informed the Soviet ambassador that he was requesting the departure of most of the Soviet advisers and technicians in Egypt. Sadat publicly announced his decision on July 18. More than ten thousand Soviet personnel would leave Egypt, precisely as Kissinger and the Israelis had hoped.

Reaction to the Expulsion of Soviet Advisers

If Sadat's primary motivation in announcing the expulsion of the Soviet advisers in Egypt was to open the way for an active U.S. diplomatic role, he had chosen a curious time for such a momentous step.[109] Nixon was in the midst of an election campaign and was not prepared to jeopardize his substantial lead over Senator George McGovern by embarking on a controversial policy in the Middle East. He and Kissinger, however, did recognize the importance of Sadat's move, and through the "back channel" they informed the Egyptian president that after the American elections were over, a new initiative would be launched. This time it would be under White House control.

A reelected president would presumably be immune to the normal pressures of domestic politics. Nixon's prestige was at its zenith, Kissinger's reputation was growing, and perhaps they could together fashion a settlement in the Middle East.

In midsummer 1972 few could have anticipated that Nixon's ability to conduct foreign policy, and eventually even his tenure in office, would be greatly affected by a seemingly minor incident on June 17. On that day five men had been apprehended inside the offices of the Democratic headquarters in the Watergate complex in Washington, D.C. Investigation of the break-in revealed that the burglars had curious connections with the Central Intelligence Agency and with the Committee to Reelect the President. Perhaps some zealous Republicans had broken the law, but no one suspected that the president himself might be involved. On June 23, 1972, however, in a conversation with his chief of staff, H. R. Haldeman, Nixon became enmeshed in the Watergate affair by ordering the CIA to block the FBI's investigation of the incident for political reasons. The conversation was recorded on the president's secret taping system. Its disclosure a little more than two years later proved fatal to Nixon's struggle to survive

Watergate. For the moment, however, Nixon and his aides had little reason to fear that the Watergate affair would not be contained.

On the eve of his reelection Nixon took pains to speak of his plans for the Middle East. "The Middle East will have a very high priority because while the Mideast has been, over the past couple of years, in a period of uneasy truce or armistice or whatever you want to call it, it can explode at any time."[110] The message to Sadat was intended to be that he should remain patient a bit longer. It would soon be his turn, once Vietnam was settled.

Nixon was reelected overwhelmingly on November 7, winning 60.8 percent of the popular vote and 97 percent of the electoral vote. But the "peace at hand" in Vietnam remained elusive. It was only after an intensive bombing campaign against North Vietnam in December that negotiations resumed. At long last, on January 13, 1973, the Paris talks were successfully concluded; on January 27 the final agreement was signed.

4 *Kissinger's Diplomacy: Stalemate and War, 1972–73*

WITH THE END of the fighting in Vietnam, Kissinger was ready to turn his attention to the Middle East. He had previously paid little attention to briefing materials prepared for him on that region; now he requested studies, perused long memoranda, and began to develop a detailed strategy of his own.

Kissinger wanted to avoid endless debates over the meaning of Resolution 242, the Rogers Plan, and the Jarring memorandum. A legalistic approach was bound to bog down rapidly. The key demands of both parties were phrased in totally incompatible terms. The Israelis wanted peace and recognition; the Arabs wanted territory and justice. Rather than try for initial agreement on these ultimate goals, Kissinger hoped to move quickly to practical agreements, but he realized the importance of some formulation that would address the end result of the negotiating process. The Jarring formulation of "peace" for "withdrawal" did not appeal to him. Instead, he preferred the formulation recommended by his aides of establishing a balance between "sovereignty" and "security." The virtue of such a formula was that it opened the door to a wide range of negotiating outcomes. For example, it might be possible to recognize Egypt's sovereignty over Sinai at an early date, while establishing special security arrangements that would allow the Israelis to maintain a presence in key areas during a lengthy transitional period.

To try out some of these new ideas, Kissinger's meeting with Sadat's national security adviser, Hafiz Ismail, was unusually important. Ismail was the first high-level Egyptian official to meet with Nixon in some time. The visit had been arranged through the "back channel." The State Department was not informed until the last moment. Nixon met with Hafiz Ismail on February 23 and appeared relaxed and self-confident. He outlined a strategy for negotiating on two levels: one would be handled in secret by Kissinger, as with Vietnam; the other would be public and would involve the State Department.[1] Nixon also mentioned the sovereignty and security formula.

Ismail's real purpose in coming to Washington, however, was to confer with Kissinger. During the next two days Hafiz Ismail met with Kissinger at a private estate in Connecticut.[2] Kissinger argued for the necessity of accepting the idea of a settlement implemented over a prolonged period. He implied that Egyptian sovereignty over Sinai could be acknowledged at an early date but that special security arrangements might be required for a long time. Ismail seemed interested, and the talks seemed to go well. He indicated that a normalization of relations with Israel might eventually be possible and that Jordan might have a role to play in solving the Palestinian issue, but he was adamant about full Israeli withdrawal from Sinai and Golan, hinting at some flexibility in the West Bank.[3]

They then discussed in detail the obligations that Egypt and Israel would undertake as part of a peace agreement, the relationship between an Egyptian-Israeli agreement and resolution of the Palestine problem, and concrete security arrangements for Israel in Sinai. Unable to resolve all these issues, Kissinger and Ismail agreed to meet again at an early date. Kissinger was in no rush. He told Ismail that little could be accomplished before the Israeli elections, scheduled for late October 1973.

The diplomatic effort launched in February had as its goal the establishment of a "negotiating framework" between Egypt and Israel. Kissinger saw this as being complemented by a U.S.-Soviet agreement on principles of a settlement, based on those tentatively drawn up in Moscow the previous May. He realized it would take time for all the pieces to fall into place.

A major preoccupation during spring 1973 was the "energy crisis" that was increasingly apparent on the horizon. The price of oil had been rising rapidly since 1971. U.S. production was stagnating, U.S. refinery capacity was insufficient to meet the demand, and shortages of gasoline and fuel oil might be felt by the end of the year. The oil companies were nervous. The president had no policy except to appear to be in control while he cast about for someone to take charge. Visitors to Saudi Arabia began to report that King Faisal, for the first time, was speaking of using the oil weapon to bring pressure on the United States unless Israel was forced to withdraw from Arab territory.

Against this background, tensions in the Middle East mounted sharply in mid-April. Lebanon was thrown into crisis by an Israeli raid into downtown Beirut that killed three top PLO leaders. More dangerous still, toward the end of the month Egyptian war preparations along the Suez Canal took on an air of determination.[4] Intelligence reports were also received that Syria had completed a detailed war plan and was prepared to attack Israel on short notice. Israel took the signs seriously and ordered a partial mobilization; by mid-May the crisis atmosphere had passed.

Meanwhile the smoldering Watergate issue had flared up. On March 21 a young lawyer working for the White House, John Dean, had informed Nixon of the extent of high-level involvement in the Watergate cover-up. He warned Nixon of a "cancer" growing on the presidency. Within weeks of this conversation Dean was telling his story to the FBI investigators dealing with Watergate. Evidence was rapidly accumulating that implicated the president's closest associates—John Mitchell, H. R. Haldeman, and John Ehrlichman. Increasingly, Nixon was obliged to devote his time and energies to the Watergate crisis. On April 30 he accepted the resignations of Haldeman and Ehrlichman. Of his closest advisers, only Kissinger now remained.

Kissinger tried to keep Middle East policy on the track charted in February, but because Nixon's authority was being undermined, it was increasingly difficult. Kissinger began to think of how he might induce the Soviet Union to cooperate with his efforts to begin a negotiating process. He wanted Moscow to endorse publicly a set of principles that would serve as guidelines for a settlement. Perhaps the Soviet Union would be more cooperative if it could be persuaded that the status quo was not working to its advantage in the Middle East. Kissinger toyed with the idea of trying to weaken the Soviets in Iraq and South Yemen as well, perhaps with the help of Iran and Saudi Arabia. In his view such anti-Soviet moves in the Middle East would not be incompatible with his objective of enlisting Soviet support for negotiations, provided U.S. involvement remained secret.

On May 4, 1973, Kissinger arrived in Moscow to prepare for the second Nixon-Brezhnev summit meeting. While there, he received a new document from Gromyko that set forth nine principles of an Arab-Israeli settlement. Gromyko's document, unlike that of the previous May, called for complete Israeli withdrawal to the June 4, 1967, lines. It also referred to the "legitimate rights" of the Palestinians. One new note was included: failure by either party to implement any part of the agreement would give the other party the right to refuse to fulfill its own obligations. On the whole, Kissinger much preferred the May 1972 document.[5]

The State Department was kept in the dark concerning these discussions, which added greatly to Secretary of State William Rogers's frustration. Rogers's exasperation was further increased when he learned by accident that Kissinger was planning to meet again with Hafiz Ismail. This time he insisted that one of his own representatives be present, and when Kissinger and Ismail met secretly outside of Paris on May 20, Alfred Atherton, the deputy assistant secretary of state for Near Eastern affairs, was part of the U.S. team.

Ismail was less interested in substance during these talks than he had been in February. He concentrated his questions instead on the role the United States intended to play. The unresolved issues from February were discussed, but inconclusively. Ismail insisted that a final peace between Egypt and Israel was contingent on a solution to the Palestinian problem.

Kissinger described to Ismail his strategy of trying for a U.S.-Soviet agreement on principles, to be followed by secret negotiations between the parties. Kissinger spoke with Ismail privately for a few minutes and felt he was making some progress. He then suggested that further talks would be desirable. Ismail promised an early reply, but when it came on June 3 it was guarded and unenthusiastic. Perhaps the Egyptians were beginning to have their doubts about Nixon's ability to produce results, given his crumbling domestic base. In any event, the promising tone of the February talks was missing in May.[6]

Brezhnev's Visit

If U.S.-Egyptian relations seemed to be stagnating, the same could not be said for U.S.-Soviet ties. Kissinger had been treated with great courtesy and attention in May, and now, in June, General Secretary Leonid Brezhnev arrived for his first visit to the United States. Talks on the Middle East were focused on the May 1972 document, with some additions from Gromyko's more recent draft. The Soviet language on full withdrawal and the "rights" of the Palestinians, however, was not accepted by the United States.

Nixon and Brezhnev, along with Kissinger and Gromyko and their staffs, discussed the Middle East at length. Brezhnev warned that the Egyptians and Syrians were intent on going to war and that the Soviet Union could not stop them. Only a new American initiative and, in particular, pressure on Israel to withdraw could prevent war.[7] The joint communiqué issued on June 25, 1973, gave little idea of the content of the talks.

Following the June summit talks, U.S. Middle East policy entered the summer doldrums. Nothing much could be done until after the Israeli elections in any case, according to Kissinger. The Arabs were clearly frustrated—Sadat called the United States the "world's biggest bully" on July 23—and King Faisal was publicly linking oil and the Arab-Israeli conflict.[8] Sadat also seemed intent on forcing the United States into an anti-Arab posture by calling for a UN debate on the Middle East crisis and then pressing for a vote on a resolution strongly condemning Israel. For the fifth time in its history, the United States cast a veto. The Arab world reacted angrily. Kissinger wondered why Sadat was seeking a confrontation. Was he merely trying to compel the United States to take a more active role?

During the third week of July 1973, Kissinger devoted considerable time to the Middle East, particularly to the question of Soviet involvement. He was concerned that the State Department's penchant for solving conflicts made the United States "lean on" its friends. His preference was to build on those friendships to look after American interests in the region.

On August 22 Nixon made a surprise announcement that he was nominating Henry Kissinger as secretary of state to replace William Rogers. Kissinger would keep his position as adviser to the president for national security affairs as well. No longer would Kissinger have to worry about the secretary of state's undercutting his strategy.

Three days after becoming secretary of state, on September 25, Kissinger met with most of the Arab ambassadors to the UN. He tried to establish his credentials as a credible mediator, joking about his own Jewish background.[9] He promised to work for a settlement but warned the ambassadors not to expect miracles. He would only promise what he could deliver, but he would deliver all that he promised. This became a common refrain in Kissinger's talks with the Arabs.

Over the next two weeks Kissinger spoke several times with the Arab and Israeli foreign ministers attending the UN General Assembly in New York. He proposed, and they seemed to agree, that serious talks between Egypt and Israel, with the United States as mediator, should begin in November. On October 5 he met with Foreign Minister Mohamed el-Zayyat of Egypt to confirm these arrangements. On the whole, he was satisfied with the results of his first foray into Middle East diplomacy as secretary of state.

The next day, Yom Kippur, Egypt and Syria launched a combined military offensive against Israeli forces in the Golan Heights and Sinai. Kissinger's policy lay in ruins, overtaken by a war that he had occasionally worried about but had not really foreseen. At the core of his misreading of Arab intentions was his belief that war would be prevented by maintaining the military balance in Israel's favor. This view, forged in the midst of the Jordan crisis, had been dangerously misleading.

A Deceptive Calm

The period between the Jordan crisis in September 1970 and the October 1973 war was deceptively calm in the Middle East. In the absence of acute crises, American policymakers paid comparatively little attention to the area. The basic frame of reference, set by Nixon and Kissinger, emphasized the U.S.-Soviet rivalry and the need to maintain the balance of power in Israel's favor. Periodically the State Department tried to launch a new initiative—the Jarring talks, the interim canal settlement, proximity talks—but the White House was only mildly supportive at best, and on occasion was distinctly negative. Bureaucratic rivalries became personalized in the Rogers-Kissinger quarrel. On the whole, Nixon sided with Kissinger.[10] As a result, United States policy during this period was particularly ineffective and inconsistent.

During the interim canal settlement talks, it was especially flawed; the Rogers-Sisco mediation left a bitter aftertaste in Israel, Egypt, and the White House. During this noncrisis period domestic politics also began to intrude on policymaking in noticeable ways. Because of election-year imperatives in 1972, no initiatives were undertaken, even in response to Sadat's expulsion of the Soviet advisers. Then, in 1973, Watergate began to divert the attention of the president from the region to which he had promised to devote highest priority in his foreign policy.

As Kissinger began to focus on the Middle East, he toyed with the idea of seeking U.S.-Soviet agreement on principles as one strand of his policy, while also talking to Egypt and Israel about both interim steps and principles for an overall settlement. Ironically, each of these approaches had been tried by Rogers and had failed. Kissinger was no more successful, but his larger purpose, in any case, seems to have been to frustrate the Arabs so that they would break with their Soviet patron and turn to the United States for help. But when Sadat began to move in this direction in 1972, Kissinger did not take him very seriously.

The most impressive shift in policy during this period concerned U.S.-Israeli relations. Despite occasional disagreements over arms, the United States and Israel entered an unusually cooperative phase in their often troubled relationship. This phase was very much the result of the Jordan crisis and Kissinger's view of Israel as a strategic asset. In fiscal years 1968, 1969, and 1970 Israel had received from the United States military credits worth $25 million, $85 million, and $30 million, respectively. After the Jordan crisis, in fiscal years 1971, 1972, and 1973, Israel received military credits of $545 million, $300 million, and $307.5 million, respectively—nearly a tenfold increase in aid.

Yet the military balance proved not to be the key to regional stability and the prevention of war. Nor did détente prevent the Soviet Union from continuing to arm Egypt, Syria, and Iraq despite the mounting signs of Arab intentions to resume hostilities. Nixon and Kissinger remained insensitive to the regional trends leading to war and ignored the growing importance of Arab oil as an element in the regional equation. The concepts guiding their policies were simply too broad to incorporate these developments; furthermore, Kissinger was not convinced of the need for a major American initiative in the Middle East.[11] It required the October war to change U.S. policy and to engage Nixon and Kissinger fully in the search for an Arab-Israeli settlement.

War and Reassessment, October 1973

The Arab-Israeli war of October 1973 had all the elements of a severe international crisis. It caught most of the world, including the United States and Israel, by surprise; it did not fit anyone's preconceptions of how a war in the Middle East was likely to develop; it threatened core values of the countries directly involved as well as those of outside powers; and it ended with a near-confrontation between the two nuclear superpowers, the United States and the Soviet Union.

Crises, by their nature, expose prevailing assumptions about reality in particularly acute ways. Faced with surprise, danger, and uncertainty, decisionmakers act from previously formulated conceptions of reality. When reality no longer conforms to these images, and policymakers are under great pressure of time and events, they are likely to restructure their perceptions with extraordinary speed. Impending failure or danger, much like the prospect of a hanging, clears the mind. Pieces of the puzzle are quickly rearranged, and new policies are tried. If the crisis is resolved successfully, the revised or restructured image is likely to endure for some time; lessons will be drawn; and a new policy framework will emerge to guide action until the next failure or crisis. The October war is therefore doubly important as an object of study, for it revealed the underlying assumptions of American policy toward the Arab-Israeli conflict from 1970 to 1973 and produced a major revision of those assumptions within a very short period.

Why the Surprise?

Shortly after 6:00 a.m. Washington time on October 6, 1973, the White House situation room received a flash cable from the American embassy in Tel Aviv. Israel finally had conclusive evidence that the Egyptians and Syrians planned to attack by 6:00 p.m. Middle East time (noon in Washington). Prime Minister Golda Meir assured the United States that Israel did not intend to preempt and asked that American efforts be directed at preventing war.

In the less than two hours remaining before the war began, Kissinger took charge, calling the Israelis to warn against preemption, urging the Soviets to use their influence to prevent war, telephoning the Egyptian ambassador to the UN with the Israeli message that Israel would not preempt, and sending messages to King Hussein and King Faisal to enlist their help on the side of moderation. Kissinger's efforts were futile, and the first word of hostilities was received shortly after 8:00 a.m.

Why was the American intelligence community caught off guard? Why was Kissinger caught by surprise?[12] Where were all the Middle East "experts"? Two basic conceptual biases led to the misperception of Egyptian-Syrian intentions. First, it was widely assumed that the "military balance" was the key to whether there would be another war in the Middle East. This had been a basic element in American policy since 1967. However strongly the Arabs might feel about the need to regain their territory, they would not go to war if they faced certain defeat. In view of Israel's qualitative advantages in the military realm, and the substantial flow of American arms after 1970, it would be an act of folly for the Arabs to initiate a war. Nor was it expected that Israel would feel the need to preempt.

A deliberate, rationally planned war was simply implausible in the light of military realities. An unintended war, caused by each side's reacting to defensive moves of the other, seemed more likely, but it would be difficult to anticipate or predict.[13] Finally, war as an irrational act might occur, but again could not be predicted with accuracy.

Second, war seemed to make sense for the Arabs only if a political alternative for recovering their territory was precluded. Although most of the U.S. bureaucracy remained uninformed, top officials were aware that Kissinger, in his talks with Israelis and Egyptians at the UN, had arranged for preliminary talks on a settlement to begin in November, after the Israeli elections. The continuation of Israeli military superiority and the option of a political alternative made an Arab-initiated war implausible. The maneuvers, threats, and warnings could all be explained away as part of a

Soviet-Arab campaign to force the United States to lean on Israel to make concessions.

Despite all the technically accurate information available in Washington about Arab war preparations, Egypt and Syria did manage to observe high standards of secrecy and deception. Well-placed Israeli intelligence agents in Egypt had been captured early in 1973.[14] Presidents Anwar Sadat and Hafiz al-Asad confided in almost no one concerning the precise moment of the attack. Communications security in the days preceding the attack was unusually good, and deliberate deception tactics were used successfully. Even so, Israel had nearly ten hours' warning.[15] But there was not enough time to take any steps to prevent war, and very little could even be done to limit the damage of the initial Arab attack.

Initial Reactions

For several hours after the outbreak of war, Washington did not know whether the Israelis or the Arabs had fired the first shots. During the rump session of the Washington Special Action Group (WSAG), convened at 9:00 a.m., the prevailing view was that Israel had probably struck first.[16] CIA director William Colby judged that, in any event, neither side had premeditated military action, but rather that the war was the result of mutual fears of actions and reactions that had escalated to hostilities.[17] The United States, it was felt, should not make accusations against either side. A multiplicity of interests was at stake—U.S.-Soviet détente, U.S.-Israeli relations, American credibility with the Arabs, and the weakened authority of the president. The initial American reaction was therefore cautious.

It soon became clear that the Egyptians and Syrians had indeed begun the hostilities, but at no point during the next three weeks did any United States official make this an issue. The public record will be searched in vain for references to Arab "aggression."[18] Unlike President Johnson, who held Nasser responsible for the 1967 war despite Israel's opening fire on June 5, Nixon and Kissinger ignored the issue of who was at fault. Among the reasons for this "evenhanded" perspective was the feeling that U.S.-Arab relations were growing in importance because of oil and this was no time for a confrontation; that an Arab attack on Israeli forces in occupied Arab territory was not the same as an attack across recognized borders; and that the status quo prevailing before the war had, in fact, given the Arabs ample incentive to try to break the "no war, no peace" stalemate by engineering an international crisis. For several days it was widely considered that the Arab action had been foolish, but not that it had been immoral.

Toward the end of the first day of fighting, a second WSAG meeting was convened, this time under Kissinger's chairmanship. For all practical purposes, he, usually in consultation with Nixon directly or through Chief of Staff Alexander Haig, made policy during the next several weeks, with occasional inputs from Defense Secretary James Schlesinger. Kissinger's initial views are therefore of particular interest.

Kissinger entered the situation room at 7:22 p.m. He reported that he had just been on the telephone to Nixon, to the Soviet ambassador, Anatoly Dobrynin, and to the Israeli foreign minister, Abba Eban.[19] The president wanted the Sixth Fleet moved east and held near Crete as a visible sign of American power. One aircraft carrier was ordered to leave port in Athens; other moves would be considered later.

Kissinger was concerned about the Soviet Union. If the Arabs suffered a real debacle, he thought, the Soviets would have a hard time staying out of the fighting. U.S. military moves should be restrained so as not to give the wrong impressions to the Soviet Union.

Discussion ensued on the diplomatic contacts made to date. In the UN the United States would try to work with the Soviet Union to reestablish the cease-fire on the basis of the status quo ante. Kissinger, expecting a reprise of June 1967, said the Arabs, in their "demented state," currently opposed that position, but they would beg for it once the Israeli counter-offensive got under way.

Israel would undoubtedly reject any cease-fire not based on a return to the status quo ante. Nixon did not want a situation in which Israel, the victim of the attack, would be condemned for rejecting a cease-fire appeal. The U.S. goal was to adopt a position that would remain consistent throughout the crisis. The war would quickly shift in Israel's favor, and what appeared to be a pro-Israel position of a cease-fire on the post-1967 lines would soon look pro-Arab. If Israel went beyond the previous lines, the United States would oppose that, thereby regaining some credit with the Arabs. Consequently the United States would propose a cease-fire status quo ante but would not push hard for it until the military realities made both parties want to accept it.

Everyone felt the crisis would be crucial for U.S.-Soviet relations. If collaboration worked, détente would take on real meaning; if it failed, the Soviets could "kiss MFN [most favored nation status] goodbye."[20] Although the Soviets might have been duplicitous in helping the Arabs plan the war, some still held the hope of working with Moscow to end it. U.S.-

Israeli relations were also on many minds. By sticking close to the Israelis during the war, the United States should be able to enhance the credibility of a future guarantee as part of a peace settlement. Eventually American and Israeli positions on a settlement would diverge, and the only way to get the Israelis to withdraw from Arab territory would be to offer some kind of formal U.S. guarantee. The president felt strongly about this issue. The Israelis must see the United States as a reliable partner during the crisis for the sake of postwar diplomacy.

On Sunday, October 7, Kissinger kept in close touch with the Soviets, Egyptians, and Israelis. Nixon sent Brezhnev a letter urging mutual restraint and calling for a meeting of the Security Council. Brezhnev's reply was conciliatory and encouraging.[21] Together with the movement of Soviet ships away from the zone of combat, this was a promising sign.

Supplementing Kissinger's talks with Foreign Minister Zayyat, the Egyptians began to send messages through the back channel that had been established in 1972. Although rejecting the idea of a cease-fire that was not linked to Israeli withdrawal to the pre-1967 lines, Sadat, communicating through his adviser, Hafiz Ismail, made it clear he did not want a confrontation with the United States.[22]

The Israelis were in a grim mood, but in communications with the United States they still appeared confident of success. Anticipating Israeli requests for arms, Kissinger made arrangements for El Al aircraft to pick up some items—ammunition, high technology products, and Sidewinder missiles—at a naval base in Virginia. Ambassador Simcha Dinitz, just arrived from Israel, met with Kissinger in the evening and, as expected, presented a list of arms that Israel needed, but the sense of urgency was not particularly great, or at least so it seemed to Kissinger and Schlesinger.[23] A modest resupply effort soon began, but Kissinger was still hoping to keep any visible involvement with Israel's war effort at a minimum.

By the time the WSAG met, shortly after 6:00 p.m. on October 7,[24] the best estimate of the CIA was that Israel would regain the initiative the following day and would go on to win the war by the end of the week. Initial concentration would be on the Syrian front, then on the Egyptian front. Kissinger voiced his perplexity about why the Arabs, if their situation was really so precarious, were refusing a cease-fire that would protect their initial gains.[25] Schlesinger felt they were being illogical; Kissinger replied that the Egyptian strategy would be to cross the canal and then sit tight. The Arabs, he thought, had attacked to upset the status quo, because they feared there would be no diplomatic movement unless there was a crisis.

By October 8 Israel was beginning to encounter military difficulties on both fronts. In Golan the Syrian air-defense system was taking a high toll of Israeli Skyhawks and Phantoms. In Sinai an Israeli effort to break through Egyptian lines with armor had been thwarted. Demands for resupply of equipment from the United States mounted. Dinitz spoke to Kissinger several times and was told that Israeli losses would be replaced. When Dinitz complained about the slow American response, Kissinger blamed it on the Defense Department, a ploy he used repeatedly with the Israeli ambassador over the next several days.[26] In fact, the U.S. position was still based on the expectation of an early end to the fighting and a desire to maintain a low profile. The arms issue was therefore handled discreetly.

The WSAG met again at 5:30 p.m. on Monday, October 8, to review the day's events.[27] The CIA reported that Israel was making rapid progress and had virtually retaken the Golan Heights. Kissinger again expressed puzzlement over why the Arabs were refusing a cease-fire. The Soviets, by contrast, were being very conciliatory. With their help, it was felt, a cease-fire could be achieved by Wednesday night. The Soviets would respond on Tuesday. Even if Israel crossed the canal, the United States would be in a good position by sticking to a call for a cease-fire based on the status quo ante. Military realities would shortly make the American proposal acceptable to Egypt, Syria, and the Soviet Union.

The basic U.S. policy, rooted in the initial assumptions of a short war with an Israeli victory, was still on the tracks, but it would not be for much longer. In the jargon of Washington it was about to be "overtaken by events."

The Crisis Deepens

From the perspective of Washington the war entered a new and acute phase on October 9. Reality was refusing to conform to the comparatively optimistic forecast on which initial U.S. policy had been based. Between October 9 and October 12 the possibility of a swift and conclusive Israeli military victory on both fronts faded; Soviet restraint began to erode; and pressure began to build for an urgent military resupply of Israeli forces. The American response was to modify gradually two aspects of policy: the call for a cease-fire based on the status quo ante was replaced by an exploration of the idea of a cease-fire in place; and arms for Israel began to flow in modest quantities, not only aboard El Al aircraft, but increasingly with direct American involvement.

In one of the most controversial decisions of the war, Nixon and Kissinger held back on a full-scale commitment of American resources to the resupply effort until the fate of the cease-fire-in-place initiative was clear and the scope of the Soviet resupply effort made further delay politically diffi- cult. Under pressure on the ground, short of supplies, and without a guar- antee of a full-scale American airlift of arms, the Israeli government reluctantly accepted a cease-fire in place on October 12. But early on Oc- tober 13 President Sadat refused the cease-fire proposal, which led to a dramatic change in American policy.

This second stage of the crisis opened on Tuesday morning, October 9, with an urgent Israeli appeal for arms.[28] Shortly thereafter Kissinger con- vened the WSAG principals for two emergency sessions before noon. The two recommendations that emerged from these sessions were presented to Nixon by Kissinger at 4:45 p.m. First, some arms must begin to reach Israel quickly, without violating the principle of maintaining a low Ameri- can profile in the conflict. Second, over the next several days a new for- mula for a cease-fire would be explored. Nixon, deeply distracted by the impending resignation of his vice president, agreed to meet most of Israel's requests.[29]

While these deliberations were going on, word began to reach Wash- ington that Israel had launched a major counteroffensive on the Syrian front. On the ground, Israeli troops had recovered virtually all the terri- tory lost during the first three days of fighting and in some areas were pushing beyond the former cease-fire line. Nonetheless, the fighting was still difficult. The Syrians were not breaking, and Iraqi reinforcements were on their way. In the air, the Israelis, thwarted in their efforts to use the air force for close support of ground troops, initiated a campaign of strategic bombing deep within Syria.

On October 9, Kissinger began to sound out the Egyptians, Soviets, and Israelis on the possibility of a cease-fire in place. Dinitz was the first to convey his government's refusal, emphasizing the need for any cease- fire to be tied to the restoration of the status quo ante.[30] Egypt's position was equally negative. Any cease-fire must be directly linked to a concrete plan calling for full Israeli withdrawal from all territories captured in 1967. Kissinger had raised the issue of a cease-fire in place through his back channel to Hafiz Ismail, stressing that Egypt had "made its point." Ismail's reply, reportedly drafted by Sadat, reached him the following day:[31]

—There should be a cease-fire followed by a withdrawal within a speci- fied period, under UN supervision, of all Israeli forces to the pre–June 5, 1967, lines.

—Freedom of navigation in the Strait of Tiran should be guaranteed by a UN presence at Sharm al-Shaykh for a specified period.

—Following the complete withdrawal of Israeli forces, the state of belligerency with Israel would be ended.

—Following the withdrawal of Israeli troops from Gaza, the area would be placed under UN supervision pending its self-determination.

—Within a specified period after the ending of the state of belligerency, a peace conference would be convened under UN auspices, to be attended by all interested parties, including the Palestinians, and all members of the Security Council. The conference would deal with all questions of sovereignty, security, and freedom of navigation.

Egypt also promised that once Israeli evacuation began, diplomatic relations with the United States would be resumed and work on clearing the Suez Canal would start.

This proposal was hardly the simple cease-fire in place that Nixon and Kissinger now envisaged. Under no circumstances were they prepared to link a cease-fire to the terms of a final settlement. Not only would the Israelis adamantly refuse such a linkage, but it also was entirely contrary to Nixon's and Kissinger's negotiating strategy.

Fortunately for Kissinger's strategy, the Soviets now seemed to be supporting the idea of a cease-fire in place, and they indicated in a message on October 10 that Egypt would most likely go along. The Soviets thought that both great powers should abstain from any Security Council Resolution calling for a cease-fire. Kissinger claims that his initial reaction was negative because he felt Israel needed more time to change things on the battlefield. In an effort to stall, he accepted the Soviet proposal "in principle" but urged the Soviets not to take any immediate action at the United Nations.[32]

The Cease-Fire Initiative

Offsetting this conciliatory gesture, however, was the first evidence that the Soviets were beginning an airlift of arms to the Middle East. On October 10, twenty-one AN-12s flew to Damascus with more than 200 tons of military equipment.[33] Late that day Washington learned that seven Soviet airborne divisions had been placed on a high state of alert. Obviously the Soviets were worried about the deteriorating situation on the Syrian front. Whether their solution to the danger posed to their interests would emphasize diplomacy or force was at the moment an unanswered question. Elements of both courses of action were visible.

Meanwhile the U.S. resupply of Israel was beginning on a modest scale. On October 9 Dinitz had been informed that a number of F-4 Phantoms would soon be on their way. In addition, El Al planes were being allowed to pick up preassembled cargoes at Oceana Naval Station near Norfolk, Virginia. The first of these resupplies had reached Israel by October 10, the same day on which the first Soviet resupplies by air reached Damascus.

The intensity of the fighting was such, however, that Israeli requests for arms could not be met simply by El Al flights. Consistent with the principle of avoiding direct official American involvement in the transport of arms to Israel, Kissinger and Schlesinger began on October 10 to explore the possibility of chartering civilian transports for that purpose. Ten to twenty flights a day were envisaged.

At this point the American and Israeli positions began to diverge. The United States wanted an early cease-fire, at least within the next two days. Israel wanted arms in sufficient quantity to ensure a military victory. Over the next forty-eight hours the United States seemed to move slowly on sending arms to Israel, either, as Kissinger maintains, because of bureaucratic confusion, or, as others believe, as a form of pressure to induce the Israelis to accept a cease-fire in place and in the conviction that the fighting was nearly over in any case.

October 11 was a day of regrouping and consolidation. Nothing extraordinary happened on the battlefield or in Washington. Israel began to transfer troops from the Syrian to the Egyptian front in order to push Egyptian forces back to the canal. U.S. diplomacy aimed at restraining King Hussein, now under pressure from Asad, Sadat, and Faisal, from joining the war and at reassuring the Israelis that the charter flights and F-4s would soon be on their way. Israel's refusal to consider a cease-fire in place was now beginning to weaken somewhat. Having made new gains on the Syrian front, Israel was prepared to consider a cease-fire coupled with a subsequent exchange of Israeli control over captured Syrian territory for a restoration of Israeli positions in Sinai.[34] Syria might see some merit in this plan, but Sadat would not; hence the United States continued to press for a simple cease-fire in place. On October 12 it seemed within grasp.

The day began with Israeli queries about the charter flights that had been promised but that had not yet begun. In an effort to retain credibility with the Israelis, Kissinger tried to accelerate the process. A message was sent at 11:09 a.m. to the Portuguese requesting the use of Lajes airbase in the Azores for chartered civilian aircraft flying military consumables to Israel. Ten to twenty flights, chartered by the Defense Department, would pass through Lajes each day.

According to Kissinger, during the morning of October 12 he was informed that Israel was prepared to accept a cease-fire in place.[35] Appar-

ently Golda Meir, in consultation with her top military leaders, but without a formal cabinet vote, had made the decision out of concern about
both the costs of continued fighting and the pressure generated by the
delay in the resupply effort.[36]

Prime Minister Meir's acceptance of the idea of a cease-fire in place
was followed by a message from Dinitz that Israel would not object if the
cease-fire idea was put to the UN immediately. Later in the evening of
October 12 Dinitz came to the White House with an urgent personal appeal from Meir to President Nixon to order an immediate resupply of
arms to Israel. She went so far as to raise the specter of an Israeli military
defeat.[37]

Meanwhile the cease-fire initiative was running into trouble. Kissinger
had urged the British to introduce the idea in the UN on October 13.
During the evening of October 12 the British told Kissinger they would
only introduce a resolution the following day if they were sure it would be
accepted by the parties. From their information, they doubted that this
would be the case. Kissinger assured them that they should proceed. But
late in the morning of October 13 the British informed Kissinger that they
had concluded that a cease-fire in place was a mirage.

The Airlift

President Nixon's role in shaping American policy during the October
war is difficult to assess accurately. He was obviously preoccupied by his
own domestic political difficulties and with the resignation in disgrace of
his hand-picked vice president, Spiro Agnew, on October 10. The president
showed little interest in the details of policy, leaving the task of day-to-day
diplomacy to Kissinger. Nixon did make key decisions, however, and it
was his authority that could be invoked to influence other governments.

Early in the morning of October 13 Schlesinger became convinced that
the only effective way to get arms to Israel would be in American military
planes. Kissinger and Haig were opposed, still preferring to keep a low
profile.[38] On the morning of October 13, having been briefed on Meir's
urgent appeal for help and Schlesinger's recommendation, and without
any positive indication that a cease-fire agreement was in sight, President
Nixon took the responsibility of ordering a full-scale airlift of military
equipment to Israel.[39]

The main considerations underlying this stage of the Nixon-Kissinger
strategy were to convince Sadat that a prolonged war of attrition, fueled

by Soviet arms, would not succeed and to demonstrate to the Kremlin that
the United States was capable of matching Soviet military deliveries to the
Middle East. Above all, for the sake of the future American position glo-
bally and in the region, Soviet arms must not be allowed to dictate the
outcome of the fighting. This did not mean that the United States now
favored a total Israeli military victory, but it did mean that Israeli success
on the battlefield had become an important factor in persuading the Arabs and the Soviets to bring the fighting to an end.[40]

Nixon and Kissinger were aware of the likelihood of adverse Arab reaction to the airlift of arms to Israel. Up to this point in the crisis there had
been no confrontation between the United States and the Arab world. The
"oil weapon" had not yet been brandished, as many had feared; American
lives were not endangered in any Arab country, including Libya, which
had been a source of early concern; no Arab country had broken diplomatic relations; and Sadat was in continuing contact with Nixon through
the back channel. U.S. influence with King Hussein had helped keep Jordan out of the war, although a token Jordanian force was now being sent
to Syria. All this might change as a result of the airlift, but Nixon and
Kissinger were prepared to take the risk. The airlift, they would argue,
was a response to prior Soviet intervention on the Arab side. Global political realities dictated that the United States respond.

By 12:30 p.m., Washington time, on October 14 (6:30 p.m. in Israel),
the first giant C-5 transport plane arrived at Lod airport. An air bridge
capable of delivering nearly 1,000 tons a day was now in operation, con-
sisting of four to five flights of C-5s and twelve to fifteen flights of C-141s.
El Al planes also continued to carry military supplies to Israel. In addition,
twelve C-130 transports were flown to Israel and were turned over to the
Israeli air force.[41] With the airlift in full swing, Washington was prepared
to wait until the new realities on the battlefield led to a change of Egyptian
and Soviet calculations.

In the meantime the United States began to plan for an anticipated
Arab oil embargo. Only 12 percent of U.S. oil consumption, or 5 percent
of total energy, consisted of crude oil and refined products received directly or indirectly from the Arab world. Through reduction of demand
for oil and some redirection of imports, the overall impact of a selective
Arab oil embargo against the United States would hardly be felt. If, however, an embargo was combined with severe cutbacks in production, then
not only the United States but also Europe and Japan would feel the pinch.
Consequently plans for the sharing of oil among allies, as well as a domestic energy plan, were required.

By the time the first C-5 had set down in Israel on the afternoon of October 14, the decisive battle of the war on the Egyptian front had been fought and won by Israel. An Egyptian offensive toward the Mitla and Giddi passes had failed, at a cost to Egypt of more than 200 tanks. It had been for the sake of this battle that Sadat had rejected the cease-fire in place offered by the British ambassador the previous day.[42] Now, with this victory behind them, the Israelis showed little interest in the cease-fire they had been prepared to accept two days earlier.[43] Instead, Israel, assured of continuing American supplies, decided to undertake a risky military operation to cross the Suez Canal. If successful, this action might result in the destruction of Egyptian missile fields, thereby exposing Egyptian ground troops to bombing by the Israeli air force. Also, Egyptian forces in Sinai ran the risk of being cut off from their lines of communication and surrounded by the Israelis. A critical moment was approaching. The Israeli operation was scheduled for the night of October 15-16.

Kissinger convened morning sessions of the WSAG on both October 14 and October 15. Besides discussing oil, the group assessed the evolving military and diplomatic situation. By October 15 the American airlift to Israel had been publicly acknowledged and widely reported. Kissinger was surprised at the moderation of the Arab response. Although he did not expect the Arab oil ministers' meeting in Kuwait the following day to cut off oil to the United States, he did feel that a plan for counterpressure on the Arabs was necessary if they did. An administration already weakened by its domestic political problems could not afford to appear susceptible to "blackmail" by Arab oil producers.

On the Soviet role in the conflict, Kissinger still reflected a certain ambivalence. The noted Washington columnist Joseph Alsop had published an article on the morning of October 15 accusing the Soviets of collusion in and extensive foreknowledge of the Arab war effort. Kissinger was suspicious, but at the same time he felt the Soviets were still interested in a diplomatic settlement. Perhaps because of the American airlift, or perhaps because of the outcome of the October 14 battle in Sinai, the Soviets early on October 15 had indicated that they were again actively trying to persuade the Arabs to accept a cease-fire. Premier Kosygin, the secretary was told, would go to Cairo the next day.

Kissinger planned to see Egyptian foreign minister Zayyat on October 16, and President Nixon would meet with four Arab foreign ministers on October 17. Diplomatic channels would thus remain open with both the Arabs and the Soviets despite the growing superpower involvement in the conflict.[44]

The Tide Begins to Turn

October 16 was a crucial day for the war and the diplomacy. Both President Sadat and Prime Minister Meir gave important public speeches outlining their policies. Israeli forces had managed to cross the Suez Canal in small numbers and were moving into the missile fields, causing havoc among the Egyptian forces. Kosygin was en route to Cairo to try to persuade Sadat to stop fighting, and Kissinger had reason to feel that the U.S. strategy was working well. Sadat's speech was fairly moderate in tone and contained an "open message" to Nixon on Egypt's peace terms. Kosygin's mission had been foreshadowed in Soviet communications during the previous day. As yet, no Arab embargo of oil had been announced. And the Israeli military successes, although not specifically designed or intended by Washington, were consistent with Kissinger's view that Sadat had to be persuaded by battlefield developments to accept a cease-fire. It was of prime importance that the fighting should be ended at the moment when all parties could still emerge from the conflict with their vital interests and self-esteem intact.

At the WSAG meeting on Tuesday morning, October 16, Kissinger further elaborated on the objectives of the airlift. He minimized its importance in the context of the Arab-Israeli conflict. Rather, he stressed, the Soviets must see that the United States could deliver more than they could. Turning its attention again to the Middle East, the WSAG addressed the question of aid to Israel to finance the arms being sent. To some, it was time to get maximum credit with Israel, because during the subsequent diplomatic effort the U.S. and Israeli positions were bound to diverge. Kissinger therefore argued for a very large aid bill for Israel—as much as $3 billion—as well as another $500 million for Cambodia and other countries, thrown in for good measure. In his view the United States had already paid its price with the Arabs, and a massive aid bill for Israel would do little further damage.

By noon he may have had some second thoughts on receiving a letter from King Faisal in response to his message on the airlift to Israel. The king was "pained" by the American action. The United States should stop sending arms and should call on Israel to withdraw. Otherwise U.S.-Saudi relations could become "lukewarm." (Nonetheless, the aid bill went forward, and on October 19 President Nixon formally requested $2.2 billion in aid for Israel. The following day King Faisal announced an embargo of oil to the United States as well as substantial production cuts. In retrospect Kissinger wondered whether he had pushed too hard on the Arabs with the $2.2 billion aid request just as the military situation was turning to Israel's advantage.)

The following day, October 17, was largely devoted to talks with the foreign ministers of Morocco, Algeria, Saudi Arabia, and Kuwait. Shortly after 10:00 a.m. Kissinger met with the four ministers in his White House office.[45] He listened while the Saudi foreign minister spelled out the Arabs' concerns: an immediate settlement of the conflict based on complete Israeli withdrawal from Arab territory seized in 1967 and restoration of Palestinian rights in accordance with UN Resolution 242. Kissinger then explained that the basic American policy was now to end the current fighting and to prevent its spread. After the war the United States would engage in a diplomatic effort for a just and lasting peace. U.S.-Arab relations should therefore remain as strong as possible. The Arabs had created a new reality in the Middle East, and the time had come for a diplomatic effort.

At 11:10 a.m. President Nixon began his talks with the four Arab foreign ministers. Omar Saqqaf, the Saudi representative, again presented their collective position, emphasizing the American responsibility to force Israel to withdraw to the 1967 lines. He evoked the long history of Arab friendship for the United States and appealed to it to uphold the principle of the territorial integrity of all states in the area. Nixon replied by referring to his visits to the Middle East, his meetings with various Arab leaders, and his desire to travel again to the area once a peace settlement had been achieved. Echoing Kissinger's themes, he said the United States was now working for a cease-fire, after which it would engage in active diplomacy. He denied that domestic politics would influence U.S. Middle East policy and urged the Arabs to trust Kissinger despite his Jewish background. He concluded by promising to work for the "implementation of Resolution 242" after a cease-fire, but emphasized that he could not promise that Israel would withdraw to the 1967 lines.

On the whole Kissinger felt the meetings had gone well. At the afternoon WSAG meeting he stated that he no longer expected the Arabs to cut off oil to the United States. Ironically, just as he was drawing this optimistic conclusion, the Arab oil ministers meeting in Kuwait were announcing that oil production would be cut by 5 percent each month until Israel had withdrawn from all Arab territories. Three days later King Faisal pushed even further, calling for a 10 percent cut immediately and an embargo of shipments of oil to the United States and the Netherlands.

On the diplomatic front the only sign of progress from the Kosygin visit to Cairo was a Soviet request for the U.S. view of a cease-fire in place linked to Resolution 242.[46] The American response was positive, but asked for a concrete proposal. The Soviet position was conveyed to Ambassador Dinitz, who passed it to Israel, where Golda Meir found it unacceptable. Rather than link a cease-fire in place to Resolution 242, the Israelis favored a link to direct negotiations between the parties.[47] The next day brought little change. Sadat was still not ready to stop.

As Kissinger had expected, the diplomacy opened up on October 19, shortly after Kosygin's return to Moscow from Cairo.[48] During the morning a message from Brezhnev reached the White House requesting urgent consultations on the Middle East crisis. Kissinger should come to Moscow "in an urgent manner." Time was of the essence.[49] Kissinger now felt that a cease-fire could be achieved quickly. In talks with Dinitz he implied that by agreeing to go to Moscow, he would be able to gain Israel a few more days to complete its military operations.[50] Dinitz emphasized the need for a link between a cease-fire and negotiations.[51]

Later that afternoon the administration sent Congress its $2.2 billion aid request, which stated that the United States was trying to reach "a very swift and honorable conclusion, measured in days, not weeks."

The Moscow Talks

Whatever he had told Dinitz, Kissinger primarily went to Moscow not to gain time for Israel's battlefield success but to obtain Soviet and Arab agreement to a cease-fire resolution that could serve as the basis for a subsequent diplomatic effort. If the Soviet and Arab position remained locked into an unacceptable formulation, then Kissinger was prepared to wait, assuming that Israeli advances on the west bank of the canal would eventually bring about a change. On the other hand, if Brezhnev and Sadat were prepared for a simple cease-fire, then Kissinger would press for a quick end to hostilities. He had no interest in seeing Sadat humiliated, especially in view of the encouraging tone of U.S.-Egyptian exchanges over the past two weeks. Nor did he want to force the Soviets to choose between standing aside to watch their clients be defeated by Israel with American arms and intervening militarily on the Arab side, with the attendant risks of nuclear confrontation.

The trick would be to get a cease-fire at just the right moment. Until then, Israel should continue to advance on the ground, but, Kissinger felt, Israel must be prepared to stop once the superpowers reached agreement on a cease-fire. After all, the stakes were no longer confined to the Middle East; they were also global. If necessary, Kissinger was prepared to lean hard on the Israelis.

During his flight to Moscow Kissinger received two important messages. One informed him of the Saudi decision to embargo oil shipments to the United States. Another, from Nixon, was a message for Brezhnev in which Nixon made it clear that Kissinger had full authority to negotiate. Kissinger claims that he resented this unusual procedure, since it deprived him of the tactic of saying that he would have to refer to Washington for final decisions.[52]

The crucial U.S.-Soviet talks began in Moscow on October 21 at about 11:00 a.m. and lasted only four hours. The Soviets, who had initially tried to link a cease-fire to some type of call for Israeli withdrawal from all Arab territory and to guarantees by the superpowers, were swift to change their negotiating position. Time was at a premium, and their client's position was in jeopardy. Ultimately Brezhnev agreed to a simple cease-fire in place, together with a call for the implementation of Security Council Resolution 242, and, at American insistence, also agreed to negotiations between the parties under appropriate auspices.[53] In addition, both sides agreed that they would serve as cochairmen of an eventual peace conference and that prisoners should be immediately exchanged by the parties after the cease-fire.

By noon, Washington time, on October 21 the United States and the Soviet Union had agreed on the text of a cease-fire resolution. It was now up to Kissinger to persuade Israel to accept it. In midafternoon Alexander Haig, now serving as Nixon's chief of staff, telephoned Ambassador Dinitz with the proposed text of the resolution. Dinitz was told that time was short and that no changes could be made. At 9:00 p.m., shortly before the UN Security Council was to convene, the Israeli cabinet decided to accept the cease-fire resolution. In her message informing Nixon of Israel's decision, Meir requested that Kissinger stop in Tel Aviv on his return from Moscow for consultations.

At 10:00 p.m. the Security Council met. Two hours and fifty minutes later, at 12:50 a.m., October 22, it adopted Resolution 338 calling for a cease-fire and negotiations.[54] Within twelve hours the fighting was to stop on all fronts.

Kissinger left Moscow on the morning of October 22 for Tel Aviv,[55] where he arrived at 12:45 p.m., Middle East time (6:45 a.m., Washington time). The cease-fire was still not in effect, but, in his talks with Meir, Kissinger was insistent that Israel move into defensive positions and not violate the cease-fire. He later claimed that he was very tough with the Israelis on this point, and that Prime Minister Meir, Defense Minister Dayan, and Foreign Minister Eban, if not the Israeli military, agreed that

Israel had nothing further to gain from fighting.[56] Kissinger emphasized that the resolution called for the first time for negotiations between Israel and the Arabs. He also assured Meir that there were no secret U.S.-Soviet understandings. Resolution 242 remained as ambiguous as ever as a guideline for the subsequent diplomacy. Israel's bargaining position was not being undercut in advance. Arms would continue to be sent. Kissinger left Israel five hours after his arrival with a feeling that Israel would abide by the cease-fire.[57] One hour after his departure, at 6:50 p.m., Middle East time, the guns fell silent, but not for long.

Toward Confrontation

With the achievement of the cease-fire on October 22, Nixon and Kissinger had reason to feel satisfied. A long and dangerous crisis had been brought to an end without a U.S.-Soviet military confrontation. The parties to the conflict had each made some gains to offset their heavy losses, so perhaps the prospects for peace negotiations would be good. Even the oil embargo seemed manageable, if irritating.

Soon after he reached his office on Tuesday morning, October 23, Kissinger was contacted by the Soviets with charges that Israel was violating the cease-fire.[58] Kissinger was worried. He had sensed the bitterness among the Israeli military at being deprived of victory. He had assured the Soviets that Israel would respect the cease-fire; hence when he called Dinitz to report the Soviet charges, he made it clear that Israel should not try to destroy the nearly surrounded Egyptian Third Army Corps.

From the onset of the crisis Kissinger had realized that American credibility with the Arabs might ultimately be tested in circumstances like these. If the United States were now to stand idly by and watch the Third Army Corps be destroyed with newly delivered American weapons, Kissinger's future role as peacemaker would be gravely jeopardized. It did not now matter which side was technically responsible for firing the first shot after the cease-fire was to have gone into effect. What was clear was that Israeli forces were advancing beyond the October 22 cease-fire lines. Despite his concern, however, Kissinger was not yet unduly alarmed.

Wednesday, October 24, began for Kissinger with a series of exchanges with the Egyptians, Israelis, and Soviets. Sadat was now in frequent communication with Nixon, even on small matters.[59] He asked for the president's help in getting the Israelis to allow medical supplies and food through to the nearly entrapped Third Army Corps. He requested that a U.S. military attaché from Tel Aviv proceed to the front lines to verify

Israel's observance of the cease-fire. Kissinger was prepared to cooperate. He called Dinitz and requested that Israel respect the cease-fire and allow supplies through to the Third Army Corps.[60]

In midafternoon word reached Washington that President Sadat had publicly appealed to the United States and the Soviet Union to send forces to the Middle East to oversee the cease-fire. The White House immediately issued a statement rejecting the idea of forces from the superpowers being sent to the area. Shortly thereafter Kissinger met with Dobrynin at the State Department to discuss the convening of a peace conference. They agreed on Geneva as the site and considered other procedural matters. Dobrynin denied that the Soviets were interested in sending a joint U.S.-Soviet force to the Middle East in response to Sadat's appeal. The meeting ended on a cordial note, and there was no hint of impending crisis.[61]

Three hours later, at 7:05 p.m., Dobrynin called Kissinger to tell him that the Soviets would support the idea of a joint U.S.-Soviet peacekeeping force if the nonaligned members of the UN were to call for one, and shortly thereafter called again to say the Soviets were considering introducing such a resolution. These messages caused deep concern in Washington. Then, at 9:35 p.m., Dobrynin called Kissinger with a "very urgent" message from Brezhnev to Nixon. He slowly read the text over the telephone. It began by noting that Israel was continuing to violate the cease-fire, thus posing a challenge to both the United States and the Soviet Union. Brezhnev stressed the need to "implement" the cease-fire resolution and "invited" the United States to join Moscow "to compel observance of the cease-fire without delay." Then came the threat: "I will say it straight that if you find it impossible to act jointly with us in this matter, we should be faced with the necessity urgently to consider the question of taking appropriate steps unilaterally. We cannot allow arbitrariness on the part of Israel."[62] Kissinger quickly relayed the message to Haig for Nixon. The president's records show that he spoke to Haig for about twenty minutes around 10:30 p.m. That was his only communication with his advisers until the next morning. Nixon reportedly empowered Kissinger to take any necessary action, including calling a military alert.[63] Kissinger then convened an ad hoc session of the National Security Council.

Unquestionably the situation was dangerous. No one knew what the Soviet Union intended to do, but Brezhnev's note unmistakably conveyed his determination not to let Israel destroy the Egyptian Third Army Corps. Kissinger understood the difficulty of the situation for the Soviets and the pressures they would be under to act. Their prestige as a superpower was on the line. This was something with which Kissinger could empathize.

But did the Soviets have the capability to intervene, whatever their intentions? The answer seemed definitely to be yes. The transport aircraft that had been flying arms to the Middle East had all returned to the Soviet Union and could be used as troop carriers. At least seven airborne divisions were on a high state of alert.[64] Two amphibious landing craft were in the eastern Mediterranean with the Soviet squadron.

Though a massive Soviet intervention was still hard to imagine, even with this combination of motives and capabilities, Moscow might yet resort to impressive displays of military power that could have explosive political, and perhaps even military, consequences. For example, a small "peacekeeping" contingent might be sent to deliver supplies to the entrapped Third Army Corps. Would the Israelis fire on Soviet forces in such circumstances? If so, the Soviets might feel compelled to react on a larger scale. If not, Soviet prestige would have gained a significant boost, precisely at a critical moment in U.S.-Arab relations.

Kissinger and the other participants in the NSC meeting reached two conclusions. The Soviets, who had seemingly not taken seriously U.S. warnings about the introduction of their forces into the area, must be under no illusion that the United States did not have the will and the ability to react to any move they might make. To underline this ability, U.S. military forces would be placed on a Def Con 3 alert, which meant that leaves would be canceled and an enhanced state of readiness would be observed worldwide. The Strategic Air Command would be on a higher state of alert than the normal Def Con 4. No change would be needed for the Sixth Fleet, which was already on a stage 3 alert. Although considerably short of a decision to go on a war footing, these visible moves should convey to the Soviets the American determination to act if necessary. If the crisis was quickly resolved, it would be easy to change the alert status.[65]

As had been true earlier in the crisis, Kissinger was concerned that the Watergate scandal not appear to impede the conduct of American foreign policy. Intentional overreaction would be better than underreaction. To underscore the meaning of the alert, Kissinger sent a message to Brezhnev in Nixon's name saying that the sending of Soviet troops to the Middle East would be considered a violation of article 2 of the agreement on the prevention of nuclear war of June 22, 1973.

Before the Soviet threat of intervention, Kissinger and his colleagues had felt that Israel must stop its advances on the Egyptian front. The Israelis had been told in no uncertain terms that the United States would not permit the destruction of the Third Army Corps.[66] But the Soviet threat introduced a new element, and apparently Kissinger signaled to the Israelis that they should be prepared to move against the Third Army if Soviet troops tried to intervene.[67]

Around midnight the first orders for the alert were issued, and at 1:30 a.m. on October 25 its scope was widened. Nixon had not participated in the deliberations of the NSC, but he had reportedly given his approval for the alert in advance.[68] Now the United States would await the Soviet reaction.

During the morning of October 25, while most Americans were first learning of the alert and wondering about its meaning, Kissinger met with Nixon for a long talk.[69] Several new bits of information were now available. Further messages had been received from Sadat, denying that Egypt was violating the cease-fire and emphasizing again that U.S. and Soviet forces were needed to enforce the cease-fire. Moreover, several ships from the Soviet squadron, including the amphibious landing craft, were steaming toward Egypt. A fragmentary piece of intelligence had been received referring to the imminent arrival of Soviet troops in Cairo. In fact, these proved to be the seventy observers and their interpreters whom the Soviets did send to Cairo, but at the time the number was unknown. All in all, the Soviets seemed to be moving toward a confrontation, and the Egyptians seemed to be encouraging it. The president ordered Kissinger to develop a plan for sending U.S. troops to the Middle East in case the Soviets did intervene. Doing so would, at a minimum, provide some leverage to get the Soviet troops out of the region after the crisis subsided. Nixon also told Kissinger to hold a press conference explaining the U.S. moves.

Shortly after noon Kissinger appeared before the press in the State Department auditorium. In a somber but restrained tone he described the various stages of the crisis and the evolution of U.S. policy. It was a brilliant performance, one of his most impressive.

After reviewing the diplomatic efforts of the first two weeks of the crisis, he spoke of the cease-fire and the alert. In the president's name he reiterated U.S. opposition to the sending of U.S.-Soviet forces to the Middle East. He was even more strongly opposed to a unilateral Soviet move into the area. He then reviewed the prospects for a peace settlement, which he termed "quite promising," and had conciliatory words for Israel, the Arabs, and even the Soviets.

In response to several questions about U.S.-Soviet détente, Kissinger emphasized the complex adversarial nature of the relationship, but he refused to condemn the Soviets for violating the spirit of détente. Asked whether the alert had been called because of the American domestic crisis, Kissinger, more in sorrow than in anger, dismissed the idea, although he went on to say that the Soviets might have acted as boldly as they did because of the weakened position of the American president. "One cannot have crises of authority in a society for a period of months without paying a price somewhere along the line."

In his concluding remarks Kissinger spelled out the principles of a new American policy toward the Arab-Israeli conflict:

> Our position is that . . . the conditions that produced this war were clearly intolerable to the Arab nations and that in the process of negotiations it will be necessary to make substantial concessions.
>
> The problem will be to relate the Arab concern for the sovereignty over the territories to the Israeli concern for secure boundaries.
>
> We believe that the process of negotiations between the parties is an essential component of this.[70]

One hour later the UN Security Council passed Resolution 340, calling for an immediate and complete cease-fire, return to the October 22 lines, dispatch of an augmented UN observer force, creation of a UN Emergency Force composed of nonpermanent members of the Security Council, and implementation of Resolution 338. This time the cease-fire did take hold, and the fourth Arab-Israeli war finally ended. A new chapter in American diplomacy was about to open, with Kissinger as the star performer.

Conclusions

American policy toward the Arab-Israeli conflict was fundamentally affected by the events of the October 1973 war. Before the outbreak of hostilities it was widely believed in Washington that stability in the Middle East was ensured by Israeli military predominance; that Arab oil could not be effectively used to pressure the West; that Sadat was not seriously interested in a peace settlement with Israel; and that Soviet influence in the region had reached its limit. The situation in the area caused concern, but not anxiety. Diplomatic initiatives were contemplated, but not with a sense of urgency or with expectations of success.

It would be wrong to maintain that the United States shifted from a pro-Israeli to a pro-Arab policy as a result of the October war. The changes that did occur were more nuanced and multidimensional than the simple Arab-versus-Israel dichotomy suggests. The war did, however, challenge several basic assumptions of U.S. policymakers that had been central to prewar policy.

First, Israeli military power had not ensured stability, as had been expected after 1967. That "lesson," reinforced in the September 1970 crisis, was shattered on October 6. This did not mean, of course, that the military balance was seen as having no importance. The latter stages of the war clearly showed that military power counted for a great deal. Israeli strength alone, however, would not lead to a political settlement, as Johnson in 1967 had hoped it would.

Second, the October war undermined the belief that U.S.-Soviet détente would serve to minimize the danger of regional conflicts. Although Nixon, Kissinger, and Schlesinger all emphasized that détente had been helpful in resolving the crisis, they were acutely aware that the two superpowers had not been able to remain aloof from the Middle East conflict. Each side was too deeply committed to allow its friends to be sacrificed for the spirit of détente. Concrete local interests won out over global abstractions when put to the test. This meant not that détente was illusory or dangerous, but rather that it was limited in scope. Superpower confrontation was still a possibility in the era of détente and negotiations, and this, above all, preoccupied the senior decisionmakers. The events of October 24–25 confirmed their worst fears.

Third, the war challenged the prevailing attitude of policymakers toward the Arab world. Despite the remarkable Israeli military achievements on both fronts, the Egyptians and Syrians had apparently fought quite well. They had also achieved surprise in the initial attack. Moreover, the degree of Arab solidarity was impressive; the use of the oil weapon was well coordinated with the diplomatic and military moves; and the tone of restraint in private and public communications was a welcome contrast to that of 1967. Sadat, in particular, was emphatic in his desire to work with Nixon and Kissinger for a post-hostilities diplomatic settlement. This was a very important new element in the picture.

Fourth, American officials, and Kissinger in particular, found themselves having to learn about petroleum economics as a part of international strategy. Kissinger had paid almost no attention to oil issues before the October crisis. He and others had a hard time distinguishing between the effects of the embargo, which was highly visible but not very important, and the curtailment of production, which sparked the dramatic price increases. Had Nixon and Kissinger been more sensitive to these issues, they might have been more discreet in their handling of the $2.2 billion aid package to Israel, announcing it after the war was over rather than in the midst of the battle. In any event, much of the subsequent diplomacy surrounding the Arab-Israeli conflict was played out under the shadow of the Arab oil weapon, which not only added a sense of urgency but also raised the specter of blackmail.

The United States would henceforth devote much more attention to the Middle East. It would be a top-priority concern for Nixon and Kissinger. Moreover, the United States would consciously try to improve its relations with the principal Arab countries, especially Egypt. This effort would be a primary element in the new American diplomatic strategy, an element that had been conspicuously lacking before October 1973. Nixon and Kissinger felt they could court the Arabs without sacrificing the U.S.-Israeli relationship. In fact, as they saw it, it was the strength of the U.S.-Israeli tie, with the obvious influence this gave Washington over Israeli policy, that would impress the Arabs and convince them that the United States held most of the diplomatic cards once the fighting was over. The Soviets could provide arms; the United States could help regain territory, provided the Arabs were prepared to make appropriate concessions of their own in the context of peace negotiations.

The shift in policy brought about by the October war was at least as important as that produced by the Jordan crisis of 1970. The result of the earlier crisis had been an inactive, status quo–oriented policy; the result of the October 1973 crisis was a much more active approach aimed at bringing about substantial change. For the first time the United States committed its top diplomatic resources to a sustained search for a settlement of the Arab-Israeli conflict.

In view of the importance of the policies forged during October 1973, one is tempted to seek explanations for them in domestic or bureaucratic politics, or in the psychological makeup of the individuals involved. After all, Watergate and the energy crisis were persistent themes throughout the crisis. And both Nixon and Kissinger had strong and unusual personalities.

Domestic politics is often linked in complex ways to foreign policy, and Nixon and Kissinger certainly took it into account as they considered policy choices. The key decisions of the crisis, however—the cease-fire proposals, the airlift to Israel, and the alert—were not responses to domestic politics. Pro-Israeli groups were not responsible for the decision to rearm Israel, largely because Kissinger skillfully persuaded the Israeli ambassador not to "unleash" Israel's supporters. Pro-Arab groups and oil companies played no role in Nixon's decisions to press Israel to accept a cease-fire on October 12 or to save the Third Army Corps. Nor does Watergate explain the military alert of October 24–25.

Crisis periods, especially, tend to isolate policymakers from domestic pressures. Decisions are often made rapidly, before public opinion can be mobilized. Information is closely held, depriving interest groups of the means for effective action. The stakes are high, and the public tends to be deferential to presidential authority, even when that authority has been weakened, as Nixon's had been.

One theme did recur in Kissinger's comments: the rest of the world must not draw the conclusion that the Watergate crisis had weakened the president's ability to conduct foreign policy. The size of the U.S. airlift to Israel, once begun, the magnitude of the aid bill for arms to Israel, and the scope of the American military alert may have been partly related to this desire to appear strong and decisive. In each case, however, the basic decision was not rooted in the fear that Watergate had led other nations to underestimate the United States. Rather, the decisions were responses to external events that seemed to require urgent action. With or without the Watergate affair, the same course almost certainly would have been taken.

Central to the decisions made during the crisis were three widely shared judgments. First, Israel must not be driven to desperation. Second, Sadat should not be humiliated. Third, the United States, not the Soviet Union, should be in the driver's seat when the crisis ended. These views lie behind each of the major decisions made by Nixon and Kissinger.

Some accounts of U.S. policy during the war have emphasized the importance of bureaucratic or personality factors. In some versions Schlesinger and Deputy Defense Secretary William Clements are portrayed as opposing the airlift to Israel; in others, Kissinger is painted as the villain.[71] The reasons given may be institutional—military men resented seeing arms taken from active U.S. units and sent to Israel; they may be linked to economic interests—Clements had ties to the oil industry; or they may be traced to personality—Kissinger and Nixon had deluded themselves with the success of détente and therefore failed to appreciate the ways in which the Soviets were manipulating the situation to their advantage.

Those perspectives, however, do not account for the fact that individuals from widely different backgrounds agreed on each of the major decisions. Whatever their subsequent relationship, Kissinger and Schlesinger did not argue over basic policy in the October war. Whatever his personal feelings toward Israel, Clements helped organize a remarkably efficient airlift to Israel once the orders were given. Bureaucratic politics was barely in evidence, so tight was Kissinger's control over the policymaking machinery. Nor did the policy changes result from the replacement of individuals with one set of views by those of contrasting persuasions. The same officials were in place, with about the same relative power, before and after the war. The difference was that they now saw the situation differently.

The key to the consensus among top officials was the ability of Kissinger to draw on President Nixon's authority—and the fact that top officials generally agreed on the stakes involved in the crisis. On occasion Nixon directly gave orders, but even when he was not present, Kissinger was clearly speaking in his name. In the principal decisions the president was involved, although sometimes rather remotely. When Kissinger would say, "The president wants" or "The president has ordered," few of the other key officials were inclined to argue. Moreover, only Kissinger—and Haig, who often relayed Kissinger's views to the president and then reported back to his former boss—had direct, continuing access to the president.[72]

American policy during the October 1973 war demonstrated once again the centrality of the authority of the president in the conduct of foreign policy, particularly in crises. In this case, Kissinger must be considered an extension of the president, for he was given an unusual margin of responsibility. It was his tie to Nixon, however, not his position as secretary of state, that ensured the acceptance of his formulations. Perhaps if the policies had been less nuanced, less complex, there might have been some overt dissension within the bureaucracy. The Nixon-Kissinger policy, however, could be seen as pro-Israel, pro-Arab, pro-détente, or anti-Soviet, depending on what one was looking for. Those who disagreed with one element of policy were likely to support other aspects. This complexity left Kissinger in a commanding position.

As the crisis came to an end, the Middle East undoubtedly had top priority in American foreign policy. American relations with allies had been damaged by the crisis; détente was under attack; the energy crisis was likely to become more acute. Progress toward an Arab-Israeli settlement would not necessarily solve these problems, but failure to defuse the Middle East situation could only complicate them. Perhaps equally important, for the first time Nixon and Kissinger sensed the opportunity to make progress toward a settlement. The Arabs were looking to Washington now, not to Moscow. The Israelis were heavily dependent on American arms and financial support, which could be translated into influence in the proper diplomatic setting. Public opinion would be supportive of a major U.S. initiative provided it did not become anti-Israeli or appear to be responsive to the Arab oil embargo.

By the time the cease-fire had gone into effect, the United States was already preparing for a new diplomatic effort. It would not be like the Rogers Plan, formal, legalistic, and worked out in U.S.-Soviet negotiations. Instead, the Soviets would be kept out of the substance of the negotiations. Their record during the war had not inspired confidence that they were prepared to play an evenhanded role in settling the conflict. Nor did Sadat seem to want them involved. Furthermore, no American plan would be presented to the parties. Instead, the United States would try to play the role of mediator, eliciting propositions from the parties, trying then to modify them, and eventually pressing for a compromise. The process would move slowly, beginning with concrete issues of particular urgency and proceeding later to more fundamental problems, such as the nature of a final peace settlement. Above all, each step must remain independent of the next; otherwise the process would never get under way, as the United States had discovered in the interim-settlement effort of 1971.

As the war came to a close, Kissinger had already decided on his new strategy—step-by-step diplomacy. Now he merely needed to persuade Israel, the Arabs, the Soviets, Congress, and the American public to give him a chance to prove his success where others had failed. For the next eight months Kissinger was accorded the opportunity to demonstrate both the strengths and limitations of his conception of how to solve the Arab-Israeli conflict.

5

Step by Step: Kissinger and the Disengagement Agreements, 1974–76

THE EIGHT MONTHS that followed the October 1973 war witnessed an unprecedented American involvement in the search for a settlement of the Arab-Israeli conflict. Henry Kissinger, before becoming secretary of state, had devoted little energy to the seemingly intractable issues dividing Israel and its Arab neighbors. Nor had he progressed far in his understanding of the "energy crisis" and the part played by Middle East oil in the international economy. Only the danger of confrontation between the superpowers growing out of tensions in the Middle East seemed capable of arousing in him a sustained interest in the affairs of the region. Now, with the October war a vivid example of the volatility of the Arab-Israeli conflict, Kissinger, with Nixon's full backing, set out to become the peacemaker, orchestrator, mediator, and catalyst in a new diplomatic initiative that would take him repeatedly to countries he had never before visited to deal with statesmen he had previously not taken seriously.

Although President Nixon was eager for the United States to play an active part in resolving the Arab-Israeli conflict, he was also increasingly preoccupied with his crumbling domestic base of support as the Watergate scandal continued to unfold.[1] Kissinger was therefore allowed extraordinary latitude in shaping the details of American diplomacy, calling on Nixon to invoke presidential authority as necessary, keeping the president informed at each stage, and on occasion ignoring his directions.

Above all, Nixon wanted results. Internationally, he worried about the consequences of other nations' concluding that the American domestic crisis had weakened the president's ability to act in foreign affairs. Domestically, he hoped that foreign-policy successes would help him through the crisis of confidence in his judgment and leadership stemming from his handling of Watergate.

Shaping an American Strategy

During the October 1973 hostilities Kissinger and Nixon had both promised an active American diplomatic initiative aimed at "implementing Resolution 242" after the war ended, but they steadfastly refused to promise any specific results, despite Sadat's pleas. The United States, they repeated, was committed to a process, not an outcome. The administration could guarantee that it would make a major effort, but it could not guarantee that Israel would withdraw from all Arab territory or that Palestinian rights would be restored. To do so would be to invite severe domestic criticism and to raise Arab hopes to an unrealistic level. Kissinger frequently mentioned that he feared the Arabs' "romanticism," their impatience, their desire for quick results.[2]

These initial perceptions, shaped by the October war, became the foundations of postwar policy. With the achievement of the shaky cease-fire of October 25, Nixon and Kissinger began to define what the contours of that policy would be. Two key elements quickly emerged. First, the United States would play an active role in trying to resolve the Arab-Israeli conflict. Unlike Johnson after 1967, and they themselves after 1970, Nixon and Kissinger now felt the situation in the Middle East was too threatening to American interests to be ignored; perhaps even more important, an opportunity for a successful American initiative existed.[3]

As Kissinger had sensed during the war, everyone was looking to the United States. He held the cards, or at least so the principal actors believed, which was what mattered. The Israelis, more isolated internationally than ever before, were in the awkward position of being heavily dependent on Washington for arms, economic aid, and diplomatic support. The Arabs, realizing the potential for U.S. influence with Israel, were anxious to turn that potential to their own advantage. As Kissinger and others had hinted, the Soviets could provide arms to the Arabs, but only the United States could produce Israeli territorial concessions through negotiations.[4]

Second, the new American strategy would try to avoid linking initial diplomatic steps with the nature of a final peace agreement. Kissinger had disliked the Rogers Plan of 1969 and was not even particularly keen on

UN Resolution 242. Such public statements of principles might provide psychic gratification to one side or the other, but in his view they did little to advance the diplomatic process. Instead they allowed each side to focus on what it rejected in the abstract plan instead of concentrating on tangible issues in the present. If an active U.S. role in the diplomacy was meant as a signal to the Arabs of a more balanced American policy, Washington's refusal to link first steps with final outcomes was meant to reassure Israel that a settlement would not be imposed against its will.

To sustain an active and effective U.S. role in the evolving diplomacy of the Arab-Israeli conflict, Kissinger felt it necessary to mitigate the international pressures created by the October 1973 war. The Arab offensive had succeeded in mobilizing European, Japanese, and third world support for a rapid settlement on essentially Arab terms. The UN could be counted on to support Egypt, Syria, and the Palestinians. The Soviets were committed to the Arab position, even at some risk to détente and U.S.-Soviet relations. The Arab oil embargo was an added source of tension, as was the continuing danger that the cease-fire would break down.

Although he admired the way in which Sadat had succeeded in marshaling his forces, Kissinger was not prepared to act under these combined pressures. He would therefore try to persuade the American allies to leave him a free hand; he would isolate the Soviets from the substance of the negotiations; he would endeavor to get the oil embargo lifted; he would build support for "moderate" Arab positions at the expense of "radical" ones; he would try to avoid a public quarrel with Israel that might have serious domestic repercussions; and he would attempt to win over the U.S. Congress and press to support his role in the diplomacy. Much of Kissinger's tactical maneuvering in succeeding months was aimed at ensuring that the United States could act free of the multiple pressures, domestic and international, generated by the October war. On the whole, he was remarkably successful.

Kissinger felt previous administrations had erred in viewing their choices as being pro-Israel or pro-Arab. In his view it was precisely the special American relationship with Israel that obliged the Arabs to deal with the United States in the diplomatic arena. Power, not sentiment, was what counted. The difficulty, of course, was that to keep the Arabs looking toward the United States, the diplomatic process had to hold out more hope to them than would another round of war. If war was seen as the answer, the Soviet Union could always provide more than the United States. Consequently, progress toward a settlement was an absolute prerequisite for maintaining the confidence of the Arabs. At a minimum, this meant the return of territory; eventually it implied some move in the direction of addressing Palestinian grievances. For the United States, it meant that Israel would have to make concessions to keep the diplomacy alive. Where possible, the United States might try to extract comparable Arab concessions, but given the kind of issues in dispute, to do so would be difficult. An additional dimension of U.S. diplomacy would therefore be offers of aid to Israel—with the implied threat of withholding it if circumstances so dictated—and promises of assistance to Egypt, Syria, and Jordan to strengthen bilateral relations through other means than delivering Israeli concessions.

U.S.-Egyptian relations were seen as the linchpin of the new American policy in the Arab world, with Jordan and Saudi Arabia playing key supportive roles in favor of Arab "moderation."[5] Only gradually did Kissinger come to perceive Syria's importance; he was even more reluctant to acknowledge the Palestinians as participants in the settlement process. For the moment the new U.S.-Egyptian relationship, already in evidence during the war, was to receive most of Nixon's and Kissinger's attention.

The role of the Soviet Union in the Middle East had long preoccupied Nixon and Kissinger. Having at one time overrated Soviet influence in the Arab world, they were now inclined to minimize the Soviet role in the settlement process. Soviet behavior in the October war, though not viewed as totally contrary to the spirit of détente, was nonetheless not encouraging.[6] Nor had previous U.S.-Soviet efforts to reach agreement on the terms of settlement been successful. The two superpowers not only had different interests in the region but also had a different concept of what a peace settlement should entail. Perhaps most important of all, the key participants in the regional conflict were not anxious to see the Soviets deeply involved in the diplomacy. Certainly the Israelis were unenthusiastic, given Soviet hostility and the lack of diplomatic relations. Jordan was still prepared to work with the United States instead of with the Soviet Union. Sadat was also ready to play his American card, and Soviet-Egyptian relations suffered as a result. Even President Asad of Syria showed a willingness to let Kissinger try his hand, although his skepticism was considerably greater than Sadat's. Finally, there was enough of the cold warrior left in both Nixon and Kissinger to produce a sense of real pleasure in demonstrating the limits of Soviet influence in the Middle East.[7]

To maintain an effective American role in the resolution of the Arab-Israeli dispute, domestic public opinion would have to be mobilized. Most Americans were sympathetic to Israel, a sentiment that was particularly strong in Congress and in the press.[8] The Arab oil embargo was doing little to change this feeling; in fact, it seemed more likely that an anti-Arab backlash might result, making it difficult to pursue the policy of building the new ties to the Arab world that were central to the Nixon-Kissinger strategy. American policy could not appear to be dictated by Arab oil pressures. Domestically and internationally, that would be an untenable posture for the administration. Consequently the new diplomatic initiatives would have to be explained to the American public and to Congress in terms of the overall objective of seeking peace in the Middle East, of strengthening U.S. ties with the Arab world without sacrificing Israel, and of minimizing the ability of the Soviets to threaten Western interests, including oil. Broad support for these objectives could be expected, especially if aid to Israel continued to flow at high levels and if the oil embargo was lifted.

If an active U.S. diplomatic role in the search for an Arab-Israeli settlement was the first principle of the new American policy, the second was the pursuit of a settlement through a step-by-step process.[9] This method soon came to be the hallmark of the Kissinger diplomacy.

Kissinger was skeptical of the American penchant for the "quick fix," the technical solution to a political problem, of negotiations carried on in the blaze of publicity, of bureaucratic compromises, and of good will as a substitute for tangible concessions. Although he would later be charged with some of these mistakes in his own conduct of diplomacy, he was at least conscious of these pitfalls, the weakness of his own role as mediator, and the sizable gap that separated the parties. Unlike other negotiations he had engaged in, the Arab-Israeli arena was one in which the United States faced the challenge of persuading adversaries to make commitments to one another. It was not enough for the United States to develop its own policies; the key to success would be to induce the parties to modify their irreconcilable positions.

Timing would be an important element of the Kissinger step-by-step diplomacy. Kissinger envisaged negotiations' probably going on for several years. The Arabs were pressing for immediate Israeli withdrawal; the Israelis were pleading for time. Kissinger was anxious to pace the negotiations so that some results could be produced at an early date, while still allowing time for all parties to adjust to a gradual, phased approach to a settlement. Most immediately, the Israelis had a national election scheduled for the end of December, and until then no serious negotiations could be expected. Somehow the Arabs would have to be persuaded to wait until early 1974 for the first Israeli withdrawals.

In the meantime it would be important to establish a negotiating frame-work, a forum that would provide the symbolic umbrella under which various diplomatic moves might be made. This forum would be a multi-lateral conference, with U.S. and Soviet participation, to be held in Geneva under UN auspices. Its primary values would be to legitimize the settle-ment process, give the Soviets enough of a sense of participation to pre-vent them from disrupting the peace effort, and provide a setting where agreements could be ratified, talks could be held, and delegations could meet. Kissinger fully expected, however, that progress toward agreements would not be made in such a cumbersome forum.

Instead of counting heavily on Geneva, Kissinger planned to deal with concrete issues through bilateral channels. Most urgent were the prob-lems on the Egyptian-Israeli front. There the armies were entangled in a dangerous fashion, constantly tempting one side or the other to resume hostilities. The Egyptian Third Army Corps was nearly cut off from sup-plies, a situation that was intolerable for Sadat. International pressure was building for Israel to pull back to the October 22 lines, which would release the Third Army. Prisoners of war (POWs) had to be exchanged, an issue of very great sensitivity to the Israelis. The Egyptian semiblockade of Bab al-Mandab at the southern entrance of the Red Sea was preventing the movement of Israeli shipping to and from Aqaba. Taken together, these issues might be negotiated in a first step that would stabilize the cease-fire through a "disengagement" of military forces.

The conceptual underpinnings of the new American policy in the Middle East, initially forged in the midst of the October war, were quickly estab-lished. Nixon and Kissinger, with virtually no opposition from the bu-reaucracy, were committing the United States to an unprecedented active role in mediating the Arab-Israeli conflict, to a step-by-step diplomatic process, and to a disengagement of Egyptian and Israeli military forces at an early date.

Setting the Stage

One result of the improved relationship between Cairo and Washington was President Sadat's frequent and urgent appeal to the United States to help the entrapped Third Army Corps. The Israelis, by contrast, were de-termined to use pressure on the corps to obtain the release of prisoners of war and the end of the naval blockade at Bab al-Mandab. The stalemate threatened to destroy the precarious cease-fire. Kissinger therefore quickly set two urgent goals: first, to stabilize the cease-fire; second, to bring about a separation of military forces. By October 27 the State Department was able to announce that Egyptian and Israeli representatives had agreed to meet to implement the cease-fire agreement. Even before the talks began on October 30, temporary arrangements had been made for the nonmilitary resupply of the Third Army Corps.

The Egyptian and Israeli positions on the terms of a cease-fire and on a military disengagement proved to be far apart. Ismail Fahmy, Egypt's new foreign minister, met with Kissinger on October 29.[10] Two days later he again met Kissinger, as well as President Nixon. Besides discussing the secretary's forthcoming trip to Egypt, Fahmy was authorized to present an eleven-point proposal. Most urgently, Egypt insisted that Israel withdraw unconditionally to the October 22 lines, as called for in UN Resolutions 339 and 340. Once that was done, Egypt would agree to release all prisoners of war.

Kissinger told Fahmy that the plan contained constructive ideas but that it seemed too ambitious at that stage. In discussions during the next two days, Kissinger raised the issue of the October 22 lines, emphasizing that it would be difficult to persuade Israel to withdraw to them and that a broader step as part of the disengagement of forces would make the October 22 lines irrelevant in any case.[11] Reflecting the new tone in U.S.-Egyptian relations, President Sadat, in a speech delivered on October 31, termed the American role "constructive."

Kissinger and Nixon then talked with Israeli prime minister Golda Meir, who arrived in Washington on October 31. Kissinger met with her on the morning of November 1.[12] She was particularly concerned about the fate of Israeli prisoners in Egypt. Continued resupply of the Third Army Corps, she argued, was conditional on the return of wounded prisoners of war, a complete list of all prisoners, and Red Cross visits to them. Israel would agree to a permanent nonmilitary supply of the Third Army Corps once the prisoners were returned and the naval blockade was lifted. Only then would Israel agree to talk to Egypt about the October 22 lines.

Shortly after noon, President Nixon met with Prime Minister Meir. Nixon offered the opinion that Sadat really wanted peace and then laid out the American strategy for the months ahead. He would try to break up the problems so they could be dealt with step by step. The United States would stand up to the Soviets, as it had done in the October war. It would try to improve its relations with Egypt and Syria, which would also help Israel. Nixon's goal would be to ensure "secure borders" for Israel. Meir was undemonstrative, emphasizing only that Israel did not want to be pressed on the October 22 lines. That evening Kissinger dined with Meir and a few others. The atmosphere was chilly, if not hostile.

Kilometer 101

With these initial talks behind him, Kissinger set off for the Middle East on November 5.[13] In Cairo, on November 7, he met President Sadat for the first time. In private talks that day Kissinger began to develop a genuine admiration for the Egyptian leader.[14] The turning point came in discussing the issue of the October 22 lines. Kissinger was in an awkward position, for he knew the Israelis could not easily be pressured, and yet he felt Sadat was right that Israeli forces should not be allowed to keep the Third Army Corps at their mercy.

Sadat was prepared to be flexible on many points, although he was still anxious for Israel to pull back to the October 22 lines. Kissinger replied that if Egypt insisted, he would agree to try to persuade the Israelis. But he offered his opinion that it might be just as easy, although it might take more time, to work out a substantial disengagement of forces that would bypass the issue of the October 22 lines. Meanwhile arrangements could be made to resupply the Third Army Corps. To Kissinger's surprise Sadat agreed with this line of argument.

On November 9 agreement on a cease-fire plan and the exchange of POWs was announced, and two days later a six-point agreement was signed by Israeli and Egyptian military representatives at a point along the Cairo to Suez road known as Kilometer 101.[15] The settlement process was off to a start, albeit a shaky one.

Meanwhile Kissinger flew to Jordan to talk with King Hussein and encouraged the king to participate in the peace negotiations. Without making firm commitments, he expressed sympathy with the king's opposition to a West Bank Palestinian state dominated by the Palestine Liberation Organization. For the moment, however, Kissinger was still concentrating on the Egyptian-Israeli front. Jordan and the Palestinians would be left for later.

In Saudi Arabia Kissinger appealed to King Faisal for support of his diplomatic effort, referring to the oil embargo as an obstacle to the American efforts.[16] He argued the logic of the step-by-step approach and appealed to Faisal for help in opening channels of communication with the Syrians.[17] Faisal gave Kissinger his standard rendition of the Zionist-communist conspiracy but also promised some help, including an easing of the oil embargo once progress began on Israeli withdrawal.[18]

On balance, Kissinger felt pleased with the results of his first trip. He had established a personal relationship with Sadat, and U.S.-Egyptian relations seemed off to a good start. The cease-fire had been stabilized. An important agreement had been signed by Israel and Egypt, with American help. Faisal had promised to relax the oil embargo. Now it was necessary to develop the broad negotiating framework in Geneva as a prelude to disengagement talks. Kissinger was in no rush, being still committed to a gradual pace under close U.S. control.

The Geneva Conference

The first Egyptian and Israeli prisoners were exchanged on November 15. The next day General Aharon Yariv of Israel and General Abd al-Ghany Gamasy of Egypt began talks at Kilometer 101 aimed at implementing the six-point agreement, particularly its second point, concerning "return to October 22 lines in the framework of agreement on the disengagement and separation of forces." On November 18 Kissinger reminded Foreign Minister Fahmy that disengagement should be the first order of business at the upcoming Geneva peace conference, but it could not become a precondition for the convening of the conference. Nor could the issue of Palestinian participation in the peace conference be settled at this stage. Only at the peace conference would the United States be able to use its full influence. In short, Kissinger was trying to build up Geneva as an important step in the process of negotiations and to keep the U.S. role central to substantive progress.

On December 6 Kissinger announced it was "extremely probable" that a conference would be convened in Geneva on December 18. But who would attend? Egypt would go, and Sadat had implied that Syria would go as well.[19] Jordan could be counted on, but since the Arab summit meeting in Algiers the previous month the PLO had been recognized by all Arab countries except Jordan as the sole legitimate representative of the Palestinian people. If the PLO attended the Geneva conference, Israel would not, nor would Israel sit with Syria unless a list of Israeli prisoners held in Syria was forthcoming.

To help overcome Israeli reluctance to attend the conference, Kissinger talked to Defense Minister Dayan in Washington on December 7. Dayan presented a long list of arms requests, and Kissinger implied that the United States would give it favorable consideration. In return, Dayan said disengagement need not await Israeli elections. He proposed a disengagement based on Israeli withdrawal to a line west of the passes, combined with substantial demilitarization of forward areas and an Egyptian commitment to reopen the Suez Canal. Kissinger urged the Israelis not to move too quickly in negotiations. Israel should not look weak. The Arabs should believe it was difficult for the United States to influence Israel; otherwise their expectations would soar.

Kissinger set off on his second trip to the Middle East on December 12, stopping in London en route to deliver an important speech.[20] During the next several days Kissinger traveled to Cairo, Riyadh, Damascus, and Tel Aviv. Only the talks with Sadat were devoid of difficulty. Sadat had already accepted a short delay in opening the Geneva conference, and he now agreed to postpone the substantive phase of disengagement negotiations until mid-January, after the Israeli elections.[21] With King Faisal the next day, December 14, Kissinger won Saudi endorsement for Sadat's approach and a promise that the oil embargo would be ended and production restored once agreement had been reached on the first stage of a settlement.

While Kissinger was lining up support for Geneva among key Arab countries, Israel was making its participation in a peace conference conditional on a number of important points. Israel opposed a strong role for the UN secretary general; it refused to discuss the issue of eventual Palestinian participation at the conference, as Sadat had proposed; and Israel's representatives would not sit in the same room with the Syrians until Syria complied with Israeli demands for a list of POWs and Red Cross visits to them. It began to appear that Israel might boycott Geneva.

At this point Nixon and Kissinger began to exert heavy pressure on Israel. At 6:45 p.m. on December 13 in Washington, Israeli minister Mordechai Shalev was handed a letter from Nixon to Meir. She had objected to the draft of a joint U.S.-USSR letter to the UN secretary general on convening the Geneva conference. Nixon said he was disturbed by her attitude and denied that the UN secretary general would have more than a symbolic role. Regarding the Palestinians, Nixon argued that the mention of Palestinian participation in the conference did not prejudice the outcome and that, in any case, the participation of additional members of the conference would require the agreement of all the initial participants. In short, Israel would not be forced to negotiate with the Palestinians. Nixon concluded his letter by warning the prime minister that the United States would not understand Israel's refusal to attend the conference and that he would no longer be able to justify support for Israel if Israel did not send its representatives to Geneva.[22]

The next day, on learning that the Israeli cabinet had not been able to reach a decision on attending Geneva, Nixon sent another message. The United States was prepared to delay the conference to December 21. Nixon referred to Israel's long-standing goal of negotiations with the Arabs, terming it inconceivable that Israel would not now take this step. In any event, the president had ordered Kissinger to attend the opening session of the Geneva conference whether Israel was present or not.[23]

While an effort was being made to obtain Israeli agreement to the Geneva conference through a combination of pressures and promises,[24] Kissinger set off for his first meeting with Syria's president, Hafiz al-Asad.[25] Kissinger found Asad to be intelligent, tough, personable, and possessed of a sense of humor. He was also the least conciliatory of all the Arab leaders Kissinger had met to date. Asad implied that he did not object to the convening of the Geneva conference on December 21, but that Syria would not attend unless a disengagement-of-forces agreement was reached first. And disengagement, he thought, should involve the entire Golan Heights. Nor was he prepared to yield to Kissinger's pleas to turn over a list of Israeli POWs. After six and one-half hours of talks with Asad, Kissinger left for Israel empty-handed.[26]

During the next two days, December 16 and 17, Kissinger used all his persuasive abilities to convince the Israelis they should attend the Geneva conference. He met with Golda Meir alone and with members of her cabinet, painting for them a grim picture of the consequences of a breakdown in the diplomatic process. Much more than the Middle East was at stake. Global stability, international economic order, the coherence of the NATO alliance, and virtually every other major issue in world politics was linked to Israel's decision. The Israelis held out for one more change in the letter of invitation—no mention of the Palestinians by name—and, subject to that condition, the cabinet met late at night to approve of Israel's attending the Geneva conference on December 21.

Kissinger now made one last try to obtain Syrian attendance. In return for a list of POWs, Israel would allow Syrian villagers to return to their homes in Israeli-controlled areas. Egypt's foreign minister, Fahmy, discussed the proposal with Asad at Kissinger's request, and the American ambassador in Beirut traveled to Damascus to take up the matter again with the Syrian leader. On December 18 Kissinger received Asad's reply, to the effect that Syria would not attend this phase of the Geneva talks but might participate later.[27]

On December 21 the Geneva conference finally convened under the auspices of the UN secretary general, with the United States and the Soviet

Union as cochairmen, and with the foreign ministers of Egypt, Jordan, and Israel in attendance. A table with Syria's nameplate on it remained unoccupied. Each foreign minister spoke, but largely for the public back home, not for one another. Kissinger tried to articulate his step-by-step strategy, stating that the goal of the conference was peace but that the urgent need was to strengthen the cease-fire by accomplishing a disengagement of forces as the "essential first step" on the path of implementing UN Resolution 242.

With these formal remarks the Geneva conference recessed, not to be convened in plenary session again for an indefinite period. A symbol now existed, however, a useful fiction perhaps, and a forum where working groups might discuss aspects of a settlement was available if needed. The endeavor had not all been in vain, but one might wonder if the results were commensurate with the effort.

Egyptian-Israeli Disengagement

Having successfully convened the Geneva conference, Kissinger now faced the challenge of producing early results on the Egyptian-Israeli front. Several related problems stood in his way. The Syrians were on a high level of military alert in late December, and a resumption of fighting seemed possible. The oil embargo was continuing, and, equally important, the Organization of Petroleum Exporting Countries (OPEC) had decided to double oil prices on December 23. More than ever, the energy crisis hung over the Arab-Israeli negotiations.

Apart from difficulties with Syria and the frustration of the continuing oil embargo, Kissinger had to confront again the fact that the positions of Egypt and Israel on disengagement were still far apart. In Israel on December 17 he had discussed disengagement with Meir and her top aides. The Israeli position was that a small Egyptian force would be allowed to remain on the east bank of the canal up to a distance of ten kilometers. A lightly armed Israeli force would control the main north-south road beyond the Egyptian forces, and the Israeli main forces would be stationed east of the Mitla and Giddi passes, beyond Egyptian artillery range. Israel would not yield the passes in the disengagement phase. On other points there was less Israeli consensus. Some cabinet members felt Egypt should end the state of belligerency in return for the pullback of Israeli forces and should allow free passage for Israeli ships in the Suez Canal and at Bab al-Mandab. Some limits on Egyptian forces on both banks of the Suez Canal were also desired. Egypt should begin work on reopening the canal and rebuilding cities along it as a sign of peaceful intentions.

Egypt's position, as conveyed to Kissinger during his pre-Geneva talks in Cairo, began with the proposition that neither Egypt nor Israel should gain military advantage in the disengagement phase. Egypt would keep its forces east of the canal on existing lines in numbers not to exceed two divisions, a reduction of three divisions from current levels. No heavy artillery and no surface-to-air missiles would be placed across the canal. Israel would retain control of the eastern ends of the passes. A demilitarized zone would be established between the Egyptian and Israeli lines, to be patrolled by UN troops. Egypt would begin work on clearing the canal and would rebuild the cities once Israeli troops had withdrawn. Israeli cargoes would be allowed to pass through the canal after it reopened.

Two gaps separated the Egyptian and Israeli positions. Egypt wanted Israeli forces to withdraw east of the passes; Israel refused. Israel wanted only a token Egyptian force on the east bank; Sadat was thinking of two infantry divisions with 100 tanks each. It would be difficult for him publicly to accept substantial force limitations in territory returned to his control. Nonetheless, the conceptual underpinnings of the two sides' positions were not very far apart, and agreement seemed possible.

Israeli elections for the Knesset were held on December 31. The opposition to Prime Minister Meir's Labor Alignment coalition gained some strength, but not to the point of making a new cabinet and prime minister necessary.

With Israeli elections out of the way, Dayan was sent to Washington for talks with Kissinger on January 4 and 5. He presented a five-zone concept for disengagement, in which each party would have two limited-force zones, separated by a UN buffer. He also specified the type of force limitations Israel could accept. Basically, each side's forces should be beyond the artillery range of the other side, and surface-to-air missiles should not be able to reach the other's aircraft. Also, the number of tanks in the limited zones should be kept very small.

During their talks Dayan urged Kissinger to return to the Middle East to aid in reaching an agreement. This idea proved to be acceptable to Sadat, and Kissinger left late on January 10. Kissinger originally expected to help establish the framework for an agreement, the details of which would be worked out by the parties at Geneva, but Sadat was anxious for results and asked Kissinger to stay in the region until an agreement was reached. Kissinger thus embarked on his first exercise in "shuttle diplomacy," flying between Egypt and Israel with proposals.

On January 13 the Israelis handed Kissinger a map of the proposed disengagement line and authorized him to show it to Sadat, which he did the next day. Sadat had already accepted, in his first talk with Kissinger, the idea of force limitations in three zones and had promised to work for the end of the oil embargo once an agreement was reached. Now he also said he would accept Israeli forces west of the passes, but he had trouble with the extent of force limits.[28] To overcome Sadat's reservations, Kissinger suggested that the United States might take the responsibility for proposing the limitations on forces. Perhaps it would be easier for Sadat to accept an American plan than an Israeli one. And instead of publicly announcing the limits in the formal documents, these could be defined in letters exchanged by Sadat and Nixon. In addition, Sadat's private assurances on Israeli cargoes transiting the canal could be handled in a secret memo of understanding. Sadat agreed.

In Israel the next day, January 15, Prime Minister Meir dropped the demand for an end of belligerency as part of the disengagement agreement. A few changes in force levels and the line of disengagement were made, wherein Dayan played an especially constructive role. With a new map in hand, Kissinger returned to Aswan to see Sadat on January 16, and Sadat agreed to scale down the Egyptian presence on the east bank to eight battalions and thirty tanks.[29] Kissinger then went back to Israel, and the next day, at 3:00 p.m., President Nixon announced that the two parties had reached an agreement on the disengagement of their military forces. The following day the chiefs of staff of Israel and Egypt signed the agreement at Kilometer 101.[30]

With the signing of the disengagement agreement on January 18, Nixon and Kissinger had entered into important and unprecedented commitments for the United States. American prestige in the Arab world was on the rise, and more than ever the United States seemed to hold the key cards. The Israelis might complain of excessive pressure, but the agreement was not bad for Israel, and U.S. aid was still flowing in large quantities. A mood of optimism, a rare occurrence, could be sensed in much of the Middle East.

Interlude between Disengagements

Kissinger's next task was to preserve this mood by translating it into new agreements that would help develop momentum toward a settlement. To do so, he set off immediately from Aswan for talks with King Hussein and President Asad. Meanwhile President Sadat, as promised, flew to Saudi Arabia to try to persuade King Faisal to take the lead in lifting the oil embargo against the United States, an act that Kissinger had termed "increasingly less appropriate" earlier in the month.[31]

Agreement on the Egyptian-Israeli front did little to dampen expectations or ease tensions elsewhere in the Middle East. Now Syria, Jordan, and perhaps even the PLO were ready to get in on the act. Israel, however, was hardly anxious to face a new set of negotiations, fearing that once more American pressure would be brought to bear to extract territorial concessions as the price of keeping diplomacy alive. Much as improved U.S.-Arab relations might be desirable in the abstract, Prime Minister Meir feared they would be purchased in Israeli coin. Timing of a second step was therefore bound to be a problem. Kissinger decided to use the unavoidable interval to consolidate the gains of the first round and to lay the basis for a next step between Syria and Israel.

Kissinger next began to try to end the oil embargo, while simultaneously laying the groundwork for a Syrian-Israeli agreement. Nixon was anxious to be able to announce the end of the embargo in his State of the Union message to Congress at the end of the month, and the Egyptians and Saudis were bombarded with messages to that effect.[32] Kissinger also began to try out an idea he had tentatively discussed during his recent trip to Syria and Israel. If Syria would give the United States a list of Israeli POWs, Israel would agree to make a concrete proposal on disengagement.

The United States proposed a plan to Asad on February 5. Syria would tell the United States the number of Israeli POWs, and the information would then be conveyed to Israel. Once it received the actual names, Israel would make a concrete proposal on the pullback of its forces. After Red Cross visits with the Israeli prisoners in Syria, Kissinger would transmit the Israeli proposal to Asad and would invite an Israeli delegation to Washington for further talks. Negotiations would then begin in Geneva in the context of the already existing Egyptian-Israeli military working group. On February 9 Asad accepted this procedure.

On February 18 Nixon and Kissinger decided to drop the issue of the embargo for the time being. The next day Nixon announced that Kissinger would make another visit to the area, and on February 25 Kissinger departed on his fourth trip in as many months.

Shuttle Diplomacy

Kissinger met with Asad for four hours on the night of February 26 and again on the following morning. The discussions were complex but basically friendly, Asad showing flexibility on procedural issues and toughness on substance. As previously agreed, Kissinger was authorized to transmit to the Israelis the list of POWs, which he had actually been given before he left Washington.[33] Red Cross visits would begin, and Israel would be expected to make a concrete proposal on disengagement. Asad made it clear that if Israel offered nothing more than a pullback to the post-1967 cease-fire lines, he would break off the talks. Kissinger was inclined to think he was serious and so told the Israelis during his stop on February 27. He then left the Israelis to develop their proposal over the next twenty-four hours before his return visit.

Meanwhile Kissinger flew to Egypt for talks with Sadat. U.S.-Egyptian ties were developing well and rapidly, and full diplomatic relations were restored on February 28. Sadat extended an invitation to Nixon to visit Egypt. Bilateral issues, including aid and the long-term prospects for U.S. arms sales to Egypt, financed by Saudi Arabia, were also discussed. By that time Kissinger was relying heavily on Sadat's advice on how to deal with other Arab leaders.

Kissinger was pleased with his talks with Sadat and began to count heavily on Egypt's leadership in the Arab world. Having once erred by underestimating Sadat and Egypt, Kissinger now seemed on the verge of making the opposite mistake.

From Egypt Kissinger flew to Israel, where he received the Israeli proposal. Basically the Israeli plan was for disengagement to be modeled on the Egyptian-Israeli agreement of January, with three zones—one Israeli, one UN, and one Syrian—all within the territory captured by Israel in October 1973. Not only would Quneitra remain entirely under Israeli control, but also Israeli forces would remain well beyond the October 6 lines.

Kissinger feared that Asad would reject the proposal and that the talks would end then and there. Therefore, when in Damascus on the evening of March 1, Kissinger did not give Asad the details of the Israeli plan. Instead he concentrated on the concept of limited-force zones and a UN buffer. He also pinned down Syrian agreement to send a representative to Washington for talks later in the month, following a similar visit by an Israeli official. Kissinger left Damascus with little in the way of substantive progress, but he did reach agreement on a further exchange of views over the next several weeks. Asad, not to be outdone by the more effusive Sadat, had embraced the secretary in Arab fashion for the first time. An improbable but genuine personal relationship was beginning to develop between these two very different men.

Kissinger's next stop was Saudi Arabia, his goal there being to urge again the removal of the oil embargo and to solicit support for a Syrian-Israeli disengagement. The secretary also discussed with the Saudis ways of strengthening bilateral economic and security relations. The idea of creating several joint commissions was put forward and eventually was implemented, symbolizing in a tangible way Kissinger's desire to use American technology and arms as complementary to his diplomatic efforts, with the aim of building a strong U.S. presence in key Arab countries.

As Kissinger flew back to Washington on March 4, the Egyptian-Israeli disengagement agreement was completed, with all parties in their new positions. Simultaneously, tensions increased on the Syrian front as Asad began to raise the danger of renewed hostilities. In the course of the next two months, negotiations on Syrian-Israeli disengagement were to be accompanied by heavy shelling and many casualties on the Syrian front. Asad was clearly going to be more difficult to deal with than Sadat had been, and the Israelis were also not in a particularly conciliatory frame of mind.

On his return to Washington Kissinger consulted with Nixon on the results of his trip. One question requiring presidential decision concerned the terms on which Israel would receive the $2.2 billion in emergency assistance to cover the purchase of military equipment. Nixon was not averse to pressuring Israel; he was unhappy with the recent Israeli proposal on disengagement. He and Kissinger therefore agreed that for the moment all $2.2 billion would be extended as credit. The president would have the option until July 1 of waiving repayment of as much as $1.5 billion. If Israel was forthcoming, it could expect favorable presidential action. Meanwhile an aid package was being put together for fiscal year 1975 which would, for the first time in years, contain a substantial sum, $250 million, for Egypt, and an unprecedented $207.5 million for Jordan.[34] Only $350 million would be requested for Israel, in the knowledge that Congress would increase that sum significantly in any event. Aid was clearly going to be an important adjunct of the Nixon-Kissinger diplomacy.

Kissinger recognized that it would be difficult to reach an agreement between Israel and Syria on disengagement. The United States alone might be able to persuade Israel to make the necessary concessions, using a combination of pressure and positive inducements, but how could Syria be brought to a more workable position? Could Sadat and other Arab leaders play a role? What about the Soviets, who seemed so anxious to be involved in the negotiations? Would Asad be influenced by the offer of American aid? Kissinger needed time to explore each of these possibilities and to let each of the parties reconsider its opening stance on disengagement.

The first order of business was to end the oil embargo. Nixon referred to this again in a press conference on March 6. The Arab oil producers would soon be meeting in Tripoli. If the embargo was not then lifted, the American diplomatic effort would be undermined. After some delays most Arab oil producers announced on March 18 that the embargo against the United States was ended, at least provisionally.

Syria had opposed the lifting of the embargo. Kissinger was now anxious to bring inter-Arab pressure to bear on Asad to accept a disengagement agreement. Egypt, Saudi Arabia, and Algeria could all play a role. If Syria refused a reasonable offer, Kissinger wanted to make sure that Asad would be isolated rather than supported by a bloc of rejectionists.

Kissinger now needed a reasonable Israeli offer to lure Asad toward an agreement. On March 15 and 19 Kissinger met with Foreign Minister Abba Eban. He explained his strategy of trying to isolate Syria from the radical Arabs and stressed the need for continued movement in the diplomatic arena. Israel would have to pull back to the October 6 lines, if not farther, and would have to give up Quneitra. Israel should not, however, be expected to abandon any settlements on the Golan Heights at this stage. Dayan should bring an Israeli proposal based on this thinking when he visited Washington later in the month.

On March 24 Kissinger set off for the Soviet Union, where, among other things, he would try to keep the Soviets from obstructing his efforts at disengagement on the Syrian-Israeli front. During a three and one-half hour meeting on March 26, described as the "toughest and most unpleasant" he had ever had with Brezhnev and his top aides, Kissinger resisted Soviet pressure to return the negotiations to Geneva. General Secretary Brezhnev hotly accused Kissinger of violating agreements that the talks would be held under joint U.S.-USSR auspices and referred to assurances given to Foreign Minister Gromyko in February that the negotiations would be conducted at Geneva. Kissinger defended his actions as being taken at the request of the regional parties. In any case, they were only paving the way for talks on a final settlement that would be held at Geneva. Obviously irritated at the growing American involvement in the Arab world, Brezhnev accurately accused Kissinger of trying to keep the Soviet Union out of the substance of the negotiations. He argued that Syria wanted the Soviets to be present.

Kissinger quickly checked with Asad on whether he did in fact want the Soviets involved at this stage. Asad replied obliquely that the agreed procedure was for Dayan to go to Washington, followed by a Syrian repre-sentative. Then Kissinger would return to the Middle East, after which a military working group could conclude the details of an agreement in Geneva with the Soviets present.

Shortly after his return from Moscow, the secretary of state met with Dayan in Washington on March 29.[35] Dayan brought a large arms re-quest—for 1,000 tanks, 4,000 armored personnel carriers, and much more—as well as an Israeli proposal for a disengagement line that would run east of the October 6 line. Israeli forces would emphatically remain in Quneitra. Kissinger was irritated by the Israeli proposal, whose only value, in his view, was the concept of a buffer zone flanked by two limited-force zones to the east and west. Kissinger warned the Israelis that Asad would not accept the line and termed their proposal inadequate, but he repeated that Israel should not give up any settlements at this stage.

Syrian-Israeli Disengagement

Having achieved enough during March and April to justify another round of shuttle diplomacy, Kissinger departed for the Middle East on April 28. Little did he realize at the time how long and difficult the negotiations would be. It was clear to Kissinger and his colleagues that a disengage-ment agreement between Syria and Israel would be much more difficult to attain than the one between Egypt and Israel. In the latter case, both sides wanted an agreement and had come close to an accord on basic issues before Kissinger began his shuttle. In the Syrian-Israeli case, the positions of the two parties were far apart, the incentives for an agreement were lacking, and the objective situation on the ground lent itself less well to an agreement than did the situation in Sinai. Moreover, both Syria and Israel were governed by somewhat shaky coalitions. Neither could afford to appear soft in the negotiations.

If the local parties had less interest in an agreement, the United States had more of a stake than before. Among other things, it must protect the Egyptian-Israeli agreement and, beyond that, the flourishing U.S.-Egyptian relationship. If Syria refused to reach a comparable disengagement agree-ment, Sadat's position would be threatened in the Arab world, and a radi-cal, rejectionist bloc might gain influence. War might resume on the Syrian front, and Egypt might well be pulled in. Apart from the intrinsic danger of another war, that situation would provide the Soviet Union with new opportunities for reasserting its presence in the region. Finally, without an agreement there might be another troublesome oil embargo.

Kissinger realized he would have great problems with the Syrians and the Israelis. To deal with the former, he counted on building strong Arab support for his efforts. With the Israelis, he would, as usual, have to combine carrot and stick. Before Kissinger's departure for the Middle East, Nixon had waived repayment on $1 billion of the $2.2 billion in aid to cover arms purchases. In normal times that might have won Kissinger a cordial reception in Israel, but these were not normal times, in part because of the continuing Watergate scandal.

Kissinger felt that Israel would have to make concessions on the line of disengagement and that the Syrians, who rejected any force limitations other than a narrow buffer zone, would have to back down as well. First he would try to win consensus on an acceptable line. Then, it might be hoped, the other elements of agreement would begin to fall into place.

His talks in Israel on May 2 did nothing to make Kissinger optimistic. The Israelis were angry at the United States for a vote it had cast in the UN and were obdurate about any alteration of the position Dayan had presented in late March. Why should Asad be rewarded for having gone to war against Israel and lost? Why now should he get a better offer than the more reasonable Sadat? Was it good for U.S. interests to appease the most militant of the Arabs? What would the world think if Israel and the United States submitted to such blackmail? And so the arguments went, until in despair Kissinger turned to Nixon for help. A letter from Nixon to Meir on May 4 warned her not to allow Israeli actions to jeopardize the favorable trends in the area. Otherwise the United States, out of friendship for Israel and a sense of responsibility, would have to reexamine the relationship between the two countries.

In Damascus the next day, Kissinger avoided precise discussion of the Israeli line of disengagement. Instead he emphasized to Asad the weakness of Prime Minister Meir's domestic position and the linkages between Israeli domestic politics and its foreign policy. He raised the issue of U.S. aid to help Syria with reconstruction. Asad remained adamant that the disengagement line would have to be west of the October 6 line but seemed to show flexibility on other issues, such as force limitations.

Over the next several days, Israel began to modify its proposal on the disengagement line.[36] Part of Quneitra would now be returned to Syria, but the western part of the city must remain under Israeli control. Kissinger told the Israelis that Asad would not accept such an arrangement. On May 7 Kissinger flew to Cyprus to brief Gromyko on the talks and found that the Soviets were prepared to remain neutral.[37]

Despite some progress in Israel on May 6 and 7, Kissinger was not optimistic. In Damascus on May 8 he disclosed some of Israel's concessions to Asad, but he withheld others so that he would have something to show on later trips. The tactic was risky, but Kissinger felt he had to avoid whetting Asad's already substantial appetite for Israeli concessions, while at the same time being able to show continued progress.[38] In any event, on May 8 Asad began to talk seriously about a line in the vicinity of that proposed by Israel.[39] Quneitra and the three surrounding hills now loomed as the main obstacle.

In his meeting with President Asad on May 11, Kissinger encountered a stalemate. Asad insisted on all of Quneitra as well as the three surrounding hills. Israel would simply not yield on the hills, the "Himalayas of General Gur," as Kissinger termed them. On May 13, however, he did get Israeli agreement to a Syrian civilian presence in all of Quneitra, along with two other minor concessions.[40] He decided on one last trip to Damascus on May 14; then he would return to Washington. In Damascus he found that Asad was not satisfied with the last Israeli proposal, insisting that the line must lie along the peak of the hills and that UN troops, not Israelis, must occupy the peaks. By now the bargaining concerned a few hundred meters, but neither side seemed prepared to yield.[41]

At this point President Nixon weighed in with Kissinger, urging him to continue to work for an agreement and promising him his full support. If Israel was intransigent, Nixon was prepared to go very far if necessary. On May 14 he asked for a list of all military and economic aid promised to Israel, as well as the total of tax-free private contributions to Israel.[42] He also asked for ideas on aid to Syria as a possible incentive.

This was what the Israelis had long feared—pressure on them and offers of aid to the Arabs. In this instance, however, Nixon did not cut aid to Israel. Instead the negotiations inched forward, as Kissinger shuttled back and forth. Encouraged by some members of the Israeli cabinet, Kissinger decided on May 15 to begin to introduce his own ideas in talks with Asad and the Israelis. As he had done in January once the gap had been narrowed, he would try to find a compromise that left each side's basic interests intact. Perhaps the Syrians would find his ideas easier to accept than Israel's.

On May 16 Kissinger succeeded in inducing the Israelis to pull back to the base of the hills. He immediately flew to Damascus to try out ideas of his own.[43] The next day he reported to Nixon that he was close to an agreement on a disengagement line. In Damascus on May 18, however, it seemed as if the remaining gap could not be bridged. Kissinger decided to leave, began drafting a departure statement, and had his luggage sent to the plane. At the last moment Asad dropped his insistence on controlling the hills west of Quneitra and urged Kissinger to keep trying for an agreement. Israel could keep the hills if Kissinger would guarantee that no heavy weapons capable of firing into Quneitra would be placed there. On May 19 Kissinger was able to obtain Israel's assent to Asad's request, and on May 20 he returned to Damascus with a map of the agreed line.

With agreement on the line of disengagement virtually assured, the problem arose of force limitations and the size of the restricted armaments zones.[44] In addition, Asad wanted Israel to give up all the positions on Mt. Hermon. Syria also wanted only a small UN force in the buffer zone, whereas Israel preferred at least 2,000 to 3,000 UN troops. After two more days of haggling over these issues, on May 22 Kissinger began to lose heart. Once again he drafted a departure statement and planned to leave the next day. Egypt, however, had sent General Gamasy to Syria, and by the time of Kissinger's next visit to Damascus, on May 23, Asad had changed his position to accept a large UN force and a wider buffer zone of ten kilometers and limited-force zones of fifteen kilometers. He was still insisting, nevertheless, on fairly sizable armaments in the limited zones, while accepting the concept developed on the Egyptian front of keeping surface-to-air missiles and heavy artillery out of range of the other side's lines. Kissinger returned on May 24 to Israel, where he faced demands that Asad commit himself to preventing terrorist attacks from his side of the lines. Israel also asked for a U.S. commitment that the UN force would not be withdrawn without the consent of both parties to the agreement. Israel also wanted reassurances on long-term military supplies. From this point on, Prime Minister Meir and Defense Minister Dayan were extremely helpful and flexible in working out the final details of an agreement.

On May 26 the drafting of the final documents began. To Kissinger's consternation, issues that he thought had been settled were now reopened by Asad. Once more it seemed as if the talks would collapse.[45] On May 27 Asad backed down, and, after ten hours of talks, Kissinger agreed to make one more trip to Israel to work out compromises on several more points. Then, on May 28, in four hours of private conversation, Asad gave Kissinger his oral commitment that he would not allow the Syrian side of the disengagement line to become a source of terrorist attacks against Israel. With that concession in hand, Kissinger flew to Israel, and on May 29 the announcement was made that Syria and Israel had reached agreement on the terms of disengagement. Two days later Syrian and Israeli military representatives signed the necessary documents in Geneva.[46]

The agreement consisted of a public document, a map, a protocol on the status of the UN forces, and several secret letters between the United States and the two parties detailing the understandings on force levels and other issues.[47] The force-limitation agreement specified a UN buffer zone paralleling the post-1967 line and including the city of Quneitra. In zones of ten kilometers east and west of the buffer zone, each party could station two brigades, with no more than 6,000 men, 75 tanks, and 36 short-range (122 mm) artillery pieces. In adjacent zones of ten kilometers, no artillery with a range of more than twenty kilometers, and no more than 162 artillery pieces, would be allowed. No surface-to-air missiles could be closer than twenty-five kilometers to the front lines. UN Disengagement Observer Forces (UNDOF) would have the right to inspect these zones, and U.S. aircraft would carry out reconnaissance flights as in the January Egyptian-Israeli accord. Agreement was reached on the exchange of prisoners, and both sides declared that disengagement was only a step toward a just and durable peace based on UN Resolution 338.

Nixon wrote to Asad on May 29 to confirm that Israel would observe the cease-fire on the hills around Quneitra, that no Israeli forces or weapons would be stationed on the eastern slopes of the hills, and that no weapons that would be capable of firing into Quneitra would be placed on the hills. Nixon also informed the Israelis that the last paragraph of the public agreement was to be interpreted to mean that guerrilla raids were contrary to the cease-fire and that the United States recognized Israel's right of self-defense in the event of violations. As usual, the Israelis also insisted on a memorandum of understanding dealing with such contingencies as a breakdown in the cease-fire at Syria's initiative and on the pacing of the negotiations. To the Syrians, the United States committed itself to work for the full implementation of UN Resolution 338.

With the signing of the agreement between Syria and Israel, together with all the side agreements conveyed through the United States, Kissinger and Nixon could point to another outstanding achievement in their Middle East diplomacy. By itself, the step was modest, but in light of the recent history of Syrian-Israeli relations it was substantial indeed. The lingering question, of course, was whether it was a step toward a more comprehensive peace agreement, or whether it would prove to be merely a pause before another round of fighting at a later date. Was Kissinger determined to continue his efforts, or, after spending one month of murderously difficult negotiations for limited results, would he conclude that no further progress was possible? Would "step-by-step" remain his preferred tactic, and, if so, where would the next step be? All these questions would have to be dealt with in the near future, but first President Nixon wanted to reap the rewards of Kissinger's efforts by staging a whirlwind tour of the Middle East. The adulation of the Egyptian crowds might take his mind off Watergate.

Nixon to the Middle East

President Nixon's trip to the Middle East was an odd affair.[48] Inevitably he was accompanied by an enormous retinue of aides, security men, and journalists. Every detail of the visit had been worked out by advance men. The local governments were nearly overwhelmed by the onslaught of American technicians, public-relations experts, TV crews, and assorted hangers-on.

Nixon himself was not in good health, his leg being inflamed and sore from a mild attack of phlebitis. Presumably his emotional state was less than serene as well.[49] For the next several days Kissinger seemed to sulk in the background as Nixon received an incredibly enthusiastic reception in Cairo and Alexandria. Sadat went to great lengths to emphasize the new chapter in U.S.-Egyptian relations that he had helped to open. The two leaders got on well, and the immense crowds almost succeeded in raising Nixon's flagging spirits.

Nixon flew to Saudi Arabia for two days of talks on June 14 and 15. Here the focus was primarily on strengthening bilateral relations and on oil. He next went on to Damascus for a somewhat restrained reception and cordial talks with President Asad. Full diplomatic relations were restored on June 16. Nixon and Asad also discussed next steps in the peacemaking process. Nixon said that the Geneva conference should be reconvened in September. Then, to an astonished and delighted Asad, he explained that the purpose of step-by-step diplomacy was to persuade the Israelis to pull back gradually on the Syrian front until they reached the edge of the Golan Heights, tumbled over, and returned to the old borders.[50] The imagery was fanciful, but the Syrians took it as a commitment to work for full Israeli withdrawal. As he left Damascus, Nixon drafted a long list of possible aid projects that might be offered to Syria. He feared that Asad might require substantial inducements to remain on good behavior.

The president was more at home on his next stop, Israel, than earlier. His counterpart, however, was no longer the worthy friend and adversary of former crises, Golda Meir, but rather Yitzhak Rabin, the new prime minister of Israel and something of an unknown quantity, despite his years in Washington as ambassador. Nixon talked at some length about the importance of dealing quickly with King Hussein on the fate of the West Bank. Better Hussein now, he observed, than Arafat later.[51] When discussing terrorism with the Israelis, Nixon startled his hosts by leaping from his seat and declaring there was only one way to deal with terrorists. Then, Chicago-gangland style, he fired an imaginary submachine gun at the assembled cabinet members. Strange behavior, strange president. Best friend or dangerous enemy of Israel? It was hard to tell.

On June 19 the president returned to Washington. Three days later, the Judiciary Committee completed its hearings, which had been watched by a fascinated television audience while Nixon was winging his way through the Middle East. On June 24 the committee issued four more subpoenas to Nixon. The next day he left for Moscow. Affairs of state continued to provide him with some relief from Watergate, and he could be sure that the Soviet leaders would not take seriously the charges against him of obstructing justice and misusing the office.

Back in Washington, Nixon agreed on the last day of the fiscal year to waive Israel's repayment of $500 million in credit for arms, a bit more carrot in anticipation of negotiations between Jordan and Israel. Throughout July Nixon and Kissinger kept up the pressure for an agreement.[52] Sadat was prepared to reverse his previous stand and endorse King Hussein as the spokesman for the Palestinians living in the Hashemite Kingdom of Jordan.[53] The Israeli cabinet, which had been toying with a formula providing for Israel to talk with the PLO if the PLO ended acts of terrorism and accepted Israel's existence, quickly reversed itself and went back to the position that Jordan was the spokesman for the Palestinians.[54] On July 21, however, the cabinet rejected the concept of disengagement along the Jordan River, and, in talks with Foreign Minister Yigal Allon the next week Kissinger was unable to persuade the Israelis to change their position.[55]

Meanwhile, in the next two and a half weeks the Watergate crisis came to a head as the House Judiciary Committee began voting on three articles of impeachment. On August 8 Nixon announced that he would resign the presidency, effective at noon the following day. His successor, Gerald Ford, was sworn in as the nation's first nonelected president.

Assessing Nixon's Middle East Policy

It is impossible to know with certainty whether American policy toward the Middle East after October 1973 would have been substantially different without the deleterious effects of the Watergate scandal. On the whole, the answer seems to be no. The policy that grew out of the October crisis had little to do with Watergate. It was aimed at ending the multiple pressures generated by the war and bringing the United States to a position of influence over the peacemaking process between Israel and its Arab neighbors. The level of commitment and the amount of energy expended in pursuit of this policy could not have been greater. Nor does it appear as if the pace of diplomacy could have been quickened or that more substantial agreements might have been reached. After all, the Israelis, Egyptians, and Syrians were operating under severe constraints. Even the modest disengagement agreements strained their political systems almost to the breaking point.

If step-by-step diplomacy as carried out by Kissinger is to be judged on its own merits, it rates high as a tactic but fails to convey any sense of long-term purpose. To gain or lose a few kilometers of Sinai or Golan was surely not worth repeated crises of confidence with Israel and substantial offers of aid to all parties. Kissinger's justification for his efforts was that without the disengagement agreements there would be another war, accompanied by another oil embargo and by a resurgence of Soviet influence in the Arab world. Preventing these upheavals was ample justification for his endless travels and his deep involvement in the disengagement negotiations.

Kissinger knew what he wanted to avoid better than he knew what positive goals he might be able to achieve. The October war was his immediate point of reference. The simple lesson from that crisis was that the status quo in the Middle East was volatile and dangerous, and it could disintegrate, with serious consequences for American global and regional interests. Consequently the status quo had to be stabilized through a combination of diplomacy and arms shipments. A political process must begin that would offer the Arabs an alternative to war, but it must be carried on at a pace the Israelis could accept. This was the extent of Nixon's and Kissinger's initial conceptualization. There was no overall American peace plan—that had been tried in 1969 and had failed.

Without a convincing picture, however, of where step-by-step diplomacy was heading, would the parties to the negotiations ever be able to address the core issues of peace, security, and the Palestinians? And would the United States be able indefinitely to remain uncommitted to outcomes? The answer was unmistakably no, and by mid-1974 Nixon found himself making private commitments to Sadat, Asad, Rabin, and Hussein on where American diplomacy was heading.

With strong presidential leadership, step-by-step diplomacy might have turned into a search for a broader settlement, including Jordan and the

Palestinians. Instead the United States was involved in an unprecedented crisis of authority, and Nixon's successor was unlikely to convey a clear sense of purpose in foreign policy. Step-by-step diplomacy therefore remained a tactic for buying more time, a tactic cut off from a larger political concept of peace in the Middle East. Unable to move beyond step-by-step diplomacy, yet fearing the loss of momentum if no results were achieved, Kissinger was obliged to continue the search for partial solutions, either on the Jordanian or the Egyptian front, whichever seemed more feasible. The chance for a more ambitious policy was lost when Nixon was forced to resign, and considerable time would have to pass before a strong American initiative in the Middle East would be resumed.[56]

Ford as President

Gerald Ford was an unlikely president. He had not sought the office. As a long-time member of the House of Representatives, his political ambition had been to become Speaker of the House—until Richard Nixon selected him as vice president in October 1973 when Vice President Spiro Agnew resigned. Less than a year later, on August 9, 1974, the final act of the Watergate scandal brought Ford to the Oval Office.

This president was different from his predecessors. He had not been elected. His initial popularity stemmed from his apparent honesty and openness, not from confidence in his ability or leadership, and even that popularity began to wane after he pardoned Richard Nixon. Foreign policy was obviously not his field of expertise, and it seemed likely that he would defer to his prestigious secretary of state and national security affairs adviser, Henry Kissinger. But could Kissinger be as effective as he had been in the past without a strong president to back his initiatives? Although Kissinger may have harbored misgivings about Nixon, he had admired Nixon's decisiveness and his willingness to take risks. Would Ford have the same attributes?

Little was known of Ford's views on foreign policy generally. As a congressman he had supported a strong defense and had backed Nixon in his Southeast Asian policy. He was known to be a good friend of Israel, but otherwise his ideas on the Middle East were uncertain. It would probably be some time before a distinctive Ford foreign policy would take shape. For the moment, Kissinger would remain in charge.[57]

Kissinger may well have had his doubts about the feasibility of continuing to seek political agreements on each Arab front separately. But what were the alternatives? A global negotiation in Geneva was sure to fail unless carefully prepared in advance. The Israelis were wary of Geneva, and Kissinger himself was opposed to bringing the Soviet Union back into the peacemaking moves. A U.S.-Soviet imposed settlement would require both a higher degree of superpower agreement than existed and a strong American president. Besides, Kissinger was opposed to such an approach to Israel. A suspension of U.S. diplomacy was a possibility, but it ran the risk of weakening the "moderate" Arab coalition Kissinger had been trying to encourage.

By a process of elimination Kissinger came back to step-by-step diplomacy, with all of its obvious limitations, as the best means to keep the peace process alive. But where to begin? The answer, never fully thought through, was the Jordan-Israel front. The unstated belief was that it was worth trying to bring Jordan into the diplomacy as a way of undercutting the more radical PLO. Kissinger would also continue to press for a second step between Egypt and Israel.[58]

A Jordanian-Israeli Settlement?

Negotiations on the Jordanian-Israeli front presented Kissinger with unprecedented problems. "Disengagement" was hardly an appropriate concept here, since there had been no military engagement between the two countries in the October war. Rather than separate military forces along cease-fire lines, Kissinger would have to deal with sensitive political issues such as sovereignty and the status of the Palestinians. Despite the tacit cooperation that existed on some levels between Jordan and Israel, the prospects for reaching agreement were unusually dim, largely because of domestic Israeli politics and inter-Arab pressures on King Hussein. Israel was now led by an untried and untested leader, Prime Minister Yitzhak Rabin. On foreign-policy matters he was obliged to work closely with his political rival and now defense minister, Shimon Peres, and his foreign minister, Yigal Allon. Unfortunately for Rabin these two key figures in his cabinet did not often see eye to eye. The only consensus Rabin was able to develop regarding the West Bank was essentially negative: he would call elections before agreeing to anything affecting the former Jordanian territory.

The pressures on Hussein were equally confining, but less focused. His own sense of responsibility and his understandable fear of being accused of selling out to the Israelis led him to insist on negotiating terms that he could defend before other Arabs and before the Palestinians. Despite Hussein's own "moderate" inclinations and his genuine acceptance of Israel's right to exist, he was not in a position to capitulate to Israeli demands. He needed to prove to his people and to the Arab world that he, like Presidents Asad and Sadat, could recover Arab territory held by Israel. Above all, he could not accede to the Israeli position of administering the populated areas of the West Bank while Israel retained military control of the area.

Within days of becoming president, Ford was conferring with Middle East diplomats and leaders, while Kissinger tried to bring him up to date on the intricacies of the Arab-Israeli negotiations. First to arrive for talks with Ford was Egyptian foreign minister Fahmy.[59] A few days later King Hussein met with Ford, Kissinger, and Secretary of Defense James Schlesinger. The king was told that the United States would accord priority to the search for a Jordanian-Israeli agreement, while also exploring possibilities for another step in Sinai. Next Syrian foreign minister Abd al-Halim Khaddam arrived to see Kissinger, on August 22. Not to be outdone, Prime Minister Rabin came to Washington on September 10 for discussions with the new president. Rabin made it clear he favored another interim step with Egypt, not one with Jordan.[60]

The upshot of all these preliminary consultations was another Kissinger trip to the Middle East. Israel was still reluctant to pull back from the Jordan River, and Hussein would accept nothing else.[61] Kissinger therefore began his travels with little chance of success. In talks with Sadat he tried to press for Egyptian support of Jordan at the forthcoming Arab summit conference in Rabat. That support had slipped somewhat during September, and the dynamics of inter-Arab politics might well produce a ringing endorsement of the PLO, to the exclusion of Jordan, which Kissinger wanted to prevent. As bait he discussed with Sadat the outlines of another agreement between Egypt and Israel. Sadat's position was firm: in a second step he must recover the Mitla and Giddi passes and the oil field at Abu Rudeis. Nothing less would justify the risks for Egypt of entering into a second agreement with Israel. Sadat was, however, willing to offer Israel many of the "operational components of nonbelligerency."[62] In Amman Kissinger and Hussein reviewed the bleak prospects for an agreement and discussed the possibility that at Rabat the PLO would be endorsed as the sole negotiator for the West Bank and as the only spokesman for the Palestinians. If that happened, the king would withdraw from the negotiations entirely. Many Jordanians would be delighted to wash their hands of the whole Palestinian problem. It would be far better to concentrate on developing the East Bank and on building ties to Syria and Saudi Arabia than to run the risk of isolation and violent opposition that might result if the king signed an unpopular agreement with Israel. For the time being

Hussein and Kissinger agreed to await the outcome of the Arab summit in Rabat. With support from Sadat, Kissinger felt sure that Hussein would emerge with a mandate to negotiate for the West Bank.

To Kissinger's considerable annoyance and dismay, the Arab heads of state who assembled in Rabat during the last week of October did not behave as he anticipated. On October 28 the conference unanimously endorsed the PLO as the sole legitimate representative of the Palestinian people. Hussein had no more right in the eyes of the Arab world to negotiate for the West Bank than any other Arab leader. Faced with such an overwhelming consensus, even Hussein had accepted the final resolution. Sadat had tried to bring about a more ambiguous outcome but had failed. Saudi Arabia, ostensibly a moderate Arab state, and Syria had been among the most vocal champions of the PLO.

The Rabat summit, followed shortly by the appearance of PLO Executive Committee chairman Yasir Arafat at the United Nations on November 13, suddenly propelled the Palestinians to the front and center of the Arab-Israeli conflict. Kissinger was unprepared for this turn of events. He had hoped to put off the Palestinian issue until later, while trying to strengthen King Hussein at the expense of the PLO. He had expected Egypt, Saudi Arabia, and perhaps even Syria to recognize the practical necessity of keeping Jordan in the negotiations. Now his carefully constructed policy had been derailed.

In fact, the Rabat action was much less decisive than it appeared at the time, but it did cause problems for Kissinger. To salvage his policy and his reputation, he needed another success. Because it could not be on the Jordan front, it would have to be in Sinai. Egypt, however, was not the strong leader of the Arab world that it had been under Nasser—the Rabat meeting had shown that to be true—and would have to move carefully in any next step. At the same time Israel was hardly in the mood to make concessions, nor did the new government seem to have any clear diplomatic strategy. Golda Meir may have been tough and difficult to deal with, but at least she was in control of the government. It was less clear that Rabin could guide the divided country through a complex set of negotiations, particularly with his defense minister, Shimon Peres, eager to take his place if he should falter.[63]

A Second Egyptian-Israeli Step

Kissinger's technique for arranging limited agreements between Israel and the Arabs was by now well developed. It began by eliciting proposals from each side, getting preliminary reactions, identifying obstacles, and then starting the diplomatic process that would eventually bridge the substantive gaps. This process would include a heavy dose of reason and persuasion, as Kissinger would explain the dire international consequences of failure to reach an agreement; it also involved marshaling forces that might influence the parties, such as other Arab countries or the U.S. Congress. Then Kissinger would commit his own prestige to bringing about an agreement, shuttling back and forth between the two sides. At this last stage Kissinger was likely to involve the president if additional pressure on Israel or commitments on future aid were needed.

Even before the Rabat meeting, Kissinger had obtained a fairly good idea of the Egyptian and Israeli objectives in a second step. Egypt wanted Israel to withdraw beyond the strategically important Mitla and Giddi passes and to relinquish control over the Abu Rudeis and Ras Sudr oil fields, which were providing Israel with about 50 percent of its total oil needs. Sadat wanted this step to be treated as another military disengagement, with only minimal political overtones. He felt he could not afford to be seen in the Arab world as having withdrawn from the conflict with Israel.

Israel's objectives in a second agreement with Egypt were quite different. Israel hoped to split Egypt from Syria and thus reduce the prospects of a combined Arab offensive such as had occurred in October 1973. To do so would require that Egypt make substantial political concessions as the price of further Israeli withdrawals. Israel would demand that Egypt renounce the state of belligerency, that the new agreement be of long duration, and that Israeli withdrawal not include the passes or the oil fields.

During November and December 1974 Kissinger was able to clarify each side's position. He was convinced that Sadat would settle for nothing less than Mitla, Giddi, and the oil fields and that he would not formally renounce the state of belligerency. He so informed the Israelis, urging them to concentrate instead on the "functional equivalents" of nonbelligerency, such as the end of the economic boycott.

As Egypt and Israel began to show readiness for a second agreement, two potentially dangerous sources of opposition appeared. The Syrians were well aware that Israel was trying to isolate Egypt, which would then leave Syria alone to confront the militarily superior Israeli forces. Asad was therefore opposed to a second step on the Egyptian front. To underscore his attitude, Asad ordered his armed forces on high alert in mid-November, just on the eve of the renewal of the mandate of the UN forces. The crisis subsided, but not before Asad had made his point.

The second source of opposition to Kissinger's strategy was the Soviet Union. By now the Soviets saw clearly that one of Kissinger's primary goals was to weaken Soviet influence in the Middle East, especially in Egypt. President Ford and General Secretary Brezhnev met in Vladivostok on November 23–24, 1974, primarily to discuss a second strategic-arms agreement but also to consider the Middle East. The two sides remained far apart, the Soviets insisting on reconvening the Geneva conference and Ford favoring a continuation of step-by-step diplomacy, at the request, of course, of Egypt and Israel.[64] On the whole, U.S.-Soviet relations were cooling, as would become clear on January 14, 1975, when the Soviet Union rejected the offer of most favored nation trading status on terms that would have required a liberalization of emigration for Soviet Jews.

In early December 1974, Foreign Minister Yigal Allon arrived in Washington for talks with Kissinger. For several hours on December 9 they discussed a ten-point proposal Allon had brought with him.[65] Kissinger and Ford were unimpressed by Israel's offer. Allon hinted that it was only a bargaining position and might be changed. For example, the duration of the agreement could be five years instead of twelve. Kissinger's main problem with the Israeli proposal, however, was the demand for nonbelligerency, which Rabin himself had termed unrealistic, and the refusal to cede on the passes and oil fields. The Israeli points were nonetheless transmitted to Sadat, and Sadat's expected rejection was duly received. Kissinger then asked the Israelis to make a new proposal.

When Allon arrived in the United States for another round of discussions with Kissinger on January 15–16, 1975, he had nothing new to offer except an invitation to Kissinger to return to the area. Kissinger repeated his warning to Allon that an agreement could not be reached on the basis of the Israeli proposal.[66] He would nonetheless make another trip to see if the gap could be narrowed. After an "exploratory" round of talks in February, he would return in March to complete the negotiations, but Israel would have to drop the demand for nonbelligerency and be more forthcoming over territory.[67]

Before Kissinger's departure Sadat publicly endorsed his efforts, adding that the United States now held virtually all the trump cards.[68] These words were precisely what Kissinger wanted to hear from Sadat. From the Syrians and the Soviets, however, he was continuing to encounter resistance to his efforts. As Sadat seemed to move forward toward another agreement, Syria began to band together with Jordan and the Palestinians in opposing him, with growing support from the Soviet Union.[69]

Kissinger's February trip was admittedly preliminary. He did not expect to reach agreement, but he did hope that Egypt and Israel would each
recognize the constraints the other was operating under and modify some
elements of their proposals. Instead he found little new. The Israelis seemed
to ease up a bit on the issue of nonbelligerency, and Sadat indicated a
willingness to end some hostile actions against Israel, but a substantial
gap remained. Nor did Kissinger succeed in persuading the Syrians to drop
their opposition to a second step in Sinai.[70]

For the next several weeks Kissinger continued to urge the parties to
moderate their positions, for he wanted an agreement, and soon. But he
did not want to embark on a third "shuttle" until he was virtually certain
of success. Assuming that the parties now understood the minimum terms
required for a successful negotiation, Kissinger left for the Middle East
once again, arriving in Egypt on March 8.[71]

Kissinger did succeed in obtaining new Egyptian proposals during the
March shuttle. Sadat was prepared to say the following: the conflict with
Israel would not be solved by military means; Egypt would not resort to
force; it would observe the cease-fire and would prevent all military and
paramilitary forces from operating against Israel from Egyptian territory;
a new agreement would remain in effect until superseded by another agreement; hostile propaganda against Israel in Egyptian-controlled media would
be reduced; and the economic boycott would be selectively eased.[72]

Israel's position, as first conveyed informally by Rabin to Kissinger on
the evening of March 9, consisted of seven points, entitled "Proposal on
Main Elements of Agreement between Israel and Egypt." Israel sought a
separate agreement with Egypt that would not depend on agreements with
other Arab parties. The agreement must be a step toward peace in some
practical aspects, such as the free passage of Israeli cargoes through the
Suez Canal, the end of the economic boycott, and the free movement of
persons between Egypt and Israel. Egypt must agree to the end of the use
of force through a "renunciation of belligerency clearly and in its appropriate legal wording." A real buffer zone must be created between the
military forces of both sides. Some solution must be found for the "dilemma of vagueness" about the duration of the agreement. An understanding must be reached on the relationship between an interim agreement
in Sinai and what might happen later at Geneva. Finally, Israel would
agree to discuss the question of the line of withdrawal only after Egypt
had responded to the first six points.[73]

Kissinger was dismayed that Israel was still holding out for nonbelligerency. Sadat was prepared to meet some of Israel's demands but insisted on

knowing whether Israel would remain in the passes. He also flatly refused to agree to nonbelligerency, though he would consider a formula based on the "nonuse of force." After several days of shuttling, Kissinger managed to persuade the Israelis to accept the nonuse-of-force formulation, but Rabin and his negotiating team were adamant that Israel would not withdraw from the passes for anything less than nonbelligerency. At best they might consider pulling back to a line halfway through the passes, but at no point in the negotiations did the Israelis provide Kissinger with a map showing a line they would accept. Complicating the bargaining further was Israel's insistence on maintaining control over an electronic intelligence station at Umm Khisheiba at the western end of the Giddi pass. Sadat would not agree to Israel's keeping the station, even if it was formally placed in the UN zone. Consequently the negotiations deadlocked on the issues of nonbelligerency and its functional equivalents, on the extent of Israeli withdrawal from the passes and the oil fields, and on the status of the Umm Khisheiba facility.

After ten days of shuttling between Egypt and Israel, with side trips to Syria, Jordan, and Saudi Arabia, Kissinger was still not able to get the Israelis out of the passes. Israel agreed to cede the oil fields but refused to give Egypt control over a road connecting the fields to the Egyptian zone. On Friday, March 21, Kissinger arrived in Israel with Sadat's final word: Israel could not keep the intelligence station, and the mandate of the UN forces would be renewed only for a second year. Without further Egyptian concessions, the Israelis would not budge. Even a tough letter from President Ford, which reached Israel on March 21, was unable to change the situation.[74] It may, in fact, have stiffened Israel's will to resist. In any event, the cabinet met Friday night and rejected virtually all Sadat's demands. Kissinger conveyed Israel's rejection to Egypt and awaited Sadat's reply.

The next day Kissinger left Israel, having announced that his negotiating effort was being suspended.[75] After Kissinger returned to Washington on March 24, President Ford ominously announced that there would now be a reassessment of U.S. policy toward the Middle East.[76]

Reassessment

Kissinger's disappointment with the Israelis for thwarting his efforts to arrange a second agreement in Sinai was genuine. He felt the Israeli leadership was shortsighted, incompetent, and weak. In his view Israel had no foreign policy, only a domestic political system that produced deadlock and stalemate. A David Ben-Gurion or a Golda Meir might be able to lead

Israel, but not the Rabin-Peres-Allon triumvirate, in which each man pulled in a different direction. In his less guarded moments Kissinger suggested that the Israelis were trying to bring him down. Reassessment, however justified, became in part an instrument for Kissinger to vent his exasperation with Israel.

President Ford, whatever his sentimental attachment to Israel might have been in the past, was also irritated at Israel and publicly blamed Rabin for his lack of flexibility.[77] He lent his weight to a serious reassessment of policy, during which new military and economic agreements with Israel were suspended. Like each of his predecessors, Ford found that his sympathies for Israel and his perception of American global and regional interests did not always mesh. When the two seemed to come into conflict, Ford was as capable as Nixon of putting pressure on Israel for concessions. The test, however, would be whether pressure could produce the desired results—and whether Israeli counterpressure might not raise the cost of the effort.

Israel, after all, was not without influential friends and supporters in the United States, nor did it lack effective spokespersons who could defend it before the American public against the charge of inflexibility. If the administration insisted on withholding needed aid, Israel could appeal to Congress to support its requests. The Israeli case did seem plausible: in return for making important economic and territorial concessions, Israel was merely asking that Egypt renounce belligerency. Why was that unreasonable or inflexible? Should Israel risk its security for anything less?

Kissinger's case against Israel was less convincing to many Americans. He claimed that the Israeli leaders had misled him into undertaking the shuttle when they knew that nonbelligerency could not be achieved, and yet they continued to insist on it. Israel had refused to make the minimal territorial concessions in the passes and around the oil fields. Kissinger argued that an agreement was necessary to preserve the delicate balances he had brought into being after the October 1973 war. On occasion, he implied that the alternative to an agreement might be war and another Arab oil embargo.

As part of the policy of reassessment, Kissinger met on April 1 with a group of prominent men from the foreign-policy establishment. Some of the group, such as George Ball, had been openly critical of Kissinger's step-by-step policy and Israel. Ball favored a more comprehensive agreement in which the United States and the Soviet Union would work out the guidelines for a settlement, which would then be negotiated by all the parties in Geneva. He had criticized Kissinger for ignoring the Soviets and trying to divide the Arabs. He did not shy away from the notion of an imposed settlement.[78] Others at the meeting also favored a return to the Geneva conference and a major effort to work out an American peace plan.

Over the next several weeks Kissinger heard essentially the same recommendations from his closest aides, from eminent academics, and from American ambassadors to the key Middle East countries.[79] The time for step-by-step diplomacy was past. A more ambitious strategy was needed. The Palestinians could no longer be ignored. The Soviets would have to be brought into the negotiations. It all sounded reasonable in the abstract, but Kissinger was haunted by the fear that this approach, too, would fail. No one could detail the steps that would be required to ensure success. And it would be costly in domestic political terms, since it would surely require heavy and sustained pressure on Israel. Ford and Kissinger were not at all certain they wanted to take on that battle unless the results were sure to warrant the effort.

By the third week of April reassessment had produced three basic options for the president. The first, supported by many in and outside the government, was a return to Geneva with a detailed American peace plan. The United States would call for Israeli withdrawal, while offering strong guarantees of Israel's security. The Soviets would be invited to cooperate. A second option would aim for a virtually complete settlement, especially on the Egyptian-Israeli front, but would fall short of calling for full withdrawal and final peace. The third option was to resume step-by-step diplomacy where it had left off in March.[80] Ford referred publicly to these three options in a general way on April 21.[81]

For several weeks it seemed as if a new American approach to peace in the Middle East might emerge, but gradually the realization set in that nothing of the sort could be expected. Kissinger's consultations with Allon, King Hussein, and the Soviets had not given him any reason to be optimistic about a new policy. American public support for a global initiative was not strong, and Congress was beginning to respond to arguments that Kissinger was exerting too much pressure on Israel. On May 21 seventy-six senators sent a letter to President Ford, urging him to be "responsive to Israel's economic and military needs." This was a clear sign that continued pressure on Israel would be politically counterproductive. Ford and Kissinger realized that the only viable strategy, in light of these realities, was to resume step-by-step diplomacy.[82] Ford himself would participate in talks with Sadat and Rabin to explore the prospects for an agreement. Sadat helped to improve the atmosphere by unexpectedly announcing that the Suez Canal would be reopened on June 5 and that the mandate of the

United Nations Emergency Force would be extended. The Egyptian president still seemed to want to reach an agreement.

On June 1–2 President Ford and Sadat met for the first time, in Salzburg. The two men got on well together, feeling relaxed in each other's company and finding it easy to talk. Sadat appealed for a public statement from Ford that Israel should withdraw to the 1967 lines, but Ford demurred, reportedly repeating instead Nixon's private commitment of the previous year to work for that goal.[83] Ford then sounded out Sadat on his willingness to try again for a limited agreement in Sinai. Sadat was favorably disposed, but his terms were still those of the previous spring: Israel must leave the passes and the oil fields and must not demand nonbelligerency. Sadat was still opposed to the idea of the Israelis' keeping the intelligence-gathering facility at Umm Khisheiba, but he did say he might accept an American presence there.[84] The idea of an American military contingent in the buffer zone had been raised earlier in the spring, but Kissinger had been unenthusiastic. The more modest concept of an American civilian presence, however, soon began to emerge as the solution to one of the problems in the negotiations.[85]

Sinai II

By the time Prime Minister Rabin reached Washington for talks with President Ford and Secretary Kissinger on June 11–12, the decision to continue with step-by-step diplomacy had basically been made. The alternative of Geneva, of a U.S.-Soviet imposed settlement, or of a withdrawal from the peacemaking effort had all been rejected. Ford and Kissinger felt the situation in the Middle East required continued diplomatic progress; as had been shown early in 1974, that could be done best through U.S. mediation. If progress toward a settlement was not made during the next few months, the United States might not be able to launch a new initiative until 1977. After all, 1976 was an American election year, and Middle East politics could hardly hope to compete for attention with a presidential campaign.

Ford, now very much involved in the conduct of Arab-Israeli diplomacy, asked Rabin to be more forthcoming in the negotiations and pressed for a new Israeli line of withdrawal to the eastern ends of the passes. Rabin was anxious to end the painful and costly confrontation with the United States.[86] His refusal of Kissinger's demands in March had contributed greatly to his prestige within Israel. Now he might be able to negotiate with more confidence. A new line therefore was drawn to demonstrate

Israel's good will, and this was seen as a modest step in the right direction. Ford reciprocated by promising that after the next interim agreement between Egypt and Israel, "the overall settlement can be pursued in a systematic and deliberate way and does not require the U.S. to put forward an overall proposal of its own in such circumstances. Should the U.S. desire in the future to put forward proposals of its own, it will make every effort to coordinate with Israel its proposals with a view to refraining from putting forth proposals that Israel would consider unsatisfactory."[87]

Despite these assurances from Ford, Rabin was unable to win cabinet authorization to make further concessions. A week later he was obliged to return to Israel's previous offer of withdrawal halfway through the passes.[88] Once again Ford and Kissinger were angry at Rabin for his apparent inflexibility and his awkwardness.

During the next six weeks Kissinger remained in Washington while Israeli and Egyptian positions were refined and transmitted through him to the other side. Sometime in the last half of June the Israeli leaders apparently decided it would be impossible to obtain the desired political concessions from Sadat and undesirable to resist the United States indefinitely. If Egypt would not make peace, then at least Israel could bargain with the United States on issues involving Israeli security. If the Americans wanted an agreement so badly, they could pay for it. Israel would agree to withdraw to the eastern slopes of the passes but would maintain control over the high ground above the passes. At the urging of Defense Minister Peres, Israel also sought to make the buffer zone between the two sides into a genuine barrier to military surprise attack by stationing American civilians there to monitor early-warning stations. The Americans could also serve as a cover for continued Israeli use of the intelligence facility. If Sadat objected, the Americans could offer to build a comparable facility for him as well.

Sadat was also prepared to be somewhat more forthcoming. He would agree to three annual renewals of the mandate of the UN forces and to the continued Israeli use of the intelligence facility, provided he was given one facing the Israeli lines. He accepted the idea of easing the boycott of some companies dealing with Israel and promised to tone down anti-Israeli propaganda. And finally, he would be willing to have most of the terms of the agreement published.

It remained for the United States and Israel to work out their own understanding of the American commitments necessary to gain Israel's consent to a new agreement. Early in July, Dinitz met with Kissinger in the Virgin Islands to present the full package of Israeli proposals and requests.[89]

In addition to a promise of about $2 billion in aid, the United States agreed to drop the idea of an interim step on the Jordan-Israel front and to accept that only "cosmetic" changes could be expected on the Golan Heights in another step. Israel also wanted a clear commitment that the United States would prevent Soviet military intervention in the Middle East.[90]

During the next several weeks further discussion of these and other points took place.[91] By the time Kissinger left for Israel on August 20, an agreement was within reach. Only the exact location of the Israeli line, the levels of U.S. aid, and the technical aspects of the American civilian presence in the passes remained to be negotiated.

Kissinger was received in Israel with unprecedented hostility, mainly from the right-wing opposition parties, and demonstrators accosted him at each stop. Nevertheless, his discussions with the leadership progressed. This time Rabin wanted an agreement. Kissinger continued to harbor misgivings about the American presence in Sinai, which by now was an essential ingredient of the Israeli package, but he was prepared to go along with the idea. Sadat was willing to accept this condition, but some quibbling still went on over the exact location of the line.[92]

By August 25 Kissinger was working with the Israelis on the language of a draft agreement. Gradually Israel began to soften its position on the line of withdrawal from the Giddi pass. Very detailed discussions on force limits and on the American presence were also required. Then, in a nonstop session in Jerusalem lasting from 9:30 p.m. August 31 to 6:00 a.m. the following day, the United States and Israel worked out the fine points of their bilateral military relationship, assurances on Israel's supply of oil, and an understanding on the need for consultations in the event of Soviet military intervention in the Middle East. Israel was disappointed with the weak language on Soviet intervention but otherwise could point to a very impressive list of American commitments. Later that afternoon both Egypt and Israel initialed the text of the agreement. It was formally signed in Geneva on September 4, 1975.

Unlike the January 1974 accord, Sinai II was greeted with a sigh of relief but with little real enthusiasm by the parties to the negotiations. Within both Israel and the Arab world, many were violently opposed to the agreement, although for entirely different reasons.

The agreement itself was modeled in part on the previous disengagement pacts.[93] The two parties committed themselves to resolve the conflict between them by peaceful means and not to resort to the threat or the use of force against each other. The UN force would continue its function, and the lines for each side's military deployments were designated on a map. Egypt agreed to allow nonmilitary cargoes destined for or coming from Israel to pass through the Suez Canal, which had been reopened to traffic the previous June. The agreement would remain in force until superseded by a new agreement.

Attached to the agreement was a detailed annex dealing with military deployments and aerial surveillance. At Sadat's insistence the forces allowed in the limited zone under the agreement were slightly larger than those permitted in January 1974: up to 8,000 men in eight battalions, with 75 tanks and 72 short-range artillery pieces. Neither party, however, was permitted to locate any weapons in areas from which they could reach each other's lines.

The arrangements for U.S. manning and supervision of the early-warning systems in the buffer zones were also spelled out in detail. Israel and Egypt would be allowed to have up to 250 technical and administrative personnel at their respective surveillance stations. U.S. civilians would operate three other smaller watch stations and would establish three unmanned sensor fields as well. Israel's willingness to implement the terms of the agreement was contingent on U.S. congressional approval of the U.S. role in Sinai. The United States also signed five secret agreements, four with Israel and one with Egypt. A sixteen-point U.S.-Israeli memorandum of understanding dealt with military assistance, oil supply, economic aid, and several political points. The United States and Israel agreed that the next step with Egypt should be a final peace agreement. The same should be true on the Jordan front. The United States also agreed to consult promptly with Israel in the event of any threat to Israel from a "world power," namely, the Soviet Union. In an addendum on arms the United States gave a vague commitment to provide a "positive response" to Israeli requests for F-16 aircraft and the Pershing missile with a conventional warhead.[94] In effect, the freeze on new arms agreements that had begun the previous April was ended.

A special memo dealing with Geneva was signed, which spelled out the policy of the United States with respect to the Palestinians: no recognition of and no negotiation with the PLO until it recognized Israel's right to exist and accepted UN Resolutions 242 and 338.[95] The United States would also carefully coordinate its strategy at Geneva with Israel and agree to keep the negotiations on a bilateral basis. In addition, Ford wrote a letter to Rabin stating: "The U.S. has not developed a final position on the borders [between Israel and Syria]. Should it do so it will give great weight to

Israel's position that any peace agreement with Syria must be predicated on Israel remaining on the Golan Heights. My view in this regard was stated in our conversation of September 13, 1974."[96]

As for Egypt, the United States merely committed itself to try to bring about further negotiations between Syria and Israel, to provide assistance for the Egyptian early-warning system in the buffer zone, and to consult with Egypt on any Israeli violations of the agreement.

Reactions to Sinai II

In his more optimistic moments Kissinger had justified step-by-step diplomacy as a process by which parties to a negotiation would gain confidence, become committed to achieving results, and be carried along by the momentum of peacemaking to resolve issues that had previously seemed intractable. But Sinai II came closer to confirming his more somber vision of the Arab-Israeli conflict. The issues were so complex, the emotions so deeply involved, that peace between the two sides was unattainable in this generation. Although some agreements might be reached, they would be modest and imperfect at best. The diplomat aspiring to mediate between Israel and the Arabs would have to be content with small achievements. These, at least, were better than nothing. The stabilization of the region, the reduction of the chances of war, and the end of the oil embargo were far preferable to renewed hostilities and superpower confrontation. Egypt, in any case, seemed firmly committed to a moderate course.

Kissinger had not consciously sought to provoke dissension among the Arabs. On the contrary, he was deeply concerned that Saudi Arabia continue to back Sadat's policies. He also recognized that Syria played a vital role in inter-Arab politics, and he genuinely wanted to draw Syria toward a moderate settlement with Israel.[97] The objective situation, however, thwarted his efforts. Golan was not Sinai, and a second step there would be difficult to manage unless Israel was prepared to give up the settlements beyond the post-1967 cease-fire lines. Israel had just demonstrated a remarkable capacity to hold out against American pressures and to exact a high price for eventual compliance. Was it worth the effort for a few kilometers on Golan? Sadat had very much wanted a second agreement, whereas Asad, by contrast, was lukewarm to the idea. He did not entirely reject the concept of a second step, but he made it clear that he was not prepared to pay much of a price for it. Instead Asad began to attack Sadat for having forsaken the struggle against Israel and to press for international recognition of the PLO. Inter-Arab politics had a dynamic of its own that was unleashed by Sinai II. Short of abandoning step-by-step diplomacy, it is not clear what Kissinger could have done to keep Egypt and Syria from drifting apart.

As the election year 1976 began, it became apparent that President Ford would be preoccupied with domestic politics. His position within his own party was precarious, and it was not certain that he would even be nominated at the Republican convention in August. Ronald Reagan, former governor of California, was mounting a strong challenge, with the support of the most conservative elements in the party. Kissinger and his foreign policy were emerging as a campaign issue for the Reagan Republicans as well as for the Democrats. And although the Middle East was not initially one of the issues in the campaign, the criticisms aimed at Ford and Kissinger did drive them to a tougher stance toward the Soviet Union, as symbolized by American policy in Angola, and precluded an ambitious new initiative in the Arab-Israeli arena.

Despite these election-year pressures, however, President Ford persevered in the attempt to improve U.S.-Egyptian relations.[98] In October 1975 Sadat had been the first Egyptian president to pay an official visit to the United States. During that visit Sadat had appealed for American economic and even military assistance. A complex debate between Congress and the administration ensued, with Ford reducing requested aid for Israel in fiscal year 1977 from $2.25 billion to $1.8 billion and simultaneously urging Congress to consider the approval of a limited sale of six C-130 transport planes to Egypt. Congress not only favored higher levels of aid to Israel but also felt that Israel should receive a supplemental grant to cover the "transitional quarter" from July 1976 to October 1, 1976, the beginning of the new fiscal year.[99]

The consideration of arms for Egypt took a new turn in mid-March 1976, when President Sadat announced the abrogation of the fifteen-year treaty of friendship and cooperation with the Soviet Union. Against the background of the news that Israel, according to CIA analysts, possessed from ten to twenty operational atomic weapons,[100] opposition to the sale to Egypt faded, although Congress preferred that it be handled purely as a commercial transaction. Eventually Egypt got the planes, worth about $50 million, and Israel received the supplementary aid, worth many times more.

Ford's willingness to take a hard line on aid to Israel and to oppose in the United Nations the Israeli policy on settlements in the occupied territories lasted through the first part of the election campaign. By the fall, however, when Governor Jimmy Carter of Georgia, the Democratic candidate, was enjoying a huge lead in the polls, the president began to play up his credentials as a strong supporter of Israel. In the last month of the campaign the Middle East became a topic of occasional debate, wherein Carter and Ford tried to outdo each other as the better friend of Israel, and Carter in particular hinted at very severe action against any future Arab oil embargo.

Carter's narrow victory over Ford on November 2, 1976, settled the issue of who would be the next president, but neither the Israelis nor the Arabs had any clear idea of what the next president's policies would be. Both expected new initiatives, and both were apprehensive.

The Kissinger Legacy

Henry Kissinger's impact on American foreign policy will be debated endlessly. Of the accomplishments credited to him, few were not also in part the product of circumstances or the actions of others. But Kissinger will undoubtedly be regarded as one of the most powerful and most successful of American statesmen in the post–World War II era. How he managed to achieve such prominence is a story in its own right, revealing Kissinger's remarkable talents as a bureaucratic maneuverer and politician. His more enduring legacy, however, will be his policies and the concepts behind them.

After several false starts Kissinger finally developed a coherent approach to the Arab-Israeli conflict after the October 1973 war. He started from the premise that the United States need not choose between a pro-Arab or a pro-Israeli policy. In fact, it was the American special relationship with Israel that compelled the Arabs to deal with Washington instead of Moscow when it came to diplomacy. Consequently, if an alternative to war could be offered to the Arabs, their interests, quite apart from their sentiments, would lead them to deal with the United States. A credible diplomatic process was therefore essential to the weakening of Soviet influence in the Middle East. This view, once stated, seems unexceptional, perhaps obvious; even so, it was often ignored, on occasion by Kissinger himself.

Kissinger's second contribution to American diplomacy in the Middle East was the development of specific negotiating techniques designed to produce limited agreements between Arabs and Israelis. If Kissinger's grand strategy often seemed fairly conventional, his tactical skills as a negotiator and mediator were unsurpassed. Here his originality, his sense of timing, his intelligence, and even his personality served him especially well.

Kissinger demonstrated that, in practice, successful negotiations require an ability to break issues into manageable pieces that can then be imaginatively recombined into viable agreements. Mastery of detail is essential to success, as is a sense of context and nuance. A sustained, high-level effort, fully supported by the president, is the only American approach to negotiations likely to produce results. Kissinger showed that such an effort could succeed, as well as how difficult it could be.

Finally, Kissinger translated into practice his belief that power and diplomacy must always go hand in hand. The United States can never rely solely on force or on negotiations in the Middle East. The test of statesmanship is to find the critical balance of the two. Arms supplies to the Israelis or the Arabs must be viewed as part of the diplomatic process, not as a technical military issue. Whatever troubles Kissinger may have had in practice with this principle, he clearly saw that political considerations outweighed narrowly military ones in decisions of this sort.

Kissinger had a blind spot toward the Palestinian issue. He knew that at some point the problem would have to be confronted. He even appeared to be tempted by the idea of dealing directly with the PLO leadership. But he geared much of his diplomacy to trying to circumvent this crucial issue, to putting off the moment of truth, and to weakening the appeal of the Palestinian movement, all the while hoping that some alternative would appear. Perhaps with time, with better luck, and with a strong president behind him, Kissinger would have helped find acceptable solutions to all these unanswered problems. But Ford's defeat brought Kissinger's public career to an end and left to the Carter administration the unenviable task of shaping an American policy toward the Arab-Israeli conflict.

PART THREE

The Carter Presidency

6 *Ambition and Realism: Carter and Camp David, 1977–78*

J IMMY C ARTER CAME to the presidency with remarkably little experience in foreign affairs. He had served one term as governor of Georgia and had earned a reputation for his strong commitment to civil rights. But as far as the Middle East was concerned, he had no known record apart from a few comments made during the campaign that offered little guide to what his policies might be.

If Carter's specific views on Arab-Israeli issues were difficult to anticipate, he had displayed certain habits of mind that might be revealing of his basic approach. Trained as an engineer, Carter seemed to believe complex problems could best be tackled by careful study, detailed planning, and comprehensive designs. To say the least, he was a problem solver more than a grand strategist.

Carter also seemed to have an optimistic streak that led him to believe problems could be resolved if leaders would simply reason together and listen to the aspirations of their people. Here he may have been consciously influenced by his experience with the civil rights movement and by his personal beliefs as a born-again Christian. None of these attributes ensured that Carter would take a strong interest in the Arab-Israeli conflict, but they did suggest that he would not be deterred from doing so by the difficulty or complexity of the issue. He might even sense a challenge in tackling a problem that had for so long defied solution.

Much would depend on his foreign-policy team, and there the evidence suggested that he would rely on mainstream figures from the Democratic party establishment. For secretary of state he selected Cyrus R. Vance, a seasoned negotiator, international lawyer, and the deputy secretary of defense during the 1967 Arab-Israeli war. Vance's views on Middle East issues were not widely known, but his would be a voice for continuity, negotiations, and steady, quiet diplomacy.

For national security adviser, Carter selected the Polish-born academic Zbigniew Brzezinski. Unlike Vance, Brzezinski had left traces, primarily in the form of numerous articles and books, mostly on Soviet-related topics, but a few on the Middle East as well. Brzezinski was an activist who believed in competing for influence with the Soviets and who saw the Arab-Israeli conflict as a source of instability and radicalism in a sensitive geostrategic region. He had publicly endorsed the idea of a Palestinian state in the West Bank and Gaza and was one of the signatories of the controversial Brookings Report.[1] Brzezinski, who clearly hoped to achieve the stature of his predecessor and academic rival, Henry Kissinger, seemed determined to put the Arab-Israeli conflict near the top of the new administration's agenda.

While other players in the policy game moved in and out of the inner circle, Carter, Vance, and Brzezinski were the key decisionmakers. On defense matters Secretary of Defense Harold Brown carried great weight and exhibited a sharp intellect, but he was not particularly forceful in pushing his views on most policy issues outside his immediate area of responsibility. Vice President Walter Mondale had close ties to the Jewish community, and he was particularly attuned to any step that would produce a negative reaction there or in Congress. From time to time he would intervene strongly in internal deliberations, but he did not have an important role in policy formulation. Nor did the "Georgia mafia" of Hamilton Jordan, Stuart Eizenstat, Jody Powell, and Robert Lipshutz have much influence, although Jordan, who eventually became chief of staff, was a shrewd tactician and had unimpeded access to Carter. He and Mondale were attentive to the domestic fallout from Carter's Middle East policy, but they were not architects as much as they were damage controllers.[2]

The Initial Assessment

Within days of reaching Washington, President Carter's foreign policy team was beginning to discuss how and whether to launch a new Middle East peace initiative. Both Secretary Vance and National Security Adviser Zbigniew Brzezinski were on record with the president as favoring a strong U.S. role in Middle East peace negotiations. Their assessment, and that of most Middle East specialists at the State Department, was that early 1977 was a good moment for the United States to exercise leadership in a new round of negotiations. The key Arab states seemed to be ready for serious talks, and a degree of consensus appeared to have been forged through Saudi mediation in the fall of 1976. The conflict in Lebanon had subsided, and the oil situation had begun to stabilize. Egypt's president, Anwar Sadat, who enjoyed great prestige in Washington, was urging the new administration to take advantage of this moment of moderation in the Arab world, a message seconded by the Saudis.

Israel also seemed to expect the United States to return to the diplomatic arena after the enforced absence of the election year. The cabinet of Prime Minister Yitzhak Rabin was to face elections in the spring and was on the defensive to an unprecedented degree. But Washington officials felt that preliminary talks could be conducted before Israelis went to the polls, and, even if they were not, any new government would be built around the Labor alignment that had ruled Israel since its birth. And Labor was a known element, likely to adopt a tough stance in negotiations but ultimately prepared to bargain and to coordinate policies with Washington. Three disengagement agreements had been hammered out with Labor governments, and American negotiators had come to respect the skills of leaders like Golda Meir, Yitzhak Rabin, Moshe Dayan, and Shimon Peres.

If political realities in the Arab world and in Israel were seen as conducive to a new round of diplomacy, the shadow of the October 1973 war served as a constant reminder of the dangers of a collapse in the peace process. Barely three years had passed since that round of hostilities, and the memories of the near-confrontation between the United States and the Soviet Union, the nuclear alert, and the oil crisis were still very much in mind. Rarely mentioned but also present was the recognition that fullscale war in the Middle East could some day involve the use of nuclear weapons. This possibility made the region exceptionally dangerous and added a strong impulse to peacemaking efforts.

Having made this initial assessment, the Carter administration spent little time on whether to accord the Arab-Israeli conflict high priority. Most of the early discussion centered on means. It was widely believed that Henry Kissinger's technique of shuttle diplomacy to achieve limited agreements had run its course with Sinai II. The United States had paid a high price for a partial Israeli withdrawal that had not opened the way for any further such agreements. Neither Syria nor Jordan was prepared to follow Sadat's lead, and even Sadat was insisting that the next step should move toward an overall settlement. And the Israelis were also disinclined to be edged back from their strategically solid positions in Sinai for less than a peace agreement and direct negotiations with Egypt.

At a meeting on February 4, 1977, the Policy Review Committee of the National Security Council agreed to recommend to the president that the Middle East should be dealt with as a matter of urgent priority and that Secretary Vance should go to the area immediately to begin discussions on procedures and substance. The president's key advisers felt the United States should promote an agreement on broad principles and then seek their staged implementation. From the Arab side the administration should seek a clear definition of peace; from the Israelis it should try to get an understanding that security could be achieved without significant territorial adjustments in the 1967 lines. At this stage in the internal discussions, there was no sense of urgency about going to Geneva for a formal conference, and the emphasis was on pre-Geneva talks to prepare for more formal negotiations at a later date. It was also agreed at the meeting that the Soviets should be kept informed of the progress of U.S. conversations with the parties but should not be involved in the negotiations at this stage.[3]

The president approved of these suggestions and noted that his own meetings with Middle East leaders over the coming few months could help lay some of the substantive groundwork before direct talks among the parties began. Already in these discussions among the president and his advisers, however, one could detect a nuance of difference between those who were more inclined to see Geneva as a desirable goal in itself, who felt cooperation with the Soviets was to some degree inevitable, and those who were more skeptical of both Geneva and Moscow. Interestingly, no one raised the argument that early U.S. initiatives might prove to be destabilizing in Israel or might raise Arab expectations to unrealistic levels.

In mid-February Vance was already in the Middle East sounding out each of the leaders on how he saw the situation, while making it clear that the United States also had some ideas of its own. Rabin, Sadat, King Hussein of Jordan, and Saudi crown prince Fahd were all invited to Washington to meet the new president, and the idea of a meeting between Carter and President Asad of Syria was also raised.

A formal meeting of the National Security Council was held after Vance's return on February 23. He reported that all the parties with whom he had consulted professed to be ready for a peace agreement. They all agreed to go to a Geneva conference in September and to discuss substance prior to those talks. All concurred that the three main issues on the agenda were the nature of peace, withdrawal, and the Palestinian question. The most difficult procedural issue was how to include representatives of the Palestinians in the negotiations. Vance seemed to believe that the Arabs might compose a single delegation, which could include members of the PLO. He had told the Arab leaders it was up to them to produce an acceptable position on this question before Geneva. Sadat had urged the United States to include the PLO, but had also raised the possibility of representing them through some other means, such as a representative of the Arab League.[4]

In talks with Israeli leaders during his first trip, Secretary Vance had been told that no Israeli government would agree to talk to the PLO as long as it remained committed to the destruction of Israel. Vance had asked Foreign Minister Yigal Allon if it would make any difference if the PLO were to accept UN Resolution 242 and Israel's right to exist as a state. He replied that a PLO that accepted Israel's existence would no longer be the PLO, and Israel's attitude would be different.[5] This answer encouraged the United States to look into the possibility that the PLO might change its formal position on 242. The Egyptians and Saudis both promised to use their influence, and the Egyptians went so far as to say that they would urge the PLO to change its covenant, which called for Israel's destruction.

The next phase of the U.S. strategy included a highly public use of presidential power to try to break the logjam on several substantive issues. Carter and his advisers had little patience with some of the conventional wisdom on how the American role should be played. The president had little sympathy for the Arab refusal to make peace with Israel, or to even use the word *peace*; and he strongly believed Israel would in some way have to come to terms with the Palestinians, and probably with the PLO, names he used almost interchangeably in his early months in office. Though he was very sympathetic to Israel's security concerns, he did not feel that territorial aggrandizement was the key to that security.

Carter was willing, even anxious, to speak out in public on all these issues, and to discuss them in private. One of his criticisms of the Kissinger style had been the emphasis on secrecy, which kept the American public in the dark about major foreign problems. Carter's inclination was to talk openly about the foreign-policy initiatives he was considering. At times this openness jangled the nerves of more traditional diplomats, and of foreign leaders, but Carter often seemed to be trying to do so deliberately. He appeared to feel he had a limited period in which to make his mark on Middle East policy and that controversial issues should be tackled early in the administration. This viewpoint led to a profusion of comprehensive plans to settle all sorts of problems, including the Middle East. On occasion, the president spoke with an awareness of the political cycle, the need to stake out strong positions during the early honeymoon phase of the administration. He knew that he might be obliged to settle for less in the end, but he hoped for a breakthrough here or there.

On March 7–8, 1977, Carter met with Prime Minister Rabin at the White House for very serious substantive discussions. The personal chemistry between the two was not particularly good, but the record of the talks shows that both leaders conducted thoughtful explorations of what might come out of the forthcoming negotiations. In retrospect, these talks stand out as one of the best substantive discussions Carter had with any Middle East leader. Shortly after the talks, however, a misunderstanding arose. Rabin publicly claimed that Carter had supported the Israeli idea of "defensible borders." Carter did not want to leave the false impression that he had offered Rabin a blank check, so the White House issued a clarification. This episode led some to conclude that a crisis had broken out in U.S.-Israeli relations, a notion that may have contributed to the Israeli Labor party's defeat at the polls two months later.[6]

Almost immediately after meeting with Rabin, and in part to counter some of the Israeli leaks about what had been discussed, Carter publicly spelled out the three basic principles, as he saw them, of a comprehensive Middle East peace. These entailed the need for concrete manifestations of peace and normal relations, such as trade and the exchange of diplomats; the need for security arrangements for all parties, but without prejudice to the establishments of recognized borders along the 1967 lines; and the need for a solution to the Palestinian problem, which had a political as well as a humanitarian dimension. A few days later, on March 16, in Clinton, Massachusetts, Carter reiterated these points, using for the first time the formulation of a "Palestinian homeland."[7] Needless to say, the Israelis were stunned and apprehensive, and the Arabs were generally encouraged.

Although the idea of a Palestinian homeland became the focus of much of the public debate, Carter's two central assumptions, which deserve careful scrutiny, were his belief that a peace settlement must evolve from previous agreement on basic principles—the comprehensive framework—rather than through piecemeal bargaining over discrete issues, and his conviction that Israel could achieve security (as well as peace and recognition) within the geographic confines of 1967, with only minor adjustments. This latter point was based on the belief that no Arab leader would ever agree to recognize Israel unless most of the territory captured in 1967 was returned and that ultimately Israel's security would be as much a function of the quality of political relationships with its neighbors as of its military might. The final judgment lying behind Carter's public statements was that Egypt, the Arab country most willing to make peace with Israel, would not do so unless some broader peace process was under way. Sadat himself was the most insistent in arguing this point.

Over the next three months Carter met with Sadat, Hussein, Fahd, and Asad. In each meeting the substantive trinity of peace, borders-security, and the Palestinian question was discussed in some depth, along with procedural questions on how to get the Palestinians represented in the upcoming negotiations. The most encouraging sign during this phase was Sadat's willingness to accept the idea that peace would entail normal relations with Israel, including the exchange of diplomats and full recognition.[8] But also, the Israeli government, while insisting that it would never accept an independent Palestinian state on the West Bank, was prepared to discuss withdrawal and was open to the idea that security would not necessarily require significant border changes beyond the 1967 lines. In addition, Rabin, Allon, and Peres all talked of the need to solve the Palestinian problem if there was to be peace in the region. And the Arab leaders were confidently predicting that the PLO would consider softening its position on the recognition of Israel.

By midyear, then, the Carter administration was well launched with its peace initiative, and the results were fairly encouraging. It is fair to say, however, that the president often felt frustrated with the seeming intractability of the issues, with the complexity of the problem, with the domestic political sensitivities aroused by his public comments, and by the sheer amount of time required to move the process forward.

Then, on June 21, 1977, the unexpected happened. Menachem Begin, whose Likud bloc had won the Knesset elections the previous month, became prime minister of Israel. Begin was an unknown figure in Washington. Insofar as administration officials knew his views, they were aware that he opposed Labor's approach to "territorial compromise" with Jordan as a means of dealing with the West Bank and the Palestinian question. Begin was known to favor an expansion of Israeli settlements, and one of his first acts that irritated the Carter administration was his visit to Elon Moreh, where he announced he would support many more such settlements. These two issues—Begin's unwillingness to accept the principle of withdrawal from the West Bank under any circumstances and his commitment to settlements—became the main sources of conflict between the United States and Israel over the next two years.[9]

Policy Reappraisal

Somewhat surprisingly, Carter's first meeting with Begin was much more cordial than the one with Rabin. Carter apparently believed Begin would become more rigid if pressured, and some of his advisers were convinced that Begin would respond best to a respectful, polite initial encounter. The personal chemistry between the two men was hardly warm, but the talks were conducted in a friendly manner.

Although Begin came prepared with procedural proposals for negotiations with the Arabs, he showed no sign of wanting to discuss substance with the United States. This, in fact, was one of the initial differences between Begin and Rabin: Begin argued that the United States should not be involved in the substance of Arab-Israeli talks but should limit its role to getting the parties together. He obviously feared that the U.S. stand on many issues would be closer to the Arab position, and therefore he wanted as little substantive role for Washington as possible. Previous Israeli governments had, by contrast, insisted on close consultation with the Americans as a way of preventing unilateral moves that might undercut Israel's bargaining position. Begin seemed to be saying that Israel did not feel the need to consult, and at the same time asked that the United States refrain from putting forward any ideas of its own on substance.

Unfortunately for Begin, the United States was already rather far down the road of trying to devise draft principles that should be agreed on before a Geneva conference. In discussions held within the administration early in July, five principles had been agreed on, and during Begin's visit these were discussed. The first point set the goal of comprehensive peace; the second reiterated the relevance of UN Resolutions 242 and 338 as the bases of negotiations; the third defined the goal of peace as involving normal relations, not just an end of belligerency; the fourth dealt with the question of borders and withdrawal in stages; and the fifth point concerned the Palestinians and their rights, including means "to permit self-determination by the Palestinians in deciding on their future status."

Vance, and then Carter, reviewed these points with Begin on July 19–20 and found, not surprisingly, that Begin entirely rejected the fifth point on the Palestinians and was insistent that on point four the United States should not say in public or private that it favored withdrawal to the 1967 lines with only minor modifications. During an evening session alone with Begin, Carter agreed not to mention the 1967 lines with minor modifications in public, and in return he asked Begin to show restraint on settlements. This compromise was part of an effort to calm the heated atmosphere before Geneva, but it also reflected a slight shift toward accepting the idea that little real progress could now be made until the parties began to talk to one another. Procedural issues began to assume greater importance, and agreement on key principles before Geneva came to be seen as unlikely, given the enormous gap between Begin and even the most moderate Arab leaders.[10]

Secretary Vance, who began to focus on the question of how the PLO might be represented at Geneva, found himself leaning increasingly toward the idea of a single Arab delegation that would include Palestinians. Israel had made it clear it would not deal directly with the PLO as a separate delegation, but would not object to Palestinians within the Jordanian delegation. Jordan, however, had no intention of representing the Palestinians and preferred the Syrian idea of a common Arab negotiating front, primarily as a way of preventing unilateral moves by Sadat. Egypt favored a PLO delegation but had shown a willingness to consider other formulations as well. During much of July, August, and September this issue was a major topic of discussion, and some progress seemed possible.

In early August 1977 Vance left on a very important trip to the Middle East. With him he took a revised set of the five principles to discuss with leaders in Egypt, Israel, Syria, Jordan, Saudi Arabia, and Lebanon. He also had with him four possible ways for the Palestinians to be included in the Geneva negotiations, and he was prepared to try out a new idea of some form of trusteeship for the West Bank and Gaza as well.

During Vance's talks in Egypt, Sadat showed considerable anxiety about the shift toward procedural discussions and away from the idea of agreement on principles before Geneva. In his view Geneva should be used for signing a pre-agreed document, little more. Sadat had little patience with the idea of negotiating with Israel, preferring that the United States present a plan to which all the parties could react. To encourage this line of thought, Sadat presented a highly secret document to Vance in Alexandria.[11] It was the draft of a peace treaty that Sadat said he would be prepared to sign, but he did not want any of the other parties to know it existed. Instead he urged Vance to ask the Israelis to put forward a draft treaty of their own; then Vance could unveil the Egyptian draft, which would lead to an eventual U.S. compromise proposal. In a tactic that he was to use repeatedly, Sadat took the Egyptian draft and wrote in the margins in his own handwriting the further concessions he would be prepared to make. These notations were intended, presumably, to convince Vance that Sadat would be flexible on most substantive points, though not on "land and sovereignty," as the Egyptian president repeatedly said.[12]

During the talks with the Egyptians, Vance was also encouraged to believe the PLO was about to change its position on UN Resolution 242. To add an incentive, Vance recommended that President Carter publicly repeat that the United States would be willing to enter into high-level talks with the PLO if the PLO accepted 242, even with a statement of reservation. Carter did so a few days later from Plains, Georgia, while Vance was in Saudi Arabia, all of which ensured that Vance's arrival in Israel was less than warm.[13] The Israelis did agree, however, to provide the United States with a draft peace treaty, and arrangements were made for further meetings between Vance and the various foreign ministers in New York in conjunction with the UN General Assembly.

September 1977 proved to be an eventful month in the evolution of Carter's Middle East strategy. American efforts were concentrated on four parallel, potentially even conflicting, goals. First was the attempt to get each of the parties to provide a written draft of a peace treaty. Israel complied, with a lengthy and legalistic document that left the delicate question of the border and the status of settlements in Sinai obscure. Jordan and even Syria eventually submitted a list of principles that should govern any peace agreement. Although the drafts per se were far from what was needed, they did provide Vance with some building blocks from which to fashion an American compromise proposal, and they had the positive effect of getting the parties to think of committing themselves to concrete positions on paper.

The second strand of policy, largely working through the Syrians but also pursued in other channels, was an attempt to find a solution to the question of how the Palestinians would be represented in upcoming negotiations in Geneva. Agreement was reached on how the PLO might express its reservation to UN Resolution 242, but the conditions demanded by the PLO for an overt acceptance of 242 were beyond what Washington was prepared to promise.[14] Nonetheless, by early October Sadat had informed Carter that the PLO would agree to be represented in a unified Arab delegation by a Palestinian who was not a PLO official. Since everyone had by then accepted the idea of a unified Arab delegation that would include Palestinians, this issue seemed to be nearly resolved.[15]

The third focus of U.S. efforts was to try to develop some understanding among the negotiating parties about the procedures of the Geneva talks. Sadat was still insistent that Geneva must be "well prepared" in advance; otherwise it could bog down and turn into a hopeless stalemate. He remained wedded to the Kissinger model of highly secret talks at the level of head of government, which would then be finalized and legitimized at Geneva. If the actual negotiating was to be done in a semipublic forum like Geneva, he seemed to fear that the other Arabs would try to restrict his freedom to maneuver and that the United States would be subject to the ever-present pro-Israeli pressures generated by American public opinion and Congress. Israel tended to share this suspicion of Geneva, and Foreign Minister Moshe Dayan warned that a unified Arab delegation was a formula for stalemate. Syria, and to a lesser extent Jordan, favored a single delegation as a way of preventing the much-feared separate Egyptian-Israeli agreement they had come to expect after Sinai II.

The American compromise proposal, largely crafted by Vance, was to get everyone to accept the idea of a unified Arab delegation. The main purpose, in his mind, was to bring the Palestinians into the peace process by that means. After a formalistic opening of the Geneva conference, at which the Arab side would appear to be a single delegation, talks would break up into subcommittees, which would essentially be bilateral, except for the discussion of the West Bank and Gaza, in which Egypt and Jordan would join the Palestinians. The American side, mistakenly, did not realize the Syrians would object to being left out of the talks on the Palestinian issue. The main problem seemed to be to get Israel to agree that the Palestinians could be at the talks in their own right, not just as members of the Jordanian or Egyptian delegations.

The fourth, and probably least carefully thought out, part of the U.S. strategy was aimed at the Soviet Union. As Geneva became more of a real concept, rather than just a symbolic umbrella for a whole series of contacts and talks, the United States had to address the question of the role to be played by the other cochairman. A number of procedures had already been worked out in December 1973, when the Geneva conference had convened in plenary session for the first and last time. To the extent possible, it was useful to adhere to those precedents. But the Soviets were clearly seeking more of a role, and in mid-September they presented a draft of a joint statement to Secretary Vance. For a Soviet document it was remarkably balanced. It did not include calls for a Palestinian state or participation by the PLO. It paid due regard to the need for security and normal peaceful relations among the states of the area. Most of the language was from UN Resolution 242. Practically the only formulation the United States had not itself used was a reference to Palestinian rights, which went a step beyond the standard American reference to Palestinian interests.

The task of trying to work out an agreed text was turned over to Ambassador Alfred L. Atherton Jr., who was advising Vance on Arab-Israeli peacemaking, and a Soviet diplomat, Mikhail Sytenko. With little effort, these two professionals produced a generally acceptable text. The question that was hardly discussed was how and when to issue this joint statement so as to advance the other efforts that were under way. At the time it was thought that a strong statement by the Soviets in conjunction with the Americans might put some pressure on Syria and the PLO to cease their haggling over procedural matters and to agree to enter negotiations on the basis of a joint invitation from the superpowers. Little thought was given to Israel's reaction, or to the need to prepare public opinion in the United States. The Israelis were shown a draft in late September, and Dayan's initial reaction was restrained.

Among the potentially controversial elements in the draft were an explicit call for reconvening the Geneva conference by the end of the year; the fact that the Soviet Union would be cochairman; the lack of explicit reference to UN Resolution 242; and a formulation the United States had not previously used referring to Palestinian *rights*. Largely because of these references the Israelis were uncomfortable with the document. But the Carter administration had not picked up any warning signals from Dayan. Thus, when the U.S.-Soviet communiqué was issued on October 1, 1977, few on the American side anticipated the storm of adverse reaction from Israel and Israel's supporters in the United States.[16]

While American efforts were aimed in these various directions, Egypt and Israel were embarking on a round of secret diplomacy. At Sadat's initiative a meeting was held between Dayan and an aide to Sadat, Hassan Touhamy, in Morocco in mid-September.[17] Similar contacts had been held over the years, including that month, between Israeli and Arab leaders, so even when the United States learned of this meeting after the fact, it was not viewed as a vote of no confidence in the ongoing U.S. strategy. In retrospect, one can see that Sadat was beginning to hedge his bets for fear that Geneva would become a straitjacket for his free-wheeling style of diplomacy. It is fair to say that the American side consistently underestimated the degree of distrust between Sadat and Asad and also tended to take Sadat at his word when he repeatedly said he could never afford to make a separate peace with Israel.

Not surprisingly, with so many initiatives under way during September, something was bound to come unstuck. The proximate cause of the explosion was the U.S.-Soviet communiqué and the firestorm of negative American and Israeli reaction it provoked. Much of the pent-up anxiety and frustration with Carter's Middle East policy now spilled over, finding willing allies in the neoconservative, pro-Israeli, anti-Soviet circles. What was in fact a political error, showing considerable amateurishness, was portrayed as a move of vast significance that would reestablish the Soviets as a major power in the Middle East. To read the text of the communiqué several years later is to wonder what all the fuss was about. The words themselves are innocuous, and even Begin used the phrase "Palestinian rights" at Camp David. Nonetheless, the political reality of early October 1977 was that Carter was under great pressure from the friends of Israel, and the Israelis played on his discomfort with extraordinary skill.

Many analysts believe Sadat went to Jerusalem in November 1977 to escape the dead end of a U.S.-Soviet sponsored Geneva conference. They often emphasize his desire to keep the Soviets out of the diplomatic arena. But the available evidence, including Sadat's own account, does not support this widely held belief.[18] When first informed of the U.S.-Soviet joint communiqué, Sadat termed it a "brilliant maneuver," since he, like some U.S. officials, thought it would soften up the Syrians.[19] In any case, he had ensured against Geneva's becoming an Arab-Soviet trap by opening his own direct channel to the Israelis, and from that contact he seemed to be assured that whenever he was ready to sign a separate peace with Israel he would recover most of Sinai. In early October Sadat was still testing to see how much more he could get with U.S. help. It was not the U.S.-Soviet communiqué that disillusioned him; it was Carter's apparent inability to stand up to Israeli pressure, coupled with evidence that Carter was tired of spending so much time on an apparently intractable problem, that seems to have convinced Sadat to strike out on his own.

If this interpretation is correct, then the crucial step along the way was the meeting between Carter and Dayan in New York on October 4, 1977.[20] Dayan began by asking if Israel was expected to accept the U.S.-Soviet communiqué as the price of going to Geneva. He termed the agreement totally unacceptable to Israel, but said Israel would still go to Geneva on the basis of 242. Carter said Israel did not have to accept the communiqué. Then Dayan upped the ante by asking Carter to reaffirm publicly all past U.S. commitments to Israel as a way of calming the crisis atmosphere set off in Israel by the communiqué. He said that if Carter did not do so, Israel might feel obliged to publish these agreements. He also asked for a statement that the United States would not use pressure on Israel to accept a Palestinian state. When Carter said he did not intend to use pressure but did not want to make any such statement, Dayan said he would therefore be obliged to say that he had asked and Carter had refused. Having issued these barely veiled threats, Dayan proceeded to deal in a businesslike way with Secretary Vance on the question of Palestinian representation, going further toward the U.S. position than Begin had probably authorized, and thus winning back for himself the reputation of being the most pragmatic and reasonable of the members of the Israeli cabinet.[21] After a formula for including Palestinians at Geneva was worked out fairly smoothly, Carter returned to the discussion.

Dayan made a strong pitch for American support for a separate Egyptian-Israeli agreement. In Dayan's words, "the future is with Egypt. If you take one wheel off a car, it won't drive. If Egypt is out of the conflict, there will be no more war." The discussion then turned to politics, and Dayan said he could help Carter quiet the fears of American Jews if Dayan could announce an agreement on Geneva between the United States and Israel. "But if we say we have to deal with the PLO or a Palestinian state, and this is bad for Israel, then there will be screaming here and in Israel. We need an agreed formula so I can say there is agreement, not confrontation, to Israel and American Jews." Secretary Vance was clearly very nervous about the image of a joint U.S.-Israeli position and suggested that both parties should state their own positions separately. Dayan objected, saying that something should be announced at the end of the meeting, or it would be very bad. President Carter then agreed that the two sides should try to issue a common statement dealing with Geneva and explaining that the U.S.-Soviet communiqué was not a precondition for Israel's participation at Geneva. After several more hours of drafting, Dayan and Vance appeared in the early morning hours of October 5 to reveal the U.S.-Israeli "working paper," as it became known.[22] To the Arabs, including the Egyptians, this document appeared to be a major retreat from the U.S.-Soviet communiqué, as well as evidence of the considerable power Israel could wield because of its strong base of support in Congress and U.S. public opinion.

In brief, the whole episode left Carter exhausted and somewhat cautious, the Israelis both distrustful and aware of their power, and the Arabs confused and alarmed at the spectacle of the United States' appearing to retreat under pressure on the eve of the Geneva conference. In retrospect, it is easy to see the significant role played by the careless handling of the U.S.-Soviet communiqué. Most of the American officials involved subsequently acknowledged that they should have been more attentive to the negative political fallout from such a joint move with the Soviets. The simple truth is that not much thought was given to the matter because so many other important developments were occurring in the Middle East arena by late September.

The next step along the way in Sadat's decision to go to Jerusalem came later in October. By then the procedural tangles of forming a unified Arab delegation had produced a near deadlock between Syria and Egypt. Progress in resolving the impasse was glacial, and Carter seemed to feel that time was running out. He repeatedly said that he and Secretary Vance had other pressing matters to attend to and could not spend all their time on the Middle East, especially when the problems were among the Arab parties themselves. In this spirit, one Friday morning toward the end of October, Carter decided to send a very personal appeal to Sadat in the form of a handwritten note to be delivered directly to the Egyptian president. In it he reminded Sadat of their mutual pledge in April to do all they could for peace. Carter came close to saying that he had little more to offer and that the time had come for a bold move from Sadat. No specifics were mentioned, but the point was clear: if further progress was to be made, Sadat would have to take the initiative.[23]

Within a week the response came, first in the form of a handwritten note from Sadat, and more formally and with more details as a cable from Cairo. Sadat's idea was to convene a super-Geneva conference in east Jerusalem, to be attended by the heads of state of all the permanent members of the Security Council, as well as by the leaders of Egypt, Syria, Jordan, Israel, and the PLO. It all seemed a bit grand and implausible, and Carter's response was cool.[24] By his own account Sadat began to think of a solo venture to Jerusalem to break the deadlock. But this time he did not bother to tell President Carter. Thus, on November 9, when Sadat publicly revealed his intention to go to Israel, Washington was caught by surprise, just as it had been by Begin's election. Once again the United States was obliged to adjust its strategy because of events in the Middle East that had proved to be beyond its control.

After Jerusalem

The initial reaction to Sadat's trip to Jerusalem in official Washington was one of admiration for the personal courage required and some puzzlement over what Sadat had in mind for an encore. He had often said that 99 percent of the cards were in American hands, but now he seemed to be ready to play his own cards without much help from Carter. No one in Washington proposed that the United States should try to thwart his moves, but there was some concern that negative Arab reactions, coupled with Begin's essential rigidity on the Palestinian issue, would cause the initiative to fall far short of the psychological breakthrough that Sadat sought. Consequently, sooner rather than later the problem would end up back in the American lap. In any case, Sadat's move would not be helped by its appearing to have been made in the United States. These considerations, coupled perhaps with some envy on the part of the politically minded members of the administration for a media-catching move they would have liked to have thought of themselves, led to a fairly reserved public posture, which was strongly criticized at the time by the friends of Israel.[25]

It took some weeks for American officials to correctly assess Sadat's reasons for going to Jerusalem. The depth of animosity between Egypt and Syria had not been recognized, but Sadat's contemptuous comments toward Asad and other Arab leaders after his trip to Israel suggested that he was determined to go it alone for the time being.

By early December the internal consensus in the administration was that Sadat's initiative should be supported strongly but that the United States should continue to use its influence to try to get as broad an agreement as possible. The administration still felt that Sadat would, in the end, not make a separate peace with Israel and that at least some measure of agreement on the Palestinian question would have to serve as a cover for any Egyptian-Israeli deal. Syria would henceforth be ignored for most practical purposes, as would the PLO, but American policy would continue to focus on some form of West Bank–Gaza accord. During the second week of December, Secretary Vance went to the Middle East to consult with the various governments and to begin the process of redefining American strategy.

Just after Vance's return from the Middle East, Begin invited himself to Washington to see President Carter. Vance had seen the prime minister only a few days before, and Begin had not put forward any new ideas, but now he said he had important proposals to discuss with the president before going to a scheduled meeting with Sadat in Ismailia on Christmas day. Some in Washington were suspicious that Begin's purpose was to try to elicit an American endorsement of his ideas before they were shown to Sadat.

Carter's talks with Begin on December 16–17 confirmed the American suspicion. Begin practically pleaded with the president to say that his proposals were a fair basis for negotiation. In fact, Carter did tell him his Sinai proposal looked promising, adding the caveat that there might be points in it that he did not fully understand yet. (This comment became a source of discord later when the Israelis claimed that Carter had approved of the Sinai proposal, knowing it included a provision that Israeli settlements would not be removed.)

If Begin's Sinai proposal was genuinely seen in positive terms, the same could not be said for his "home rule" proposal for "Judea, Samaria, and the Gaza District."[26] In lengthy discussions with Begin, the president, the vice president, Vance, and Brzezinski all tried to encourage Begin to modify his plan. Several points stood out. The home rule proposal was intended as a permanent arrangement, not as a transition to the return of the territory to Arab political control once a peace agreement had been reached. The plan also contained the type of detail that would be bound to irritate Sadat, and Begin was urged to present a simpler set of principles, perhaps only orally. But Begin seemed to be proud of his creation and rather arrogantly told the American side that he did not need their advice on how to negotiate with Sadat. Begin was so eager to win U.S. endorsement, however, that he did imply he would make some improvements in the plan after consulting with his cabinet. With that, he promptly went public with a statement that came very close to saying the president had approved of his plan, which required a clarification from the American side to the effect that the plan was a positive step in the direction of negotiations.

Some in the administration saw merit in Begin's proposal, in part because they thought he could be tricked into turning it into a proposal for only a transitional period.[27] They saw as positive elements Begin's willingness to leave Israel's claim to sovereignty over the West Bank and Gaza in abeyance for five years; his acceptance of the idea that a special administrative regime would go into effect in all the territory of the West Bank and Gaza; and his suggestions about equality of rights and obligations for Arabs and Israelis. (Some of the most attractive points were dropped a few days later from the proposal that was actually presented to Sadat, which left the American negotiators feeling that Begin had used the meeting with Carter just as they had expected and that their entreaties for greater moderation and flexibility had fallen on deaf ears.)[28]

Indicative of the gap between the Egyptian and Israeli positions was the difference in Begin's and Sadat's accounts of their meeting in Ismailia. According to the Israeli version, Sadat was on the verge of accepting the Israeli proposals and issuing a common declaration of principles but was persuaded not to do so by his hard-line advisers from the Foreign Ministry. Sadat's account, by contrast, said that Begin had not grasped the importance of his Jerusalem visit and that the Israelis were trying to haggle and tread on sovereignty. He was quite caustic in his remarks, suggesting there was little point in going on with direct negotiations.

Carter and Vance, who had worried that Sadat and Begin would find it difficult to reach agreement in direct talks, believed an ongoing negotiating process was essential if the United States was to use its influence. Consequently a meeting of the so-called political committee was arranged in January at the level of foreign ministers. For Egypt this meant that Muhammad Ibrahim Kamel, Sadat's new foreign minister, would make his first visit to Jerusalem, something he obviously did not welcome. In fact, the talks seemed to proceed fairly well on the technical level, with the objective of drafting a declaration of principles. (By now the United States was pushing a formula calling for "the right of the Palestinians to participate in the determination of their own future.") For reasons still not entirely clear, but perhaps reflecting Kamel's anger at a toast delivered by Begin at a dinner the first night, Sadat suddenly called his delegation home. Vance, who had seen many negotiations go through such moments, termed it "a bump in the road" and returned to Washington to help forge a new approach in light of events that once again seemed to have taken a somewhat alarming turn.

U.S.-Egyptian Coordination

Discussions within the American negotiating team in January led to a strategy of trying to change two key elements in Begin's position: to achieve a freeze on the construction of new settlements in the occupied territories, an issue of special concern after Begin blatantly allowed new settlements to be started in Sinai within days of his talks in Ismailia with Sadat; and to convince Begin to return to the previous Israeli formula for the West Bank and Gaza by offering to withdraw, at least partially, as the quid pro quo for peace and recognition. This latter point was put in terms of Begin's unwillingness to accept the fact that the withdrawal provision of UN Resolution 242 applied to the West Bank and Gaza. The Labor party, in formally accepting 242 in mid-1970, had interpreted the resolution as requiring "peace for withdrawal" on all fronts, and because of this Begin had left the national unity government that existed at the time.[29]

The Americans thought that the two issues of settlements and withdrawal were intrinsically important if there was to be any chance of a negotiated peace, and that on these issues Begin was vulnerable at home and in the American Jewish community. They therefore decided to mount a campaign of public pressure against Begin on these two points, and to that end they prepared a very comprehensive "white paper," which showed conclusively that Begin did not accept 242 in the same terms as previous Israeli governments had. The document was never released, but it was used for judicious leaking to the press. On settlements, the administration in public and private tried to get a settlements freeze, and indeed the record of 1978 shows very few new settlements being established that year, even though Begin never formally agreed to a freeze until the Camp David talks.

The Carter administration felt it was on sure ground on the two issues of settlements and withdrawal, provided the United States remained clearly committed to Israel's security and supported the Israeli idea that peace should entail normal relations. But Carter felt that Sadat should help the campaign to pressure Israel and worried that Sadat's decision to pull out of the political talks in Jerusalem would weaken the case against Begin. Consequently Carter decided to invite the Egyptian president to Washington in February for a serious review of strategy.

One idea discussed before Sadat's arrival was to try to work out with the Egyptians a series of coordinated moves that would maximize the pressure on Begin. The risk of appearing to collude with the Egyptians was obvious, but Sadat's reputation for making sudden and sometimes unhelpful moves was very much on the Americans' minds. It was also thought that Sadat would be delighted at the prospect of playing a somewhat Machiavellian game aimed at Begin.

A second American effort in early 1978 was to redraft Begin's autonomy proposal into a number of general principles that might be agreed on between Egypt and Israel as a formula for a transitional period of three to five years. By the time of Sadat's arrival at Camp David in the first week of February 1978, a nine-point document had been developed.[30]

Sadat and Carter spent the weekend at Camp David alone. The weather was cold and there was snow on the ground. Sadat was not in good health and clearly disliked the setting, so far from his normal winter refuge of Aswan. By the time the sessions with advisers began, Sadat had convinced Carter that his initiative had nearly reached an end and that he saw no point in going on. Sadat, it must be remembered, was a consummate actor, and some of his posture was no doubt theater, but some was also real. After a lengthy exposé by Carter of all the areas of disagreement, during which Sadat looked despondent, the president asked his pipe-smoking guest if he had any comment to make. Sadat puffed on his pipe, looked grave, and finally said he had only one question to ask: would there be an American proposal? The answer from Carter was yes, and much of the rest of the day was spent developing an agreed strategy that would culminate in a U.S. proposal.

The Americans insisted that Sadat must first return to the negotiating table and reiterate his commitment to the peace process. Then Begin would be invited to Washington, and Carter would privately press hard on the issues of settlements and Resolution 242, issues that the Egyptians would also stress. The United States would also present the nine-point plan as a basis for a possible joint declaration. Part of the strategy also meant getting a formal Egyptian counterproposal to Begin's home rule plan before an American proposal would be put forward. Sadat was urged to make his initial proposal fairly tough, even at the risk of creating a crisis in the negotiations, so that the United States could be in a position of arguing with both Israel and Egypt over aspects of their proposals. To be in that position would help protect Carter's flank at home, since one-sided pressure on Israel could not easily be sustained. The key point in this strategy was that Sadat would, at the appropriate point in the crisis, moderate his position and accept American compromise proposals, making it possible for U.S. pressure then to turn on Israel. The strategy was complex, a bit devious, and only partly internalized by the American and Egyptian officials who were supposed to carry it out. But Sadat loved it. His long-sought goal of forging a joint U.S.-Egyptian strategy seemed to be at hand.[31]

What happened to the Sadat-Carter accord of February 1978? First, the agreed-upon calendar, which envisaged an American proposal by mid-year, was thrown off by the decision to seek congressional approval for the sale of advanced aircraft to Saudi Arabia, Egypt, and Israel. The F-15s for Saudi Arabia proved to be very controversial, and the administration had to spend large amounts of time and political capital to get the sale through. This issue arose right at the moment when the first stage of the joint U.S.-Egyptian strategy should have been taking shape. Second, Sadat was a bit shaky in carrying out his side of the bargain. He tended to ignore the themes of 242 and Israeli settlements in his public statements, making it appear that Carter was being more pro-Arab than Sadat himself. In addition, when he finally did send the United States a proposal, it was very general and did not really serve as a counter to Begin's autonomy plan. Third, Vance decided to ask the Israelis to clarify their views on what would happen at the end of the five-year period of autonomy, and the Israelis took a long time to answer. When they did so, they basically confirmed what was already known of Begin's annexationist intentions.

By midsummer neither Carter nor Vance seemed to feel that the more manipulative aspects of the strategy discussed with Sadat could be made to work, although both remained wedded to the idea that a U.S. proposal should be developed. But no one seemed to relish the idea of a showdown with Begin, except perhaps Brzezinski, who felt Begin was manipulating the United States and needed to be reminded that Washington was capable of pursuing its national interests in a vigorous way and would not always succumb to domestic pressures.

While the American side was edging away from a joint U.S.-Egyptian strategy by mid-1978, Sadat seemed to be operating on the assumption that the general outline of what had been discussed at Camp David was still valid. Thus he periodically adopted extreme positions in public, threatened to call off talks with Israel, talked ominously of October 1978 as the expiration date of the Sinai II agreement (not true), and generally seemed to be trying to engineer an Egyptian-Israeli crisis into which Carter could step with a compromise proposal. Though prepared to go along with the stage setting insisted on by the Americans, such as the Leeds Castle talks at the level of foreign minister in July, Sadat was clearly getting impatient for the showdown with Begin.

Through the spring and summer of 1978 little substantive progress was made in an endless series of contacts with Egyptian and Israeli leaders. Carter was impatient with the slow pace of diplomacy and seemed to feel a desire to get more directly into the act. During much of July a highly secret planning group began to develop a U.S. proposal under Vance's supervision, and the president followed the progress with interest. On July 20 he discussed with his advisers an idea he had been toying with for some time—a summit meeting at Camp David with both Begin and Sadat.[32] Carter seemed to view a summit as the only way to force decisions to a head, and he doubtless counted on his own role as mediator to bridge the still very large gaps. His view of a summit was psychological and political: once the leaders were committed, they could not afford to fail, and he counted on the special atmosphere of Camp David, away from the press and the burdens of everyday governing, to help produce a positive result. The rest of the foreign-policy team was somewhat more wary of the summit idea, tending to focus on the need for very careful substantive preparations. In early August Vance went to the Middle East to invite Begin and Sadat to Camp David in early September. Both accepted readily, and no doubt Sadat saw this event as the much-awaited moment of truth when he and Carter would corner Begin.

The Camp David Summit

Carter, Sadat, and Begin, along with their top advisers, isolated themselves at the president's mountaintop retreat, Camp David, from September

5 to September 17. Little information reached the outside world of these deliberations at the time, so many were surprised by the news on the last day that agreement had been reached on two frameworks for negotiations. The first dealt with the principles of an Egyptian-Israeli agreement; the second, more complex and less precise, consisted of a formula for an interim period of self-government for Palestinians living in the West Bank and Gaza. The outcome was not quite what anyone had expected at the beginning of the historic summit.

Carter prepared himself meticulously for the talks. His briefing book contained an analytical paper entitled "The Pivotal Issue," which focused on the question of "linkage" between agreements on Sinai and on the West Bank.[33] The point was made that Begin would seek to ensure that any agreement he might reach with Sadat concerning Egyptian-Israeli relations should in no way be dependent on resolving the Palestinian question. Sadat, by contrast, would want some relationship between the two so as to protect himself from the charge that he had abandoned the Palestinians and had accepted a separate peace with Israel. The problem for Carter would be to see if an agreement could be reached at the summit that would make it possible to use the incentive of reaching peace with Egypt to moderate Begin's position on the Palestinian question, without at the same time making Egyptian-Israeli relations entirely subject to whether a solution could be found to the most difficult part of the Arab-Israeli conflict.

The American delegation had identified several specific issues that were likely to be obstacles to a successful agreement at Camp David. First was Begin's unwillingness to accept that the principle of withdrawal from occupied territory, as called for in Resolution 242, should apply to the West Bank and Gaza at the end of a transitional period. Second was the problem of Israeli settlements in Sinai and in the West Bank. Third was the question of how to associate Jordan and the Palestinians with subsequent rounds of negotiations.

The American team felt it was pointless at Camp David to try to resolve the question of the border between Israel and a Palestinian-Jordanian entity.[34] Not only would Begin be at his most intransigent, but also the Arab parties most directly concerned would not be present. Similarly the Americans felt the questions of sovereignty over the West Bank and Gaza, as well as the status of Jerusalem, should be deferred. Instead they thought that Egypt and Israel could make some headway on outlining a transitional regime for the West Bank, building on Dayan's idea of dismantling the military occupation and replacing it with an elected Palestinian body with broad responsibility for day-to-day affairs, perhaps including control over state lands (which would have effectively foreclosed the possibility of extensive new Israeli settlement activity during the transitional period).

No one on the American side anticipated insurmountable problems in reaching a general agreement on principles regarding Sinai. Israel was expected to leave the settlements and the airfields, provided firm security arrangements could be worked out. Sadat was taken seriously when he said that he could not bargain over land or sovereignty, but that everything else could be negotiated.

These assessments led the American team to think in terms of seeking agreement between Begin and Sadat on general principles regarding both Sinai and the West Bank and Gaza. Begin would have to cede on the applicability of 242 to the West Bank and Gaza in any final settlement and to a freeze on settlement activity, in return for which he could expect Sadat to be forthcoming on Israeli security requirements in Sinai and the West Bank, and to accept a very loose linkage between negotiations on the two fronts. In Vance's view an agreement of this sort would guide the efforts of the foreign ministers as they sought to translate the principles agreed on by the political leaders into a concrete document leading to an Egyptian-Israeli peace treaty and to a formula for Palestinian self-government for a transitional period.

President Carter's initial reaction to the advice of his team was that it should have aimed higher.[35] Rather than just seek agreement on principles concerning an overall settlement, he wanted to work out the details of an Egyptian-Israeli peace treaty, including specific security arrangements. At Camp David this became his special project, and the first draft of the Egyptian-Israeli accord was done in his hand.[36] Carter, it is fair to say, was less concerned with the so-called linkage problem than were other members of the American team, and he was also more optimistic about the chances of reaching a satisfactory agreement through direct talks with Begin and Sadat.

Carter's views proved to be partly correct and partly wrong. He was right in sensing that the best avenue for real progress lay in getting a detailed understanding between Begin and Sadat on Sinai and on the basic elements of an Egyptian-Israeli peace treaty. Begin skillfully withheld his final concessions on removal from Sinai of Israeli settlements and return of three airfields to Egypt until the very end, but from the outset it was clear that an agreement was possible. Carter was wrong, however, in believing that the talks could be concluded quickly and that the three leaders could work well together to solve problems. After only two sessions with both Begin and Sadat in the same room, the president realized it would be better to keep them apart.[37]

Sadat arrived at Camp David ready for a fight with Begin. To ensure that it would happen, he presented to Carter and Begin an Egyptian draft of a fairly tough agreement. Begin reacted sharply, and the Israelis began to write a counterdraft. At the same time, however, Sadat privately told Carter that he was prepared to be flexible on most points, except for land and sovereignty, but that Carter should put forward proposals for both delegations to react to.[38] On the Israeli side, Attorney General Aharon Barak had also reached the conclusions that the time had come for the United States to put forward proposals of its own and that Begin and Sadat should be kept apart. Thus, by the first weekend, the American team began to polish the first of many negotiating drafts.

Over the next ten days a pattern developed whereby the U.S. delegation, and often just the president and Secretary Vance, would meet separately with the Israeli and Egyptian leaders. They would work from nonbinding written drafts, each time trying to elicit concrete reactions to proposals. These would then be discussed within the American team, and a new draft would be produced, often only marginally different from the previous one. By this means the main issues of disagreement surfaced quickly.

On Sinai there were essentially two problems: settlements and airfields. Both were resolved satisfactorily toward the end of the talks, with Begin reserving his position on settlements by saying the issue would have to be put to a vote of the Knesset. Predictably, the final status of the West Bank and Gaza and the question of linkage were the main stumbling blocks. In addition, the Egyptians insisted on including language from Resolution 242 on the nonacquisition of territory by war. The Israelis refused, even though the language was found in 242, which Begin professed to accept. The not-very-elegant solution was to append the full text of 242 to the Camp David Accords, but not to single out that phrase in the text. For Begin this was a minor victory, typical of his tenacious concern for words and principles, and also indicative of Sadat's comparative indifference to precise language.

Two central issues seemed likely to prevent agreement as the days wore on. First was the bedeviling question of what would happen on the West Bank and Gaza after a five-year transitional period. The Egyptians, supported by the Americans, wanted to make it clear that a final agreement would be negotiated during the transitional period that would resolve the questions of borders, sovereignty, security, and recognition according to the same principles of 242 that would govern agreements on other fronts, such as Sinai. In other words, the "peace for withdrawal" formula would remain intact even if the details might be worked out somewhat differently and over a longer period. Begin would have none of it, but instead of fighting the issue head on, he preferred to focus on other matters until the very last days of the negotiations.

Begin, more than any of the other negotiators, seemed to have a feel for the strategic use of time, taking the negotiations to the brink of collapse over secondary issues to avoid being pressed on key problems. Sadat, by contrast, simply refused to negotiate at all over those matters of deepest concern to him—Egyptian land and sovereignty—while leaving to his aides the unhappy task of trying to stand up to Begin on the Palestinian issue. Carter, who often grew impatient with Sadat's subordinates, frequently went directly to Sadat to get them overruled, something that did not recommend itself on the Israeli side, since there it was Dayan, Defense Minister Ezer Weizman, and Barak who showed flexibility, while Begin was the hard-liner (a much stronger negotiating position to be in, as the results showed).[39] Begin's position was also strengthened by his willingness to accept a failure in the talks. Both Sadat and Carter were more committed to a positive outcome, and Begin could therefore credibly use the threat of walking out, as he did, to extract some concessions.

The second difficult issue was the question of settlements: the American and Egyptian teams wanted to get a freeze on them during the negotiations over Palestinian self-government. Again, Begin deferred the discussion of this issue until near the end of the talks.

September 16, a Saturday, proved to be the crucial day for addressing the hard issues involving the West Bank and Gaza.[40] Until that time all of the American drafts contained language on the applicability of 242, including the principle of withdrawal, to the final negotiation on the West Bank and Gaza. And a paragraph calling for a freeze on settlements had always been included. That morning Dayan and Barak met with Vance. The Israelis explained why Begin would never accept the language on 242 and withdrawal. Barak added that he felt a solution could be found, but only if they were all prepared to continue negotiating for another week or so. Prophetically, he said that if agreement had to be reached that day, all they could hope to do was to paper over some very major problems that would come back to haunt them.

Apart from Barak and a few others, however, no one had the stomach for another week in the claustrophobic environment of Camp David. As a result, in the course of the day on Saturday, the American draft was fundamentally changed. The elements of 242, including withdrawal, which had previously been spelled out were deleted. The language was changed to make it clear that the negotiations, but not necessarily the results of the negotiations, would be based on the principles of 242. And the negotiations about the West Bank and Gaza were artfully obfuscated by creating two tracks, one involving peace-treaty negotiations between Israel and Jordan and the other involving talks between Israel and representatives of the Palestinians about the West Bank and Gaza.

Israel had no objection to saying that 242 should be the basis for negotiations with Jordan. In Begin's view Jordan had no right to the West Bank, and saying that did not imply a commitment to the "peace for withdrawal" formula. In the Israeli view, 242 did not apply to the talks on the final status of the West Bank and Gaza. A careful reader of paragraph 1(c) of the "Framework for Peace in the Middle East" signed on September 17, 1978, will see language about "two separate but related committees," and "the negotiations shall be based on all the provisions and principles of UN Security Council Resolution 242." It may take a lawyer to explain how, but Begin successfully protected his position of principle that 242 did not apply to the negotiations over the West Bank's future; the Americans accepted the ambiguity; and Sadat may well have wondered what all the verbal gymnastics were about. In any case, Begin won this round as well.

Later on Saturday evening Carter and Vance thought they had finally won a round with Begin. At a late-night session Carter insisted that Begin agree to a freeze on settlement activity in the West Bank and Gaza for the duration of the negotiations over autonomy. Carter agreed to delete the paragraph in the draft text and to substitute a letter from Begin to him, and he dropped his insistence that existing settlements should not be thickened. But he clearly thought a commitment had been made not to construct new settlements during the autonomy talks. Vance also understood Begin to have made such a promise, although he was concerned about Begin's hesitation to accept an open-ended commitment to a freeze.[41]

In any event, the issue should have been settled on Sunday morning, when Begin sent a draft letter on the topic to Carter. By this time Sadat had already been informed that Begin had agreed to a freeze on settlements. But the actual letter did not conform to Carter's understanding, and, without speaking directly to Begin, Carter sent it back. Begin had promised to freeze settlements for three months, a time period he had mentioned the previous evening. Now, however, Begin was linking the freeze to the duration of the Egyptian-Israeli negotiations, not to the autonomy talks, which was an entirely inappropriate and unprecedented step. Alarm bells should have gone off, but so many other issues were on the agenda that day, especially a diversionary argument over Jerusalem which erupted in the afternoon, that both Carter and Vance continued to act as if there had merely been a misunderstanding that would be cleared up as soon as Begin sent back a new draft.

The final version of the letter did not arrive until after the Camp David Accords had been signed, and in it Begin held stubbornly to his position that the freeze would last only through the three-month period of the Egyptian-Israeli talks. Another round went to Begin, and this round was on a position of considerable importance to the skeptical Arab audience that was waiting to see what, if anything, would be offered to the Palestinians as a result of the separate Egyptian-Israeli peace apparently in the making. Carter never got over the feeling that Begin had misled him, and this episode caused deep mutual distrust between the two leaders.

Late in the afternoon of September 17 Sadat and Carter met for the last time to discuss the agreement that was nearing completion. Sadat was reserved, and his mood was not one of pleasure at a job well done. The American team also realized that many problems lay ahead, but in the end it had made the political decision to get the best agreement then available, while hoping that the next stage of talks would fill in some of the gaps and clarify areas of ambiguity.

Conclusions

During the lengthy talks that preceded Camp David and at Camp David itself, U.S. policy constantly had to adjust to two realities: events in the Middle East cannot be easily controlled or influenced, so developments there frequently caught the Americans by surprise and obliged them to revise their strategies; and domestic American political realities intrude with particular force on the decisionmaking process regarding the Middle East. A president must simultaneously adjust his plans to the unpredictable twists and turns of Middle East politics and keep an eye on his domestic political base. What seems possible and desirable in the first year of a president's term is likely to be seen as hopelessly ambitious by the third year.

The result of these Middle East and domestic pressures is to move American policy away from grand designs with strong ideological content toward a less controversial, and less ambitious, middle ground that can win bipartisan public support as well as acceptance by Arabs and Israelis. To do so, of course, is not always possible, as much as it might be politically desirable, so American policy toward the Middle East rarely manages to satisfy everyone who has an interest in shaping it. Presidents seem to tire of all the controversy generated by Middle East problems, and the intractability of the issues is a source of much frustration.

The Camp David Accords amply demonstrate the limits of what in fact can be achieved, even with a massive commitment of effort.[42] But they are also a reminder that diplomacy can produce results, if the will, the energy, and the creativity are there. The historical verdict on Camp David cannot be fully rendered, although with each passing year it seems to be more widely accepted as part of the new reality of the Middle East. By any standard, however, this remarkable adventure in summit diplomacy achieved more than most of its detractors have been willing to acknowledge and less than its most ardent proponents have claimed.

7 *Forging Egyptian-Israeli Peace*

THE TWO AGREEMENTS reached at Camp David marked an important watershed in the peace negotiations, but much remained to be done before peace would actually be achieved. Many of the blanks in the Camp David Accords had to be filled in, and many of the ambiguities had to be resolved one way or another. Along the way there would be pauses, detours, some backtracking, and many dead ends. Egypt and Israel would finally reach their goal of a formal peace treaty, but the broader objective of finding a peaceful resolution to the Palestinian question remained elusive.

The phase of detailed drafting was now to begin, a seemingly technical task, but in fact a complex process during which major political battles were still fought and attempts to revise the basic framework of negotiations were still made. Although the technicians were sitting at the table drafting documents, the political leaders were still deeply involved.

Menachem Begin, Anwar Sadat, and Jimmy Carter each devised strategies for this phase of negotiations, but the special circumstances of the summit could not be recreated. Isolating the leaders from the press and their own public opinion had no doubt been a prime factor in reaching the two framework agreements. Now, however, each leader would have to return to the real world in which domestic constituencies would have their say.

As each of the Camp David participants felt compelled to justify what he had done at the summit, the gap separating them began to widen again.

By the time of the self-imposed target of three months for negotiating the peace treaty between Egypt and Israel, the talks had come to a halt.

Post-Summit Strategies

Carter left Camp David with a feeling of real satisfaction. The reaction in Congress, the press, and the public at large to the news of an agreement between Begin and Sadat was overwhelmingly positive. Carter received much of the credit, and his political fortunes seemed to improve significantly as a result.

To sustain this political boost, however, Carter needed to make sure that the Camp David frameworks did not remain dead letters. Time was of the essence in reaching a formal peace treaty. Among other considerations, midterm congressional elections were scheduled for early November, and it would probably help Democratic candidates, and therefore Carter, if a peace treaty could be signed by then.

Although Carter was no doubt pleased by the domestic American reaction, he was worried by the early signs of disenchantment in the Arab world. He had implied to Sadat that he would make a serious effort to win support from Jordan and Saudi Arabia, and in his more careless moments he had said that anything he and Sadat agreed to would have to be accepted by King Hussein and the Saudis. But Hussein was wary of the accords reached at Camp David and refused to meet with Sadat on the Egyptian president's return trip to Cairo.

Carter's clear priority after Camp David was to conclude the treaty negotiations as quickly as possible, literally within days. As usual, the president tended to see the remaining issues as technical and therefore susceptible to rapid resolution. The deeper political problems faced by both Begin and Sadat were harder for him to fathom. Carter found it difficult to accept the fact that neither shared his own sense of urgency.

Not only did Begin not share Carter's feeling that time was of the essence, but he also wanted to slow down the pace of negotiations for fear that too much pressure would otherwise be put on Israel. Whenever Carter showed himself too eager for quick results, Begin seemed to dig in his heels to resist demands for Israeli concessions. He was particularly recalcitrant about the settlements in the West Bank and Gaza. As hard as Carter might press to resolve this issue, Begin simply said no to the idea of a prolonged freeze on new settlements. And that was that.

If Begin was attentive to the rhythms of American politics, and surely he was, he must have realized it would be increasingly difficult for Carter to play a strong role in the negotiations as 1979 unfolded. At some point the preelection atmosphere would take hold, and Carter would have to turn to shoring up his political position. He would not then want to engage in confrontations with Israel. Begin was well aware that Carter tended to side with Sadat on the Palestinian question and that the negotiations over the West Bank and Gaza would be extremely difficult. It would be far better, then, not to begin talks on autonomy until sometime well into 1979, when Carter would have other preoccupations.

In many ways Sadat was in a weaker position than Begin, which inevitably influenced the outcome of the negotiations. If the talks now broke down, Israel would stay put in Sinai. Sadat would have nothing to show for his "historic initiative." And his hope for American economic, military, and technological assistance would fade if the peace negotiations collapsed because of his actions. Carter had already warned him of that at Camp David. Sadat worried less about time than Carter, but he too must have understood that Carter's role would have to change as the election year of 1980 approached.[1] Sadat also knew, however, that any show by him of impatience or eagerness to conclude the negotiations would be used by Begin to try to extract further concessions.

From the perspectives of Carter, Sadat, and Begin, the post-summit phase of negotiations was bound to be difficult. The unique circumstances of the thirteen days at Camp David had facilitated reaching agreement, but now most of the pressures were working in the opposite direction. It was not a propitious atmosphere in which to resume the talks.

Preparing for the Next Round

Carter was not content to sit and wait for the results of the Knesset vote on the Camp David Accords, scheduled for two weeks later. There was one item of unfinished business. On Monday, September 18, 1978, Begin had sent Carter the promised letter on the settlements in the West Bank and Gaza. The text was identical to the one Carter had rejected the previous day. Referring to his notes of the Saturday night conversation, Carter wrote down what he thought had been agreed to and had Assistant Secretary of State Harold Saunders deliver his version to the Israelis, along with the original of Begin's letter, which Carter refused to accept.

Carter continued to look for ways to push Begin into agreeing to a freeze on settlements for the duration of the negotiations on self-government for the Palestinians. For example, he dispatched an oral message to Begin, repeating his view on what had been agreed on and warning that "the settlements could become a serious obstacle to peace. Construction of new settlements during the negotiations could have a most serious consequence for the successful fulfillment of the agreement."

When Begin met with the American ambassador to Israel, Samuel W. Lewis, on September 27, 1978, he provided the text of Attorney General Aharon Barak's notes from the meeting on the night of September 16. According to Begin, the notes proved that he had not agreed to the freeze Carter had requested. He had agreed only to consider it.

Neither Carter nor Begin would budge, but soon Carter turned to other matters. To the many bystanders who were waiting to see the outcome of this dispute, round one seemed to go to Begin—not an encouraging sign for Sadat or King Hussein, who had been following the negotiations carefully.

While Carter was trying to untangle the controversy over settlements, Secretary of State Cyrus Vance was traveling in the Middle East. His goal was to try to win Jordanian and Saudi support for the Camp David Accords. What he found instead was deep skepticism, coated only with a formal politeness that some Americans interpreted as an expression of hope that the next round of negotiations would succeed.[2]

Carter and Vance both felt that some of Begin's public interpretations of the Camp David Accords were making it difficult for King Hussein and the Saudis not to reject them.[3] The Americans were also frustrated by Sadat's seeming unwillingness to communicate with either the Jordanians or the Saudis.[4]

Despite all these problems, Carter remained somewhat optimistic that Jordan would join the negotiations.[5] Vance was more skeptical, especially after his visits to Amman and Riyadh. King Hussein had raised many questions, and Vance knew it would be difficult to overcome his doubts. In an attempt to do so, however, Vance did agree to give the king written answers to questions he might have about the accords.[6]

Meanwhile the PLO was making queries through intelligence channels to Washington about the meaning of the agreements. Arafat was skeptical, but he showed a serious interest in finding out if there might be more to Camp David than met the eye. Although the Americans had no reason for optimism, they could see that an Arab consensus had not yet formed. If the Arabs took Begin's interpretations, or Sadat's contemptuous expressions, as the final words on the matter, the case would be closed. But the Americans hoped they might succeed in giving a more open-ended interpretation to the framework dealing with the Palestinians and thus prevent a strongly negative Arab reaction. They therefore decided to use the questions from King Hussein as the means of offering a liberal American interpretation of Camp David.

While the Americans were working to convince other Arabs to be open-minded about Camp David, the Israeli Knesset met on September 27, 1978, to vote on the Camp David Accords, including the provision for withdrawing settlements from Sinai. After lengthy arguments, the vote was 84 in favor and 19 opposed, with 17 abstentions.

Carter phoned Begin the next day to congratulate him on the outcome of the Knesset debate. He also mentioned his hope that the "difference of opinion" between them over settlements in the West Bank and Gaza would soon be resolved. Begin said he had already sent the president a letter on the topic. Carter added that he would like to see a Sinai agreement within days. Begin said it should be possible if everyone agreed to use the standard form of a peace treaty and just fill in the blanks with appropriate details.

Carter then called Sadat, and the two agreed that negotiations on the peace treaty could begin in mid-October. With these conversations Carter seems to have given up the idea of trying to force Begin to change his position on West Bank and Gaza settlements. By continuing to dwell on that topic, Carter would risk the Sinai agreement he so badly wanted. He would also be reminding the other Arabs of one of the flaws in the Camp David framework. Instead, he apparently decided to end the public debate over the issue. For three months, in any case, there would be no more Israeli settlements, and during that period Carter hoped that a solution might be found. So that same day, September 28, he authorized Secretary of Defense Harold Brown to sign a letter to Israeli defense minister Ezer Weizman promising American support in building two airfields in the Negev.

The Blair House Talks

To prepare for the next phase of negotiations, the American team had drawn up a draft of an Egyptian-Israeli peace treaty. Vance wanted to use the same procedure that had proved successful at Camp David. Each side would be asked to comment on the American draft, but changes in the text would be made only by the American side after consulting with the others. The device of a "single negotiating text" was one of the methodological devices the Americans had found useful, and both the Egyptians and Israelis had come to accept it.

Carter reviewed the draft treaty on October 9. His only comment was that Israel should withdraw fully from Sinai in two, not three, years. The draft treaty was a fairly simple document. It formally ended the state of war and established a relationship of peace. Israel would withdraw to the international border according to details to be worked out by the parties. On the completion of an interim phase of withdrawal, diplomatic relations would be established. The border between the two countries was defined as the former international boundary between Egypt and mandated Palestine. Article 3 of the treaty called for normal peaceful relations, the details of which were to be spelled out in an annex. Article 4 called for security arrangements in Sinai and along the border. Article 5 dealt with freedom of navigation. And article 6 spelled out the relation between this treaty and other international obligations of the parties.

From the beginning the Americans realized that several issues would be contentious. For Israel, there was the question of the timing of withdrawal. Israel's fear was that Egypt might get most or all of its territory back before entering into any form of peaceful relations with Israel. For the Israeli public, all the concessions would then seem to be coming from the Israeli side. Israel therefore insisted that Egypt establish diplomatic relations before final withdrawal and that some aspects of normal relations should begin at an early date. For Egypt, this timing posed a problem. Sadat wanted to withhold the exchange of ambassadors until Israel had at least carried out the provisions of the Camp David Accords that called for elections for the Palestinians in the West Bank and Gaza to establish their own self-governing authority. This was the famous issue of linkage, which here boiled down to when Egypt would send its ambassador to Israel. Since that was a matter of great importance to Begin, it acquired significance for Sadat as well. A test of wills quickly developed over the issue.

A second issue of likely contention was the so-called priority of obligations. Israel wanted the treaty to contain a clear statement that it superseded other Egyptian commitments, such as Egypt's many mutual defense pacts with Arab countries. Sadat found it intolerable to say in public that commitments to Israel counted for more than commitments to Arab states. For example, if Israel carried out aggression against an Arab state allied to Egypt, Sadat did not feel it would be a violation of the treaty if he went to the aid of that state. In reality, of course, whatever was written on paper would not guarantee what would happen in some future conflict, but these were issues of high symbolic importance for each party, and each was trying to make its position clear to the United States in the event of future disputes. Much more was to be heard about the priority of obligations.

Vance, the experienced international lawyer, realized from the outset that this issue would be a sticking point.

Perhaps most difficult was the question of how the two parties would express their continuing determination to work for a solution to the Palestinian question after they had signed the treaty. Begin wanted only a vague commitment to negotiate, whereas Sadat insisted on deadlines and specific commitments that would demonstrate that Egypt had not concluded a "separate peace." Here, again, was the linkage issue in its pure form.

Besides these difficult conceptual problems, there were also some complicated details. Israel wanted to retain access to Sinai oil, and it wanted some form of guarantee from the United States if Egypt later refused to supply the oil. Some of the specific issues involving security arrangements in Sinai might also prove difficult, even though the military men on both sides had a good record of finding concrete compromise solutions.

This phase of the negotiations differed from Camp David not only in content but also in format and personnel. On the American side, Carter was less involved. He felt he had spent too much time on the Middle East and that he now had to turn his attention to other issues.

Normalization of relations with China and the conclusion of SALT II with the Soviet Union were high on his foreign-policy agenda. Vance was designated as the principal negotiator on the American side, though he too had other responsibilities. He hoped to delegate much of the day-to-day work to Alfred Atherton, the U.S. ambassador for the peace talks.

The Egyptian team was also somewhat different. In the past Carter had relied heavily on his ability to deal directly with Sadat, over the heads of the Egyptian delegation. Now that the time had come to put words to paper in a peace treaty, the Egyptian lawyers would have their chance again to push Sadat toward harder positions. The new minister of foreign affairs and head of the Egyptian delegation was Kamal Hassan Ali, who was assisted in the negotiations by Boutros Boutros-Ghali and Usama al-Baz, both veterans of Camp David. Sadat also soon named a new prime minister, Mustafa Khalil, who had played no previous part in the negotiations.

The Israeli participants were more familiar, most of them having been at Camp David. Foreign Minister Dayan and Defense Minister Weizman led the negotiating team to Washington, accompanied by Attorney General Barak and Meir Rosenne, a legal adviser to the foreign minister. Begin refused to delegate much authority to the team, however, and the Israeli cabinet as a whole wanted to be kept abreast of most of the details of the talks. As a result, the comparative moderation of the negotiating team meant little.

The delegations arrived in Washington in the second week of October, and the first sessions were scheduled for October 12. Carter met with both the Israelis and the Egyptians before the formal resumption of the talks in order to urge both sides to move toward agreement quickly. In his talks with the Egyptians on October 11, Carter said the negotiations in Washington should be used to deal with the problems of Sinai and the West Bank and Gaza. He urged the Egyptians not to give up on the Jordanians and Palestinians. At the same time, he said, the issues involving the West Bank and Gaza should not be allowed to impede progress toward an Egyptian-Israeli peace treaty.

In the meeting with Carter, Boutros-Ghali took the floor for the Egyptians to make the case for linkage, or the "correlation" between the two agreements, as he was fond of calling it. After Egypt and Israel reached agreement, he asked, what pressure would there be on Israel to do anything about the West Bank and Gaza? If Egypt received some advantages in Sinai, the Palestinians must also have something. Otherwise Egypt would be isolated in the Arab world. This could jeopardize the approximately $2 billion that Egypt was receiving from Saudi Arabia. Al-Baz interjected the thought that the opposition to Camp David had already peaked in the Arab world and that within a few months King Hussein would be ready to join the talks. Carter concluded by repeating that he was committed to finding a solution to the West Bank and Gaza but he did not want to risk the treaty between Egypt and Israel because of problems with Jordan or the Palestinians.

Opening Bids

For several days after these initial meetings the talks dragged on without any breakthroughs. The technicians were able to make some headway on the annexes, but the problems at the political level remained. Carter began to show signs of impatience. He was thinking of flying to the Middle East in late October and even hoped, unrealistically, to be able to preside over the signing of the Egyptian-Israeli peace treaty at that time. An Arab summit was being talked about for early November, and Carter wanted to pin down the treaty before it convened. He also had his eye on the congressional elections.[7]

To speed up the talks, Carter decided to meet both delegations on October 17. Dayan complained about three issues: the language on priority of obligations in the treaty; the linkage between the treaty talks and the West Bank–Gaza issues; and Egypt's reluctance to speed up normalization.

Then, in a shrewd gesture seemingly calculated to win Carter's support, Dayan announced that Israel was prepared to accelerate withdrawal to the interim line in Sinai. (The Camp David Accords called on Israel to pull back its forces from about two-thirds of Sinai within nine months of signing a peace treaty.) The town of Al-Arish, which had great symbolic value to Sadat, could be returned within two months instead of the nine envisaged in the framework agreement. Carter was pleased and saw the offer as a welcome sign of Israeli flexibility. In return, Carter agreed to talk to the Egyptians about moving quickly on normalization; he undertook to resolve a technical problem involving the location of the interim line; and he agreed to consider helping to finance the withdrawal of the Israeli military from Sinai, but not the cost of removing the settlers.

A few hours later Carter met with the Egyptian delegation. Kamal Hassan Ali informed the president that agreement had been reached on the delineation of limited-force zones in Sinai. Boutros-Ghali then argued the case for some correlation between the treaty negotiations and the Palestinian question. In particular, he put forward the idea of establishing diplomatic relations in stages that would somehow be related to progress on the West Bank and Gaza. Carter was unhappy with this proposal and reminded the Egyptians that Sadat had orally agreed at Camp David that ambassadors would be exchanged at the time of the interim withdrawal. He then gave the Egyptians copies of his answers to King Hussein's questions and said they should help deal with the problem of linkage.

Carter also informed the Egyptians that the Israelis were prepared to accelerate withdrawal to Al-Arish. Now, he said, the Egyptians seemed to be backsliding on the timing of sending their ambassador to Tel Aviv. He argued that Egypt should reciprocate Israel's constructive attitude on withdrawal by agreeing to an early exchange of ambassadors. Carter ended the talks by asking the Egyptians to tell President Sadat of his desire to visit the Middle East, before November 1 if possible.

Carter was now back in the middle of the negotiations. On October 20 he held a sometimes acrimonious meeting with the Israeli delegation. He charged that Israel was ignoring the fact that the Egyptian-Israeli framework was part of a broader commitment to work for a settlement on the West Bank and Gaza as well. Barak asked if Carter thought the treaty should be made contingent on whether an agreement could be reached on the West Bank. Carter said that was not his intention. After all, the West Bank formula might fail because of the actions or inactions of third parties, in particular the Jordanians or Palestinians. But, Carter asked, what if Israel was the party responsible for the failure of the West Bank framework?

Did Israel think that in those circumstances the treaty would be unaffected? Barak answered that the treaty must be legally independent of whatever happened on the West Bank and Gaza, even though some degree of political linkage might exist. Carter then told the Israelis that he was sure he could get Sadat to agree to an exchange of ambassadors within one month of the interim withdrawal. Dayan asked if the United States could write a letter guaranteeing that the treaty would be carried out.

After further discussion, agreement *ad referendum* was reached on the text of the treaty. Each delegation had to refer back to its own capital for final approval, but the basic elements of the treaty were seemingly all in place. The Egyptians, however, had proposed during the talks that a parallel letter be signed by Sadat and Begin dealing with the West Bank and Gaza. The letter should coincide with the treaty and would commit the two parties to conclude the negotiations on the West Bank and Gaza by a fixed date, with elections to be held within three months after the treaty was signed.

Egypt also mentioned in the negotiations its special responsibility for Gaza, a reminder of Sadat's interest in the "Gaza-first" option, whereby self-government would be established first in Gaza and only later in the West Bank, after King Hussein joined the negotiations. Al-Baz referred to this as a ploy to scare King Hussein and the Palestinians, in essence telling them that if they did not get into the negotiations soon they would be left out.

Carter wrote to Sadat on October 22, spelling out the terms of the treaty as negotiated in Washington. He asked that Sadat accept the text in its current form and that in addition he agree to a letter committing Egypt to send an ambassador to Israel within one month of the interim withdrawal. Carter repeated that he had asked the Israelis to withdraw more rapidly to the interim line than was called for at Camp David. Carter concluded the letter by saying he would like to visit the Middle East for the treaty signing, which he hoped could be at a very early date. A similar letter was sent to Begin. Carter noted that he did not yet have Sadat's approval to send an ambassador to Israel within one month of the interim withdrawal, but he hoped that Sadat would have a positive attitude.

Sadat's reply came on October 24. He was willing to accommodate Carter on several points, including the exchange of ambassadors, provided some changes could be made in the text of the treaty. Egypt could not agree to permanent force limits in Sinai. Up to twenty-five years would be acceptable. (Carter noted, "Not a problem.") Second, article 6 of the treaty, the priority of obligations issue, made it seem as if Egypt's commitments to Israel were greater than those to the Arab League.[8] The language of the treaty should not downgrade Egypt's obligations under previous agreements. (Carter noted, "A problem.") Third, the treaty must clearly say that Egypt has sovereignty over Sinai. (Carter wrote, "Okay.")

A letter from Begin arrived the same day. In it the Israeli prime minister complained at length about the answers provided to King Hussein. Then Begin reviewed the dispute over settlements in the West Bank and Gaza, noting that he had told the president there were plans to add several hundred families to the settlements in Judea and Samaria, even during the three-month moratorium.

Meanwhile Dayan and Weizman were in Israel seeking to win cabinet approval for the draft treaty. They ran into considerable criticism, but nonetheless Begin pressed for cabinet support of the existing draft and won a sizable majority on October 26. For reasons of his own, and perhaps as a reward to some of the hard-line cabinet members, Begin accompanied the announcement of the cabinet's decision on the treaty with a decision to "thicken" settlements in the West Bank.

Carter was furious. He perfunctorily congratulated Begin on the cabinet vote and then commented on the decision to thicken settlements: "At a time when we are trying to organize the negotiations dealing with the West Bank and Gaza, no step by the Israeli government could be more damaging." In his own handwriting Carter added, "I have to tell you with gravest concern and regret that taking this step at this time will have the most serious consequences for our relationship."

In light of these developments, it was somewhat ironic that the Nobel peace prize was awarded the next day to both Begin and Sadat. Some of Carter's aides were bitter that the president was not included, but for the moment the more important problem was that peace itself seemed to be slipping away. Reports had even reached Washington that Sadat was about to withdraw his delegation and break off the talks. Carter contacted him and convinced him not to take any rash action, but the mood at the White House was gloomy. At a minimum, Carter would not be able to make his hoped-for trip to the Middle East before the end of the month.

During the last days of October the American team became increasingly aware that the Israelis were insisting on a very narrow definition of self-government for the Palestinians in the West Bank and Gaza. Dayan, in an unusually frank session with Vance on October 30, conveyed the most recent Israeli cabinet decisions on the treaty, and then went on to talk about the West Bank problem. Israel, he said, was prepared to talk to Egypt only about the "modalities" for holding elections. It would be a mistake to get into the question of the "powers and responsibilities" of the elected self-governing authority. To do so would open a Pandora's box. Far better to limit the talks to holding elections; then Israel could work out with the Palestinians the powers of the body to which they had been elected.

The next day Dayan made many of these same points before the Egyptian delegation. He presented a strong case for limiting the discussions between Egypt and Israel to the question of how to organize the elections in the West Bank and Gaza. Otherwise the talks would drag on indefinitely. Al-Baz, speaking for the Egyptians, disagreed. The Palestinians had to know, he argued, what they were voting for. Unless the powers and responsibilities were defined in advance, the elections would be seen as a fraud. It would not be easier to grapple with this problem later. Dayan, who knew his prime minister well, said he would refer this issue to Begin if the Egyptians insisted. But he could tell them now that if Israel did consent to discuss powers and responsibilities, the negotiators would spend years trying to reach agreement.

When Carter read the accounts of these meetings, he was outraged. He saw them as further evidence of Israeli backsliding from the commitments made at Camp David. Carter's top advisers were called to the White House on November 1 for a strategy session. They decided to slow down the pace of the negotiations, to review Israel's commitments under the Camp David Accords, and to develop a series of steps to bring pressure on Begin to live up to those commitments. Responses to Israeli requests for arms could be delayed, and several other steps could be taken.

The next day Vance flew to New York for a brief meeting with Begin, who happened to be in town on his way to Canada. Dayan had earlier made it clear that Begin and the cabinet had ultimate authority and that he could do little more to resolve the disputes on remaining issues. Now, Begin found most of the treaty text acceptable but had problems with the side letter dealing with the West Bank and Gaza. Dayan and Weizman had said it should be possible to mention a target date for the holding of elections, but they did not want that date to coincide precisely with the interim withdrawal in Sinai. That would give the appearance of too much linkage. Begin, however, now said that Israel was adamantly opposed to the idea of any target date for elections. He argued that if for some reason beyond the control of Egypt and Israel the elections could not be held, that would call into question everything else, including the peace treaty. By contrast, Begin, always the legalist, found no problem in agreeing to the Egyptian request that powers and responsibilities of the self-governing authority be defined in advance of elections. On both these crucial issues, Begin ignored Dayan's advice. This was the first concrete evidence that Dayan's authority in this phase of the negotiations was much less than it had been in the preceding year.

Then Begin turned to bilateral issues. Israel would need $3.37 billion from the United States to help finance the withdrawal from Sinai, including the removal of the settlers. This aid should take the form of a loan at low interest rates. The cabinet would never approve the treaty, he said, unless the question of aid was solved first. Vance was noncommittal, refusing to give up one of the few elements of leverage the United States possessed.

As tensions rose in the U.S.-Israeli relationship, largely over the perception that Begin was diluting his already modest commitments concerning the Palestinians, pressure was mounting on Egypt to adopt a tougher position in support of Palestinian rights. The Arabs had held a summit meeting in Baghdad, and on November 5 they announced their conclusions. They criticized the Camp David Accords, and they decided that the headquarters of the Arab League was to be moved from Cairo if Egypt and Israel reached a peace treaty. The conference participants sent a small delegation to Cairo to meet with Sadat to dissuade him from continuing with the peace negotiations, but the Egyptian president refused to meet it. Instead, he publicly referred to the summit participants as "cowards and dwarfs." He would not pay any attention, he said, to "the hissing of snakes."

Still, within days the Egyptian position seemed to harden.[9] Sadat sent a message to Carter on November 8 saying there must be unequivocal agreement on what was to take place on the West Bank and Gaza. Otherwise he would be accused of making a separate deal with the Israelis and abandoning the Palestinians.

Carter met with his senior aides to review the negotiations on November 8. He was in a bad mood. Brzezinski was arguing for a tough line with Begin. He urged Carter to consider reducing aid to Israel by a certain amount for each new settlement that Begin authorized. "We do not intend to subsidize illegal settlements and we will so inform Congress." No decisions on aid should be made until Begin accepted a target date for elections.

Carter decided Vance should not go to the Middle East again as had been proposed. It was pointless for him to spend full time on a nonproductive effort. Carter had concluded that Israel wanted a separate treaty with Egypt, while keeping the West Bank and Gaza permanently. The creation of new settlements, he thought, was deliberately done to prevent Jordan and the Palestinians from joining the negotiations.[10] Carter and

Vance now felt they must try to pin down the agenda for the West Bank and Gaza, even if that meant delaying the signing of an Egyptian-Israeli treaty. As usual, their sympathies were more with Sadat than with Begin.

Over the next few days the American side worked to complete the text of the treaty and all its annexes, as well as a letter on the West Bank and Gaza. Carter reviewed the entire package, and it was ready to present to the Israelis and Egyptians on November 11. In a late session at the State Department that same evening, Vance and Dayan tried to resolve some remaining issues in anticipation of a meeting between Vance and Begin in New York the next day. Dayan informed Vance that the Israeli cabinet was adamant against agreeing to accelerate withdrawal to the interim line. He personally was inclined to accept a target date for elections in the West Bank and Gaza, but the date should not correspond to the interim withdrawal. As for the text of the treaty, Dayan seemed to be satisfied.[11]

Begin, however, was not in a conciliatory frame of mind. He refused to accept the idea of a target date, telling Vance on November 12 that Dayan had no authority to imply otherwise. He repeated his refusal to consider accelerated withdrawal. And as if he should be rewarded for his intransigence, he demanded that the aid for the withdrawal from Sinai take the form of a grant, not a loan. He had made a mistake, he said, when he earlier requested a loan and had promised that every penny of it would be repaid.

Sadat Loses Patience

Meanwhile Carter telephoned Sadat in Cairo to urge him to accept the same package. Sadat was more agitated than usual. He argued at great length that the Baghdad rejectionists should not get the upper hand. He must show that he had gotten something for the Palestinians, at least in Gaza, before Israel completed the interim withdrawal. He would even be willing to have the withdrawal delayed by a few months if that would allow the elections for Palestinian self-government to be held at the same time as the return of most of Sinai. Somewhat awkwardly, Sadat said he would not agree to the first phase of withdrawal without at least the beginning of self-government in Gaza. Carter made it clear he did not favor treating Gaza differently from the West Bank. Elections should be held in both areas by the end of 1979, he said.

Sadat repeated that the first phase of withdrawal should coincide with the day the Palestinians started their self-government in the West Bank and Gaza, or at least in Gaza. He accused Begin of trying to delay everything until the start of the American elections.

Carter then called Begin in New York, pointing out that the prospect of agreement was now quite remote. Begin responded by saying that Israel had broken no promise in refusing to accelerate the withdrawal. Weizman should never have agreed to such an idea. In any case, Egypt had no right to use the Israeli decision as a pretext to refuse to send an ambassador to Israel, as Boutros-Ghali had implied. Carter reassured him that Sadat would stand by his agreement to send an ambassador within one month of the interim withdrawal.

Several days later, on November 21, Begin telephoned Carter to say that the Israeli cabinet had voted to accept the text of the treaty and its annexes. Carter was pleased, but asked about the letter on the West Bank and Gaza. Begin replied that the cabinet had rejected the idea of setting a target date at the end of 1979 for elections in the West Bank and Gaza. And he added that there were also other problems. First, Israel wanted to resolve the question of a grant from the United States to help cover the costs of withdrawal from Sinai. Second, Israel needed assurances on oil, especially in light of the turmoil in Iran, the country from which Israel normally received its oil.

On November 30, U.S. Ambassador to Egypt Hermann Eilts was handed a letter from Sadat to Carter strongly criticizing Begin for wanting only a separate peace. The talks had reached a crossroads. An Egyptian presence in Gaza was now essential. Article 6 of the treaty on priority of obligations was impossible to accept, and article 4 needed to be revised so that it did not imply permanent limits on Egyptian forces in Sinai. When Israel reneged on accelerated withdrawal, Sadat said, this upset the equation on an early exchange of ambassadors. He could no longer agree to send an ambassador to Israel one month after the interim withdrawal. Sadat also provided the Americans with the text of a sixteen-page letter he was sending to Begin.

More constructive was Sadat's decision to send his prime minister, Mustafa Khalil, to Washington to consult with Carter. Khalil made a good impression on the Americans as a man of reason and as an able spokesman for the Egyptian side. In a meeting with Carter on December 1, Khalil pressed hard on the importance of simultaneity of Israeli withdrawal to the interim line and establishment of the self-governing authority. He also wanted to revise article 6 of the treaty. Carter objected to the idea of revising the treaty but did suggest that interpretive notes could be appended to it.

Several days later, on December 4, Carter met with his Middle East team to review the details of the proposals Khalil had brought with him.

Carter and Vance were both eager to know what Sadat's bottom line was. Would he insist on a fixed date for elections in the West Bank and Gaza? Carter favored a less precise formulation of a target date. On article 6, Carter thought Sadat might settle for some cosmetic change of words. But Carter was convinced that Sadat would insist on some explicit relationship between the implementation of the Sinai agreement and the establishment of self-government in the West Bank and Gaza. Brzezinski noted that the Camp David Accords were ambiguous on this issue of linkage, but Carter responded that Sadat was correct that some degree of linkage was implied by the agreements.[12]

Hamilton Jordan added the thought that at this point only success in the negotiations could help Carter politically. Once the treaty was signed, Carter would be in a stronger position to deal with the West Bank and Gaza issues. Carter seemed to be willing to take some political risks. He told Vance to press Israel hard, even if that ended up costing him the election and Jewish support.[13]

Vance to the Middle East

Vance set off for Cairo on December 9, 1978, with two clear objectives and one new proposal. First, he wanted to complete negotiations on the text of the treaty. Second, he wanted to make sure that the letter on the West Bank and Gaza would mention a target date of the end of 1979 for the establishment of self-government, or at least for the conclusion of the negotiations before the holding of elections.

Vance's new idea was one that originated with Carter in response to his belief that Sadat would be adamant about some form of linkage. The Camp David Accords had specified that diplomatic relations would be established after the interim withdrawal in Sinai, but there was no mention in writing about when ambassadors should be exchanged. Carter had earlier convinced Sadat that the exchange should be made right away, but after the Israelis dropped the idea of an accelerated withdrawal, the Egyptian position had become less certain.

Carter now felt it would be justified for Sadat to say that he would establish diplomatic relations after the interim withdrawal, but that the actual exchange of ambassadors would not take place until the self-governing authority in the West Bank and Gaza had been established. Sadat was likely to see considerable merit in this form of linkage, and Begin would inevitably react with horror.

Vance met privately with Sadat on December 10 and reviewed the new position on the timing of the exchange of ambassadors. As predicted, Sadat was pleased. In return, he showed some flexibility in accepting a target date instead of a fixed date for setting up the self-governing authority. He also agreed that article 6 could remain essentially unchanged, provided an interpretive note could be added making clear that this treaty did not prevail over other treaties to which Egypt was a party. In the side letter Sadat also wanted to mention the possibility that the self-governing authority might start first in Gaza, and he also inserted a provision for Egyptian liaison officers to be stationed in Gaza because of Egypt's former administrative role there.

On the evening of December 12, Sadat and Vance met again to go over the entire package. Sadat said he was willing to accept everything, but he stressed to Vance that this was as far as he could go. He pleaded with Vance not to come back to him to ask for more concessions. In his words, there was no further room for compromise. He wanted the United States at his side in this final round. Vance said he would do his best.

As he set off for Israel Vance was aware that the three-month deadline for completing the negotiations was approaching. If at all possible, he wanted to have a package agreed on by December 17. He knew there would be some tough bargaining in Israel, but he had Carter's clear instructions to press the Israelis hard.

Vance began his meeting with Begin and his colleagues by reviewing the recent evolution of the Egyptian position. He explained that he had convinced Sadat to drop demands for changing the treaty and for a fixed date for establishing self-government. There would, however, have to be some interpretive notes to articles 4 and 6. Vance also mentioned the idea of a target date and the possibility of reaching agreement first on Gaza. Then he explained Sadat's new position on not exchanging ambassadors until after the self-governing authority was established.

Begin, always suspicious of U.S.-Egyptian collusion, looked tense during this presentation. When Vance was done, Begin did little to hide his anger. He accused Sadat of deviating from Camp David, especially on his promise to exchange ambassadors after the interim withdrawal. He rejected the idea that Egypt should have any special role in Gaza, and he maintained that Israel would never accept a target date for setting up the self-governing authority. Nor did he like the idea of interpretive notes. These seemed to dilute the strength of the peace treaty and might open loopholes for Egypt not to live up to its obligations.

Begin then went on at length to review all the concessions he had made and all the risks Israel was required to take. The United States, he said, was unfairly siding with Egypt, when it should instead be supporting Israel.

Vance eventually managed to defuse the Israeli concern over the minor issue of an interpretive note to article 4 of the treaty. Dayan even showed some interest in the idea of proceeding with autonomy in Gaza first. He also privately told Vance that there might be a way for Israel to accept the delay in the exchange of ambassadors, but that this point should not be spelled out in a letter. Any delay in exchanging ambassadors should be left vague until after the treaty was signed, and then Sadat could say whatever he wanted. On this suggestion, however, Dayan was clearly not speaking for Begin.

Vance was obliged to leave the Middle East somewhat ahead of schedule. The decision had been made to announce the normalization of relations with China, and Carter wanted him to be in Washington for the occasion. Vance had time to make only a quick stop in Cairo before he left. There he informed Sadat of Begin's angry reaction. Sadat smiled and expressed his pleasure. Vance said he had told Begin in private that the United States supported the Egyptian position.

While flying back to Washington, Vance received word that the Israeli cabinet had met and had issued the following statement: "The Government of Israel rejects the attitude and the interpretation of the U.S. government with regard to the Egyptian proposals." For once, Vance was genuinely angry. His inclination was to let the negotiations remain temporarily in limbo. An impasse had been reached, and nothing more could be done for the moment.

Impasse

As 1978 came to an end, the prospects for peace anywhere in the Middle East looked dim. Not only were the Egyptian-Israeli talks at an impasse, but also Iran was in turmoil. The shah's regime was on the verge of collapse, and no one in Washington seemed to know what to do about it.[14]

For the next several months American thinking about the Camp David negotiations was colored by what was happening in Iran. The strategic balance of power in the region was changing, and the positions of the negotiating parties were hardening. Israel seemed to be reacting by becoming even more insistent that the peace treaty with Egypt be independent of any commitments involving the Palestinians. Furthermore, access to Egyptian oil assumed special importance as Iranian production, hitherto Israel's main source of supply, dried up. And the spectacle of a pro-American regime in a Muslim country being swept aside by religious extremists did little to increase Israeli confidence in the long-term value of Sadat's promises.

As usual, the United States was pulled in several directions. The Iranian revolution made it increasingly important to conclude the peace negotiations between Begin and Sadat successfully. Not only was a peace treaty desirable for strategic reasons; Carter also needed a political success to offset the enormous failure in Iran. At the same time Carter sympathized with the Egyptian argument that Egypt should not be isolated from the rest of the region because of peace with Israel. If possible, Carter still wanted Sadat to be able to defend his dealings with Israel before the moderate Arab regimes. Egypt's potential role as a stabilizing force in the Arab world seemed essential now that Iran had become a new source of unrest in the region.

In brief, the American role in this last phase of the peace negotiations was heavily influenced both by Iran and by the domestic political clock. Iran provided a strategic rationale for pressing for a quick conclusion of the Camp David process; the political calendar told Carter that he would soon have to turn his attention to other matters, namely reelection. Either he needed a quick and dramatic success, or he would have to back away from further involvement in the negotiations and hope that the electorate would not accuse him of losing the chance for peace between Israel and the largest Arab country. Carter had invested so heavily in the peace process by this time that he was determined to make one last stab at agreement.

Going for Broke

After returning to Washington in mid-December 1978, Vance spent the weekend at Camp David with Carter to discuss the foreign policy agenda for 1979. The president felt things were falling apart in the Middle East. Dealing with that region had also become his heaviest political burden. And it was incredibly time-consuming. But the stakes were too high to let the negotiations drop. Carter decided to "continue to move aggressively on it and not postpone the difficult discussions, even though they were costly to us in domestic politics."[15]

On January 23, 1979, Brzezinski sent a memorandum to the president spelling out his concerns on the Arab-Israeli issue.

Events may make it difficult for us to pursue such a strategy, but I am firmly convinced for the good of the Democratic Party we must avoid a situation where we continue agitating the most neuralgic problem with the American Jewish community (the West Bank, the Palestinians, the PLO) without a breakthrough to a solution. I do not believe that in the approaching election year we will be able to convince the Israelis that we have significant leverage over them, particularly on those issues. . . . We have little time left.[16]

On February 6 Carter wrote to Begin and Sadat asking them to agree to a meeting in Washington involving Dayan, Khalil, and Vance. The talks would begin on February 21 and be held at Camp David.

Camp David Talks

In preparation for the talks at Camp David, the Middle East team undertook one of its periodic assessments. It seemed clear that at some point Carter would have to deal directly with Begin and Sadat. Arabs and Israelis were both concerned that the United States had lost its way. The only conceivable success on the horizon for Carter in foreign policy was an Egyptian-Israeli peace treaty. Both Egypt and Israel knew the United States needed a success after Iran, and Israel had concluded that Carter would not fight hard for the West Bank.

Carter realized he would probably have to meet again with the Egyptian and Israeli leaders. As he cast around for new ideas, he argued that Sadat should not try to speak for the West Bank. The president even speculated in front of his Middle East advisers that Sadat really "did not give a damn about the West Bank." He was more concerned with Gaza. If he would drop his interest in the West Bank, he could have his separate treaty with Israel, get something in Gaza, and embarrass Hussein.

Carter stated clearly that he did not want a public confrontation with Israel. This was a time for progress on the overall negotiation, with details to be resolved later. Carter acknowledged that he had to take some of the blame for urging Sadat to link the exchange of ambassadors to the establishment of self-government, but Sadat would now have to drop that demand for linkage. Carter also said two mistakes had been made at Camp David. Too much emphasis had been placed on the timing of the exchange of ambassadors, and Sadat should not have agreed to negotiate in place of King Hussein if Jordan refused to join the talks.

The second round of talks at Camp David began on February 21. Vance, Dayan, and Khalil were the principal participants, and each was accompanied by several aides. Khalil continued to insist that Egypt could not afford to be isolated, especially with the turmoil in Iran. Any treaty must be defensible before reasonable Arab opinion. On specifics, Khalil showed some interest in holding elections only in Gaza, and he implied that the exchange of ambassadors need not necessarily be tied to West Bank and Gaza developments.

Dayan had little room for negotiating, and he repeatedly said Vance would have to deal directly with Begin on the outstanding issues. He did, however, imply that Israel might be able to make some unilateral gestures toward the Palestinians, a point the Egyptians had pressed hard.

Talks at this level seemed to hold little promise of further progress. Khalil had authority to negotiate, but Dayan did not. So Carter invited Begin to join the talks. On February 27 the Israeli cabinet rejected Dayan's recommendation that the prime minister attend, saying Begin would not participate in a summit with Khalil. Only Sadat would do. Carter was irritated but decided to ask Begin to come to Washington to meet with him. Things now seemed to be working toward a climax.

Carter and Begin in Washington

To prepare for his meeting with Begin, on February 28, 1979, Carter called together his top advisers—Vice President Walter Mondale, Vance, Brzezinski, and Hamilton Jordan. Brzezinski bluntly stated that Israel seemed to want a separate peace and wanted Carter not to be reelected. Jordan agreed. Mondale drew the conclusion that Carter should therefore not confront Begin but should stand back and let things take their natural course.[17]

The first session between Carter and Begin took place on Friday, March 2, 1979. Begin opened with a strong argument that the United States should help Israel because only Israel stood in the path of a Soviet takeover of the whole Middle East. He maintained that Israel could help prevent a communist takeover in Saudi Arabia, and even went so far as to offer the United States an airbase in Sinai that he had already promised to return to Egypt. None of these remarks had much effect on Carter.

Next Begin turned to the outstanding issues in the negotiations. He said the talks were in a deep crisis. The American interpretative notes to article 6 on the priority of obligations were tantamount to making peace between Egypt and Israel contingent on the achievement of a comprehensive peace in the region. Such linkage would allow Egypt to use any pretext to tear up the treaty. Begin added that he was sure that some future Egyptian leader would recommend doing so. No interpretations would be acceptable. The text of the treaty must stand unchanged, whether Sadat liked it or not.

Begin then raised his objections to the side letter dealing with the West Bank and Gaza. It contained deviations from Camp David. There was no reason to separate Gaza from the West Bank, as Sadat now wanted to do, though if Egypt was prepared to drop all interest in the West Bank, Israel might consider discussing Gaza alone with Egypt. But Gaza would not then be a precedent for what might later be done on the West Bank.

Next on the list of Begin's objections was the idea of setting a target date for elections to the self-governing authority. If for some reason the date was not met, Israel might be accused of violating the treaty with Egypt, and Egypt might then break some of its commitments. Israel could not accept such linkage between the treaty and the future of the West Bank and Gaza.

Finally, Begin turned to the question of oil. Since signing the Camp David Accords, he said, Israel had lost access to Iranian oil. More than ever, Israel needed a firm guarantee from both Egypt and the United States that its oil supply would be met. If Egypt refused, Israel would not evacuate the oil fields in Sinai.

Carter was very discouraged by this meeting. There seemed to be no openings. Still, Vance was prepared to continue the talks over lunch at the State Department.

Vance and his team took some time on Saturday to develop new language on article 6 and on the target date for elections in the West Bank and Gaza. The most significant alteration was tying the target date to the conclusion of the negotiations between Egypt and Israel rather than to the actual holding of elections. Meanwhile Carter had another session with his top advisers, in which he raised the possibility of going to the Middle East to bring the negotiations to a dramatic conclusion. Hamilton Jordan, in particular, favored it. As Carter was later to say, "My proposal was an act of desperation."[18] Later in the evening Carter had another unproductive private meeting with Begin.

A final session between the two leaders was scheduled for Sunday morning, March 4. They met against a backdrop provided by a message from Sadat, who said he was planning to go to Washington to denounce Begin for his intransigence. Carter had already begun to think the best way to proceed was for him to go to the Middle East, and he hardly welcomed the telegenic Sadat's stealing the show in Washington with ringing denunciations of Israel. So an effort was made to resolve some of the issues and therefore to justify a trip by the president to the region.

Somewhat surprisingly, Begin was in a rather conciliatory mood on Sunday morning. Vance reviewed the new formulations on article 6, and after a brief discussion among the members of the Israeli delegation in Hebrew, Begin made a minor suggestion for a change in wording and agreed to seek cabinet approval, provided the United States formally withdrew its previous legal opinion on article 6. Similarly, Begin said the new American proposal on setting a target date for concluding the negotiations on autonomy was serious and would be considered by the cabinet.

The problem of oil supplies remained, along with the timing of the exchange of ambassadors, but Carter implied that he would deal directly with Sadat on both issues to find a satisfactory solution. To his surprise Carter found that the United States and Israel were now in agreement on most issues. The reason, it seemed, was not so much that Begin had been won over by Carter's argument, but rather that the new American formulations went just far enough to overcome Israeli suspicions. Begin must have also realized that the moment had come to clinch the bilateral deal with Sadat.

As soon as the meeting was over, Carter sent a message to Sadat informing him that some progress had been made in the talks and that he did not want Sadat to say anything further in public, and especially not to commit himself to coming to Washington. In fact, said the president, he was considering a trip to the Middle East himself in the next few days.

The following day, March 5, 1979, the Israeli cabinet approved all the new American proposals. Carter now felt that success was at hand. A trip by him to the Middle East would produce a peace treaty and a much needed political boost.

Carter immediately decided to send Brzezinski to Cairo to see Sadat. He wanted Brzezinski to have a broad strategic review with the Egyptian president, to inform him of the new proposals and ask for his support of them, and to tell Sadat "very privately that the President's domestic political situation was becoming more difficult and that Begin might even wish to see the President defeated."[19]

Brzezinski met with Sadat on March 6 and delivered the president's messages. Sadat made it clear that the new formulations would pose no problem for him. He was, however, reluctant to go back to the idea of sending an ambassador to Israel after the interim withdrawal.

Sadat then told Brzezinski of his most important "secret weapon"—a proposal that Carter would be allowed to convey to Begin for building a pipeline from the Sinai oil fields directly to Israel. Sadat denounced the Israelis as idiots for ignoring his proposal on Gaza, but nonetheless said he would do everything possible to make Carter's visit a big success. The treaty should be signed while Carter was in the Middle East. If all went well, Sadat would even invite Begin to Cairo for the signing. Carter was very pleased by this prospect.

Carter to the Middle East

By the time Carter arrived in Cairo on March 7, 1979, he had every reason to believe his trip would be crowned with success. Sadat had essentially said Carter would have carte blanche to negotiate the final text of the treaty with Israel.[20]

Carter spent much of his time in Egypt celebrating the close ties between Egypt and the United States. Sadat put on an impressive show, including a train ride to Alexandria, which exposed the American president to larger and friendlier crowds than he was used to seeing at home.

Just before leaving for Israel, Carter and Secretary Vance met with Sadat and his top advisers at the Maamoura rest house near Alexandria. Carter pledged to get the best possible agreement for Egypt while in Israel and spoke as if he had Sadat's proxy in hand. Once the treaty was a reality, the United States and Egypt could plan for a "massive" government-to-government relationship in the military and economic fields. Carter also expressed the hope that the American private sector would invest in Egypt after the peace treaty was signed. In addition, Carter promised to use his maximum influence to get Jordan and Saudi Arabia to back the fait accompli of the treaty.[21]

While Carter and Sadat were congratulating each other on the achievement of peace, the Egyptian foreign ministry officials were showing anxiety. They still wanted Carter to persuade the Israelis to make some unilateral gestures to the Palestinians, and they hoped that Israel would agree to some form of special status for Egypt in Gaza. They also wanted a few minor changes in the treaty, including the replacement of a word in the notes to article 6 that they did not like. Carter and Vance promised to do their best.

Carter arrived in Israel after sundown on Saturday, March 10, 1979. He immediately drove to Jerusalem for a private dinner with Begin. To Carter's surprise, Begin made it clear that there was no chance of concluding the negotiations and signing the peace treaty while Carter was in the

Middle East. The president was angry and suspected Begin of wanting him to fail. Begin was standing on procedure, arguing that the Knesset must have a chance to debate the agreement before it could be signed. Carter reminded Begin that this had not been necessary at Camp David, but Begin would not be rushed.

Carter had little sympathy for Begin in the best of times. It was a bad start for what proved to be a difficult few days. The upbeat mood of Cairo had suddenly been replaced in Jerusalem by mutual suspicions and recriminations. In that atmosphere, once again it seemed as if the chance for peace might be lost.

On Sunday, March 11, Carter and Begin met with their full delegations. Carter began by sketching his preferred scenario. Negotiations on the treaty text should be concluded within the next day or so; Sadat would fly to Jerusalem to sign; then Begin, Sadat, and Carter would all travel to Cairo together for a second signing ceremony.

Begin immediately poured cold water on the president's idea. The cabinet, he explained, would have to debate the matter fully, and then the Knesset would have to vote before any signature could be put on so solemn a document as a peace treaty. All this would take at least two weeks. Then Begin asked to hear the new Egyptian proposals.

Sadat and his advisers had not liked the wording of the proposed notes to article 6. The notes had been included to meet Sadat's desire to portray the Egyptian-Israeli treaty as part of the comprehensive peace mentioned in the Camp David Accords. To this end, the notes had said that article 6 of the treaty did not contravene the framework for peace agreed on at Camp David and that the treaty was not to be seen as prevailing over any other treaties to which the parties were bound. But to meet Israeli concerns, the notes went on to say these provisions did "not derogate from" the language of article 6, which in essence said that the provisions of the Egyptian-Israeli treaty would be respected without regard to actions of other parties even if a conflict arose with other obligations.

The Egyptians were bothered by the word "derogate." Carter therefore suggested that Israel accept the substitution of the following phrase: "The foregoing [the notes to article 6] is not to be construed as inconsistent with the provisions of article 6." From the Americans' standpoint, there was no substantive difference. The point was that the notes to article 6 should not be seen as changing the meaning of the treaty.

Carter also said Egypt was insisting on having liaison officers in Gaza to help prepare for self-government there. Vance then passed around the new texts of the notes to article 6 and the letter on the West Bank and Gaza.

Begin frostily replied that the United States and Israel had already agreed on the language of the notes when he was recently in Washington. Sadat had the right to object, but Begin would not budge. He rejected the new language and expected Carter to stand by the text that had been worked out in Washington. The two phrases "does not derogate from" and "is not inconsistent with" were worlds apart, he said. Article 6 was the heart of the treaty. Without it the treaty would be a sham document. Israel would not knowingly sign a sham document. At one point he said that if the words "is not inconsistent with" were used instead of "does not derogate from," it would mean that Egypt would start a war while it had a peace treaty with Israel.

Carter then asked if Begin had any counterproposals to make. Begin said no. He would stand by what had been agreed on in Washington. Begin went on to make a lengthy critique of the new note to article 6, paragraph 2. He had agreed in Washington to say in a note to the article that it should not be construed as contravening the framework for peace in the Middle East agreed to at Camp David. Sadat had wanted to add that Camp David had called for a "comprehensive peace," as in fact it did. Begin argued that by adding these two words, "comprehensive peace," Sadat was seeking a pretext to violate the treaty with Israel by making it contingent on other Arab states also making peace with Israel. Syria, he said, would then be able to render the treaty null and void by refusing to negotiate.

Toward noon Begin turned his impressive critical powers to the new letter concerning the West Bank and Gaza. He strongly objected to the possibility of implementing autonomy in Gaza first. Nor would he accept Egyptian liaison officers there. Then, for what must have been the tenth time, he objected to the term West Bank, giving a lesson to the president on the geographic and historical inappropriateness of the term and the importance of using the words Judea and Samaria. Only if Sadat were to renounce entirely his interest in those two areas, said Begin, would he agree to discuss Gaza alone with Egypt.

After a break for lunch, the talks resumed at 3:00 p.m. Carter tried to regain Begin's confidence by promising an American guarantee of Israel's oil supply. He also said he was sure he could persuade Sadat to exchange ambassadors after the interim withdrawal if Israel would expedite the withdrawal, as originally agreed the previous November. He also said the United States would sign a memorandum of understanding with Israel on steps to be taken if Egypt violated the treaty.

Turning to bilateral U.S.-Israeli relations, Carter maintained that the two countries were equal partners. He added that what the United States did for Israel was more than balanced by what Israel did for the United States, a point that Begin had long been pressing on American audiences and that Carter did not really believe. Israel, he said, was a tremendous strategic asset to the United States, especially if it was at peace with Egypt, the other major regional friend of the United States. With these sweeteners, Carter urged the Israelis to try to find words to resolve the dispute over article 6, which eventually was done.

During a late afternoon session Begin told Carter that the Israeli cabinet would meet that evening to make its formal decisions on the matters under discussion. Then Vance could go to Cairo, and Carter could return home. In about two weeks, if all was proceeding smoothly, the Israelis might be ready to sign the treaty.

Carter responded by saying that Vance would not go to Cairo. The Egyptian position was already known to the Americans. They could conclude the negotiations right now. Begin replied that he was very tired and that the meeting should now be adjourned. Once again, the Americans felt Begin was deliberately trying to keep Carter from enjoying the fruits of his high-stakes trip to the Middle East.

Just before the meeting broke up, Carter again pleaded with Begin to try to reach agreement in the next day or so. Begin replied that the sky would not fall if agreement was not reached.

The next morning Carter and Begin and their advisers met again at 10:20 a.m. The cabinet had been in session all night, breaking up at 5:30 a.m. The Israelis looked exhausted. Carter began by making a strong case for the strategic benefits to Israel of peace with Egypt. He argued that the U.S.-Israeli relationship would grow even stronger and the United States could be even more forthcoming on aid if the peace treaty was concluded. Egypt and Israel could work together to prevent the kind of radicalism seen in Iran from spreading to the rest of the region. If the opportunity for peace was now lost, it would be hard to recover.

The Israeli cabinet had essentially confirmed the new wording of the notes to article 6, and Carter was satisfied. But the cabinet had adamantly refused to consider giving Egypt any special status in Gaza. Carter argued that its refusal would be hard for Egypt to accept. He pleaded with Begin to reconsider, but Begin refused.

Vance was scheduled to have one more session with the Israeli delegation on Monday afternoon, March 12. Carter hoped that the remaining problems on Gaza, on oil, and on the timing of withdrawal from Sinai and the exchange of ambassadors could all be settled.

Begin opened the meeting by saying that the cabinet had been in session for two hours and had decided to reconfirm its position on all issues. There would be no further changes from the Israeli side. Israel needed, he said, a clear-cut Egyptian promise to sell 2.5 million tons of oil to Israel each year. Begin did say he would agree to consider an Egyptian proposal to start the autonomy talks in Gaza, but this issue could not be included in the side letter. Nor could any mention be made of Egyptian liaison officers. Even on article 6 Begin insisted that the words "comprehensive peace" be removed from one of the notes, arguing that otherwise the treaty would appear to depend on the action of other Arab parties in making peace with Israel. Begin did suggest that some expedited withdrawal to the interim line might be possible, but only if Sadat agreed to send an ambassador to Israel shortly thereafter.

Vance tried to salvage the situation by urging that both the Gaza and oil issues be dropped from the agreement. Neither had been included in the Camp David Accords, and both could be dealt with later. Begin said oil was a matter of life and death and could not be left out of the agreement. Nor would Israel agree now to put in writing its willingness to accelerate withdrawal to the interim line.

To the surprise of the Americans, Begin then said that the talks were over and a joint communiqué should be issued announcing that some progress had been made, but that some questions still needed to be resolved. A text to this effect, obviously prepared well in advance, was passed over to Vance for his agreement.

Carter was immediately informed of the outcome of the talks. He decided there was no point for him to stay in Israel any longer. Begin clearly did not want an agreement at this time. The president ordered his plane to be prepared to return directly to Washington. But the hour was late, and to get all the presidential party and its luggage assembled in time would be difficult. Reluctantly Carter agreed to spend the night in Jerusalem, but he was a bitterly disappointed man.

Finale

When the Americans reconvened at the King David Hotel, the mood was gloomy. No one saw much point in trying to come up with new formulations on the outstanding issues.

Toward 9:00 p.m. one of Dayan's associates called Vance to suggest that the secretary should invite Dayan over for an informal talk. Dayan, it turned out, had been caucusing with members of the cabinet who were unhappy with the way the negotiations seemed to be ending. Dayan had got Begin's permission to see Vance. Weizman was apparently threatening to resign if the peace treaty was jeopardized by Begin's obstinacy.

Dayan made several suggestions and confirmed that most of the cabinet would accept the U.S. proposals on guaranteeing Israel's supply of oil and for accelerated Israeli withdrawal to an interim line in Sinai. In return for those concessions, Dayan suggested that the side letter should omit reference to Gaza as a special case and to a role for Egyptian liaison officers there. He urged Carter to meet again with Begin the next morning to put these proposals forward as new American suggestions. Meanwhile Dayan would try to prepare the way with Begin. Vance agreed to try, and for several hours the American team worked on a new set of proposals.

Carter met with Begin alone on Tuesday morning; they were then joined by Dayan and Vance. Begin, as usual, held back from making a complete commitment to the new proposals. If Egypt accepted them, and if Sadat agreed to an early exchange of ambassadors, Begin would recommend the new proposals to the Knesset. Carter knew that was tantamount to having Begin's agreement. Pressing his luck a bit, he asked Begin if Israel would agree to undertake some unilateral gestures to improve the atmosphere for the Palestinians in the West Bank and Gaza. This issue was of great importance to the Egyptians. Begin said he would sympathetically consider this request. Carter finally knew he had an agreement in hand.

Carter then flew directly to Cairo, where he met with Sadat at the airport. Sadat's aides still had some objections, but Sadat was in no mood to quibble.[22] He had promised the president a success, and he was prepared to say that agreement had now been reached on all issues. At 5:00 p.m. Carter said that full agreement had been reached, and he placed a call to Begin from the airport to tell him so. Begin agreed to go to the cabinet the next day for final approval, but the outcome was no longer in doubt. Carter and Sadat then walked out on the tarmac to tell the awaiting press corps that a peace agreement had been concluded.

On the plane back to Washington Carter's political aides were ecstatic. At long last Carter could point to a major foreign-policy achievement that would be genuinely welcomed by most Americans. The foreign-policy advisers were a bit less jubilant, thinking as always of the many problems that lay ahead. Most of all, they were exhausted and grateful that the

talks were over, at least for the moment. When they arrived at Andrews
Air Force Base later that evening, a large crowd was waiting to congratulate Carter and Vance. It had been quite a day, starting in Jerusalem and
ending in Washington.

Signing the Peace Treaty

The comprehensive Middle East peace that Carter had originally hoped
for was still far off, but the largest of the building blocks in that design,
the Egyptian-Israeli peace, was nearly a reality. Carter was ambivalent
about whether the peace treaty would by itself bring stability to the Middle
East, or whether it would set in motion an inevitable process that would
widen the circle of peace around Israel. He certainly did not believe it
could make matters worse than they already were.

Despite a few remaining drafting problems, a signing ceremony was
scheduled for March 26, 1979. Carter was joined by Begin and Sadat on
the north lawn of the White House. A large audience was invited to attend. Many political debts were paid that day. Egyptians and Israelis
mingled freely and expressed hopes that peace might be at hand. The day
was one of optimism and good feeling, and it was crowned that evening
by a magnificent banquet on the south lawn of the White House.

The formal Egyptian-Israeli agreement consisted of a thick file of documents that few people would ever read in its entirety.[23] Besides the text of
the treaty, there were three annexes dealing with security arrangements,
maps, and normal relations between the parties. Seven interpretive notes
were attached to the basic documents. Sadat and Begin also signed a letter
to Carter concerning negotiations on the West Bank and Gaza issues. Carter
added in his own handwriting an explanatory note to the letter saying, "I
have been informed that the expression 'West Bank' is understood by the
Government of Israel to mean 'Judea and Samaria.'"

Sadat signed another letter to Carter promising that a resident ambassador would be sent to Israel within one month of the interim withdrawal.
Carter conveyed this information to Begin in a letter, and Begin acknowledged its receipt. Carter also wrote to both Sadat and Begin to spell out
what the United States would do to help monitor the security arrangements
in Sinai and how the United States would use its best efforts to organize a
multinational peacekeeping force if UN troops were unavailable.

On the day of the signing of the peace treaty, Vance and Dayan also put
their signatures to a memorandum of agreement. Most of the commitments made in this document were hedged with qualifications, but it put

the weight of the United States behind Israel in the event that Egypt violated the treaty. Promises made as part of previous memorandums of understanding were reaffirmed. An agreement on oil supply was signed at the same time.[24]

As for military aid to Israel, Secretary Brown wrote to Weizman committing the United States to $3 billion to help construct new airfields in the Negev. Of that amount, $800 million would be in the form of grants. The United States also informed Israel that it was prepared to act positively on a number of weapons systems that had been requested earlier. (During the negotiations Carter had deliberately held off making major decisions on arms so that he would have some remaining leverage over both Israel and Egypt.)

Brown wrote a similar letter to the Egyptian minister of defense, promising $1.5 billion in aid over the next three years. A list of military equipment that Egypt would be allowed to purchase was appended to this letter. Inevitably, a few loose ends were handled by memorandums for the record written by the legal adviser or other participants in the negotiations. None of the memos changed the basic outline of what had been agreed on.

At the last minute Carter was also required to write a secret letter to Begin, affirming what Begin and Sadat had orally agreed upon on March 26 concerning oil supplies. Carter also wrote to Egyptian prime minister Khalil to inform him of the results of his discussions with Begin about unilateral gestures toward Palestinians in the West Bank and Gaza.

Assessing the Treaty Negotiations

Complex diplomatic initiatives rarely work out in quite the way their authors anticipate. Midcourse corrections are part of the normal negotiating process. For American presidents, in particular, the intrusion of domestic political considerations is also part of the game. In light of these realities, one cannot judge results by the standard of initial designs or theoretical abstractions.

Instead one must look at the Egyptian-Israeli peace treaty in its political context. What more might have been achieved, given the very real constraints operating on all the parties? Could positive aspects of the agreement have been enhanced? Could the negative ones have been minimized? Why was Carter unable to make headway on the West Bank and Gaza? Why did he seem to care less about those areas than he did about Sinai?

First, Egypt and Israel were talking to each other and were ready to make decisions. The other Arabs were either opposed to the process or were sitting on the sidelines to see what would be offered them. Carter felt more of an obligation to Sadat because Sadat had taken risks for peace.

Second, the chance for a successful negotiation between Egypt and Israel was much greater than between Israel and any of the other Arab parties. Two disengagement agreements had already been signed in 1974 and 1975. Direct talks between the parties had shown that the distance between them on bilateral issues was not large. Carter's involvement could plausibly help bridge the remaining gap.

Third, Egypt was the most powerful Arab country. Peace between Egypt and Israel would not make war impossible in the Middle East, but it would dramatically change its nature. The danger of U.S.-Soviet confrontation would be reduced as well. On these grounds even a separate peace had immense strategic value for the United States.

Finally, one must frankly admit, the American political system makes it difficult for a president to tackle a problem like that of the Palestinians. Presidential authority in foreign affairs is theoretically extensive, but in practice it is circumscribed by political realities. And the Palestinian question has proved to be so controversial that most presidents have been reluctant to get deeply involved in it. Sadat, who was genuinely popular with the American public, was, in Carter's view, worth a fight with Begin. But the Palestinians had no domestic constituency, and when Sadat seemed less concerned about their fate than about Sinai, Carter found it impossible to be more demanding than the leader of the largest Arab country.

Among the participants, Carter had come to the negotiations with the least knowledge of the issues and with the greatest capacity to evolve in his understanding. The Middle East was important in his view, but he did not have fixed ideas on exactly how the problems should be solved. The engineer in him seemed to want the grand design of a comprehensive peace; left to his own devices, he might have remained wedded to that appealing notion. But he could not build the edifice alone, and so he began to concentrate on the part that was most feasible.

The idealist in Carter also played a role. The president deeply believed that men of goodwill could resolve problems by talking to one another. At Camp David he initially thought he would need only to get Sadat and Begin together and help them to overcome their mutual dislike. The agreement itself would then be worked out by the two leaders in a spirit of compromise and accommodation. The depth of their distrust, even hatred, was hard for him to understand. Begin's fixation on Judea and Samaria was especially hard for him to grasp. Finally, it was Carter who was forced to reexamine his assumptions and change his approach in the face of Begin's intransigence and Sadat's apparent willingness to settle for a bilateral deal.

The politician in Carter was slow to make his entry into the negotiations. For most of the first year domestic politics rarely seemed to concern the president as he tackled the Middle East problem. He was sometimes reckless in his disregard for public opinion, and he probably would have done better to engage in less controversy with Israel in public in the first months of his term. In retrospect, his behavior gained him little on the Arab side and may have helped marginally in Begin's rise to power. As time wore on, Carter, and especially his advisers, came to believe he was paying a heavy price for his involvement in the Arab-Israeli imbroglio. They also saw the Egyptian-Israeli peace treaty as one of the few potential successes that could boost the president's prestige at home and abroad.[25] By early 1979 politics had come to the fore in the decisions leading to the final push for peace. Soon after the peace treaty was signed, Carter turned over the next phase of Middle East diplomacy to a special negotiator, Robert Strauss, fully expecting him to help cover the president's political flanks as the campaign for reelection got under way.

The Autonomy Talks

The negotiations concerning the West Bank and Gaza were bound to be complicated. First of all, the Palestinians (and Jordanians) were adamant that they would not participate in the talks, so Egypt had to play the part of uninvited stand-in for them. Second, Egypt and Israel could not agree what they were negotiating about. Sadat was not very concerned with details or language, but he and his colleagues saw the negotiations as preparing the way, in stages, for the Palestinians to govern themselves, with limits on their control over foreign and defense policy only. Not surprisingly, the Egyptians fastened on those parts of Camp David that spoke of an elected "self-governing authority"; an interim period that should serve as a transition to a final agreement based on UN resolution 242; the withdrawal of Israeli forces to designated locations; and the "powers and responsibilities" of the elected Palestinian authority.

Begin, who felt that he had originated the idea of Palestinian "autonomy"—he did not like the term "self-governing authority"—had a very different notion of what the negotiations were all about. While he had agreed to postpone an Israeli claim to sovereignty during an interim period, he had not agreed to abandon such a claim. Indeed, when asked what would come after five years of Palestinian autonomy, Begin had a simple answer. Israel would at that point assert its claim to sovereignty; if the Arabs agreed, that would settle the matter. If they did not agree, autonomy would continue indefinitely. And during this prolonged period of autonomy, Israeli settlements would continue to be built in "Judea and Samaria"; East Jerusalem was not to be part of the autonomy plan at all; land and water resources would not automatically come under the control of the self-governing authority, since autonomy applied only to persons, in Begin's view, not to territory.

Insofar as Carter and Vance had developed their thinking on Palestinian issues, they tended to agree more with the Egyptian interpretation of Palestinian self-government as a transitional stage. Carter was on record as supporting the right of Palestinians from East Jerusalem to participate in elections for the self-governing authority; his views on the importance of a freeze on settlement activity were well known; and his interpretation of 242 was that Israel was obliged to withdraw, at the end of the transitional period, from most, if not all, of the West Bank and Gaza as the quid pro quo for Palestinian recognition of Israel's right to live in peace within secure and recognized boundaries. For some of the Americans involved in the negotiations, the fact that autonomy would apply to the entire West Bank and Gaza would provide the Palestinians with a sort of presumptive territorial claim when the time came to settle the "final status" of the territories. This was a point also made by some of Begin's right-wing critics, who saw in the autonomy idea the germ of a Palestinian state.

Whatever Carter's views on these matters might be, he was not inclined to engage his time and efforts in this next round of negotiations. Vice President Mondale and Hamilton Jordan had long urged Carter to find a more "political" negotiator, and Robert Strauss, fresh from his success as special trade negotiator, seemed to fit the bill. The fact that he knew little about the Middle East was not seen as a major problem.

Strauss's tenure as special negotiator was brief and uneventful. At one point he thought the problem of Jerusalem should be tackled head on, presumably on the theory that if the toughest problem could be solved first, all else would fall into place. But by fall 1979, with Carter's reelection prospects in question, Strauss left to head the reelection effort.

If Carter needed any reminding that the Palestinian issue was political dynamite at home, he had only to reflect on the fate of his UN ambassador, Andrew Young. In August discussions were taking place about the possibility of amending UN Resolution 242 to make it more palatable to the Palestinians. Needless to say, the Israelis were intensely suspicious of any such move.

In his capacity as head of the Security Council, Young met with the PLO representative to see if a formula could be found that would bring the PLO to accept UN Resolution 242. Neither Carter nor Vance was informed of the meeting. Young personally appealed to the Israeli UN ambassador to keep the meeting quiet, but that was not to be. Vance was furious that Young had told the Israeli ambassador about the meeting before informing Washington and insisted to Carter that Young be replaced, which he was by his deputy, Donald McHenry.

The Andrew Young affair may have angered Israel's supporters, but it was the Iranian seizure of American hostages at the U.S. embassy in Tehran on November 4, 1979, that accelerated Carter's political decline. Unable to win their release by diplomacy and hesitant to use force, the president soon found himself trapped in the White House with the unresolved hostage problem confronting him day in and day out. Every night on the evening news the countdown went on—"This is day xxx of the hostages' captivity in Iran." As he struggled to cope with this most debilitating of foreign-policy crises, Carter had little time for Palestinian autonomy.

To replace Strauss, Carter selected another lawyer-negotiator with good credentials in the Jewish community, Sol Linowitz. With the experience of negotiating the Panama Canal treaty to his credit, Linowitz was a skilled professional, but he lacked familiarity with the complex details of the Arab-Israeli peace process. He also found himself dealing with an Israeli cabinet minus Moshe Dayan, who broke with Begin precisely over the latter's restrictive view of autonomy.[26] Similarly on the Egyptian side, the negotiators, except for Mustafa Khalil, showed little flexibility, correctly arguing that they had no mandate from the Palestinians to decide on details. At most, they were prepared to develop broad principles for the transitional period, setting in motion a process that would lead to some form of Palestinian self-determination, a far cry from Begin's vision of perpetual autonomy.

Not surprisingly, little progress was made on the toughest issues, although Linowitz had some success in resolving many of the more technical ones.[27] In the spring of 1980, while Linowitz was struggling to find common ground between Egypt and Israel on Palestinian autonomy, Carter's fortunes hit a new low with the abortive mission to rescue the hostages in Tehran. Vance, who had recommended against the operation, resigned and was replaced as secretary of state by Edmund Muskie, a senator from Maine.

Toward the end of the Carter administration, Linowitz reached the point where he felt that substantial progress had been made. But no agreement

had been reached on such sensitive issues as whether East Jerusalem Palestinians could participate in the elections to the self-governing authority or
whether there would be a freeze on constructing new settlements, and
only a hint had been given that some degree of shared authority over
future development of water and land resources might be possible. In brief,
on issues of vital importance to the Palestinians, the negotiations had not
produced much. Without the direct participation of the Palestinians in the
negotiations, Egypt would be reluctant to go much further in dealings
with Israel. Thus for much of the next ten years, until finally the Palestinians joined the peace talks as full participants in 1991, the part of Camp
David that dealt with the future of the West Bank and Gaza remained
essentially a dead letter.

Carter's overwhelming defeat in November 1980 rendered hypothetical the notion that a reelected Carter might have turned his considerable
abilities to completing the process started at Camp David. Instead, on
January 20, 1981, a few minutes before the hostages were finally released
from their captivity in Tehran, Carter turned over the office of the president to Ronald Reagan, like him a former governor and an outsider to the
world of Washington. But in most other ways Reagan was to be a very
different kind of president.

Conclusions

Jimmy Carter was unique among American presidents in the depth of his
concern to find a peaceful resolution of the conflict between Israel and its
Arab neighbors. More than any other foreign-policy issue, the Middle
East occupied his time and energies.

At the beginning of his administration he knew little about the intricacies of the problem. But he felt the challenge of tackling an issue that had
eluded solutions in the past, and he no doubt felt that American interests
would be well served if peace could be brought to the Middle East.

As time went on Carter came to know many of the leaders in the Middle
East, and he turned his extraordinary capacity for mastering detail to the
negotiations between Egypt and Israel. He pored over maps of Sinai to
identify lines for the interim withdrawal. He personally drafted the first
version of the Egyptian-Israeli framework agreement at Camp David. Twice
he put his political reputation on the line by engaging in summit negotiations that could easily have failed.

In the end Carter was able to preside over the signing of the Egyptian-
Israeli peace treaty, perhaps the most noteworthy foreign-policy achieve-

ment of his administration. Yet he gained little in domestic political terms for these efforts, and some would argue that he even weakened his political base.

It does nothing to diminish Carter's achievement in the Middle East to acknowledge that he built on firm foundations laid by Presidents Richard Nixon and Gerald Ford, and especially by the remarkable diplomatic efforts of Henry Kissinger in brokering three Arab-Israeli agreements during 1974–75. Carter was also ably served by his secretary of state, Cyrus Vance, who deserves much of the credit for patiently shaping the Camp David Accords and the text of the peace treaty.

Carter's initiatives would have come to naught had the leaders of Egypt and Israel been unwilling to accept American mediation and to make peace between their two countries. At no point did Carter forcefully impose American views on either side, though often he was able to change the positions of either Prime Minister Begin or President Sadat, especially Sadat. American leadership was certainly a necessary condition for the success of the negotiations, but it was not sufficient. The parties to the conflict had to be ready for agreement.

Throughout the Egyptian-Israeli peace negotiations, Sadat maintained he needed to demonstrate that he had achieved something for the Palestinians. He repeatedly said he was not prepared for a "separate peace." What he wanted from Begin was a simple statement that Israel was willing to return Arab territory captured in the 1967 war in exchange for peace, recognition, and security from the Arabs. Also, he hoped for some form of commitment from Israel to Palestinian rights, including the right of self-determination. This commitment, of course, Begin would not give.

In retrospect, it is clear that Sadat and Carter both overestimated the role that Egypt could play in laying the groundwork for a negotiated settlement of the Palestinian issue. Both misread the attitudes of King Hussein and the Palestinian leaders. Both misjudged the part that the Saudis might be willing to take in the negotiations. Neither took Syria sufficiently into account.

Even with these errors it might have been possible to carry out the provisions of the Camp David Accords if the idea of self-government for the Palestinians in the West Bank and Gaza could have been given real content. For example, if Carter had succeeded in getting Begin's agreement to a freeze on settlement activity; if the self-governing authority had been given control over land and water resources; if genuinely free elections, including the right to vote, for Palestinians living in East Jerusalem, had been promised; and if the military occupation authority had been abolished, then it might have been possible to attract Palestinians into the negotiating process.

But none of these measures proved feasible while Begin was prime minister, and thus the concept of autonomy was devalued in the eyes of those who were most crucial in determining its viability. When Begin refused to budge on these matters, neither Sadat nor Carter could find a way to persuade him to change his mind. It remained to be seen if Ronald Reagan would choose to pick up where Carter had left off, or whether he had other ideas in mind. In light of the deterioration in U.S.-Soviet relations after the Soviet invasion of Afghanistan late in 1979, it seemed likely that Reagan would accord much more attention to East-West issues than to Arab-Israeli peace talks.

Carter had been slow to recognize the depth of Begin's attachment to the West Bank and Gaza. He had also been slow to understand the linkage issue.[28] Once Egypt and Israel were at peace, Begin had few remaining incentives to deal constructively with the Palestinian question. Sadat did feel strongly about the need for linkage, and for many months he had tried to establish some explicit connection between what would happen in bilateral Egyptian-Israeli relations and the Palestinian negotiations. But when put under pressure by Carter, in the face of Begin's intransigence, and when confronted with hostility from other Arab leaders, Sadat resigned himself to accepting the separate agreement that he had hoped to avoid when he first set off for Jerusalem in November 1977.

PART FOUR

THE REAGAN AND BUSH PRESIDENCIES

8 *Cold War Revival:*
Who's in Charge?

THE ELECTION OF Ronald Reagan as president in No-
vember 1980 was a watershed event in American politics. Rarely had a
campaign pitted against each other two such different candidates as Reagan
and Jimmy Carter. Reagan, a two-term governor of California and a moderately successful movie actor, came from the conservative wing of the
Republican party. He propounded two main themes: the federal government was too big and inefficient, and communism was an evil that should
be fought relentlessly. Increases in defense spending were central to his
foreign-policy program.

Apart from these broad principles, it was hard to know what Reagan
would bring to the presidency, especially in the field of international affairs. But he certainly implied that he would break with Carter's approach
to the world. No more embracing of Brezhnev, appeasing of dictators,
courting of leftists, pressuring of friends. Reagan even seemed prepared to
reverse course on relations with China, speaking admiringly of Taiwan in
contrast to "Red China."

Even if Reagan had not come to the presidency as a determined anticommunist, recent events would have ensured that U.S.-Soviet relations
would be strained. The invasion of Afghanistan late in 1979 by the Soviets
was one worrisome sign that they were embarking on a more aggressive
foreign policy, with implications for the Persian Gulf region in particular.
In addition, war between Iran and Iraq had broken out in September 1980,
and many in Washington feared that the Soviets would try to exploit the

conflict to advance into the sensitive gulf region. With these concerns in mind, Reagan and his entourage were not inclined to press hard for movement in the Arab-Israeli peace process. In any event, Reagan's sympathies were with Israel, and Israel was in no hurry to move.

Reagan's familiarity with Hollywood seems to have introduced him, if only superficially, to personalities close to Israel. But his views on the Middle East were otherwise virtually unknown, except for a ghost-written opinion piece that had appeared during the campaign. There Reagan had displayed a strong commitment to Israel as the only reliable friend of the United States in the Middle East, because of both its democratic values and its military prowess. The contest in the Middle East was described almost exclusively in cold war terms, with scant mention of the peace process.

The only reference to the Palestinians in the article came in a warning against the creation of a radical Palestinian state on Israel's borders. The words "Camp David," "peace process," and "negotiations" were nowhere to be found. The idea of Israel and Egypt as partners in peace was missing, replaced by a description of Israel as a formidable strategic asset. Egypt, it was noted, might also be prepared to "take a front-line position in defense of Western security interests," but this possibility was clearly viewed as a "secondary" link that could not "substitute for a strong Israel in the ever-turbulent Middle East."[1]

On the surface, then, Reagan seemed likely to shift American policy in the region away from the Camp David approach toward a more muscular competition with Moscow for influence. Israel would be regarded as a strategic partner. Engaging in peace talks would be accorded lower priority than bolstering American influence in the gulf region. American arms sales to some Arab countries, such as Jordan, might be reduced, while arms might continue to flow to Saudi Arabia. In view of campaign promises, it seemed possible that Reagan would also order the American embassy in Israel to move from Tel Aviv to Jerusalem, a highly symbolic act. In short, the Reagan agenda appeared likely to reflect the neoconservative, pro-Israeli views that were widespread among his advisers and senior officials.[2]

But Reagan was not only a pro-Israeli, anticommunist ideologue.[3] He was also remarkably uninterested in the kind of detail that fascinated his predecessor. He would seemingly be content with setting the broad lines of policy, leaving to his associates the fine points of interpretation and implementation.[4]

To say the least, Reagan evinced little interest in the nuances of Middle East policy.[5] Perhaps more than any other president, Reagan was very dependent on his staff—and on his wife, who was a keen judge of people and was fiercely determined that her husband should be protected from criticism. To get to the president, it was thought, one had to pierce the wall created by Nancy Reagan and the troika of his closest advisers— Edwin Meese, Michael Deaver, and James A. Baker III. Even a powerful cabinet member like Secretary of State Alexander M. Haig Jr. felt frustrated in his efforts to deal with Reagan. The national security adviser, Richard Allen, was relegated to the White House basement and sent his memos to the president through the notoriously inefficient Meese. Among this group, only Secretary of Defense Caspar W. Weinberger seemed to have the kind of personal relationship with the president that allowed him regular direct access.

These three men, Haig, Weinberger, and Allen, who occupied the key foreign-policy positions in the Reagan administration, would presumably have considerable influence on how Reagan tackled Middle East issues. Haig had served in the military, as Kissinger's deputy at the White House, and as Nixon's chief of staff. He could be expected to be strongly pro-Israeli, somewhat skeptical of the peace process, and deeply suspicious of Soviet intentions in the region. On the face of it, his views and Reagan's did not seem to differ much.

Weinberger's foreign-policy views were less predictable. His prior government service had involved economic issues, and his business experience had been with Bechtel, a large construction company with extensive experience in the Middle East, including Saudi Arabia. Weinberger had spent time in Saudi Arabia and was presumably aware of Arab views. Sharing the president's conservative, anticommunist perspective, he might be counted on to boost the Saudis as a force for stability and moderation in the region.[6]

Assuming that Haig and Weinberger did indeed tilt in different directions on Middle East issues, it was anybody's guess how Reagan might decide concrete cases in the event of divided counsel. His national security adviser seemed too weak to be an effective referee between such powerful figures as Haig and Weinberger. Similarly, Reagan's ambassador to the United Nations, Jeane Kirkpatrick, was unlikely to wield the kind of influence that comes with proximity to the president. Nonetheless, as one of the few intellectuals in the Reagan entourage, and as a committed neoconservative, her voice would be heard on occasion.[7]

Less visible, but quite important, was William J. Casey, Reagan's director of Central Intelligence. Casey had a background in intelligence from World War II, had written books on how to make money, and, by all accounts, had a penchant for covert action and an omnivorous appetite for facts and information. Rare among Reaganites, he read books. His was not, however, a reflective intelligence. He was a man of action. He had little use for abstract theorizing.[8] Given this background, one might expect that Casey would see in Israel a model ally—muscular, action oriented, anti-Soviet, and with a highly reputed intelligence service.

Unvarnished Reaganism: The First Year

At one point during his campaign for the presidency, Reagan was quoted as saying, "Let's not delude ourselves. The Soviet Union underlies all the unrest that is going on. If they weren't engaged in this game of dominoes, there wouldn't be any hot spots in the world."[9] Such a perspective, if really an accurate reflection of Reagan's thinking, would have profound implications for his dealing with problems of the Middle East.

As president, Reagan's contribution to shaping American Middle East policy consisted primarily of injecting this theme of the Soviet instigation of regional unrest into the thinking of his subordinates. Secretary Haig, while much more attuned to nuances than the president, shared Reagan's view that the Middle East should be viewed primarily through the prism of the U.S.-Soviet rivalry.[10] Surrounding him at the State Department, and clustered at the White House and the Defense Department, was a group of like-minded newcomers with very little experience in making foreign policy. It was common to hear top officials arguing that the most serious problem in the Middle East was the presence of twenty-plus Soviet divisions on Iran's northern border.

Early in the Reagan administration Haig began to speak of the need to try to forge a "consensus of strategic concerns" among the pro-Western regimes in the Middle East. If that meant anything at all—and the phrase was never explained clearly—it presumably meant trying to focus the attention of "our friends" in the region on the Soviet threat, while simultaneously attempting to push parochial local conflicts to the back burner. An early test case arose in the form of a decision to sell a sophisticated radar plane, called airborne warning and control system (AWACS) aircraft, to Saudi Arabia.

In normal circumstances one would expect the Israelis to put up quite a fight, arguing that the presence of AWACS in Saudi Arabia could threaten their security. But if Israel and Saudi Arabia were both parts of the U.S.-sponsored strategic consensus, and if both saw the Soviet Union as the primary threat to their security, then the Israelis might be persuaded to allow the sale to go forward in the interests of strengthening the common front against the Soviets and their clients. But there was no such luck. Israel and its supporters in the United States decided to make it an all-out fight. In the end they lost. The AWACS aircraft were sold, but only after Reagan had put his prestige on the line and had gone some distance toward meeting Israeli concerns.[11] After the AWACS battle one heard far less talk of strategic consensus, and Haig himself repeatedly said the concept had never been correctly understood.

The AWACS debate was not the only sign that the pro-Israeli Reagan administration would nonetheless have disagreements with Israel. In mid-1981, on the eve of the Israeli national elections, Prime Minister Menachem Begin ordered the bombing of the Iraqi nuclear reactor on the outskirts of Baghdad. Although many in official Washington were no doubt impressed by Israel's technical prowess, and were quietly cheering Begin's bold action, open endorsement of this form of "nonproliferation" policy toward Iraq, a member state of the International Atomic Energy Agency (IAEA), would be hard to explain. So, for a moment, the United States rapped Israel's knuckles symbolically by holding up the delivery of F-16 aircraft.

In the midst of these unanticipated challenges the Reagan administration had taken comfort in the fact that Egypt under Anwar Sadat's rule seemed to be stable and friendly. But that assumption was dramatically challenged on October 6, 1981, when Sadat was gunned down by Islamic extremists. Among the charges they made against him was his orientation toward the West and his peace agreement with Israel. Sadat's successor, Husni Mubarak, was well known to the Americans, but no one could be sure if Egypt would remain stable. At worst, the peace with Israel, and therefore the final phases of Israeli withdrawal from Sinai, could be called into question, to say nothing of the Palestinian autonomy talks.

In these troubled circumstances another crisis erupted in December 1981, when Israel decided to extend Israeli law to the Golan Heights, a step just short of annexation. The Reagan administration had just signed an anti-Soviet strategic cooperation agreement with Israel at the end of November, but the agreement was suspended on December 18 as a sign of Washington's disapproval of Israel's action on Golan.[12]

In light of these developments, one might have begun to wonder wherein lay the substance of the vaunted strategic relationship with Israel. The answer was soon to be provided, at least from the Israeli perspective, by Begin's assertive defense minister, Ariel Sharon. Lebanon was to be the testing ground.

Crisis in Lebanon

In the world of pure Reaganism, chronic problems such as those in Lebanon either were not worth much attention or were symptoms of Soviet mischief-making. No wonder White House aides had little patience for arcane discussions of the internal political dynamics of Lebanon. Who, they seemed to be saying, could keep track of all the sects and their leaders with unpronounceable names?

But Lebanon had a way of forcing itself onto the American agenda because of Israeli concerns. In early 1981 Israeli-PLO clashes had intensified across Israel's northern border. Syria had been drawn into the fray. The veteran diplomat Philip C. Habib was then called on by Reagan to try to calm things down. The United States thus found itself negotiating a cease-fire between the two archenemies, and after mid-1981 the Lebanese-Israeli border was quiet, although no one was confident that the calm could last for long.

Israeli leaders, and especially Sharon, had grander plans in Lebanon. For years the Israelis had been secretly cultivating the tough leader of one of the Christian Lebanese militias, Bashir Gemayel. With presidential elections in Lebanon slated for the second half of 1982, they saw a chance to help bring their man to power. Sharon and his colleagues were also determined to crush the PLO's military presence in southern Lebanon. In some of the most dramatic scenarios, Israel might also try to drive Syrian forces out of Lebanon, inflicting a heavy blow on the leading client of the Soviet Union in the process.[13]

These possibilities were risky enough to require careful planning and an attempt at coordination with the United States. On visits to Washington, D.C., in early 1982, Israeli officials outlined their ambitious plan for Lebanon in great detail. Some State Department officials were appalled and were afraid that Sharon would get the impression from Haig's lack of objection that the United States was encouraging, or at least acquiescing, in his plan. What Haig did say, repeatedly, was that the United States would understand such a military move only in response to an "internationally recognized provocation," whatever that might mean.[14] To some, that sounded like an invitation to find a pretext to go to war. Some Israelis have claimed that Haig's statements were indeed interpreted as a "green light."[15]

During the early part of 1982 one of the key concerns in Washington was that the Egyptian-Israeli peace treaty be implemented smoothly. This was by no means a foregone conclusion. Sadat's assassination had raised questions in Israeli minds about the durability of commitments given by Sadat. Some analysts thought Begin might be looking for a pretext to postpone the last phase of Israeli withdrawal from Sinai, particularly since such a move would put off the politically painful moment of dismantling Israeli settlements around Al-Arish and forcing the 15,000 Israelis living there to leave their homes. No one in Washington wanted a flare-up in Lebanon to dampen the prospects for full implementation of the Egyptian-Israeli peace. So for several months considerable diplomatic effort went into containing the potential for conflict in Lebanon and facilitating the final withdrawal of Israeli troops from Sinai. Except for a small disputed area named Taba, all Israeli forces were removed from Sinai on April 25. When the United Nations proved unwilling to provide a peacekeeping force for Sinai, the United States took the lead in creating a multinational force, including U.S. troops. Both Egypt and Israel were satisfied with the arrangement, and it worked smoothly in ensuing years. Without much fanfare American diplomats successfully contributed to keeping Egyptian-Israeli relations on track.

As part of this effort Haig had even traveled to the region twice in January 1982 to try to breathe life into the stalled autonomy talks. But here Mubarak was showing great caution, and those efforts soon petered out. Thus, as tensions rose on the Lebanese-Israeli front, the peace between Egypt and Israel was cool, at best, and a broader negotiating process was not in sight.

Soon rumors of an Israeli move against the PLO and Syria in Lebanon were being heard regularly. By May 1982 those Americans most in the know seemed to accept the inevitability, if not desirability, of such a move.[16] All that was needed was a pretext. That came on June 3, 1982, in the form of an assassination attempt against the Israeli ambassador in London. Almost immediately it was clear that this exploit had been ordered by the notorious renegade terrorist Abu Nidal. Whether it constituted the "internationally recognized provocation" that Haig had spoken of or not, Israel did not wait to find out. Israel struck at PLO ammunition dumps in Beirut, and the PLO retaliated by shelling towns inside Israel. Six Israeli divisions then crossed into Lebanon on June 6—"Operation Peace for Galilee"— and it was immediately clear that more than a small retaliatory raid was under way.[17]

When the Israeli invasion began, Reagan was traveling in Europe. His relations with Haig were already somewhat strained, and others in Reagan's entourage seemed to be looking for a pretext to ease out the prickly secretary of state. Tactical differences over how to deal with Israel during the

Lebanon crisis quickly emerged. One faction formed around Haig, who felt that Israel, whatever the original justification for Israel's intervention in Lebanon, should not be stopped short of destroying the PLO. Somewhat uncharacteristically, Jeane Kirkpatrick sided with Haig, normally her bitterest rival.[18] Opposed to Israel's grand design were Vice President George Bush, who was in charge of crisis management in the White House, and his close ally, Chief of Staff James Baker.[19] William Clark, who had replaced Allen as national security adviser early in 1982, also favored reining Israel in, as did Secretary of Defense Weinberger.

As the early days of the crisis passed, Sharon seemed intent on cutting off the Syrian forces and leaving them no option but a humiliating withdrawal. In this scenario President Asad might even be toppled. At a minimum, Lebanon would be out from under the Syrian thumb. This is what the Phalangist allies of Israel were most eager to see coming out of the Israeli invasion. By contrast, a defeat of the PLO that left Syria still in Lebanon was of lesser interest to the Phalange.

Sharon seems not to have counted on strong intervention from Reagan. That was a mistake. Reagan, for all his passivity, could be aroused by his advisers. When scenes of violence were brought to his attention, he would sometimes react quite emotionally. Thus, on June 9, Reagan wrote one of the harshest notes ever delivered to an Israeli prime minister:

> I am extremely concerned by the latest reports of additional advances of Israel into central Lebanon and the escalation of violence between Israel and Syria. Your forces moved significantly beyond the objectives that you have described to me. The tactical advantages may be apparent, but a much more important need is to avoid a wider war with Syrian involvement, and possibly with that of the Soviets as well.
>
> Today I received a letter from President Brezhnev which voices grave concern that a very serious situation has been created that entails the possibility of wider acts of hostility. Of course, I did not accept most of the points in his letter, but the danger of further escalation does exist.
>
> It is now clear that escalation of Syrian-Israeli violence has occurred. I now call on you to accept a ceasefire as of 6:00 a.m. on Thursday June 10, 1982. I implore you to recommend to your government the acceptance of my proposal.
>
> Menachem, a refusal by Israel to accept a ceasefire will aggravate further the serious threat to world peace and will create extreme tension in our relations.[20]

It is hard to believe that Reagan personally took the initiative to send such a message. More likely his aides made the case that Israel should be forced to stop, and Reagan went along.

By all accounts Haig was furious that his advice to let the Israelis finish the job was not being taken. On a whole series of issues, Reagan seemed to be ignoring his views. As early as June 14 Haig had hinted that he might resign unless Reagan gave him a clear vote of confidence. Finally, on June 25 Reagan met with Haig to accept a letter of resignation that had not been written.[21] But Haig hung on as acting secretary of state for some time, trying to steer the course of U.S. diplomacy from his retreat at the Greenbrier resort in West Virginia. Reagan, who had no stomach for confrontations, finally asked his designated secretary of state, George P. Shultz, to call Haig on July 5 and tell him to stop acting as if he were still in charge.[22]

This bizarre episode demonstrated clearly that Reagan was not only very susceptible to the influence of his advisers but was also reluctant to exercise much discipline over them. He apparently found personal confrontations unpleasant and tried hard to avoid them. With Haig's departure the Israelis feared that they had lost one of their best friends.

George Shultz, who had been Weinberger's boss at Bechtel, was viewed by Israelis with suspicion. A former secretary of both labor and the treasury, Shultz had been on Reagan's short list for secretary of state at the outset of the administration, but Richard Nixon had argued effectively on Haig's behalf.[23] During his initial confirmation hearings before the Senate in July, Shultz showed himself to be a careful, well-informed person, who seemed attentive to the nuances of the Middle East regional setting. He addressed the Palestinian issue in a forthright manner, thus confirming for some his pro-Arab reputation.[24]

As secretary of state, Shultz immediately turned his attention to the long-neglected peace process. In his view the Israeli invasion of Lebanon would destroy the chance for peace unless the United States took a new initiative. He was also worried about the impact of the invasion on the still-fragile Egyptian-Israeli relationship. Thus on July 17 he quietly convened a working group of senior officials to start planning for a "fresh start" on Arab-Israeli peacemaking.[25]

While supporting a resumption of peace diplomacy, Shultz did not look favorably on Yasir Arafat and the PLO. In his view Arafat should get no reward for leaving Beirut. But the moment the fighting in Lebanon was over and the PLO was on its way to a new location, Shultz was determined to have a peace initiative in place, and the initiative would not be postponed until the problems of Lebanon were resolved. Also, it would bear the imprint of the president, thereby giving it more authority. Reagan's willingness to go along with this approach was growing as he witnessed the Israeli shelling of Beirut. On July 30 Shultz showed Reagan a draft of the new peace initiative. Later that afternoon, National Security Adviser Clark called Shultz to say, "The president's friendship for Israel is slipping. Enough is enough."[26]

During much of August 1982 the United States, once again with the energetic assistance of Philip Habib, tried to bring the fighting in Lebanon to an end and to arrange for the evacuation of PLO fighters from Beirut.[27] An American military contingent was even sent to Lebanon as part of an international force to help oversee the PLO departure. Habib not only helped to end the bloodshed but also successfully pressed for the election of Bashir Gemayel as Lebanon's next president. To secure the PLO's departure from Lebanon, he also made explicit written commitments to the PLO that assurances had been obtained from the Israelis about the safety of Palestinian civilians left behind after the PLO's departure.[28]

The Reagan Plan

By late August 1982 the Reagan administration seemed to be on the verge of success in the midst of the Lebanese agony, with a pro-Western president about to be inaugurated in Beirut, the Syrians badly battered in the Bekaa valley of eastern Lebanon, and the PLO driven from the country. (The Soviets, meanwhile, had shown themselves unable to do much to help their clients and suffered a loss of political prestige at a crucial moment in the revived cold war atmosphere of the early 1980s.)

Already on August 13 Shultz had won the president's approval of his "fresh start" initiative. Shultz felt Reagan was finally getting involved in Middle East policymaking. The following day he even arranged to have senior officials "role play" the likely reactions of Begin, Mubarak, and King Hussein to the new initiative. Watching the president's awakened interest, Meese observed that Reagan had been ready for this moment a year earlier, but Haig had kept him away from Middle East issues.[29]

With the PLO on its way out of Beirut, and the United States in a position of apparent diplomatic strength, Shultz urged the president to seize the moment to outline the new plan for a diplomatic settlement of the Israeli-Palestinian conflict. Shultz anticipated that the Israelis, in particular, would react negatively, but he nonetheless felt the United States could help to shape the postwar agenda. On September 1, 1982, Reagan gave his first and only major speech on the Arab-Israeli conflict.[30]

The core of the initiative was still Camp David, but with important substantive additions. Whereas Camp David had been vague on the so-called final status of the West Bank and Gaza after a transitional period, Reagan said the United States would oppose both Israeli annexation and an independent Palestinian state. The U.S. preference, he said, was for some form of association between the West Bank, Gaza, and Jordan. Lest any doubt remain, Reagan said the United States believed that the withdrawal provision of UN Resolution 242 should apply to the West Bank and Gaza, a position completely at odds with the policy of Begin and the Likud party.

Within days the United States spelled out its views in greater detail. During the transitional period, for example, the United States would support a freeze on Israeli settlements. Palestinians should have real authority over land and resources; and Palestinians living in East Jerusalem should be allowed to vote in elections for a self-governing authority. As for the "final status" negotiations, the United States went on record as favoring the view that the extent of Israeli withdrawal from occupied territories should be influenced by the extent and nature of the peace and security arrangements offered in return. These were not positions likely to win approval from Begin. They did not. Begin reacted angrily to the Reagan Plan, as it inevitably was dubbed.[31]

The Reagan initiative clearly shifted the spotlight from Egypt to Jordan and the Palestinians. Syria was left out in the cold. Begin rejected the proposal immediately because it called for eventual Israeli relinquishment of most of the occupied territories as the price for peace. The Arab response was, on the whole, less categorical. Questions were asked, some positive noises were heard, and it was widely rumored that King Hussein (and Arafat as well) had been briefed in advance on the initiative and had indicated general approval.[32]

Shortly after the Reagan initiative the Arab states held a summit meeting in Fez, Morocco, and adopted a Saudi proposal that came to be known as the Fez plan. Though different in content from the Reagan proposal, the Fez plan at least gave the United States and the Arabs something to talk about.

The Reagan administration's decision to launch an initiative on the Palestinian issue, albeit with a strong Jordanian tilt, was predicated on the belief that the problems of Lebanon were on their way toward solution. Even before the war in Lebanon, some in the bureaucracy had been making the case for a revived peace effort. Sharon had told the Americans he would solve the Palestinian issue his way—by moving tanks into Lebanon. Once the PLO was crushed, the Palestinians in the West Bank would become pragmatic and ready to deal with existing realities.

The shortcomings of Sharon's vision became abundantly clear within weeks of the Reagan initiative. The comforting belief that Lebanon's travails were nearly over was literally and figuratively blown away with the assassination by pro-Syrian elements of Bashir Gemayel on September 14, 1982. General Sharon, who had discussed with Gemayel a plan for "cleansing" Lebanon of Palestinians, now saw a danger that Israel's long-term investment would be lost with Bashir's death. He pressed the leadership of the Lebanese Forces (a Christian militia) and the Phalange party to respect the deals he had arranged with Bashir and to prepare for "immediate action." In the circumstances Israel had great leverage over the Phalange, including the ability to withhold or grant support for the candidacy of Bashir's brother, Amin, as president.[33]

Some of the details of what happened next are not entirely clear, but the broad outline is known. Units of the Lebanese Forces militia under the command of Eli Hobeika moved into two Palestinian refugee camps, Sabra and Shatila, on the southern outskirts of Beirut. There, under the eyes of their Israeli allies, they systematically murdered as many as eight hundred Palestinian civilians. This massacre led to a strong reaction everywhere, including in Israel. Five months later Sharon and several other officers were censured for their role in not preventing the massacres and were removed from their posts.[34]

The American response to the Sabra and Shatila massacres was to put Lebanon and its ills back at the top of the agenda. American military forces, which had been withdrawn after the departure of the PLO, were returned to the Beirut area to protect the refugee camps and to provide visible backing for the embattled Lebanese government. To negotiate an Israeli-Lebanese agreement that would lead to the withdrawal of both Israeli and Syrian forces became a priority of U.S. diplomacy, to be pursued in parallel, or even before, the Reagan Plan for the West Bank and Gaza.[35] Shultz's hope that Arab-Israeli peace talks could avoid becoming hostage to Lebanon's ills was increasingly in doubt.

Courting King Hussein

King Hussein, the object of the Reagan initiative in its first phase, began to watch how the Americans handled the Lebanese imbroglio as a test of how serious they were likely to be in dealing with the Palestinian issue. He, like many Arabs, felt that unless the Americans could get the Israelis out of Lebanon, there would be little chance of dislodging them from the West Bank. President Reagan further undermined the chances of success for his initiative by saying publicly that nothing could be done on the Palestinian question until agreement was reached on Lebanon.[36] For those who had opposed the Reagan initiative from the outset—and that included Begin, Asad, and the Soviets—this statement was an invitation to make things in Lebanon as difficult as possible, to ensure that "another Camp David," as the Syrians labeled the Reagan initiative, would not succeed.

King Hussein visited Washington in December 1982 for talks with President Reagan. In an effort to persuade the king to support the Reagan initiative, the president wrote two letters to him spelling out promises and commitments, including a supply of arms, if Hussein would agree to enter negotiations. Reagan also promised that he would convince Israel to freeze settlement activity in the West Bank once negotiations with Jordan began and that the transitional period might be shortened to less than five years.

By all accounts, Hussein was tempted, but he felt the need for Palestinian support. On occasion, however, the king left the impression that he would proceed without Arafat if the latter proved to be intransigent. Shultz, who was primarily in charge of the negotiations, was never quite sure what to make of King Hussein's comments. But he felt that the State Department "Arabists" tended to be too optimistic in their assessments.[37]

Talks between Jordan and the PLO took place over the next several months. Finally, in April 1983, the king concluded that there was no basis for developing a joint negotiating position with the PLO. The Jordanians blamed pro-Soviet hard-liners in Arafat's entourage for this inability to reach an agreement. Jordan, too, came under direct Soviet pressure not to go along.[38] On April 10, 1983, the king called Reagan to tell him that his talks with Arafat had failed. He was not prepared to move on his own. The same day he officially announced that Jordan could not accept the Reagan initiative, stating, "We in Jordan, having refused from the beginning to negotiate on behalf of the Palestinians, will neither act separately nor in lieu of anybody in Middle East peace negotiations."[39] For the moment, the Reagan Plan seemed dead.

Lebanese-Israeli Peace?

For much of the remainder of 1983, Arab-Israeli peacemaking became, from the American perspective, synonymous with trying to forge a viable

Lebanese-Israeli agreement as a step toward the withdrawal of both Is-raeli and Syrian forces from Lebanon. Secretary Shultz, who had shown reluctance to engage directly in the shuttle-style travels of his predeces-sors, went to the Middle East to put the final touches on the Lebanese-Israeli accord. In part he did so to respond to the expressed concerns of Egyptian president Mubarak. Shultz was skeptical about Syria's role and tried to enlist Saudi support to pressure Damascus. He also ran into prob-lems with the Israelis, who were unwilling to abandon their ally Major Saad Haddad in southern Lebanon. Despite all the obstacles, however, Shultz's shuttle seemed to pay off. On May 17, 1983, Lebanon and Israel signed an agreement that was just short of a peace treaty.

But the agreement was stillborn. Israeli withdrawal was made depen-dent on Syrian withdrawal, and Asad (who commanded a sizable con-stituency inside Lebanon) would not tolerate such a condition. Already the United States and Syria seemed to be on a collision course. In April the American embassy had been bombed with devastating effectiveness.[40] Americans traced the bombing to Lebanese allies of Iran, perhaps with some Syrian involvement as well. During the summer, fighting resumed in Beirut, and Arafat defiantly returned to the northern Lebanese city of Tri-poli. Syria, by now fully rearmed by the Soviets, became increasingly as-sertive in Lebanon, including against the PLO.

As the violence mounted, the Israelis began to disengage from the Shouf mountains overlooking Beirut, leaving the American contingent near the airport exposed to hostile attacks. Before long the U.S. Marines found themselves, in their lightly defended positions, drawn into intra-Lebanese battles. The peacekeeping mission was gradually being eroded, and the United States was becoming a cobelligerent on the side of the Lebanese Christian forces. On October 23, at a time of mounting tension between the United States and Syria, a truck loaded with explosives drove into the compound of the American contingent of the multinational peacekeeping force. The effect was devastating. Two hundred and forty-one American servicemen were killed.[41] Simultaneously, French and Israeli units were attacked by suicide truck bombs.

Within days of the attack on the American troops in Beirut, President Reagan signed National Security Decision Directive 111, thereby reviving the strategic cooperation agreement that had been suspended in Decem-ber 1981.[42] According to some accounts, Under Secretary of State Lawrence S. Eagleburger had concluded earlier in the year that close cooperation with Israel was essential for American policy in Lebanon to succeed. In reaching this conclusion, he was influenced by the decision made by the new Israeli defense minister, Moshe Arens, to withdraw Israeli troops from central Lebanon, an action of great strategic importance that had been undertaken without coordination with Washington. Eagleburger seemed to hope that by restoring the strategic cooperation agreement, the Reagan administration would be better able to influence Israeli decisions that impinged on American interests. By November 1983, Joint Political-Military Group meetings had been agreed on to develop areas of strategic cooperation.

Adding urgency to the rebuilding of U.S.-Israeli ties was the emergence of new leadership in Israel. To the surprise of many, on September 15, 1983, Menachem Begin, suffering from the recent death of his wife and seemingly depressed over the outcome of the war in Lebanon, announced his resignation and entered a period of seclusion that continued until his death in 1992. His replacement was Yitzhak Shamir, whose early political career had been with the Stern Group (Lehi), which had won him a reputation for extremism and violence. Relegated to the margins of Israeli political life in the early years of independence, Shamir spent some years in the Israeli intelligence service, Mossad, returning to politics in the 1970s as a member of Begin's party. At the time of the Camp David Accords he served as speaker of the Knesset; after Dayan resigned as foreign minister in October 1979, Begin had hesitated before offering the post to Shamir, but eventually did so in March 1980.[43]

Now, with Begin's departure from the scene, Shamir won Likud's endorsement to take his place. Instead of Begin and Sharon, the Americans now found themselves dealing with Shamir and Arens, a change that some felt would be for the better.

Whatever the prospect for improved relations with Israel might have been, the situation in Lebanon offered little hope for Reagan and Shultz. After the October bombings, American policy became more overtly aimed at punishing Syria. On December 4, 1983, two American planes were shot down by the Syrians, with one pilot killed and one captured.[44]

By early 1984, when the politics of reelection were uppermost in the minds of some of the president's advisers, Reagan made a decision, over the opposition of Shultz, that the Marines should be "redeployed offshore." Critics termed the decision "cut and run." Whichever words one chose, the facts were the same. Reagan, who had pinned American prestige on a stable settlement in Lebanon, was removing the most tangible sign of that commitment.[45] Henceforth Lebanon would be left primarily to the squabbles of its internal factions and its two powerful neighbors.

A Missed Opportunity?

Election years rarely witness serious initiatives for Arab-Israeli peace by American presidents. Their priorities lie elsewhere. Controversy, an inevitable corollary of any serious U.S. initiative in the region, is shunned. Pleas from Arab regimes for arms and diplomatic support are put off until after the elections.[46]

The year 1984 did not, however, prove to be entirely wasted. Early in 1984 Egypt was readmitted to the Islamic Conference, a sign that it was no longer isolated because of its peace agreement with Israel. A month later Mubarak and King Hussein made a joint appearance in Washington with President Reagan, which was symbolically important, even if Egypt's overt support for the PLO caused some ill feeling in American circles. In Israel, midyear elections produced a near standoff between Labor and Likud, resulting in a unity coalition of both parties and a rotating premiership. For the first two years Shimon Peres would be in the top job. Beginning in October 1986 Yitzhak Shamir would serve out the remaining two years of the term as prime minister. Throughout, Yitzhak Rabin would serve as minister of defense. As unusual as such an arrangement might seem, it did mean that the second Reagan administration would be dealing with Israelis in power who did not automatically exclude the key elements of Resolution 242 and its practical interpretation as spelled out by Reagan in September 1982. Indeed, it soon became clear that Peres and King Hussein were eager to explore areas for cooperation and were looking to Washington for help against the common adversaries of the Reagan Plan—Likud, Syria, and the PLO.

This combination of regional developments, plus Reagan's extraordinary electoral victory over Walter Mondale in November 1984, seemed to set the stage for a new round of American involvement in the peace process. Rarely had conditions been better for trying to press forward with some version of an Israeli-Jordanian deal, provided that enough Palestinian support could be found to give the exercise an aura of legitimacy in Arab eyes.

During the fall of 1984 the new assistant secretary of state for Near Eastern affairs, Richard Murphy, had spent six weeks in the region probing for possible openings on the peace front. King Hussein gave the impression of being ready to proceed, perhaps without the PLO, and for the first time he did not insist on knowing the outcome of negotiations before joining the process. If that became a solid Jordanian position, it could radically change the prospects for peace, especially with a Labor-led coalition in power in Israel. Shultz began to be more hopeful about the long-stalled peace diplomacy.[47]

Arab leaders had often expressed the hope that they could deal with a reelected Republican president. This nostalgic view stemmed largely from the perception of the second Eisenhower term, and especially Dwight D. Eisenhower's tough treatment of the Israelis during and after the Suez crisis of 1956. Now, in 1985, the Arabs were again dealing with a popular, reelected Republican. So, one by one, Arab leaders trekked to Washington in the first half of 1985. First came King Fahd of Saudi Arabia, followed a month later by Egyptian president Husni Mubarak. Most important, King Hussein arrived in Washington at the end of May.

Much of Egyptian and Jordanian policy at the time was aimed at evoking a positive American response to a joint Jordanian-PLO position that had been formalized in a carefully worded statement signed on February 11, 1985.[48] In many ways the Jordanian-PLO position could be construed as a new attempt to respond belatedly to the 1982 Reagan initiative. Both parties announced that their common goal was the creation of a Jordanian-Palestinian confederation, to be established once Israel had fully withdrawn from occupied territory. They pledged to negotiate as a joint delegation within the framework of an international conference.

Shultz was wary of the idea of an international conference. As envisaged by the Arabs, such a conference could become a lopsided means of pressuring Israel for concessions. Even Peres would not accept such an arrangement, and his Likud partners were much more hostile to the idea. At most, Shultz would consider a symbolic conference to open the way to direct negotiations. Until Jordan made clear that the PLO would remain in the shadows and the international conference would not become a barrier to direct negotiations, Shultz would show little interest in the new Jordanian-PLO accord.[49]

Although the February 11, 1985, agreement raised more questions than it answered in the minds of the Reagan administration, the Jordanian attempt at clarification was reassuring. During their visit to Washington in May, Jordanian officials stated that the concept of confederation was really much closer to "federation," with responsibility for foreign affairs and defense clearly understood by both parties to be vested in Amman. The Jordanians, moreover, played down the importance of the international conference, stressing instead the need for U.S. contact with a group of Jordanians and Palestinians. They also made it clear that they thought the PLO could be brought to the point of accepting Resolution 242, perhaps in return for some form of American recognition of Palestinian self-determination within the framework of a confederation with Jordan.[50]

However tempted some American officials may have been to press forward with an initiative in these seemingly propitious circumstances, there were three offsetting considerations. In the first place, President Reagan was on record saying, in March 1985, that the United States did not want to participate in Arab-Israeli peace negotiations, despite the Camp David commitment for the United States to be a "full partner" in subsequent phases of the peace talks.[51] Reagan and Shultz repeatedly said that the problem was not for the United States to talk to the parties but to get the parties to talk to each other. Direct negotiations became something of a slogan, especially among key senators and representatives. The administration could not ignore these sentiments. Indeed, Hussein was told there was no chance of congressional approval of an arms package for Jordan unless he committed himself to direct negotiations with Israel.

A second problem in bringing the United States into a more active role in support of King Hussein's approach was reportedly Secretary Shultz's sense of disillusionment with most of the Arab leaders he had dealt with during 1982–83. He seemed to think that they wasted the opportunity provided by the Reagan Plan and that their words could not always be counted on. The PLO, in particular, was not a fit partner for peace talks, in his view, although he did believe that Palestinians from the West Bank and Gaza would have to be included in a Jordanian delegation. But the idea of having Assistant Secretary Murphy meet with a joint Jordanian-Palestinian delegation proved to be controversial. As King Hussein saw it, such a meeting would set the stage for the PLO to accept UN Resolution 242; there would then be further contacts between the United States and a Jordanian-PLO delegation; next, there would be an international conference; and only at that point would there be negotiations with Israel. Shultz, in contrast, insisted that any American meeting with a Jordanian-Palestinian delegation should be followed immediately by contacts with the Israelis.[52]

A third inhibition to American policy came from a concern for the political standing of Prime Minister Peres. During his first year in office he had become popular. The withdrawal of Israeli forces from Lebanon had been welcomed by a war-weary populace. Efforts to curb raging inflation were progressing, though with considerable pain. His management of the economy was turning out well for Peres. Quiet diplomacy with Jordan seemed to be laying the groundwork for a kind of condominium over the West Bank and Gaza at the expense of the PLO. Some American officials wanted to help Peres position himself for a showdown with Likud. This desire led them to advise against anything that could be viewed as causing a strain in U.S.-Israeli relations, such as American dealings with the PLO or American support for Palestinian self-determination.

A practical test of American policy emerged during the summer. The Jordanians wanted to proceed with the idea of an American exploratory meeting with a joint Jordanian-PLO delegation. On July 19 King Hussein had met secretly with Peres in London to discuss his strategy. He had gone over a long list of possible Palestinian participants who might be part of a joint Jordanian-Palestinian delegation. Shultz was informed of the meeting by the Israelis on August 5. Peres was not enthusiastic about a preliminary U.S.-Jordanian-Palestinian meeting but would not oppose it strongly so long as no PLO members participated.

On August 9 Shultz informed Reagan of the state of play. Reagan was firm in his opposition to American officials meeting with anyone even vaguely connected to the PLO. Meanwhile, Foreign Minister Shamir sent a message to the White House expressing his adamant opposition to the idea of the Americans' meeting with any Palestinians. Shultz pressed Reagan for a decision, and finally was given authority to allow Murphy to meet with a joint Jordanian-Palestinian delegation only if that led immediately to direct negotiations with Israel.[53]

The Jordanian response was noncommittal. Essentially the Jordanians said that an initial meeting should take place, and then next steps could be considered. As the Jordanians were quick to point out, their reply was almost a verbatim repetition of a long-standing American response to the Arabs' question of what would happen once negotiations with Israel began.

To try to organize a preliminary meeting between the United States and a joint Jordanian-Palestinian delegation, the Jordanians forwarded a list of seven names of possible Palestinian members of the delegation, from which the Americans were expected to select four. The Israelis had said they had no objection to two of the seven names but were quick to label the others as PLO. The Americans objected to at least three of the names, but, more important, they kept asking for assurances that any preliminary talks would be accompanied by a clear Jordanian-Palestinian commitment to direct negotiations with Israel.[54] Jordan, eager not to offend Syria, was not prepared to abandon the idea of an international conference in favor of U.S.-sponsored direct bilateral negotiations.

Despite these difficulties, for a moment in the summer of 1985 the United States seemed about to take the plunge. Assistant Secretary Murphy was sent to the Middle East, and members of a joint Jordanian-Palestinian team were assembled in Amman to meet him; but at the last moment he was told not to proceed with the meeting. Reagan's conditions could not be met, and Shultz therefore had to scrap the idea of a meeting. According to Shultz, Reagan had been immovable on the points of excluding the PLO and insisting on direct negotiations. But it is far from clear how hard anyone tried to persuade Reagan, and in any event Shultz was beginning to detect signs that the situation in the region was moving away from the possibility of productive peace talks.[55]

King Hussein made a final effort to persuade the Americans in the fall. He had been told that there was no chance of winning congressional support for a big new arms package for Jordan—something Reagan had promised the king in writing in December 1982—unless Jordan committed itself to direct negotiations. At his speech to the UN General Assembly, the king did make such a commitment, saying, "We are ready to negotiate with Israel under suitable, acceptable supervision, directly and as soon as possible, in accordance with Security Council Resolutions 242 and 338."[56] One month later the U.S. Senate rebuffed the king's request on arms, stipulating that no major sale could be concluded until "direct and meaningful" negotiations with Israel had begun. In the face of continuing congressional hostility to the sale, the administration finally withdrew the nearly $2 billion arms package for Jordan on February 3, 1986.

October proved to be a disastrous month for Jordanian-PLO relations, as well as for Hussein's initiative. The month began with a spectacular Israeli bombing attack on Arafat's headquarters in Tunis, ostensibly in retaliation for a PLO attack on several Israelis in Cyprus a few days earlier. On October 5 King Hussein and Prime Minister Peres met secretly in London to develop a plan for joint rule in the West Bank.[57]

While Arafat was being abandoned by King Hussein, he was also being challenged by radicals from within his own organization. On October 7 a minor faction of the PLO—the Palestine Liberation Front of Abul Abbas—had the idea to hijack an Italian cruise ship, the *Achille Lauro*. Before the incident was over, one elderly American, confined to his wheelchair, had been murdered and thrown overboard. (The Syrians, eager to discredit the PLO, recovered the body on their coast and dutifully returned it to the American government, thus providing conclusive proof that the victim had been shot.)[58] At about the same time Jordan and the PLO failed to reach agreement on terms that would have allowed for a meeting of a joint Jordanian-PLO delegation with the British foreign secretary.

President Asad must have watched all these events with great satisfaction. He had opposed the February 11, 1985, agreement from the outset. He had labeled the U.S. efforts to arrange direct talks under its own auspices tantamount to another Camp David, and now he found the Jordanian-PLO alliance coming apart. So Asad, working closely with the Jordanian prime minister, Zaid al-Rifai, encouraged the development of a working alliance with Jordan. The king was obliged to acknowledge past Jordanian misdeeds in allowing anti-Syrian terrorist groups to operate from his territory. Thus the stage was set for a Syrian-Jordanian rapprochement and a break between Jordan and the PLO, which was not long in coming.[59] On February 19, 1986, the king spelled out in graphic detail the reasons for the breakdown of coordination with the PLO.[60] The February 11, 1985, accord had lasted barely one year.

In retrospect, it seems clear that the Americans had never been enthusiastic about dealing with a joint Jordanian–PLO delegation. As one Jordanian minister put it early in the discussions in Washington, Jordan tried to stress that the PLO was relatively weak and therefore could be pressured to make concessions. The American reply, he said, was that if the PLO was weak, it should be excluded entirely from the diplomatic process.[61] Finally, when King Hussein began to conclude that the PLO was a liability in his dealings with Israel, Syria, and Washington and that it was recreating a substantial presence in Jordan, he moved to sever the tie. In retrospect, Shultz concluded that neither Hussein nor Peres was politically strong enough to deliver the concessions needed to make the peace process work, even though their own thinking was not far apart.[62]

Covert Dealings with Iran

American involvement with the Arab-Israeli conflict can never be entirely isolated from other developments in the Middle East. In complex ways, events in Lebanon, Libya, and Iran all came to be entwined with Arab-Israeli diplomacy. If there was a connecting thread among these geographically remote locations, it was terrorism. By the mid-1980s the Reagan administration had become obsessed with the battle against terrorism, especially of the state-sponsored variety. And the three states topping the list of suspects were Syria, Iran, and Libya. All were actively involved in Lebanon, some with Lebanese groups and some with militant Shiites.

Already in 1984 Americans were falling victim to terrorist attacks. Malcolm Kerr, the president of the American University of Beirut and a leading specialist on Middle East affairs, was gunned down in cold blood in January 1984. Two months later the head of the CIA station in Lebanon, William Buckley, was kidnapped. In succeeding months, on into 1985, 1986, and 1987, fourteen more Americans were kidnapped from the streets of Beirut and held hostage. And terrorist attacks on airlines and airports claimed more lives.

Given the tough rhetoric of the Reagan administration against terrorism, the United States might have been expected to lash out at the states thought to be sponsoring such attacks. But only once did that happen, when Libya was held responsible for the bombing in Berlin that took two American lives. On April 14, 1986, American planes bombed Tripoli, nearly killing President Muammar Qaddafi in the process.

Curiously, Iran was treated quite differently from Libya, even though its involvement with the hostage takers in Lebanon was beyond doubt. During the spring of 1985, just as the joint Jordanian-PLO strategy was getting off the ground, some officials in Washington were beginning to debate the merits of trying to improve relations with Iran.[63] The rationale at the outset was presented in anti-Soviet terms. Iran was a large, important country that had not chosen sides in the cold war rivalry. After Ayatollah Khomeini left the scene, some argued, there would be a struggle for power, with pro-Soviet elements having a chance to gain the upper hand. The United States should therefore find some way to establish contacts with Iranians who were not pro-Soviet.[64]

On July 3, 1985, David Kimche, the director general of the Israeli Foreign Ministry, met at the White House with Robert McFarlane, Reagan's most recent national security adviser.[65] Israel had maintained some useful contacts in Iran after the revolution, and Kimche now offered to put these at the disposal of the United States in pursuit of the policy of improving relations with Iran. He told the Americans that at some point the Iranians, who were locked into a costly war with Iraq, would almost certainly ask for arms.[66] Within days of this conversation President Reagan was briefed on the Kimche conversation and reportedly gave general approval to the policy of cultivating "moderate" elements in Iran. During August Israel made a large shipment of American-made antitank missiles to Iran, and several weeks later an American hostage was released in Beirut. The "arms for hostages" exchange had begun.

Throughout most of 1986 the United States became more and more involved with Iran. Over the opposition of both his secretary of state and secretary of defense (who rarely agreed on much at all), and without their knowledge, Reagan signed an intelligence finding on January 17 that authorized the sale of American arms to Iran. Israel was to serve as the conduit. The moment of high drama—and even strange humor—came in May when McFarlane, accompanied by his National Security Council staff

aides Oliver North and Howard Teicher, as well as Peres's adviser on terrorist affairs, Amiram Nir, traveled secretly to Tehran. As a symbol of
their desire for a new relationship with the "moderates" in Iran, they took
with them a chocolate cake with a small gold key on top of it—direct from
a Tel Aviv bakery!

McFarlane soon learned that his Iranian counterparts were interested
only in getting more arms and had no desire to discuss broad strategic
issues or to deliver more hostages as a sign of their good intentions. He
returned to Washington empty handed, although his energetic assistant
Oliver North continued to press forward with the policy, developing in
the process an innovative way of financing another of the president's pet
projects, aid to the Nicaraguan Contras, which Congress had prohibited.

Finally, after the release of two more American hostages in Beirut and
the taking of an additional three, the news of McFarlane's secret visit to
Tehran the previous May was published, and on November 25, 1986, the
White House was obliged to confirm that arms had been sent to Iran, with
the proceeds illegally diverted to the Contras. A political scandal of unprecedented proportions ensued, leading eventually to indictments against
McFarlane; his successor as national security adviser, John Poindexter;
and Oliver North. Reagan, who professed ignorance about the diversion
of funds to the Contras, was weakened by the affair.

How, if at all, did the Iran-Contra affair affect American policy toward
the Arab-Israeli conflict? First, just as the Jordanian-Palestinian initiative
was getting off the ground in 1985, the attention of the White House was
turning to the sensitive issue of the opening to Iran, and Israel was to play
a key part in the strategy. This was no time to press the Israelis to be
particularly forthcoming toward the Jordanians or Palestinians. In fact,
the Israelis were in an excellent position to embarrass the Reagan administration if they ever had reason to do so.

Second, as the flow of arms from Israel to Iran got under way in 1985,
Arab governments began to take notice and assumed a degree of American complicity. Simultaneously, the United States was openly tilting toward Iraq in the Iran-Iraq war. How could the two strands of policy be
reconciled? At a time when American credibility was important for the
possible success of the peace process, Egypt and Jordan seem to have developed doubts about the reliability of the United States.

Third, the initiative toward Iran caused deep divisions in the upper
echelons of the American government, which Reagan was unwilling or
unable to resolve. Divided counsels on the Middle East undermined a

coherent policy toward the peace process. In the end, however, the Iran-Contra affair cannot be credited with causing the failure to exploit a possible opening in the peace process in 1985–86. But it did contribute to the erosion of American credibility at a crucial moment, weakening the president and perhaps leading to his further disengagement from foreign-policy issues as he approached the end of his second term.

9 *Back to Basics: Shultz Tries Again*

FROM THE MOMENT he became secretary of state in 1982, George Shultz had been the dominant architect of the Reagan administration's approach to the Arab-Israeli peace process. But on related matters in the Middle East, such as Lebanon and the Iran-Iraq war, he was not able to get his way so easily. Secretary of Defense Weinberger had persuaded the president to withdraw American troops from Lebanon early in 1984, a move that Shultz had opposed; and Casey, McFarlane, Poindexter, and North had been able to conduct the covert "arms-for-hostages" operation in 1985 and 1986, to which both Shultz and Weinberger had objected.

The Iran-Contra scandal clearly strengthened Shultz's hand in dealing with the White House. After firing Poindexter and North, Reagan could hardly afford to lose his respected secretary of state as well. The new national security adviser, Frank Carlucci, who took over in January 1987, was an experienced team player. He brought a degree of professionalism to the National Security Council that had been sorely lacking in previous years.

One sign of the new coherence in top-level policy circles came with the decision to support Kuwait's request early in 1987 to provide protection for its tankers from Iranian air attacks. For several years the United States had been tilting toward Iraq, and considerable concern had developed late in 1986 that Iran might be able to mount a major ground offensive in southern Iraq that would bring Iranian troops to the borders of Kuwait and Saudi Arabia. Shultz and Weinberger saw in the Kuwaiti request for

269

"reflagging" of eleven of their tankers a chance to erase the stain of Iran-Contra and to signal to the Iranians that a threat to the oil-rich states of the Arabian peninsula would be of direct concern to the United States.

Besides wanting to restrain Iran, the United States was hoping to rebuild its damaged credibility with a number of Arab states. The fact that Kuwait had also requested, and received, Soviet help was another reason for a swift American response. By mid-July 1987 the United States was routinely escorting Kuwaiti tankers to the northern end of the Persian Gulf and, equally surprising, was hard at work with the Soviet Union on a UN Security Council resolution calling for a cease-fire in the seven-year-old war. Resolution 598 was passed the same day that the first U.S.-escorted Kuwaiti convoy sailed through the gulf.[1]

On the whole, the reflagging operation was remarkably successful. At modest cost, and with relatively few risks, the United States helped to create conditions in which Iran finally felt compelled to accept a cease-fire—or in the words of Ayatollah Khomeini, "to drink poison"—thus ending the Middle East's costliest war to date. American prestige in the Arab world, which had sunk to a low point after the Iran-Contra revelations, was at least partially restored. Adding to the improved atmosphere in U.S.-Arab relations was an appreciation, especially in Jordan, that the United States had gradually been adjusting its position on the question of convening an Arab-Israeli peace conference.

Rediscovering the International Conference

In early 1986, after the break between Jordan and the Palestine Liberation Organization, King Hussein had placed renewed emphasis on the idea of an international conference. He had always maintained that he needed either the PLO or Syria to provide cover for his talks with Israel. If the PLO was now out of the picture, it was all the more important that Syria be given an incentive to go along with any diplomatic efforts. Hence the need for an international conference of some sort. Inevitably, that would mean some degree of Soviet participation as well, an issue the Reaganites were still unenthusiastic about. American hostility to the idea of an international conference was partly rooted in the notion that such an arrangement would bring the Soviet Union back into the Middle East, from which it had supposedly been absent since Kissinger's maneuvering of 1973–74.[2]

In late 1985 Shimon Peres, still in the role of prime minister, had begun to speak positively about some type of international forum or sponsorship of direct Arab-Israeli negotiations. His expressed conditions for a conference were that it not be empowered to impose solutions and that the Soviet Union should restore diplomatic relations with Israel before the conference.

About the same time as the modification in the Israeli position, Shultz also began to hint that the administration's previous opposition to the idea of an international conference was weakening. As early as September 23, 1985, Shultz had tried out some ideas on King Hussein, who at that moment was not much interested. But Shultz was clearly edging toward the idea of some type of international "event" to accommodate Arab concerns. He was also beginning to think about how the idea of sovereignty could be reconceptualized to accommodate the complexities of the relations binding Israel, the Palestinians, and Jordan. Various forms of mixed and overlapping sovereignty seemed to him the key to overcoming the impasse over Israeli withdrawal from occupied territories.[3]

Without much fanfare, the international conference reappeared on the Arab-Israeli diplomatic scene as a potentially live issue. Quiet diplomacy then took over, with professional American diplomats trying to develop a basis of agreement between Israel and Jordan.

During much of 1986 Jordanian-Israeli contacts increased. King Hussein met secretly with Defense Minister Yitzhak Rabin near Strasbourg in April.[4] Subsequently Jordan closed down PLO offices in Amman, and Jordan and Israel both encouraged the development of "Village Leagues" as alternative sources of leadership to the PLO-oriented nationalist leadership in the West Bank. Branches of the Cairo-Amman bank were opened in the West Bank, and a pro-Jordanian newspaper was set up in Jerusalem. The United States threw its support behind so-called quality-of-life measures, presumably on the theory that improved living standards would produce Palestinian political moderation.[5]

On the political front, however, the international conference remained of importance to Jordan, if only to help legitimize the de facto arrangements that were under way with Israel. In October 1986, as part of the rotation agreement between Labor and Likud, Yitzhak Shamir became prime minister. Peres took over as foreign minister, and Rabin stayed on as defense minister. Shamir had been kept informed of the contacts with Jordan but was unlikely to share Peres's enthusiasm for dealing with the king. Peres, however, was determined to press ahead, and by the spring of 1987 was within sight of an important breakthrough.

Jordan had firmed up its ties with Syria, to the point that an emissary of King Hussein met with Shultz on April 7, 1987, to say that Syria was prepared to attend an international conference of the sort Jordan had been proposing. Shultz was skeptical, but he realized that the Soviets might now be ready to help.[6]

Meanwhile King Hussein and Israeli foreign minister Peres met secretly in London to work out the principles for convening an international conference. Agreement was reached on April 11, 1987. Jordan and Israel both supported the idea that a conference would not have plenary powers. It could not impose its views or veto the results of bilateral negotiations that would take place under the umbrella of the conference. Both countries agreed there would be a ceremonial opening with representatives of the permanent members of the UN Security Council and those regional parties to the conflict that had accepted Resolution 242. One sticky issue, the question of what would happen in the event of a deadlock in the bilateral negotiations, the so-called referral issue, was finessed for the moment.[7]

On the day that Peres and Hussein reached agreement, an aide to Peres met with Shultz to plead with him to make the new document the core of an American initiative. Only in that way might Shamir be persuaded to accept it. Shultz refused to play this kind of game and insisted that Peres present his own agreement to Shamir before the United States would take any position on it. On April 20 Peres told Shultz that Shamir had been briefed, and two days later Shamir told Shultz that he totally rejected the London document.[8]

Shamir's rejection of the idea of a nonbinding international conference was rooted in his determination never to cede an inch of the historic Land of Israel—in practice, this meant no Israeli withdrawal from the West Bank. Moreover, the fact that Peres had negotiated the agreement behind Shamir's back ensured its frosty reception. Shultz was simply not prepared to take sides in this internal dispute, and a visit by Moshe Arens on Shamir's behalf on April 24 seems to have convinced Shultz not to embrace the London document. Still, he felt that Shamir had made a mistake, and he was encouraged to see that Hussein's idea of a conference was approaching his own.[9]

As a coda to this phase of diplomacy, a final effort was made, this time in collaboration with Shamir, to find some form of international sponsorship for Israeli-Jordanian talks. In mid-June Shamir had hinted to Shultz that he might consider some type of international meeting to endorse direct negotiations with Jordan. Shultz sent his aide, Charles Hill, to Israel in late July to explore this idea further. On August 6 an emissary from Shamir came to see Shultz to inform him that Shamir had met with Hussein. Shamir was still opposed to an international conference, but he would not object if the permanent members of the UN Security Council met to endorse direct Arab-Israeli negotiations. Shamir reported that his meeting with Hussein had gone well. Shortly thereafter, however, Shultz heard from Hussein about the same meeting. Hussein characterized Shamir as "hopeless."[10]

In September Peres suggested to Hill the idea that Mikhail Gorbachev and Ronald Reagan, as part of their upcoming summit meeting, might invite Shamir and King Hussein to meet with them. Shultz was well disposed toward the idea, and Reagan was briefed on it on September 11. The president did not immediately agree, and Shultz sensed he was growing weary of the Middle East. Finally, on September 23 Reagan gave the green light.[11]

Shultz flew to the Middle East in October 1987 while en route to Moscow to put the finishing touches on arrangements for a U.S.-Soviet summit meeting in Washington before the end of the year. While in Jerusalem he persuaded Shamir to agree in principle to the idea of an American-Soviet invitation to come to Washington at the time of the summit, along with King Hussein, to receive a joint U.S.-Soviet blessing for direct negotiations.

The next day, October 19, Shultz presented the idea to King Hussein in London. The United States had made little advance preparation with Jordan, in contrast to its numerous exchanges during the fall with the Israelis. The king, who was about to host an Arab summit in Amman, was politically unable even to hint at an interest in an idea that would be ridiculed by the other Arabs. He also had no reason to think the Soviets would agree to the idea, and the Syrians, who were only mentioned as an afterthought as possible participants in the adventure, would certainly say no. So the king found himself put in the position of saying no to the Americans, a fact that was duly leaked to a pro-Israeli columnist a few months later.[12]

In normal times Hussein's hesitation would have been the last word on the peace process for the Reagan administration. With both American and Israeli elections slated for November 1988, Washington had little appetite for continuing to grapple with the seemingly intractable Arab-Israeli conflict. When the Arab summit was held in Amman in early November, it even seemed as if the Arabs had turned their backs on the Palestinian question. The Persian Gulf, it appeared, was a much greater worry, and Arafat found himself the odd man out among the assembled Arab potentates. Even the acceptance of Egypt back into the fold, which most members of the Arab League endorsed, seemed driven more by gulf concerns than by a desire to coordinate the diplomacy of Arab-Israeli peacemaking with Cairo.

The Intifada and the Shultz Initiative

During Israel's twenty-year domination of the West Bank and Gaza, there had never been trouble-free times. But the costs of the occupation had not been judged excessive by Israeli governments, and a semblance of normal life existed on most days for the growing numbers of Israeli settlers, and for the Palestinians, some 100,000 of whom had jobs in the Israeli economy as of 1988. Then on December 9, 1987, an unusually nasty series of incidents took place in Gaza, sparking large-scale Palestinian protests. Within days West Bank Palestinians joined the "uprising," or *intifada*,[13] as it was to be called, and even Israeli Arabs showed support. It soon became clear that something qualitatively new was happening. The previously quiescent Palestinians of the West Bank and Gaza were coming of political age, and with a vengeance.[14]

Though caught by surprise by the timing of the uprising and by how quickly it spread, the PLO had long been cultivating support in the occupied territories, and pro-PLO networks existed and were backed by the generally pro-PLO sentiment of the population. Before long, coordination between the Unified National Leadership of the Uprising, as the internal leadership referred to itself, and the PLO seemed to be far reaching.[15]

By January 1988 the Israelis were acknowledging that they had an unprecedented situation on their hands. Defense Minister Rabin took a strong law-and-order approach, publicly sanctioning a policy of beatings and breaking of bones as part of an attempt to frighten the young Palestinians who threw rocks and Molotov cocktails at heavily armed soldiers. Within days images of savage Israeli beatings of Palestinian youngsters were a part of the American evening television news. Public reaction was strong. Even from within the normally pro-Israeli American Jewish community there was an outpouring of criticism and concern.

Several developments then took place that convinced Secretary of State Shultz to reengage his prestige in trying to get Arab-Israeli peace talks started.[16] First, in a six and one-half page letter to Shultz dated January 17, 1988, Shamir hinted that the Israeli position on "autonomy" for the Palestinians might be softening. Second, American Jewish leaders, as well as some Israeli politicians, began to urge Shultz to become more actively involved. Third, President Husni Mubarak of Egypt came to Washington to make a forceful and convincing plea that American leadership was urgently needed to ward off a radicalization of the entire region.

Shultz approached the challenge methodically. He did not make a flamboyant speech, nor did he hold out great hopes of a breakthrough. But he did begin to explore ideas with all the parties, this time including Syria, the Soviets, and some individual Palestinians, as well as with Jordan and the Israelis. At the end of his second trip to the region in as many months, on March 4, 1988, Shultz formalized his initiative in a proposal he described as a "blend of ideas" designed to repackage and streamline the Camp David Accords.[17]

The Shultz initiative, as it was immediately labeled, was certainly the most important U.S. involvement in Arab-Israeli peacemaking since Reagan's peace initiative in September 1982. In essence, Shultz outlined the conventional goal of a comprehensive peace to be achieved through direct bilateral negotiations based on Resolutions 242 and 338. But Shultz added a new element with what he called the "interlock" between the negotiations on the transitional period for the West Bank and Gaza and the negotiations on "final status." Shultz had long felt that the time scale envisioned in Camp David should be compressed, and his initiative explicitly ensured that it would be.

The Palestinian issue, according to Shultz, should be addressed in negotiations between an Israeli delegation and a Jordanian-Palestinian delegation. Six months would be set aside for negotiating transitional arrangements. In the seventh month negotiations on the final status of the West Bank and Gaza would start—regardless of the outcome of the first phase of negotiations. A target date of one year for negotiating the final status of the territories was mentioned. Assuming that agreement could be reached on transitional arrangements, a transitional period would begin at an early date and would continue for three years. The United States, Shultz said, would participate in both sets of negotiations and would put forward a draft agreement on transitional arrangements for the consideration of the parties.

Preceding the bilateral negotiations between Israel and a Jordanian-Palestinian delegation, there would be an international conference. The secretary general of the United Nations would invite the regional parties and the permanent members of the Security Council.[18] All participants in the conference would have to accept Resolutions 242 and 338. Although the negotiating parties, by agreement, might report to the conference from time to time, the conference would have no power to impose its views or to veto the results of the negotiations.

Shultz also said that Palestinians should be represented in a combined Jordanian-Palestinian delegation. That delegation would deal with the Palestinian issue in its entirety, and those negotiations would be independent of any other negotiation.

In the months that followed his initiative, Shultz doggedly tried to wear down the opponents of his initiative in both Israel and the Arab world. His biggest problem was Prime Minister Shamir, who blasted the idea of an international conference—which Shultz saw as a marginal part of his initiative—in no uncertain terms. Shamir also rejected the "interlock" concept, claiming it was contrary to Camp David. As Shamir correctly noted, the Camp David Accords had made the "final status" talks dependent on prior success in reaching agreement on transitional arrangements. Under Shultz's proposal the talks on final status would begin whether or not agreement had been reached on an interim period, thus providing little incentive for the Palestinians to negotiate seriously on the initial transitional stage. The prospects for success in resolving the final-status issues were not bright, since, as Shamir said publicly, the exchange of territory for peace was foreign to him.[19]

Israeli criticism of the Shultz initiative was well publicized, even though Peres publicly welcomed the American effort. On the Arab side, King Hussein went to great lengths not to be put in the position of saying no to Shultz. He asked questions, sought clarifications, played hard to get, referred publicly to the importance of including the PLO in the game, and generally tried to keep his shrinking options open.

The Palestinian response was more categorical. Though pleased to see the United States responding to the uprising, the Palestinian leaders were unhappy with the second-class treatment they were given in the Shultz plan. They saw themselves as being assigned, at best, to the role of junior partner to Jordan.

The Soviet Union was also unenthusiastic about a central feature of the Shultz plan, the international conference. Whereas Shamir professed fears that the conference would become authoritative and would work to undermine the Israeli position, the Soviet concern was just the opposite. The international conference, as envisaged by the Americans, appeared to the Soviets to be only symbolic. The Soviets wanted a real role in the negotiating process, not just an opportunity to legitimize a made-in-America initiative that would ultimately leave them on the sidelines. Syria, likewise, was cool to the Shultz proposal. Only Mubarak, whose country was already at peace with Israel, openly endorsed the new American plan.[20]

In the face of these obstacles the Shultz plan never had much chance of complete success. Nonetheless, it had wide support in American public opinion. There was little criticism of any features of the proposal, except for some sour words from Henry Kissinger about the whole idea of an international conference. Shultz and his colleagues were no doubt hopeful that they would get a lucky break and that a negotiating process might be started on their watch. But they also spoke of other purposes behind the initiative. Most important, they wanted to influence Israeli public opinion. With the prospect of peace negotiations with their Arab neighbors, the Israeli public, it was hoped, would vote in the scheduled fall 1988 elections for a leadership committed to compromise positions. That possibility might, of course, prove to be wishful thinking; much would depend on Shultz's producing an acceptable Arab partner for peace talks. Still, the American intention was to help shape the political debate in Israel so that the elections would become a referendum, of sorts, on peace.

The Shultz plan depended crucially on cooperation with King Hussein. During four trips to the Middle East in the first half of 1988, Shultz had tried to persuade Hussein, and had even reached out, without much success, to Palestinians in the West Bank. On July 31, however, the foundations of the Shultz initiative collapsed, when King Hussein, in an official statement, relinquished all Jordanian legal and administrative ties to the West Bank, stating bluntly that henceforth the PLO would be responsible for the Palestinians living there.[21]

A U.S.-PLO Dialogue?

With Jordan at least temporarily out of the picture, one might have thought the United States would lose interest in pursuing Arab-Israeli peace initiatives. Especially in an election year, attention was bound to be focused elsewhere. But each day the news from Israel brought more images of violence and radicalization of the Palestinians, particularly among the youth, as well as signs of increasing Islamic militancy. No one in Washington was comfortable with the worsening situation between Israel and the Palestinians. But what could be done, especially prior to both Israeli and American elections?

The idea of establishing direct contacts between Washington and the PLO had frequently been explored in previous years. Insofar as there was episodic interest in the idea among American officials, the goal was to moderate the PLO position on peace with Israel and open the way for direct participation by legitimate Palestinian representatives in negotiations.[22] At least grudgingly, most American policymakers accepted the fact that the PLO was the most widely supported spokesman for the Palestinians. Only King Hussein was ever seen as a possible alternative. So, in one way or another, most administrations had tried to develop some contacts with the PLO.

As early as 1974 Kissinger had authorized meetings between the PLO and Vernon Walters, then with the CIA. In Beirut, U.S. and PLO intelligence operatives had maintained contacts for purposes of exchanging information on security. On occasion, diplomatic messages were exchanged in these channels. But after Kissinger's 1975 pledge that the United States would not recognize or negotiate with the PLO unless the PLO acknowledged Israel's right to exist and accepted Resolution 242, official contacts had been rare. The pledge had not stopped intermediaries from exchanging messages, sometimes with authorization and sometimes on their own.[23] But no ongoing, high-level, openly acknowledged relationship had ever existed between the United States and the PLO.

Few would have expected the pro-Israeli Reagan or the equally pro-Israeli Shultz to alter this policy. And these two men would probably argue that, in fact, they did not. Yet it was on their watch, in the waning days of the Reagan presidency, that the United States finally agreed to begin an official dialogue with the PLO.

According to the standard version of what happened, the PLO, in danger of being marginalized as the *intifada* gained momentum, and under pressure from both the Arab states and the Soviets, finally met the well-known American conditions, and therefore the dialogue began.[24] That is only part of the story.

As early as April 1988 a small group of American Jewish leaders began to explore the possibility with the Swedish government of meeting with the PLO to formulate a well-developed statement of the PLO's commitment to a peace settlement with Israel.[25] The Swedish foreign minister, Sten Andersson, had been a good friend of Israel during his career, but had been appalled by what he had seen during a visit to Israel and the occupied territories. Thus he set about trying to build bridges between Palestinians and Israelis, but soon settled on the idea of starting with a meeting between PLO leaders and prominent American Jews. He informed George Shultz of his intentions. Hearing no objections, Andersson quietly went forward with his plans.

By his own account Shultz was not much interested in this exercise in private diplomacy, apparently paying little attention to it until later in the year.[26] He did, however, hold Andersson in high regard and took him seriously as a professional diplomat who could be trusted. This recognition proved to be important in the last phases of establishing the dialogue.

Meanwhile another track of private diplomacy began to explore formulations the PLO and the United States might agree on, initially in private, that would meet the political needs of both sides for beginning talks. The impetus for this initiative came from a Palestinian American, Mohamed Rabie, shortly after King Hussein announced his decision to break legal ties to the West Bank.[27] Rabie was convinced that the PLO would now be ready to accept the American conditions if it could be assured in advance that an official dialogue would ensue, along with some expression of American support for the idea of Palestinian self-determination.[28]

By mid-August this initiative had been reviewed with the State Department. Draft statements that the PLO might make, and a corresponding American reply, had been reviewed.[29] The American attitude toward the initiative, to be conveyed to the PLO, was spelled out as follows:

—There has been no change in what it will take for the United States to agree to deal with the PLO.

—The United States and the PLO have come close to agreement in the past, only to see the chance slip away. If a serious effort is to be made now, there must be clarity on both sides. Ambiguity would be counterproductive, especially on the eve of Israeli elections.

—If the PLO made the kind of statement the United States required, talks could begin right away. For political reasons certain things may be easier to do after the U.S. elections, but there is no need to wait.

—Any conditional clause accompanying a statement of acceptance of Resolution 242 will not be accepted by the United States. Whatever conditions the PLO wishes to state should be done in a separate paragraph. The United States needs a "clean" acceptance of 242.

—The proposed U.S. statement seems fairly close to what the United States might be willing to say, but it will have to be reviewed personally by Secretary Shultz at the appropriate time.

—This initiative is worthwhile "if the PLO is serious." A very small group will be in charge of the initiative on the American side and will be available at all times. No other channel is pursuing this course.[30]

Shortly thereafter Rabie left for Tunis, where he presented the documents and the idea of the initiative to Arafat and other top PLO leaders. After lengthy talks he returned to Washington in early September with PLO approval of a slightly revised formulation, conditional on the United States' making a statement that would approximate the sample that had been discussed with, but not yet approved by, Washington.[31] This information was immediately passed to State and was received with interest. Shultz felt he could help the next administration by starting the dialogue, but he was not prepared to endorse Palestinian self-determination, which he saw as a code word for a Palestinian state, as the necessary price.

For the Reagan administration the issue now arose of whether to tip its hand on what it would say in exchange for the PLO's acceptance of 242, its recognition of Israel's right to exist, and its renunciation of terrorism. Over the ensuing weeks news came from Tunis of impatience to hear the official American position. In mid-September the Soviets were informed by the PLO of the initiative, which they reportedly supported.

On September 16 Shultz made a major speech to a pro-Israeli group at the Wye Plantation in Maryland. He explained why the United States would not endorse the idea of Palestinian self-determination if it were seen as meaning an automatic right to statehood. He did add, however, that in negotiations the Palestinians were "free to argue for independence." But negotiations were the key thing.[32]

As frustrations began to mount on both sides, Shultz authorized an oral message to be conveyed to Rabie for Arafat on September 23, 1988. It stated: "We welcomed the receipt of the initiative, which we recognize as a serious effort. This issue has been given careful consideration and will continue to be seriously discussed. We expect to provide our reaction in six weeks or so." In brief, the American response to the proposed PLO statement would be sent after the Israeli and American elections.[33] But already one could detect that the Reagan administration was not passively awaiting PLO compliance. It was signaling a positive attitude and was reiterating that talks would in fact begin as soon as the well-known conditions were met. Previously, the stated policy was that talks could not take place unless the PLO accepted the American conditions, but even PLO acceptance of those conditions would not necessarily result in an official dialogue. Now it was explicitly stated that talks would follow immediately on the PLO's acceptance of the American terms.

In an effort to avoid having this initiative wither in the intervening weeks, the PLO provided a glimpse of its plans. On October 19 the PLO conveyed the position that it intended to take at the upcoming meeting of the Palestine National Congress (PNC). It would accept the principle of a two-state solution to the conflict, anchoring its acceptance in UN Resolution 181 of 1947, which had called for the partition of Palestine into two states and had been rejected by the Arabs at the time. In addition, the PLO would accept UN resolutions 242 and 338 as the basis for an international conference, along with the recognition of the rights of the Palestinian people, including their right to self-determination. The PLO would also condemn terrorism. After adopting these positions officially, the PLO would make the statement the United States wanted, and then the United States should respond.

On the basis of this information, several problems could be foreseen. The PLO still seemed to be insisting on American acceptance of Palestinian self-determination as the price for accepting 242. While condemning terrorism, the PLO was not willing to renounce it. Also, Israel's right to exist was not explicitly mentioned.

Shortly after receiving this message, the administration was told by the Jordanians that Arafat was no longer insisting on recognition of the Palestinian right to self-determination. If Israeli withdrawal could be achieved, and with the Jordanian legal claim to the territories annulled, the Palestinians would become the ruling authority in any territory vacated by Israel. While logical, the Jordanian position was not automatically credited as an accurate reflection of the PLO position.

With the Palestine National Congress scheduled to meet in November, Arafat conveyed some uneasiness about the reliability of the channel being used to communicate between Washington and Tunis.[34] More to the point, most likely, he was disappointed by what he was hearing. Shultz was not willing to tip his hand until after the PNC had met.

As that meeting approached, results of the Israeli and American elections came in. The Israeli elections again produced a standoff between the Likud and Labor parties, which in due course led to a Likud-dominated coalition with Labor, but this time without a rotation of the premiership and with Moshe Arens as foreign minister instead of the more dovish Shimon Peres, who moved over to the finance ministry. Rabin stayed on as defense minister, so Labor continued to hold influential posts in the cabinet. But foreign-policy decisions would henceforth be solidly under Shamir's control.

The American elections were more conclusive than those in Israel just a few days earlier. Vice President George Bush defeated Governor Michael Dukakis of Massachusetts in a landslide. A narrow window was now open during which a U.S.-PLO agreement might still be reached before the Reagan administration left office. Bush was especially eager that this be done before he was sworn in, but he did not play an important role in the decisions concerning the PLO.

When Arafat convened the PNC from November 12 to 15, he succeeded in pushing through his political program and in declaring the existence of a Palestinian state with himself as president.[35] The state was presumably to be established alongside Israel in the West Bank and Gaza. The PLO appeared to be accepting UN resolution 242, but not unconditionally. And some of the language in the political document continued to express old slogans. Shultz was unimpressed.

Meanwhile the Swedish initiative was beginning to bear fruit. An initial meeting of PLO representatives and American Jewish leaders had been held in late November, and agreement had been reached on a general political statement. It took the form of an agreed interpretation of the recent PNC resolutions. The culmination of this effort was to be a public meeting of the American Jewish leaders with Arafat in Stockholm, during which the new statement would be released. Before the meeting Andersson contacted Shultz to ask if he could convey anything of importance to Arafat. Shultz, who had just turned down Arafat's request for a visa to come to the United Nations on grounds that the PLO was a terrorist group, decided nonetheless to respond to Andersson.[36]

Getting the Words Right

In a letter dated December 3, 1988, Shultz conveyed the long-awaited American position, along with a text of exactly what Arafat would have to say to meet the American conditions. In his letter Shultz made it clear he would not bargain further over the language. He also noted that the PLO could add other points to the basic statement, but that these should not condition or contradict its acceptance of the U.S. conditions. Finally, Shultz added that nothing in his letter should imply that the United States was prepared to recognize an independent Palestinian state.[37]

The proposed PLO statement conveyed to Arafat by Andersson on December 7 read as follows:

> As its contribution to the search for a just and lasting peace in the Middle East, the Executive Committee of the Palestine Liberation Organization wishes to issue the following official statement:
>
> 1. That it is prepared to negotiate with Israel a comprehensive peace settlement of the Arab-Israeli conflict on the basis of United Nations Resolutions 242 and 338.
>
> 2. That it undertakes to live in peace with Israel and its other neighbors and to respect their right to exist in peace within secure and internationally recognized borders, as will the democratic Palestinian state which it seeks to establish in the West Bank and the Gaza Strip.
>
> 3. That it condemns individual, group and state terrorism in all its forms, and will not resort to it.
>
> 4. That it is prepared for a moratorium on all forms of violence, on a mutual basis, once negotiations begin.[38]

In return, Shultz promised, the United States would announce that it was prepared to begin substantive discussions with the PLO. The United States would recognize that the representatives of the Palestinians would have the right in the course of negotiations to raise all subjects of interest to them. Then, Shultz said, an American official would answer a planted question about whether the Palestinians could table their position on statehood, to which the answer would be "Yes, the Palestinians, as far as we are concerned, have the right to pursue an independent state through negotiations." This response was as close as Shultz would go to saying that Palestinians had a right to self-determination. In response to a PLO request, Shultz also agreed to answer a question on the international conference as follows: "The U.S. has long made its support for direct negotiations clear, but we remain prepared to consider any suggestion that may lead to direct negotiations toward a comprehensive peace. The initiative proposed by Secretary Shultz in the beginning of the year called for an international conference to begin direct negotiations. Any conference of this type must be organized so that it does not become an alternative to direct negotiations."

Arafat responded in two ways to Shultz's message. He told Andersson that he personally agreed to the language proposed by Shultz, and he even put his signature to the proposed text.[39] But he added that he would have to seek agreement from the other members of the PLO Executive Committee. Then, in public, Arafat issued the statement that had been worked out between his representatives and the American Jewish leaders on November 21. Its operational language came close to meeting Shultz's concerns, but not quite. Instead of unconditionally accepting UN Resolutions 242 and 338 as the basis for negotiations with Israel, Arafat added the right of the Palestinians to self-determination as another basis for the conference, implying that this condition would have to be accepted in advance by the other participants, something that neither the United States nor Israel was prepared to do. Furthermore, though Arafat did "reject and condemn" terrorism in all its forms, he did not renounce it or pledge not to engage in it in the future. These may have seemed like verbal squabbles to some, but to Shultz they mattered. Perhaps most positive and significant, Arafat did state openly that the PLO "accepted the existence of Israel as a state in the region," a formulation he had not used before.

The next step in the process of trying to get Arafat to utter the magic words came during his appearance before a special session of the United Nations held in Geneva on December 13, 1988. Arafat had encountered some opposition within the PLO Executive Committee to the idea of using the precise language that Shultz had provided to Andersson. Nayif Hawatmeh was particularly hostile to the idea. Thus Arafat sent word to the Swedes that he would use the Shultz formulation in his speech, but it would be scattered throughout the text.[40] This message was apparently not clearly conveyed to the Americans, who were expecting to hear the exact words they had agreed on.

As Arafat worked his way through his long and rambling speech, he made the point about "rejecting" and "condemning" terrorism in all its forms, but he did not "renounce" it.[41] Toward the end of the speech, Arafat addressed the issues of 242 and Israel's right to exist. The wording was complicated in Arabic but is probably best translated as follows:

> The PLO will work to achieve a comprehensive peaceful settlement among the parties to the Arab-Israeli conflict, including the Palestinian state, Israel, and other neighboring states, within the framework of the international conference for peace in the Middle East, in order to achieve equality and a balance of interests, especially the right of our people to liberation and national independence, and respect for everyone's right to exist, to peace, and to security, according to Resolutions 242 and 338.

Some State Department officials listening to the speech felt that though Arafat had come close to doing so, he had not specifically mentioned negotiations with Israel or Israel's right to exist, nor had he renounced terrorism. Shultz and his influential assistant, Charles Hill, reacted negatively.[42] They had expected verbatim compliance and felt the speech was another sign that Arafat could not be trusted. The Swedes acknowledged that the speech did not meet the American conditions, but they felt it had almost done so. All Shultz would agree to was that Arafat could try one more time.

During the day on December 14 many people weighed in with Arafat— the president of Egypt, the Saudis, the Swedes, individual Americans—to try to persuade him to utter the exact words that Shultz was insisting on. Finally, in the company of several rich Palestinian businessmen who were in telephone contact with the State Department to check on acceptable wording, Arafat agreed to hold a press conference, where he finally said, in English:

> Yesterday . . . I made a reference to our acceptance of resolutions 242 and 338 as the basis for negotiations with Israel within the framework of the international conference. . . . In my speech also yesterday, it was clear that we mean . . . the right of all parties concerned

in the Middle East conflict to exist in peace and security and, as I have mentioned, including the state of Palestine, Israel, and other neighbors according to the resolution 242 and 338.

As for terrorism, I renounced it yesterday in no uncertain terms, and yet I repeat for the record that we totally and absolutely renounce all forms of terrorism, including individual, group, and state terrorism.[43]

Shultz finally agreed that Arafat had met the American conditions and so informed Colin Powell, the national security adviser, who then sought the president's approval to announce that the U.S.-PLO discussions could begin at the level of the American ambassador in Tunisia. Reagan reportedly gave his consent quite easily. On December 14 the United States finally lifted the ban on dealing with the PLO.[44] At least the incoming Bush administration would not have to wrestle with the problem of opening a dialogue. It, however, would face the equally daunting task of giving substance to the talks and relating them to the broader peace process.

Assessing the Reagan Era

Reagan remained a popular figure throughout most of his presidency. He was widely credited with restoring American self-confidence after the gloom of the Carter years. More tangibly, he presided over the last phase of the cold war. By the time he left office, the world seemed a safer place, as the two great nuclear powers began to reduce their bloated arsenals of weapons of mass destruction. On the economic front, many Americans were better off as the 1980s came to an end, but many at the lower rungs of the economic ladder were poorer than ever. By most measures the gap between rich and poor had grown significantly. And then there was the deficit. For all of Reagan's talk about the virtues of a balanced budget, never once did he submit one, nor did Congress come close to passing one. As a result, interest on the national debt had become the second largest item in the budget by 1989.

For most Americans these were the bread-and-butter issues that counted as they thought about the 1980s. But they were also aware that Reagan had blundered badly with his "arms for hostages" initiative in 1985–86. Some might even remember the horrifying scenes of Beirut being bombed, the Sabra and Shatila massacres, and the explosions in Beirut in 1983 that took the lives of more than three hundred Americans, more than died in any other Middle East situation under any American administration.

Reagan and his top officials, however, never seemed to be blamed for such disasters, which led to the accusation that this was a "Teflon presidency."

Few broad overviews of the Reagan presidency take note of his Arab-Israeli diplomacy. No such monument as Camp David sticks in collective memory when Reagan's Middle East policy is evoked. Some would even say that there was no policy toward Arab-Israeli peace during the Reagan period. But that is manifestly untrue. Reagan, with Shultz as his mentor, gave one of the most carefully crafted speeches ever on American policy toward the Arab-Israeli conflict. A decade later it still set the parameters of American policy by both embracing and extending the Camp David Accords. At the time it enjoyed broad bipartisan support. Even the American Israel Public Affairs Committee (AIPAC) felt compelled to praise the speech, despite Begin's ferocious rejection of it. But if Reagan was unexcelled as a speechmaker, he and his aides failed to devise a strategy for translating words into practical diplomatic steps. In their defense, it can be said that even a brilliant strategist might have found it difficult to move the Likud governments of Begin and Shamir from their entrenched positions.

Still, in both 1983 and 1985, and especially the latter, Reagan and Shultz might have inched the peace process forward had they shown more drive and determination. Nothing like Kissinger's intense shuttle diplomacy, or Carter's summitry, was tried until early 1988, by which point time was running out. So the Reagan period produced little in the way of tangible progress toward Arab-Israeli peace, although several helpful additions to the Camp David framework were put forward by Shultz. On balance, Israel and its neighbors were no closer to agreement in 1988 than they had been in 1980.

Perhaps the most one can say is that things had not deteriorated beyond repair. Egypt and Israel were still at peace, even though the temperature of the relationship was tepid. The Palestinians were engaged in a sustained rebellion against the Israeli occupation, which convinced Jordan's King Hussein to pull back from the exposed position he had adopted in 1987. The long-pursued Jordan option was dead. But the Palestinians were signaling a willingness to accept explicitly Israel's existence as a state in the region, provided they could establish their own ministate alongside it in the West Bank and Gaza. This position, long discussed by Palestinians in private, finally came into the open in 1988 and, through a tortuous diplomatic effort cautiously encouraged by Shultz, led to the opening of a U.S.-PLO dialogue, one of the greatest surprises of the Reagan era.

The prospects for Arab-Israeli peace, however, did not advance during the 1980s under Reagan, and in one dimension the objective situation became more difficult. At the time of the signing of the Camp David Accords, about 10,000 Israeli settlers lived in the West Bank and Gaza (in addition to another 100,000 or so in the Greater Jerusalem area). Before Reagan, all American presidents had maintained that Israeli settlement activities in the occupied territories were not only illegal under the terms of the Fourth Geneva Convention but were obstacles to peace. Reagan, apparently influenced by the legal arguments of Eugene Rostow, professor of international law at Yale and a prominent spokesman for neoconservative, pro-Israeli views, switched position on settlements.[45] Henceforth American policy was that Israeli settlements in the occupied territories were not illegal, although they were still viewed as obstacles to peace.

Reagan's change of policy on settlements was not the reason that the number of Israeli settlers in the occupied territories grew to nearly 100,000 by 1992. But the permissive American attitude certainly encouraged the determined settlement policy of Shamir and Sharon. Some even concluded in the early 1980s that settlement activity had gone so far that a negotiated Israeli-Palestinian agreement was no longer possible.[46] Even those who resisted this conclusion acknowledged the difficulty of dealing with the large number of Israeli settlers living beyond the "green line." Reagan personally never seemed to worry much about this issue, because he was essentially uninvolved with the details of trying to advance the peace process. But his successor was to inherit the settlements issue as a major complication both in U.S.-Israeli relations and in the revived peace process of the 1990s.

It is hard not to conclude that Reagan's disengaged style as president, his lack of curiosity, and his passivity on issues related to the Middle East were impediments to creative U.S. peace diplomacy.[47] He was unwilling or unable to discipline his quarreling subordinates (Lebanon); he tolerated actions taken in his name that seemed to undercut his ostensible policies (Iran-Contra); he had no sense of strategy for dealing with Arabs and Israelis, except to make the Israelis feel secure and the Arabs almost desperate. Fortunately, during his watch the Soviet Union began to unravel, so his weaknesses and oversimplifications did not prove to be disastrous. And in his way he did lend his prestige to steps that his successor might build on.

When a president is passive and uninvolved, how much can his secretary of state hope to achieve? Shultz clearly dominated diplomatic moves toward the Arab-Israeli conflict throughout his tenure. During the last two years he was in charge of all aspects of foreign policy and was heading a team of considerable ability. Bureaucratic bickering came to an end. On some Middle East issues, such as the reflagging of Kuwaiti tankers, a policy of nuance was carried out successfully. But on Arab-Israeli matters Shultz seemed to hesitate when opportunities opened up, as in 1985. He stuck doggedly to his belief that King Hussein could be drawn into peace talks and reassessed the situation only when his policy had clearly failed. His own formulation on an international conference was so convoluted that it failed to win support from either Arabs or Israelis, although some of the points survived in a different form under President Bush and his secretary of state, James Baker.

How much of Shultz's hesitation came from a realization that he could not count on much help from the president he served? How much came from a conviction that the Arabs needed to face up convincingly to the reality of Israel before the United States could help them? How much stemmed from a genuine admiration for the tough, pro-American Israelis with whom he dealt? How much can be attributed to domestic politics and the role of the pro-Israeli lobby? Shultz has not been communicative about his own motives, and those who worked most closely with him often found him enigmatic. But it seems fair to conclude that he admired the Israelis and was reluctant to pressure them; he became frustrated with the Arab leaders with whom he dealt and was skeptical about the wisdom of running after them unless they developed a strong commitment of their own to peace with Israel; and he shared Reagan's distrust of Soviet motives, although less so by the end of his tenure.

For both Reagan and Shultz—and they were the two key figures who counted on Arab-Israeli issues—policies emerged more often as reactions to events in the Middle East region than as part of a grand design. The Reagan initiative of 1982 was sparked by the Israeli invasion of Lebanon; the ill-conceived May 17, 1983, agreement between Israel and Lebanon was largely sponsored at Israel's behest; and the Israelis helped to plant the idea of the opening to Iran, which was then twisted and distorted by too zealous, insufficiently supervised Reaganites into an "arms for hostages" scheme and a slick means of avoiding the congressional ban on aid to the Contras in Nicaragua.

In much the same vein, the Shultz initiative of 1988 was a reaction to the *intifada*. Without the eruption of violence in the occupied territories, Shultz would probably not have devised his plan. And the opening to the PLO was a grudging reaction to King Hussein's announced relinquishment of responsibility for the West Bank.

When Reagan had strong convictions, as on how to deal with the Soviet Union, some elements of strategy became visible in the unfolding policies. But when Reagan was indifferent or uncertain, and when his advisers disagreed or were hesitant to act, policy became derivative or reactive. Not surprisingly, the record of promoting Arab-Israeli accommodation was unimpressive.

Even in the realm of U.S.-Israeli relations the legacy of the Reagan era is uncertain. Aid continued to flow at unprecedentedly high levels; Congress was unusually sympathetic to Israel; potential quarrels, such as the Pollard spying affair,[48] were treated as aberrations; revelations about Israel's nuclear capabilities were ignored;[49] and the entire relationship was given a strategic rationale that had previously been missing, or had at least been less central.[50]

Many Israelis were delighted with the result. They basked in the glow of being treated as a "non-NATO ally"; American aid to the Israeli defense industry was welcomed; intelligence cooperation reached new heights. But without a vigorous peace process, the United States and Israel risked losing one of the solid links of the past. After all, the major steps in forging close U.S.-Israeli ties had come in the context of moves toward peace. Over time, would the American public and future administrations continue to provide generous support to an Israel that was not making moves toward peace with its neighbors? If the blame for the lack of peace was clearly on the Arab side, the answer might still be yes. But what if the perception was less clear? What if Israel was seen as more of an obstacle to peace than the Arabs were?[51] What if Israel's occupation of the West Bank and Gaza was seen as unjustified by a younger generation of Americans who no longer felt such close ties to Israel and who had no memory of how the conflict had come about?

President Reagan and the Likud party seemed to feel that a strong strategic alliance against the Soviet Union and its regional allies would provide enough support for U.S.-Israeli relations even without an active peace process. But what if the cold war ended and the Soviet Union was no longer a threat to the region? What then would bind the United States and Israel if not the more conventional shared values and common purposes? Could the pro-Israeli lobby alone keep the relationship intact if its strategic and moral premises were called into question? These matters never seemed to be considered during the Reagan period, and yet within a short time U.S.-Israeli relations entered a very difficult period. Some would place the blame on Reagan's and Shultz's successors. Others would point to the overvaluation of the strategic relationship with Israel and the underinvestment in peacemaking during the Reagan era.

10 *Getting to the Table:*
Bush and Baker, 1989–92

R<small>ARELY, IF EVER,</small> has a president assumed office with a more impressive foreign affairs résumé than George Bush. Before coming to the White House in January 1989, he had been director of Central Intelligence, head of the American diplomatic mission to China, and ambassador to the United Nations, and he had spent eight years as vice president under Ronald Reagan, with special responsibility for crisis management for the National Security Council. In addition, Bush was from a political family, had served with distinction as a pilot in World War II, was a graduate of Yale, had been elected to Congress, was a successful businessman in the Texas oil patch, and had been national chairman of the Republican party.

While Bush's credentials were impressive, they gave little clue to his own deeply held views on foreign affairs. He had not been in positions where he had primary responsibility for making and articulating policy. Except for his long stint as vice president, during which he kept any views that differed from Reagan's closely guarded, he had not, in fact, held most of his jobs for long. During his unsuccessful bid for the presidency in 1980, he had presented himself as a moderately conservative Republican but had not spelled out his views on foreign policy. For a man of wide experience, he had left few traces.

Unlike Reagan, Bush was not a skilled communicator, at least not on television. He seemed to prefer informal meetings and off-the-cuff dealings with the press to set-piece speeches. Early on it became clear he would be a hands-on president when it came to foreign policy. He, after all, knew dozens of foreign leaders; he was reasonably conversant with most major foreign-policy issues; he had an appetite for dealing with the details and personalities involved in world affairs; he was inclined to pick up the telephone at a moment's notice and talk to leaders around the world.

Bush was clearly an internationalist who saw a continuing role for American leadership as the world entered the ambiguities of the post–cold war era. Initially his internationalism was tinged with a skeptical view of the Soviet Union and its leader, Mikhail Gorbachev. Bush's hard-line stance was rather surprising in light of Reagan's own mellowing toward Gorbachev in 1987–88.

One might have concluded from Bush's background that he would use the unique powers of the presidency to conduct a foreign policy that was active in pursuit of American interests, internationalist in tone, practical in execution, and essentially aimed at upholding the status quo. Nothing in Bush's past suggested that he had a radical vision for transforming international politics. He was, in fact, often criticized for not having "the vision thing." His aides described his style as "principled pragmatism." Others saw in Bush's views a familiar state-centered, balance-of-power approach to world affairs.[1]

With respect to the Middle East, Bush had left few hints during his career of how he felt about the Arab-Israeli conflict. It was commonly known that he had urged Reagan to take a tough line against the Israeli invasion of Lebanon in 1982. As vice president he had gone to Saudi Arabia in the mid-1980s to urge the Saudis not to let the price of oil drop too low. He was on good terms with the Saudi ambassador to Washington, Prince Bandar ibn Sultan. And it was rumored that he did not share Reagan's emotional attachment to Israel. But none of these observations added up to much with respect to policy toward the Arab-Israeli conflict.

As secretary of state, Bush selected a close friend and political ally, James A. Baker III, formerly Reagan's chief of staff and treasury secretary, as well as the manager of Bush's successful bid for the presidency in 1988. Baker, though he never ran for office himself, was a quintessential politician. His strengths were alleged to be found in "deal making." If politics was the art of the possible, then Baker was a supreme politician. And he would doubtless approach diplomacy in much the same way. His lack of experience in foreign affairs counted for little compared with the excellent rapport, sometimes tinged with friendly rivalry, that he had with the president.[2] Besides, he was a quick study. Bush and Baker seemed likely to form a team that might not include many other players. Both men prized secrecy and played their cards close to the vest.

Baker had a reputation among Republicans as a "moderate." Whether this label was deserved or not, Baker was clearly not cut from neoconservative cloth. Like Bush, he was likely to be problem-oriented, tactical in his approach, and suspicious of grand theory and strategy—a manager more than a conceptualizer. Rumor had it that Baker harbored ambitions of one day becoming president, which might mean he would seek to use his time as secretary of state to preside over a series of international successes, while avoiding anything that seemed destined for failure or aroused too much controversy.[3] Like the president, Baker had given few hints of his views on Arab-Israeli issues. An article on Baker, published in February 1989, portrayed him as a man of great self-control and manipulative skills. His favorite pastime, it seemed, was turkey shooting, which, in Baker's words, consists of "getting them where you want them, on your terms. Then *you* control the situation, not them. *You* have the options. Pull the trigger or don't. It doesn't matter once you've got them where you want them. The important thing is knowing that it's in your hands, that you can do whatever you determine is in your interest to do."[4]

Asked in an interview shortly before his confirmation as secretary of state what leverage the United States had in the Middle East, Baker replied:

> The U.S. is and can be the most influential player. But it is important that we not permit the perception to develop that we can deliver peace, that we can deliver Israeli concessions. If there is going to be lasting peace, it will be the result of direct negotiations between the parties, not something mandated or delivered by anybody from the outside, including the U.S. We must do whatever we can to enhance the prospect of the parties negotiating the problem out among themselves. It is not the role of the U.S. to pressure Israel. At the same time, it is in Israel's interest to resolve the issue. Both sides have got to find a way to give something.[5]

The other member of Bush's core foreign-policy team was Brent Scowcroft, his national security adviser. Having served in this same role for President Ford, and before that as deputy to Henry Kissinger, in addition to his career in the Air Force, Scowcroft brought to the job experience and common sense. He was not known for any particular views on the Middle East, but he was a thorough professional whose views were widely respected.

Most new administrations take their bearings in foreign policy from the experiences of their immediate predecessors. In the case of Bush and Baker, they had been members of an administration whose record on Arab-Israeli peacemaking was hardly distinguished. It had produced plans and initiatives but few concrete achievements. It was a fair guess that Baker, in particular, would avoid launching new substantive plans, preferring to explore procedural openings and biding his time until the parties to the conflict showed a willingness to move. Part of this cautious stance was a matter of tactics; part was no doubt politics; and part was due to competing priorities, especially in the rapidly changing arena of East-West relations.[6]

Working Assumptions

If Bush and Baker shared certain ways of looking at foreign policy, including the Middle East, they certainly did not seem to have a fully developed rationale for their low-key approach to Arab-Israeli peacemaking. That was provided by a small group of like-minded aides at the State Department and the National Security Council. Most important was Dennis Ross, head of Baker's policy planning staff, a specialist on U.S.-Soviet relations with a strong interest in the Middle East. Ross had worked at the Pentagon, at the NSC under Reagan, and had then joined the Bush campaign in 1988 as a foreign-policy adviser. During the summer of 1988, just before joining the campaign, he had played an important part in developing the logic of how a new administration should tackle the Arab-Israeli conflict.

As a member of the grandly labeled Presidential Study Group that produced an influential pamphlet entitled *Building for Peace*, Ross associated himself with an incrementalist approach to Arab-Israeli peacemaking. From this perspective the United States should be wary of substantive plans, international conferences, and highly visible initiatives. Instead the new administration should start from the realization that the Arab-Israeli conflict was not "ripe" for resolution. The differences between the parties were too great. A premature move to negotiations would doubtless fail. So, small steps to change the political environment should receive attention. The parties should be encouraged to engage in a prenegotiation phase of confidence-building measures. And the Soviets should be left on the sidelines until they had demonstrated by their actions a willingness and an ability to play a constructive role in peacemaking by putting pressure on the Arabs and reassuring the Israelis.[7]

Another important contributor to *Building for Peace* was Richard Haass, author of a book called *Conflicts Unending*, which promoted the thesis of "ripeness" as the key to negotiations.[8] Haass became the head of the Middle East office on the National Security Council staff. His views, if followed, would lead to a low-profile American approach to the region. In his analysis of the Arab-Israeli conflict, the United States could err by being too active in trying to promote a settlement. That, he argued, could make a difficult situation even worse. Until the parties to the conflict were ready to negotiate, the United States should concentrate on small steps to improve the environment.[9]

This "gardening" metaphor for Middle East policy seemed founded on a belief that previous bouts of American activism had been counterproductive. They had raised Arab expectations about American pressures on Israel, had caused the Israelis to adopt a defensive stance to ward off such pressures, and had made Washington the centerpiece of all diplomatic moves, instead of placing emphasis on the need for the parties to deal directly with one another. Like an attentive gardener, the United States might help the ripening process by watering the plants and weeding and fertilizing, but that was pretty much the proper extent of Washington's involvement until the fruit was ripe and ready to harvest.

Critics of the "ripening" approach thought the fruit might well rot before it ever got harvested. Time did not seem to matter to the gardeners. They appeared to believe that by concentrating on procedural issues first, the hard substantive issues could be dealt with more easily at a later date. Ripening seemed to be a natural process, not something that could be advanced or impeded by political action. But what if the parties to the conflict were not uniformly hostile to the idea of a settlement, had mixed feelings, or were evenly divided? In such circumstances, should the United States sit back and wait until things were clarified, or should it try to accelerate the ripening process by deliberate interventions of its own? These questions were all unanswerable in theory. Time would tell whether they received answers in practice.

Implicit in this approach was an anti-Carter, anti-Kissinger perspective. No comprehensive plans, no high-level shuttle diplomacy were warranted in this phase of the conflict. To many Israelis this was long-awaited music; for the Arabs, this approach led to intense suspicions.[10] It was not long before these initial assumptions were put to the test.[11]

On the surface the views articulated by Bush's Middle East team seemed to indicate strong support for Israel. But there was a catch. If and when the Palestinians or Syrians ever agreed to negotiate seriously with Israel, the United States might press Israel hard to reciprocate. At the outset of the administration, however, the assumption seemed to be that it was up to the Arab parties to move further. Prime Minister Yitzhak Shamir was viewed as a tough leader who could not be expected to make any concessions to the Arabs as a down payment for negotiations. Only if negotiations were under way was there a chance of moving Shamir off dead center.

No one in the Bush administration seemed sure whether Shamir's hardline policy toward the Arabs was primarily a tactical ploy or an accurate reflection of his deepest beliefs. On balance, the judgment seemed to be that Shamir could be moved, but only slowly and carefully. In any event, the administration's first initiative was built on the assumption that Shamir was interested in peace and could best be dealt with by pursuing ideas that bore his prior stamp of approval.

The paradox of the Bush presidency was that this initial agenda was probably more consonant with Israeli views than that of any previous president. And yet this same administration was soon widely viewed as the most hostile ever to Israel. The change, insofar as it was real, did not reflect a change of sentiment on the part of the top decisionmakers and their advisers.

The Team

All along, Bush, Baker, and Scowcroft were thought to be less emotionally involved with Israel than either Reagan or George Shultz had been. But no one in 1989 would have accused them of being anti-Israeli. And apart from Bush and Baker, the top echelons of the administration were filled with figures friendly to Israel, including the secretary of defense, Richard Cheney; the deputy secretary of state, Lawrence Eagleburger; and the entire Middle East team of Ross, Haass, Daniel Kurtzer, and Aaron Miller. Several members of the team could speak Hebrew quite well. But no one who knew them felt that their sympathies were with the Likud party or Shamir. Rather, the Labor party, and especially Yitzhak Rabin, the Israeli defense minister, seemed more to their liking.

During most of 1989, as the new administration was developing its approach to the Middle East, other international issues demanded much attention. Relations with the Soviet Union and Gorbachev were of particular importance, and only toward the end of 1989 were Baker and Soviet foreign minister Eduard Shevardnadze beginning to develop an especially close bond. Meanwhile relations with China quickly soured after the Tiananmen crackdown in June 1989. Shortly thereafter the amazing sequence of events that resulted in the collapse of all the communist regimes of eastern Europe began, culminating in the dramatic execution of the Romanian dictator Nicolai Ceauşescu in the last days of 1989. With so many significant international developments taking place in 1989, it was a wonder that the administration had time left over for the Arab-Israeli conflict. Not surprisingly, caution was the watchword of the new "confidence-building" approach to Middle East peacemaking.

Early in 1989 Shamir and Rabin were told that the Bush administration would be interested in hearing new ideas on how to revive the peace process. Rabin, in particular, saw this as an invitation to Israel to set the agenda for the next round of diplomacy. By the time Shamir arrived in Washington in early April for his first meeting with President Bush, the Israeli cabinet had adopted a four-point proposal. Its centerpiece was a call for elections in the West Bank and Gaza to select non-PLO Palestinians with whom Israel would then negotiate, according to the Camp David formula, an interim agreement on self-government.[12] Implicit in this approach was that no international conference on the Middle East would take place, a point on which Likud and Labor differed and on which the Bush administration seemed to side with Shamir, at least for the moment. Washington's initial response to these ideas was sympathetic.

On May 22, 1989, Baker spoke at the annual AIPAC convention in Washington, D.C. Baker's remarks were predictably friendly toward Israel at the outset, noting the shared commitment to democratic values and the strong strategic partnership. Baker welcomed the Shamir initiative as "an important and positive start down the road toward constructing workable negotiations." He endorsed the idea of a prenegotiations phase of talks. Only when Baker turned to the missing element in the Shamir plan, the fate of the occupied territories, did he hit a discordant note. Interpreting UN Resolution 242 as requiring the exchange of land for peace, Baker referred to "territorial withdrawal" as a probable outcome of negotiations. Then, in a pointed reference to Shamir's ideology, Baker said: "For Israel, now is the time to lay aside, once and for all, the unrealistic vision of a greater Israel. Israeli interests in the West Bank and Gaza—security and otherwise—can be accommodated in a settlement based on Resolution 242. Forswear annexation. Stop settlement activity. Allow schools to reopen. Reach out to the Palestinians as neighbors who deserve political rights." The fact that Baker immediately enunciated a comparable list of requirements for the Palestinians did nothing to warm the chilly atmosphere that descended over the pro-Israeli crowd, which only a few years earlier had heard George Shultz, from the same platform, lead the chant "Hell no, PLO."[13]

Baker's speech, besides raising Israeli worries, marked a subtle shift toward a more active effort by the Bush administration to redesign the Shamir initiative into something that might be acceptable to the Palestinians. Doing so without losing Israeli support would be difficult, to say the least. Over the next several months Baker became increasingly involved in Arab-Israeli diplomacy, probing through his diplomatic contacts for any opening.

As of mid-1989 the operational goal of American policy was to persuade the PLO to allow negotiations with Israel to begin with Palestinians who were not from within the ranks of the PLO leadership per se. The reason was simple: Shamir, it was believed, would never agree to negotiate with the PLO.[14] At the same time it would be difficult for Washington to convince the PLO to stay entirely on the sidelines. After all, the PLO's claim to be the "sole, legitimate representative of the Palestinian people" was part of the bedrock of its position. Still, by the summer of 1989 the PLO was showing signs of flexibility on this score. The PLO could stay in the shadows on two conditions: if it could select any Palestinian delegation, and if at least one delegation member was from outside the West Bank and Gaza. The PLO also felt strongly that Palestinians residing in East Jerusalem could not be excluded from the list of eligible representatives, a point on which the United States had previously expressed its agreement.

Just as the United States was trying to win PLO acceptance of Shamir's election proposal as a starting point, strains began to develop in the bilateral U.S.-PLO talks that were being conducted in Tunis. First, a leak to the press revealed that the American ambassador had been meeting with Salah Khalaf (Abu Iyad), a man associated in the minds of many Americans and Israelis with terrorism, but also one who had been instrumental in bringing about the shift of PLO policy toward greater pragmatism.[15] Shortly thereafter the Fatah Congress adopted a tough line. The Palestinians thought a U.S.-PLO meeting on August 14 had involved an American ultimatum that no Palestinians from outside the occupied territories could be included in a Palestinian delegation. That was not, in fact, a correct perception of American policy, but it contributed to a growing lack of mutual confidence.

As the U.S.-PLO dialogue faded during the summer, Egypt and Sweden stepped in to try to improve the prospects for getting the PLO to go along with Baker's approach. Because President Husni Mubarak could deal directly with the PLO leader, Yasir Arafat, officials in Washington soon found this was a more effective channel than the formal U.S.-PLO dialogue, from

which Arafat was excluded. Egypt thus became instrumental in crystalliz-
ing the PLO position. Mubarak, for example, spelled out, on behalf of the
PLO, ten points that should govern elections in the West Bank and Gaza.
Baker then responded, initially through diplomatic channels, to see if common ground could be found.[16]

By late in 1989 the Egyptians had indicated that Arafat had accepted
Baker's five points.[17] The most important of these points was the notion
that the Palestinians could bring to the negotiations any position related
to the peace process. The precise makeup of the list of Palestinian negotiators had not been settled, but a procedure had been agreed on that
would give Israel a virtual veto, although without calling it that. In short,
the United States and Egypt would produce a list of Palestinians, after
consultations with the PLO, that satisfied criteria laid down by the Israelis.
Israel, in turn, would not ask too many questions about the origin of the
list, provided the names were acceptable. No one knew for sure if Palestinians from East Jerusalem would be acceptable to Shamir, or whether
someone from outside the territories might be included. But Baker was
exploring all sorts of possibilities, including Palestinians with one resi-
dence in Jerusalem and one elsewhere; Palestinians who had recently
been deported by Israel, but had normally been residents of the West
Bank; and so on.

Israeli Reactions

Early in 1990 Baker seemed to feel he had Egyptian and Palestinian support for his basic approach. Now he turned up the heat on Shamir to
accept what Baker kept insisting was Shamir's own plan. To start the process, Baker suggested that he meet with the Israeli and Egyptian foreign
ministers in Cairo. The prime minister, by now, must have had his own
reservations about taking this first step onto the slippery slope, but he also
had ample domestic political reasons for balking. His right-wing allies,
for example, were planning to bolt the coalition if Shamir accepted the
American plan; Labor was threatening to withdraw from the national
unity government if he did not.

In the midst of this political acrimony the Americans became alarmed
at reports of large numbers of new immigrants from the Soviet Union
going to live in the occupied territories. Shamir had minimized the issue,
but in so doing he had made no mention of the large number of new
immigrants moving into neighborhoods of East Jerusalem. President Bush,
who felt strongly that settlements were an obstacle to peace, was fully

briefed, with maps, on the location of new settlers, and he apparently believed Shamir had deliberately lied to him.

Meanwhile a powerful Likud voice, that of Benjamin Begin, son of the redoubtable Menachem, came out publicly against the Baker plan. The Likud establishment then met and recommended that Shamir not accept the plan. Just after that recommendation, word came from Washington that Bush had spoken critically of Israeli settlements in the West Bank and East Jerusalem.[18] This was no slip of the tongue. American policy had long considered East Jerusalem to be part of the occupied territories,[19] but no previous president had singled out East Jerusalem for special comment when discussing settlements. The Israeli reaction was harsh. Shamir, who almost certainly had already decided to reject the Baker plan, now had a pretext for doing so, claiming that the United States had revealed its lack of objectivity as a potential mediator. With Shamir's blunt "no," the first phase of the Bush administration's peacemaking effort was put on hold.[20] For a few weeks Israeli internal politics was so uncertain that it seemed possible that Labor party leader Shimon Peres might be able to form a narrow coalition without Likud. Had that occurred, there would have been widespread satisfaction in the Bush administration. But try as he might, Peres could not lure the religious parties away from Shamir, and when the dust had settled in May 1990, Shamir was still prime minister, but this time at the head of a very right-wing cabinet from which Labor was excluded.

Challenges

While the Israelis were absorbed in their internal crisis, the Arab world seemed similarly disoriented. But there the proximate cause was the end of the cold war and the loss of Soviet patronage. Iraqi president Saddam Hussein chose the occasion of a meeting in Amman, Jordan, in late February 1990 to reflect on how the end of the cold war might lead to a Pax Americana-Hebraica in the Middle East.[21] For a leader who was receiving economic and political support from the United States, and who had been quietly assisted by Washington during much of his eight-year-long struggle against Iran, such comments might have been considered reckless. King Hussein, among others, thought the Iraqi leader was going too far in attacking Washington, but anti-American sentiment was on the rise in the Arab world, fueled, perhaps, by a sense of vulnerability in a one-superpower world, and reflecting as well the growing appeal of Islamic radicalism, with its anti-Western, anti-Israeli overtones. Whatever the cause of these sentiments, Saddam seemed to be gambling on finding a positive Arab response to his increasingly strident attacks on the United States and Israel.[22] With the peace process in limbo and anti-American sentiment being fanned from Baghdad, it was perhaps inevitable that the U.S.-PLO relationship would unravel. How it happened revealed the fragile underpinnings of the dialogue on both sides. First came an unusually bloody incident in Israel, where a deranged soldier shot and killed seven Palestinians at Rishon le Zion. Subsequent riots resulted in more Palestinian dead. The PLO, with strong international backing, launched an appeal in the United Nations to take some action to prevent further violence against Palestinians in the occupied territories. Arafat was keen to come to New York to address a session of the UN. Bush and Baker did not share his enthusiasm, and a compromise deal seems to have been worked out. A special session of the UN would be held in Geneva, Arafat would be allowed to make his appeal, and the United States would support a resolution calling on the secretary general to send an envoy to the territories.

Just as the vote was about to be held on the resolution in Geneva, a Palestinian commando unit landed on the beach outside Tel Aviv. The Israelis managed to intercept and neutralize the group, which consisted of members of Abul Abbas' Palestine Liberation Front (the same group that had been responsible for the *Achille Lauro* affair), before any civilians were hurt, but it clearly seemed to be an intended terrorist action, at least as defined by Israelis and Americans.[23] As such, this event seemed to constitute a breach of the PLO pledge to renounce terrorism. In Israel and in the United States a cry went out for the United States to break off the dialogue with the PLO.

Under considerable political pressure at home, Bush authorized his representative at the UN to veto the resolution on conditions in the occupied territories, a step that infuriated Arafat and many other Palestinians. But Bush was reluctant to take the next step of ending the dialogue. Instead he insisted that the PLO condemn the commando raid and discipline those responsible for it. In particular, the United States wanted action taken against Abul Abbas, who was still a member of the PLO executive committee, although his membership was apparently frozen, which meant that he did not participate in decisionmaking.

Arafat seemed to be in no mood to meet the American conditions. Instead he began to spend increasing amounts of time in Baghdad, and reports were even received that he was thinking of moving his political headquarters there from Tunis. In mid-June, Arafat's deputy, Abu Iyad, expressed his concern that Arafat was coming under Saddam's influence. The Abul Abbas raid, he maintained, had been an Iraqi operation. Its goal was to put an end to the PLO's policy of moderation and to its links with both Washington and Cairo. Saddam had something in mind, said Abu Iyad, something big. And he was maneuvering to get the PLO into his corner. This could only be bad, he thought, for the Palestinians. He was eager to find some way to prevent a break with Washington.[24] But it was too late. On June 20 Bush announced, more in sorrow than in anger, the suspension of the U.S.-PLO dialogue.[25] The summer of 1990 found American Middle East policy seemingly adrift. No one could see much future for the peace process, with an Israeli government bent on settling the occupied territories as rapidly as possible and a Palestinian movement drifting toward an alignment with an increasingly militant Iraq. And no one seemed to know what Saddam Hussein had in mind. He was making demands on the Gulf states for money and threatening Israel with chemical weapons if he was ever attacked, and by late July he began to move troops toward the Kuwaiti border to back up his demands for money. Within the region the prevailing interpretation was that Saddam was out to blackmail the Kuwaitis and Saudis by displaying his power. Egyptians, Jordanians, and leaders of the Gulf states all advised Washington not to provoke Saddam by overreacting to his bullying. Instead talks would be held in Saudi Arabia, a deal would be struck, and Saddam would back off. But he did not. On August 2 his troops poured into Kuwait, occupying the country in a matter of hours and then annexing it, thus changing for years to come the politics of the region.

The Gulf Crisis: America Goes to War

This is not the place to analyze Saddam Hussein's motives for invading Kuwait. Nor is George Bush's response the center of this study.[26] Suffice it to say that Saddam must have calculated that Bush would not react militarily. In reaching such a conclusion, he may well have hoped that the force of Arab opinion would run so strongly against Western intervention that no Arab regime would dare collude with Washington to force Iraq to back down. This was a misreading of the Saudis and Egyptians in particular, both of whom agreed to cooperate with a massive deployment of Western, mostly American, forces in the region. And it was a misreading of George Bush, who had been raised on the lessons of Munich and did not need much coaching to conclude that American interests would suffer if Saddam Hussein got away with his bid for power.

If Saddam controlled Iraqi and Kuwaiti oil supplies directly, and if he kept troops on the Saudi border, he would in fact dominate the Persian Gulf's vast reserves of oil and would become a one-man OPEC, able to manipulate supply to achieve whatever price he wanted. With his enormous oil revenues, he would also be able to accelerate his buildup of arms, including nuclear, chemical, and biological weapons. Before long the stage would be set for another war in the Middle East, this one involving Israel and Iraq, both possibly armed with nuclear weapons. Added to these tangible concerns were the matters of American leadership in the post–cold war world, of resistance to aggression, and of domestic political pressures on Bush to act.

While Bush methodically prepared for a war that America and its allies could not lose, Saddam tried to link his occupation of Kuwait to the Israeli occupation of Arab territories (and the Syrian occupation of Lebanon). Before asking Iraq to withdraw from territory that was rightfully Iraqi, Saddam implied, Israel and Syria should withdraw their forces. This stance was designed to win support from many in the Arab world who were inclined to see no particular difference among the three occupations and who held no special brief for the overly rich Kuwaitis in any case. Palestinians were particularly prone to grasp at Saddam's effort to link these issues, sensing the possibility that a powerful Arab savior, an echo of the great Nasser, might save them at a time when no one else seemed able to do so. Thus in Jordan and in the occupied territories, an outpouring of support for Saddam could be registered, if only briefly.

None of that support made much difference to Bush and his top aides in Washington. They were determined to oust Saddam from Kuwait, to destroy his war-making capability, to remove his weapons of mass destruction, and to do so with minimal American casualties, quickly, and under the guise of UN legitimacy. On January 16, 1991, the American-led coalition launched massive air strikes against Iraq. Almost immediately it was clear the Iraqi fighting force was doomed. Saddam tried to drag Israel into the war by firing SCUD missiles at Tel Aviv. If the Israelis came into the war, Saddam presumably believed, the Saudis, Egyptians, and Syrians would switch sides. But under considerable American pressure, Israel did not retaliate; the Arab allies in the coalition held firm; and Saddam's forces, faced with a ground offensive, beat a hasty retreat from Kuwait at the end of February. Throughout, the Soviet Union did nothing to protect the Iraqi regime. In fact, the Soviets voted in the UN with the United States, in a graphic display of post–cold war cooperation.

What would the American-led victory, Saddam's defeat, Israeli restraint, and Palestinian support for Saddam mean for the stagnant peace process?

Bush had refused to accept Saddam's effort to link the occupation of Kuwait with the Israeli occupation of the West Bank, but in a gesture toward the Arabs he had hinted on October 1, 1990, that when he had settled accounts with Saddam, he would turn his attention back toward Arab-Israeli peacemaking.[27] In March 1991 many wondered if Bush's comment had been more than idle rhetoric. Within weeks evidence began to accumulate that Bush and Baker saw an opportunity coming out of the Gulf crisis to relaunch the peace process. Indeed, Baker began to resemble a former secretary of state, Henry Kissinger, who had rushed to the region in the aftermath of another war, in 1973. Between March and October 1991 Baker made eight trips to the region, spending endless hours huddled with Syria's Hafiz al-Asad and Israel's Yitzhak Shamir. As Kissinger had done, he also touched base in Saudi Arabia and other Arab countries. But his most interesting innovation was that he began to talk with Palestinians from within the occupied territories who were known to have close ties to the PLO. Faisal Husseini and Hanan Ashrawi became his interlocutors of choice on the Palestinian side. It proved to be an important procedural shift, opening the way for Palestinian participation in the peace process despite some residual ill-feeling on both sides about the Gulf war.

Return of Diplomacy

During the war against Iraq the Middle East team at the State Department began to think the outcome of the war might create conditions in which Arab-Israeli peace negotiations would prove possible. The reasoning went as follows. The defeat of Iraq would convince even the most die-hard Arab militants that a military solution to the Arab-Israeli conflict was impossible. The fact that the Soviet Union had cooperated with the United States during the crisis would further demonstrate that the old cold war rules of the game were being rewritten, and that the United States, more than ever, occupied the key diplomatic position. Palestinians and Jordanians, who had allowed their emotions to draw them to Saddam's side, would now realize that they had lost support among Arab regimes and that time was working against their interests. Out of weakness, therefore, the Palestinians might be expected to respond positively to any serious diplomatic overture. Thus was born the idea of a peace conference in Madrid, Spain.

American officials also hoped that patterns of cooperation forged during the Gulf war might carry over into the postwar diplomacy. On the Arab side, this would mean that Egypt, Syria, and Saudi Arabia might be expected to work in tandem to support the peace process, something that had not happened since 1974. Indeed, one of the main debates within the Bush administration was over the role to be accorded Syria in the postwar era. In public many opinion leaders were warning of the danger of embracing Hafiz al-Asad, as if he were nothing more than a somewhat shrewder version of Saddam Hussein. Asad's past record on Arab-Israeli peace provided little comfort to those who thought he might be more flexible in this round. But the weight of consensus was that Asad should be put to the test. If he agreed to negotiate with Israel, the Palestinians would almost certainly follow suit. And if Israel saw the chance of talking directly with Syria, that might provide a positive incentive to join the process. By contrast, Shamir seemed to believe nothing good could come of talking just with the Palestinians.

Shamir remained something of an enigma to the Americans. On the one hand, he had surprised many by showing great self-control during the Iraqi SCUD attacks on Israel. At the American request, he sat tight, resisting the advice of some of his own military to strike back at Iraq. On the other hand, nothing in Shamir's personality gave reason to think that the issues on which the peace process had foundered a year earlier could now be easily swept away. Still, a judgment was made that objectively Israel was more secure than it had ever been. Furthermore, the fact that the United States had rushed Patriot missiles to help defend against the SCUDs, followed by infusions of aid to offset war-related losses, would presumably create conditions in which Shamir would be reluctant to say no to George Bush.

Finally, the Middle East team realized that the American-led victory in the Persian Gulf would inevitably enhance the leadership potential of President Bush, at least for the near term. Bush was enjoying unprecedented popularity at home. No one would seriously question his judgment in turning from the victory to Arab-Israeli peacemaking.

One lingering question remained. What national interest would the United States now serve by tackling the congealed Arab-Israeli conflict? In the Persian Gulf, Americans could be persuaded that the combination of oil and potential Iraqi nuclear capabilities justified the expenditure of lives and money to defeat Saddam. But why should the United States, especially in the post–cold war era, take another run at the impossibly complex dispute between Israel and its Arab neighbors? Was there really any chance of success? Was the stalemate so threatening to American interests? Only a few years earlier any answer to these questions would have noted the possibility of Soviet gains and of threats to oil supplies as reasons to tackle the Arab-Israeli conflict. But the Soviet threat was now gone, and oil supplies bore no obvious relationship to the course of the Arab-Israeli dispute, at least not in 1991.

If some old answers were no longer credible, others were. For example, it had long been assumed that the Egyptian-Israeli peace would be strengthened if the peace process could be revived. In the absence of further movement in the peace process, the cool relations between Egypt and Israel might collapse altogether, at great cost to the prospects for regional stability. That remained a valid concern. Another concern was that a prolonged stalemate in the Arab-Israeli arena would result in a radicalization of opinion both in Israel and among the Palestinians. In the worst of circumstances, the conflict would be defined increasingly in religious terms, Jews against Muslims, and destroy the prospects for any settlement.

Some within the administration were also worried about the effect of a prolonged stalemate on U.S.-Israeli relations. Would the American public continue to support large outlays of aid to Israel now that the "strategic asset" argument carried so little weight? What would the effect on American opinion be of more years of TV images of heavily armed Israelis shooting at Palestinian stone throwers? Without a peace settlement Israel would look more and more like a colonial state ruling over a restless people with its own national aspirations. No one believed Israel would offer the Palestinians equal rights within the Israeli political system, since that would radically dilute the Jewishness of the state. The only alternatives to a peace settlement with territorial withdrawal would then be prolonged second-class status for the Palestinians or their expulsion from the occupied territories. Neither option seemed compatible with strong U.S.-Israeli relations. Unless the two countries could again be seen as cooperating in pursuit of peace, some felt Israel ran the risk of a sudden loss of American public support.

The clinching argument for the Middle East team, however, seems to have been more related to the prospect of a future war in the region. Without a peace settlement, some feared, another war between Israel and some coalition of Arab states was still possible. The danger of such a war had been hinted at in the recent conflict with Iraq. Surface-to-surface missiles may not have been very effective in 1991, but who could be sure that accuracies would not be improved within the decade? And what about nonconventional weapons? This time Iraq had refrained from using its chemical weapons, and it did not yet possess nuclear weapons. But would the same apply to an Arab-Israeli war fought later in the decade? No one could be sure, but it seemed prudent to try to avoid another test of arms if at all possible.

With these arguments at hand, and with a legacy of past commitments in mind, the Bush administration moved quickly to explore the new terrain in the Arab-Israeli arena. From previous experience one could presume that there would be no grand design; that the emphasis would be on procedures for getting the parties to the negotiating table; and that big, new commitments of aid would not be part of the diplomacy. The main cost to the United States was likely to be the time and energy of the secretary of state and his top aides.

On March 6, 1991, Bush addressed a joint session of Congress, saying: "We must do all that we can to close the gap between Israel and the Arab states and between Israelis and Palestinians. . . . A comprehensive peace must be grounded in United Nations Security Council Resolutions 242 and 338 and the principle of territory for peace. This principle must be elaborated to provide for Israel's security and recognition, and at the same time for legitimate Palestinian political rights. Anything else would fail the twin tests of fairness and security. The time has come to put an end to Arab-Israeli conflict."[28]

Within days of the president's speech Baker was on his way to the Middle East for what proved to be the first of eight such trips in 1991. He stopped in Saudi Arabia, moved on to Israel, where he also met with Palestinians, and then went to Damascus. Shortly thereafter Mubarak and Asad issued a call for an international peace conference on the Arab-Israeli conflict, and Shamir responded by saying that Israel might agree to a regional conference under U.S.-Soviet sponsorship.

From this first round of talks it seemed as if an effort was under way to bring Syria into the process. The price for doing so would be some form of international conference. To win Israeli support, any such conference would have to be stripped of coercive authority, providing little more than a venue for the parties to negotiate directly. Israel would resist any UN role as well. Nor was Israel enthusiastic about European participation. All these latter points would be matters for endless hours of argumentation with Asad, but none seemed insoluble. Baker's strategy seemed to be to win Asad's agreement first, on the assumption that Israel would not then want to say no. In his talks with leaders in the region, Baker urged each one not to be responsible for the breakdown of the peace process. He made it clear that he was prepared, in his words, to leave the "dead cat on the doorstep" of the intransigent party if talks failed.

Baker made two more trips to the region in April, without visible results. In contrast to previous forays into Arab-Israeli diplomacy, however, this time Baker did not let his frustrations show, and he did not repeatedly threaten to drop the whole matter if the parties refused to cooperate. Both he and the president gave the impression of steady determination to get the answers they wanted.[29] During May 1991 a potentially difficult issue surfaced. The Israeli ambassador in Washington announced that Israel would be requesting $10 billion in American loan guarantees over the next five years to help with the absorption of new immigrants from the Soviet Union.[30] At a time when Israel was building new settlements at breakneck speed in the West Bank (and around Jerusalem), this demand raised a question in Washington of how to respond. The previous U.S.-Israeli agreement on $400 million in loan guarantees for housing had left a bitter aftertaste in Washington, since the Israelis immediately rejected the notion that these funds could not be spent beyond the green line in East Jerusalem.[31] Neither Bush nor Baker wanted to be in a position of subsidizing Israeli settlements, which they genuinely believed to be an obstacle to any future agreement between Israel and the Palestinians. Needless to say, in his many meetings with Palestinian leaders Baker was told that negotiations could not succeed unless Israeli settlements were stopped. Appearing before a House Foreign Affairs Subcommittee on May 22, Baker labeled Israeli settlement activity a major obstacle to peace. Bush echoed this view the following day.[32]

During the summer Baker tried to strengthen the architecture of prospective peace talks, avoiding substance but developing a structure that had substantive implications. On May 29 the administration launched a proposal on regional arms control. This, it seemed, was designed to appeal to the Israelis by drawing several Arab states, such as Saudi Arabia, into discussions on limiting arms in the region. But the most difficult issue for Baker was to work out an acceptable formula for Palestinian representation in the peace talks. No one had ever succeeded at this task. Shamir was adamant in his refusal to deal directly with the PLO, and even a veiled role for Arafat was more than he seemed willing to accept. By contrast, most Palestinians seemed to feel that only the PLO could validate the idea of negotiating with Israel, just as in 1988 only the PLO could have legitimized the idea that Israel had a right to exist as a state within a part of the former Palestine mandate.

Conceptually, a solution to this problem was not too hard to imagine, but it would require considerable political skill to find the right balance. The starting point in the quest seemed to be the point where Baker had left off in the spring of 1990. Then the PLO had already agreed that no one from the organization would be present in the negotiations with Israel. The idea had been explored that a list of names would be drawn up by the PLO but would be put forward by Egypt. Now, in 1991, the idea of the PLO's forwarding a list through Palestinians within the occupied territories gained favor. But who would be on the list? Shamir made his views clear. No one from East Jerusalem; no one from outside the occupied territories; and no one involved in terrorist actions.

A year earlier Baker had supported the Palestinians in their desire to have someone from Jerusalem and from outside the territories, but now he would not do so. The PLO had lost ground because of the Gulf war. Arafat's apparent support for Saddam Hussein on the eve of the Iraqi invasion of Kuwait left many Americans, and some Arabs, with a strong feeling that the PLO leader should be punished. For a while, at least, the Palestinians could not count on much support in Washington.

Baker was enough of a realist to know that the PLO could not be entirely excluded from the diplomacy. So he devised a formula for a joint Jordanian-Palestinian delegation, with all the Palestinians coming from the occupied territories. At the same time they would all be selected by the PLO, whose role would only barely be disguised.

On the American side, some felt that the decline of the PLO would be a desirable development in itself, not just because Shamir objected to its inclusion in the talks. The idea was widespread in Washington that the Palestinians inside the territories were more moderate, more realistic, than those on the outside. The latter, it was believed, would always feel the need to defend the rights of the exiled Palestinians, including their right to return to their original homes, an issue on which the Israelis were immovable. Although this view had some merit, it missed the point that the so-called moderates in the West Bank and Gaza had very little mass following. Insofar as they could claim to speak for the Palestinians, it was because they were seen as representing the PLO. The grass-roots leaders, by contrast, were often more radical than the PLO, sometimes on the left, sometimes as part of the growing Islamic movement. So to get the moderate Palestinians into the game, and to give them political cover, the PLO was still necessary.

Early in June Bush sent letters to Shamir, Asad, King Hussein, King Fahd of Saudi Arabia, and Mubarak spelling out his ideas for convening a peace conference in Madrid in the fall. The first positive reply came on July 14—from Damascus. Within days Baker was in Syria for talks with Asad, then on to Jordan, where King Hussein agreed to the conference idea. Hussein also publicly endorsed an idea that Mubarak had suggested: the Arabs would drop the secondary boycott of Israel once Israel agreed to stop settlements in the occupied territories.

Now Baker turned to trying to win Shamir's agreement. As an inducement Baker told Shamir that the United States would continue to honor
the terms of the letter sent by President Ford to Prime Minister Rabin on
September 1, 1975. That letter had promised to "give great weight to
Israel's position that any peace agreement with Syria must be predicated
on Israel remaining on the Golan Heights."[33] Some suspected that Baker
had probably made a commitment to Asad along the lines that the United
States did not recognize Israel's annexation of the Golan and felt that the
terms of UN Resolution 242 should be applied there. Both American promises were tenable, although one could foresee a possible contradiction somewhere down the road. But diplomats eager to make deals are often drawn
to such parallel assurances. The question is not why they are given; rather,
one wonders why they are so highly valued.

Lest anyone have any doubt about his views on substance, Shamir joined
the debate on July 24, 1991, stating: "I don't believe in territorial compromise. Our country is very tiny. The territory is connected to our entire
life—to our security, water, economy. I believe with my entire soul that we
are forever connected to this entire homeland. Peace and security go together. Security, territory and homeland are one entity."[34] In short, Shamir
would not go into negotiations with any prior commitment to withdrawal.
A few days later, on August 1, Shamir announced his conditional acceptance of the American proposal for a peace conference in October. All that
remained was to get a list of Palestinian negotiators with whom Israel
would agree to meet.

What could the Palestinians hope for from the negotiations if the PLO
was to be excluded and Shamir seemed unwilling to budge on withdrawal?
Perhaps the Americans could at least try to stop the Israeli settlements, or
at least refuse to subsidize them. Palestinian hopes may have been raised
earlier in the year when Bush had postponed the decision on the Israeli
request for a $10 billion loan guarantee. For the Palestinian establishment
this issue was a crucial indicator of whether Bush could be a credible
intermediary. If the United States was actively subsidizing new Israeli settlements, possibly on a massive scale, Palestinians would question whether
American-brokered negotiations could yield them any of their rights. By
contrast, if Bush could hold the line, perhaps he could be trusted.

During August an attempted coup against Gorbachev set the stage for
dramatic change in the Soviet Union. Whatever slight chance there might
have been for the Soviets to play an effective role as cochairman in the
peace talks came to an end. Gorbachev's own position was irretrievably
weakened, and the Soviet Union began to break apart. By year's end the

Communist party had been banned, Gorbachev was out of power, and each of the constituent parts of the former Soviet Union was on its way toward independence. Boris Yeltsin was the new ruler of Russia. For the Palestinians and Syrians these dramatic events were further reminders that they now stood on their own, with no major power behind them.

But Bush was gaining credibility in Arab eyes, just as the Soviets were dropping off the map. On September 6, 1991, Bush asked Congress for a 120-day delay before considering the Israeli loan request. After encountering congressional resistance, Bush went public on September 12. He spoke out forcefully against Israeli settlements and against the Israeli lobby. Within days polls showed that a large majority of the American public supported the president in his stand on the Israeli aid request.[35] By contrast, many American Jews were deeply offended by what they saw as Bush's questioning of their right to lobby on behalf of issues they believed in.

During the next few weeks Baker made additional trips to the Middle East. One could sense the beginning of the endgame. Letters of assurances were being demanded and offered.[36] Symbolic gestures, such as Bush's call for the repeal of the UN resolution on Zionism as a form of racism, were freely made.

Finally, on October 18 Baker was given a list of members of the prospective Palestinian negotiating team. On October 20 the Israeli cabinet voted to go to the conference. On October 22 Faisal Husseini announced the names of the Palestinian negotiating team, along with those, including himself, who would form an advisory group. One member of the Jordanian part of the joint team was a Palestinian from outside the territories with close family ties to Jerusalem. So the Palestinians could finally say that they had chosen a representative negotiating team, while the Israelis could say that they were not dealing with the PLO and had not recognized East Jerusalem as having the same status as the rest of the occupied territories.

The Madrid Conference

On October 30, under the joint chairmanship of Bush and Gorbachev, the Middle East peace conference opened in Madrid.[37] Israel, Syria, Lebanon, and a joint Jordanian-Palestinian delegation were all in attendance; so was a representative of the UN secretary general and a representative of the European Community, but far from center stage. Of greater symbolic importance was the presence of Prince Bandar ibn Sultan, the Saudi ambassador to Washington, dressed in traditional garb.

The formal speeches were unlikely to be long remembered, with the possible exception of the unusually eloquent Palestinian speech.[38] But no one could ignore the symbolic—and therefore political—importance of the parties' sitting together at the negotiating table. And for the first time in recent history, the Palestinians were present, speaking on their own behalf. To prove that the formal ceremonies were not the end of the road, all the parties were even persuaded to engage in a few days of face-to-face talks. The fact that no substantive progress had been made was hardly surprising. The important point was that a commitment to an ongoing negotiating process seemed to exist.

After the procedural breakthrough of getting all the parties to the negotiating table, what did Bush and Baker have in mind? They had not even hinted at any new substantive ideas, although by getting the Palestinians to the table as an almost independent party, the administration had done what no other had done before. And Bush had strongly implied that any increase in aid to Israel would be accompanied by some conditions to slow down the pace of settlements. Otherwise Washington seemed determined to play the part of convener, but not yet that of mediator. The parties would repeatedly be brought to the negotiating table—first in Washington in December 1991, then in January, in March, and again in April 1992, to be followed by more meetings in Rome. But despite appeals from the Arabs for more substantive American involvement, Bush and Baker held back.

The reason for their reticence was not hard to discern. The Americans had always been worried about raising Arab expectations that Israeli concessions would simply be delivered by Washington. This was not going to happen. The Arab parties would have to develop positions of their own and negotiate seriously before the United States would seek to bridge differences with proposals of its own.[39] In addition, on many of the points in dispute, the Americans had no strong views of how the issues should be resolved. What they wanted was a workable agreement. Whatever the parties could agree on would easily pass muster in Washington. At most, the administration had views of workable compromises, but it was not eager to tip its hand prematurely. So it envisaged a prolonged phase of bilateral negotiations.

Complementing the bilateral talks would be the multilateral meetings on arms control, economic development, water, refugees, and the environment. No one expected any immediate results from these talks, but some useful ideas might be explored at the expert level that would then be available to feed into the political talks at appropriate moments. In a gesture to the Russians the first round of the multilateral talks took place in Moscow on January 28, 1992. Syria did not attend, but that did not prevent some other Arab parties from participating. In the follow-on talks Israel chose not to participate in the meetings on refugees and economics because of the presence of Palestinians from outside the territories, but the meetings proceeded in any event. No party's absence from a single session, it seemed, could now torpedo the negotiating process.

If the Israelis had reason to feel gratified that the United States was not intervening in the substance of the negotiations, they had less reason for joy on the matter of the postponed loan guarantees. The 120-day deadline came and went without a decision. By mid-January 1992 congressional leaders were exploring possible compromises. In one version, Israel would receive the first year of loan guarantees, some $2 billion, but any funds spent on settlements in the occupied territories would be deducted from future amounts. A well-informed *New York Times* columnist wrote on January 17, 1992, that Shamir would be wrong to think Bush would settle for such a compromise. One way or another, Bush wanted Shamir to agree to stop settlements.[40] A few days later Shamir said there was no chance that Israel would agree to a freeze.

Domestic political realities were clearly beginning to play a role in both Washington and Jerusalem. Israeli elections were now scheduled for June 1992, as a result of the defection of small right-wing parties from Shamir's coalition. Shamir was unlikely to make concessions on settlements in the best of times, but certainly not on the eve of elections.

Normally one would expect an American president going into a reelection campaign to avoid a showdown with Congress and Israel. But foreign aid was unpopular. Bush would not lose many votes by saying no to Shamir. And it already seemed obvious that Bush would not win many votes from the American Jewish community, which increasingly saw both the president and Baker as hostile to Israel. Still, Bush did not want to alienate Israelis across the political spectrum. Instead he decided to attach conditions to the loan guarantees that he knew Shamir, but not all Israelis, would find difficult to accept. Apparently Bush hoped that Shamir's unwillingness to accept the American conditions would lead Israelis to debate the wisdom of pursuing an unrestrained policy of settling the territories. Many of the new immigrants, in particular, might blame Shamir for missing the opportunity to secure assistance that would benefit them.

Few who knew Bush and Baker believed they were indifferent to the outcome of the Israeli elections. Shamir had been a difficult leader for them to deal with. His policy on settlements and his refusal to countenance withdrawal were genuine concerns as the administration tried to foresee the future of the peace process. And Labor, after a hard-fought internal campaign, was united behind Yitzhak Rabin, a man who just might be regarded by Israelis as combining the right dose of realism and toughness to see them through the next phase of the negotiating process. To grant the loans to Shamir without conditions might well ensure Shamir's victory at the polls. That Bush and Baker did not want to do.[41] On February 24, 1992, shortly after Rabin's victory within the Labor party, Baker laid out the conditions for granting the $10 billion in loan guarantees.[42] Efforts by Congress to find a compromise were rejected by Bush on March 17. For the moment, the issue of loan guarantees seemed dead.[43] Until the Israeli and American elections were over, the negotiating process would probably be on hold as well.[44]

The Israeli Elections

Israelis went to the polls on June 23 and delivered a stunning defeat to the Likud party that had ruled, almost without interruption, since 1977. Only 25 percent of the electorate cast ballots for Likud, yielding thirty-two Knesset seats, down from forty in the 1988 elections. The defeat for Shamir was so great that he announced his intention to step down as party leader. Moshe Arens, sometimes thought to be the heir apparent, decided to retire from politics, criticizing Shamir's views on Greater Israel as he left.[45]

If Likud was the clear loser, Rabin and his Labor party were the winners. With nearly 35 percent of the popular vote, and forty-four Knesset seats, Rabin was in a position to forge a narrow coalition without any of the right-wing parties. Although he spent some time exploring the possibilities of creating a broad coalition, on July 13 he presented a cabinet to the Knesset that represented a coalition of Labor, the left-wing Meretz bloc, and the Shas religious party. Together these three parties held sixty-two seats, and the coalition could probably count on five Arab Knesset members as well in a future vote of confidence.

Rabin moved quickly to assert his authority. He kept the Defense portfolio for himself. As foreign minister he named Shimon Peres, his long-time rival. But he made it clear that he, not Peres, would oversee the peace process. As head of the Israeli team negotiating with the Syrians he named a respected Tel Aviv University academic specialist on Syria, Itamar Rabinovitch. No such change was made at the head of the Israeli team dealing with Jordan and the Palestinians.

Within days of Rabin's investiture Baker arrived in Israel to push for a resumption of peace negotiations and to prepare the way for a Rabin visit to the United States. Shortly thereafter, in a trip that symbolized the new era, Rabin traveled to Egypt for a cordial meeting with President Mubarak. Two days later Rabin announced that more than 6,000 housing units planned for the West Bank would be canceled, and subsidies on the remainder would be reduced. (Some 10,000 units well on the way to completion would be finished, so a "freeze" on settlement activity was still not in sight.)

Rabin also injected into his rhetoric a sense of urgency about finding a negotiated settlement, especially with the Palestinians. But before long he was also expressing optimism that progress could be made on the Syrian front as well.[46] Meanwhile Shamir confirmed the worst suspicions of many when he allegedly said that if he had been reelected, he would have strung out the negotiating process for at least another ten years.[47]

The changes in Israel were warmly welcomed by Bush and Baker. By playing the issue of the loan guarantees as they had, they had contributed in some degree to Shamir's defeat. Not surprisingly, then, Bush received Rabin on August 10 in Maine with a degree of warmth that had been noticeably missing from his encounters with Shamir. Although details remained to be worked out, Bush was able to tell Rabin that he would now support the loan guarantees to Israel. On October 5 both houses of Congress voted for a foreign aid appropriations bill that contained the $10 billion in loan guarantees, with Israel covering the reserve costs of some $400 million. The president retained the authority to deduct from these funds amounts that Israel might spend on settlements beyond completion of the 10,000 housing units already under way. On the whole, most Israelis had every reason to be very pleased with the outcome of this year-long struggle over aid.

Bush's Declining Fortunes

Throughout the early part of 1992 Bush had pressed ahead with his foreign-policy agenda, including the Middle East, as if 1992 were not an election year. After all, he faced no serious opposition for his party's nomination. His support in the polls in mid-1991, after the Gulf war victory, had been at all-time highs, and the Democratic field of candidates did not look very impressive. The cloud on the horizon was the weak state of the economy and signs of growing disenchantment with Bush's leadership.

During the primaries Bush faced a surprisingly sharp challenge from Patrick Buchanan, a conservative columnist who was able to win about one-third of the votes in the early Republican primaries. Unlike Bush, he was essentially an isolationist, a protectionist on trade issues, an opponent of foreign aid, and a sometime critic of Israel. The net effect of his challenge was probably to push Bush more to the right on domestic political issues—so-called family values.

On the Democratic side, it was clear by late spring that Governor Bill Clinton of Arkansas would be the candidate after the July party convention. Clinton had a fairly good record of governing a small, poor state, but his views on foreign policy were almost unknown. As the campaign gained momentum, Clinton launched some criticism at Bush for being too tough on Israel and for attaching conditions to the loan guarantees. But Rabin's election and the renewed warmth of U.S.-Israeli relations during the summer removed the loans as a major campaign issue. Indeed, most foreign-policy issues were ignored by both parties in favor of debates over domestic priorities or questions of character. Clinton spent more time attacking Bush's role in the Iran-Contra affair and his support of Saddam Hussein before the invasion of Kuwait than on any contemporary issue of foreign policy.

The Democratic Convention in New York proved to be surprisingly harmonious. Clinton chose as his running mate Senator Albert Gore Jr. of Tennessee. These young Democratic candidates presented themselves as the agents of change. Initial public opinion polls showed them with a commanding lead over President Bush.

Normally the Republican Convention, which nominated Bush easily, should have given the president a significant boost in the polls. But his campaign seemed disorganized and lacking focus. Rumors began to spread that the president would call on his friend and adviser James Baker to take charge. On August 13 the announcement was made that Baker would become chief of staff as of August 23. As he took his farewell from the State Department, Baker seemed to be speaking with a heavy heart. He had clearly relished the role of statesman and was unhappy about leaving the Arab-Israeli peace process, in particular, at a sensitive moment.

The sixth round of peace talks convened in Washington the day after Baker and his entire top team left for the White House. Middle East policy would now be technically in the hands of Acting Secretary Lawrence Eagleburger, assisted by Assistant Secretary Edward Djerejian. Few expected much of a push from the American side as negotiations resumed on August 24.[48]

During most of September and October Bush was fully occupied with running for reelection. Despite his and Baker's absence from the negotiating process, some modest gains were made on the Syrian-Israeli front.

Asad spoke publicly of the need for a "peace of the brave," consciously echoing the words of former French president Charles de Gaulle.[49] Asad's foreign minister then spoke of "total peace for total withdrawal," which for the first time indicated that Syria might go beyond merely ending the state of belligerency with Israel. By the seventh round of negotiations, in late October, the Israelis had reciprocated by using the word "withdrawal" in a formal document referring to the Golan front. And Israel was working with a Syrian draft paper to try to develop a statement of joint principles to guide the negotiations. All this was fairly encouraging, but both Asad and Rabin seemed frustrated that the United States was not helping to close the deal. Also, the Palestinians, who were seeing no comparable progress in their own negotiations with Israel, were getting nervous about the possibility of Syria's concluding a separate peace.

Some observers believed the conditions in the fall of 1992 were such that a major commitment of time and energy by the Bush administration might have produced significant results. But precisely because of election-year imperatives, the United States was in no position to play the role of mediator, full partner, or deal maker that it had in the past.

Finally, on November 3, 1992, the long election campaign came to an end. Despite his foreign-policy achievements, his experience, and the doubts he had raised about his opponent's character, Bush was solidly defeated in his bid for reelection. The popular vote divided 43 percent for Clinton, 38 percent for Bush, and 19 percent for independent candidate Ross Perot, resulting in a one-sided victory for the Democratic candidate in the electoral college. Once again domestic politics intruded on the conduct of American policy in the Middle East, forcing a hiatus of several months before American leadership in the peace process might once again be expected.

Unfortunately, events in the Middle East rarely conform to the needs of the American electoral calendar. During the lame-duck period from the election on November 3, 1992, to January 20, 1993, when Bill Clinton was inaugurated as president, the tensions between Israelis and Palestinians mounted rapidly. During December alone, Palestinians killed more Israelis, and Israelis killed more Palestinians, than in much of the previous year. Rabin, under domestic pressures, struck back with an unprecedented decision to deport more than 400 suspected Islamic activists to Lebanon. In another unprecedented move, Lebanon, finally governed by a cabinet with considerable popular support, refused to allow the Palestinians into Lebanon. Thus, in difficult conditions, the Palestinians remained in a sort of no-man's-land in southern Lebanon.

Coming on the last days of the eighth round of peace talks in Washington, this action cast a pall over the negotiations. Palestinian spokesmen asserted that talks would not be resumed until the deportees were returned to their homes. Rabin refused to budge. Bush could do nothing, thus ensuring that the Clinton administration would inherit a stalled peace process in need of resuscitation rather than the ongoing, institutionalized one that had continued through most of 1992.

Conclusions

Bush and Baker had come to power with an interest in the Arab-Israeli conflict, but with a determination to avoid some of the mistakes of their predecessors. They would offer no big plans, no special negotiators, no heightened expectations. The administration would probe cautiously to see if the parties were ready to move. If not, it would hold back. It would wait for the conflict to ripen.

Events in the Middle East prove to be powerful teachers. Theories do not hold up well in the face of swiftly moving realities. So it is not surprising that the administration found itself drawn into an increasingly assertive role in late 1989 and early 1990, trying to break the impasse with a proposal for Israeli-Palestinian talks on holding elections in the West Bank and Gaza. This effort failed, and failure is also part of the learning process.

The Bush administration's greatest foreign-policy error, its misreading of Saddam Hussein before his invasion of Kuwait, also set the stage for one of its greatest triumphs—the mobilization of a broad international coalition to defeat Iraq and restore Kuwait's independence. This success, in turn, opened the way for a revived and improved effort to bring Arabs and Israelis to the peace table. Bush and Baker hit on an effective division of roles. Baker was the negotiator, the deal maker, the master of details. Bush held back, but he made the hard decisions on loan guarantees and lent his constant support to his secretary of state. With considerable effort, and at some cost to Bush's domestic position, the administration attained its initial goal. Despite his defeat in November 1992, Bush was successful in winning bipartisan support for his success in bringing Arabs and Israelis to the negotiating table.[50] Clinton promised to pursue the same policy.

Bush and Baker were widely credited with realizing that the end of the cold war and the defeat of Saddam Hussein created a new opportunity for Arab-Israeli peace diplomacy. Not everyone at the time thought a major American initiative was warranted or could succeed.[51] Baker's persistence in working out the procedures for the Madrid conference also won high marks, as did his tactical skills as a negotiator. When he left to become chief of staff in August 1992, many believed his absence would be felt. And, in fact, little further progress was made over the ensuing several months.

Bush and Baker were not as widely credited for their handling of the loan guarantee issue. Democrats tended to criticize Bush for one-sided pressure against Israel. Yet to link the provision of aid to a curtailment of settlement activity may well have been one of Bush's most important decisions. Without it, Shamir might well have been reelected, which would have cast serious doubt on the chances for the peace process. Bush's critics, most of whom were happy to see Shamir replaced by Rabin, did not seem to notice the contradiction in their own stance.

Where Bush and Baker may fairly be criticized was in their initial caution. Throughout much of 1989 they acted as if the Soviet Union still represented a serious competitor in the Middle East. They also took the comfortable path of trying to work with Shamir on structuring the peace negotiations, seeming to believe he could be cajoled toward more moderate positions. Given the short time available to any president to tackle foreign-policy issues, the loss of most of 1989 on misguided Arab-Israeli initiatives is regrettable. By the time Bush and Baker were back on track, they were already well into their third year, leaving little time to bring their efforts to fruition.

Ultimately, no president can conduct a successful foreign policy, least of all on complex matters such as Arab-Israeli negotiations, without a strong domestic base. By allowing his domestic support to fade from the historic highs of spring 1991 to the abysmal lows of late 1992, Bush ensured that he would not be able to provide the leadership necessary to move beyond the first phase of the Madrid peace talks. Fortunately, the foundations that he and Baker constructed were robust enough to survive the absence of strong American leadership, at least for a while. Because support for the negotiations was fairly strong—in the region, internationally, and in the United States—Clinton did not have to face the challenge of forging a new policy toward the Arab-Israeli conflict. Instead he could work with the structure left to him by Bush and Baker. His challenge would be to add substance to the process, to move toward concrete agreements, and to use time and circumstances to make major steps toward Arab-Israeli peace.

PART FIVE

THE CLINTON
PRESIDENCY

11 *Clinton*
the Facilitator

NO PRESIDENT EVER came to office with a more promising set of circumstances for promoting peace between Israel and its Arab neighbors than did Bill Clinton. Peace between Egypt and Israel was already well anchored, having endured the regional turmoil of the 1980s. Radical Arab nationalism, as represented by Iraqi leader Saddam Hussein, had been discredited. Israeli hard-liners had lost the 1992 election, returning the experienced pragmatist Yitzhak Rabin to power. True, Islamic militants were hostile to the notion of Arab-Israeli peace negotiations, but they still represented primarily an opposition current, and governmental authority in most Arab states was still in the hands of nationalists who, with varying degrees of enthusiasm, supported the so-called Madrid process of peacemaking.

While regional circumstances seemed hopeful, the new president was quite new to foreign policy. Like other governors who had become president—one thinks of Jimmy Carter and Ronald Reagan—Clinton had made his name tackling domestic issues, not foreign policy. Unlike Richard Nixon and George Bush, he had not had a long apprenticeship in Washington that included the intricacies of national security issues. The term of the governor of Arkansas is only two years, so to hold onto the office Clinton was required to run for reelection every other year. He had done so six times, losing only once. It was not much of an exaggeration to say that Clinton's political life had been a perpetual campaign since the late 1970s.[1] He was smart, telegenic, empathetic, and ambitious. Few in 1991 could imagine any Democrat beating the hugely popular George Bush. But Clinton saw an opening, and against great odds managed to win the 1992 election with about 40 percent of the popular vote in a three-way race that included the eccentric Ross Perot. How he would deal with foreign policy in general, and the Middle East in particular, was a mystery.

One foreign-policy adviser who met with Clinton during the transition told him that he could be the president who helped produce four Arab-Israeli peace agreements. Clinton's response was that he would like to do that, but that he did not yet know enough about the issues to be in a position to judge if that was really possible—an honest statement in the circumstances. More than for many presidents, Clinton's approach to the challenge of Arab-Israeli peacemaking would thus depend on his advisers and his own political calculus as he began to learn about the positions of the various parties. No one questioned that Clinton was a quick study and was quite capable of impressing even the most experienced foreign-policy experts. But no one could be sure whether he had a clear idea of where he wanted to go with foreign policy in the uncertain post–cold war era.

Clinton's vice president, Al Gore, had served in the Congress and was known to be quite pro-Israeli. What that might mean in the circumstances of 1993 was not at all clear. For secretary of state, Clinton turned to a veteran of the Carter administration—one of the few in his inner circle—Warren Christopher, former deputy secretary of state, respected lawyer, and probably best known for his role in negotiating the deal that resulted in the release of the American hostages held in Iran in 1980–81. Christopher's strengths lay in his experience and good sense; but his ability to play a leadership role in foreign policy was more uncertain, in part because of a rather diffident personal style.[2]

Clinton's choice for national security adviser was Anthony Lake, a professor with considerable experience in the world of foreign policymaking, but no particular background on the Middle East. Lake's deputy, Samuel "Sandy" Berger, was a skilled political operative who had known Clinton for years and was reputedly sympathetic to the dovish "Peace Now" movement in Israel.

What Middle East expertise there was at a senior level in the new administration came largely from four individuals, Dennis Ross, Martin Indyk, Samuel Lewis, and Edward Djerejian. Ross had served at the White House, the Pentagon, and the State Department during the Reagan and Bush presidencies. He had accompanied James Baker to the White House in August 1992 when Baker took over the Bush reelection campaign. Thus it was something of a surprise that Ross was asked to stay on by the new secretary of state as his special counselor for the Middle East. Ross had been slated to take over the very influential pro-Israeli think tank, the Washington Institute for Near East Policy (WINEP), whose former director, Indyk, had just been asked by Lake to run the Middle East office of the National Security Council. Both Indyk and Ross were well known in Washington, their views had been widely disseminated in WINEP's publications, and both were thought to be strong admirers of Rabin.[3]

Sam Lewis was named head of the policy planning staff at State. He had served for years as ambassador to Israel and knew the nuances of the Israeli political scene as few other Americans did. Christopher asked Edward Djerijian to stay on as assistant secretary for Near East affairs. He was a professional foreign service officer with particular experience in Syria, where he had served as ambassador. Both Lewis and Djerejian played important roles in Clinton's first year before moving on to other positions outside government.

One could expect that Clinton's advisers would support the Madrid approach to negotiations, with strong emphasis on letting Rabin set the pace, while providing him with full backing on security issues. When phrases were later heard to the effect that "the United States could not want peace more than the parties," that the American role was "to facilitate negotiations between the parties, not to impose its own views," and that the United States would try to help "reduce the risks for Israel" as it moved toward peace, many detected the words of Ross and Indyk. These two were, in many ways, the intellectual architects of policy, even if Clinton and Christopher made the final decisions.

Clinton's campaign for the presidency had revealed many of his strengths as well as some of his potential vulnerabilities. He was clearly articulate, masterful in using the media, at ease with people from all walks of life, and full of energy. Bush, by contrast, had seemed tired and bored. But Clinton had also been confronted with charges of adultery, draft evasion, and pot smoking, and his elaborate explanations of his behavior had done little to establish a reputation for straightforwardness. His critics had found weak spots, even though his personal vulnerabilities had not proved to be fatal. More than any president since Nixon, however, Clinton would have to deal with attacks on his basic integrity and character.

During the election campaign, Clinton had adopted a fairly standard position of supporting the Madrid peace talks on the Middle East, but criticized Bush and Baker for one-sided pressure on Israel. A specific point of criticism was the $10 billion loan guarantee program to which Bush had attached conditions. Clinton termed this unfair pressure on an ally, implying that he would not do such a thing in similar circumstances. Fortunately for Clinton, however, by the time he became president, Rabin was prime minister, and the loan guarantee program was already back on track. All that was needed, it seemed, was to get the parties back to the negotiating table following the hiatus caused by the American elections and by Rabin's decision to expel hundreds of activists belonging to Hamas, a radical Palestinian Islamist group, from Gaza to south Lebanon. This issue had to be resolved before negotiations could begin, but no one in official Washington seemed to think that there was much need for a fundamentally new strategy.

Each new president in recent memory has started his term with a review of the major foreign and domestic issues confronting the country. Frequently the incoming secretary of state makes the round of major world capitals, and then leaders wend their way to Washington for "face time" with the new president. Much familiar ground is covered, but these initial contacts are often important, helping top policymakers to decide where they want to place their bets, which leaders they think they can work with, and how to proceed. Clinton followed this well-worn pattern, sending Christopher to Europe and the Middle East almost immediately. One concrete result was an easing of the impasse over the expelled Hamas activists.

Competing with the Middle East for attention in early 1993 was the simmering crisis in Bosnia, which had grown out of the breakup of Yugoslavia. Some hoped that Europe would take the lead in dealing with the Bosnian crisis, but there was little reason to believe that Europeans could bring themselves to act in the absence of some American involvement. During the early months of the Clinton presidency, this issue commanded a great deal of attention, as did the question of how to deal with Russia now that the cold war was apparently over. Given the importance of these European security issues, it was not at all obvious that Arab-Israeli peace would figure high on Clinton's agenda. Christopher, however, did see an opportunity, and persuaded the new administration to devote time and resources to the Middle East. But the American role, in his opinion, was to help the parties to reach agreements, not to do the heavy lifting for them. That sounded reasonable, especially to a president who was on shaky ground in dealing with the highly charged issues of the Middle East.

One announced goal of Christopher's trip was to get the negotiating process back on track. In practice, this came to mean tending to several different strands of negotiations, each with a somewhat different logic and tempo. Most attention was paid to the Israeli-Palestinian track, which was technically part of the broader Israeli-Jordanian-Palestinian negotiation. Here the major problem was that the Palestinians who were actually talking to the Israelis were not given much authority by the Palestine Liberation Organization, which insisted that only it could act on behalf of the Palestinian people. In public, the Israelis were reluctant to deal directly with PLO chairman Yasir Arafat and his colleagues, although one could detect some softening in the position of the government of Prime Minister Yitzhak Rabin and Foreign Minister Shimon Peres. For example, early in 1993 the Knesset passed a bill ending legal sanctions against Israelis who might talk to PLO officials. The Meretz faction within Rabin's coalition was openly calling for talks with the PLO and recognition of the Palestinian right to self-determination. Unofficial contacts between Israelis and PLO-affiliated individuals were becoming commonplace in conferences and public meetings in Europe and elsewhere. Still, the Israeli-Palestinian talks in Washington in early 1993 seemed endlessly stalled over the issue of whether the PLO would be allowed out of the antechamber into the front parlor. Little substantive progress was made.

The other tracks of the Madrid negotiations involved Syria, Lebanon, and Jordan, as well as multilateral talks dealing with arms control, economic cooperation, security, the environment, and refugees. Experts met at regular intervals, and some reports of progress were heard, but no one expected that agreements could be reached in the multilaterals until the bilateral talks had overcome the central political obstacles in the way of peace. Still, a great deal of energy was being devoted to a wide range of peace-related activities, and one did not have to be a starry-eyed optimist to see merit in building these networks of expertise from Israel, Arab countries, Europe, Japan, and the United States.

The Syrian-Israeli track was never seen as similar to the Israeli-Palestinian one.[4] First, it was clear from the outset of the Clinton administration that Syrian president Hafiz al-Asad and Rabin would not delegate much authority to their negotiating teams. If headway were to be made, it would be through American mediation between these two powerful leaders. Christopher quickly established that he was prepared to be the go-between, turning to Clinton for support when necessary. Over his four years as secretary of state, Christopher made some twenty trips to the Middle East in pursuit of a breakthrough on the Israeli-Syrian front. Clinton also met with Asad and Rabin and was in frequent phone conversation with both. From time to time, the negotiating teams in Washington made some headway. But the big decisions were always reserved for Asad and Rabin.

Peace talks between Israel and Lebanon, it soon became obvious, could go nowhere until Israel and Syria were well on their way to peace. Asad

was simply not prepared to give up his Lebanese card until he had the concessions from Israel on the Golan Heights that he had long sought. Similarly, Jordan was not prepared to reach an agreement with Israel ahead of
the Palestinians, but here the issues were much less complex, and it was
clear that negotiations would not be particularly difficult once the political
conditions made Israeli-Jordanian peace a possibility. Most important, there
was no significant territorial issue separating the two parties, since Jordan
no longer had any claim of sovereignty to the West Bank or Jerusalem.[5]

With these realities in mind, American policy concentrated on promoting Israeli-Palestinian talks in Washington, with the fairly clear subtext of
trying to find a "respectable" Palestinian negotiating partner for Israel
other than the PLO. Assuming that Israel would not deal with the PLO,
Americans tried to encourage a non-PLO Palestinian alternative. Faisal
Husseini and Hanan Ashrawi were frequently contacted as part of an effort to build up the reputation of these supposedly independent Palestinian personalities.[6] Arafat, of course, saw the game for what it was and
made sure that they made no moves that he did not sanction. The result
was deadlock in the Washington negotiating channel by spring 1993.

Another reason for the impasse in the Israeli-Palestinian track was that
the two parties were approaching the negotiations from very different
angles. The Israelis were interested in a time-buying interim agreement
that might calm things down and allow a moderate West Bank Palestinian
leadership to emerge. This could all be done, they thought, within the
context of the five-year transitional arrangement envisaged at Camp David
in 1978. The so-called final-status issues, which were so potentially divisive in Israeli society, could be postponed until later. For the Palestinians,
by contrast, the important point was to gain recognition of the PLO as the
sole representative of the Palestinian people and to force the issue of statehood as the ultimate goal as soon as possible. In addition, to meet the
concerns of the West Bank and Gaza populations, the PLO needed to
demonstrate that it could end Israeli occupation and limit land confisca-
tion and building of new settlements.

Faced with these very different goals in the negotiations, the Americans
firmly sided with the Israelis, insisting that small practical steps needed to
be taken first (confidence-building measures), to be followed by agreement on a transitional period, and only later on the final-status issues that
were uppermost in the minds of Palestinians. Since the Palestinians were
the weak party, the ones with the most to gain, they would simply have to
go along with the Israeli-American approach. Or so it was thought in
Washington.[7]

The Israeli-Syrian track had a different logic altogether. Both sides understood that the basic trade-off would resemble that made on the Egyptian-Israeli front. Israel would ask for peace, normal relations, security, arrangements concerning water—and time. The Syrians would insist on recovering their sovereignty over the Golan Heights. Once these general principles were agreed upon, the details of trade-offs and phasing of an agreement could be negotiated. In short, the negotiators would focus initially on the end point of the process, then work backward.[8] By contrast, the Israeli-Palestinian talks would proceed without an explicit understanding of where they were headed.

By the spring of 1993, officials in Washington were beginning to worry about the lack of movement in the Israeli-Palestinian talks. Both sides seemed to be posturing, playing for the home audience, refraining from the serious give-and-take of negotiations. It was becoming clear that Arafat was not giving his team in Washington any room for maneuver. It was as if he were determined to show that no progress could be made until the Americans—and Israelis—agreed to deal directly with him. That is exactly what the Israelis were beginning to do, but in secret, and at one step removed from Arafat himself.

During the spring of 1993, Rabin and Peres had agreed to allow several Israelis to meet under Norwegian auspices with Palestinians who were clearly acting on Arafat's behalf.[9] What began as a semiofficial channel soon acquired official standing as aides to Peres and Rabin joined the discussions in the spring. Soon a framework agreement was largely negotiated, and during the summer the Norwegian foreign minister, Johann Holst, helped to persuade the parties to overcome their remaining obstacles and to agree on a declaration of mutual recognition. All of this was done in deep secrecy, although the Americans were kept informed of the general picture.

In the first days of August 1993, Rabin faced a decision of whether to proceed on the promising, but still secret, Palestinian front, or to try to conclude a framework agreement with Syria. He was convinced that he could not move on both fronts at once, an assumption that the Americans never seem to have questioned. Christopher went to Damascus on August 4 to try out Rabin's "hypothetical" offer to return Golan in exchange for peace and security. The Americans saw Asad's response as encouraging, and they were eager to continue on the Syrian-Israeli track. Rabin, however, felt otherwise. Asad had attached too many conditions for his taste.[10] The Israeli prime minister therefore abruptly decided to put the Syrian talks on hold and to move on the Palestinian front instead.

It was not until late August 1993, however, that Peres and Holst flew to California to inform a surprised Christopher that an actual agreement had been reached. This was the famous Oslo Accord, the first Arab-Israeli agreement since 1967 to be negotiated without significant involvement by the United States. Was this a sign that the American role was no longer needed, that direct talks between the parties could now be relied on to bring the peace process to a successful conclusion? Some thought the answer was yes, that Oslo proved the wisdom of the American strategy of holding back, of facilitating but not mediating. Others doubted that the road ahead would be so smooth. But skeptics and optimists alike flocked to the south lawn of the White House on September 13, 1993, to see Bill Clinton preside over the signing of the first Israeli-Palestinian peace agreement and to urge Arafat and Rabin to shake hands.

Clinton may not have done much to produce the Oslo Accord, but he was a gracious host and a marvelous impresario. The United States, he implied, would be ready and willing to lend its help for further steps on the way to Arab-Israeli peace, a peace that now seemed to some to be an inevitability.[11] Indeed, shortly after the White House ceremony, Clinton helped to mobilize international economic support of about $2 billion over several years for development in the West Bank and Gaza, including a $500 million contribution from the United States.

The Oslo Accord and Its Aftermath

Much of what the Israelis and Palestinians agreed to in the Oslo Accord was consistent with the Camp David approach of starting with a five-year transitional period and then moving on to discuss the final-status issues of borders, sovereignty, arms control, refugees, and Jerusalem.[12] This had the theoretical advantage of letting the parties defer debate on the truly difficult issues, while gaining experience in managing their new relationship by tackling practical administrative and security arrangements that would have to be mastered before a lasting peace could be forged.

Oslo also went beyond Camp David in several ways. First, it included Israeli recognition of the PLO as the legitimate representative of the Palestinian people. While Likud was in power, this had been inconceivable. Second, Oslo transferred to direct PLO control a small amount of territory, starting in Gaza and the town of Jericho. Thus at an early date the Palestinians had a territorial base in which they could begin to organize the future state that they dreamed of. True, the territory was entirely surrounded by Israelis, was minute in size, and was teeming with economically distressed Palestinians. It was a start, however. And if all went well, within a short period there would be additional Israeli withdrawals from Palestinian cities and towns, the economy would benefit from external assistance, Israeli settlement activity would be frozen, and before long negotiations on a final agreement would begin. Everyone knew that the remaining issues would be terribly difficult to resolve, but a taboo had been broken, successful negotiations had occurred, and optimists had reason to believe that history was on their side.[13]

Just as Carter had seemed a bit dismayed when Egyptian president Anwar Sadat had gone off on his own to Jerusalem in November 1977, Clinton did not seem sure of what his role should be after hosting Arafat and Rabin at the White House. A strong argument could be made that Oslo was their agreement and that it was now up to them to figure out how to make it work. The United States would try to help mobilize support in the international community, would contribute money to the new Palestinian authority, would resume its suspended relationship with the PLO, and might even offer to help with the next phase of negotiations. Many of the issues that now had to be decided were of a very technical nature, however. The United States had no comparative expertise on how Israel might best hand over authority in Gaza, on what size police force the PLO should be allowed to have, or on what the fate of nearby Israeli settlements should be. Even the territorial outline of Gaza and Jericho had to be determined, but this was hardly an issue on which the United States could be expected to have an opinion. At best, Clinton and Christopher might urge the parties not to give up when the going got difficult and perhaps suggest some compromises once the negotiators had already narrowed differences sufficiently. But Oslo, unlike Camp David, was not an American-designed agreement, and therefore the parties had less reason to turn to Washington when disputes arose. In any case, they had already shown an impressive capacity to deal with one another. American efforts could better be deployed on other fronts, such as the stalemated Syrian-Israeli track.[14]

Confidence that the Israelis and Palestinians could indeed push the negotiations forward was not misplaced. By early May 1994 agreement was reached, with only modest American help, on how Oslo should be implemented. This was the so-called Cairo Accord, the nomenclature reflecting Egypt's helpful role in this stage of peacemaking.[15] The practical significance of the Cairo agreement was that it started the clock ticking on the five-year transitional period. Final-status talks were to begin no later than May 1996, with May 1999 as the envisaged end of the transitional period.[16] In addition, the new agreement opened the way for Arafat's return to Gaza along with many of his PLO colleagues. Slowly but surely, the PLO would now have the chance to start building the institutions of the future state that it talked so much about. Israelis would begin to get used to having a mini-Palestinian entity as their next-door neighbor.

As the Cairo Accord went into effect, the negotiating strategies of the Israelis and Palestinians inevitably diverged, and both turned to the United States for support. Rabin wanted to slow things down, to allow his constituents to get used to the new realities, and to concentrate on the Syrian-Israeli track, which had considerable strategic importance. He was in no rush to make further withdrawals in the West Bank, especially faced with the risk that Palestinian opponents of peace might try to stage attacks against Israel from recently evacuated territory. Furthermore, Rabin knew that some Israelis would object to ceding any of what they believed to be "the Land of Israel," and he wanted to be sure of his domestic base before confronting that challenge. In any case, Rabin had a reputation for moving cautiously, and he certainly wanted to test Arafat before making further concessions.

Rabin had long been interested in the possibility of reaching an agreement with Asad, despite his disappointment with Asad's position in August 1993. Peres and his inner circle had really been the enthusiasts for a deal with the PLO, and Rabin had come along somewhat reluctantly. The Syrian front, however, was potentially of great strategic importance. Syria had a large standing army, tanks, missiles, and chemical weapons. No other immediate neighbor posed such a military threat to Israel.

Rabin was beginning to justify the peace process primarily in strategic terms. An agreement with Syria would clearly advance Israel's security. His argument went as follows: in the future, the threat to Israel was likely to come from Islamic radicalism and take the form of missiles and nuclear weapons. It was not likely that Israel's immediate neighbors would be as big a threat as Iran or Iraq. In order to face such distant threats—as Israel had found in 1991—it would be important to have regional allies, such as Egypt, Turkey, and Jordan, and perhaps even Syria. After all, in Israel's confrontation with Iraq a few years earlier, Syria had been a tacit ally. Peace with Syria would not only reduce the immediate threat from the north, but also could open the way for peace with Lebanon and better relations with other Arab countries in North Africa and the Persian Gulf as well. At least this was the argument that Rabin was making in support of his far-reaching strategy of negotiating a comprehensive peace with Israel's neighbors.

Rabin knew, and the Americans agreed, that Asad was a serious leader who could be dealt with. The Golan agreement of 1974 had been scrupulously respected for twenty years. Asad, however, was also cautious, tough, and quite parochial in his outlook. He would not be moved by appeals to history or to visions of a new Middle East. His position was clear: he insisted on the return of the Golan Heights in their entirety, a privileged position in Lebanon, and removal of Israeli settlements from Golan; in exchange he was reluctant to go much beyond the formal end of the state of war, which he would equate with peace. Rabin, in turn, would stick to his demand for far-reaching security arrangements, a guarantee that the headwaters of the Jordan would not be tampered with, a stretched-out timetable for implementation, and as many of the visible symbols of peace as possible, including some forms of public diplomacy to help persuade Israeli public opinion that peace with Syria was a possibility.[17]

Clinton met with Asad in Geneva on January 16, 1994. During a joint press conference, Asad was reluctant to go beyond his rhetoric of the "peace of the brave," but Clinton had stood next to him and spelled out that he understood Asad to mean a full peace with normal relations. Clinton had been criticized for putting words in Asad's mouth, but those who knew Asad did not doubt that he had made the decision in principle to work with the Americans to see if a deal on his terms could be found. In private, Clinton did get from Asad some movement on the timing of normalization of relations.[18] Rabin's immediate response to these developments had been wary, but not entirely negative. He had indicated that at some point he would hold a national referendum on returning the Golan Heights to Syria. The Syrians saw this as one more unacceptable condition, but for many Israelis it was a signal that withdrawal from Golan might indeed be a future possibility.

A Syrian-Israeli agreement based on the exchange of land for peace was familiar to American diplomats. In most ways, it would be similar to the deal forged in 1978–79 between Sadat and Israeli prime minister Menachem Begin. Since Asad and Rabin were not yet on speaking terms, American mediation seemed essential. One way or another, the U.S. role would be crucial in shaping the agreement in principle and probably in working out the details as well. Henry Kissinger and Baker had proved that it was possible to negotiate with Asad, but neither would claim that it would be easy. Nevertheless, Christopher was prepared to devote a great deal of time and energy over the next year to forging an agreement between these adversaries.

In August 1993 Rabin had made a crucial move that helped open the negotiations on the Syrian front by holding out the prospect of the return of Golan, no matter how carefully conditioned by other Israeli demands. After a delay of some months, Christopher was ready in the spring of 1994 to resume the talks with Asad and Rabin. From July 18 to 21, 1994, Christopher shuttled from Israel to Syria and succeeded in producing a clarification of the territorial issue, now known as "the June 4 issue," referring to the armistice demarcation line that had preceded the Six-Day War.[19] This was meant to satisfy the Syrian demand for full withdrawal. It left unclear how quickly Israeli troops would actually leave Golan, what the security arrangements would have to be, and the stages to peace that would go hand in hand with the Israeli pullback. But the Syrians recognized the importance of Rabin's message, and the pace of negotiations picked up.

Christopher made the trip to Damascus to see Asad again in August and in October. On October 27 Clinton, who had come to the Middle East to preside over the signing of the Jordan-Israel treaty the previous day, arrived in Damascus to see Asad. The meeting was not a success, as Clinton felt that Asad reneged on a promise to speak out publicly against terrorism. Nonetheless, one month later, Rabin was in Washington for further talks, and during Rabin's visit Clinton said that he would work to persuade Congress to support American peacekeeping troops on the Golan if this proved to be necessary to secure an Israeli-Syrian peace.[20] This was a strong indicator that the talks were concentrating on crucial issues of security. Within a few weeks, Christopher was back in Damascus, and by the end of December regular negotiations were taking place in Washington between Israeli and Syrian teams. From all appearances, an Israeli-Syrian deal was in the works, but the details were proving to be agonizingly difficult.

Israeli-Jordanian Peace

Immediately after the signing of the Oslo Accord, Israel and Jordan had initialed an outline agreement that was to serve as a framework for peace negotiations. Over the next several months, diplomats from the two sides met, sometimes with help from the Americans, to work out the text of a peace treaty. On October 26, 1994, the peace treaty was signed, with Clinton in attendance. Almost immediately, one could sense that the tone of the relationship between Israel and Jordan would be warmer than Israel was likely to encounter with any of its other neighbors. The reasons were twofold. First, King Hussein and Yitzhak Rabin had been meeting in secret for years and had developed a high degree of mutual esteem.[21] Second, once King Hussein had dropped Jordan's claim to the West Bank and Jerusalem, the territorial issues between Israel and Jordan became insignificant. To be sure, negotiators still needed to resolve a number of difficult issues, but the main problem had been to find a political setting in which King Hussein could sign a peace treaty with Israel without being accused by other Arabs of being a traitor. The fact that the PLO had already signed two agreements, that Asad was actively engaged in negotiations with Israel, and that Iraq's Saddam Hussein was still licking his wounds from the Gulf war of 1991 meant that few voices were heard in the Arab world in opposition to the new peace. To a large degree, the treaty confirmed what many already knew—a de facto state of peace between Israel and Jordan had long existed. Now, however, citizens of the two countries could easily travel back and forth, which led to a flood of Israeli tourists and some negative reaction among Jordanians who still felt bitter toward Israel. The king, it seemed clear, was ahead of his populace in his readiness to open a new page in relations with Israel.

Some saw in the Israeli-Jordanian peace a model of how to negotiate and resolve conflict.[22] The American role had been modest, the parties had dealt directly and straightforwardly with one another, they had made mutual concessions, and they had built on common interests. If there was something to be learned here of broader relevance, it would most likely not be for the Syrian or Palestinian fronts, where the issues remained much more tangled and the lack of trust was still palpable. Instead, the Lebanese front might follow a similar course. The fate of the 1983 agreement, which was abrogated within a year of being signed, had shown that a bilateral deal could not stand up to Syrian opposition, but if Syria were to make peace, then an Israeli-Lebanese treaty would not be far behind. As was true between Israel and Jordan, the absence of fundamental disagreements over legitimacy and territory would make the negotiation relatively easy.

Toward Oslo II

The Israeli and, by extension, the American negotiating strategy began to incorporate explicit political considerations during 1995. Both Rabin and Clinton would have to face the electorate again in 1996. It would be good politics to show that the peace process was alive and well. A serious effort would be made during 1995. But on which front, Palestinian or Syrian? If the negotiations were not moving quickly enough, might there not be a temptation to put things on hold until Rabin had renewed his mandate?

Israelis themselves were curiously divided over whether another move with the Palestinians or an agreement with Syria would be more welcome. Many in the Labor party were more inclined to negotiate with Arafat, since they genuinely believed that Israel needed to extricate itself from running the daily lives of Palestinians in the West Bank. Many of those who opposed further withdrawals in the West Bank were right-wing or religious supporters of Likud in any case. By contrast, the Golan was of strategic importance, and most of the settlers there were Labor supporters. In addition, Asad had still not shown any willingness to deal directly with Israel. Any number of attempts to arrange a direct meeting between Rabin and Asad had been brushed aside. What seemed clear was that Rabin wanted the peace process to continue, but was not eager to face his electorate having made major concessions on both the West Bank and Golan. As in August 1993, one or the other would get priority.

While American diplomats probably hoped to see progress on both fronts, they seemed to accept that there was greater urgency about reaching another agreement on further withdrawal in the West Bank. The Golan front, after all, was stable, which could not be said of the nascent Israeli-PLO relationship. Indeed, the lack of a sense of urgency concerning negotiations on the Golan front had always been a problem since 1974.

The next basket of issues that had to be addressed between Israel and the PLO was both territorial and political. Israel was prepared to withdraw from the major towns of the West Bank—Nablus, Hebron, Ramallah, Bethlehem, Jenin, and so forth—which would extend the authority of the PLO to most of the inhabitants of the West Bank, while not yet dealing with the sensitive issue of Israeli settlers, who now numbered some 150,000, not including those in East Jerusalem. Once the Israelis were out of the towns, elections could be held for a "Palestinian authority," which would help to provide Arafat with the legitimacy he would need to continue the negotiating process. Then Arafat would undertake to revoke the clauses in the PLO National Charter that called for Israel's destruction, a symbolically important step in the eyes of many Israelis. If all went well, Rabin would then be able to go into elections in mid-1996 with an impressive record of negotiating with the Palestinians behind him.

Rabin and the Americans saw an advantage in keeping both the Palestinian and Syrian tracks of negotiation alive for some time. After all, Asad might prove to be more conciliatory if he saw that movement was being made on the Palestinian front, and Arafat would not want to see Syria go first. No one, it was thought, would want to be last in line. During much of the first part of 1995, both Asad and Arafat were courted, and progress seemed to be made on both fronts.

In March, for example, Christopher met again with Asad, and shortly thereafter the press reported that Syria had agreed to establish some form of diplomatic relations with Israel before complete Israeli withdrawal from Golan.[23] In May American officials reported that Syria had dropped its demand that Israeli and Syrian areas of demilitarization on the Golan front should be of equal size. Soon thereafter, Israeli officials confirmed that Golan was seen as Syrian territory.[24] Neither party seemed ready to move quickly to agreement, however, and Washington did nothing to break the impasse.

Early in July, it seemed as if the Palestinian track was progressing rapidly. Peres and Arafat spoke of July 25 as a target date for signing an agreement. Then, on July 24, a suicide bomber detonated a bomb in Tel Aviv, killing five Israelis. Hamas, the radical Palestinian Islamist group, claimed credit for the attack. Israel responded by suspending negotiations and sealing its borders, a pattern that would be repeated in the future and a reminder that each step forward in peacemaking would be met with opposition.

Over the next several months, Israel and the PLO managed to work out the details of a complex agreement that came to be known as Oslo II. The territories of the West Bank and Gaza were divided into three zones. About 3 percent, including all of the major towns, would be under full Palestinian control. Another 24 percent, mostly surrounding the towns and including many villages, would be under Palestinian civilian control, but Israel would still have the upper hand on security matters; and finally, the majority of the territories, including all Israeli settlements, would remain under exclusive Israeli control. Israel would withdraw within three months except from Hebron, where the proximity of Israeli settlers posed special problems. Three further withdrawals of unspecified extent would take place during the next several years before the final-status agreement. Elections would be held in January 1996 for the Palestinian authority, a legislative body of sorts, and for a Palestinian president. The jurisdiction of the new Palestinian authority would not extend to East Jerusalem, but Palestinians living there would be able to vote, under a complex formula. Finally, Israel would release Palestinian prisoners. On September 28, 1995, Rabin and Arafat signed the agreement in Washington, with Clinton, Egyptian president Husni Mubarak, and King Hussein looking on.[25]

With this agreement, Rabin had set his course for reelection. There would be no further move on the Syrian front until after his reelection.

Asad, never in much of a rush, seemed to accept this tactic calmly. Israeli troops began to withdraw from West Bank towns in October. Then, toward the end of the month, Israeli agents killed a leader of Islamic Jihad, and a few days later a bomb exploded, wounding a number of Israelis. In this tense atmosphere, Rabin and Peres attended a rally for peace in Tel Aviv. The usually stiff Rabin even joined the crowd in singing a song for peace. As he left the stage and was about to get into his car, Yigal Amir, an Israeli religious extremist who opposed the peace process, shot Rabin in the back. The Israeli prime minister died minutes later, leaving the country in shock at this unexpected act of violence and the peace process without one of its most crucial players.

After Rabin

Rabin's successor, Shimon Peres, was as committed to peace as anyone in Israeli political life. He had served as prime minister in the mid-1980s and possessed a wealth of experience, but he had never led his party to an electoral victory. Still, in the atmosphere following Rabin's assassination, the right wing of the political spectrum was widely condemned for creating an atmosphere conducive to violence, and few doubted that Peres could be elected on his own. Meanwhile, the Israeli-Palestinian accord was to be carried out.

In order to prepare the way for the eventual final-status talks, scheduled to begin in May 1996, Peres designated one of his aides, Yossi Beilin, to meet with Arafat's deputy, Mahmoud Abbas (Abu Mazin). The two men met in secret and explored in broad outline the shape of an eventual agreement. These were not formal negotiations, and one should not exaggerate the significance of what they accomplished. Still, their talks went further than any others of an official nature in bridging some of the most difficult differences between the two sides. If peace had been achieved while Peres was prime minister and Arafat was head of the PLO, it would have resembled this.

According to Beilin's own summary, Israel would recognize a demilitarized Palestinian state with all the attributes of sovereignty. Israel would annex a portion of the West Bank along the 1967 lines that would thereby incorporate many settlements and the large majority of Israeli settlers (approximately 100,000 of the 140,000) under full Israeli sovereignty; these settlements would be as Israeli as Tel Aviv and Beersheba. The annexation would occur in the framework of an exchange of territories, in which Israel's narrow waist would be widened and the Palestinians would receive extra territory along the Gaza Strip. Israeli settlers not annexed to Israel would have the option of compensation or living in the Palestinian state, with special security arrangements for them. As for refugees, none would return to Israeli territory, but there would be no limitation on immigration to the Palestinian state.

Jerusalem was the toughest issue of all. There Beilin and Abu Mazin reached a tentative understanding as follows: Palestinians would recognize West Jerusalem as sovereign Israeli territory and Israel's capital; this would bring world recognition of West Jerusalem as Israel's capital. For Palestinians, the geographic area of "al-Quds" (Jerusalem in Arabic) is in fact much larger than the municipal boundaries of Israeli Jerusalem. Therefore, Israel would recognize a Palestinian capital in "al-Quds," which would actually be in an area like Abu Dis, currently a Jerusalem suburb. East Jerusalem would be designated by both parties as disputed territory, with the status quo remaining in place for the indefinite future; Israel would still operate there as de facto sovereign, but without being recognized as such. The Palestinians would have extraterritorial status over the Haram al-Sharif (the Temple Mount), which essentially mirrors the current situation, in which the Muslim authorities control the site. The city of Jerusalem itself would be divided into boroughs, with each borough (for example, Arab, ultra-orthodox Jewish Israeli, secular Israeli) enjoying significant autonomy under a "roof municipality." Arab residents within Israeli borders could be citizens of the Palestinian state.[26]

Transition

Peres had apparently been unaware of how much progress had been made in the Syrian-Israeli negotiations, and soon after he took over he tried to resume those talks.[27] During a trip to Washington in December, he publicly called on Asad to resume talks. A few days later, Christopher again met Asad in Damascus and was able to announce that Syrian and Israeli negotiators would meet by the end of the month in Washington. On December 27, Uri Savir, who had helped to negotiate the Oslo Accord, met at the Wye Plantation outside of Washington with the Syrian ambassador, Walid Muallam. These talks, in which the Americans were closely involved, wrestled with security issues and seemed to make some headway.

In January the Palestinians proceeded to hold elections, and Arafat and his Fatah supporters won handily in a carefully monitored and essentially honest election. Soon thereafter, the new Palestinian authority voted to remove those clauses of the Charter that challenged Israel's right to exist.

Everything seemed to be on track, except for the lingering threat from extremists. Peres, perhaps hoping to show he could be as tough as Rabin, ordered the assassination of Yahya Ayyash, a Hamas extremist also known as "the bombmaker."

In February and early March 1996, Hamas struck back, with devastating results. In Jerusalem and in Tel Aviv, suicide bombers set off their explosives on buses and in public places. When the bombs finally fell silent, more than fifty Israelis had been killed, some in the heart of Tel Aviv's Dizengoff Center. The effect on public opinion was dramatic, and Peres was unable to reassure ordinary Israelis, even when he ordered a massive attack into Lebanon in an attempt to strike at Israel's enemies. By mistake, his military ended up killing more than one hundred innocent Lebanese civilians huddling for protection in a UN camp. Many of Israel's Arab voters were appalled, and they showed their anger by refusing to vote for Peres when elections were held in May.

The events of February and March brought the Israeli-Syrian talks to a halt, and Israeli-Palestinian peace also seemed endangered. Peres, the candidate of peace, could no longer assume that he would win an easy victory against his Likud opponent, Benjamin Netanyahu, who presented himself as "Mr. Security." The 1996 elections would be the first ones held under new rules that allowed Israeli voters to choose the next prime minister in a direct head-to-head contest. When the votes were tallied on May 29, Netanyahu had won by less than one-half of one percent, and his Likud party actually won fewer seats in the Knesset than did Labor. Few observers doubted that the peace process would be put on hold for some time, perhaps indefinitely.

Could Clinton Have Done More?

The period 1992–96 is striking for the progress made—Oslo I and II, peace between Israel and Jordan, progress on the Syrian front—and the relatively modest part played by the United States in bringing the parties to agreement.[28] It was not that Clinton and Christopher and Ross were not involved. On the contrary, they talked and traveled and prodded and encouraged. They played the role they thought most appropriate, that of facilitator. They were prepared to support peace with aid, and they even hinted that American troops might go to Golan as part of a peacekeeping force. All of this was appreciated by the negotiating parties, and one finds little overt criticism of the American role during this period. The PLO always hoped for more from the United States, but could not really expect to compete with Israel for American support, so Arafat tried to build a good working relationship with Clinton in the expectation that the Americans would play their part in the final-status negotiations.

If Rabin had lived to see his strategy through, the Clinton approach of letting Israel set the pace for negotiations might have made sense. But time is often of the essence in the Middle East, and the United States did little to impart its own sense of urgency. On the Syrian front in particular, it was unable to close a deal that seemed ripe for the making. Precisely why this was the case is hard to determine, but one sees little sign of an American effort to persuade either Asad or Rabin to cast aside their normal caution and go for broke. Nothing happened in Clinton's first term comparable to the Kissinger shuttles, Camp David, or Baker's organization of the Madrid conference. No one can say that such tactics would have worked, but it is striking that they were not tried, given the historic role that the United States had played and the momentum that had developed in the peace talks in 1993.

At no time did Clinton allow himself to get out in front of Rabin, certainly not in public. Before Oslo, the Clinton administration made no contact with the PLO, fearing that doing so would undermine more moderate Palestinians. Rabin and Peres, of course, saw things for what they were and proceeded to deal with Arafat. Clinton was quick to follow suit after the signing of Oslo. Even then, however, Clinton adhered to the policy that the United States did not support the creation of a Palestinian state. If the parties themselves were to agree on such an outcome, then of course the United States would not object. But it was as if Clinton had no views of his own, or as if the United States had no independent national interest at stake in the peace process. Had Clinton spoken positively of a democratic Palestinian state as a possible outcome, it might well have strengthened Palestinian moderates, who still had little to show the people of the West Bank and Gaza, and it might have eased the transition to an Israeli acceptance of the outcome that Rabin and Peres privately acknowledged was inevitable.[29]

Clinton's unwillingness to take any steps that might be seen as undermining Rabin was perhaps understandable and was certainly consistent with the views of Ross and Indyk. It fit the domestic landscape of Washington politics, where Congress, now under the control of the Republicans, was poised to jump on Clinton at every turn for being insufficiently supportive of Israel.[30] Until February 1996, one had little concrete reason to think that Clinton and his team were on the wrong track. But what would they do with Netanyahu as prime minister? Could the Clinton team devise a strategy to keep the peace process alive with a hard-line Israeli prime minister? Would they continue to eschew pressure of any sort? Or would they see a strategic interest in preserving the gains of the past years and come up with some mix of incentives to persuade the new Israeli leadership that negotiation based on the "land for peace" formula was in Israel's national interest? Nothing in Clinton's first term gave any reason to expect a significant change of strategy, but the situation on the ground was soon to change in fundamental ways.

12 *Clinton's Finale: Distractions, Hesitation, and Frustration*

THE NEWS IN late May 1996 of Benjamin Netanyahu's election as prime minister of Israel must have been something of a shock to President Bill Clinton and his closest foreign policy advisers. They had forged close links with Yitzhak Rabin, and subsequently with Shimon Peres, and their policy for promoting Arab-Israeli peace rested solidly on the assumption that Israel would eventually relinquish most of the territories it had taken in 1967 once it could be assured of peace and security from its neighbors. Now, with a Likud-led government back in power, Clinton would have to figure out how to deal with an Israeli government that was skeptical about the Arabs, reluctant to cede territory under any conditions, and tough about being dictated to by the United States.

In theory Clinton, who had invested a great deal of time already in Arab-Israeli peacemaking but had thus far avoided controversy by limiting his role to that of facilitator, could continue along the same line in the hope that Netanyahu would turn out to be a pragmatist. Alternatively, he could back off from diplomatic initiatives in the Middle East for a while, forcing the parties to come to terms with the consequences of less American involvement. Perhaps in time they would invite the United States back in, giving Clinton added leverage. Or Clinton could decide that the United States had a deep interest in seeing the conflict brought to an end for reasons of its own and could try to pressure and cajole both sides—especially the more powerful Israelis—to make the concessions needed for peace. This latter strategy would clearly be costly in domestic political terms, and Clinton had to tend to his own reelection before even thinking of such a course.

Propping Up Oslo

Netanyahu had campaigned as "Mr. Security," claiming that the Oslo Accords were a danger to Israel, that Yasir Arafat was little more than a terrorist, and that Israel would make no further territorial concessions. Without some moderating of these views, Clinton would witness the unraveling of much of the progress that he had helped produce in the preceding several years. Therefore, the first item of business was to persuade the new Israeli government to stick to its commitments and to deal in a constructive manner with Arafat. For Clinton and his team, Arafat might well have an unsavory past, but he was the only leader on the Palestinian side who seemed capable of delivering on his promises. If not Arafat at the helm, some feared, it would be the more radical leaders of Hamas. More was at stake than Oslo; the ideological tenor of Arab and Muslim politics could shift in a dangerous direction if Israeli-Palestinian peace were placed in doubt. Further, the peace between Israel and Egypt and Israel and Jordan could be undermined by a prolonged stalemate in the Oslo process.

Early in July 1996, Clinton held his first meeting in the Oval Office with the new Israeli leader. At this point his goal seemed to be the seemingly modest one of keeping the negotiating process on track. Clinton was on fairly strong ground. Netanyahu might disagree with Oslo, but he could not really afford to renounce it. More likely, he would prove to be a stickler concerning Palestinian obligations under Oslo, making any further Israeli withdrawals dependent on Arafat's scrupulous compliance with the security provisions. Indeed, Netanyahu spoke of "security" and "reciprocity" as the central ingredients of Oslo, spelling out a list of Palestinian violations that would have to be remedied before he would resume contacts with the Palestine Liberation Organization.

Clinton and his team realized that Netanyahu placed considerable value on Israel's relations with Egypt and Jordan, however much he might object to their support for Arafat. Thus both President Husni Mubarak and King Hussein were encouraged to deal directly with Netanyahu, to treat him respectfully, to give him the benefit of the doubt, and thereby to help persuade him to soften his opposition to the Oslo Accords. King Hussein was willing and went so far as to invite the new Israeli prime minister to Amman, much to the chagrin of the vocal Jordanian opposition. Mubarak had a harder time concealing his distaste for the new Israeli leader.

It soon became clear that one specific part of the Oslo Accords was going to be difficult to carry out. Rabin and Peres had already agreed that Israeli forces would withdraw from most of the city of Hebron, but Peres had postponed the implementation of that written agreement in the weeks preceding the election in May. Now Netanyahu made clear that he would not carry out the Hebron agreement as signed; it would have to be renegotiated. Arafat objected, claiming that renegotiating would set a terrible precedent. A deadlock ensued, lasting nearly a month.

Finally, in early October, with considerable encouragement from the United States, Netanyahu and Arafat met face to face. Shortly thereafter, Clinton and Netanyahu met again, ostensibly to talk about how best to resume the Syrian-Israeli talks, but also to get Oslo back on track. A few days later, Israel and the Palestinian Authority opened negotiations on a revised approach to Israel's withdrawal from Hebron.

In a pattern that soon became familiar, Netanyahu offset his nod in the direction of the PLO, which had exposed him to some criticism within his own party, with an action that seemed designed to appeal to his hard-line supporters. For years an issue had simmered of whether Israel should open an ancient tunnel that ran alongside the Temple Mount (Haram al-Sharif) area. If opened, the tunnel would allow people to go directly from the Western Wall to one of the entrances to the Dome of the Rock Mosque in the Muslim Quarter of Jerusalem. Like so much else in Jerusalem, religious sensitivities were involved, and previous Israeli governments had simply decided not to risk inflaming Muslim opinion, whatever the legal rights of the matter might be. Netanyahu, however, decided to act unilaterally, without much previous warning to his own security forces, to say nothing of the Palestinians. Demonstrations ensued in the next few days, and for the first time the Palestinian police joined the fray. Israeli troops firing on Palestinian demonstrators were met not just with rocks, but also with automatic weapons fire. There were casualties on both sides. Netanyahu was outraged, claiming that the Palestinian Authority, which was responsible for maintaining security, had shown its true colors in the crisis. The Palestinians, needless to say, blamed Netanyahu for the provocative act of opening the tunnel.

Clinton was sufficiently worried by the outburst of violence that he invited Arafat and Netanyahu, along with King Hussein, to Washington; Mubarak was unable or unwilling to participate. Always a believer in the virtue of talk, Clinton brought the two antagonists together in the White House, hosted a lunch for them and King Hussein, and then left them alone—as if all they needed was time together to patch up their quarrel.

This was vintage Clinton—always the facilitator, but hesitant to get involved in substance. The result of this peculiar summit was a decision to resume talks on Hebron.

Clinton's Reelection

Whatever Clinton's shortcomings as a foreign policy strategist, no one could say that the president was not a masterful campaigner. Compared to his opponent, Republican Bob Dole, he came across as energetic, personable, and optimistic about the future. The fact that the economy was doing well also worked to his great advantage. Dole's effort to seem more pro-Israeli than Clinton was to no avail. Jewish voters overwhelmingly supported the president, who was introduced at campaign rallies as the best friend Israel had ever had. With so much in his favor, Clinton was assured of a sizable victory when voters finally went to the polls in November. For the first time since 1964, an incumbent Democrat had been reelected—quite an accomplishment for Clinton in his last-ever campaign. Now, no longer facing the prospect of yet another election, what would he do with his final term?

Clinton's personal victory at the polls did not lead to a Democratic victory in Congress. There the Republicans stayed in control of both houses, placing a serious constraint on the president in both domestic and foreign affairs. Heading up the Senate Foreign Relations committee was the formidable Jesse Helms, a strong critic of the United Nations, foreign aid, multilateralism, the State Department, and—in his current incarnation, though not always in the past—an ardent fan of Israel. Chairing the House Committee on International Relations was Ben Gilman, also a stalwart supporter of the Jewish state. Nevertheless, a popular president, with a strong reputation as a friend of Israel, could afford to take a few risks of disagreeing with Netanyahu, provided that he remained attentive to Israeli security needs and wrapped himself in the mantle of Oslo and the peace process.

The Hebron Agreement

Warren Christopher's swan song as secretary of state consisted of bringing the negotiation on Israeli redeployment from Hebron to a successful conclusion. It was almost as if he wanted to clear the agenda before the new term began.

After months of difficult negotiations, Israel and the PLO finally initialed the Hebron agreement on January 15, 1997.[1] Soon thereafter it was ratified by the Israeli Knesset and the Palestinian Legislative Council, in each case by large majorities. Since this was the first agreement ever reached between a Likud-led Israeli government and the PLO, it was seen by many as a watershed, and the Clinton administration was quick to take its share of credit. Optimists also claimed that the agreement proved that Netanyahu would not cling to all of Judea and Samaria, as the right wing in his party insisted.

Before this agreement, Israel had withdrawn its troops from all the major cities and towns of the West Bank except Hebron under provisions of the Oslo II Accord. In this so-called Zone A—comprising about 3 percent of the territory of the West Bank and Gaza—the Palestinian police were fully responsible for security. No Israelis lived anywhere within Zone A. Hebron differed from the other West Bank cities because about four to five hundred Israeli Jewish settlers, mostly zealots associated with the right-wing Gush Emunim movement, had moved into houses within the city boundaries, close to the sensitive religious site of the Ibrahimi Mosque/ Tomb of the Patriarchs. Surrounded by Arabs, this tiny community required constant Israeli military protection. The Palestinians wanted the settlers to leave the city entirely; Labor had refused to evacuate the settlement and had worked out an arrangement that would allow the settlers to stay under Israeli military protection during the interim period. This would mean that Israel would withdraw from 80 percent of the city, while keeping control over 20 percent. This latter area held the Jewish settlers as well as some 30,000 Palestinians.

The Hebron agreement confirmed the basic elements of the Oslo II Accord concerning Hebron. In a few instances, however, the security arrangements were strengthened in Israel's favor, as Netanyahu had insisted. The agreement also included quite specific arrangements for security at various holy sites, the most important being the Ibrahimi Mosque/Tomb of the Patriarchs, where both Israelis and Palestinians worshiped in close proximity to one another.

One of the innovations in the Hebron agreement was the inclusion of a "Note for the Record" written by the American special Middle East coordinator, Dennis Ross. Apparently Netanyahu was reluctant to put his name directly to a document committing Israel to carry out further withdrawals, as called for in Oslo II, but he was prepared to let Ross write a note stating that Israel would remain committed to Oslo II "on the basis of reciprocity." This issue of reciprocity had been a major theme in Netanyahu's rhetoric, and he frequently said that Israel could not be expected to carry out its obligations under the Oslo Accords if the Palestinians were not in compliance on such matters as providing security and revising their National Charter. In fact, neither side was in full compliance with all of the details of the Oslo Accords: Israel had not released all prisoners, as promised, and the PLO had not formally made the final revisions of the National Charter. In theory, the reciprocity argument could be used to justify a suspension of the Oslo Accords by either side, but only Israel would stand to gain by doing so at this stage.

Ross specifically delineated Israel's responsibilities under Oslo II as follows:[2]

—Further redeployment of Israeli forces from parts of Zones B and C would begin during the first week of March 1997.

—Prisoner release issues would be dealt with according to the provisions of Oslo II.

—Negotiations would be resumed on a variety of outstanding issues, including safe passage from Gaza to the West Bank, an airport and a seaport for Gaza, and a basket of economic and security issues.

—The negotiations on final status, which technically began in March 1996 but were immediately suspended, would resume "within two months," in other words, sometime in March 1997.

Note that this statement of Israeli responsibilities said nothing about any subsequent Israeli withdrawals after Hebron. Nor did it specify the amount of territory in the rest of the West Bank from which Israel would withdraw. The Oslo II agreement, by contrast, had specified three stages of withdrawal at six-month intervals, with specific target dates for their completion. The amount of territory was not delineated there either, but a general understanding had been reached on this issue between Israeli and Palestinian negotiators. That common understanding no longer existed.

As part of the Hebron agreement package, Secretary of State Christopher wrote to each leader spelling out additional points. The text of his letter to Netanyahu was released.[3] The letter contained four American understandings, each of which must have been welcomed by Netanyahu. First, Christopher accepted the "reciprocity" language used by Netanyahu and stated that he had told Arafat that the Palestinians must be serious about making every effort to uphold order and security. Without that, the implementation of the interim agreement could be called into doubt. Second, Christopher stated as his belief that "all three phases of the further redeployments should be completed within twelve months from the implementation of the first phase of the further redeployments but not later than mid-1998." In other words, the United States expected Netanyahu to proceed with the three-stage withdrawal plan, but it was only stated as Christopher's "belief," not as a solemn commitment by Netanyahu.

More important, Christopher explicitly said to Netanyahu, "I have advised Chairman Arafat of U.S. views on Israel's process of redeploying its forces, designating specified military locations, and transferring additional powers and responsibilities to the Palestinian authority." In other words, Israel would decide on its own the extent and location of further withdrawals. These issues would not be subject to negotiation with the Palestinians. Christopher later publicly confirmed this interpretation.

Finally, Christopher used a phrase that was music to Israeli ears, saying at the end of the letter, "Israel is entitled to secure and defensible borders, which should be directly negotiated and agreed with its neighbors." The language of UN Resolution 242 called for "secure and recognized" borders. Israeli hawks preferred to speak of "secure and defensible" borders, and now the United States was using the same language.

While many praised Netanyahu for breaking with rigid Likud ideology by agreeing to withdraw from most of Hebron, it seemed likely that further withdrawals would not be as extensive as the Palestinians hoped, nor would they be as complete. It was widely reported in the Israeli press that Netanyahu intended to pull back from no more than 40–50 percent of the total territory of the West Bank, and that in any case these redeployments would not mean that Palestinians had full authority in the evacuated areas. Instead, Netanyahu seemed to have in mind some withdrawals from Zone C, turning these areas into Zone B for purposes of security. In other words, both Israelis and Palestinians would have security responsibilities in these areas. The total area under exclusive Palestinian control might not be much more than the urban areas of Zone A. This would mean that the Palestinian population would remain in enclaves surrounded by Israeli security forces, Palestinian islands in an Israeli sea. This was quite different from the image of a Palestinian sea with Israeli islands (the Israeli settlements under Israeli military protection) that the Labor party had seemingly held out as the likely outcome in the West Bank once the three phases of withdrawal were completed. As this image began to be understood as a real possibility, the word "Bantustans" was increasingly heard, a reference to the failed homelands policy in white-ruled South Africa.

New Faces

Presidents often start their second term by reshuffling their cabinet. Some key players have burned out; some have done poorly; some have lost the

president's confidence. Presidents need not explain. They have full authority to surround themselves with the advisers of their choice, subject only
to Senate confirmation in the case of cabinet officials and senior department heads (but not the National Security adviser or his staff). To no one's
surprise, the respected but bland Warren Christopher was replaced by the
fiercely competitive and articulate UN ambassador, Madeleine Albright.
Tony Lake left the post of National Security adviser, to be replaced by his
deputy and Clinton's old friend, Samuel "Sandy" Berger. At Defense, a
moderate Republican, William Cohen, was appointed. Most of the Middle
East team remained intact, although Martin Indyk eventually returned
from Israel to assume the position of assistant secretary of state for Near
Eastern affairs. Dennis Ross and Aaron Miller stayed on with responsibility for shepherding the negotiations. One possibly important newcomer at
State was the under secretary for political affairs, Thomas Pickering, who
had served as ambassador to both Jordan and Israel and had been at the
United Nations during the Gulf war. A talented and respected diplomat,
he could be expected to play some role on Arab-Israeli matters.

Albright was an interesting choice for secretary of state. The first woman
to hold this position, and a respected academic, she enjoyed considerable
bipartisan support at the outset. Her particular expertise was in European
affairs. A native of Czechoslovakia, she was multilingual, at ease in other
cultures, and an initial hit on the lecture circuit, where her predecessor
had been so disappointing. She seemed to want to make foreign affairs
interesting to the new generation of students who were coming of age in
the post–cold war era. All of a sudden, the State Department and foreign
policy seemed to have an outspoken defender. She even set out to charm
Senator Jesse Helms into opening the congressional purse a bit. Albright
had spent years in the Carter administration dealing with Congress, so she
could be expected to be well tuned to the mood on the Hill. Few secretaries of state came to the job with a stronger grounding in domestic American politics. Some worried that she looked at foreign policy too much
through a domestic lens, simply compounding an inclination of her boss,
but no one doubted that she would be a forceful presence.

Now in the limelight as never before, Albright was asked about her
background. A practicing Episcopalian who had been raised Catholic, she
was confronted with evidence that all of her grandparents were Jewish,
and three of them had died in the Holocaust. Strangely, she professed not
to know these details of her family history. Some Israelis wondered if she
was embarrassed by her origins; some Arabs wondered if this would mean
that she might tilt toward Israel. But in the end, her family history seemed

to have less bearing on her Middle East views than did her strong feel for domestic politics, her loyalty to Clinton, and her plausible hope to serve on as secretary of state in a future Gore administration. All of this was enough to ensure that she would not relish a fight with Netanyahu. Whether she would choose to engage at all on the peace process was an open question. Christopher had been mocked for traveling dozens of times to the Middle East with little to show for his efforts. Albright seemed eager to focus on other matters, leaving the peace process until it was "ripe" for her attention.

The Second Term

It has always been difficult to get a focus on what makes a president's second term different from his first term. There is the obvious point that he is no longer accountable to the electorate in the same way. Short of being impeached and convicted for "high crimes and misdemeanors," a president can expect to serve out his second four years even if he loses public and congressional support. In theory, this could mean that he would be free to pursue unpopular policies. For example, if he felt that taxes needed to be raised in order to expand social programs, reelection concerns would not prevent him from making such a proposal. Congress, of course, might still balk, and members of his party might plead for restraint, but the president could, in theory, do as he wished. In foreign policy, now would be the time for tackling unpopular issues. In the Middle East, Clinton might consider rebuilding ties with Iran and stepping up criticism of the Netanyahu government for undermining the Oslo process.

Presidents in their second terms are not really such free agents, however. If they are thinking of their place in history—and it is hard to imagine that a president does not care about how future generations will look at his record—they still need to govern effectively, which means working with Congress. This becomes particularly difficult if Congress is controlled by the opposition party. Then there is the so-called "lame duck" phenomenon. At some point in the second term, the political clout of a president is bound to fade as the public and the political establishment begin to focus on the next presidential contest. In foreign policy, this is likely to mean that foreign leaders will want to wait and see who the next president will be rather than make hard decisions under pressure from an outgoing president.

In the Middle East case, any attempt by Clinton at the very end of his term to exert heavy pressure on Israel would likely be ineffectual. In practical terms, the realities of the second term meant that the first two years were likely to see the president at the peak of his powers. By the spring of his last year, as presidential primary season got under way, his influence was likely to begin to fade.

A few weeks after his inauguration in January 1997, Clinton met with Netanyahu again to discuss further steps in the Oslo process. Hebron was now behind them, and Netanyahu was being criticized by some in his party for accepting the principle of giving up land. Clinton wanted to persuade the Israelis to go ahead with the envisaged further interim withdrawals. Here the problem was that Netanyahu was not committed to the principle, the schedule, or the extent of withdrawal that had been worked out by the preceding government. His insistence on reciprocity and security meant that any Palestinian lapse in living up to Oslo would become an excuse for not implementing further withdrawals.

Once again Netanyahu, when pressured by Washington, responded by appeasing his right wing. In this instance, the issue at stake was the building of 6,500 new housing units on land in East Jerusalem whose ownership was disputed. The Israeli government referred to the area as Har Homa and rejected the idea that it did not have the right to make unilateral decisions there. Arabs called the area Jabal Abu Ghunaym and claimed that it was mostly owned by Arabs.

In the tense atmosphere created by the prolonged stalemate in the peace process, the Israeli announcement of new housing in East Jerusalem set off a major reaction among Palestinians, in the Arab world, and internationally. In early March the UN Security Council met to consider a resolution critical of Israel. The United States cast a veto, even though it agreed that Netanyahu's decision had been provocative.

For several months in mid-1997, Israeli-Palestinian tensions remained high and no further progress was made in negotiations. The Israeli cabinet did come up with a proposal for another stage of withdrawal, but it was rejected by Palestinians as being insufficient. Finally, in early August 1997, Secretary Albright broke her silence on the Middle East and announced that the United States would become more deeply involved in pushing the parties toward agreement. In an effort to address Palestinian concerns, she spoke of accelerating the talks on interim steps; to respond to Netanyahu's approach, she spoke of moving quickly to the issues of a final settlement. She did not spell out American views on substance, but seemed to suggest an active mediating role for Washington.[4] In addition, the United States organized a tripartite group—Israelis, Palestinians, and Americans—to coordinate efforts to boost security. The American representative was from the Central Intelligence Agency and soon developed a reputation for professionalism in working with both parties. Albright's first trip to the region as secretary of state took place the following month, on September 10, 1997.

Shortly thereafter, Israel carried out a botched assassination attempt on a Hamas activist in Jordan, leading King Hussein to react strongly. He insisted, among other things, that Netanyahu release the jailed and ailing head of Hamas, Sheikh Ahmed Yassin. Yassin soon returned to Gaza, which boosted morale among the Palestinian opponents of Oslo.

As those critical of negotiations seemed to be gaining ground in both Israel and Palestine, Albright met again in November with Netanyahu and Arafat, this time in Europe. She floated the idea of one more Israeli withdrawal, instead of three, before the final agreement, and implied that the United States might put forward a plan of its own. Her irritation with the Israeli prime minister was noticeable.[5]

1998

A year that should have seen Clinton at the zenith of his influence started badly for him. As governor of Arkansas Clinton was frequently rumored to have had intimate relations with women other than his wife. During his first campaign for president, these rumors had nearly cost him the nomination, but, with the support of his wife, he had confronted the media and ridden out the mini-storm. In early 1998, however, a more serious charge was laid at his door. Reportedly, the president had been sexually involved with a young White House intern, Monica Lewinsky, since 1996. The issue had come to light during a lawsuit against the president for sexual harassment that had been filed by another woman, Paula Jones. As part of the judicial process, the president had been asked to make a deposition under oath in this case. There he was asked explicitly if he had had sexual relations with Monica Lewinsky. He denied it, and he repeated the denial emphatically in public. Ms. Lewinsky filed a false deposition denying the affair and soon thereafter was helped to find a job by a close associate of the president.

Suspicions that Clinton had lied lingered on, as did the rumor that he had tried to persuade Ms. Lewinsky to lie under oath (which she did) and to conceal evidence that would give credence to their affair. All this was tawdry and titillating to many, but it also raised the more important and nagging issue of Clinton's character and judgment. A special prosecutor, filled with anti-Clinton zeal, seemed determined to prove that Clinton was guilty of serious crimes. At the outset, few thought that impeachment might result, but a cloud was hanging over the presidency during much of the early part of 1998.

Despite the distractions of the "Monica affair," as it soon came to be known, Clinton and his team persisted in trying to bridge the gap between Arafat and Netanyahu. Meeting with Netanyahu in the Oval Office in January, Clinton spelled out the ideas that would go into an American plan. There would be concrete efforts to improve Palestinian performance on security and an American proposal on Israeli withdrawal. By March the details of the plan were reported: Israel would be expected to withdraw from an additional 13.1 percent of the West Bank and Gaza, including territory in both Zone C and Zone B.

Albright met the Israeli and Palestinian leaders in London in May to get their response to the American plan. Arafat, without many cards to play at this point, accepted the plan in its entirety. Netanyahu did not. Albright then set a deadline, saying that if Netanyahu did not accept, the United States would "reexamine its approach to the peace process."[6] This sounded like an ultimatum, although no one knew what would happen if Netanyahu simply sat tight. At a minimum, some thought, the United States would then go public with its proposal and would try to mobilize pressure on Netanyahu to accept it, even going over his head to the Israeli public to make the case that Israel was not being asked to make unreasonable concessions.

But the deadline came and went, with no consequences. Apparently Clinton, with urging from Berger and Vice President Al Gore, decided to avoid a confrontation and to rely instead on more quiet diplomacy.[7] As a result, much of the summer slipped by without any further movement on the peace front.

The same could not be said, however, of the president's personal and political situation. As evidence mounted that his denials of an affair with Ms. Lewinsky were untrue, on August 17, 1998, the president was subjected to detailed questioning by the special prosecutor and then went public with a brief statement acknowledging that he had misled the American public and had indeed had an "improper" relationship with Ms. Lewinsky. He struck out harshly at the special prosecutor and argued that his personal life was off limits to public scrutiny. In a lawyerly manner that had little credibility with the general public, he denied having earlier lied under oath when he said he had not had sexual relations with Lewinsky. Within weeks, the special prosecutor had sent to the House of Representatives a detailed report suggesting that the president had indeed committed perjury and obstruction of justice. In early October, the House Judiciary Committee voted to proceed with impeachment hearings. Over the next two months, the American public witnessed the somewhat surreal spectacle of congressional elections showing considerable support for the president's party and major involvement by Clinton in Middle East diplomacy, while at the same time the impeachment process moved ineluctably forward.

Wye River Summit

During September 1998 Albright and Clinton began to turn up the heat on Netanyahu and Arafat to break the nearly two-year-old negotiating deadlock. The basic trade-off seemed fairly straightforward. Arafat would have to make a major effort on security and perhaps once again reject the parts of the National Charter that challenged Israel's right to exist; and Netanyahu would have to agree to further withdrawals from Zones B and C, totaling at least another 13 percent of the West Bank and Gaza.

By mid-October, Clinton was ready to go for broke, resorting to the Carter model of summit diplomacy. Arafat and Netanyahu were invited to meet with the president over a period of days at the Wye River Plantation in eastern Maryland. The president and his colleagues would play a direct role, mediating where necessary, to try to bring the parties to agreement.

Clinton's political stock seemed surprisingly high as the Wye talks began. Public opinion polls showed that most Americans blamed Congress and the special prosecutor for making such a big thing out of Clinton's dalliances. Either the legal issues were too complex to understand or the evidence was too shaky to be convincing. Clinton also benefited from the booming American economy. With budget surpluses anticipated over the next several years, Congress was in a spending mood. The Federal Reserve cut interest rates just as the Wye talks began, and the stock market responded by going up 330 points. Perhaps Clinton's famous luck would hold. Somehow, his flaws seemed to make him human, vulnerable, and therefore worthy of sympathy and support, if not respect.

Unlike Carter at Camp David, Clinton did not remain at the negotiating site each day. On several occasions, he rushed off for fund-raising events on behalf of Democratic candidates. Finally, after days of stalemate and ill will in the talks, Clinton threw himself into the end game, "pulling an all-nighter," in the adolescent idiom of his staff, on October 22–23.[8] Late in the afternoon on October 23, Arafat and Netanyahu signed the Wye Agreement, in the presence of Clinton and King Hussein, who had come from his sick bed to try to help.[9]

The substance of the Wye Agreement was not particularly surprising. Palestinians committed themselves to further steps on security and revocation of parts of the National Charter; Israel undertook to make a series of gradual withdrawals as Palestinians carried out their side of the bargain. Israel also promised to release a number of prisoners. The whole process would take several months, after which the parties would begin final-status talks.

The Israelis did go ahead with an initial pullback, turning over a small area in the northern West Bank to Palestinian control. Netanyahu was reluctant to go further, however, claiming that the Palestinians first had to come into compliance on security. Quarrels over the release of prisoners erupted immediately. Wye was not off to a great start. Israeli internal politics added to the difficulty, as Netanyahu lost support in his own cabinet from the right wing.

Impeachment Comes—and Goes

Wye was just enough of a plus for Clinton on the domestic front to ensure that his popularity would remain high. As a result, the November elections were something of a setback for his Republican adversaries. In the House, the Republicans actually lost five seats, unusual in an off-year election. While retaining a majority in the House and in the Senate, where there was no net change, the Republicans could not claim a clear popular mandate as they forged ahead with the impeachment process. Among the biggest surprises after the election was the announcement by Newt Gingrich that he would step down as Speaker of the House.

As part of the Wye negotiations, Clinton had promised Arafat that he would visit Gaza at the time the Palestine National Council revoked the Charter. Symbolically, this was of considerable interest. The most pro-Israeli of presidents would also be the first president to make an official visit to Palestinian-controlled territory.[10] For Arafat, this strengthening of relations with Israel's closest supporter was a major achievement, provided that he could show results in future negotiations. Indeed, the improvement in U.S.-Palestinian ties was perhaps the most enduring legacy of the Wye negotiations, helped immeasurably by Netanyahu's poor chemistry with the American president.

From December 13 to 15, 1998, Clinton visited Israel and Gaza, trying to keep some momentum behind the now-stalled Wye Agreement. While Clinton was in the Middle East, the House Judiciary Committee voted four articles of impeachment to be considered by the full House. A few days later Clinton struck out at Iraq, where a dispute over weapons inspection had been simmering for some time. Foreign policy and domestic politics were inevitably intertwined as commentators speculated that Clinton's Middle East moves were attempts to distract attention from his embarrassing position at home.

On December 19, the House voted two articles of impeachment. Those articles were sent to the Senate, where the Senate convened as a trial court for the second time in its history to consider removing a president from office. As the trial began, Netanyahu, facing domestic problems of his own, suspended implementation of Wye and called new elections for mid-May 1999, conveniently just past the date of expiration of the Oslo Accord and the date by which Arafat had threatened to declare unilaterally a Palestinian state.

The new Congress began its work in January, and the Senate spent much of the next six weeks listening to arguments about Clinton's misdeeds and whether or not they rose to the level of "high crimes and misdemeanors," as specified in the Constitution. To convict and remove the president, a majority of two-thirds would be needed and that could not be attained without significant defections among Democrats. That did not happen. In fact, not a single Democrat voted to convict when the tally was taken on February 12. Humiliated by the prolonged public discussion of his personal life and questionable morals, Clinton nevertheless survived, with his popular support seemingly intact. Even so, time was running out for him as election-year political calculations began to make themselves felt. As much as he might like to redeem himself by accomplishing something on the foreign policy front, especially a Middle East peace agreement, little could be done until after Israeli elections, and even then much would depend on the outcome. If Netanyahu were reelected, progress would be difficult, at best. A more moderate Israeli prime minister would be easier to deal with, but Clinton's ability to push negotiations forward was bound to fade by early in the new millennium.

The Kosovo Crisis

As the Israeli election campaign got under way, another international crisis erupted that demanded much of the president's attention during the spring of 1999. Kosovo, an impoverished province of Yugoslavia comprising about 90 percent Albanians and 10 percent Serbs, had been drifting toward crisis for many months. As in Bosnia, the hard-line policies of Serb president Slobodan Milosevic made political compromise difficult. Many suspected that the Serb leader was planning a major campaign of ethnic cleansing against the Albanians in Kosovo. Defenders of the Serb

position placed the blame on an increasingly militant armed Kosovo liberation movement. Negotiations were begun in France, the result of which
was an ultimatum to Milosevic to accept conditions in Kosovo that would
have protected the Albanian majority and set the stage for possible self-
determination and independence. Milosevic rejected these terms, and in
retaliation the United States and its major NATO allies began to bomb
targets throughout Yugoslavia in late March 1999.[11]

Since most Albanians are Muslim, the Kosovo conflict aroused more
than usual interest in the Middle East. Most Arab countries sympathized
with the Kosovars, noting the similarities of their plight to that of the
Palestinians, especially as large numbers of refugees fled to neighboring
countries. A few Arab countries, especially Iraq, deplored the precedent of
NATO forces intervening in the internal affairs of a sovereign country.
Similarly, Israelis were somewhat torn, with the official line showing sympathy for the Kosovars, but some people also worrying about the precedent being set by the UN and NATO.

For the first two months of the air campaign against Serbia, there were
many voices raised in America in criticism of Clinton's policy. Henry
Kissinger, as was his wont, grumbled that there was no strategic thinking
behind the well-intentioned humanitarian impulse to help the Kosovars.[12]
As the evidence mounted that hundreds of thousands of Albanians were
being forced from their homes, it seemed as if the net effect of the NATO
intervention had been to make things worse. Images of bomb damage on
Serbian targets, including innocent civilians, began to raise the inevitable
questions of the morality of bombing civilian targets to achieve poorly
defined strategic goals.

The only part of the campaign that seemed to go well for Clinton was
the total lack of combat casualties on the part of the NATO allies. The
bombing was carried out day after day with no adverse consequences for
American forces. Still, many doubted that bombing alone could persuade
Milosevic to back down and withdraw his troops from what was, after
all, a province of his own country. Clinton hesitated to make the decision
on ground troops, turning instead to the Russians for diplomatic help.
And, amazingly, it worked. In early June an agreement was reached that
called for withdrawal of all Serb forces from Kosovo, the return of the
Albanian refugees to their homes, and the introduction of a multilateral
force, including Russians, to preserve the peace. How this would end politically in Kosovo remained an open question, but for Clinton it was another stroke of good luck. What had seemed to have the potential of a
foreign policy disaster—or at least a major distraction—was over, and the
president was free to turn his attention to other matters.

The Israeli Elections and the End of Oslo

While the Kosovo campaign was under way, two important events took place in the Israel-Palestine arena. The first was the formal end of the five-year interim period of the Oslo Accord. Arafat had made a big issue of declaring Palestinian statehood on May 4, 1999; Netanyahu had responded with threats to annex the Israeli-controlled areas of the West Bank if such a declaration were made. Considerable time and effort went into avoiding a clash over this looming crisis. The fear on the American side was that Netanyahu might turn such a confrontation with Arafat to political advantage, and with Israeli elections scheduled for May 17, no one in official Washington wanted to give Netanyahu a boost in the polls. So Clinton sent Arafat a letter promising that the United States would make a major push for a final-status agreement within a reasonable period of time, culminating in a Washington summit meeting.[13] In addition, Clinton repeated his support for "the aspirations of the Palestinian people to determine their own future on their own land," a formulation that seemed to move close to the Palestinian hope for a state of their own. In coordination with the United States, the Europeans went even further in their support for the Palestinians. With these gestures from the western powers in hand, Arafat withdrew his threat to declare statehood, at least until after Israeli elections.

The Israeli election pitted Benjamin Netanyahu against Ehud Barak, a much-decorated general, a protégé of Yitzhak Rabin, reputedly tough, pragmatic, and smart. For the second time, Israelis would cast two ballots, one for prime minister and one for a party list for the Knesset.

When votes were counted on May 17, 1999, the results were striking but difficult to interpret. Barak scored a remarkable victory over Netanyahu, winning some 56 percent of the total vote. Netanyahu was so disgraced that he announced that he would resign from his party and leave politics altogether—at least for a while. The Knesset vote, however, was much more ambiguous, as here the Israeli electorate voted its more narrowly defined interests. Neither of the two large parties managed to avoid losing seats. Indeed, the only significant gain was for the Shas party, representing primarily Orthodox Sephardic voters. Barak's first challenge before he could turn to diplomacy was to form a coalition government out of the motley array of secular and religious, left and right parties that would hold seats in the new Knesset.

Even before Barak managed to present his government for Knesset approbation, however, the response in official Washington to Barak's election was barely suppressed delight. U.S.-Israeli relations had soured during the last months of Netanyahu's tenure, and high expectations existed that

Barak would be a prime minister in the Rabin mold. Clinton had never disguised his admiration for Rabin, and he seemed eager to meet the new Israeli prime minister.

Barak set about putting his cabinet together in a methodical manner. He met with nearly all the parties, played his cards very close to his chest, hinted that he would include his Likud rivals, then switched signals and indicated that Shas would have a favored spot. All of this took time, and Barak seemed intent on demonstrating his mastery of the domestic political arena before tipping his hand on his final choices. It was not until early July that he finally put his coalition in place. It consisted of his own party, One Israel, the leftist Meretz party, Shas, the Center party, and several others. In all, Barak could count on more than seventy members of the Knesset on any issue, and even more when the ten members of Arab parties were taken into account. Combined with impressive support in public opinion polls, this degree of strength in the Knesset placed Barak in an enviable position to resume negotiations.

During June an interesting signal occurred in an exchange of mutual compliments between Syria's Hafiz al-Asad and Barak. In interviews with a well-known specialist on Syria, Patrick Seale, Asad termed Barak "honest and strong." Barak reciprocated in remarks to Seale that strongly suggested that he was eager to reach a deal with Asad, especially since he had committed to a withdrawal of Israeli troops from Lebanon within one year, and to achieve that goal he would need Syrian help, or so he seemed to think.[14]

Barak's inaugural address to the Knesset reinforced the view that peacemaking would be high on his agenda. He spoke movingly of a soldier's knowing war and seeking peace. He referred in respectful terms to his adversaries, even acknowledging that Israel had caused the Palestinian people to suffer.

Barak's first foreign meetings were with Egyptian president Husni Mubarak, followed by visits with Yasir Arafat and King Abdallah of Jordan. Then he set out for the United States to meet Clinton, who described himself as being as "eager as a kid with a new toy" as he looked forward to his talks with Barak.

Clinton and Barak met at the White House on July 15, then spent the night of July 16 at Camp David with their wives. A gala dinner was held at the White House on July 18, and the two men met again the following day. Out of all this time together, several themes emerged.

Barak seemed intent on securing a new type of American engagement, more strategic and less involved in details.[15] He publicly criticized the United States for becoming too involved in the minutiae of the Wye Agreement, acting sometimes as judge and arbitrator. He specifically singled out the role of the CIA in Gaza as inappropriate. More fundamentally, Barak seemed to be questioning the value of the incrementalist approach, which assumed that confidence could be built through a series of small steps. Oslo had been built on such a notion, and Barak, it was known, was not a great fan of Oslo. Instead, he seemed to want to know what the overall design of an agreement would be, to determine if the other side was ready to make the hard decisions, and then to seek agreement on basic principles first, leaving the details for later.

Clinton, eager to adapt to Barak's preferences, quickly restated that the United States sought only to be a facilitator, helping the parties to reach agreement, but not seeking to impose its views. Barak, however, obviously sought more from Clinton than America's good offices. He asked for, and received, promises of more military support.[16] He seemed particularly intent on getting the Americans to resume their dialogue with Asad to help determine if peace on the Syrian front could be concluded expeditiously.

Barak's election appeared to give Clinton a last chance to achieve a foreign-policy success before his time ran out. On the face of it, a Syrian-Israeli agreement did not seem beyond reach. Both parties had discussed the issues extensively in the 1993–96 period.[17] Barak had even participated in those talks as chief of staff. Rabin had made the essential concession when he offered to return the Golan to Syria, provided issues of security and peace could be resolved. Clinton, who had spent more time with Asad than had any other president, might well be able to help persuade the aging Syrian leader to move toward agreement at something other than his usual snail-like pace. The United States could also help by providing some form of security and monitoring presence on the Golan.[18]

The Israeli-Palestinian front was likely to be more complex. First, the issues themselves were difficult. Little in the known positions of the parties suggested that compromises could be forged easily on Jerusalem, borders, settlements, water, or refugee claims. The easier issues, security and Palestinian statehood, might be the subjects of early agreement in principle, but even there the sensitivities on both sides were considerable. The United States, which had historically taken positions on many of these sensitive matters, was now reluctant to reaffirm those stances, arguing that it was up to the parties to reach agreement through direct negotiations. But what would happen when the inevitable deadlocks were reached? Would the United States go beyond "facilitating"?

As Clinton approached his last year in office, he seemed to be torn by several competing impulses. There was the natural desire to leave a historical legacy of which he could be proud.[19] In the domestic arena, his chance to launch new initiatives was limited by the realities of congressional and electoral politics. In the foreign policy realm, however, he might still hope for a breakthrough that would allow him to play the coveted role of states-man. Over the years, Clinton had reportedly gained self-confidence in his ability to deal with international issues, and he had become particularly intent on trying to achieve a breakthrough in the Arab-Israeli arena. He was on good terms with most of the leaders in the region and was familiar with the issues.

Offsetting the temptation to make Arab-Israeli peacemaking a top pri-ority were two factors. First, the chances of success were not great. The gap between the parties, especially between Israelis and Palestinians, was large, and it might take much more than American encouragement to reach agreement. Second, a high-profile presidential commitment might result in considerable domestic controversy, particularly if it seemed that the United States was putting pressure on Israel to make concessions, which frequently had happened in previous rounds of peacemaking. Even though Clinton was not up for reelection, his vice president, Al Gore, who was hoping to succeed Clinton, would not welcome any moves that might weaken his support among Israel's many friends in the United States. Clinton's wife, Hillary, was also running for the Senate in New York and would not want her husband to tackle publicly such controversial issues as Jerusalem, refugee claims, settlements, or borders.[20]

Clinton's apparent resolution of these cross-pressures was initially to do everything short of engaging in high-powered public diplomacy to get the Israelis, Palestinians, and Syrians moving toward agreements. He and his aides would engage in serious prodding and cajoling, but Barak, as the new player in the game, would be given time to set his agenda. The results of this modest approach were, not surprisingly, modest—at least for the first year of the Barak period.

Considerable time was spent trying to get the Wye Agreement back on track. Netanyahu had effectively suspended it on the grounds that the Palestinians were not living up to their commitments. Arafat, whose po-litical base of support was fading, felt the need to show that Israeli troops were gradually leaving Palestinian areas as called for in Wye. In early September 1999, Arafat and Barak met at Sharm al-Shaykh and seemed to agree on next steps, including an ambitious set of target dates for fur-ther agreements. Secretary of State Albright, in a memorable phrase, de-scribed her role as that of a "handmaiden" in helping to broker the accord.[21]

Albright's next achievement was to persuade Syrian leader Hafiz al-

Asad to agree to resume negotiations with Israel at a high level. In mid-December, Clinton presided over talks in Washington with Barak and Syrian foreign minister Farouk Sharaa. A few weeks later, those talks resumed in Shepherdstown, West Virginia, and on January 7, 2000, the United States actually put forward a draft accord.[22]

Agreement between Israel and Syria now seemed within reach, despite the fact that Barak had not yet met the Syrian demand for recognition of the June 4, 1967, line as the future border. Even on that sensitive issue, however, it seemed as if progress was possible. Late in February 2000, Barak told his cabinet that Rabin had agreed to withdraw from the Golan Heights to the June 4, 1967, lines—with specified conditions—and that his government was not about "to erase the past."[23]

Clinton was sufficiently encouraged by Barak's apparent move toward the Syrian position that he decided to meet with Asad in Geneva on his way back from a trip to South Asia in late March. Clinton had called Asad in advance and told the ailing Syrian president that he had good news. Barak, however, had still not agreed to accept the June 4 line, and instead had asked Clinton to explore some compromise proposals directly with Asad.[24] When the two leaders met on March 26, 2000, Clinton tried to explain that Barak could not afford politically to go back all the way to the June 4 line, but that he had some alternative proposals to put forward. Asad would have nothing to do with this approach. Within minutes, the discussion was at a dead end. Clinton left Geneva empty handed, and the chance for a breakthrough on the Syrian-Israeli front seemed dim. Barak, in response, decided to withdraw all Israeli troops from South Lebanon where the number of casualties among his troops had been a growing concern. By May 24, 2000, the last Israeli troops had left Lebanese territory. Without any agreement with Syria, however, it was uncertain whether the border would remain quiet.[25]

On June 10, 2000, Hafiz al-Asad died suddenly, apparently of a heart attack. His son, Bashar, who had been groomed to succeed him, was an unknown political figure and many wondered how and whether he could fill his father's shoes. Eventually, he might turn out to be a more flexible negotiator, but his first order of business would be to shore up his political position within Syria. As a result, the chance for Clinton to do much in his remaining months to advance the prospects of Israeli-Syrian peace seemed very slim.

Clinton's last sustained opportunity to make an impact on Middle East peace began on June 14, 2000, when he met at the White House with Yasir Arafat. Both Arafat and Barak were under considerable domestic political pressure from their opponents, and it was by no means clear that either was prepared to make the hard decisions that would be needed for peace to be achieved. Nor was it clear how Clinton could help. The anodyne advice offered to the president by Henry Kissinger was: "I would tell him to stay calm and be available as a facilitator. And I would tell him not to be more interested than the parties themselves."[26] This, of course, was precisely the course that Clinton had followed to date, with little to show for it.

Camp David II

Soon after the failure of his summit meeting with Asad, Clinton turned his attention to the Israeli-Palestinian front. Talks were organized among Israeli, Palestinian, and American diplomats; Clinton worked the phones with Barak and Arafat; and Secretary Albright traveled again to the Middle East to see if the time was ripe for a summit meeting. Arafat was reluctant to agree, maintaining that more preparation was needed if a full agreement was to be negotiated.[27] Barak, by contrast, seemed eager to plunge into the last round of peacemaking, even though his coalition government was crumbling around him.

Finally, with an eye on the clock, Clinton invited the Israeli and Palestinian leaders to join him at Camp David on July 11, 2000, for a final effort to bridge the quite substantial gaps that still existed between the positions of the two sides. By all accounts, this was not a summit that was guaranteed to succeed. But episodes of violence the preceding May, plus the impending September 13 deadline, convinced the administration to take the risk.

Camp David II, as the new round of diplomacy was soon labeled, bore many resemblances to the original. Once again, the negotiating teams would be sequestered at the presidential retreat; there would be a near total news blackout; the president would be deeply involved in trying to forge compromises; and the promise of substantial American aid might help to pry loose compromise positions.

The two summits also had significant differences. First, each of the regional leaders was considerably weaker than Menachem Begin and Anwar al-Sadat had been in 1978. Barak's coalition government was unraveling as he traveled to the presidential retreat in the mountains of Maryland. Whereas Begin could count on support from opposition parties for the concessions he would have to make to win peace with Egypt, Barak could expect to face fierce opposition if he were to come close to meeting the minimum demands of the Palestinians. Similarly, Arafat was widely suspected by his constituents of being too eager to become the first president of a Palestinian state. If the price were major territorial concessions to Israel or a relinquishment of rights in Jerusalem or concerning refugees, many Palestinians would oppose the deal. For most Palestinians, the acceptance of Israel within the 1967 lines was already a huge concession and should not be the starting point for further concessions. In 1978, by comparison, Sadat was assured of domestic support if he could recover Egyptian territory, although many in the Arab world would condemn him for short-changing Palestinian rights.

Clinton's own role at Camp David was surprisingly strong. Although he was approaching the end of his tenure in office, both negotiating parties seemed to have a degree of confidence in him and were unsure about his successor. Some thought this might give him unusual leverage for a lame-duck president. Clinton also remained surprisingly popular within the United States and could count on bipartisan support for his Middle East efforts, at least up to the point where he might feel it necessary to press the Israelis on sensitive issues or ask Congress for a very large aid package.

Clinton had a remarkable ability to persuade both Israelis and Palestinians that he sympathized with them. He had avoided taking stands on many of the most controversial issues, urging the parties to reach compromises, but hesitating to put forward an American plan. If Camp David II were to follow the pattern of the original, this posture would come under pressure as each side tried to win American support for its own stance. Based on his previous record, Clinton could be expected to side with Barak more than with Arafat. Carter, by comparison, had been much more willing to take stands on substance, often to the irritation of both his guests. He sided with Begin on the issue of full peace and with Sadat on the question of full withdrawal from Sinai. He did not hesitate to use fairly blunt pressure to get them to budge from positions that he judged to be unreasonable. On one occasion he told Begin that he would have to denounce his intransigence in public if the talks failed, and he had bluntly told Sadat that the U.S.-Egyptian relationship would be finished if Sadat walked away from the negotiating table. Clinton seemed unlikely to use such harsh tactics, but it was unclear if his more conciliatory manner would be enough to budge the parties from their firm positions.

As the Israelis and Palestinians convened at Camp David on July 11, their known positions on the key issues were quite far apart. Barak maintained that there would be no withdrawal to the 1967 lines, no recognition of a right of return for Palestinian refugees, no removal of all the settlements beyond the 1967 line, no remilitarization of the West Bank and Gaza, and no relinquishment of the parts of Jerusalem taken in the 1967 war. Arafat, not surprisingly, insisted on full Israeli withdrawal from all occupied territory, including East Jerusalem; the establishment of a Palestinian state with East Jerusalem as its capital; and recognition of the right of Palestinian refugees to return to their homes or to compensation. The only issue on which the two sides seemed likely to agree was that a Palestinian state of some sort would be part of the final agreement. If these positions were engraved in stone, it seemed unlikely that a deal could be reached.

Many expected that the talks at Camp David II would fail because of the incompatibility of these stances. Some thought that another interim agreement, leaving some issues for later resolution, was the best that could be hoped for. But both Barak and Arafat showed little interest in another interim agreement. For the Palestinians, such a deal would simply postpone the time when they might expect a normal life within their own state. For the Israelis, an agreement that failed to resolve the conflict once and for all would leave them having made concessions with little in the way of a quid pro quo. The logic of small, confidence-building steps as the way to reach peace seemed to have exhausted itself. In Clinton's words, it was time for a "Hail Mary pass," one dramatic effort to score a touchdown.[28]

During the first week of the summit, it became clear that Barak was prepared to go further toward meeting some of the Palestinian demands than many had expected. As much as 90–95 percent of the West Bank and Gaza could eventually be returned to Palestinian control; a number of Palestinian refugees, perhaps in the tens of thousands, would be allowed to return to their homes under the family reunification policy; and Palestinian statehood would be recognized, provided the state was essentially demilitarized. All of these positions reflected a relatively moderate Israeli stance in accord with the earlier Beilin–Abu Mazin discussions.[29] On Jerusalem, however, there was much less sign of flexibility.

Clinton was scheduled to leave for a meeting with the leaders of other industrial countries in Japan on July 20. On Wednesday, just before his departure, the summit nearly ended in failure over the Jerusalem issue. Barak wrote a letter to Clinton saying that there was no point continuing; that Arafat had shown himself not to be a fit partner for peace; and that he was preparing his delegation for departure without agreement. An announcement that the summit was over was in fact made, but Arafat was unwilling to see things end on such a negative note and said that he was prepared to stay on until the president returned from Japan. Clinton then urged Barak not to leave, and the two delegations settled in for desultory talks presided over by the secretary of state until Clinton returned late on Sunday, July 23.

The Jerusalem issue was particularly complex for both symbolic and substantive reasons (see map). East Jerusalem had been annexed by Israel immediately after the 1967 war, and settlements had been built all around the eastern part of the city with the avowed purpose of cutting it off from the rest of the West Bank. Barak seemed to think that he might be able to persuade Arafat to give up most of East Jerusalem if Israel made a fairly generous offer to return other parts of the West Bank and would agree to a form of Palestinian civilian control in some of the Arab-populated neighborhoods of East Jerusalem. He was not, however, prepared to recognize full Palestinian sovereignty over any part of the old walled city, and this, of course, was the portion of the city that counted most in the eyes of many Palestinians and Muslims.

The Americans reportedly proposed a number of possible compromises, all premised on breaking down the notion of sovereignty so that each side could claim to exercise some degree of control over areas that were of special importance. Ideas of shared or joint sovereignty sounded plausible in the abstract, but were likely to be difficult to translate into realities on the ground. Late on Monday, the president made a final effort to persuade Arafat to show flexibility, but a few hours later the Palestinian leader sent Clinton a note saying that he could not accept the compromises suggested by the American side. At midday on Tuesday, July 25, 2000, a weary and disappointed President Clinton announced that the summit had ended without agreement. He also made clear that he thought Prime Minister Barak had shown more flexibility and seriousness of purpose than his Palestinian counterpart.[30]

Some observers thought that the failure of the Camp David summit would be a fatal blow to the prospects for Israeli-Palestinian peace. Others argued that the dark cloud had a silver lining. At least the hard issues had finally been broached at the highest level, and some movement had been registered on a whole range of topics, although full agreement was not reached on any of the core problems. Perhaps each side needed more time to absorb the realities of what would be required for peace to be achieved. Perhaps each needed to bolster domestic support. Indeed, American officials were quick to conclude that Arafat had probably not intended to reach a final agreement at Camp David, preferring instead a crisis that would show his own people that he had stood firm against American and Israeli pressures. Perhaps after strengthening his fragile political base, he would be ready to resume negotiations in a more constructive mood.[31]

Old Walled City of Jerusalem

Barak left Camp David in Clinton's good graces. As he departed, he asked if the president could say something that might help him back home, especially concerning Jerusalem. He seemed concerned that leaks from the negotiations about how far he had been prepared to go might hurt him with the Israeli public. As a result, on July 28, 2000, Clinton gave an interview to Israeli television in which he repeated his support for Barak, defended him against the charge of selling Israeli security short, warned Arafat not to think of a unilateral declaration of statehood, and stated that he might consider moving the American embassy from Tel Aviv to Jerusalem before the end of the year.[32] Palestinians saw this as a blatant attempt to punish Arafat and reacted by rallying behind their leader.

Why did Camp David II fail? The easy answer is to blame one party or the other for intransigence, and there is doubtless some blame to be apportioned. But the negotiators were dealing with extraordinarily difficult issues that required a great deal of nuanced discussion and compromise. One of the problems with the Oslo approach was that it had put off consideration of these issues in the belief that a gradual process of partial agreements would help to build confidence between the two sides.

The "Oslo theory" was not entirely wrong. Some issues did seem to become easier with the passage of time, such as the eventual establishment of a Palestinian state. On a human level, Israel and Palestinian negotiators did manage to forge cordial personal relations, and neither side reverted to blunt threats of resorting to violence if negotiations failed.

It is nonetheless striking that the participants at Camp David II could say with a straight face that Jerusalem had not really been discussed until the last day or so. If that were true, it is no surprise that compromise positions could not be agreed upon. Indeed, much of what took place at Camp David II had a rather informal, improvised quality about it. Nothing was put on paper, for fear that it might leak and embarrass one party or the other. Verbal understandings, however, had a way of dissolving when the Americans tried to translate them into concrete terms for a deal. The technique used at Camp David I—of a "single negotiating text" that was regularly revised in light of the reactions of each side— was not used at Camp David II, and as a result it was hard to know at the end of the talks what, if anything, had actually been agreed upon. Since nothing was final until everything was agreed, especially Jerusalem, it was technically accurate to say that no agreement had been reached on anything. In reality, of course, the conditional compromise positions considered at Camp David would not be so easily swept from the table and would provide a benchmark of sorts for negotiators whenever talks resumed.

Clinton emerged from Camp David with credit for having tackled the challenging issue of Israeli-Palestinian peace. Few felt that the effort was not worthwhile, and few Americans criticized him for the way he played his part. Israelis on the whole seemed reassured that Clinton was a close friend. Palestinians were not so sure, although Arafat was careful not to attack Clinton personally. Still, Clinton had gambled and failed, even if the failure was not attributed by most observers to anything that he did or did not do. If there were a criticism that seemed valid, it would be not so much that Clinton mishandled the negotiations at Camp David, but that so little of the preceding seven years had been used to lay the basis for the substantive discussion of the issues that finally came into focus at the summit. Clinton's penchant for relying on all-nighters had perhaps served him well in the past, but it did not this time.

Although Camp David II ended without an overall agreement, and both Barak and Clinton had raised questions about Arafat's willingness to negotiate in good faith, no one was yet ready to declare the peace process dead. In fact, all parties seemed to agree that some progress had been made on the extremely difficult issues of Jerusalem, settlements, borders, refugees, and security. So Clinton persevered, urging the resumption of negotiations and holding out the possibility of another summit if the gaps could be sufficiently narrowed.

The Palestinian negotiators, who had been frustrated at the July summit by what they thought was American bias in Israel's favor, spoke openly of the need for the United States to be an honest broker, to put forward compromise proposals of its own, not just warmed-over Israeli ideas. Barak, who had begun his tenure as prime minister dismissing an active American mediating role, also spoke of the need for American proposals if there were to be a final agreement. Clinton made clear that he was prepared to present such ideas, but only if the parties resumed talks and made initial headway on their own.

Time, of course, was a growing concern for both Barak and Clinton. Barak's support in the Knesset was razor thin, and when Israel's lawmakers reconvened in late October, there was a real chance that a bill calling for new elections might be passed. Clinton also had to face the reality that his time in office was growing short. He had warded off the symptoms of being a lame duck longer than most of his predecessors, but with the passage of time he too would be constrained from playing an effective role as peacemaker.

A *New* Intifada

Toward the end of September, there seemed to be a glimmer of hope that the negotiations might get back on track. Barak and Arafat came together for what both sides described as an unusually cordial meeting. Within days, however, a new and dangerous cycle of violence began.

On Thursday, September 28, 2000, Likud opposition leader Ariel Sharon waded into one of the most sensitive issues in the negotiations by insisting on visiting the Haram al-Sharif/Temple Mount area. Hundreds of Israeli police accompanied him. Palestinians reacted angrily to what they viewed as a deliberate provocation, a flaunting of Israeli power and claim to control over the holy sites. After noon prayers the next day, large numbers of young Palestinians poured out of the mosques and began to throw stones at Jews praying at the Western Wall below the compound. As this was the eve of Rosh Hashanah, the Jewish new year, there was an unusually large number of worshippers. Israeli police fired at the Palestinian crowd, killing several and wounding many others. Thus began several months of violence that came close to destroying the chance for peace.

During the first weeks of October, clashes between Palestinian stone throwers and Israeli police spread to include the Palestinian police force, armed with automatic weapons, and regular units of the Israeli military, using tanks and helicopter gunships. Before long, armed Israeli settlers and Israeli Arab citizens joined the fray in what seemed another *intifada*, if not quite an all-out war. Casualties rose daily, reaching more than three hundred and fifty dead by year's end, over 90 percent of whom were Palestinians, including some Arab citizens of Israel.

During the fighting, Secretary Albright met with Barak and Arafat in Paris to try to arrange a truce. Arafat was reluctant to issue a call for an end to the fighting unless Israel agreed to an international inquiry into the origins of the clashes. Verbal commitments were reportedly made to ease the tensions, but within a few days the violence resumed, including a particularly provocative act by Palestinians who destroyed a Jewish religious site in Nablus shortly after Israeli soldiers had abandoned it. Barak then issued a forty-eight-hour ultimatum, due to expire just after Yom Kippur. Arafat was told to stop the violence. Many Israelis had reached the conclusion that he was deliberately instigating the crowds as part of his broader strategy to rally Arab and international support to his side. Clinton was reluctant to point the finger so directly at Arafat, but many in his entourage reported that they were beginning to wonder what Arafat was doing and whether he was still someone they could work with.

A climactic day in the crisis came on October 12. Two Israeli soldiers somehow approached a Palestinian funeral procession in the midst of Ramallah. The crowd was calling for revenge, and the soldiers were seized and taken to the nearby police station. A huge mob gathered, broke into the station, and murdered the soldiers, desecrating the body of one and parading it through the streets. Israelis were enraged, and Barak ordered helicopter gunships to fire on the police station in Ramallah, as well as near Arafat's residential compound in Gaza. The same day, a small boat approached an American destroyer, the USS *Cole*, in Aden harbor in Yemen and exploded, killing seventeen sailors. Whether the attack was directly related to the events to the north was unknown, but it brought home to Americans the extraordinary speed with which the Middle Eastern scene seemed to be shifting from impending peace to all-out conflict.

During this prolonged, tragic crisis, Clinton and his team worked the phones relentlessly, trying to urge an end to the fighting and a resumption of high-level negotiations. This time, however, unlike many earlier occasions, both Israelis and Palestinians, as well as other Arab leaders, were slow to answer the president's appeals. Having invested heavily in his relations with both Barak and Arafat, Clinton now found himself frustrated as the violence eroded his hopes for being a peacemaker. Others joined the effort to restore a ceasefire. UN secretary general Kofi Annan and Egypt's president Mubarak were particularly active.

Finally, Arafat and Barak agreed to a summit meeting on October 16 in Sharm al-Sheik with Clinton, as well as with Kofi Annan, King Abdallah II of Jordan, Mubarak, and a representative of the European Union, but now the focus was on reestablishing a truce more than on advancing the search for a comprehensive agreement. By midday on October 17, Clinton emerged from the marathon negotiations to announce that the parties had agreed to try to end the violence and that there would be a commission of inquiry into the crisis.

Clinton's last phase of peacemaking was colored by political drama in the United States, Israel, and among the Palestinians. Americans went to the polls in November and split their votes almost evenly between Vice President Al Gore and Texas Governor George W. Bush. Gore won the popular vote by more than 500,000, but the electoral college vote came down to the tally in one state, Florida, where the margin was so close that a final determination of who won the election could not be made until mid-December, when the Supreme Court finally put an end to the squabble of how to count the ballots. George W. Bush emerged as the victor and seemed eager to encourage Clinton to pursue his long-shot obsession of trying to forge an Israeli-Palestinian agreement in the weeks that remained for his presidency.

In Israel, meanwhile, Barak's governing coalition was about to collapse, and, in a move to preempt his rivals, Barak resigned, forcing new elections for prime minister by February 6, 2001. In the interim, Barak would hang on as prime minister and try to conclude negotiations so that he could make the election a referendum on peace. Whether his high-risk strategy could work was debatable, but many agreed with him that the election of his rival, Ariel Sharon, would put an end to peacemaking.

Arafat's political stance was harder to assess. In some ways the *intifada* seemed to have strengthened his shaky position, but it had also radicalized popular opinion and weakened support for the idea of peace with Israel. Within Arafat's own Fatah movement, younger leaders were outspokenly critical of the whole idea of negotiating.

Still, Clinton persuaded both sides to make another effort in late December. After lengthy preliminaries and endless telephone conversations with the principals, Clinton finally met with Israeli and Palestinian negotiators at the White House on December 23, 2000, to put forward his own suggestions for a compromise.[33] The Clinton plan, as it was soon dubbed, envisaged a Palestinian state in about 95 percent of the West Bank and Gaza, with vague notions of land swaps to allow Israel to incorporate most settlers into Israeli sovereign territory, while compensating Palestinians with additional land in the vicinity of Gaza.

On the sensitive issue of Jerusalem, Clinton put forward a compromise that would give Arab neighborhoods to the Palestinians, including the Muslim and Christian parts of the Old City, and most importantly the Haram al-Sharif compound. Israel would retain the Jewish quarter and a passageway through the Armenian quarter and would retain control over the Western Wall and the Temple Mount beneath the Haram al-Sharif.

While at Camp David II the Jerusalem issue had proved to be the stumbling block, this time both parties seemed close to accepting the Clinton compromise, although many within their constituencies were still bitterly opposed. The intractable issue now seemed to be the proposal for dealing with the right of return of refugees. The public portrayal of the Clinton plan was that in exchange for Arab Jerusalem, the Palestinians would have to give up the "right of return." This was not quite a fair reading of the plan, but Clinton did state that Israel could not be expected to accept an unrestricted right of return of refugees, and that the most realistic option for refugees would be return to the new state of Palestine, not to their original homes. Palestinian reaction to this formulation on refugee rights was generally negative.

Barak seemed to feel that his only hope was to go into elections with some kind of deal in hand. He therefore convened his cabinet and won acceptance of a conditional approval of the Clinton proposals. In effect, he stated that if Arafat were to accept them as the basis for negotiation, so would he. Arafat was initially less forthcoming. He and his negotiators complained that many crucial details still needed to be clarified. They did not want to be forced by artificial deadlines to make fateful (and probably unpopular) decisions.

Arafat must have known that even if he were to accept, there would still have to be a very long and difficult negotiation before a final agreement could be reached, and Clinton would not be around for that phase. Arafat seemed not to worry that the new president, George W. Bush, would be less supportive of a fair peace settlement than Clinton. Indeed, many Arabs seemed to have high hopes that Bush, with his well-known connections to the oil industry, would be more sympathetic to their concerns.

Arafat did have a tough calculation to make concerning Barak, whom he did not exactly trust, but who was certainly a preferred partner to Ariel Sharon. If Arafat were to flatly reject the Clinton plan, Barak stood little chance of being reelected in February. On the other hand, even if Arafat did say yes, or maybe, there was a good chance that Barak would be defeated, and in that case Arafat's concessions might expose him to severe criticism from his own camp.

On January 2, 2001, Arafat met Clinton in the White House for a lengthy discussion. The following day his spokesmen said that the Palestinians were ready to accept the proposals, with conditions, as the basis for further negotiations. This left Clinton at the end of his term with both parties reluctantly accepting his general framework, but without time to push for a full agreement. And the mood in both Israel and among Palestinians was far from supportive of the Clinton plan. Ironically, the president who had devoted so much of his last months to Middle East peace passed on to his successor a region filled with explosive potential.

Clinton's Legacy

Clinton's legacy in the Middle East will be a curiously mixed one. He came so close to being the president who helped bring the region to peace that some will want to give him a good grade for effort. In politics, however, good intentions rarely count for much. Nevertheless, Clinton did succeed in establishing a serious relationship with most of the key leaders in the Arab-Israeli arena; he gave legitimacy to the idea that peace would eventually involve the creation of a Palestinian state; his December 2000 proposals provided a serious and substantive framework for eventual negotiations; and his efforts underscored the centrality of American interests in Middle East peace. His policy was largely backed by American public opinion, and both parties were generally supportive. Whenever negotiations do resume, they are likely to build on the forward positions explored by Clinton in his last year of hyperactive involvement in the peace process.

The puzzle about the Clinton presidency and Arab-Israeli peacemaking is whether Clinton could realistically have achieved more than he did, especially in the period when Rabin and Barak were prime ministers. The record is not easy to read. There were moments of hope and real accomplishment, including the Oslo Accords and their sequels, the Jordan-Israel peace treaty and the Hebron and Wye agreements. Even the unsuccessful Camp David II summit and the Clinton plan were widely credited with having advanced the consideration of the most difficult of the substantive issues in dispute. To varying degrees, the United States played an essential role in promoting these steps along the path to peace.

Clinton and his team spent considerable time and energy on these issues. One cannot blame him for ignoring the region, especially in light of the many other international crises that demanded attention during his presidency. And yet, there is a nagging sense that Clinton and his colleagues could have done more, especially in his first term. They might have helped accelerate the pace of diplomacy when Rabin was at the peak of his influence, a uniquely propitious time for peacemaking; they might have helped clinch the deal between Israel and Syria; they might have held Netanyahu to the terms of Oslo more effectively; they might have persuaded Arafat to move to final-status talks more rapidly and to live up to his part of Oslo without ambiguity; they might have urged Barak to move more quickly toward establishing the "land for peace" framework with Asad; and they might have started the discussions on Jerusalem well before the Camp David II summit.

While any analysis of why Clinton did not achieve more is bound to be hypothetical, it is still a valuable exercise to look at the main competing hypotheses. Four come to mind. First, there is the issue of presidential character. Second, one can point the finger at Congress and the influence of pro-Israeli groups. Third, one can examine the underlying assumptions behind the strategy developed by the Middle East team. Fourth, one can place the blame for the stalemate clearly on the parties to the conflict, arguing that there is a limit to what the United States can be expected to do when the regional players are unwilling to take risks for peace. Let us examine each of these arguments.

Those who knew Clinton best would frequently argue that his strengths and weaknesses were inseparable.[34] He was intelligent, but not focused; personable, but not loyal; politically skillful, but deeply self-centered; flexible, but without a solid core of conviction. Some saw in Clinton a product of his generation, the result of a troubled childhood, the offspring of addictive and abusive parents. Psychology can only take one so far in understanding a complex figure such as Clinton, but it does seem clear that Clinton had a deep need for recognition and success; was inclined toward compromise rather than principled stands; and was skillful with words and relationships to build broad coalitions of support for himself and his policies.

The advantage of these qualities in conducting Middle East policy was that Clinton had the ability to impress his many visitors—Arabs and Israelis alike—with his intelligence and seriousness of purpose. No president has been more trusted than Clinton by mainstream Israelis, for he was able to persuade them that he understood their unique security dilemmas and their historical trauma. Bush's less empathic personality, by comparison, left Israelis cold. Amazingly, by Clinton's second term, some Palestinians were also claiming that Clinton was the first president to understand them. This ability to reach over barriers, to appeal to both sides of a conflict, was vintage Clinton, but so was his inability to take firm stands with either party, especially the politically potent Israelis. Deadlines would come and go, agreements would be broken, and Clinton would find it hard to draw a firm line or to threaten sanctions. Nor would he risk controversy by taking positions that might offend the Israelis in particular. Part, at least, of Clinton's inclination to go slow, to hesitate rather than to confront, seems to have been rooted in his character.

The second possible explanation for Clinton's cautious approach to Arab-Israeli peacemaking involves Congress. Without a doubt, Congress was a problem for him. The Republicans controlled both houses; and pro-Israeli resolutions regularly commanded nearly unanimous support in the Senate and House. Still, the American public mood, while supportive of Israel, was not strongly enamored of Netanyahu. Many Jewish groups, including the famed American Israel Public Affairs Committee, were under relatively moderate leadership. Issues such as expansion of settlements and refusal to carry out Oslo and Wye were not ones where Netanyahu could count on much American support if the president had taken a firm stand. True, Clinton would have had to use some of his precious political capital in any real showdown with Netanyahu, but in his second term he could afford to draw down a bit in order to bolster his historical legacy. Yet he kept going to fundraisers, and in early 1999 was speaking of his last major political goal as the election of Al Gore in 2000. The permanent campaign would apparently continue. Congress and domestic politics were no doubt an impediment to Clinton's Middle East policy, but he came nowhere close to testing the limits of the possible or engaging in an effort to ease the constraints under which any president must operate in dealing with Congress.

From early in his presidency, Clinton bought the comforting "ripeness" theory propounded by his advisers, notably Dennis Ross and Martin Indyk. This placed him in the role of a facilitator, helping well-meaning parties to make peace whenever they were so inclined to do so. As long as Rabin, Peres, and Barak were in power in Israel, this seemed to be a viable stance. Oslo gave it validity. Clinton could bask in the glow of the peacemakers without having to do much heavy lifting. But this way of understanding the Arab-Israeli conflict, so congenial to Clinton, seemed to assume that the United States had only a modest stake of its own; that time was on the side of peace; and that the United States could do little to accelerate the ripening process by adding to the calculus of gains and losses of the parties to the conflict.

By the time Clinton seemed to become aware of the need for a more forceful approach, namely during the Wye negotiations, he was already midway through his second term. Here his failure was not so much one of character, but one of his learning curve. He remained dependent for too long on an approach that was comfortable but strategically weak. He surrounded himself with like-minded advisers who had proved themselves competent, but regularly lagging behind events. For instance, only after Oslo was the Clinton team ready to renew ties to the PLO; a more forceful push on the Syria front in 1993 or 1995 might have paid real dividends; the early "benefit of the doubt" phase with Netanyahu seems to have been largely wasted; and earlier efforts to promote Palestinian economic development and efficient and professional security measures might have produced significant dividends. The reassuring mantras—"we cannot want peace more than the parties do"—were intellectually empty, a fact that Clinton was slow to recognize. Indeed, the very special features of Israeli-Palestinian peacemaking, where asymmetries abounded, where power imbalances were so acute, and where American interests were complex, required a particularly sophisticated diplomacy, something Clinton was unable to bring to it and his advisers did not offer.

Finally, it is always easy to blame the lack of progress in the Arab-Israeli peace process on the intransigence of the parties themselves. It is certainly true that every American president and secretary of state who has tackled this problem has felt frustrated by the rigidity of the parties at one time or another. There is ample evidence, however, that breakthroughs such as the disengagement agreements of 1974, Camp David in 1978, and Madrid in 1991 were able to succeed in the face of very considerable reluctance on the part of Arabs and Israelis. The parties were nudged to do things they would have preferred to postpone. The United States not only helped to reduce the risks, but also tried to sharpen the focus, identify trade-offs, apply discreet pressure, and mount a campaign that peace in the Middle East was both an American national interest and a regional imperative. Had Clinton looked to these models instead of Oslo—where the parties had indeed come together out of a sense of mutual need—he might have been more ambitious, less hesitant, less prone to equivocate. Then he might have been able to point to an enduring legacy as a Middle East peacemaker. As it was, he came close, but his character and his concepts—and his monumental, self-inflicted distraction during most of 1998—kept him from making an all-out effort when the time was most promising for Arab-Israeli peace.

Fortunately for Clinton, he was lucky, along with all his other qualities and defects, and Barak's election in May 1999 gave him another chance to do what he excelled at in the Middle East. He could help persuade the parties to get on with the tough job of negotiation. But in light of the difficulty of resolving the issues in the Israeli-Palestinian conflict, it required more than friendly persuasion. A real restructuring of incentives through active mediation and the use of carrots and sticks was needed. Faced with comparable challenges, Nixon and Kissinger, Carter and Vance, and Bush and Baker had asserted an American interest and pressed reluctant parties to move forward.[35] The results were impressive and provided the foundations for subsequent peace efforts. Clinton, for all his efforts, was only able to bring the parties to the brink of peace, and at that crucial moment, the violence that erupted late in 2000 came close to unraveling much of what had been achieved in previous years. The legacy that he had sought, that of presiding over a comprehensive Middle East peace, eluded him, at least in part because of his own hesitant political style, and thus it will fall to his successor, George W. Bush, to try to secure the elusive goal of peace between Israel and its Arab neighbors.

PART SIX

CONCLUSION

13 Challenges Facing
Future Administrations

WITH ALARMING REGULARITY since 1967, American presidents have found themselves dealing with Middle East crises for which they were poorly prepared. Many, but not all, of these crises have been related to the Arab-Israeli conflict. The June 1967 war, the war of attrition in 1969–70, the Jordan crisis of September 1970, the October 1973 war, the Iranian revolution in 1978–79, the Iran-Iraq war from 1980 to 1988, the Israeli invasion of Lebanon in 1982–83, the early years of the Palestinian *intifada* in 1987–88, the Iraqi invasion of Kuwait in 1990, the subsequent war against Saddam Hussein in 1991, and the "second *intifada*" late in 2000 were enormous challenges for American foreign policy. Each evoked serious debate in Washington over the proper course of action. Each seemed to threaten important American interests in the region. Each, to some extent, caught Washington by surprise.

Future administrations will most likely find themselves in the position of dealing with some form of ongoing Arab-Israeli peace negotiation. Since the Madrid conference in October 1991 the parties to the conflict have been in broad agreement on procedures for peace talks. What has been needed, besides direct negotiations, has been an effective mediator who could steer the negotiating teams toward realistic agreements, engage with political decisionmakers to extract command decisions, and offer both reassurance and pressure when necessary. President Bill Clinton tried to play this role at the very end of his presidency, but fell short of his goal as his term came to an end.

The Balance Sheet

The American record of managing Arab-Israeli crises and their aftermaths is mixed. On the whole, the United States has done best when it has tried hardest. From 1968 onward, successive administrations laid the foundations for peace between Israel and Egypt. In 1979 the two countries signed a peace treaty, which they have observed ever since. As its contribution to this historic achievement, the United States, under seven presidents, has invested important resources—time, energy, imagination, money, military equipment—to establish a framework for peace, to get the parties involved in a negotiating process, to clinch the formal deal, and to continue to bolster the normalization of relations well after the signing of the peace treaty between the two countries.

Peace between Israel and Egypt did not come cheaply, nor was the path smooth. Several wars were fought before serious negotiations began in 1974. The bilateral peace between Israel and its most powerful Arab neighbor left many other issues unresolved. It also probably exacerbated the problems of Lebanon and initially made the Israeli-Palestinian relationship even more intractable than it had been. But the Israeli-Egyptian peace also changed the strategic picture of the region, provided something of a model for negotiations on other fronts, bolstered American influence, and ultimately helped to persuade other Arabs that diplomacy offered a better course for redressing grievances than military threats.

For the United States the economic cost of Israeli-Egyptian peace has been substantial. Since the peace treaty was signed, Congress has allocated more than $5 billion a year to the two countries. In special circumstances, additional sums have been offered. Of this total, more than half has gone to the purchase of American military equipment. Since 1985 almost all aid has been on a grant basis. In 1990 Congress even took the unusual step of agreeing to write off nearly $7 billion of Egypt's military debt from earlier years. Congress also supported $10 billion in loan guarantees to Israel to assist with housing and absorption of immigrants in the 1990s. When agreement between Israelis and Palestinians seemed close in mid-2000, rumors were spread that the price tag might be tens of billions of additional dollars in aid. Suffice it to say that no other countries in the Middle East, or anywhere else for that matter, come even close to receiving such openhanded assistance.

Apart from the important achievement of peace between Israel and Egypt, the American record is less impressive. The most promising step has been the Oslo agreement of 1993 and its sequels, which commit Israel and the Palestine Liberation Organization to a peaceful settlement of their conflict. Even optimists, however, acknowledge that the negotiations will be difficult, especially as the issues of Jerusalem, refugees, and final borders have yet to be resolved, and mutual suspicions were deepened by the tragic events of late 2000.

On the other side of the ledger are the failures and fiascoes of American Middle East policy. Some have entered the popular jargon of politics— "Irangate," for the misguided attempt to trade arms for hostages in the mid-1980s, and subsequently "Iraqgate," for the policy of trying to accommodate Saddam Hussein before his invasion of Kuwait in August 1990. No simple phrase encapsulates the multiple disasters of American policy in Lebanon during the early 1980s, but the bombs that blew up the American embassy in Beirut and the Marine barracks in 1983 left graphic and tragic reminders that American failures in the Middle East can carry a heavy price tag in American lives. More Americans were killed in Lebanon in 1983 than in the massive war against Iraq in 1991. The tally of the costs of failed policies is even higher if it includes the prolonged agony of American hostages held in Iran and in Lebanon.

Protecting National Interests

Still, for all the shortcomings of American policy in the Middle East generally, and toward the Arab-Israeli conflict in particular, American interests in the Middle East have fared surprisingly well. The great fear of Soviet dominance in the region never materialized, nor did the possibility of direct military confrontation between the two nuclear superpowers. Despite the prevalence of images of a "Middle East tinderbox," the region did not play the part of the Balkans earlier in the century in igniting a global conflagration. Regional conflicts, on the whole, remained confined to the region. Nuclear weapons, though present, remained in the background. Terrorism, though a persistent threat, never succeeded in changing the course of events in fundamental ways. Revolution, though often talked about, took place only in Iran. Elsewhere the state system has proved to be remarkably resilient, despite its seeming artificiality.

With respect to oil, American interests have not gone unscathed, but part of the blame must be assigned to shortsighted policies on the home front. Disruptions of oil supplies in the Middle East were bound to have some impact on price, but the exaggerated effects of the 1973–74 and 1978–79 cutbacks were due in part to flawed domestic policies and the failure to purchase adequate insurance in the form of a strategic petro-

leum reserve. During the 1980s and early 1990s interruptions of oil supplies from the Middle East also occurred in conjunction with Persian Gulf
crises, but better policies were in place and the impact was smaller. Whatever the reason, the United States and the rest of the world were dealt a
heavy economic blow in the 1970s and early 1980s as a result of Middle
East oil-supply disruptions. The recessions of the 1970s and early 1980s
were directly related to the higher costs of energy. While oil prices dipped
in the late 1990s, they spiked again in 2000, exceeding $30 a barrel for the
first time in many years.

Finally, as regards the third main American interest, Israel's security has
greatly increased in the post-1967 era. By the end of the 1990s Israel was
more secure than at any previous time in its history. More Arabs were reconciled to the idea of a Jewish state in at least a part of historic Palestine
than ever before. Many Arab states were on speaking terms with Israel for
the first time. New immigrants from the former Soviet Union held out the
promise of a renewal of social and economic vitality into the next century.
Economic and social problems existed, but the survival of the state seemed
more assured than one could have imagined thirty years earlier. Although
peace with the Palestinians and the Syrians still remained over the horizon,
its general contours seemed fairly clear after the efforts of the Clinton years.

Despite this relatively positive overview of how American interests have
fared in the Middle East since 1967, one should not conclude that all is
well. The region remains volatile; most regimes have little mass support;
and opposition movements that reject the present order are widespread
and are often intensely anti-American, as was seen in the mass protests in
much of the Arab world in late 2000 during the "second *intifada*." Economic development has been disappointing, except in the oil sheikhdoms
and recently in Egypt, and population growth puts an almost unmanage-
able burden on weak governments.

The Arab-Israeli conflict still generates strong passions, and the achievements of the past could be lost if, for example, the regime in Egypt changed
suddenly, if radical Palestinian sentiment gained ground, or if Israeli extremists tried to achieve their goals by force. The region is still overarmed;
weapons of mass destruction are already in the arsenals of many states in
the region, along with surface-to-surface missiles. Although the danger of
superpower confrontation is now gone, the risk of war is still present, and
in such a war American interests could still be threatened. To reconcile the
American commitment to a secure Israel with the long-term need for Middle
East oil, future administrations will no doubt continue to see the peace
process as an important part of their broader regional policy.

Ingredients of Success

To deal effectively with these challenges in the Middle East in years to come, future administrations would do well to learn from the past record of success and failure. For policies to produce desirable results—such as in the drafting of UN Resolution 242 in 1967, the 1974–75 disengagement talks, the Camp David and peace treaty negotiations in 1978–79, the diplomacy leading to the Madrid conference in 1991, and some aspects of the post-Oslo negotiations—certain conditions must be met.

There must be a realistic appraisal of the regional situation. To influence governments in the Middle East, politicians in Washington must be keenly aware of what is taking place there. Sustained dialogue with the parties to the conflict is the best way to develop the necessary sensitivity to the real political constraints. Dealing with the Middle East parties through intermediaries does not work well. Wishful thinking, ideological blinders, and indifference are the enemies of success in trying to take the measure of the parties to the Arab-Israeli conflict. As with medicine, correct diagnosis is the key to effective prescription. Presidents and their advisers should also pause periodically to question their assumptions and their analysis. It is far too easy to wall oneself off from critical views, dismissing them as "unhelpful" or "ill-informed." Critics are often in tune with a part of a complex reality, however, and should not be so readily ignored.

The president and his top advisers must be involved and must work in harmony. Unless the prestige and power of the White House are clearly behind American policy initiatives, leaders in the Middle East will not take them seriously. This is one reason that special envoys from Washington rarely succeed. Bureaucratic rivalries and presidential disengagement will also weaken the credibility of any U.S. policy. When policies did succeed, Nixon and Kissinger, Carter and Vance, Bush and Baker were seen to be working closely together. Failures were associated with the Kissinger-Rogers rivalry, the Brzezinski-Vance disagreement over Iran in 1978, and the long-running Shultz-Weinberger arguments over policy toward Lebanon and arms to Arab countries. In these latter cases presidents who were ambivalent or uninterested allowed those quarrels to undermine their policies. Had he cared enough, however, each president had the power to end these feuds. One of the few unquestioned powers of a president is to fire any top adviser who does not meet his standards. Bureaucratic rivalries are commonplace, but presidents do not have to put up with them indefinitely.

The domestic basis of support for American policy in the region must be constantly developed. Presidents must work with Congress and must explain their purposes to the American public, especially if the costs of the policy are likely to be substantial. Presidents who are unskillful in managing the domestic politics of foreign policy will undermine their own purposes. The ability to mobilize support seems to be very much tied to context: Lyndon Johnson had broad backing for his Middle East policy in 1967, while he was losing support for his Vietnam policy; Richard Nixon won praise for his foreign policy, while losing his base over Watergate; Jimmy Carter succeeded in his Arab-Israeli diplomacy, while simultaneously losing ground over Iran and the hostage crisis; Ronald Reagan was widely praised for his September 1, 1982, speech on the Middle East, and generally criticized for the Iran-Contra fiasco; George Bush won domestic laurels in the war against Iraq, only to see his standing in the polls drop within a matter of months; Bill Clinton remained remarkably popular during his two terms, but was distracted from Middle East diplomacy in 1998 and 1999 by domestic scandal and other international crises. The lesson must surely be that high-level attention to the home front is a constant preoccupation. No president can assume that Congress and public opinion will back him for long. At the same time policy toward the Arab-Israeli conflict cannot simply reflect the pro-Israeli tone of domestic politics without losing credibility with the Arab parties to the conflict. The president should seek a domestically sustainable policy of evenhandedness, even if it will always be somewhat precarious unless the peace process is moving forward.

Success as a mediator requires a feeling both for process—the procedures for bringing the parties to the negotiations—and for substance. Issues rarely arise that are devoid of substantive implications. The questions of who comes to the negotiating table, the structure of the agenda, and the symbols associated with the peace process are all likely to convey powerful substantive messages to the parties in the Middle East. The United States cannot advance the search for peace between Israel and the Arabs by simply playing the role of mailman; nor can it design a blueprint and impose it on reluctant parties. In between these extremes lie the proper roles for the United States—catalyst, energizer, friend, nag, technician, architect. Some of each of these roles has been necessary whenever the United States has succeeded in bridging the gaps between Arabs and Israelis. Carrots and sticks must both be used, sometimes together, to influence reluctant parties. Public acrimony is usually counterproductive, although a display of presidential temper is sometimes useful to underscore serious intent. Threats to abandon the peace process are effective only with the weakest parties, and they often lack credibility in any case.

There must be a substantial investment in quiet diplomacy, in "pre-negotiation" exploration of the terrain, before deals can be cut. Formal settings, conferences, and direct negotiations are important for symbolic purposes, but most progress is made in secret talks with the top leadership in the region. Presidential letters, memorandums of understandings, and private commitments will all be part of the process of nudging parties toward agreement. Leaks of sensitive information and offhand remarks can complicate delicate negotiations. Tight discipline is needed. Words have consequences. Not everything can be discussed in public, although excessive secrecy can also backfire. Each participant in the negotiating process need not be told exactly the same thing, but any deliberate deception will prove counterproductive. One should assume that much of what one says will eventually be leaked by someone. All the more reason to avoid duplicity.

Pressure sometimes succeeds, but it must be skillfully exerted. Part of the conventional wisdom about U.S.-Israeli relations is that pressure on Israeli governments is bound to backfire. But the record suggests a much more complex reality. True, pressures do not always produce desired results and may sometimes stiffen resistance. Pressure on Israel can also produce domestic controversy and adverse congressional reactions. At one time or another, however, each president has tried to persuade Israel to take some action by implying that refusal would be costly. In a surprising number of instances, such efforts at influence have succeeded, often with an added sweetener of rewards for compliance. The same has been true of dealings with Arab parties, with the added twist that it is often difficult to twist the arm of an apparently weak party such as the Palestinians. When the PLO leader said "no" to Bill Clinton in late 2000, Arafat's domestic support seemed to rise. To succeed in influencing parties to the Arab-Israeli conflict, the United States must ask for feasible concessions, while wielding both carrots and sticks as incentives.

Timing is crucial for successful negotiations. The American political calendar does not allow much time for launching initiatives and seeing them through to completion. Also, the parties in the region may not be ready to move when the politicians in Washington are. One reason crises are so often followed by initiatives is that crises tend to persuade all parties to agree that something new must be tried. Those who argue for a passive stance, in the belief that time will work in favor of accommodation, have the burden of evidence against them. The deliberate policy of doing nothing in the period 1970–73 led to a major war; the stalemate of the 1980s led to the *intifada* and may have helped create the atmosphere in the Arab world that led Saddam Hussein to believe he could get away with his invasion of Kuwait. To say that each of these crises was followed by peace initiatives is hardly a recommendation for deliberately provoking crises. Policy that reacts only to crises is extremely dangerous. Carter demonstrated in 1977 that it was not necessary to wait for an explosion before taking an initiative. Too often, however, initiatives have come only in the aftermath of wars or violence. Clinton, who seemed to want to advance Arab-Israeli peace even without the prod of an imminent crisis, turned his full attention to the issues too late in his second term and finally went to his Camp David summit with insufficient previous agreement on major issues.

Changing of the Guard

These guidelines may seem noncontroversial, even banal, but translating them into practice proves to be extremely difficult. One reason is the relatively rapid turnover in top positions in the U.S. government. Little experience is accumulated; continuity is rare. Even the record of past commitments is often hard to discover after a new administration takes over.

Between 1967 and 2000, seven presidents occupied the Oval Office. Only Reagan and Clinton managed to complete two full terms. These seven presidents appointed eleven secretaries of state and a similar number of directors of central intelligence, secretaries of defense, national security advisers, assistant secretaries for Near Eastern and South Asian Affairs, and directors of the Middle East office of the National Security Council. On average, then, the top personnel in charge of Middle East policy changes about every three or four years. Ambassadors to key Middle East countries are rotated with about the same frequency.

Since 1989 only one position central to Middle East policymaking has seen continuity. The counselor for Middle East policy at the State Department, Dennis Ross, has occupied the post during three presidential terms, with similar continuity in his immediate staff. Ross has been the most knowledgeable member of the team, and his views, especially on process, have carried great weight.

The turnover in high places in Washington contrasts starkly with the amazing continuity sometimes found in the Middle East. Yitzhak Rabin was chief of staff in Israel during the 1967 war, ambassador to Washington during the Jordan crisis, prime minister during the second disengagement negotiations, defense minister during the *intifada*, and again prime minister from 1992 until his assassination in 1995. As a result he knew more about the history of American involvement in Arab-Israeli diplomacy than most American diplomats. Similarly, Syria's Hafiz al-Asad ruled without interruption as president from 1970 until his death in 2000. He also knew intimately the dossier of recent peace diplomacy, most of which he had opposed and often helped to undermine. King Hussein was acquainted with every American president from Eisenhower to Clinton and often seemed to despair that every few years he had to invest all over again in winning the trust of a new team in Washington. Even the indomitable Yasir Arafat has managed to stay on top of the PLO since 1969. He has outlasted most American peace initiatives.

Initial Predispositions

If Americans cannot compete with Middle Easterners in the length of their tenure, the depth of their direct knowledge of the issues, and their study of history, where can they get their bearings? This book places emphasis on two main sources: the predispositions that policymakers bring with them to office, and the views that they acquire on the job. Because of the short tenure in high positions, American policymaking reflects an almost continual process of bringing in new people and educating them in the realities of the Middle East (and the ways of Washington concerning the Middle East). Formal positions on substantive issues change relatively little, but policies, representing tactical judgments, change quite often.

Predispositions relevant to Arab-Israeli diplomacy come in many forms, but for analytical purposes they can be grouped into three clusters. Do the president and his team tend to see Arab-Israeli issues in their regional context or in a broader global context? Are they inclined to attach a high priority to Arab-Israeli issues, or would they prefer to leave these issues on the back burner? Are their sympathies primarily with Israel, or are they relatively evenhanded in their views? These predispositions may be related to other views that have to do with the state of U.S.-Soviet relations (for earlier presidents), the possibility of finding a solution to age-old disputes, the role of force in diplomacy, and the place of domestic politics in the management of Arab-Israeli diplomacy. But context, salience, strategic inclinations, and sympathies are good starting points for characterizing the views of the presidential team that deals with Arab-Israeli issues.

Nixon and Reagan were clearly globalists in their approach to the Middle East. The contest with Moscow was never far from their thoughts. Carter was much more of a regionalist. Bush, Johnson, and Ford were somewhere in between. Clinton saw the issues in regional terms, but always with an eye toward his domestic position.

For Johnson and Reagan the Middle East was rarely a top priority, except in moments of crisis. Nixon tended to see the Middle East as explosive, but Kissinger persuaded him not to be too eager to push for a settlement. After the October 1973 war Nixon, Ford, and Carter were all prepared to deal with the Arab-Israeli issue as a matter of top priority, as was Bush after the war against Iraq. Clinton was slow to throw himself into the vortex of Arab-Israeli diplomacy, but during his last year that all changed, and he spent more time with Barak and Arafat than with any other foreign leaders.

Johnson, Reagan, and Clinton were no doubt the most pro-Israeli presidents. Nixon, Ford, Carter, and Bush seemed more evenhanded. Among secretaries of state, Henry Kissinger, Alexander Haig, George Shultz, and Warren Christopher were strong supporters of Israel as an important ally, whereas Dean Rusk, William Rogers, Cyrus Vance, James Baker, and Madeleine Albright took a more evenhanded stance. Baker and Albright dealt with Likud prime ministers with whom they often clashed over settlements and other matters, giving them a reputation in some circles of being critical of Israeli policies. It would be unfair, however, to describe either of them as hostile to Israel, and Albright was very supportive of Israeli positions once Barak became prime minister.

If these characterizations of initial predispositions are fairly accurate, they nonetheless cannot convey a full sense of the views of these key decisionmakers. Over time, nuances are added, more information is absorbed, personal relations develop, commitments are made, and lessons are drawn that modify these initial views. Shultz, for example, began his tenure as secretary of state with a reputation for being evenhanded, but later he was seen by the Israelis as their closest friend. And yet it was also Shultz who, in his last weeks as secretary of state, opened the dialogue with the PLO.

The easiest of these predispositions to change is the sense of priority one brings to the analysis of the Arab-Israeli situation. When tensions rise, or violence erupts, it is quite easy for presidents and secretaries of state to turn their attention to the Arab-Israeli conflict. Nixon and Kissinger immediately changed their assessment of the priority due to the Arab-Israeli dispute when war broke out on October 6, 1973. Alternatively, if the costs of activism seem too great, a president can try to disengage from Arab-Israeli diplomacy, as Carter did in mid-1979.

It seems to be somewhat harder for leaders to shift from a globalist to a regionalist perspective, or vice versa. Such views tend to be fairly well established as part of an overall approach to foreign policy. Nevertheless, Kissinger, the quintessential globalist, found himself avidly absorbing information about Middle East politics once he decided to engage in sustained negotiations with the parties to the conflict. Similarly, Bush was initially fairly hard line in dealing with the Soviet Union in the Middle East, but suddenly the Soviet Union collapsed, and Bush and Baker found a regionalist perspective quite congenial. Only Carter moved somewhat in the opposite direction. After the Iranian revolution and the Soviet invasion of Afghanistan in 1979, and in the midst of his own reelection campaign, Carter adopted a tough anti-Soviet line. He termed Israel a strategic asset in the struggle to contain Soviet influence, said he opposed a Palestinian state because it would be an outpost of Soviet influence, and generally adopted a position closer to that of Ronald Reagan than to his own earlier stance. With the end of the cold war, this dimension of policy analysis ceased to be so important.

Sympathies seem to change least of all. Pro-Israeli officials do not stop sympathizing with Israel, but they may come to appreciate the need to cultivate relations with Arab leaders as well. This seems to have been true of Reagan, who never wavered in his support for Israel, but who also sold AWACS aircraft to Saudi Arabia, tilted toward Iraq, and authorized the opening of a dialogue with the PLO. Nixon, who seemed to have little emotional affinity for the Jewish state, nonetheless adopted policies, in large measure because of his global outlook, that were very pro-Israeli. Bush, who developed a reputation for being anti-Israeli, endorsed an Israeli proposal for Palestinian elections; crushed Iraq, Israel's principal Arab foe; sidelined the PLO from the official negotiations; continued economic and military support for Israel at all-time high levels despite the end of the cold war; and found no trouble in patching up quarrels with Israel once Shamir had been replaced as prime minister by Rabin. Finally Clinton, the most pro-Israeli of all presidents, also became the first president to develop a friendly relationship with Yasir Arafat, to visit Gaza, and to speak sympathetically of Palestinians' aspirations to rule themselves on their own land. He all but endorsed the idea of a Palestinian state.

In short, no president or secretary of state has remained narrowly bound by initial sympathies. All have come to realize that effective mediation requires an ability to deal with leaders on both sides of the conflict, whatever one's personal preferences might be. Thus, although such preferences resist the kind of change that other views may undergo, they also seem least important in the setting of policy. It will long be debated by serious Israelis, for example, whether the ostensibly pro-Israeli Kissinger and Reagan did more for Israel's long-term security than Carter and Bush did.

On-the-Job Training

In learning how to deal with the Middle East, American officials must assess past performance and draw lessons about what has worked and what has failed. On the whole, Americans agree on the successful cases: the adoption of UN Resolution 242; the Egyptian and Syrian disengagement agreements; Camp David and the Egyptian-Israeli peace treaty; the Madrid conference; and the Oslo agreement and its aftermath. The problem with these successes is that they cannot easily be replicated. The lessons to be learned tend to be general ones, not specifically related to the context of existing problems. By their nature, successes change the environment, leaving new problems in their wake.

Failures are another matter. They leave strong impressions about what not to do. Once a tactic is judged to have failed in one context, it will be hard to argue that it should be tried again in another. In the annals of Arab-Israeli diplomacy it is widely believed that the Rogers Plan of 1969 was a mistake; that the U.S.-Soviet joint communiqué of October 1, 1977, calling for a resumption of the Geneva conference, was an error; that the May 17, 1983, agreement between Lebanon and Israel was fatally flawed; and that the deployment of U.S. forces to Lebanon in 1982 should never be repeated. No one has made a career in Washington in recent years by trying to argue that the Rogers Plan had some positive elements that eventually led to the Egyptian-Israeli peace treaty, or that it failed because it was undercut from within the Nixon administration as much as for any other reason. Few have questioned that the October 1, 1977, communiqué was misguided, and for years the standard rebuff to anyone suggesting that the Soviet Union should be involved in Middle East diplomacy was the example of the fate of that effort. The successful Camp David talks of 1978 were a model for Clinton's Camp David II, but when those failed there was no rush for a Camp David III. The new watchword was that careful preparations should precede the convening of a summit to ensure its success. Equally important is a sound strategy that takes into account the most fundamental interests of both sides.

Other Middle East cases are harder to judge. Was the Jordan crisis a success or a failure? Some of both, one could contend. King Hussein was strengthened; allies of the Soviet Union were checked; the crisis was contained. But the lessons drawn were the source of subsequent problems. Complacency set in; confidence grew in Israeli military prowess as the key to stability; and Arab frustrations were ignored. The "success" in handling the Jordan crisis led, in part, to the "failure" to anticipate the October 1973 war. That "failure" in turn set the stage for the "success" of the disengagement talks. In brief, lessons of history are invariably drawn, but they involve highly subjective judgments. Nevertheless, they serve as powerful guidelines in intrabureaucratic discussions.

Accumulated experience with Middle East diplomacy does not suggest a single correct method for pursuing the peace process. Each president has had a somewhat distinctive style. Johnson limited himself to spelling out the general principles for a peace settlement, while insisting that Israel should be allowed to hold captured Arab lands as bargaining leverage to achieve peace. The logic of that approach has rarely been questioned by his successors. Nixon, influenced by Kissinger, initially opted for a policy of confronting the Soviets in the region before tackling the Arab-Israeli conflict. Then, after the 1973 war, Nixon and Kissinger developed the technique of step-by-step shuttle diplomacy. Carter began with a comprehensive design but was obliged to scale back to a more modest, though still impressive, goal of peace on one front. Reagan and Haig preached a doctrine of strategic consensus, which had few regional supporters; then in 1982 Reagan gave a speech that spelled out as clearly as has ever been done what the United States would support in an Arab-Israeli settlement. The speech was not connected to a strategy, and the Reagan years saw little real progress in peacemaking, but the vision spelled out in that speech has informed policymaking ever since. Bush and Baker, after one false start, perfected the art of the deal, bringing all the parties to accept the architecture of a negotiating process. Finally, Clinton's initial contribution to Arab-Israeli peacemaking was modest, but with time he helped all parties to get used to the idea of dealing with the Palestinians as a full party to the peace process. He helped bring Arab-Israeli peace closer than ever before, but his own distractions and hesitations, at least in part, kept him from bridging the final gaps.

Substantive Building Blocks

Over time presidents and their advisers have spoken less about the substance of an Arab-Israeli agreement and more about process. This "procedural bias" stems from a belief that big plans do not work, that they are too controversial, that they become targets of opposition rather than frameworks for agreement. Yet many of the most impressive monuments of American peacemaking in the Middle East are in fact sketches of both the content of peace and the process for achieving it. UN Resolution 242, which is still seen as a foundation for any Arab-Israeli peace, is essentially a statement of the main substantive trade-off that will have to be negotiated: the withdrawal of Israeli forces from territory occupied in 1967 in return for recognition, peace, and security arrangements for Israel. If 242 had flaws, they were primarily the total disregard of the Palestinians (a substantive issue that was dealt with through procedural arrangements in later years) and the feeble mechanism designed to promote peace (a UN-designated envoy without any powers). Besides providing the basis for the Egyptian-Israeli peace, UN Resolution 242 and its "land for peace" trade-off will almost certainly be at the core of a future Syrian-Israeli agreement.

The Camp David Accords went further than Resolution 242 in addressing the Palestinian issue. Their chief innovation was to call for an interim agreement between Israel and the Palestinians based on the concept of self-government, or autonomy. The reason for this approach was that neither Israelis nor Palestinians seemed able to agree on more than such an interim step. The architects of Camp David also hoped that the experience of the "transitional" period would make the issues of a final settlement more tractable. Although Camp David is not explicitly the agreed basis for the negotiations between Israel and the Palestinians, the central idea of a two-stage negotiation, starting with interim self-government for the Palestinians, was built into the Oslo agreement.

Reagan's substantive legacy was his elaboration on the missing part of Camp David—namely, what lay beyond the transitional period. Without going into great detail, Reagan said that the United States would not support Israeli annexation of the West Bank and Gaza or a fully independent Palestinian state. Instead the United States would favor some form of association between the occupied territories and Jordan. The *intifada*, however, eroded much of Jordan's support in the West Bank, and since 1988 it has become increasingly clear that the Palestinians will eventually have some form of state of their own, although it will inevitably have a close association with Jordan.

The main substantive contribution of the Bush administration did not come in the form of plans or speeches. In the course of organizing the Madrid conference, Bush and Baker began to deal with the Palestinians as a full partner in the negotiations. This ostensibly procedural step had substantive implications, although these remain to be elaborated in the course of negotiations. Bush also returned to the emphasis on freezing Israeli settlement activity during the negotiating process. Carter had tried and failed to win this point. Bush, wielding the big stick of $10 billion in loan guarantees, was taken more seriously. Indeed, one of Bush's major contributions to the peace process was the boost he gave to the unseating of the ideologically rigid Yitzhak Shamir and his replacement by the more pragmatic Yitzhak Rabin. For the first time since 1977, Israel was governed by a cabinet committed to UN Resolution 242 in its original meaning—the exchange of land for peace, in conditions of security and mutual recognition, on all fronts of the conflict. Even Bill Clinton noted that Rabin's election was the most important contribution to the peace process in the year following the Madrid conference, although he gave George Bush no credit for pushing Shamir to the sidelines.[1]

Clinton's own contribution is hard to assess. Many agreements were signed during his two terms—Oslo I and II, the Israel-Jordan peace treaty, the Hebron agreement, the Wye agreement—and in each case he played some role, encouraging the parties to reach agreement and helping to ease the way. He may well be remembered as the facilitator par excellence, but Clinton was reluctant until the last month of his incumbency to spell out the details of his vision of an Israeli-Palestinian peace. On the Israeli-Syrian track, which ultimately failed to result in agreement, one could detect a steady American effort to press the parties toward a package deal based on the return of Golan to Syria, an American security presence, and full normalization of relations over a number of years. On the Palestinian front, Clinton finally proposed a demilitarized Palestinian state in most of the West Bank and Gaza, with Palestinian control in parts of East Jerusalem, and with limits on the Palestinian "right of return." A consensus seemed to emerge that a Palestinian state would be part of the future architecture of the Middle East. But the final pieces of the design never quite fell into place on his watch. The devil, to say the least, was in the details.

Future Prospects

As the new millennium begins, the United States has succeeded in institutionalizing the process of Arab-Israeli negotiations, but full peace remains elusive. A design can be detected in the series of previous agreements, but nothing really tells us how and when the complex issues between Israelis and Palestinians and between Israelis and Syrians will ultimately be resolved. Almost certainly, however, the United States will be called on to help elaborate the contents of future peace agreements if negotiations are to succeed. Nothing in the historical record suggests that the parties will reach agreement on final-status issues if left alone in direct negotiations.

In many ways the American role in the future should be easier to play than in the past. The Soviet Union as a rival and potential spoiler is no more. The globalist bias that often adversely affected American policy in the Middle East has lost its rationale. With it has gone the notion that Israel is a strategic ally of such importance that it must be supported at all costs.[2] Public backing for Israel remains high, but the White House is under little pressure to offer Israel a blank check. Public opinion, if not Congress, is more prone than ever to support an evenhanded stance toward the Arab-Israeli conflict. Such an atmosphere provides a degree of tactical flexibility for a president seeking to find common ground between Arabs and Israelis.

The record of the peace process since 1967 shows that progress is not incremental or continuous. More frequently, long periods of stalemate have been succeeded by bursts of activity that have produced substantial changes in the nature of the Arab-Israeli conflict. Then the parties seem to need some time to absorb the results, to ready themselves for another major move, to build support on the domestic front.

One can credibly argue that the 1980s represented an unusually long lull in the peace process and that the stage is set in the new millennium for significant breakthroughs. One possibility would be moves toward a Syrian-Israeli treaty, based on full peace and recognition for Israel, extensive security arrangements to reduce the chance of surprise attack, and Israeli recognition of Syrian sovereignty on the Golan Heights. All these principles could be implemented over a period of years. Israel and Syria came close to such an agreement in 1995 and again early in 2000, and they might resume negotiations along these lines in the future.

On the Israeli-Palestinian front the prospects for an overall agreement are more difficult to assess. The post-Wye status quo seems unlikely to last indefinitely. The outline of future agreements depends very much on the balance of opinion within the Israeli body politic. The moderate Israeli view, represented by Prime Minister Ehud Barak in 2000, provided a plausible base for a negotiated agreement, assuming that the impasse over Jerusalem and refugees could ever be resolved. Likud's vision, by contrast, seems to go little beyond the leopard-spot map of Wye, leaving the Palestinians with limited authority over less than half the land of the West Bank and Gaza, in conditions of questionable economic viability. It is hard to see this as a pattern for peace. Domestic Israeli politics will be a major determinant of how and whether negotiations resume. In addition, the frayed nerves from the confrontation of late 2000 will need some time to heal.

For the peace process to move ahead, American leadership will be needed. That prospect is somewhat challenged by a revival of isolationist sentiment in the United States. This attitude affects Middle East policy less than other foreign-policy issue areas, but it places a limit on any initiative that is likely to require substantial resources. As a result the United States, while still playing the key mediating role, will have to find partners who can help underwrite steps toward peace, toward regional development, and toward arms control.

As the peace process moves along, the United States will also be confronting other, related challenges in the Middle East. How should the next president deal with assertive Islamic movements? What is the place for democracy in this part of the world? Can economic development be accelerated, as in east Asia, as a complement to peacemaking and democratization? Can arms control make headway in a region where conflicts are so endemic? And can anything be done to prevent the proliferation of weapons of mass destruction in the region? All these concerns will demand attention alongside the traditional peace process agenda. Even that agenda will have to address in creative ways the problems of regional security, refugee claims, settlements, and the future of Jerusalem, issues that have thus far bedeviled negotiators.

Time is still of the essence, not so much because peace must be achieved suddenly or not at all. Rather, the process is likely to take time, even in the best of circumstances, which means that political leaders in the region must be able to show results early and often if they are to retain the necessary support. The way in which domestic support for Ehud Barak eroded from 1999 to 2000 should be a warning to those who believe time is on the side of peace. A prolonged stalemate in the peace process will frustrate moderates on both sides of the conflict, as was seen in late 2000, and could eventually lead to public disinterest in the United States and set the stage for future crises in a radicalized Middle East whose oil resources will be increasingly important for the industrialized West.

Thus the peace process, with an emphasis now on the most difficult substantive elements of future peace agreements, is likely to be a priority for future presidents. The record suggests that their own predispositions will matter in the shaping of policy toward the Arab-Israeli conflict, even though by now there is a fairly strong American consensus on the peace process and its rationale. Nevertheless, in those moments when judgment is called for, when crises clarify choices, when trade-offs must be made, and when priorities must be set, the person occupying the Oval Office makes a difference.

If presidents play their part well, they can help advance the peace process. If they falter, they risk jeopardizing American interests. For better or worse, they will not be allowed to ignore the region for long. Their understanding of the basic issues of the Arab-Israeli conflict and their ability to learn from experience will be the keys to whether presidents become statesmen. If they do, they stand a good chance of contributing to the long-sought goal of Arab-Israeli peace.

Notes

Chapter 1

1. For the texts of UN Resolutions 242 and 338, see www.brookings.edu/press/appendix/peace_process.htm.

2. The formative works on bureaucratic politics are Graham Allison, *Essence of Decision: Explaining the Cuban Missile Crisis* (Little, Brown, 1971); and Morton Halperin, *Bureaucratic Politics and Foreign Policy* (Brookings, 1974). For an excellent critique, see Robert Art, "Bureaucratic Politics and American Foreign Policy: A Critique," *Policy Sciences*, vol. 4 (1973), pp. 467–90.

3. See Mitchell Geoffrey Bard, *The Water's Edge and Beyond: Defining the Limits to Domestic Influence on United States Middle East Policy* (New Brunswick, N.J.: Transaction Publishers, 1991).

4. See William B. Quandt, *Camp David: Peacemaking and Politics* (Brookings, 1986), pp. 6–29.

5. For a more detailed discussion of these three approaches, see William B. Quandt, *Decade of Decisions: American Policy toward the Arab-Israeli Conflict, 1967–1976* (University of California Press, 1977), pp. 3–28.

6. See Daniel Yergin, *The Prize: The Epic Quest for Oil, Money and Power* (Simon and Schuster, 1991).

7. See Raymond A. Bauer and Kenneth J. Gergen, eds., *The Study of Policy Formulation* (Free Press, 1968), p. 15.

8. Charles E. Lindblom, "The Science of 'Muddling Through,'" *Public Administration Review*, vol. 19 (Spring 1959), pp. 79–88.

9. John Steinbruner, *The Cybernetic Theory of Decision: New Dimensions of Political Analysis* (Princeton University Press, 1974), pp. 109–24.

10. Ernest May, *"Lessons" of the Past: The Use and Misuse of History in American Foreign Policy* (Oxford University Press, 1973).

11. Merle Miller, *Plain Speaking: An Oral Biography of Harry S. Truman* (Berkley Publishing, 1973).

12. Lynn E. Davis, *The Cold War Begins: Soviet-American Conflict over Eastern Europe* (Princeton University Press, 1974).

13. Alexander L. George, "The Case for Multiple Advocacy in Making Foreign Policy," *American Political Science Review*, vol. 66 (September 1972), pp. 751–85; and Irving L. Janis, *Victims of Groupthink: A Psychological Study of Foreign Policy Decisions and Fiascoes* (Houghton Mifflin, 1972).

Chapter 2

1. Abba Eban, *An Autobiography* (Random House, 1977), pp. 354–55, gives an account of Johnson's early concern with Israel. Among Johnson's close friends who were strong supporters of Israel were Arthur Krim, president of United Artists and chairman of the Democratic National Party Finance Committee, and his wife Mathilde; Abraham Feinberg, president of the American Bank and Trust of New York; Abraham Fortas, Supreme Court Justice; and Arthur Goldberg, ambassador to the United Nations. See Donald Neff, *Warriors for Jerusalem: The Six Days That Changed the Middle East* (Simon and Schuster, 1984), pp. 80–85, 156–58.

2. The report prepared in the fall of 1966 by Ambassador Julius Holmes contained this theme.

3. See Michael Brecher, *Decisions in Israel's Foreign Policy* (Yale University Press, 1975), pp. 359–61, for a review of these threats. The best documented, and the one that was carried by UPI and showed up in the *New York Times* on May 13, consisted of a background briefing on May 12, 1967, by the Israeli head of military intelligence, Aharon Yariv. John Cooley, *Green March, Black September: The Story of the Palestinian Arabs* (London: Frank Cass, 1973), p. 160, quotes from a tape of the briefing: "I could say we must use force in order to have the Egyptians convince the Syrians that it doesn't pay [to let the Palestinians carry out attacks across Syria's borders]. . . . I think that the only sure and safe answer to the problem is a military operation of great size and strength." Some analysts have mistakenly assumed that it was Chief of Staff Yitzhak Rabin who made the "threat" against Syria. See *Middle East Record, 1967*, vol. 3 (Jerusalem: Israel Universities Press, 1971), p. 187.

4. Although Israeli threats to take action against Syria were not very precise in this period, it does appear that some retaliatory action was contemplated. Michael Brecher, *Decisions in Crisis: Israel, 1967 and 1973* (University of California Press, 1980), p. 36, states that on May 7, 1967, "Israel's Cabinet decided that if Syria did not heed her public warnings and if all other noncoercive methods of persuasion failed, Israel would launch a limited retaliation raid." For the Egyptian reaction, see Mohamed Heikal (in Arabic, Muhammad Hassanayn Haykal), *1967: Al-Infijar* (Cairo: Markaz al-Ahram, 1990), pp. 445–56. For a discussion of the Israeli threats and the Soviet role by participants in the conflict, see Richard B. Parker, ed., *The Six-Day War: A Retrospective* (University Press of Florida, 1996) pp. 13–73.

5. Heikal, *1967: Al-Infijar*, pp. 371–72, greatly exaggerates when he implies that Johnson was obsessed with Nasser and engaged in a conspiracy to bring him down.

6. On this incident, which, in the words of Yitzhak Rabin, caught Israel "with its pants down," see Avner Yaniv, *Deterrence without the Bomb: The Politics of Israeli Strategy* (Lexington, Mass.: Lexington Books, 1987), pp. 84–85.

7. Some, including Egypt's foreign minister, Mahmoud Riad, have maintained that Egypt only asked that the UNEF be withdrawn from the border area, not from Sharm al-Shaykh. That may have been the intention behind the initial requests, but Egyptian commanders in the field made it clear that the UNEF contingent at Sharm al-Shaykh should also leave. Riad's own letter to UN Secretary General U Thant on May 18 requested the removal of the UNEF from the territory of the UAR [United Arab Republic, or Egypt]. See Mahmoud Riad, *The Struggle for Peace in the Middle East* (Quartet Books, 1981), p. 18; and "Report of the Secretary-General on the Withdrawal of the United Nations Emergency Force, June 26, 1967," reprinted in John Norton Moore, ed., *The Arab-Israeli Conflict*, vol. 3: *Documents* (Princeton University Press, 1974), p. 756. U Thant has been criticized for acceding too hastily to the Egyptian request, for not referring the question to the General Assembly—in short, for not calling Nasser's bluff. See, for example, Nadav Safran, *Israel: The Embattled Ally* (Harvard University Press, 1978), pp. 394–95. Heikal, *1967: Al-Infijar*, pp. 457–74, argues that Nasser did initially favor only a partial withdrawal of the UNEF, while Abd al-Hakim Amr ['Amir], the head of the armed forces, wanted the UNEF to leave completely. There are many indications from Egyptian sources that the Nasser-Amr rivalry was a serious problem throughout this whole period. For a good overview of the relevant facts, see Richard B. Parker, "The June 1967 War: Some Mysteries Explored," *Middle East Journal*, vol. 46 (Spring 1992), pp. 184–96.

8. Lyndon Baines Johnson, *The Vantage Point: Perspectives of the Presidency, 1963–1969* (Holt, Rinehart, and Winston, 1971), p. 290; and M. Gilboa, *Six Years, Six Days* (in Hebrew) (Tel Aviv: Am Oved, 1968), p. 144.

9. Harold Saunders, a staff member of the National Security Council (NSC) at this time, was responsible for compiling the White House documents on the 1967 crisis for the Johnson Library. In a reflective cover memorandum entitled "The Middle East Crisis: Preface," December 20, 1968, top secret (declassified October 14, 1983), Saunders notes that "we 'decided' at the outset of the crisis to try to restrain Israel from trying to settle its own problems militarily. . . . The alternative was to let the Israelis do as they had so often done before—respond militarily on their own. This alternative was rejected, almost out of hand. . . . I had the impression that President Johnson himself, though he wanted to avoid war, was profoundly skeptical that we would succeed in rallying practical international support for keeping the Straits open. If we failed, our last hope was to negotiate with Nasser's Vice President. If that didn't work, we would be left to open the Straits in direct confrontation with the whole Arab world."

10. Gilboa, *Six Years, Six Days*, p. 145; and *Middle East Record, 1967*, vol. 3, pp. 194, 196.

11. The text of the February 11, 1957, aide-mémoire can be found in Moore, *Arab-Israeli Conflict*, vol. 3: *Documents*, pp. 638–39. On February 24, 1957, Eban sought a clarification from Secretary of State John Foster Dulles to the effect that Israel could invoke the right to self-defense under article 51 of the UN Charter if its ships were attacked. Dulles agreed with Eban's position. The public mani-

festation of this "assent" was somewhat vague. Golda Meir spoke at the UN on March 1 and stated that Israel would exercise its inherent right of self-defense if armed force were used to interfere with Israeli shipping in the Strait of Tiran. Henry Cabot Lodge, the American ambassador to the United Nations, took note of this declaration and said that it did not seem "unreasonable." Eban was unhappy with this formulation, and therefore Eisenhower wrote to Ben Gurion on March 2, 1957, saying that Israel would "have no cause to regret" its withdrawal from Sinai and that the expressed Israeli views were "reasonable." All the relevant texts can be found in Nina J. Noring, ed., *Foreign Relations of the United States, 1955–1957: Arab-Israeli Dispute, 1957* (Government Printing Office, 1990), pp. 254–348.

12. On May 21, Johnson did send Eshkol a letter. Gilboa, *Six Years, Six Days*, p. 145; Brecher, *Decisions in Israel's Foreign Policy*, p. 375; Michael Bar-Zohar, *Embassies in Crisis: Diplomats and Demagogues behind the Six-Day War* (Prentice-Hall, 1970), p. 68. The full text of the Johnson letter is in Department of State telegram 198955, May 21, 1967, secret (declassified May 24, 1990). In mid-October 1969 Abba Eban submitted an article to the *New York Times Magazine* that was prepared for publication but was withdrawn at the last moment. A copy of the galley proofs is in the author's possession, and it differs in significant ways from Eban's later account in his autobiography. His words concerning the May 21 letter in the draft were: "Nothing could have been less promising than these early reports. Indeed, it was their lack of virile purpose and Johnsonian authenticity which had swayed my decision to go to Washington. This was not Johnson language; a frightened bureaucrat bleated from every line. Nothing except the signature seemed to have anything to do with the firm and candid personality which Israel had respected throughout all of his vicissitudes—and ours—at home and in the world."

13. The original draft of the letter, with Johnson's own corrections and additions, is available from the Johnson Library (declassified May 8, 1981). See also Mohamed Heikal, *The Cairo Documents: The Inside Story of Nasser and His Relationship with World Leaders, Rebels, and Statesmen* (Doubleday, 1973), p. 243. Nolte delivered the letter, plus a more substantive "note verbale," which warned of war by miscalculation, to the Egyptian foreign minister, Mahmoud Riad. Three areas of concern were emphasized: continuing guerrilla activities against Israel from Syrian territory, withdrawal of the UNEF, and troop buildups. The note went on to say, "We are convinced that any interference whatever with these international rights [of free and innocent passage in the strait for ships of all nations] could have the gravest international consequences." For the "note verbale," see Department of State telegram 199710, May 22, 1967, confidential (declassified January 4, 1990).

14. Rusk added a message to the Israelis suggesting that the UNEF be transferred to the Israeli side of the border.

15. Johnson, *Vantage Point*, pp. 290–91.

16. Johnson did take one step on May 22 that had continuing importance during the crisis: he ordered the Sixth Fleet, with two aircraft carriers, the *Saratoga* and the *America*, to the eastern Mediterranean.

17. Brecher, *Decisions in Israel's Foreign Policy*, p. 378.

18. "President's Decisions: Israeli Aid Package 23 May 1967," top secret (declassified May 9, 1983). A subsequent decision was made to approve the sale of gas masks. See *The Department of State during the Administration of President Lyndon B. Johnson, November 1963–January 1969*, vol. 1: *Administrative History*, pt. 4, chap. 4, section H-1, secret (declassified September 16, 1983), pp. 20, 33. According to the same source (p. 45), Eugene Rostow believed the United States had pulled the Israelis back from preemptive strikes on May 23. The United States had also asked Israel not to test the closure of the strait by sending its flagships through. Therefore, Rostow felt, an enormous responsibility fell on the United States.

19. "The United States Calls for Restraint in the Near East: Statement by President Johnson," *Department of State Bulletin*, vol. 56 (June 12, 1967), p. 870.

20. Brecher, *Decisions in Israel's Foreign Policy*, p. 381, refers to Evron's cable on why the United States was planning to take its case to the United Nations.

21. Johnson, *Vantage Point*, pp. 291–92.

22. Johnson was quite aware that his policy might fail. See "Record of National Security Council Meeting held on May 24, 1967 at 12 noon—Discussion of Middle East Crisis," top secret (declassified October 14, 1983). On September 10, 1992, additional portions of this document were declassified. The intriguing points are that CIA director Helms categorically asserted that there were no nuclear weapons in the area, while General Earle Wheeler, chairman of the Joint Chiefs, was "more skeptical." Later in the discussion the president returned to the question of "what we would do after relying on Israeli forces. General Wheeler noted that a long war would hurt the Israeli economy. At that point we would have to decide whether we were going to send in forces and confront Nasser directly." The next section of the transcript is still classified.

23. Johnson, *Vantage Point*, p. 292; Gilboa, *Six Years, Six Days*, p. 143; and Bar-Zohar, *Embassies in Crisis*, p. 98.

24. Bar-Zohar, *Embassies in Crisis*, p. 125.

25. These messages were sent at the instigation of the chief of staff, Yitzhak Rabin, who was eager to force an American decision. Either Johnson would have to commit himself to concrete action or Israel would be free to act on its own. See Yitzhak Rabin, *The Rabin Memoirs* (Little, Brown, 1979), pp. 86–89; Gideon Rafael, *Destination Peace: Three Decades of Israeli Foreign Policy. A Personal Memoir* (Stein and Day, 1981), pp. 144–45; Eban, *Autobiography*, pp. 348–49; and Steven L. Spiegel, *The Other Arab Israeli Conflict: Making America's Middle East Policy from Truman to Reagan* (University of Chicago Press, 1985), p. 450, note 95, for a slightly different version.

26. Brecher, *Decisions in Israel's Foreign Policy*, p. 386; and, with more detail, Brecher, *Decisions in Crisis*, pp. 130–32; Bar-Zohar, *Embassies in Crisis*, p. 109; and Moshe Dayan, *Moshe Dayan: Story of My Life* (William Morrow, 1976), p. 329.

27. Brecher, *Decisions in Israel's Foreign Policy*, pp. 386–87; and Bar-Zohar, *Embassies in Crisis*, pp. 112–13. Eugene Rostow called in the Egyptian ambassador and warned that Egypt must not attack Israel. The Soviets were also asked to use their influence to restrain Nasser, which they reportedly did. Heikal, *Cairo Documents*, p. 244; Gilboa, *Six Years, Six Days*, pp. 145–46; Brecher, *Decisions*

in Israel's Foreign Policy, p. 387; and Bar-Zohar, *Embassies in Crisis*, pp. 111–12. While Eban was making his pitch at the State Department, the CIA had received an alarmist report presented by an Israeli intelligence official to the CIA station chief in Tel Aviv. It warned of a Soviet takeover of the region if Nasser was not forced to back down. Interview with Richard Helms, June 8, 1992.

28. Brecher, *Decisions in Israel's Foreign Policy*, pp. 387–88. Harman saw Eugene Rostow and Joseph Sisco.

29. Bar-Zohar, *Embassies in Crisis*, p. 114–15. We now know that the Egyptian military, in particular Abd al-Hakim Amr, had issued orders for the Egyptian air force to carry out air strikes on the morning of May 27. The Israelis must have gotten wind of this. According to Egyptian sources, Nasser countermanded the order on May 26. See Muhammad Fawzi, *Harb al-Thalatha Sanawat, 1967–70: Mudhakirat al-Fariq Awal Muhammad Fawzi* (The Three-Year War, 1967–70: Memoirs of General Muhammad Fawzi) (Cairo: Dar al-Mustaqbal al-Arabi, 1984), p. 123; and Abd al-Muhsin Kamil Murtaji, *Al-Fariq Murtaji Yarwa al-Haqa'iq* (General Murtaji Narrates the Facts) (Beirut: Al-Watan al-Arabi, 1976), pp. 79–81. Also, Heikal, *1967: Al-Infijar*, pp. 573–75.

30. See Tom Wicker, *JFK and LBJ: The Influence of Personality upon Politics* (William Morrow, 1968), pp. 195–99.

31. Eban, *Autobiography*, pp. 349–51; Brecher, *Decisions in Israel's Foreign Policy*, pp. 389–90; and Bar-Zohar, *Embassies in Crisis*, p. 115. The previous evening, May 25, 1967, Johnson had met with Helms and Wheeler to discuss a recent Israeli intelligence assessment that was viewed as alarmist. The president had asked for the Israeli assessment to be "scrubbed down." On May 26 a joint CIA-DIA (Defense Intelligence Agency) assessment was ready. It concluded that Israel would gain air superiority in Sinai within twenty-four hours if Israel took the initiative, and within two to three days if Egypt struck first. The assessment went on to conclude that the Egyptian defense lines would be breached within several days. Interview with Richard Helms, June 5, 1992.

32. "Memorandum for the President: Your Conversation with the Israeli Foreign Minister," May 26, 1967, secret (declassified and sanitized, August 30, 1982).

33. McNamara did not oppose the president's policy, however.

34. See Rusk's handwritten draft using these words, Johnson Library (declassified June 27, 1983). This key sentence was used frequently in later communications, sometimes in slightly different forms. The Israelis spent considerable time trying to figure out if the message constituted a subtle form of encouragement to act on their own. To Rusk, it seems, it did not. Rusk's handwritten draft was edited by Johnson, who added the phrase "We cannot imagine that it will make this decision" right after the "go alone" sentence. This became the aide-mémoire handed to Eban during the meeting that evening. See marked-up draft of the aide-mémoire, Johnson Library, May 26, 1967, secret (declassified September 21, 1983).

35. The view was expressed that no overt act of aggression had yet occurred. Until Egypt resorted to the use of armed force, according to this argument, the U.S. commitment to Israel would not be activated.

36. The above summary is from rough notes of the meeting taken by Harold Saunders, May 26, 1967. See also Neff, *Warriors for Jerusalem*, pp. 142–43, especially for the text of Walt Rostow's memo for the president in preparation for this

meeting. Rostow stated, among other things, that Eban would want to know "what can you offer right now better than a pre-emptive [Israeli] strike."

37. Jonathan Trumbull Howe, *Multicrises: Sea Power and Global Politics in the Missile Age* (MIT Press, 1971), pp. 362–67. Howe interviewed an unnamed White House source (John Roche), who stated that Johnson was stalling Eban because he had just been shown the memo of the Dulles-Eban talks of 1957 and wanted to check its authenticity.

38. Evron recalled Johnson as having said that without congressional approval for any action taken, Johnson would be "just a six-foot-four-inch friend of Israel." He went on to say that "Israel is not a satellite of the United States. Nor is the United States a satellite of Israel." In retrospect, Evron felt that this was Johnson's way of saying that Israel was on its own. The message was less clear, he believed, when Johnson spoke to Eban, relying on the State Department briefing papers, shortly after this meeting. Interview with Ephraim Evron, June 4, 1992.

39. Brecher, *Decisions in Israel's Foreign Policy*, pp. 390–91, provides the full text of Evron's official account of his meeting with Johnson.

40. "Memorandum of Conversation, May 26, 1967," secret/nodis (drafted by Joseph Sisco, sanitized and declassified September 21, 1983). See also Brecher, *Decision in Israel's Foreign Policy*, p. 392. Johnson, *Vantage Point*, p. 293, says he told Eban the United States would use "any and all means" to open the strait. The official transcript reports on pp. 7–8 that Eban, choosing his words carefully, said, "I would not be wrong if I told the Prime Minister that your disposition is to make every possible effort to assure that the Strait and the Gulf will remain open to free and innocent passage? The President responded, yes." Earlier in the conversation, however, Johnson did say that the United States would pursue "any and all means" to reopen the strait. The difference between these two formulations—"every possible effort" and "any and all means"—became a source of controversy between the two governments a few days later.

41. The aide-mémoire said, in part: "I have already publicly stated this week our views on the safety of Israel and on the Strait of Tiran. Regarding the Strait, we plan to pursue vigorously the measures which can be taken by maritime nations to assure that the Strait and the Gulf remain open to free and innocent passage of the vessels of all nations.

"I must emphasize the necessity for Israel not to make itself responsible for the initiation of hostilities. Israel will not be alone unless it decides to go alone. We cannot imagine that it will make this decision."

42. Interview with Eugene Rostow, February 17, 1969; and Howe, *Multicrises*, pp. 362–67. Howe quotes White House aide John Roche to the effect that Johnson said after his meeting with Eban: "[Israel is] going to hit them." Roche's account can be found in his oral history interview with the Johnson Library, July 16, 1970, tape 2, p. 68. Just after the meeting with Eban, Johnson took a call from Ambassador Arthur Goldberg in New York. This conversation must have led Goldberg to ask for an urgent meeting of his own with Eban, who was transiting New York on his way back to Tel Aviv. The two met at the Waldorf Astoria. Goldberg, speaking authoritatively, underscored the point the president had made about the necessity for congressional support for any U.S. action. Goldberg offered his personal opinion that this meant that the United States could do nothing

militarily to help Israel. Rafael, *Destination Peace*, p. 145, provides part of this story. In addition, see the oral history interview with Arthur Goldberg, LBJ Library, March 23, 1983, p. 22. In the same interview Goldberg claims that Johnson had asked him to take charge of the crisis because Rusk had disqualified himself by making anti-Israel remarks earlier in his career (p. 16).

43. Brecher, *Decisions in Israel's Foreign Policy*, pp. 398, provides the text of this message: "The Soviets stated that if Israel starts military action, the Soviet Union will extend help to the attacked States. . . . As your friend, I repeat even more strongly what I said yesterday to Mr. Eban: Israel just must not take preemptive military action and thereby make itself responsible for the initiation of hostilities." Johnson then requested a two- to three-week delay before Israel would resort to force to open the strait. The original draft of the message had said "It is essential that Israel not. . . ." From his Texas ranch, Johnson strengthened this to read "Israel just must not. . . ." He also suggested including the following language: "Without exception our Congressional leaders have made it clear that preemptive actions would find no support here." Memorandum from Jim Jones to Walt Rostow, May 27, 1967 (declassified and sanitized, September 21, 1983).

44. Brecher, *Decisions in Israel's Foreign Policy*, p. 400. Brecher, *Decisions in Crisis*, p. 146, claims that this message had a significant impact on Eshkol's thinking and probably kept the cabinet from deciding on war that day.

45. Interview with Daniel P. Levitt, law clerk for Justice Fortas in 1967, on August 8, 1991. Levitt indicated that he believed but could not confirm that Johnson had asked Fortas to play the role of "informal intermediary" with Israel.

46. See Laura Kalman, *Abe Fortas: A Biography* (Yale University Press, 1990), p. 301; and, from the same source (Levitt), Robert Shogan, *A Question of Judgment: The Fortas Case and the Struggle for the Supreme Court* (Bobbs-Merrill, 1972), p. 139.

47. Just as the Israelis were setting out to determine Johnson's views with precision, Johnson left town for a long weekend at his Texas ranch. None of his foreign policy advisers accompanied him, although they were able to stay in regular touch by telephone and cables. Much of his time over the Memorial Day weekend—which extended from Saturday, May 27, until his return to the White House very early Wednesday morning, May 31—was spent in the company of Arthur and Mathilde Krim, Mary Lasker, and Jake Jacobsen, a former legal adviser. All were involved in party politics, and the Krims and Mrs. Lasker were large contributors to the Democratic party.

48. Interview with Walt Rostow, October 16, 1991; and Walt Rostow, *The Diffusion of Power: An Essay in Recent History* (Macmillan, 1972), pp. 417–19.

49. Johnson, *Vantage Point*, p. 294; Bar-Zohar, *Embassies in Crisis*, pp. 159–60; and Brecher, *Decisions in Israel's Foreign Policy*, pp. 338, 413. The full text of Eshkol's message, which Walt Rostow characterized as "somber" in a covering note to Johnson, has never been published. According to one source, Eshkol did refer to "the intelligence cooperation which you have authorized." Brecher, who has seen the letter, quotes the following sentences from it: "One of the difficulties that I face is that I must call on my people to meet sacrifices and dangers without being able fully to reveal certain compensatory factors such as the United States commitment and the full scope of your determination on the matter of the Straits

of Tiran" (p. 338). Eshkol also referred to the need to stand up to Nasser soon, noting the effect he was having on Jordan. "President Nasser's rising prestige has already had serious effects in Jordan. . . . The time is ripe for confronting Nasser with a more intense and effective policy of resistance" (p. 413). This latter point impressed Rostow, and probably the president as well. Reacting to this same Eshkol message, Harold Saunders wrote to Walt Rostow on May 31 and urged him to consider a "quite different alternative," presumably to that of the multilateral fleet. In a recently declassified portion of the message, Saunders notes that the British and Canadians "are wobbling" and that "Eshkol's message suggests that we may be up against this choice sooner rather than later." "Memorandum for WWR," secret (declassified, October 14, 1992).

50. Transmittal of "Yost's First Report" from Walt Rostow to the president, received LBJ Communications Center in Texas, May 30, 1967, at 2:17 p.m., secret (declassified June 27, 1983).

51. Heikal, *Cairo Documents*, p. 245; Brecher, *Decisions in Israel's Foreign Policy*, p. 420; and Bar-Zohar, *Embassies in Crisis*, p. 168. Anderson's report of his talk with Nasser reached Washington on June 2. See Department of State telegram, Lisbon 1517, June 2, 1967, top secret (declassified September 3, 1982). Nasser told Anderson that Egypt would not attack, but expected the Israelis to strike. Nasser said that "he was confident of the outcome of a conflict between Arabs and Israelis."

52. Bar-Zohar, *Embassies in Crisis*, pp. 160–61.

53. Interview with Evron, November 5, 1991.

54. Bar-Zohar, *Embassies in Crisis*, p. 157, states that on May 30, after Jordan threw in its lot with Egypt, Walt Rostow expressed the opinion that he no longer saw a political solution.

55. Brecher, *Decisions in Israel's Foreign Policy*, p. 417. See also Ian Black and Benny Morris, *Israel's Secret Wars: A History of Israel's Intelligence Services* (Grove Weidenfield, 1991), p. 537, referring to an interview with Amit, who claims he went to Washington "to tell [the Americans] that we were going to war, and to hear their reaction."

56. Letter to William B. Quandt from Abba Eban, July 26, 1990. Eban, *Autobiography*, pp. 384–85, gives a more extensive account of this message but without any mention of Evron or Fortas by name. According to Eban, an American close to Johnson (Fortas) reportedly said, "If Israel had acted alone without exhausting political efforts it would have made a catastrophic error. It would then have been almost impossible for the United States to help Israel and the ensuing relationship would have been tense. The war might be long and costly for Israel if it broke out. If Israel had fired the first shot before the United Nations discussion she would have negated any possibility of the United States helping her. Israelis should not criticize Eshkol and Eban; they should realize that their restraint and well-considered procedures would have a decisive influence when the United States came to consider the measure of its involvement." Fortas reportedly understood that "time was running out and that it was a matter of days or even hours." But Fortas believed that "if the measures being taken by the United States prove ineffective, the United States would now back Israel." Abba Eban, *Personal Witness: Israel through My Eyes* (Putnam's, 1993), p. 405, repeats this account, this time

naming Fortas. Johnson and Fortas spoke at 8:43 p.m. on May 28, according to the president's daily calendar. Johnson tried again to call Fortas on May 31, but Fortas was in Puerto Rico. See also Shimon Peres, *David's Sling* (Random House, 1970), p. 236, where he writes: "As the month of May approached its end, it became clear that there was no longer any prospect of a maritime operation through the Straits. Even in certain circles in Washington the view was heard that the only one able to find a way out of the impasse was Israel herself. This view reached the ears of Jerusalem."

57. Brecher, *Decisions in Israel's Foreign Policy*, p. 417, indicates that Eban had also seen Amit's report, with its judgment that "there is a growing chance for American political backing if we act on our own." Eitan Haber, *Today War Will Break Out: The Reminiscences of Brigadier General Israel Lior* (Jerusalem: Edanim/Yedi'ot Aharonot, 1987) (in Hebrew), p. 213, notes that on June 1 Eban concluded that there was no longer any need to wait for U.S. action. His change of mind was seen by some as providing a green light for military action. According to Haber, Yariv had already reached the conclusion that the United States was not serious about the maritime fleet and that therefore Israel was free to act on its own (pp. 205–06).

58. Johnson, *Vantage Point*, p. 294, without naming Evron, reveals part of this incident. The rest is based on interviews with participants.

59. By contrast, the American embassy in Cairo strongly felt that the Egyptians would react militarily to any attempt to reopen the strait. See cables on May 26, 1967 (Cairo 8007, secret), May 28, 1967 (Cairo 8093, secret), and June 3, 1967 (Cairo 8432, secret), all declassified on January 4, 1990.

60. Interview with Evron, December 30, 1974. Notes of this meeting were made by Harold Saunders, who was present, and have been consulted as well.

61. Evron was busy on June 3. Early in the morning, he presented a long list of Israel's military needs to McNamara, who implied that the arms could never get to Israel in time, since the war would be quickly over. Evron read this as a hint that the United States was confident that Israel would win and that there was no need to wait for American action. Later in the day Evron saw Rusk, who, during a very cordial meeting, gave him Johnson's letter to Eshkol. That same evening he dined with Walt Rostow, who talked at some length about what should be done in the region after the war was over. In his view, these three senior American officials, all aware of his and Amit's messages, had several chances that day to warn Israel not to take military action, but instead they talked as if war was a foregone conclusion. Interview with Evron, November 5, 1991.

62. According to Evron, this was the closest Johnson came to responding to the messages from him and Amit that time was running out and Israel might have to act soon. By acknowledging these signals, he thought Johnson was saying to Israel that "the red light has turned to amber." Interview with Evron, October 22, 1991.

63. Interview with Richard Helms, June 8, 1992. Amit told Helms that Israel needed nothing from the United States except the supply of arms already agreed on, diplomatic support, and holding the Soviets at bay if necessary. Amit interpreted his and Ambassador Harman's recall to Jerusalem on June 1 as an indication that the decision for war was imminent. In Amit's view, Nasser was not

planning a ground attack, but Israel could not afford to wait for his next move. The economic costs were too great, and the political pressures on Eshkol were intense. In addition, there was the possibility of an Egyptian air strike, perhaps at the Dimona nuclear reactor. According to Shlomo Aronson, *The Politics and Strategy of Nuclear Weapons in the Middle East: Opacity, Theory, and Reality, 1960–1991. An Israeli Perspective* (State University of New York Press, 1992), p. 109, an Egyptian aircraft had overflown Dimona on May 17, 1967, on a reconnaissance flight. Aronson makes an elaborate argument that Nasser's primary objective in the crisis that led to the June 1967 war was to put Egypt in a position to strike at Dimona before Israel acquired nuclear-tipped surface-to-surface missiles. Eshkol was reportedly preoccupied with the possible threat to Dimona. See Haber, *Today War Will Break Out*, p. 161.

64. Letter from President Johnson to Prime Minister Eshkol. Available with cover memorandum, June 3, 1967, from the Johnson Library, secret (declassified April 5, 1982), with the intriguing note from Walt Rostow that "It may be urgent that we put this letter on record soon." See also Brecher, *Decisions in Israel's Foreign Policy*, p. 420. Bar-Zohar, *Embassies in Crisis*, p. 175, also printed part of this text. Dayan, *Moshe Dayan*, pp. 345–46, states that a letter from Johnson was read to the ministerial defense committee meeting on June 4 at which the decision for war was made.

65. Department of State telegram 297977, June 3, 1967, p. 3, secret (declassified January 9, 1990).

66. Levitt to Quandt, August 8, 1991; and Kalman, *Abe Fortas*, p. 301.

67. Nasser had sent Johnson a letter on June 2, which reached the president the following day, that agreed to the visit of Muhieddin, but was, in the words of Walt Rostow, otherwise "quite uncompromising." See Rostow memo to Johnson, June 3, 1967, with text of Nasser letter, secret (declassified August 27, 1982), Johnson Library. Anderson's discouraging report of his talk with Nasser also reached the president at about this time.

68. Gilboa, *Six Years, Six Days*, p. 199. A participant in the meeting noted that Amit reported that the United States would bless whatever Israel did if it succeeded in getting rid of Nasser. See also Andrew Cockburn and Leslie Cockburn, *Dangerous Liaison: The Inside Story of the U.S.-Israeli Covert Relationship* (HarperCollins Publishers, 1991), pp. 145–46, quoting from Eshkol's cabinet secretary. For the original source, see Haber, *Today War Will Break Out*, pp. 216–18. Amit's own version is that he said something to the effect that the United States would not mourn if Israel struck at Egypt (interview, June 4, 1992). Amit also told the cabinet members that the "Red Sea Regatta" should not be taken seriously. During the subsequent June 4 cabinet meeting, when the decision to go to war was officially made, Eshkol said that Johnson had now softened his stand and would give Israel political support. See Brecher, *Decisions in Crisis*, p. 167.

69. Outgoing telegram, Department of State, Circular to Arab Capitals, Eyes Only for Ambassador from Secretary, June 3, 1967, 7:17 p.m., secret (declassified January 4, 1990). "You should not assume that the United States can order Israel not to fight for what it considers to be its most vital interests. We have used the utmost restraint and, thus far, have been able to hold Israel back. But the 'Holy War' psychology of the Arab world is matched by an apocalyptic psychology

within Israel. Israel may make a decision that it must resort to force to protect its vital interests. In dealing with the issues involved, therefore, we must keep in mind the necessity for finding a solution with which Israel can be restrained. . . . It will do no good to ask Israel to accept the present status quo in the Strait because Israel will fight and we could not restrain her. We cannot throw up our hands and say that, in that event, let them fight while we try to remain neutral."

70. Merle Miller, *Lyndon: An Oral Biography* (Putnam's, 1980), p. 480. The formal Israeli cabinet decision to go to war was taken at the end of a seven-hour meeting on June 4, which ended about mid-afternoon Israeli time. If this anecdote is true, Feinberg must have based his report to Johnson on the prior decision in principle to go to war on June 5 taken by the Israeli "inner cabinet," first on June 2 and again on June 3. Evron termed the Feinberg story "bunk" in an interview on October 22, 1991. No one in the United States, he said, knew at that point when exactly the war would begin.

71. On the second day of the war, Arthur Goldberg forwarded to the White House a message from Israeli Prime Minister Eshkol, conveyed to him through the chief justice of Israel: "Eshkol 'hopes you understand' the action taken by Israel; that it resulted from a judgment that their security situation had so deteriorated that their national existence was imperiled. Eshkol strongly hopes that we will take no action that would limit Israeli action in achieving freedom of passage through the Gulf of Aqaba. They understand your difficulties in achieving this result; and are prepared to handle the matter themselves." See memo from Rostow to Johnson, June 6, 1967, 11:00 a.m., secret (declassified August 23, 1982).

72. Memorandum for the record, National Security Council Meeting, June 7, 1967, secret (declassified August 27, 1982). "The president said 'he was not sure we were out of our troubles.' He could not visualize the USSR saying it had miscalculated, and then walking away. Our objective should be to 'develop as few heroes and as few heels as we can.' It is important for everybody to know we are not for aggression. We are sorry this has taken place. We are in as good a position as we could be given the complexities of the situation. We thought we had a commitment from those governments, but it went up in smoke very quickly. The President said that by the time we get through with all the festering problems we are going to wish the war had not happened."

73. "Memorandum for the Record: Walt Rostow's Recollections of June 5, 1967," November 17, 1968, top secret (declassified October 23, 1984), p. 3: "I might just say parenthetically that President Johnson has never believed that this war was ever anything else than a mistake by the Israelis. A brilliant quick victory he never regarded as an occasion for elation or satisfaction. He so told the Israeli representatives on a number of occasions. However, at the time, I should say that, war having been initiated against our advice, there was a certain relief that things were going well for the Israelis. . . . It did look as though we would not be put in a position of having to make a choice of engaging ourselves or seeing Israel thrown into the sea or defeated. That would have been a most painful moment and, of course, with the Soviet presence in the Middle East, a moment of great general danger."

74. Interview with McGeorge Bundy, December 11, 1968.

75. Jonathan Trumbull Howe, *Multicrises: Sea Power and Global Politics in the Missile Age* (MIT Press, 1971), p. 90 (interview with Rusk).

76. Ibid., pp. 91, 93, where Rusk states that an immediate cease-fire, favored by the United States, would have left Israel only fifty miles inside Sinai.

77. Johnson was informed on June 7, 1967, of the views of a high-ranking Israeli official who had informed his American counterpart that "the Syrians will get their blow as we deal with each country in turn." The same official raised the question of what the United States had in mind for Nasser when the war was over. This was taken as more than a veiled hint that Israel would like to consider joint action to remove Nasser from power.

78. Clark Clifford, a member of the President's Foreign Intelligence Advisory Board, was asked to determine who was responsible for the *Liberty* attack. According to the notes of the NSC Special Committee meeting on June 9, 1967, Clifford reported that it was "inconceivable that it was an accident." A marginal note says that "President agreed 100%" (declassified August 12, 1985). For more on the *Liberty* affair, see James M. Ennes Jr., *Assault on the Liberty: The True Story of the Israeli Attack on an American Intelligence Ship* (Random House, 1979); James Bamford, *The Puzzle Palace: A Report on America's Most Secret Agency* (Houghton Mifflin, 1982), pp. 217–29; Hirsch Goodman and Ze'ev Schiff, "The Attack on the *Liberty*," *Atlantic Monthly*, September 1984, pp. 78–84; and letters to the editor, *Atlantic Monthly*, December 1984, pp. 7–8. Many American officials believed at the time of the *Liberty* attack that Israel had acted deliberately. In later years some participants in the crisis claimed that intelligence information showed that the Israeli pilots knew they were attacking a ship flying the American flag. Several motives have been suggested by those who believe the attack was deliberate. The one most frequently cited is that Israel was planning its assault on the Golan Heights and did not want the United States to have evidence that Israel was deliberately breaking the UN cease-fire.

79. Johnson, *Vantage Point*, pp. 301–02.

80. See "Memorandum for the Record: Hot Line Meeting June 10, 1967," top secret, October 22, 1968 (partially declassified February 22, 1982, and February 2, 1993).

81. Stephen Green, *Taking Sides: America's Secret Relations with a Militant Israel* (William Morrow, 1984), pp. 204–10, maintains that an American airforce reconnaissance unit was sent to Israel a few days before the outbreak of war to assist with the gathering of intelligence. This is the only concrete charge of direct American participation in military operations on the Israeli side, apart from the apocryphal charge made by president Nasser that American planes joined Israel in the initial preemptive strike. For a complete and convincing rebuttal of Green's charges, based on extensive interviews with those who allegedly participated in this operation, see Richard B. Parker, "USAF in the Sinai in the 1967 War: Fact or Fiction?" *Journal of Palestine Studies*, vol. 27, no. 1 (Autumn 1997), pp. 67–75.

82. As early as June 6, 1967, Walt Rostow had noted to the president that a simple cease-fire that left Israel in control of territory would mean that "we could use the *de facto* situation on the ground to try to negotiate not a return to armi-

stice lines but a definitive peace in the Middle East" (declassified March 3, 1982). The following day, in a handwritten memo to the president, Walt Rostow wrote that "Bill Moyers reports via Fineberg [sic] from Eban: 1. When USSR asks withdrawal from cease-fire lines, Eban will say: NO DRAW-BACK WITHOUT DEFINITIVE PEACE. . . . 3. Fineberg says this is route for the President totally to *retrieve* position after 'neutrality' and all that." Rostow was referring to a statement made on the first day of the war by the State Department spokesman that the United States was "neutral in thought, word and deed." This had set off a firestorm in the pro-Israeli community, which read it as a statement of indifference.

83. Evron conveyed this point to Walt Rostow on June 5.

84. By chance, the Israeli cabinet decided that same day that it would be prepared to pull back to the international border with Egypt and Syria in return for peace and demilitarization. This decision was conveyed by Rabin to Rusk on June 22, 1967. See Rabin, *Rabin Memoirs*, p. 135. The West Bank would be subject to negotiations, but Israel would not commit itself to full withdrawal, and East Jerusalem had already been annexed within the expanded municipal borders of Greater Jerusalem.

85. For an excellent summary of the diplomacy of this period at the UN, see David A. Korn, *Stalemate: The War of Attrition and Great Power Diplomacy in the Middle East, 1967–1970* (Boulder, Colo.: Westview Press, 1992), pp. 31–45.

86. Ibid., pp. 84–86.

87. The text of the "agreed minute" was transmitted to the Department of State in telegram 1278, October 9, 1967, from USUN New York (secret/exdis). Reference can be found in Nina J. Noring and Walter B. Smith, "The Withdrawal Clause in UN Security Council Resolution 242 of 1967: Its Legislative History and the Attitudes of the United States and Israel since 1967," February 4, 1978 (secret), p. 5.

88. For the texts of UN Resolutions 242 and 338, see www.brookings.edu/press/appendix/peace_process.htm.

89. Dean Rusk, *As I Saw It* (Norton, 1990), p. 389, said that "we never contemplated any significant grant of territory to Israel as a result of the June 1967 war." See also Donald Neff, "The Differing Interpretations of Resolution 242," *Middle East International*, September 13, 1991, pp. 16–17, which draws on classified documents from the time, including Ambassador Goldberg's commitment to King Hussein that was conveyed on November 3, 1967. To obtain Jordan's acceptance of the resolution, Goldberg gave assurances to the Jordanians that the United States would work for the return of the West Bank to Jordanian authority. When George Ball, who became U.S. ambassador to the UN in June 1968, visited the Middle East in mid-July, he was authorized by the Israelis to convey to King Hussein that they were prepared to return the West Bank, with minor modifications, to his authority in return for peace.

90. On October 24, 1967, the State Department announced that forty-eight A-4 Skyhawk jets, agreed on in February 1966, would be delivered to Israel. This came one day after the Egyptian sinking of the Israeli naval ship *Elath*. Eventually the Johnson administration agreed to sell one hundred A-4s to Israel.

91. Israeli Prime Minister Eshkol stated in *Davar*, January 24, 1969, that Johnson had effectively given him a veto over whether the United States should sell tanks to Jordan.

92. Johnson reportedly delayed announcing his tentative decision on the F-4s in the hope of interesting the Soviets in an arms-limitation agreement for the Middle East. The Soviet position was consistent and negative: before a political settlement, there could be no agreement to limit arms to the area. Just before leaving office in January 1969, Johnson finally authorized the sale of the F-4s. See Korn, *Stalemate*, p. 66, for the differing American and Israeli versions of what Johnson promised.

93. The most authoritative account of Israeli nuclear developments and doctrine up to the 1970s is Avner Cohen, *Israel and the Bomb* (Columbia University Press, 1998).

94. The announcement came after unsuccessful talks earlier in October between Rusk and Gromyko on limiting arms to the Middle East. The atmosphere created by the Soviet invasion of Czechoslovakia in August had made agreement in such talks unlikely. In addition, on October 8 Israeli Foreign Minister Eban presented a nine-point "peace plan" to the UN. Eban, consistent with American preferences, subsequently downplayed the need for direct negotiations and endorsed Resolution 242 as a useful set of principles "which can help the parties and guide them in their search for a solution."

95. Riad, *Struggle for Peace*, pp. 90–92; and Rabin, *Rabin Memoirs*, p. 140.

96. For evidence of Fortas's strong pro-Israeli sentiments, see Kalman, *Abe Fortas*, p. 302.

97. See Joseph A. Califano Jr., *The Triumph and Tragedy of Lyndon Johnson: The White House Years* (Simon and Schuster, 1991), pp. 204–05. Johnson's pro-Israeli sentiment did not keep him from exploding when he thought his efforts on behalf of the Jewish state were not appreciated by Israel's friends. Many American Jews had been angry at a State Department statement on June 5 that defined the U.S. position as "neutral in thought, word and deed." Johnson came under immense pressure to distance himself from that statement, and some of his advisers urged him to address a pro-Israel mass rally in front of the White House on June 7. Unless he did, said some, it could turn anti-Johnson. Spotting one such aide in the hallway outside the Oval Office, Johnson shouted at him: "You Zionist dupe! You and [Ben] Wattenberg are Zionist dupes in the White House! Why can't you see I'm doing all I can for Israel. That's what you should be telling people when they ask for a message from the President for their rally."

98. According to a high-ranking intelligence official, Angleton and the CIA chief of station in Amman tried, on the second or third day of the war, to warn the political leaders in Washington that something should be done immediately to bring about an Israeli-Jordanian understanding on Jerusalem. Otherwise, they feared, this would become an insoluble problem. Their advice was ignored.

99. On President Johnson's relationship with Robert Kennedy, see Jeff Shesol, *Mutual Contempt: Lyndon Johnson, Robert Kennedy, and the Feud That Defined a Decade,* (W. W. Norton, 1997), especially pp. 370–421.

100. The United States was not heavily dependent in 1967 on Arab oil. Walter Levy, acting as adviser to the State Department, correctly predicted that an Arab oil embargo would not be very effective.

101. Some new faces were added to the circle of Johnson's advisers once war broke out, in particular, McGeorge Bundy, who was named chairman of the Ex-

ecutive Committee of the National Security Council to deal with the Middle East on June 6, 1967.

Chapter 3

1. LBJ Library, June 5, 1967 (declassified December 22, 1982).

2. Richard M. Nixon, *RN: The Memoirs of Richard Nixon* (Grosset and Dunlap, 1978), p. 435. Nixon received about 17 percent of the Jewish vote in the 1968 election, compared with about 80 percent for Hubert Humphrey.

3. See I. M. Destler, *Presidents, Bureaucrats and Foreign Policy: The Politics of Organizational Reform* (Princeton University Press, 1972), pp. 121–27, for a description of the NSC under Nixon.

4. Initially this was called the Interdepartmental Group (IG).

5. Kissinger's staff consisted of several close personal assistants as well as specialists in certain geographic and functional areas. Those who participated in Middle East policy included his deputy, Alexander Haig, two special assistants, Peter Rodman and Winston Lord, and his senior Middle East specialist, Harold H. Saunders, who had been on the NSC staff since the Kennedy administration.

6. Nixon, *RN*, p. 477. Nixon expressed concern that Kissinger would have difficulty working with Arabs because of his Jewish background. Henry Kissinger, *White House Years* (Little, Brown, 1979), p. 348, said that Nixon "suspected that my Jewish origin might cause me to lean too much toward Israel."

7. Kissinger, *White House Years*, p. 348. Nixon "calculated that almost any active policy would fail; in addition, it would almost certainly incur the wrath of Israel's supporters. So he found it useful to get the White House as much out of the direct line of fire as possible."

8. Two other office directors were influential in the shaping of Middle East policy during this period: Richard Parker, in charge of Egyptian affairs, and Talcott Seelye, office director for Arab Republic Affairs (ARA), which covered Jordan, Lebanon, Syria, and Iraq. Deputy Assistant Secretary Rodger Davies was also involved in most of the policy deliberations during this period.

9. Before being named to his White House post, Kissinger had spelled out a middle-of-the-road strategy for negotiations and the disengagement of American troops from Vietnam. In an article published in January 1969, he expressed a concern that was to haunt the Nixon administration throughout its first term: "what is involved now is confidence in American promises. However fashionable it is to ridicule the terms 'credibility' and 'prestige,' they are not empty phrases; other nations can gear their actions to ours only if they can count on our steadiness." "The Viet Nam Negotiations," *Foreign Affairs*, vol. 47 (January 1969), pp. 211–34.

10. Kissinger, *White House Years*, pp. 562–64, provides his clearest assessment of the differences between his own views on the Middle East and those of Nixon. Most significantly, Nixon believed that the Soviets were strengthening their position in the region in the aftermath of the June 1967 war; Kissinger felt that their position would be undermined as long as Israel was kept strong and the Soviets' inability to satisfy Arab demands was repeatedly demonstrated.

11. Kissinger, *White House Years*, p. 347.

12. The "Nixon Doctrine" was outlined by the president on July 25, 1969, during a news conference on Guam. The first practical manifestation of the policy, "Vietnamization," was announced by Nixon in a speech delivered November 3, 1969.

13. See Nixon, *RN*, p. 343, for the "powder keg" analogy.

14. The administration's opposition to an imposed settlement was twofold: it probably would not last for long, because the parties would have little sense of commitment to its terms and outside powers would tire of trying to enforce it; and it would be unfavorably received in this country.

15. Kissinger, *White House Years*, pp. 349–52. "I . . . doubted the advisability of American pressure for a general settlement until we could see more clearly what concessions the Arabs would make and until those who would benefit from it would be America's friends, not Soviet clients. . . . I thought the prerequisite of effective Middle East diplomacy was to reduce the Soviet influence so that progress could not be ascribed to its pressures and moderate governments gained some maneuvering room."

16. Nixon, news conference on January 27, 1969, *Department of State Bulletin*, vol. 60 (February 17, 1969), pp. 142–43.

17. This account was obtained in interviews with participants in the first NSC policy review of the Middle East. Kissinger's reaction to these State Department initiatives is found in *White House Years*, pp. 352–53. For background on the State Department proposals, including evidence that the Soviet position began to show signs of flexibility in mid-1969, see David A. Korn, *Stalemate: The War of Attrition and Great Power Diplomacy in the Middle East, 1967–1979* (Boulder, Colo.: Westview Press, 1992), pp. 150–56.

18. Prime Minister Eshkol died on February 26, 1969. Golda Meir was sworn in as head of government on March 17, 1969.

19. Hedrick Smith, "Big Four May Meet on Mideast Soon," *New York Times*, March 26, 1969, p. 11.

20. See Yaacov Bar-Siman-Tov, *The Israeli-Egyptian War of Attrition, 1969–1970: A Case Study of a Limited War* (Columbia University Press, 1980); and Korn, *Stalemate*, pp. 165–88.

21. See Kissinger, *White House Years*, p. 362-63. According to Kissinger, King Hussein was prepared to agree to fairly substantial rectifications in the borders of the West Bank if he could gain Gaza.

22. Ibid., pp. 360–62.

23. Between July 31 and August 25 the Soviets commented on Sisco's July 15 proposals in talks held in Moscow with Ambassador Beam. No new Soviet position was forthcoming, however.

24. Israel made the formal request for the one hundred A-4s and twenty-five F-4s on September 15, 1969.

25. Kissinger, *White House Years*, pp. 370–71; Golda Meir, *My Life: The Autobiography of Golda Meir* (London: Futura, 1976), pp. 326–30; and Yitzhak Rabin, *The Rabin Memoirs* (Little, Brown, 1979), pp. 150–57. Meir mentions a request for 80 Skyhawks, but the number was, in fact, 100.

26. Rabin, *Rabin Memoirs*, pp. 156–57; Abba Eban, *An Autobiography* (Random House, 1977), pp. 464–65; and Gideon Rafael, *Destination Peace: Three*

Decades of Israeli Foreign Policy. A Personal Memoir (Stein and Day, 1981), pp. 210–11.

27. Kissinger, *White House Years*, p. 372. Nixon's own account differs. "I knew that the Rogers Plan could never be implemented, but I believed that it was important to let the Arab world know that the United States did not automatically dismiss its case regarding the occupied territories or rule out a compromise settlement of the conflicting claims. With the Rogers Plan on the record, I thought it would be easier for the Arab leaders to propose reopening relations with the United States without coming under attack from the hawks and pro-Soviet elements in their own countries." Nixon, *RN*, p. 479.

28. For the full text of the Rogers Plan, see www.brookings.edu/press/appendix/peace_process.htm.

29. Mahmoud Riad, *The Struggle for Peace in the Middle East* (Quartet Books, 1981), pp. 110–11.

30. The December 9, 1969, speech by Rogers contained most of the points in the October 28 document. He described United States policy as "balanced," emphasizing friendly ties to both Arabs and Israelis. He referred to three principal elements of a prospective peace agreement:

—binding commitments by the parties to peace, including the obligation to prevent hostile acts originating from their respective territories.

—Rhodes-style negotiations to work out details of an agreement. Issues to be negotiated between Egypt and Israel would include safeguards in the area of Sharm al-Shaykh, the establishment of demilitarized zones, and final arrangements in Gaza.

—in the context of peace and agreements on security, Israeli forces would be required to withdraw to the international border between Egypt and Israel.

The full text of the speech can be found in "Text of Speech by Secretary Rogers on U.S. Policy in Middle East," *New York Times*, December 10, 1969, p. 8. See also Korn, *Stalemate*, pp. 158–61.

31. Nixon had authorized the presentation of the proposals for an Israeli-Jordanian agreement on December 17, but, according to Kissinger, *White House Years*, p. 376, at the same time he conveyed private assurance to Golda Meir via Leonard Garment "that we would go no further and that we would not press our proposal."

32. Points 1, 2, 4, 5, 7, 8, 9, and 10 of the October 28 document were essentially repeated in the December 18 proposal.

33. A summary of the text of the December 18 document appears in *Arab Report and Record*, December 16–31, 1969.

34. Ibid., p. 549.

35. The Soviet note was published in the *New York Times*, January 13, 1970. According to Egypt's foreign minister, once Israel had rejected the proposals, there was little reason for Egypt to accept, "for it would mean further concessions within the framework of a settlement which we were doubtful the US could get Israel to accept." Riad, *Struggle for Peace*, p. 114. Moscow's rejection of the Rogers Plan came after extensive consultations with Egyptian officials in Moscow, including Vice President Anwar Sadat, Minister of War Fawzi, and Foreign Minister Riad. According to Riad, the Soviets were worried by the escalating

fighting along the Suez Canal but saw no contradiction between providing arms to Egypt to liberate the Sinai and pursuing a political settlement. In fact, Leonid Brezhnev reportedly made far-reaching promises during these meetings, offering sixty Soviet pilots and SAM-3 missile batteries with their crews. Riad, *Struggle for Peace*, p. 113.

36. Korn, *Stalemate*, pp. 174–92.

37. Dayan was quoted in Raymond H. Anderson, "Israeli Jets Raid Suburbs of Cairo; Shoppers Watch," *New York Times*, January 29, 1970, p. 1, as saying that one of the purposes of the bombing raids against Egypt was to bring home to the Egyptian people the truth about the war. "We are saying, 'Now look here. Your leaders are not doing you any good.'" The same theme is picked up in comments by Prime Minister Meir, *Le Monde*, January 18–19, 1970.

38. A debate exists over what was actually decided during Sadat's visit to Moscow in December and what Nasser accomplished by his visit the following month. See Mohamed Heikal, *The Road to Ramadan* (Quadrangle Books, 1975), pp. 83–90. See also Uri Ra'anan, "The USSR and the Middle East: Some Reflections on the Soviet Decision-Making Process," *ORBIS*, vol. 17 (Fall 1973), pp. 946–77, for the case in favor of the decision to send Soviet forces being made before Nasser's visit. Whatever the facts, most officials in Washington seemed to believe that Israel's deep penetration bombing was the cause of the stepped-up Soviet role in the fighting. They were, therefore, hesitant to support the Israeli request for more F-4s during the spring, despite the Soviet buildup. See Korn, *Stalemate*, pp. 189–97.

39. The full text of the Soviet note appears in "Nixon-Kosygin Letters," *Arab Report and Record*, March 1–15, 1970, p. 167.

40. Kissinger, *White House Years*, pp. 560–61.

41. The chairman of the Joint Chiefs took the position that the 100 A-4s should be sold but not the F-4s.

42. Rabin, *Rabin Memoirs*, pp. 169–72; and Kissinger, *White House Years*, pp. 568–70.

43. Also, Nasser had warned in mid-February that the United States would lose its economic interests in the Arab world within two years if it agreed to sell additional Phantom jets to Israel. James Reston, "Excerpts from Interview with President Gamal Abdel Nasser of the U.A.R.," *New York Times*, February 15, 1970, p. 18.

44. The record of Sisco's April 12, 1970, meeting with Nasser shows the Egyptian leader in a very bitter frame of mind. According to Sisco's report, Nasser said that he had "no confidence in the USG. US is strong and UAR sees its only security in Soviet Union, on whom it must depend completely. Nasser said he therefore prefers to have dialogue through Soviets than directly with US." Despite the harsh words, Nasser, as usual, was cordial to Sisco and said that he wanted to keep the door open. He said that he was prepared to make peace with Israel but only if all Arab demands were met. See Sisco's cable reporting on the April 12, 1970, meeting, Department of State telegram, Cairo 803, April 13, 1970, secret/nodis (declassified April 3, 1990).

45. Nasser's "final" appeal, repeated in a letter to President Nixon the following day, stated: "The USA, in taking one more step on the path of securing mili-

tary superiority for Israel, will impose on the Arab nation an irrevocable course from which we must draw the necessary conclusion. This will affect the relations of the USA and the Arab nation for decades, and, maybe, for hundreds of years. ... We will not close the door finally on the USA, in spite of the offences against us, in spite of the bombs, the napalm and the Phantoms. . . . I say to President Nixon that there is a forthcoming decisive moment in Arab-American relations. There will be either rupture forever, or there will be another serious and defined beginning. The forthcoming developments will not only affect Arab-American relations alone, but will have wider and more far-reaching effects." Part of the text appears in "Nasser Appeals to Nixon on U.S. Arab Relations," *Arab Report and Record*, May 1–15, 1970, p. 276.

46. This point was repeated in a letter from President Nixon to Prime Minister Meir dated June 20, 1970, just after the second Rogers initiative had been launched. See Eban, *Autobiography*, p. 466.

47. Meir did not believe that Israel had ever accepted UN Resolution 242, although Israel's ambassador at the UN had publicly done so in 1968. Rafael, *Destination Peace*, p. 215.

48. During the second week of June a minicrisis erupted in Jordan as the Popular Front for the Liberation of Palestine, led by George Habash, seized hostages, including Americans, in two Amman hotels. On June 12 President Nixon ordered the 82d Airborne Division on alert.

49. See text of Rogers's letter to Egyptian foreign minister Riad, dated June 19, 1970, *New York Times*, July 23, 1970, p. 2; and "U.S. Initiative toward Peace in the Middle East," *Department of State Bulletin*, vol. 63 (August 10, 1970), pp. 178–79.

50. See Michael Brecher, *Decisions in Israel's Foreign Policy* (Yale University Press, 1975), chap. 8, for details of the Israeli response.

51. Marvin Kalb and Bernard Kalb, *Kissinger* (Little, Brown, 1974), p. 193.

52. All the jets promised under the December 1968 contract had been delivered by the end of August 1970. According to Tad Szulc, "U.S. Mideast Plan Urges Both Sides to 'Start Talking,'" *New York Times*, June 26, 1970, p. 1, the Israelis were reassured that they would be allowed to purchase additional aircraft if the cease-fire proposal of June 19 were to fail or to break down.

53. Heikal, *Road to Ramadan*, pp. 93–95.

54. Egypt orally accepted the U.S. proposal "unconditionally." The subsequent formal written reply was somewhat more guarded.

55. Inasmuch as Jordan and Israel were formally respecting the cease-fire, one might ask why Jordan was included in the second Rogers initiative. The answer seems to be that the United States wanted to ensure that both Egypt and Jordan would be committed to controlling the fedayeen, who were expected to oppose any political settlement based on the Rogers plan. In accepting the Rogers proposal of June 19, King Hussein clearly understood that he would be held responsible for preventing all acts of force from his territory. He informed his cabinet before his acceptance that this might mean further military clashes with the fedayeen.

56. Brecher, *Decisions in Israel's Foreign Policy*, p. 495. In addition, President Nixon stated at a news conference on July 30 that the United States was

committed to "maintaining the balance of power in the Mideast. Seventy-one Senators have endorsed that proposition in a letter to me which I received today." Nixon further reassured Israel that it would face no risk of a military buildup during the cease-fire because there would be a military standstill during that period. Text of the interview in "President Nixon's News Conference of July 30," *Department of State Bulletin*, vol. 63 (August 17, 1970), pp. 185-87. A letter signed by seventy-three senators had been sent to Secretary Rogers on June 1, 1970, urging the sale of one hundred A-4s and F-4s. The text of that letter and the signatures appear in *Congressional Quarterly Weekly Report*, vol. 28 (June 5, 1970), p. 1475.

57. See Prime Minister Meir's speech to the Knesset, August 4, 1970, printed in *Jerusalem Post*, August 5, 1970, p. 3.

58. See the text of the cease-fire agreement in *Arab Report and Record*, August 1–15, 1970, p. 457; and the Egyptian, Jordanian, and Israeli replies to Rogers's proposal of June 19, ibid., pp. 458–60.

59. For example, in his news conference on July 20, 1970, Nixon emphasized the importance of the peace initiative then under way, stating, "That is why we have not announced any sale of planes or delivery of planes to Israel at this time because we want to give that peace initiative every chance to succeed." *New York Times*, July 21, 1970, p. 16.

60. See William Safire, *Before the Fall: An Inside View of the Pre-Watergate White House* (Doubleday, 1975), p. 394.

61. See William B. Quandt and others, *The Politics of Palestinian Nationalism* (University of California Press, 1973), pp. 124–28.

62. The PLO temporarily suspended the PFLP from the Central Committee because of the unauthorized hijackings, but welcomed it back once the fighting broke out on September 16.

63. Kissinger, *White House Years*, p. 597.

64. Ibid., pp. 602–06; and Seymour M. Hersh, *The Price of Power: Kissinger in the Nixon White House* (Summit Books, 1983), p. 235.

65. Elmo R. Zumwalt Jr., *On Watch: A Memoir* (Quadrangle, 1976), pp. 295–96, provides a brief account of a WSAG meeting on September 10 at which David Packard, deputy secretary of defense, argued against any form of ground involvement in the crisis by American troops.

66. Kalb and Kalb, *Kissinger*, p. 197; Henry Brandon, *The Retreat of American Power: The Inside Story of How Nixon and Kissinger Changed American Foreign Policy for Years to Come* (Doubleday, 1973), p. 133; Frank Van der Linden, *Nixon's Quest for Peace* (Robert B. Luce, 1972), p. 77; and Kissinger, *White House Years*, pp. 610–12.

67. *Chicago Sun-Times*, September 17, 1970; and Hedrick Smith, "Nixon Hints He May Act If Outsiders Join the Fight," *New York Times*, September 19, 1970, p. 1.

68. Brandon, *Retreat of American Power*, p. 134.

69. Terence Smith, "Washington Reported Weighing $500-Million in Aid for Israelis," *New York Times*, September 18, 1970, p. 1.

70. Kissinger, *White House Years*, p. 618. The Syrians went to considerable lengths to make their intervention appear to consist of units of the Palestine Liberation Army. Tanks were hastily painted with PLA symbols.

71. The most damaging evidence of Soviet complicity in the intervention came from reports that Soviet military advisers had accompanied Syrian tank units as far as the Jordanian border.

72. Communications in Amman between the American embassy and the royal palace were extremely difficult. Radio and walkie-talkie were used, and the fedayeen often eavesdropped on sensitive conversations.

73. Kissinger, *White House Years*, p. 620.

74. Van der Linden, *Nixon's Quest for Peace*, pp. 81–82; and Kissinger, *White House Years*, p. 621.

75. Kissinger, *White House Years*, p. 622.

76. Ibid., p. 623. Rabin, *The Rabin Memoirs*, p. 187, gives a somewhat different version. Rabin claims that Kissinger conveyed the king's request for Israeli air strikes and asked for an immediate Israeli reply. Rabin then asked what the U.S. was recommending, and Kissinger said he would have to call back. An hour later, according to Rabin, Kissinger called, saying, "The request is approved and supported by the United States government." "Do *you* advise Israel to do it?" Rabin asked. "Yes, subject to your own considerations," replied Kissinger.

77. Kissinger, *White House Years*, p. 623. See also Kalb and Kalb, *Kissinger*, pp. 202–07; and Benjamin Welles, "U.S.-Israeli Military Action on Jordan Was Envisioned," *New York Times*, October 8, 1970, p. 1.

78. Kissinger, *White House Years*, p. 625.

79. The United States had no independent aerial intelligence–collection capabilities to follow the course of the battle. It had to rely on Israeli reconnaissance flights and Israeli and Jordanian accounts of what was happening on the ground.

80. Kissinger, *White House Years*, p. 626. Kissinger asserts that he was not entirely happy with this decision, since it might have been impossible to contact King Hussein to determine his views if the situation deteriorated sharply.

81. The Syrian air force, commanded by General Hafiz al-Asad, did not intervene, nor did the Iraqi troops in Jordan, confronted as they were by a full division of the Jordanian army.

82. Kalb and Kalb, *Kissinger*, p. 204, misinterpret the meaning of this message.

83. Alone among analysts of the Jordan crisis, Alexander Haig maintains that Israeli air strikes did, in fact, occur and were instrumental in turning the tide of battle. Haig initially states that Israel "may" have destroyed some Syrian tanks, but two paragraphs later states: "The Israeli air strikes, together with strong American diplomacy backed by credible military maneuvers suggesting that overwhelming United States air, sea, and ground power would be committed to the conflict if necessary, preserved King Hussein's regime, and, with it, the frazzled peace in the region." Alexander M. Haig Jr. with Charles McCarry, *Inner Circles: How America Changed the World. A Memoir* (Warner Books, 1992), p. 251. Interviews with Joseph Sisco, Alfred L. Atherton, Harold H. Saunders, Richard Helms, and information from Israeli general Aharon Yariv, all confirm that no Israeli air strikes took place. William Bundy, *A Tangled Web: The Making of Foreign Policy in the Nixon Presidency* (Hill and Wang, 1998), p. 187, mistakenly gives credence to Haig's account.

Nixon's own recollection of the Jordan crisis is reflected in the following anecdote. Talking to Kissinger by phone during the October 1973 war, Nixon said about the Jordan crisis: "We really—with no cards at all . . . played a hell of a game." Walter Isaacson, *Kissinger: A Biography* (Simon and Schuster, 1992), p. 517.

84. According to Kissinger, *White House Years*, p. 631, on September 25 Israel was formally notified that "all aspects of the exchanges between us with regard to this Syrian invasion of Jordan are no longer applicable. . . . If a new situation arises, there will have to be a fresh exchange."

85. The British had announced in 1968 that they would remove their military presence east of Suez by the end of 1971. This led to considerable planning within the bureaucracy on how to fill the ensuing vacuum.

86. See Henry Kissinger, *The White House Years* (Little, Brown, 1979), p. 1285. "What finally got me involved in the execution of Middle East diplomacy was that Nixon did not believe he could risk recurrent crises in the Middle East in an election year. He therefore asked me to step in, if only to keep things quiet."

87. On October 12, 1970, Kissinger and Sisco gave a background briefing to the press on the post–Jordan crisis situation in the Middle East. Sisco addressed the question of the Palestinians in the following terms: "more and more the Palestinians are thinking in terms of a given entity, wherever that may be. . . . So that if I were to look ahead over the next five years, assuming that we can stabilize this area, it would be on the basis of the Arabs having adopted a live and let live attitude, that is, willing to live alongside of Israel; Israel's meeting at least part of the Arab demands insofar as the occupied territories are concerned; and, lastly, giving expression to the Palestinian movement and very likely in the form of some entity."

88. The administration sought an understanding on the conditions under which Israel might use the new weapons.

89. William Beecher, "U.S. Officials Say Israelis Will Get 180 Modern Tanks," *New York Times*, October 24, 1970, p. 1. The supplemental defense appropriation, including $500 million in credits for Israel, was signed by Nixon on January 11, 1971.

90. Meir speech to the Knesset, as cited in Lawrence L. Whetten, *The Canal War: Four-Power Conflict in the Middle East* (MIT Press, 1974), p. 142; and Tad Szulc, "U.S. Officials Say a Series of Commitments Won Israelis' Return to Mideast Peace Talks at the U.N.," *New York Times*, January 1, 1971, p. 8. Shlomo Aronson, *The Politics and Strategy of Nuclear Weapons in the Middle East: Opacity, Theory, and Reality, 1960-1991. An Israeli Perspective* (State University of New York Press, 1992), p. 146, may have these understandings in mind when he refers to a 1971 agreement on "secure boundaries" that included American recognition of Israel's nuclear potential. But Aronson has only an interview with former ambassador Simcha Dinitz to rely on, and no other account mentions anything about nuclear weapons.

91. Little was known in Washington about Sadat when he became president. The biography prepared by the CIA was less than flattering. It prominently mentioned that Sadat had gone to the cinema on the night of the Egyptian revolution in 1952, implying that this was typical of his political style. Sadat openly discusses the incident in *Revolt on the Nile* (John Day, 1957).

92. The text of Sadat's February 4, 1971, speech can be found in *New Middle East*, March 1971, pp. 32–35.

93. For Jarring's memorandum, along with the Egyptian and Israeli replies, see *Arab Report and Record*, March 1-15, 1971, pp. 158–59. The United States had strongly urged Israel not to include the sentence on refusing to withdraw to the pre–June 5, 1967, lines.

94. Hedrick Smith, "Israel Denounces Plans of Jarring and U.S. on Sinai," *New York Times*, March 11, 1971, p. 1.

95. Meir interview in *The Times* (London), March 13, 1971, p. 1. Meir's comments set off a lively debate within Israel. The right-wing Gahal party accused her of being too conciliatory.

96. William Beecher, "U.S. Selling Israel 12 More F-14 Jets; Weighs New Bid," *New York Times*, April 20, 1971, p. 1.

97. Whetten, *Canal War*, pp. 182–83; Peter Grose, "Israeli Cabinet Briefed on Rogers Talks," *New York Times*, May 10, 1971, p. 3; and Meir speech of June 9, 1971, reported in "Israel Asks U.S. for New Arms Deal," *New York Times*, June 10, 1971, p. 9.

98. Sadat claimed subsequently in his interview with Arnaud de Borchgrave, "Sadat: 'We Are Now Back to Square One,'" *Newsweek*, December 13, 1971, pp. 43–47, that Sisco had illustratively sketched lines on a map of Sinai indicating the depth of Israeli withdrawal. Sadat suggested that UN peacekeeping forces should be stationed between the Egyptian and Israeli line.

99. These ministers included Sami Sharaf, in charge of presidential security; Sharawi Guma, minister of interior; and General Mohammed Fawzi, minister of defense.

100. For Kissinger's critique of the effort to revive the Jarring talks, see Kissinger, *White House Years*, pp. 1278–80. He termed the effort "activity for its own sake amid self-generated deadlines that could be met only by papering over irreconcilable differences that, in turn, made a blowup all the more inevitable. . . . My aim was to produce a stalemate until Moscow urged compromise or until, even better, some moderate Arab regime decided that the route to progress was through Washington."

101. Kissinger, *White House Years*, p. 1285, dates his operational control over Middle East policy from this point. He notes that Rabin approached him in October 1971 to urge that he get personally involved in the interim accord negotiations: "He told me confidentially that Israel might be more flexible in its terms if I were involved and it had Presidential assurances that the demands would not be open-ended" (p. 1287). Kissinger was simultaneously being asked by an Egyptian emissary to meet with Heikal.

102. Henry Tanner, "U.S. Assures Israel on Sinai Memo," *New York Times*, June 30, 1971, p. 3.

103. Kissinger, *White House Years*, pp. 1280–89.

104. See Heikal, *Road to Ramadan*, pp. 140, 152–55. Kissinger, *White House Years*, p. 1276, dates the beginning of the back-channel contacts with Sadat to the spring of 1972.

105. Tad Szulc, "Behind the Vietnam Cease-Fire Agreement," *Foreign Policy*, no. 15 (Summer 1974), pp. 34–41.

106. See Kissinger, *White House Years*, p. 1494, for the text of the agreement. Elsewhere Kissinger minimizes the importance of these principles, saying that he

conducted a "delaying tactic" in his talks with Gromyko (pp. 1247–48). My impression is that Kissinger took the exercise somewhat more seriously, and almost certainly Nixon did. And though written in general terms, the principles did not simply parrot UN resolutions, as Kissinger implies.

107. The text of the joint communiqué is found in *United States Foreign Policy, 1972: A Report of the Secretary of State* (April 1973), pp. 598–603.

108. Heikal, *Road to Ramadan*, pp. 183–84; and "Arab Aide's Talk with Nixon Called Factor in Sadat's Decision," *New York Times*, July 24, 1972, p. 2.

109. Uri Ra'anan, "The USSR and the Middle East: Some Reflections on the Soviet Decision-Making Process," *ORBIS*, vol. 17 (Fall 1973), pp. 946–77, has called into question whether Sadat took the initiative in asking the advisers to leave. Ra'anan raises some intriguing points but seems to underestimate Sadat's anger at the Soviets. See also David Kimche, *The Last Option: After Nasser, Arafat and Saddam Hussein. The Quest for Peace in the Middle East* (Scribner's, 1991), pp. 22–24, for another argument that Sadat and the Soviets colluded on the withdrawal of Soviet advisers as a step in Egypt's plan to go to war.

110. Nixon interview with Garnett D. Horner of the *Washington Star*, November 5, 1972; and "Statements from Pre-Election Interview with Nixon Outlining 2d-Term Plans," *New York Times*, November 10, 1972, p. 20.

Chapter 4

1. Mohamed Heikal, *The Road to Ramadan* (Quadrangle Books, 1975), pp. 200–02; and Henry Kissinger, *Years of Upheaval* (Little, Brown, 1982), p. 213.

2. Heikal, *Road to Ramadan*, pp. 202–03. The estate belonged to the chairman of the board of Pepsi-Cola, Donald Kendall, who was an ardent Nixon supporter and a proponent of improved U.S-Egyptian relations.

3. Kissinger, *Years of Upheaval*, pp. 214–15.

4. Kissinger, *Years of Upheaval*, p. 225. On March 26, 1973, Sadat had formed a "war cabinet" with himself as prime minister. Three days later he told Arnaud de Borchgrave of *Newsweek* that war was imminent. De Borchgrave rushed the text of the interview to Kissinger before its publication on April 9, 1973.

5. After returning from Moscow, Kissinger consulted with Israeli officials on Israel's reaction to the May 1972 principles. He was told that Israel was opposed to the idea altogether, but that if such principles were announced they should call for negotiations and should speak only of Israeli withdrawal to secure and recognized borders.

6. Kissinger, *Years of Upheaval*, pp. 226–27. Kissinger concludes that Sadat had already made his decision for war in the summer of 1972 and that the meetings with Hafiz Ismail were essentially a diversionary tactic. According to a well-informed Israeli source, Kissinger had reason to believe that Egypt had decided on war. According to Moshe Zak, King Hussein had told him of the Egyptian-Syrian plan for war, and Kissinger had told the Israelis. On May 21, 1973, Dayan informed the general staff: "The IDF must prepare, by the end of the summer, for Egypt and Syria launching war against Israel, without Jordan." See *Jerusalem Post*, September 22, 1991, p. 5.

7. Richard Nixon, *RN: The Memoirs of Richard Nixon* (Grosset and Dunlap, 1978), pp. 884–86.

8. Kissinger was concerned by signs of Faisal's growing involvement in the Arab-Israeli conflict. He feared that Saudi activism would ultimately bring down the monarchy, which might then be replaced by a Qaddafi-like regime. Each time King Faisal made some reference to the use of oil as a weapon against the West, however, one of his aides would hasten to inform U.S. officials that such remarks were meant only for domestic Arab consumption.

9. Edward R. F. Sheehan, *The Arabs, Israelis, and Kissinger* (Reader's Digest Press, 1976), pp. 27–28.

10. See Kissinger, *Years of Upheaval*, pp. 202–03, 211–12, for a comparison of Kissinger's and Nixon's views. According to Kissinger, Nixon "deep down wanted . . . to impose a comprehensive settlement sometime during his term in office" (p. 202). For a detailed account of how Nixon saw the Arab-Israeli conflict in the early 1990s, which tends to confirm the view that he favored a comprehensive settlement, see Richard M. Nixon, *Seize the Moment: America's Challenge in a One-Superpower World* (Simon and Schuster, 1992), pp. 217–30.

11. By contrast, Nixon seemed eager to press forward on Middle East peace, warning on one occasion in early 1973 that "this thing is getting ready to blow." See Kissinger, *Years of Upheaval*, p. 211.

12. Conor Cruise O'Brien, *The Siege: The Saga of Israel and Zionism* (Simon and Schuster, 1986), pp. 512–17, argues at length that Kissinger, perhaps implicitly or indirectly, encouraged Sadat to go to war. His evidence is meager, but he does rely heavily on Mohamed Heikal, *Autumn of Fury: The Assassination of Sadat* (Random House, 1983), pp. 49–50. Heikal argues that information reached Egypt through Saudi intelligence channels that Kissinger favored a "heating up" of the situation before he would be prepared to tackle it. This was supposedly confirmed in the meetings between Hafiz Ismail and Kissinger. I do not believe that Kissinger wanted Egypt to go to war. He did, on occasion, talk about the circumstances that would convince him to tackle the Arab-Israeli conflict. Those circumstances included a deterioration of the situation that would threaten American interests or an opening that would make a diplomatic effort productive. And Nixon had, of course, written an entire book, *Six Crises* (Doubleday, 1962), with the subtheme that crises could provide opportunities for solving problems. Although it may be true that Sadat calculated, correctly, that a resort to war would unblock the frozen diplomatic landscape, I do not believe that either Nixon or Kissinger deliberately encouraged Sadat to go to war.

13. Some analysts at the CIA reportedly played down evidence of Egyptian and Syrian preparations for hostilities, fearing that any such conclusions might be communicated to the Israelis and serve as a reason for a preemptive attack.

14. Interview with high-ranking Israeli intelligence official, December 1975.

15. Israel received confirmation that the Arabs planned to attack at about 4:00 a.m. Israeli time, October 6. It was expected that hostilities would begin about 6:00 p.m. See Chaim Herzog, *The War of Atonement, October 1973* (Little, Brown, 1975), pp. 52–54.

16. This meeting was chaired by Kissinger's deputy, General Brent Scowcroft, and was attended by Defense Secretary James Schlesinger, Chairman of the Joint

Chiefs of Staff Admiral Thomas Moorer, Deputy Secretary of State Kenneth Rush, CIA director William Colby, Deputy Assistant Secretary of State for the Near East Alfred Atherton, Deputy Assistant Secretary of Defense for International Security Affairs James Noyes, and several staff members. As a member of the National Security Council staff during this period, I attended most of the WSAG meetings. The accounts of these sessions included here are based on memory, interviews with participants, and brief notes on the main substantive topics discussed at each meeting. Kissinger's memoirs, *Years of Upheaval* (Little, Brown, 1982), also discuss these meetings in some detail. The full record is, of course, still classified, and the sources I have been able to use are in no way definitive. I have tried to concentrate on recording the themes that recurred in the discussions, on the major concepts that participants relied on in reaching judgments, and on the mood that existed on each day of the crisis. Decisions were not usually made at WSAG meetings. Their real value lay in keeping top-level decisionmakers on the same wavelength. There was very little controversy or argument during any of the meetings.

17. See the same version in the Watch Committee report, October 6, 9:00 a.m., printed in *Village Voice*, February 16, 1976, p. 78, note 305. "We can find no hard evidence of a major, coordinated Egyptian/Syrian offensive across the Canal and in the Golan Heights area. Rather, the weight of evidence indicates an action-reaction situation where a series of responses by each side to preconceived threats created an increasingly dangerous potential for confrontation."

18. Kissinger made a point of this in his discussion with Mohamed Heikal, November 7, 1973, as translated from *Al-Anwar*, November 16, 1973, in "Interviews: Kissinger Meets Haikal," *Journal of Palestine Studies*, vol. 3 (Winter 1974), p. 213.

19. The president's phone logs do not show any conversations with Kissinger on October 6, and Kissinger makes no such reference in his memoirs. But Kissinger was adept at invoking Nixon's authority in front of other members of the administration. He presumably was in touch with Haig, but Haig himself did not talk to Nixon after noon on that day. See President Richard Nixon's daily diary, October 6, 1973.

20. Granting the Soviets most-favored nation (MFN) trading status was a key issue in the fall of 1973. Senator Henry Jackson had introduced an amendment that would withhold MFN treatment for the Soviet Union unless Soviet Jews were allowed to emigrate freely. Nixon and Kissinger opposed the amendment, arguing that quiet diplomacy would be more effective and that the Soviets would not accept such interference in their internal affairs. Ultimately the Soviets refused MFN tied to free emigration.

21. Matti Golan, *The Secret Conversations of Henry Kissinger: Step-by-Step Diplomacy in the Middle East* (Quadrangle Books, 1976), p. 64; and Marvin Kalb and Bernard Kalb, *Kissinger* (Little, Brown, 1974), pp. 462–63.

22. Kissinger subsequently told Egyptian officials that he was very impressed when they began to send messages through the back channel shortly after the war began. Interview with high-level Egyptian diplomat, April 1976. Nixon and Kissinger attached considerable importance to the possibility of improving U.S.-Arab relations after the war was over. See Kissinger, *Years of Upheaval*, pp. 481–

82. Until receiving this back-channel message, says Kissinger, "I had not taken Sadat seriously."

23. Golan, *Secret Conversations of Kissinger*, p. 45.

24. Membership at WSAG meetings varied, but the following members were usually present: Kissinger, Schlesinger, Moorer, Colby, Scowcroft, Rush, Sisco, Clements, and several staff assistants. When oil was discussed, Deputy Secretary William Simon, former governor John Love of Colorado, and Charles di Bona might participate.

25. Kissinger apparently was aware that the Soviets, six hours after the war had begun, had suggested to Sadat that he accept a simple cease-fire at an early date. The Soviets had repeated the request on October 7. See William B. Quandt, "Soviet Policy in the October Middle East War," *International Affairs*, vol. 53 (July 1977), pp. 377–89, and vol. 53 (October 1977), pp. 587–603; and Sadat's own account in *Al-Hawadith*, March 19, 1975, and *Al-Jumhuriyyah*, October 24, 1975. See also Heikal, *Road to Ramadan*, pp. 209, 212–15.

26. Kalb and Kalb, *Kissinger*, p. 466. See also Edward N. Luttwak and Walter Laqueur, "Kissinger and the Yom Kippur War," *Commentary*, vol. 58 (September 1974), p. 36. Kissinger, in *Years of Upheaval*, p. 485, writes, "When I had bad news for Dinitz, I was not above ascribing it to bureaucratic stalemates or unfortunate decisions by superiors."

27. Kissinger arrived at 5:55 p.m. and was already well briefed on the course of the day's fighting.

28. Kissinger, *Years of Upheaval*, pp. 491–93; and Kalb and Kalb, *Kissinger*, pp. 466–67.

29. See Kissinger, *Years of Upheaval*, pp. 495–96, including the content of his message to Dinitz informing him of the president's decision on resupply. At this point there was still no talk of an American airlift, unless an emergency need for tanks arose. Kissinger told Dinitz that everything on Israel's list except laser bombs was approved and that all losses in planes and tanks would be made up. According to Alan Dowty, *Middle East Crisis: U.S. Decisionmaking in 1958, 1970, and 1973* (University of California Press, 1974), p. 238, Kissinger mentioned to Dinitz that the United States intended to keep a low profile and that charters might be used by Israel to carry supplies.

30. Insight Team of the London Sunday Times, *Yom Kippur War* (Doubleday, 1974), p. 279. Kissinger, *Years of Upheaval*, p. 499, says that around midday on October 10 he spoke to Dinitz, who conveyed Meir's thanks for Nixon's decision on resupply. Kissinger urged Israel to push back to the prewar lines "as quickly as possible, or beyond them on at least one front. We could not stall a cease-fire proposal forever."

31. Heikal, *Road to Ramadan*, pp. 223–24; and Kissinger, *Years of Upheaval*, pp. 499–500.

32. Kissinger, *Years of Upheaval*, p. 498.

33. Quandt, "Soviet Policy in the October Middle East 1973 War" (both parts), summarizes available data on the Soviet delivery of military equipment by air and sea during the war.

34. Insight Team, *Yom Kippur War*, p. 279. This has been confirmed by a highly placed Israeli source.

35. Kissinger, *Years of Upheaval,* p. 509. The Israelis were told that a vote in the United Nations would not be scheduled before late afternoon October 13.

36. Brecher, *Decisions in Crisis,* p. 214. The decision was made on October 12 in the afternoon, Israeli time. Earlier in the day the inner cabinet had decided to postpone a decision on an attempted crossing of the canal. Ibid., p. 173.

37. Kissinger, *Years of Upheaval,* pp. 512–13, describes in detail his meeting with Dinitz at 11:20 p.m., October 12. Kissinger was surprised that Israel had not launched its offensive. Dinitz attributed this to a shortage of supplies. By 1:00 p.m., with no guidance from Nixon (the presidential logs show no calls from either Kissinger or Haig in this time period), Kissinger decided on some initial steps to speed the delivery of arms. Kalb and Kalb, *Kissinger,* p. 474; Golan, *Secret Conversations of Kissinger,* pp. 53, 61, 66–67; and Insight Team, *Yom Kippur War,* pp. 279–80. According to Defense Secretary Schlesinger, "Kissinger called me Friday night. . . . He indicated Israel was running short. To say the least, he was a little bit concerned." Interview with James Schlesinger, *Jewish Telegraphic Agency Daily Bulletin,* July 1, 1974, p. 4. In his October 26, 1973, news conference, Schlesinger stated that on October 13 "there were some who believed that the existence of the state of Israel was seriously compromised." At least one author, Nadav Safran, *Israel: The Embattled Ally* (Harvard University Press, 1978), p. 483, assumes that Kissinger was motivated by a fear that Israel might resort to nuclear weapons.

38. See Walter Isaacson, *Kissinger: A Biography* (Simon and Schuster, 1992), p. 521, quoting from the transcript of a Kissinger-Haig telephone conversation early on October 13. Haig said, "He's [Schlesinger] ready to move MAC [Military Assistance Command] aircraft in there immediately. I think that would be foolish." "That would be disaster, Al," Kissinger replied. "How can he fuck everything up for a week—he can't now recoup it the day the diplomacy is supposed to start." This exchange tends to confirm the view that Kissinger did see a link between the airlift and the possibility of an early cease-fire.

39. Kissinger, *Years of Upheaval,* pp. 514, 515. At 12:30 p.m. on October 13 Kissinger was able to tell Dinitz that giant C-5As would fly directly to Israel until the charter issue was sorted out. Fourteen F-4s would also soon be on their way. See also Edward N. Luttwak and Walter Laqueur, "Kissinger and the Yom Kippur War," *Commentary,* vol. 58 (September 1974), p. 37; and Isaacson, *Kissinger,* p. 522. See also Leonard Garment, *Crazy Rhythm : My Journey from Brooklyn, Jazz, and Wall Street to Nixon's White House, Watergate, and Beyond* (New York: Times Books, 1997), pp.196–99. He credits Nixon with overcoming the hesitancy of his advisers.

40. It is extremely difficult to ascertain the degree to which the U.S. airlift affected Israeli strategy. From interviews with top Israeli officials, I have concluded that the impact of the airlift on strategic decisions was minimal on the Syrian front and only slightly more significant on the Egyptian front. The crossing of the canal had been seriously recommended by Bar Lev on October 12. (See Herzog, *War of Atonement,* pp. 202–07.) After the Israeli victory in Sinai on October 14, it would have been ordered even without the assurance of U.S. supplies. However, the crossing might not have been exploited so aggressively if arms had not been on their way. Some items, such as TOW and Maverick missiles, were

being used to good effect in the last few days of the fighting and may have raised the prospect of a full defeat of the Third Army Corps. Ironically, the U.S. resupply put Israel in a position to do something that Kissinger was determined to prevent.

41. From October 14 until the October 25 cease-fire, the U.S. resupply effort delivered approximately 11,000 tons of equipment, forty F-4 Phantoms, thirty-six A-4 Skyhawks and twelve C-130 transports. Included were only four tanks on the early C-5 flight, and fewer than twenty were sent during the entire airlift. From October 26 until the airlift ended on November 15 another 11,000 tons of equipment were delivered. In all, 147 sorties were flown by C-5s, with 10,800 tons aboard, and 421 sorties by C-141s with 11,500 tons. During the same period, El Al aircraft carried about 11,000 tons of military supplies to Israel in more than 200 sorties. By November 15, the first ships were beginning to reach Israel with supplies, and the airlift became superfluous. *Aviation Week and Space Technology*, vol. 99 (December 10, 1973), pp. 16–19, contains information on the airlift.

42. Heikal, *Road to Ramadan*, p. 224.

43. Golan, *Secret Conversations of Kissinger*, p. 67.

44. Impromptu comments by Nixon on October 15 at a Medal of Honor ceremony caused some consternation in Arab diplomatic circles. U.S. policy, he stated, is "like the policy that we followed in 1958 when Lebanon was involved, it is like the policy we followed in 1970 when Jordan was involved. The policy of the United States in the Mideast, very simply stated, is this: We stand for the right of every nation in the Mideast to maintain its independence and security. We want this fighting to end. We want the fighting to end on a basis where we can build a lasting peace." *Weekly Compilation of Presidential Documents*, vol. 9 (October 22, 1973), p. 1251. The president's reference to Lebanon and Jordan raised the specter of U.S. military intervention. Nixon was presumably simply mentioning the two other Middle East crises in which he had been personally involved.

45. Heikal, *Road to Ramadan*, pp. 232–34, gives a somewhat distorted version of these talks but covers most of the main points.

46. Golan, *Secret Conversations of Kissinger*, p. 70.

47. Ibid., p. 72.

48. Kosygin left Cairo at 2:55 a.m., Washington time, on October 19.

49. Kissinger, *Years of Upheaval*, p. 542.

50. Golan, *Secret Conversations of Kissinger*, p. 75.

51. Kalb and Kalb, *Kissinger*, pp. 481, 483; and Ze'ev Schiff, *October Earthquake: Yom Kippur, 1973* (Tel Aviv: University Publishing Projects, 1974), p. 264.

52. Kissinger, *Years of Upheaval*, pp. 546–48.

53. In a side agreement both parties agreed that "appropriate auspices" meant that "the negotiations between the parties concerned will take place with the active participation of the United States and the Soviet Union at the beginning and thereafter in the course of negotiations when key issues of a settlement are dealt with." Ibid., p. 559.

54. For the texts of UN Resolutions 242 and 338, see www.brookings.edu/press/appendix/peace_process.htm.

55. On learning that Kissinger was stopping in Israel, Sadat invited him to come to Egypt as well. Kissinger declined, but expressed hope that he would be able to visit Cairo soon. Heikal, *Road to Ramadan*, pp. 248–49.

56. Golan, *Secret Conversations of Kissinger*, pp. 84–87, states that Kissinger hinted that Israel would not be held to strict observance of the cease-fire. Kissinger, *Years of Upheaval*, p. 569, says that he told the Israelis that a few hours' "slippage" in the cease-fire deadline while he was flying home would not be a problem. Joseph Sisco, testifying before the Committee on Foreign Affairs of the House of Representatives, December 3, 1973, stated, "The Israelis were anxious for a cease-fire at the time [October 22] the cease-fire was concluded as were the Egyptians." *Emergency Security Assistance Act of 1973*, Hearings before the Committee of Foreign Affairs of the House of Representatives, 93 Cong. 1 sess. (GPO, 1973), p. 56. See also Walter Laqueur, *Confrontation* (Quadrangle, 1974), p. 194; and *Maariv*, October 26, 1973.

57. During a stopover in London Kissinger called the Soviets, urging them to press the Syrians to call off an offensive planned for the following day.

58. Kalb and Kalb, *Kissinger*, p. 486.

59. Heikal, *Road to Ramadan*, pp. 251–52, prints the text of two of Nixon's letters to Sadat on October 24. In addition, Nixon wrote Sadat on October 23 to make it clear that the United States had only committed itself to engage in a process designed to make possible a political settlement but had not guaranteed any specific outcome of that process.

60. Kalb and Kalb, *Kissinger*, p. 488.

61. Ibid., p. 489.

62. See Kissinger, *Years of Upheaval*, pp. 575–83.

63. Richard M. Nixon, *RN: The Memoirs of Richard Nixon* (Grosset and Dunlap, 1978), p. 938.

64. An enhanced alert status of seven Soviet airborne divisions was first noted on October 11; the alert status was altered on October 23. See "Secretary of Defense Schlesinger's News Conference of October 26," pp. 617–26.

65. One other consideration that may have contributed to the decision to call a global alert was the arrival during the evening of October 24 of an intelligence report that a suspicious Soviet ship had given off neutron emissions as it transited the Bosporus on October 22 on its way to Alexandria. Some thought this might indicate that the Soviets were introducing nuclear warheads into Egypt. Kissinger, *Years of Upheaval*, p. 584, mentions some "ominous signs," probably referring to this report. See also "Secretary Schlesinger's News Conference of October 26"; Raymond L. Garthoff, *Détente and Confrontation: American-Soviet Relations from Nixon to Reagan* (Brookings, 1985), p. 378; and Dowty, *Middle East Crisis*, p. 275. For a Soviet participant's perspective, see Anatoly Dobrynin, *In Confidence: Moscow's Ambassador to America's Six Cold-War Presidents* (Times Books, 1995), pp. 296–99, where he claims that Kissinger told him privately that the alert was mostly determined by "domestic considerations."

66. Dayan was subsequently quoted as saying that Kissinger threatened to send U.S. forces to resupply the Third Army Corps. Other Israelis, including Eban, have contended that Kissinger stated that the Soviets might try to resupply the Egyptian forces. The latter seems more plausible, perhaps with the addition of an implied threat not to help the Israelis if they found themselves in confrontation with the Soviets over the fate of the Third Army Corps. This issue is discussed by Theodore Draper, "The United States and Israel: Tilt in the Middle East," *Com-*

mentary, vol. 59 (April 1975), pp. 29–45, and the exchange of letters in *Commentary*, vol. 60 (September 1975), pp. 18–24. Moshe Dayan, *Moshe Dayan: Story of My Life* (William Morrow, 1976), p. 544, says the Americans "more or less" gave Israel an ultimatum to allow supplies through to the Third Army Corps but does not go into details.

67. See Richard Ned Lebow and Janice Gross Stein, *We All Lost the Cold War*, (Princeton University Press, 1994) p. 307.

68. Ibid., pp. 247 and 480–81, reviews the evidence that Nixon was unable to participate in the meeting because he had drunk too much that evening. According to the authors, Kissinger refused to comment when asked about these allegations in an interview.

69. Kissinger, *Years of Upheaval*, p. 593. This meeting was the first that Nixon learned of the measures taken overnight.

70. See "Secretary Kissinger's News Conference of October 25," *Department of State Bulletin*, vol. 69 (November 12, 1973), pp. 585–94, for the complete text. The following day, October 26, Nixon held a press conference in which he discussed the alert: "We obtained information which led us to believe that the Soviet Union was planning to send a very substantial force into the Mideast, a military force. . . . When I received that information, I ordered, shortly after midnight on Thursday morning, an alert for all American forces around the world. This was a precautionary alert. The purpose of that was to indicate to the Soviet Union that we could not accept any unilateral move on their part to move military forces into the Mideast. . . . The outlook for a permanent peace is the best that it has been in twenty years. . . . Without détente, we might have had a major conflict in the Middle East. With détente, we avoided it." "The President's News Conference of October 26, 1973," *Weekly Compilation of Presidential Documents*, vol. 9 (October 29, 1973), pp. 1287–94.

71. The debate over Kissinger's role in the October war has spawned a remarkably partisan body of writing. Kalb and Kalb, *Kissinger*, are favorable to Kissinger and erroneously portray Schlesinger as the obstacle to the airlift to Israel. Tad Szulc, "Is He Indispensable? Answers to the Kissinger Riddle," *New York*, July 1, 1974, pp. 33–39, points the finger at Kissinger instead. Luttwak and Laqueur, "Kissinger and the Yom Kippur War," try to set the record straight, but overlook the importance of the cease-fire effort of October 10–13. Gil Carl AlRoy, *The Kissinger Experience: American Policy in the Middle East* (Horizon Press, 1975), is a bitterly anti-Kissinger polemic. Golan, *Secret Conversations of Kissinger*, is better informed, but equally hostile to Kissinger. Edward R. F. Sheehan, *The Arabs, Israelis, and Kissinger: A Secret History of American Diplomacy in the Middle East* (Reader's Digest Press, 1976), is sympathetic to him. Very few writers have been able to discern Nixon's role in the formulation of U.S. policy during the war or to distinguish between those aspects of policy designed to preserve détente and those aimed at promoting a new relationship with Egypt.

72. The president's daily diary provides a detailed log of all meetings and telephone calls. For the seventeen days of the crisis that Kissinger was in Washington, he spent on average thirty-four minutes each day in private or very restricted meetings with Nixon. (This excludes cabinet meetings and briefings of congres-

sional leaders where Kissinger was present.) In addition, they spoke by telephone about two times each day, each call averaging some six minutes. Altogether, Kissinger was in direct touch with the president for about three-quarters of an hour a day, or nearly an hour each day if the larger meetings are also counted. As chief of staff, Haig probably spent more time with Nixon, but much of that must have involved the Watergate mess.

Chapter 5

1. Nixon was more inclined than Kissinger to consider a forceful American role in imposing a settlement in the region and was not reluctant to talk of pressuring Israel. But he was neither able nor determined to follow through on these sentiments.

2. He expressed this concern to Mohamed Heikal in Cairo on November 7, as reported by Heikal in a lengthy account of his talk with Kissinger in *Al-Anwar*, November 16, 1973, translated in "Interviews: Kissinger Meets Haikal," *Journal of Palestine Studies*, vol. 3 (Winter 1974), pp. 210–15.

3. See "Interviews: Kissinger Meets Haikal," pp. 211–12. Kissinger reportedly told Heikal that he had not dealt with the Middle East crisis before October 1973 because of his fear of failure. Not enough elements of the situation were under his control to ensure success.

4. Ibid., p. 214. "The USSR can give you arms, but the United States can give you a just solution which will give you back your territories, especially as you [the Arabs] have been able to really change the situation in the Middle East. . . . Politics in our age is not a question of emotions; it is the facts of power."

5. Edward R. F. Sheehan, *The Arabs, Israelis, and Kissinger: A Secret History of American Diplomacy in the Middle East* (Reader's Digest Press, 1976), p. 51, refers to a coherent Arab policy based on a "quasi-alliance" between Washington and Cairo and on the promotion of American technology as a means of increasing American influence in the Arab world.

6. See William B. Quandt, "Soviet Policy in the October Middle East War," *International Affairs*, vol. 53 (July 1977), pp. 377–89, and vol. 53 (October 1977), pp. 587–603.

7. Nixon and Kissinger may also have been irritated by Moscow's unwillingness to live up to the commitment it undertook on October 20–21 to work for the immediate release of Israeli prisoners held in Egypt and Syria.

8. William B. Quandt, "Domestic Influences on U.S. Foreign Policy in the Middle East: The View from Washington," in Willard A. Beling, ed., *The Middle East: Quest for an American Policy* (State University of New York Press, 1973), pp. 263–85.

9. See Henry A. Kissinger, *Years of Upheaval* (Little, Brown, 1982), pp. 615–16.

10. In his first meeting with Kissinger, Fahmy agreed that the Third Army Corps would be resupplied only with nonmilitary items if Israel agreed to pull back to the October 22 lines. Fahmy at the time was acting foreign minister. He was named foreign minister on October 31.

11. Kissinger, *Years of Upheaval*, pp. 616–17. Kissinger did promise that Israel would not launch a military offensive from its position on the west bank of the Suez Canal. He also agreed to send a high-level representative to Cairo at an early date.

12. Ibid., pp. 619–24.

13. Kissinger had seen the Syrian representative to the United Nations on November 2, but there was still no channel for continuing contacts between Washington and Damascus.

14. Kissinger, *Years of Upheaval*, pp. 636–41. See also Sheehan, *Arabs, Israelis*, pp. 48–51.

15. The text of the agreement can be found in Kissinger, *Years of Upheaval*, p. 641.

16. Ibid., p. 664, states, "Had I understood the mechanism of oil pricing better, I would have realized that Saudi production cutbacks were more dangerous than the embargo since they critically affected world supply and therefore provided the precondition for the impoverishing price rise."

17. Sheehan, *Arabs, Israelis*, pp. 70–73, contains a partial transcript of the Kissinger-Faisal meeting. See also Kissinger, *Years of Upheaval*, pp. 659–66.

18. Several days later, in Peking, Kissinger spoke of Israeli "withdrawals" as part of a settlement, in a deliberate effort to signal his good intentions to the Saudis. The Israelis were not particularly pleased; they worried about Kissinger's mention of U.S. guarantees, fearing that external guarantees would become a substitute for Arab concessions. See "Secretary Kissinger's News Conference of November 12, 1973," *Department of State Bulletin*, vol. 69 (December 10, 1973), p. 713.

19. Sadat's reply to Nixon's invitation, dated December 8, confirmed Egypt's willingness to go to Geneva but did not mention Syria.

20. Kissinger's speech before the Pilgrims of Great Britain on December 12 discussed the October war and the energy crisis. It contained the revealing admission that "it is fair to state . . . that the United States did not do all that it might have done before the war to promote a permanent settlement in the Middle East." *Department of State Bulletin*, vol. 69 (December 31, 1973), p. 780.

21. Kissinger spent four hours with Sadat on December 13 and five hours on December 14. They discussed what they might do if Israel refused to attend the Geneva conference. Sadat also promised to work for the lifting of the oil embargo in early January.

22. Kissinger, *Years of Upheaval*, p. 759, quotes from the letter.

23. Nixon's tone in these letters was reflected in remarks he reportedly made to a group of seventeen governors on December 13. "The only way we're going to solve the crisis is to end the oil embargo, and the only way we're going to end the embargo is to get the Israelis to act reasonable. I hate to use the word blackmail, but we've got to do some things to get them to behave." Thomas O'Toole and Lou Cannon, "Jobs, Oil Put Ahead of Environment, Israel," *Washington Post*, December 22, 1973, p. A1.

24. These promises were codified in a memorandum of understanding. See David Landau, "Kissinger Obtains Jerusalem's Consent to Attend Geneva Parley," *Jerusalem Post*, December 18, 1973, p. 1

25. Kissinger, *Years of Upheaval*, pp. 777–86. Sheehan, *Arabs, Israelis*, pp. 95–97, includes transcripts of portions of these talks.

26. Asad did agree to the opening of an American-manned interests section in Damascus. Thomas Scotes was sent to head the mission.

27. Kissinger, *Years of Upheaval*, pp. 1249–50, reproduces the text of a memorandum that he sent to Nixon on December 19, 1973, summing up the positions of the parties on the eve of the conference.

28. Ibid., pp. 821–29; and Marvin Kalb and Bernard Kalb, *Kissinger* (Little, Brown, 1974), pp. 534–35.

29. Kalb and Kalb, *Kissinger*, p. 539.

30. The text and map appear in "The Agreement: New Deployment of Forces along the Suez Canal," *Jerusalem Post*, January 20, 1974, p. 1, and in Kissinger, *Years of Upheaval*, p. 839 (map) and p. 1250.

31. "Secretary Kissinger's News Conference of January 3, 1974," *Department of State Bulletin*, vol. 70 (January 28, 1974), p. 78. On January 6, 1974, Defense Secretary Schlesinger raised for the first time the possible use of force if the oil embargo should continue indefinitely.

32. These messages, which seemed to imply that Nixon wanted the embargo lifted for domestic political reasons, later proved an embarrassment to him. When the Saudis failed to live up to their promises to lift the embargo, Kissinger hinted that he might be obliged to release the texts of the commitments undertaken by Faisal. The Saudis responded by suggesting that they, too, might have some embarrassing messages to release. The issue was quickly dropped. See Kissinger, *Years of Upheaval*, p. 947: "In the tenth month of his [Nixon's] torment he was still in thrall to the idea that a dramatic lifting of the embargo under his personal leadership was the cure-all for his Watergate agonies."

33. Bernard Gwertzman, "Israel and Syria to Confer in U.S.," *New York Times*, March 3, 1974, p. 1. There were sixty-five names on the list, more than some observers had expected.

34. During his visit to Washington on March 12, King Hussein had requested $130 million in budget support, in addition to other sums for military assistance. The administration at the time was considering $100 million, which was about twice the amount provided the previous year. The formal aid request for the Middle East for fiscal year 1975 was sent to Congress on April 24 and contained an uncommitted $100 million, presumably to be used as aid for Syria if diplomatic relations were resumed.

35. Dayan's visit had nearly been called off by the Israelis in protest over what they viewed as Egypt's violations of the terms of the disengagement agreement. The dispute over the violations is mentioned in "Arabs Assess Talks Progress," *Washington Post*, March 26, 1974, p. A13.

36. Kissinger, *Years of Upheaval*, pp. 1052–1110, gives a detailed account of the Damascus-Jerusalem shuttle. Sheehan, *Arabs, Israelis*, pp. 94–106, covers this period, including texts of some of the conversations between Kissinger and Meir. See also Matti Golan, *The Secret Conversations of Henry Kissinger: Step-by-Step Diplomacy in the Middle East* (Quadrangle Books, 1976), p. 194.

37. *Pravda*, May 20, 1974, did, however, warn Asad not to settle for half-measures.

38. Sadat fully endorsed this approach to Asad.

39. Golan, *Secret Conversations of Kissinger*, p. 196; and Bernard Gwertzman, "Syria-Israel Gain Seen by Kissinger," *New York Times*, May 9, 1974, p. 1.

40. Nixon had sent Meir a letter on May 10 expressing his concern that an agreement be reached.

41. The Americans had anticipated difficult negotiating around Quneitra and had come armed with large aerial photographs of the area. The photographs were actually used for drawing the final lines instead of maps because of their extraordinarily accurate detail.

42. Kissinger, *Years of Upheaval*, p. 1078, recounts Nixon's orders to cut off all aid to Israel. In the context of the Palestinian terrorist attack on Israelis at Ma'alot that occurred on May 15, Kissinger felt such action would be particularly inappropriate, and he opposed it.

43. After four hours with Prime Minister Meir and eight with President Asad, Kissinger reported to Nixon that May 16 had been his toughest day yet. The previous day Israel had been traumatized by the Ma'alot massacre, which had resulted in the deaths of numerous schoolchildren. This contributed to the defiant mood in Israel concerning concessions to Syria and added to the difficulty of Kissinger's task.

44. "Two Issues Said to Delay Troop-Separation Accord," *New York Times*, May 23, 1974, p. 1.

45. Sheehan, *Arabs, Israelis*, p. 126.

46. As late as June 2, Syria was still trying to make changes in the disengagement line. Israel refused.

47. For the text of the agreement, see *Arab Report and Record*, May 16–31, 1974, p. 215.

48. Kissinger, *Years of Upheaval*, pp. 1123–43; and Richard M. Nixon, *RN: The Memoirs of Richard Nixon* (Grosset and Dunlap, 1978), pp. 1007–18.

49. Nixon reportedly spent his free time listening to the possibly incriminating Watergate tapes. The House Judiciary Committee was holding hearings on whether there was sufficient evidence to warrant his impeachment. Subpoenas for evidence had been issued, Nixon had refused to comply, and the Supreme Court would have to decide the matter.

50. Kissinger, *Years of Upheaval*, p. 1134.

51. Golan, *Secret Conversations of Kissinger*, pp. 214–17.

52. Golan, *Secret Conversations of Kissinger*, pp. 220–21, claims that arms shipments were delayed as a form of pressure on Israel.

53. Egyptian-Jordanian Joint Communiqué, July 19, 1974, in Foreign Broadcast Information Service, *Daily Report: Middle East and North Africa*, July 19, 1974, p. D1.

54. Information Minister Aharon Yariv stated in July 1974, "Negotiations with the PLO would be possible should the PLO . . . declare its readiness to enter into negotiations while acknowledging the existence of the Jewish state in Israel and calling off all hostile acts against it." "Israel for the First Time, Gives Basis of Talks with Palestinians," *New York Times*, July 13, 1974, p. 1.

55. Golan, *Secret Conversations of Kissinger*, pp. 220–22.

56. Kissinger, *Years of Upheaval*, p. 1247, note 1, recognizes this criticism but argues that in the immediate aftermath of the October 1973 war nothing more than a step-by-step approach could have worked. I agree for that period, but I think more might have been done to build on the second disengagement agreement if presidential authority had not been so badly undermined. In brief, American influence might have made a difference, but it was not available from mid-1974 on.

57. Ford shared Kissinger's suspicion of the Soviet Union. See Gerald R. Ford, *A Time to Heal: The Autobiography of Gerald R. Ford* (Harper and Row, 1979), p. 183: "Even before I became President, Kissinger had achieved significant success in easing the Soviets out of the Middle East. I thought they didn't want a bona fide settlement there and that their only aim was to promote instability, so I wanted to keep them out."

58. See Cecilia Albin and Harold H. Saunders, "Sinai II: The Politics of International Mediation," FPI Case Study 17, Johns Hopkins University, School of Advanced International Studies, Washington, 1991, for a detailed account of these negotiations. The authors point out that Ford himself was inclined to concentrate on the Egyptian-Israeli front, in part because it seemed more feasible in political terms (pp. 37–38). Also, Henry A. Kissinger, *Years of Renewal* (Simon & Schuster, 1999), pp. 347–459.

59. Fahmy told Ford that Egypt was prepared to go ahead with another partial agreement with Israel before an Israeli-Jordanian agreement was reached. He also expressed the opinion that simultaneous negotiations on these two fronts was impossible. Albin and Saunders, "Sinai II," pp. 29–30.

60. Kissinger, *Years of Renewal*, pp. 368–69, notes that both Israel and Egypt worked to undermine the Jordan option.

61. Albin and Saunders, "Sinai II," p. 30, indicates that King Hussein made an important concession by accepting the idea that Israeli forces could remain behind in designated locations along the Jordan River after a disengagement agreement. This is referred to as the "leopard spots" concept.

62. Kissinger, *Years of Renewal*, p. 382.

63. Ibid., pp. 380–81, notes that Rabin and Ford did not develop a close relationship and that Rabin at this stage was not particularly flexible.

64. The joint communiqué issued on November 24, 1974, said that the search for peace in the Middle East should be based on UN Resolution 338, "taking into account the legitimate interests of all the peoples of the area, including the Palestinian people, and respect for the right to independent existence of all States in the area." *Department of State Bulletin*, vol. 71 (December 23, 1974), p. 880.

65. Golan, *Secret Conversations of Kissinger*, pp. 229–30; *Haaretz*, December 17, 1974; and Kissinger, *Years of Renewal*, pp. 389–91.

66. Ford also weighed in with advice to the Israelis to be more flexible. See Ford, *Time to Heal*, pp. 245–46, for his view that Israel was sufficiently strong to be able to make concessions.

67. Kissinger, *Years of Renewal*, pp. 393–97.

68. *Le Monde*, January 21, 1975.

69. On February 3, 1975, Syria and the Soviet Union issued a joint communiqué calling for the reconvening of the Geneva conference.

70. Asad's position on a second step in the Golan Height remained ambiguous. He did not appear particularly anxious for such an agreement, but neither did he preclude it.

71. Kissinger, *Years of Renewal*, pp. 397–421.

72. Wolf I. Blitzer, "Kissinger Reveals Sadat's Twelve 'Concessions,' " *Jerusalem Post*, May 12, 1975, p. 1. According to Albin and Saunders, "Sinai II," p. 58, Sadat also gave Kissinger a fallback position to use as needed. This became a standard Sadat tactic in later negotiations.

73. Sheehan, *Arabs, Israelis*, p. 156. See also Albin and Saunders, "Sinai II," pp. 56–58 for a summary of these points.

74. See Golan, *Secret Conversations of Kissinger*, pp. 236–38, although he incorrectly gives the date of the letter as March 19. Yitzhak Rabin, *The Rabin Memoirs* (Little, Brown, 1979), p. 256, provides a partial text of the letter, in which Ford threatens "reassessment" of U.S. policy, including relations with Israel. Ford, *Time to Heal*, p. 247, said that he was "mad as hell" at the Israelis over their negotiating tactics. Kissinger, *Years of Renewal*, pp. 418–21, makes no mention of Ford's letter, but notes Ford's anger at Israeli "intransigence."

75. Before his departure Kissinger called on Golda Meir. Although she publicly supported Rabin, she privately implied to Kissinger that Rabin had mishandled the negotiations and that she would have known how to get the cabinet and the Knesset to support an agreement.

76. Ford met with Max Fisher on March 27, 1975, to express his irritation with Israeli policy. Fisher was a wealthy Detroit businessman, a Republican, and a leader in the American Jewish community. He often served as an informal channel of communication between the United States and the American Jewish community. See Ford, *Time to Heal*, pp. 247, 286. Kissinger, *Years of Renewal*, p. 425.

77. Ford interview with the Hearst newspaper chain, March 27, 1975. See Bernard Gwertzman, "Ford Says Israel Lacked Flexibility in Negotiations," *New York Times*, March 28, 1975, p. 1.

78. George Ball, "How to Avert a Middle East War," *Atlantic Monthly*, January 1975, pp. 6–11.

79. During this period Stanley Hoffmann brilliantly argued the case that it was in Israel's own interest to come up with a comprehensive peace initiative. The major flaw in his argument was that such a policy would require a strong Israeli government backed by a broad public consensus. That apparently was lacking. See "A New Policy for Israel," *Foreign Affairs*, vol. 53 (April 1975), pp. 405–31.

80. Sheehan, *Arabs, Israelis*, p. 166; and Albin and Saunders, "Sinai II," p. 79. Kissinger, *Years of Renewal*, p. 428, says that in the weeks after Indochina's collapse, he made a private pact with himself: "if the step-by-step approach had to be abandoned and the United States was driven to state terms for a settlement, I would resign. The disparity between Israel's perception of its margin of survival and ours would become too difficult to bridge. If we prevailed, we would break Israel's back psychologically; if we failed, we would have doomed our role in the Middle East."

81. He also referred to U.S. policy as "evenhanded."

82. Ford, *Time to Heal*, p. 287, says that he publicly welcomed the letter from the senators, but "in truth it really bugged me. The Senators claimed the letter was

'spontaneous,' but there was no doubt in my mind that it was inspired by Israel. We had given vast amounts of military and economic assistance to Israel over the years and we had never asked for anything in return."

83. Sheehan, *Arabs, Israelis*, pp. 176–77.

84. Golan, *Secret Conversations of Kissinger*, p. 59; and Ford, *Time to Heal*, pp. 290–91.

85. Ford, *Time to Heal*, p. 291, says that he also offered Sadat significant amounts of economic assistance ($800 million) and C-130 transports. Offensive military equipment was ruled out because of Israel's strong objections.

86. Kissinger, *Years of Renewal*, pp. 441–42, says Rabin made an impressive strategic argument, which he reproduces in full on pp. 1095–97.

87. Ford letter to Rabin, September 1, 1975, referring to their meeting of June 12, 1975. Reproduced in Michael Widlanski, ed., *Can Israel Survive a Palestinian State?* (Jerusalem: Institute for Advanced Strategic and Political Studies, 1990), pp. 120–21. According to Albin and Saunders, "Sinai II," p. 92, Ford told Rabin that he was inclined to put forward a U.S. plan.

88. Golan, *Secret Conversations of Kissinger*, p. 245; and Terence Smith, "Israel Offers Compromise to Egyptian Sinai Accords," *New York Times*, June 25, 1975, p. 1. Rabin, *Rabin Memoirs*, p. 267, states that the proposed map was approved by the Israeli negotiating team and conveyed to Egypt, where it was rejected. The issue seems to have been how one defined the "eastern end of the passes."

89. Golan, *Secret Conversations of Kissinger*, p. 248, although he mistakenly gives the date of this meeting as early August. Bernard Gwertzman, "Kissinger Visited by Israeli Envoy for Secret Talks," *New York Times*, July 4, 1975, p. 1.

90. Albin and Saunders, "Sinai II," p. 86, note that Israel was very intent on getting more military assistance to fund its ten-year modernization program called Matmon-B.

91. Rabin and Kissinger met near Bonn on July 12, after which the Israeli cabinet authorized a new negotiating position. Kissinger, *Years of Renewal*, p. 449. See also *Arab Report and Record*, July 1–15, 1975, p. 401; Terence Smith, "U.S. Is Considering Proposal That It Man Posts in Sinai," *New York Times*, July 13, 1975, p. 1; and Kathleen Teltsch, "Kissinger Warns Majority in UN on U.S. Support," *New York Times*, July 15, 1975, p. 1. Egypt's reply was forthcoming on July 21, but was rejected by Israel on July 27. Israel then presented an "absolutely final" position to Kissinger, who transmitted it to Sadat via Eilts on July 31. The Egyptian response reached Kissinger in Belgrade on August 3, and by August 7 Dinitz had responded with the Israeli position. During the next few days, further exchanges took place, and by mid-August United States and Israeli officials had completed work on a draft agreement. Ford then instructed Kissinger to undertake another trip to the Middle East to pin down the details of an agreement.

92. Sheehan, *Arabs, Israelis*, p. 184.

93. The text of the agreement can be found in *Department of State Bulletin*, vol. 73 (September 22, 1975), pp. 466–70. The secret part of the agreement was published in "U.S. Documents Accompanying the Sinai Accord," *New York Times*, September 17, 1975, p. 4, and "U.S.-Israeli Pact on Geneva," *New York Times*, September 18, 1975, p. 16. The map was also released by the Department of State

94. Kissinger had kept Sadat informed of most of the commitments he was making to Israel but did not mention the Pershing missile. This irritated the Egyptians and raised doubts about other secret agreements that Kissinger might not have mentioned.

95. According to Albin and Saunders, "Sinai II," p. 100, the Israelis had sought much stronger language. The American negotiating team at the time interpreted this commitment as leaving room for contacts with the PLO. See also Kissinger, *Years of Renewal*, p. 456. "What we put in writing with respect to both the PLO and the Golan was not so much a new commitment as a formal statement of existing American policy."

96. This letter remained secret until published in Widlanski, ed., *Can Israel Survive?* pp. 120–21. See www.brookings.edu/press/appendix/peace_process.htm.

97. On September 29, 1975, Kissinger spoke to the Arab representatives at the United Nations. He said that the United States was prepared to work for a Syrian-Israeli second step, if that was wanted; that the United States would consider ways of working for an overall settlement; and that he would begin to refine his thinking on how the legitimate interests of the Palestinian people could be met. "Furthering Peace in the Middle East," Toast by Secretary Kissinger, *Department of State Bulletin*, vol. 73 (October 20, 1975), pp. 581–84.

98. Kissinger, *Years of Renewal*, p. 454, gives Ford considerable credit for his "persistence" in working for Egyptian-Israeli peace.

99. Even without Sinai II, of course, the level of aid for Israel and Egypt would have been substantial. The marginal cost of Sinai II should be measured as several hundreds of million dollars, not several billion. For an account of the congressional debate on Sinai II, see Bernard Gwertzman, "Senate Unit Asks Word from Ford," *New York Times*, October 1, 1975, p. 14. The House and Senate voted in favor of United States technicians in Sinai by large majorities, on October 8 and 9, respectively. Ford, *Time to Heal*, pp. 308–09, provides his rationale for increased aid to Israel: "If we provided the hardware, we could convince Israelis that they were secure. Then they might be willing to accept some risks in the search for peace."

100. Bernard Gwertzman, "Israel Indicates a Cool Reaction to Egypt's Ideas," *New York Times*, March 15, 1975, p. 1.

Chapter 6

1. *Toward Peace in the Middle East*, Report of a Study Group (Brookings, 1975). This report was subsequently credited with steering the Carter administration toward a comprehensive approach to an Arab-Israeli peace agreement, with the Geneva Conference as the centerpiece of the strategy. It is true that Vance and Carter both read the report, and many of its suggestions were incorporated into policy, but it would be an exaggeration to say that the report served as a blueprint for the policies of the first year.

2. The rest of the Middle East team consisted of Alfred L. Atherton Jr., the assistant secretary of state for Near Eastern and South Asian affairs and later ambassador-at-large for the peace talks; Harold H. Saunders, the director of intelligence and research at State and later the assistant secretary for Near Eastern

affairs; and me as staff member of the National Security Council. All of us had been involved with Kissinger's shuttle diplomacy and were personally well acquainted, which helped to reduce the normal State-NSC frictions and ensured a large measure of continuity with past negotiating efforts. Two other people came to play important roles as the negotiating process got under way: Hermann F. Eilts, ambassador to Cairo and an experienced Middle East hand; and Samuel W. Lewis, ambassador to Israel, who had considerable experience with the United Nations and proved to be a very popular and influential envoy to Israel.

3. For more detail, see William B. Quandt, *Camp David: Peacemaking and Politics* (Brookings, 1986), pp. 38–40.

4. Ibid., pp. 41–43.

5. Cyrus Vance, *Hard Choices: Critical Years in America's Foreign Policy* (Simon and Schuster, 1983), p. 171.

6. See Yitzhak Rabin, *The Rabin Memoirs* (Little, Brown, 1979), pp. 292-99, for his version of the meeting. See also Jimmy Carter, *Keeping Faith: Memoirs of a President* (Bantam Books), 1982, p. 280; Zbigniew Brzezinski, *Power and Principle: Memoirs of the National Security Adviser, 1977–1981* (Farrar, Strauss, Giroux, 1983), pp. 90–91; and Vance, *Hard Choices*, p. 173.

7. "Clinton, Massachusetts: Remarks and a Question-and-Answer Session at the Clinton Town Meeting, March 16, 1977," *Public Papers of the President: Carter, 1977*, vol. 1 (Government Printing Office, 1977), p. 387.

8. Quandt, *Camp David*, p. 51.

9. See Carter, *Keeping Faith*, pp. 284–88, for his reaction to Begin. About this time, Hamilton Jordan wrote a highly confidential forty-three page memo for the president to inform him of the basic facts of life about the "Jewish lobby" and to urge him to develop a strategy to win support from Jewish political figures. See Hamilton Jordan, Confidential File, Box 34, File "Foreign Policy/Domestic Politics Memo, HJ memo, 6/77," declassified June 12, 1990.

10. See Quandt, *Camp David*, pp. 77–82; Moshe Dayan, *Breakthrough: A Personal Account of the Egypt-Israel Peace Negotiations* (Knopf, 1981), pp. 19–20; and Carter, *Keeping Faith*, p. 290.

11. Ismail Fahmy, *Negotiating for Peace in the Middle East* (Johns Hopkins University Press, 1983), pp. 216–19.

12. Quandt, *Camp David*, p. 90.

13. Ibid., p. 91.

14. Ibid., pp. 101–03.

15. Fahmy, *Negotiating for Peace*, p. 252.

16. Quandt, *Camp David*, pp. 122–23. For the text of the joint communiqué of the U.S. and Soviet governments, see www.brookings.edu/press/appendix/peace_process.htm.

17. Dayan, *Breakthrough*, pp. 38–54.

18. For a review of the evidence, see Martin Indyk, *"To the Ends of the Earth": Sadat's Jerusalem Initiative* (Harvard University, Center for Middle Eastern Studies, 1984), pp. 41–43; and Quandt, *Camp David*, pp. 123–25.

19. See the letter written by Ambassador Hermann Eilts, "The Syrians Have Been Their Own Worst Enemies," *New York Times*, January 12, 1982, p. A14.

20. Quandt, *Camp David*, pp. 125–31.

21. Dayan, *Breakthrough*, p. 71.

22. Ibid., pp. 70–71.

23. Quandt, *Camp David*, pp. 139–41.

24. Fahmy, *Negotiating for Peace*, pp. 262–63.

25. See Steven L. Spiegel, *The Other Arab-Israeli Conflict: Making America's Middle East Policy, from Truman to Reagan* (University of Chicago Press, 1985), pp. 341–44.

26. Ibid., p. 156; and Vance, *Hard Choices*, p. 199.

27. Brzezinski, *Power and Principle*, pp. 115–20.

28. See Quandt, *Camp David*, p. 158; Carter, *Keeping Faith*, p. 300; and Dayan, *Breakthrough*, pp. 359–61, for the revised text of the Self-Rule proposal.

29. On August 5, 1970, Begin explained before the Knesset why he was resigning from the cabinet: "As far as we are concerned, what do the words 'withdrawal from territories administered since 1967 by Israel' mean other than giving up Judea and Samaria. Not all the territories; but by all opinion, most of them."

30. Quandt, *Camp David*, pp. 171–72.

31. Ibid., pp. 173–76.

32. Ibid., p. 201.

33. Ibid., pp. 212–14.

34. Ibid., pp. 216–17.

35. Ibid., p. 218.

36. Ibid., appendix F, p. 369.

37. Ibid., pp. 222–25.

38. Ibid., p. 222.

39. See Shibley Telhami, *Power and Leadership in International Bargaining: The Path to the Camp David Accords* (Columbia University Press, 1990), pp. 162–67.

40. Quandt, *Camp David*, pp. 242–47.

41. Ibid., pp. 247–51.

42. For the text of the Camp David Accords, see www.brookings.edu/press/appendix/peace_process.htm.

Chapter 7

1. On Sadat's political position at this time, see William B. Quandt, *Camp David: Peacemaking and Politics* (Brookings, 1986), p. 262.

2. On September 19, 1978, the Saudi News Agency released an official Saudi cabinet statement critical of the Camp David Accords because they did not call for full Israeli withdrawal and did not provide for Palestinian self-determination. Nonetheless, the cabinet statement went on to say that it did not dispute Egypt's right to recover Sinai. See FBIS, *Daily Report: Middle East and Africa*, September 20, 1978, p. C3.

3. See Jimmy Carter, *Keeping Faith: Memoirs of a President* (Bantam Books, 1982), p. 405, in which he notes that Begin seemed to want to keep both the peace with Egypt and the West Bank; and Cyrus Vance, *Hard Choices: Critical Years in America's Foreign Policy* (Simon and Schuster, 1983), p. 229. Begin had made some particularly hard-line public comments on the day after signing the Camp David Accords. Carter was so angry that he took Begin aside during their joint appearance before the U.S. Congress and told him, in Sadat's presence, that his

remarks could cause serious problems. Interview with President Jimmy Carter, Plains, Georgia, May 22, 1985.

4. Sadat had the impression from Carter that the United States would deliver Saudi support for Camp David. See Hermann Frederick Eilts, "Improve the Framework," *Foreign Policy*, no. 41 (Winter 1980–81), p. 9.

5. Zbigniew Brzezinski, *Power and Principle: Memoirs of the National Security Adviser, 1977–1981* (Farrar, Straus and Giroux, 1983), p. 274.

6. For the text of Carter's answers to King Hussein, see www.brookings.edu/press/appendix/peace_process.htm.

7. Brzezinski, *Power and Principle*, p. 276, says that Carter had hoped to have the treaty signed by election day.

8. According to Ambassador Eilts, Sadat was irritated with the way his negotiating team in Washington had handled the language of article 6 of the treaty. This was one of the reasons he brought Mustafa Khalil more directly into the negotiations from that point on. Interview with Hermann Eilts on November 30, 1984.

9. According to Kamal Hassan Ali, after the Baghdad summit Sadat was very sensitive to the priority-of-obligations issue. This slowed up the negotiations on the Egyptian side. Interview in Cairo, February 4, 1985.

10. Carter, *Keeping Faith*, p. 409; Brzezinski, *Power and Principle*, pp. 276–77; and Vance, *Hard Choices*, p. 238.

11. The text of the November 11, 1978, draft of the treaty was leaked to the press by the Egyptians and Israelis. It is available in Meron Medzini, ed., *Israel's Foreign Relations: Selected Documents, 1977–1979*, vol. 5 (Jerusalem: Ministry of Foreign Affairs, 1981), pp. 577–81.

12. Ezer Weizman, *The Battle for Peace* (Bantam Books, 1981), p. 375, essentially agreed with Carter and Sadat when he wrote that it was naive to believe there was no link at all between the two agreements. After all, they were signed together.

13. Brzezinski, *Power and Principle*, pp. 277–78.

14. See Gary Sick, *All Fall Down: America's Tragic Encounter with Iran* (Random House, 1985), pp. 130-40.

15. Jimmy Carter, *Keeping Faith: Memoirs of a President* (Bantam Books, 1982), p. 412.

16. Memorandum from Brzezinski to Carter, January 23, 1979.

17. See Zbigniew Brzezinski, *Power and Principle: Memoirs of the National Security Adviser, 1977–1981* (Farrar, Straus and Giroux, 1983), p. 279. Brzezinski thought that Iran made it impossible for Carter to stand aside. "To let the Camp David Accords slip away would be to turn a triumph into disaster, with unforeseeable consequences for the Middle East as a whole." Carter by this time had also concluded that all that could be attained was a separate peace, followed by prolonged negotiations on the West Bank and Gaza. Carter, *Keeping Faith*, p. 413. In a memorandum to Carter written on February 28, 1979, Brzezinski had said that Begin believed he could afford a failure and Carter could not. "He believes that election year realities will increasingly weaken our hand in the negotiations." It was also clear that the United States would have to be very forthcoming on aid to get Israel to budge on the remaining issues of the treaty. Bilateral issues were now as important as Egyptian-Israeli differences.

18. Carter, *Keeping Faith*, p. 416.

19. Brzezinski, *Power and Principle*, p. 282. Carter, in an interview on May 22, 1985, did not recall having sent any such message to Sadat. Brzezinski, in an interview on June 3, 1985, recalled in some detail his conversation with Carter. Because Brzezinski was carrying a "political" message to Sadat from Carter, Vance did not object to his going to Cairo.

20. Carter had called Sadat on March 5 to tell him of Brzezinski's visit, and Sadat had promised him that the president's trip would be a great success. Carter felt he had a guarantee from Sadat that the negotiations would not fail because of any U.S.-Egyptian differences. As Carter later wrote. "Once more, I wanted Begin to have his way with particular phrases and depended on Sadat to be flexible on language and to take the long view concerning the effect of the agreement." Carter, *Keeping Faith*, p. 417.

21. While in Cairo, Carter had a strained meeting with his ambassador to Saudi Arabia, John C. West. He told West in no uncertain terms that he was disappointed with the Saudis and instructed him to be blunt in telling Crown Prince Fahd that he expected Saudi support in the future.

22. When Khalil asked Carter to try to change the text of the agreement in several places, the president replied: "For the last 18 months, I, the president of the most powerful nation on earth, have acted the postman. I am not a proud man— I have done the best I could—but I cannot go back to try to change the language."

23. For the text of the Egyptian-Israeli Peace Treaty, see www.brookings.edu/ press/appendix/peace_process.htm.

24. See Moshe Dayan, *Breakthrough: A Personal Account of the Egypt-Israel Peace Negotiations* (Knopf, 1981), pp. 356–58, for the texts of these two memoranda.

25. Ironically, according to public opinion polls, Carter gained very little as a result of the peace treaty. See Jody Powell, *The Other Side of the Story* (William Morrow, 1984), p. 102.

26. Dayan, *Breakthrough*, pp. 303–04.

27. For a solid account, including the texts of the Israeli and Egyptian proposals, see Harvey Sicherman, *Palestinian Self-Government (Autonomy): Its Past and Its Future* (Washington: Washington Institute for Near East Policy, 1991), pp. 21–34, and appendixes 6 and 7. Sicherman also includes the text of Linowitz's report to the president on the autonomy talks, dated January 14, 1981 (appendix 7). Linowitz provides an additional perspective in "The Prospects for the Camp David Peace Process," *SAIS Review*, no. 2 (Summer 1981), pp. 93–100. In a news conference on September 6, 1989, Linowitz claimed that "some 80% of the areas of responsibility to be conveyed to the self-governing authority" had been agreed on. See "Ambassador Sol M. Linowitz's Press Conference: Middle East Peace Negotiations," *Department of State Bulletin*, vol. 80 (December 1980), p. 51.

28. Carter later showed that he understood the linkage issue quite well. *In The Blood of Abraham* (Houghton Mifflin, 1985), p. 45, he wrote: "From Begin's point of view, the peace agreement with Egypt was the significant act for Israel; the references to the West Bank and Palestinians were to be finessed. With the bilateral treaty, he removed Egypt's considerable strength from the military equation of the Middle East and thus gave the Israelis renewed freedom to pursue their

goals of fortifying and settling the occupied territories and removing perceived threats by preemptive military strikes against some of their neighbors."

Chapter 8

1. Ronald Reagan, "Recognizing the Israeli Asset," *Washington Post*, August 15, 1979, p. A25. The rhetorical flourishes and the line of argument suggest the influence of Joseph Churba, who became an adviser to Reagan during his 1980 campaign for the presidency. Churba may well have been the ghostwriter for this piece. See Joseph Churba, *The Politics of Defeat: America's Decline in the Middle East* (Cyrco Press, 1977), p. 97, in which the author speaks of "the conflict and tension endemic to the [Middle East] region. This condition is traceable largely to the sectarian and fragmented nature of Middle East society." Reagan's article says, "The Carter administration has yet to grasp that in this region conflict and tension are endemic, a condition traceable largely to the fragmented sectarian nature of Middle Eastern society." See also Ronald Reagan, *An American Life* (Simon and Schuster, 1990), p. 410, on his reasons for supporting Israel. There he stresses "moral responsibility," not Israel's importance as a strategic asset.

2. Reagan won an unusually large proportion of Jewish American votes, some 39 percent, in the 1980 election. See Steven L. Spiegel, *The Other Arab-Israeli Conflict: Making America's Middle East Policy from Truman to Reagan* (University of Chicago Press, 1985), p. 397. Normally, Democratic presidential candidates can count on winning about 80 percent of the Jewish vote.

3. According to Lou Cannon, *President Reagan: The Role of a Lifetime* (Simon and Schuster, 1991), pp. 288–91, Reagan was also fascinated by the Biblical story of Armageddon, and attached special importance to the founding of the Jewish state in 1948 as a portent that Armageddon was approaching.

4. Ibid., p. 35, where Cannon states: "He could act decisively when presented with clear options, but he rarely initiated a meeting, a phone call, a proposal or an idea. He thought his staff would tell him anything he ought to know and invested most of his energy and interest in the public performances of the presidency. . . . He thought of himself as a man of principle, and he was difficult to push on the issues that mattered most to him. As president, he was at once the most malleable and least movable of men."

5. See Raymond Tanter, *Who's at the Helm? Lessons of Lebanon* (Boulder, Colo.: Westview Press, 1990), a book written by a member of the National Security Council staff. Reagan is hardly mentioned as a participant in the policy process.

6. Weinberger's views on the Middle East are best spelled out in "Defense Chief Weinberger on Peace Prospects Now," *U.S. News & World Report*, September 27, 1982, pp. 26–28. Among other points, Weinberger said, "We need several friends in the Mideast—not Israel alone, but clearly our relationship with Israel should be maintained."

7. Jeane Kirkpatrick, formerly a Democrat, attracted considerable attention in conservative circles with her article "Dictatorship and Double Standards," *Commentary*, vol. 68 (November 1979), pp. 34–45.

8. See Bob Woodward, *Veil: The Secret Wars of the CIA, 1981-1987* (Simon and Schuster, 1987), pp. 35–49, 71–88.

9. From an interview cited in Karen Elliott House, "Reagan's World," *Wall Street Journal*, June 3, 1980, p. 1.

10. On Haig's views generally, see Alexander M. Haig Jr., *Caveat: Realism, Reagan and Foreign Policy* (Macmillan, 1984), especially pp. 20–33.

11. See Spiegel, *Other Arab-Israeli Conflict*, pp. 407–11; and Reagan, *American Life*, pp. 412, 415–16, on the AWACs fight and his anger at Begin for lobbying on Capitol Hill against the president's policy after having promised not to do so.

12. Helena Cobban, *The Superpowers and the Syrian-Israeli Conflict: Beyond Crisis Management?* (Praeger, 1991), pp. 83–84; for the text of the memorandum of understanding, see Nimrod Novik, *Encounter with Reality: Reagan and the Middle East (The First Term)* (Boulder, Colo.: Westview Press for the Jaffee Center for Strategic Studies, 1985), pp. 86–88.

13. See Ze'ev Schiff and Ehud Ya'ari, *Israel's Lebanon War* (Simon and Schuster, 1984); Itamar Rabinovich, *The War for Lebanon, 1970–1983* (Cornell University Press, 1984); and Yair Evron, *War and Intervention in Lebanon: The Israeli-Syrian Deterrence Dialogue* (Johns Hopkins University Press, 1987).

14. Haig, *Caveat*, pp. 332–35.

15. Schiff and Ya'ari, *Israel's Lebanon War*, pp. 62-77. See also David Kimche, *The Last Option: After Nasser, Arafat and Saddam Hussein. The Quest for Peace in the Middle East* (Scribner's, 1991), p. 145: "Israel's political leaders, especially Prime Minister Begin and Defence Minister Sharon, had become convinced, during those spring months of 1982, that the Reagan administration was not averse to an operation in which the PLO, and perhaps even the Soviet-aligned Syrians, would be taught a lesson." Kimche states bluntly, on his own considerable authority, that there was no strong resistance to Sharon's plans in Washington. He quotes both Haig and Reagan as being understanding of Israel's objectives. "When Begin sent an oral message to Reagan in May 1982 warning that it might become 'imperative and inevitable' to remove this PLO threat, Haig's reaction was that the United States would probably not be able to stop Israel from attacking. And when Sharon met Haig in Washington later that month, Haig was reported to have told him: 'We understand your aims. We can't tell you not to defend your interests.'"

16. Just a week before the Israeli invasion, on May 26, 1982, Haig gave a major speech on the Middle East in which he focused on the Iran-Iraq conflict, the autonomy negotiations, and the explosive situation in Lebanon.

17. See Cobban, *Superpowers*, pp. 35–40.

18. Allan Gerson, *The Kirkpatrick Mission: Diplomacy without Apology. America at the United Nations, 1981–1985* (Free Press, 1991), pp. 138–55.

19. Ibid., p. 134.

20. Translated from the Hebrew version of the letter from Reagan to Begin, June 9, 1982, as published by Arye Naor, *Cabinet at War* (in Hebrew) (Tel Aviv: Lahav, 1986), p. 76. American officials have confirmed the essential accuracy of this version but add that Brezhnev's message was not particularly menacing. They imply that Reagan deliberately exaggerated the danger of escalation to make an impression on Begin.

21. Alexander M. Haig Jr., *Inner Circles: How America Changed the World. A Memoir* (Warner Books, 1992), p. 547.

22. Cannon, *President Reagan*, pp. 202–04; and Haig, *Inner Circles*, pp. 547–

48. Haig claims that he was on the verge of achieving agreement on PLO withdrawal from Lebanon in early July and that this effort fell apart when he was suddenly dismissed.

23. Cannon, *President Reagan*, pp. 202–05.

24. Bernard Gwertzman, "Shultz Declares Palestinian Needs Must Be Resolved," *New York Times*, July 14, 1982, p. A1.

25. George Shultz, *Turmoil and Triumph: My Years as Secretary of State* (Scribner's, 1993), pp. 85–86. The working group consisted of Robert McFarlane, Lawrence Eagleburger, Nicholas Veliotes, Robert Ames, Paul Wolfowitz, Charles Hill, William Kirby, and Alan Kreczko.

26. Ibid., p. 87.

27. Reagan, *American Life*, pp. 425–29; and Michael Deaver, *Behind the Scenes: In Which the Author Talks about Ronald and Nancy Reagan . . . and Himself* (William Morrow, 1987), pp. 165–66. Deaver takes credit for persuading Reagan, against the advice of the NSC staff, to call Begin to tell him to stop the bombing of Beirut. When Begin agreed, Reagan reportedly turned to Deaver and said, "I didn't know I had that kind of power." Also see Gerson, *Kirkpatrick Mission*, pp. 164–69, on the UN diplomacy in this period, especially the delaying tactics on the French-Egyptian proposal, which called for mutual Israeli-PLO recognition.

28. See Rashid Khalidi, *Under Siege: P.L.O. Decisionmaking during the 1982 War* (Columbia University Press, 1986), p. 177.

29. Shultz, *Turmoil and Triumph*, p. 90.

30. For the text of Reagan's speech and talking points, see www.brookings.edu/press/appendix/peace_process.htm.

31. See Kimche, *Last Option*, p. 157, where he quotes Begin speaking to his Israeli colleagues on September 1: "We have been betrayed by the Americans, the biggest betrayal since the state was established. They have stabbed us in the back. We now have a completely different fight on our hands."

32. Veliotes had made a secret trip to Amman to brief King Hussein on August 20. Arafat was also given an advance briefing on the speech while still in Beirut. Begin was briefed by Ambassador Lewis only on August 31. Shultz, *Turmoil and Triumph*, pp. 91–92, discloses the Veliotes mission and describes Shultz's rationale for going ahead in the face of probable Israeli opposition.

33. According to notes, made available to the author, of Sharon's meeting with Pierre Gemayal in Bikfaya on September 16, 1982, Sharon referred to his discussions with Bashir and again called for "the necessity of immediate action to prevent establishment of new facts by the present government in its final days, and the danger that hostile elements would try and modify political processes desirable to us." Some of the relevant background to this meeting is covered by Schiff and Ya'ari, *Israel's Lebanon War*, pp. 246–58.

34. For the results of the official Israeli inquiry, see *The Beirut Massacre: The Complete Kahan Commission Report* (Princeton, N.J.: Karz-Cohl, 1983).

35. See Geoffrey Kemp, "Lessons of Lebanon: A Guideline for Future U.S. Policy," *Middle East Insight*, vol. 6 (Summer 1988), pp. 57–68, on debates over the role of the multinational force from September 1982 until the withdrawal of the American contingent in February 1984.

36. See William B. Quandt, "Reagan's Lebanon Policy: Trial and Error," *Middle East Journal*, vol. 38 (Spring 1984), pp. 241–42.

37. Shultz, *Turmoil and Triumph*, p. 440.

38. The best account of the background to the king's decision can be found in two Pulitzer-prize-winning articles by Karen Elliott House: "Hussein's Decision: King Had U.S. Pledges on Peace Talks but Met a Maze of Arab Foes," *Wall Street Journal*, April 14, 1983, p.1, and "Hussein's Decision: Fears for His Kingdom, Sense of History Drove Monarch to Seek Talks," *Wall Street Journal*, April 15, 1983, p. 1. According to the king, General Secretary Yuri V. Andropov had taken him aside in early December 1982 during a visit to Moscow to warn, "I shall oppose the Reagan plan, and we will use all our resources to oppose it. With due respect, all the weight will be on your shoulders, and they aren't broad enough to bear it."

39. Text of "Jordan's Statement on Its Refusal to Join the Reagan Peace Initiative," *New York Times*, April 11, 1983, p. A12.

40. Among the victims of the bombing was Robert Ames, one of the top CIA officials with responsibility for the Middle East, and one of the core group of officials who had worked closely with Secretary Shultz at the inception of the Reagan initiative.

41. For an inquiry into the reasons for the vulnerability of the U.S. Marine compound, see *Report of the DOD Commission on Beirut International Airport Terrorist Act, October 23, 1983* (Department of Defense, 1983). Before the bombing of the Marine compound, the Israelis had begun to withdraw from the Shouf area, a step on the way toward the new Israeli policy of consolidating a security presence in southern Lebanon only.

42. Cobban, *Superpowers*, pp. 87–88.

43. On Shamir, see Avishai Margalit, "The Violent Life of Yitzhak Shamir," *New York Review of Books*, May 14, 1992, pp. 18–24.

44. See John K. Cooley, *Payback: America's Long War in the Middle East* (Brassey's, 1991), pp. 94–97.

45. Kemp, "Lessons of Lebanon," p. 67. Kemp concludes that only a strong president can put a stop to squabbling between powerful cabinet members such as Shultz and Weinberger. In his words, "In the case of Lebanon the President never once ordered the Secretary of Defense to play a more assertive role in supporting U.S. policy in Lebanon. Indeed, at the height of the debate within the White House over whether or not the marines should be redeployed to ships in February 1984, Reagan's own viewpoint was difficult to discern. The decision in favor of withdrawal was made by a simple majority within the inner circle of advisors."

46. See William B. Quandt, *Camp David: Peacemaking and Politics* (Brookings, 1986), pp. 25–27.

47. Shultz, *Turmoil and Triumph*, pp. 439–40.

48. See Quandt, ed., *Middle East*, p. 473, for the text of the February 11 agreement. Both Jordanian and Palestinian sources say that some amendments were later made to the basic text. The authorized English translation of the first principle called for "total withdrawal from the territories occupied in 1967 for comprehensive peace." The Arabic text simply said "land in exchange for peace."

49. Shultz, *Turmoil and Triumph*, pp. 444–45.

50. On Israeli-Jordanian contacts during this period, see Adam Garfinkle, *Israel and Jordan in the Shadow of War: Functional Ties and Futile Diplomacy in a Small Place* (St. Martin's Press, 1992), pp. 109–20.

51. Text of "President's News Conference on Foreign and Domestic Issues," *New York Times*, March 22, 1985, p. A12.

52. Shultz, *Turmoil and Triumph*, pp. 446–47.

53. Ibid., pp. 453–54.

54. Garfinkle, *Israel and Jordan*, p. 120, provides four of the names: Hanna Siniora (Jerusalem-based editor of *Al-Fajr*), Fayez Abu Rahme (a lawyer from Gaza), Sheik Abd al-Hamid Sayah (the speaker of the Palestine National Council), and Nabil Sha'ath (a political adviser to Arafat and prominent member of the Palestine National Council). In addition, the list mentioned Khalid al-Hassan (prominent in Fatah and occasional emissary to Washington), Hatem Husseini (former PLO representative in Washington), and Salah Ta'amari (Fatah activist who had been imprisoned by Israel and had the distinction of being married to a former wife of King Hussein). Jerusalem Domestic Service, July 19, 1985, in Foreign Broadcast Information Service (FBIS), *Daily Report: Middle East and Africa*, p. I1. Neither the Americans nor the Israelis had any objections to Siniora and Abu Rahmeh. Nabil Sha'ath presented the most complicated case. For the PLO, his inclusion was essential. For Israel, it was out of the question. The Americans vacillated.

55. Shultz, *Turmoil and Triumph*, p. 454.

56. See the text of the September 27, 1985, speech in Amman Domestic Service, FBIS, *Daily Report: Middle East and Africa*, September 30, 1985, p. F3.

57. Garfinkle, *Israel and Jordan*, pp. 122–23.

58. In the denouement of the *Achille Lauro* affair, U.S.-Egyptian relations were strained as American F-14s intercepted an Egyptian airliner carrying the hijackers to Tunis, where the PLO would have allegedly put them on trial. The Egyptian plane was forced to land at a NATO base in Sicily, which caused a great outpouring of anger in Cairo and self-congratulations and boasting in the United States. On the *Achille Lauro* affair and its aftermath, see David C. Martin and John Walcott, *Best Laid Plans: The Inside Story of America's War against Terrorism* (Harper and Row, 1988), pp. 235–57; and Woodward, *Veil*, pp. 414–16.

59. Garfinkle, *Israel and Jordan*, p. 124, credits King Hussein with initiating the move toward Syria as a means of preventing Arafat from winning Syrian support while Jordan pursued its new strategy with Israel. Peres had reportedly accepted the idea of an international conference in order to give the king something to use with Syria.

60. The full text is found in Amman Television Service, February 19, 1986, FBIS, *Daily Report: Middle East and North Africa*, February 20, 1986, pp. F1–F16. According to American sources that were closely involved in the diplomacy of early 1986, a last-ditch effort was made to find a formula whereby the PLO would accept Resolution 242 unambiguously as the basis for negotiations with Israel and then would spell out its additional demands. King Hussein told the Americans that the PLO needed a quid pro quo for such a step, and the United States therefore made some concessions on how the PLO would be invited to, and represented at, an international conference. The PLO was still not prepared to

accept Resolution 242. Arafat insisted that the United States endorse the Palestinian right of self-determination and open direct channels of communication to the PLO instead of negotiating through the Jordanians. The Jordanians had told the PLO that the United States would not budge on the issue of self-determination and urged the PLO to accept 242 anyway. The final meeting between Hussein and Arafat ended acrimoniously. The Jordanians and Americans concluded that the PLO was neither serious nor trustworthy. This conclusion had a significant impact on subsequent diplomatic moves. Hussein's public account does not cover all of these points, but the tone and substance of his remarks give credence to this interpretation.

61. Garfinkle, *Israel and Jordan*, p. 121, states that Jordan wanted to co-opt a weak Arafat, and Israel, much like the United States, wanted to eliminate him.

62. Shultz, *Turmoil and Triumph*, pp. 461–62.

63. According to Kemp, "Lessons of Lebanon," p. 67, the Shultz-Weinberger deadlock over Lebanon had convinced some Reaganites, especially Casey and NSC staffer Oliver North, that a capability should be developed to carry out covert actions "outside the system."

64. Many sources provide the basic chronology of what came to be known as the Iran-Contra affair. See especially *The Tower Commission Report: The Full Text of the President's Special Review Board* (Random House, 1987). Woodward, *Veil*, pp. 413–501, provides insider detail, as does Martin and Walcott, *Best Laid Plans*, pp. 227–34, 323–61. See also Kimche, *Last Option*, pp. 208–20, for his own and Israel's role in the opening to Iran.

65. McFarlane served as national security adviser from October 1982 until the end of 1985. After his retirement he remained involved with the arms for hostages affair, and when he made his infamous trip to Tehran in May 1986, he no longer held an official position in the government. By then, the national security adviser was the intensely secretive John Poindexter. See Martin and Walcott, *Best Laid Plans*, p. 331.

66. Kimche, *Last Option*, pp. 211–13.

Chapter 9

1. See Thomas L. McNaugher, "Walking Tightropes in the Gulf," in Efraim Karsh, ed., *The Iran-Iraq War: Impact and Implications* (St. Martin's Press, 1989), pp. 171–99.

2. For additional reasons to be skeptical of an international conference, see Peter W. Rodman, "Middle East Diplomacy after the Gulf War," *Foreign Affairs*, vol. 70 (Spring 1991), pp. 10–18.

3. George Shultz, *Turmoil and Triumph: My Years as Secretary of State* (Scribner's, 1993), pp. 454–57.

4. Adam Garfinkle, *Israel and Jordan in the Shadow of War: Functional Ties and Futile Diplomacy in a Small Place* (St. Martin's Press, 1992), pp. 128–29.

5. For more information on the efforts to create a sort of Israeli-Jordanian condominium, see Yossi Melman and Dan Raviv, *Behind the Uprising: Israelis, Jordanians, and Palestinians* (Greenwood Press, 1989), pp. 187–200.

6. Shultz, *Turmoil and Triumph*, p. 937.

7. For the text of the London Document, see William B. Quandt, ed., *The Middle East: Ten Years after Camp David* (Brookings, 1988), pp. 475–76.

8. Shultz, *Turmoil and Triumph*, pp. 938, 940.

9. Ibid., p. 941.

10. Ibid., p. 943.

11. Ibid., pp. 943–45.

12. See William Safire, "The Little King," *New York Times*, January 13, 1988, p. A23.

13. The word *intifada* in Arabic means "shaking off," as in shaking off the occupation.

14. Two seasoned Israeli journalists give their account of the early phase of the *intifada* in Ze'ev Schiff and Ehud Ya'ari, *Intifada: The Palestinian Uprising. Israel's Third Front* (Simon and Schuster, 1989).

15. See Helena Cobban, "The PLO and the Intifada," *Middle East Journal*, vol. 44 (Spring 1990), pp. 207–33.

16. By this time Shultz was fully in charge of the foreign policy of the United States. Weinberger had left in November 1987, to be replaced by Frank Carlucci. General Colin Powell then took over the job as national security adviser, Reagan's sixth in seven years. Also, Casey had died in January 1987.

17. Shultz, *Turmoil and Triumph*, pp. 1028–29, for the text of his initiative. See www.brookings.edu/press/appendix/peace_process.htm.

18. The use of the word "parties" instead of "states" suggested that the Palestine Liberation Organization might be invited to the conference.

19. Shamir's statement prompted Senators Rudy Boschwitz, Carl Levin, and twenty-eight other senators, including many friends of Israel, to write a letter to Shultz, dated March 3, 1988, expressing their concern about the Israeli position. Shamir's reply was published in "Text of Letter from Shamir on Criticism from Senators," *New York Times*, March 10, 1988, p. A10.

20. Shultz, *Turmoil and Triumph*, pp. 1030–31, states, "I was frustrated by Shamir's inflexibility and by the fact that divided government, as had existed in Israel since late 1984, meant that no one could be held responsible and accountable." His comments on King Hussein were that he was "candid and gloomy: he again gave me nothing but wanted me to 'persevere.'" Asad put Shultz through an "exercise in agony," concluding by saying, "I can give you nothing but 'continue.'"

21. See the text of the king's speech of July 31, 1988, in Foreign Broadcast Information Service, *Daily Report: Middle East and North Africa*, August 1, 1988, pp. 39–41.

22. At the Algiers Arab Summit meeting in Algiers in June 1988, the PLO had circulated a document entitled "PLO View: Prospects of a Palestinian-Israeli Settlement." Bassam Abu Sharif, a close adviser of Arafat's, soon claimed authorship. Most American officials who took note of the document were encouraged by its content and tone but were unsure whether it truly represented a new, more moderate tendency within the PLO. For the text, see Quandt, ed., *Middle East*, pp. 490–93.

23. John Mroz, from the International Peace Academy in New York, had many talks with Arafat in 1981-82 that were conveyed to the State Department. According to Harvey Sicherman, *Palestinian Self-Government (Autonomy): Its Past*

and Its Future (Washington: Washington Institute for Near East Policy, 1991), p. 37, Haig never used the channel for any official messages.

24. Congress in August 1985 added one more condition of its own. No American official could negotiate with the PLO unless the PLO met the conditions laid down in 1975—acceptance of UN Resolutions 242 and 338 and Israel's right to exist—and renounced the use of terrorism. Public Law 99-83, section 1302, August 8, 1985.

25. Among the Jewish personalities involved were Rita Hauser, a New York attorney; Stanley Sheinbaum, an economist and publisher from Los Angeles; Menachem Rosensaft, a Holocaust survivor who later regretted his participation; Drora Kass, from the American branch of the Israeli International Center for Peace in the Middle East; and A. L. Udovitch, professor of Middle Eastern history at Princeton University, who joined the group just before the Stockholm meeting.

26. Shultz interview with Swedish reporter Susanne Palme, March 30, 1992 (made available to the author).

27. Mohamed Rabie is an economist by training and the author of a number of books, including *The New World Order: A Perspective on the Post-Cold War Era* (Vantage Press, 1992).

28. Rabie approached me on August 2, 1988, with his idea. As far as I knew then or know now, it was his own proposal, not one initiated by the PLO in Tunis. At this initial meeting we agreed to try to develop language that would meet the requirements of both sides. Rabie assumed that I had contacts in the State Department, and he assured me that he could communicate easily with the PLO leadership. Over the next several months he dealt exclusively with the PLO leadership, especially Abu Mazin, and I dealt with a handful of people in the State Department and NSC who were aware of this initiative. Rabie and I would then convey to each other whatever we had learned of importance to the success of the initiative. The main result of this effort, I believe, was to establish that both sides were interested in beginning a dialogue before the end of the Reagan administration and in demonstrating that mutually acceptable language would not be too difficult to develop. See Mohamed Rabie, "The U.S.-PLO Dialogue: The Swedish Connection," *Journal of Palestine Studies*, vol. 21 (Summer 1992), pp. 54-66; and his longer study, *U.S.-PLO Dialogue: Secret Diplomacy and Conflict Resolution* (University Press of Florida, 1995).

29. The proposed text of what the PLO might say, as conveyed to the State Department on August 12, was as follows:

As its contribution to the search for a just and lasting peace in the Middle East, the Executive Committee of the Palestine Liberation Organization has met and decided to issue the following official statement:

1. That it is prepared to negotiate a comprehensive peace settlement of the Arab-Israeli conflict on the basis of United Nations resolutions 242 and 338.

2. That it considers the convening of an international conference under the auspices of the United Nations as an appropriate framework for negotiating a political settlement and ultimately achieving peace in the Middle East.

3. That it seeks to establish a democratic Palestinian state in the West Bank and Gaza strip and to live in peace with its neighbors and respect their right to live in peace.

4. That it condemns terrorism in all its forms and is prepared for a moratorium on all forms of violence, on a mutual basis, once negotiations under the auspices of an international conference begin.

These points are derived from the PLO's commitment to the following principles: all the states in the region—including Israel and a Palestinian state—are entitled to live in peace within secure and internationally recognized borders; that all peoples in the region—including the Israelis and the Palestinians—must enjoy the right of self-determination; and that no state should violate the rights of others, acquire land by force, or determine its future by coercion.

Israel's acceptance of these same principle is a precondition for meaningful negotiations to begin.

After talking at length with Rabie, the PLO made a few minor changes, most important of which was the addition of the idea that "all parties to the conflict, including the PLO, should participate in the international conference on an equal basis."

30. I conveyed these points, on behalf of the State Department, to Mohamed Rabie on August 13, 1988. I was told that they had been cleared by Shultz's office, which meant, at a minimum, Shultz's aide, Charles Hill, had cleared them and that Shultz was informed. I did not at any point deal directly with Shultz or Hill, although my interlocutors regularly did. See Shultz, *Turmoil and Triumph*, pp. 1034–36, for his account of these developments.

31. The PLO wanted the United States to say:

The U.S. Government welcomes the new PLO initiative and wishes to make the following statement:

1. The United States considers the PLO statement as a commitment to seek a political settlement of the Arab-Israeli conflict through peaceful means.

2. Recognizing the right of all peoples to self-determination as called for in the charter of the U.N., the United States believes that the Palestinian people have the right to self-determination, and should be enabled to do so through negotiations leading to a comprehensive peace settlement.

3. The United States believes that U.N. resolutions 242 and 338 embody the basic principle upon which a political settlement to the Arab-Israeli conflict can be established.

4. The United States considers the PLO's endorsement of U.N. resolutions 242 and 338, its condemnation of terrorism, its commitment to a political settlement through peaceful means as having removed the obstacles which in the past prevented the United States from having official contacts with the PLO.

Consequently, the U.S. government is prepared to meet with designated representatives of the PLO, the legitimate representatives of the Palestinian people, as soon as the Executive Committee names its representatives. Finally, the United States calls upon all parties to seize the opportunity to renew the search for peace without delay.

32. Shultz had been disappointed by Arafat's speech in Strasbourg on September 13. The PLO had signaled that this speech would not contain the new PLO

position, but Shultz was still critical. For the text of Shultz's remarks, see "The First George P. Shultz Lecture on Middle East Diplomacy," Washington Institute for Near East Policy, September 16, 1988.

33. About this time consultations took place between the United States and the Soviet Union, and the Soviets made it clear that they were supporting the initiative. Shultz, *Turmoil and Triumph*, p.1036, implies that he did not authorize the sending of a message to the PLO, but in fact one was sent.

34. Shultz, *Turmoil and Triumph*, p. 1036, notes that the PLO was able to communicate with him through the CIA. Arafat used this channel on occasion to clarify points but not for ongoing negotiations.

35. For an English translation of the resolutions of the Nineteenth PNC, see *Journal of Palestine Studies*, vol. 18 (Winter 1989), pp. 213–23.

36. In his interview with Susanne Palme, on March 30, 1992, Shultz said: "[The Swedish ambassador] came to me [on December 2] and asked: Sten Andersson wants to know what the PLO could say that would cause us to be willing to have a dialogue with them and what kind of response we would make if they made these statements. And so I produced a statement and an answer and [the Swedish ambassador] came to my home and got it and I told him this is strictly for Sten Andersson. I have nothing to do with the American Jews that are there, I don't want them to see it, the dialogue between them and the Palestinians is something you are running, it's something totally separate from this. . . . Sten was a person I trusted and had confidence in and so I thought if he is going to talk to Arafat and if he seems to think this is a serious possibility we will get him a statement. And we had learned some things about some PLO sensibilities from the Quandt [and Rabie] interchange. So that helped I think a little bit in the phraseology of what we said." See Shultz, *Turmoil and Triumph*, pp. 1038–39, for more on these developments, especially his reasoning in denying a visa for Arafat to come to the United Nations.

37. For Shultz's letter, see www.brookings.edu/press/appendix/peace_process.htm.

38. This document was quite close to the draft that Rabie had brought back from Tunis in September with PLO approval, with the addition of several key words referring to not engaging in terrorism in the future. For reasons that are not clear, the PLO objected to the fourth point on the moratorium on violence—after having accepted it the previous September—and Shultz accepted this deletion. A few other word changes were also agreed on through the Swedes, including the addition to point one that negotiations should take place "within the framework of an international conference."

39. This led American officials to believe, for a brief moment on December 7, that the breakthrough had been achieved. For Arafat's response see www.brookings.edu/press/appendix/peace_process.htm

40. A PLO internal account of this incident reads as follows: "Many voices were raised warning of the outcome of embarking on this step. And here too Hawatmeh played a disruptive role. He tried to contact Kuwait and others to incite our brothers to refuse it. He did the same thing within his organization; he began to dispatch letters and messengers. All of that led Abu Ammar (Arafat) to work to distance himself from the step, and for that reason he took another look at his speech to remove most of the commentary that it contained and that complied with the proposed text from the Americans. Abu Ammar feared for national

unity and imagined that the DFLP [Hawatmeh's group] and the PFLP [of George Habbash] might leave the PLO which might influence the *intifada*, just as it would affect the total credibility of the PLO which desired an acceptable democratic appearance." From an internal PLO document in Arabic, p. 195.

41. In Arabic, he used the verbs *abaa* and *rafada* (condemn and reject), not *nabadha* (renounce, abandon, or forsake). Shultz felt that rejecting or condemning terrorism did not involve admitting that one had been engaged in it. In one form or another, he wanted the PLO to say that it would stop doing something that it had been doing previously.

42. Shultz, *Turmoil and Triumph*, p. 1043, revealingly notes that he told Reagan that Arafat, in his speech, was saying in one place "'Unc, unc, unc,' and in another he was saying, 'cle, cle, cle,' but nowhere will he yet bring himself to say, 'Uncle.'"

43. For the text of Arafat's statement, see www.brookings.edu/press/appendix/peace_process.htm.

44. For the text of Shultz's statement, see www.brookings.edu/press/appendix/peace_process.htm.

45. See Eugene Rostow, "Palestinian Self-Determination: Possible Futures for the Unallocated Territories of the Palestine Mandate," *Yale Law Studies in World Public Order*, vol. 5 (1979), p. 147. Rostow has made the same point about the legality of Israeli settlements in a number of other publications. This theme was picked up and popularized by George Will in his syndicated column in the early 1980s.

46. Meron Benvenisti wrote in 1983 that the clock had struck midnight. For an example of his thinking, see his essay "Demographic, Economic, Legal, Social and Political Developments in the West Bank," in *The 1987 Report: The West Bank Data Base Project* (Boulder, Colo.: Westview Press, 1987), pp. 67–80. See also Meron Benvenisti, *Conflicts and Contradictions* (Villard Books, 1986), pp. 169–82.

47. Reagan's memoirs, *An American Life* (Simon and Schuster, 1990), give many examples of his lack of care with details in discussing the Middle East. For example, Reagan says that UN Resolution 242 called on Israel "to withdraw from all the territories it had claimed after the 1967 war, including the West Bank" (p. 414); he casually interprets his September 1, 1982, initiative as supporting the right of Palestinians to "self-determination and self-government" (p. 430); and he states that Israeli settlements, which he had said were not illegal, were "in continued violation of UN Security Council Resolution 242" (p. 441). All three statements are inaccurate.

48. See Wolf Blitzer, *Territory of Lies: The Exclusive Story of Jonathan Jay Pollard. The American Who Spied on His Country for Israel and How He Was Betrayed* (Harper and Row, 1989).

49. The first account of the information provided by Mordechai Vanunu appeared in Peter Hounam and others, "Revealed: The Secrets of Israel's Nuclear Arsenal," *Sunday Times* (London), October 5, 1986, p. 1. See also Seymour M. Hersh, *The Samson Option: Israel's Nuclear Arsenal and American Foreign Policy* (Random House, 1991), pp. 307–12.

50. See Karen L. Puschel, *US-Israeli Strategic Cooperation in the Post-Cold War Era: An American Perspective* (Boulder, Colo.: Westview Press, 1992), chaps. 2–4.

51. For the first time, in November 1991, poll results showed that more Americans blamed Israel than the Arabs for the lack of progress in making peace. See

Gerald F. Seib, "On Day One of Mideast Talks, Calm Prevails amid Ceremony," *Wall Street Journal*, October 31, 1991, p. A18.

Chapter 10

1. The fullest account of Bush's views can be found in George Bush and Brent Scowcroft, *A World Transformed* (Knopf, 1998).

2. On the Bush-Baker relationship, see Marjorie Williams, "His Master's Voice," *Vanity Fair*, October 1992; and John Newhouse, "Shunning the Losers," *New Yorker*, October 26, 1992, pp. 40–52. Also, see James A. Baker III with Thomas M. De Frank, *The Politics of Diplomacy: Revolution, War and Peace, 1989–1992* (Putnam, 1995), esp. pp. 17–36.

3. Baker, *The Politics of Diplomacy*, pp. 41–46.

4. Some Israelis saw this article on Baker as an early sign of his hostility to Israel. Early in the stream-of-conscious musings, Baker is quoted as wondering if it will ever be possible to get peace in the Middle East. Then, right after the comment on turkey-shooting tactics, he mentions Israel and notes that Israel is internally divided. "But creating something productive when Israel is divided internally is going to be real tough. Who knows?" See Michael Kramer, "Playing for the Edge," *Time*, February 13, 1989, p. 44. For an Israeli interpretation of how this shows Baker's hostility toward Israel, see Dore Gold, "US and Israel Enter New Era," *Jerusalem Post*, February 28, 1992, p. 9A.

5. Kramer, "Playing for the Edge," p. 30.

6. Bush's other key foreign policy appointment, Secretary of Defense Richard Cheney, was not known to have strong views on the Middle East and seemed most likely to wield influence on U.S.-Soviet relations and arms control issues.

7. Washington Institute's Presidential Study Group, *Building for Peace: An American Strategy for the Middle East* (Washington: Washington Institute for Near East Policy, 1988).

8. Richard Haass, *Conflicts Unending: The United States and Regional Disputes* (Yale University Press, 1990), pp. 30–56.

9. Haass's views did apparently evolve somewhat. On September 13, 1991, he said that "one of the things we've learned, and it has affected a lot of my thinking, is that even when you try to think small and avoid some of the most sensitive, final status issues, a kind of step-by-step approach, you find that people see precedents everywhere." See "The Impact of Global Developments on U.S. Policy in the Middle East," *From War to Peace in the Middle East? Sixth Annual Policy Conference* (Washington: Washington Institute for Near East Policy, 1991), p. 10.

10. Arab suspicions were also heightened by the fact that the four top advisers to Bush and Baker on the Middle East were all Jewish—Dennis Ross, Richard Haass, Aaron Miller on the Policy Planning staff, and Daniel Kurtzer in the Near East Bureau. Somewhat ironically, the presence of Jews in such prominent positions did not seem to reassure some Israelis, especially Likud supporters, who soon were speaking crudely of "Baker's Jew boys" as responsible for the strains in U.S.-Israeli relations. See Margaret G. Warner, "Whose Side Are You On?" *Newsweek*, June 1, 1992.

11. One significant development had taken place after the publication of the Presidential Study Group's *Building for Peace*. That was the onset of the U.S.-PLO dialogue. Those who had contributed to the report had taken a very skeptical attitude toward the PLO, indicating that the prospects were much better for finding a Palestinian negotiating partner for Israel from within the West Bank and Gaza, where objective circumstances imposed a kind of realism and pragmatism. But in December 1988 Shultz, with the support of both Bush and Baker, had agreed to the opening of a U.S.-PLO dialogue. From the outset Bush and Baker made it clear that they wanted the dialogue to continue, albeit with discretion. In addition, Bush and Baker rejected the proposal of the report that a special negotiator for the Middle East should be named.

12. The other three points of the Israeli proposal, which received less attention because they were less original, emphasized the need for negotiations with Arab states to conclude peace treaties, the importance of settling the refugee problem, and the necessity for the Camp David partners to renew their commitment to the agreements and to peace. For the text of the initial plan, see *Jerusalem Post*, April 14, 1989, p. 8. On May 15, 1989, *Jerusalem Post*, p. 2, published an expanded twenty-point version of the government's peace plan. This latter document is sometimes referred to as the May 14, 1989, initiative. Baker, *The Politics of Diplomacy*, p. 120, termed Shamir's plan "weak," but "With a bit of creative window dressing and diplomatic sleight of hand, we now had *something* with which to challenge the Palestinians. . . . " See also Avi Shlaim, *The Iron Wall: Israel and the Arab World* (Norton, 1999), pp. 443–46.

13. Address by Secretary Baker, "Principles and Pragmatism: American Policy toward the Arab-Israeli Conflict," *Department of State Bulletin*, vol. 89 (July 1989), p. 24. One of the members of the Baker Middle East team called the speech "reality therapy." Another said that "slight tension with Israel is the price we pay for having credibility with the Arab side."

14. Baker, *The Politics of Diplomacy*, p. 118. "In effect, we were asking Arafat to disenfranchise himself on the grounds of political expediency: there was no way a Shamir-led government would ever negotiate with the PLO." Shamir may not have been prepared to negotiate with the PLO, but he did apparently establish contact in early 1989. According to Salah Khalaf (Abu Iyad), in an interview with the author in February 1989, Shamir had sent a message to him via an Arab leader. Shamir wanted to know if Abu Iyad continued to believe that a Palestinian state in the West Bank would simply be a stage on the way to the elimination of Israel. Shamir followed up by sending one of his political allies to Morocco to engage in lengthy discussions with Abu Iyad. Subsequent meetings were envisaged but never took place.

15. See, for example, Salah Khalaf (Abu Iyad), "Lowering the Sword," *Foreign Policy*, no. 78 (Spring 1990), pp. 91–112. Somewhat earlier Abu Iyad had videotaped a statement to Israelis that indicated a shift in his views toward acceptance of a two-state settlement. The tape was shown in Israel and produced extensive commentary, especially in the peace camp.

16. Baker also tried to enlist the help of the Iraqi government. On November 9, 1989, he sent a message to the Iraqi foreign minister informing him that the administration had decided to act favorably on grain credits for Iraq. Baker went on

to say: "We are at a critical point in our diplomacy. The Government of Egypt is working closely with Palestinians to respond positively to our five-point framework, enabling us to get an Israeli-Palestinian dialogue launched. It would be useful if you could weigh in with them and urge them to give a positive response to Egypt's suggestions." Elaine Sciolino, "Baker Telling Iraqis of Loan Aid, Asks Help on Palestinian Talks," *New York Times*, October 26, 1992, p. A6.

17. For the text of Baker's five points, see Thomas L. Friedman, "Advance Reported on Mideast Talks," *New York Times*, December 7, 1989, p. A11.

18. See David Makovsky, *Jerusalem Post* (International Edition), March 24, 1990, p. 2. Baker, *The Politics of Diplomacy*, p. 128, says John Sununu, Bush's Chief of Staff, was responsible "in large measure" for the president's controversial remarks.

19. In a letter attached to the Camp David Accords, Jimmy Carter had reiterated (albeit obliquely) the official policy that the United States considered East Jerusalem to be occupied territory to which the fourth Geneva Convention should apply. See William B. Quandt, *Camp David: Peacemaking and Politics* (Brookings, 1986), p. 386.

20. Baker, *The Politics of Diplomacy*, p. 132.

21. For the text of Saddam Hussein's speech, see Foreign Broadcast Information Service (FBIS), *Daily Report: Near East and South Asia*, February 27, 1990, pp. 1–5.

22. See Saddam's speech in which he said Iraq possessed binary chemical weapons and threatened their use against Israel if Israel were to attack Iraq. FBIS, *Daily Report: Near East and South Asia*, April 3, 1990, pp. 32–35.

23. Some Palestinians and their supporters argued that the intended target was military, that no one was hurt, and that the action had not been authorized by Arafat. Therefore, it should not be seen as a violation of the PLO's pledge not to engage in terrorism. Such arguments fell on deaf ears in Washington, partly because at about the same time an Israeli had been killed in a bomb explosion that intelligence sources traced directly to Fatah.

24. Author's interview with Abu Iyad, June 15, 1990.

25. Baker, *The Politics of Diplomacy*, p. 130.

26. For a generally convincing account, see, Bob Woodward, *The Commanders* (Simon and Schuster, 1991). See also, Bush and Scowcroft, *A World Transformed*, pp. 450–87 on Desert Storm.

27. See Bush's speech before the UN General Assembly, reprinted in *New York Times*, October 2, 1990, p. A12, where he says that "in the aftermath of Iraq's unconditional departure from Kuwait, I truly believe there may be opportunities for Iraq and Kuwait to settle their differences permanently, for the states of the gulf themselves to build new arrangements for stability and for all the states and the peoples of the region to settle the conflicts that divide the Arabs from Israel." Baker, *The Politics of Diplomacy*, pp. 414–15, said that after the Gulf war Scowcroft was reluctant to get involved in the Arab-Israeli conflict; Bush was "eager" for Baker to try; and Baker's own earlier skepticism had been fundamentally altered by the war. The United States, he believed, now had much more leverage.

28. For the text of Bush's speech on March 6, 1991, see www.brookings.edu/press/appendix/peace_process.htm.

29. Baker, *The Politics of Diplomacy*, pp. 415–29.

30. The actual budgetary impact of granting the loan guarantees was difficult to assess. A small percentage of the total value of the loan—an amount to be determined on the basis of risk assessment—would have to be appropriated and set aside in a reserve fund. This amount could run from $50 to $800 million. Assuming that Israel repaid all the loans on time, there would be no further costs to the taxpayer. But if Israel defaulted, the costs would, of course, be substantial at a later date.

31. Baker and Israeli Foreign Minister Levy concluded agreement on a $400 million housing loan guarantee, after lengthy discussions, in October 1990. Within days, however, it became clear that Israel did not accept the American condition that no funds should be used in East Jerusalem. See "Israel Retracts Pledges to U.S. on East Jerusalem Housing," *New York Times*, October 19, 1990, p. A16. In the spring of 1992 a National Security Council staff member, Richard Haass, was quoted as saying that Israel had not given the administration a satisfactory reply about how it had spent the $400 million in loan guarantees. See *Haaretz*, April 15, 1992, p. A1, as reported in FBIS, *Daily Report: Near East and South Asia*, April 16, 1992, p. 36. See also David Makovsky and Allison Kaplan, "What Went Wrong with the U.S. Aliya Loan Guarantees," *Jerusalem Post*, March 20, 1992, p. 5A, for further evidence that the Israeli government deliberately withheld cooperation in providing information on how the $400 million loan was being used.

32. Thomas L. Friedman, "Baker Cites Israel for Settlements," *New York Times*, May 23, 1991, p. A5. Thomas L. Friedman, "Bush Backs Baker View of Mideast Peace Barriers," *New York Times*, 24, 1991, p. A3. According to one source, Shamir gave Baker a commitment in February 1991 not to build beyond a "baseline" rate of settlement growth in the West Bank. See *Report on Israeli Settlement in the Occupied Territories*, vol. 2 (Washington, July 1992), p. 1, quoting a report from the Jewish Telegraphic Agency giving Baker's comments to a delegation of leaders from the American Jewish Congress on May 10, 1992.

33. See Martin Indyk, "Israel's Grand Bargain," *New York Times*, July 24, 1991, p. A21. The text of Ford's letter can be found at www.brookings.edu/press/appendix/peace_process.htm. Baker, *The Politics of Diplomacy*, p. 424, also notes that he raised the possibility with Shamir of American troops on the Golan Heights.

34. Linda Gradstein, "Shamir Bars Losing Territory," *Washington Post*, July 25, 1991 p. A27.

35. See "Excerpts from President Bush's News Session on Israeli Loan Guarantees," *New York Times*, September 13, 1991, p. A10. Thomas Dine of AIPAC later called September 12 a "day of infamy."

36. For the text of the U.S. "letter of understanding" given to the Israelis, see *Yedi'ot Aharonot*, September 17, 1991, p. 17, as reported in FBIS, *Daily Report: Near East and South Asia*, September 17, 1991, p. 28. For the text of Baker's letter of assurance to the Palestinians, see www.brookings.edu/press/appendix/peace_process.htm. For the Palestinian reply to Baker, see *Al-Dustur* (Amman), October 26, 1991, p. 26, as reported in FBIS, *Daily Report: Near East and South Asia*, October 28, 1991, p. 1.

37. For the U.S.-Soviet invitation to the peace conference, see www.brookings.edu/press/appendix/peace_process.htm.

38. For excerpts from the speeches, see "3 Speeches: The Area Is a 'Dangerous Battleground,'" *New York Times*, November 1, 1991, p. A10. A *Wall Street Journal*/ABC poll showed that 37 percent of Americans identified Israel as the main obstacle to peace, while 35 percent so labeled the Arabs. See Gerald F. Seib, "On Day One of Mideast Talks, Calm Prevails amid Ceremony," *Wall Street Journal*, October 31, 1991, p. A8. For the text of President Bush's address, see www.brookings.edu/press/appendix/peace_process.htm.

39. The Palestinians put forward an initial proposal for an interim self-governing authority on January 14, 1992, and then developed a more elaborate version on March 3, 1992.

40. Leslie H. Gelb, "Bush's Ultimatum to Shamir," *New York Times*, January 17, 1992, p. A29.

41. Baker, *The Politics of Diplomacy*, pp. 540–57, for his account of the loan guarantee debate.

42. Thomas L. Friedman, "U.S. Details Terms Israel Must Meet for Deal on Loans," *New York Times*, February 25, 1992, p. A1.

43. Thomas L. Friedman, "Bush Rejects Israel Loan Guarantees," *New York Times*, March 18, 1992, p. A11. At the same time, Baker met with Arens on March 17, 1992, to discuss reports of military technology transfers from Israel to China. A General Accounting Office report, *Report of Audit: Department of State Defense Trade Controls*, on the same topic was released in March 1992 by Sherman M. Funk, inspector general, Department of State. Some saw a mounting campaign by Bush and Baker against Israel, but the administration soon pulled back, perhaps fearing that the Israeli electorate would rally around Shamir if too much pressure was applied. For a detailed analysis of U.S.-Israeli relations in early 1992, see Leon T. Hadar, "The Last Days of Likud: The American-Israeli Big Chill," *Journal of Palestine Studies*, vol. 21 (Summer 1992), pp. 80–94.

44. Talks were held in Washington in April 1992 without results, but it was now commonplace for a PLO-related person to be in the background, coordinating with Tunis. In May 1992 multilateral talks were held: on environmental issues in Tokyo, on arms control in Washington, on economic issues in Brussels, on water in Vienna, and on refugees in Ottawa.

45. See Clyde Haberman, "Arens Faults Prime Minister's 'Greater Israel' Concept," *New York Times*, June 29, 1992, p. A3.

46. Indicative of Rabin's new tone were remarks that he made on September 3, 1992: "We should back away from illusions and seek compromises in order to reach peace or, at least, make practical moves to promote it. We should drop the illusions of the religion of Greater Israel and remember that we must take care of the Israeli people, society, culture, and economy. We should remember that a nation's strength is not measured by the territories it holds but by its faith and its ability to cultivate its social, economic, and security systems." FBIS, *Daily Report: Near East and South Asia*, September 3, 1992, p. 26. Also indicative of a new tone from Rabin was his view of Israel's importance to the United States. Rather than emphasizing the "strategic asset" argument, Rabin stressed the "peace partner" role. "The more the U.S. can say it is bringing peace to the area—assisted by Israel acting in its own interests—the more Israel will serve the mutual interest in creating stability and leaving less room for the extremists." Leslie H. Gelb, "America in Israel," *New York Times*, June 15, 1992, p. A19.

47. See Clyde Haberman, "Shamir Is Said to Admit Plan to Stall Talks 'for 10 Years,'" *New York Times*, June 27, 1992, p. A1. Subsequently, Shamir claimed that he had been misinterpreted. But even his clarifications indicated that he envisaged the "interim" agreement as lasting an indefinite time, during which Israel would continue to build settlements.

48. Bush and Baker had indicated that they would remain deeply involved in the negotiations, despite Baker's change of title. But according to Eagleburger, Baker played little role in foreign policy after going to the White House. See Don Oberdorfer, "Baker-less State Department Not in Idle, Officials Say," *Washington Post*, October 16, 1992, p. A23.

49. Asad, speaking to a delegation from the Golan Heights, reported on Syrian Radio, September 9, 1992, in FBIS, *Daily Report: Near East and South Asia*, September 9, 1992, p. 41.

50. Newhouse, "Shunning the Losers," pp. 50–51, in an otherwise quite critical article on Bush's foreign policy. Michael Kramer, "Bush's Reward for Courage," *Time*, August 3, 1992, p. 44, also gave Bush and Baker "considerable credit" for their handling of the loan guarantees and the negotiations more generally.

51. Kissinger expressed the view that the United States should not spend so much effort trying to organize negotiations that are destined to fail. Later he softened his views somewhat. See Henry Kissinger, "Land for Time in the Middle East," *Washington Post*, June 2, 1991, p. D7, and "If Not Peace, at Least Progress," *Washington Post*, October 31, 1991, p. A21. See also the harsh judgment of neoconservative thinker Irving Kristol, "'Peace Process' That Heads Nowhere," *Wall Street Journal*, June 18, 1992, p. A16.

Chapter 11

1. David Maraniss, *First in His Class: The Biography of Bill Clinton* (Simon & Schuster, 1995), pp. 387–418. The idea of the "permanent campaign" was apparently devised in the 1982–84 period, when Clinton was briefly out of office and was planning his return with the help of political consultant Dick Morris.

2. For more on his views, see Warren Christopher, *In the Stream of History: Shaping Foreign Policy for a New Era* (Stanford University Press, 1998), largely a compilation of his speeches, but with some revealing commentary on the Middle East, as in chs. 4, 13, 14, 34.

3. The most influential WINEP study, to which both Ross and Indyk contributed, was *Building for Peace: An American Strategy for the Middle East* (Washington Institute for Near East Policy, 1988). See the discussion in chapter 10 above.

4. For an authoritative Israeli account of the Syrian-Israeli negotiations, written by Rabin's ambassador to Washington and top adviser on Syrian affairs, see Itamar Rabinovich, *The Brink of Peace: The Israeli-Syrian Negotiations* (Princeton University Press, 1998); and Helena Cobban, *The Israeli-Syrian Peace Talks: 1991–96 and Beyond* (Washington, D.C.: U.S. Institute of Peace, 1999).

5. The only territorial issue between Jordan and Israel after 1988 involved the actual delineation of the border in the Dead Sea area, a dispute involving a few hundred acres only.

6. See Hanan Ashrawi, *This Side of Peace: A Personal Account* (Simon & Schuster, 1995), pp. 229–49.

7. Clinton deferred to Rabin from their first meeting. See Samuel W. Lewis, "The United States and Israel: Evolution of an Unwritten Alliance," *Middle East Journal*, vol. 53 (Summer 1999), p. 370, where he writes of Rabin and Clinton: "Their official relationship quickly ripened into a close friendship, one in which the older, more experienced Rabin assumed seniority, outlining to Clinton the diplomatic strategy he wanted to follow and readily obtaining Clinton's support."

8. Rabinovich, *The Brink of Peace*, pp. 104–05. Rabin told Christopher on August 3, 1993, that he should explore with Asad what Syria would do on matters of peace and security, assuming that "his own demand would be satisfied," presumably meaning that Israel was conditionally willing to consider withdrawal from Golan as the quid pro quo for peace and security.

9. Several accounts of the Oslo negotiations exist: Jane Corbin, *The Norway Channel: The Secret Talks That Led to the Middle East Peace Accord* (Atlantic Monthly Press, 1994); David Makovsky, *Making Peace with the PLO: The Rabin Government's Road to the Oslo Accord* (Boulder, Colo.: Westview Press, 1995); Mark Perry, *A Fire in Zion: The Israeli-Palestinian Search for Peace* (New York: Morrow, 1994); and, most authoritative, Uri Savir, *The Process: 1,100 Days That Changed the Middle East* (New York: Random House, 1998).

10. Rabinovich, *The Brink of Peace*, pp. 106–08.

11. Clinton told Rabin when he invited him to the White House for the signing ceremony that the American role henceforth would be to help reduce the risks that Israel was running in making peace. Clinton also was quick to see the political significance of having Rabin and Arafat meet face to face. Some of Clinton's advisers had opposed the idea. (Interview with former White House official, May 13, 1999.)

12. For the text of the Oslo Accord, see www.brookings.edu/press/appendix/peace_process.htm.

13. Public opinion polls showed that both Israelis and West Bank–Gaza Palestinians supported the Oslo Accord at the outset. See Asher Arian, *The Second Republic: Politics in Israel* (Chatham, N.J.: Chatham House Publishers, 1998), p. 365; and Khalil Shikaki, "Peace Now or Hamas Later," *Foreign Affairs* (July/August 1998).

14. Christopher, *In the Stream of History*, p. 80, says that in a speech on September 20, 1993, he tried to signal to the Syrians that "engaging Syria could not be the immediate priority."

15. For the text, see www.brookings.edu/press/appendix/peace_process.htm.

16. One ambiguity in the Cairo Accord was that it did not explicitly address the question of what would happen if no agreement on final status were reached by the end of the interim period. This became a contentious issue in early 1999, as Palestinians stated that they had the right to declare statehood after May 4, 1999, while the Israeli government countered that such action would be a violation of the agreement and would open the way for Israel to respond by annexing territory in the West Bank.

17. Rabinovich, *The Brink of Peace*, p. 121, refers to the American position at this time as support for full Israeli withdrawal from Golan in return for a diluted

version of the Syrian package envisaged by Rabin in August 1993. The early part of 1994 was one of U.S.-Israeli acrimony over the Syrian track.

18. Interview with former White House official, May 13, 1999.

19. Itamar Rabinovich, *Waging Peace: Israel and the Arabs at the End of the Century* (New York: Farrar, Straus and Giroux, 1999), p. 64: "By July 19, [1994] a formula had been found for grafting the lines of June 4 onto the original hypothetical, conditional suggestion made in August 1993." The most thorough analysis of the June 4, 1967, line can be found in Frederic C. Hof, *Line of Battle, Border of Peace? The Line of June 4, 1967* (Washington, D.C.: Middle East Insight, 1999). For Israelis, the June 4, 1967, line poses problems because it touches on the Sea of Galilee in the northeast quadrant and might therefore be seen as conveying to Syria riparian rights to the water itself.

20. Rabinovich, *The Brink of Peace*, p. 165–67, notes that Likud lobbied hard with the American Congress to oppose the idea of American troops on the Golan.

21. See Avi Shlaim, *The Iron Wall: Israel and the Arab World since 1948* (New York: W. W. Norton, 1999), especially chapter 13.

22. Laura Zittrain Eisenberg and Neil Caplan, *Negotiating Arab-Israeli Peace: Patterns, Problems, Possibilities* (Indiana University Press, 1998), pp. 90–100, sees the Jordan-Israel negotiations as a model worthy of emulation.

23. *New York Times*, April 1, 1995.

24. *New York Times*, May 25 and 29, 1995. *Financial Times* (London) July 4, 1995, claimed that Syria has accepted a six-to-ten ratio in the size of demilitarized zones.

25. For the text of Oslo II, see www.brookings.edu/press/appendix/peace_process.htm.

26. From Yossi Beilin, "The Past, Present, and Future of the Oslo Process: View from the Labor Party," special policy forum report to the Washington Institute for Near East Policy, *Peacewatch*, no. 112 (December 11, 1996), p. 2. The draft of the Beilin–Abu Mazin agreement was leaked in September 2000. It had reportedly been an important point of reference for the negotiations that took place at Camp David in July 2000. The full text can be found at www.brookings.edu/press/appendix/peace_process.htm.

27. Savir, *The Process*, pp. 266–83.

28. Rabinovich, *The Brink of Peace*, p. 259, describes the American role as follows: "The Middle East peace process had been one of the most important areas of the administration's foreign policy during Bill Clinton's first term, *where considerable success was achieved in return for a comparatively small investment and limited risks*" (emphasis added).

29. William B. Quandt, "The Urge for Democracy," *Foreign Affairs*, vol. 73 (July/August 1994), pp. 2–7.

30. In the 1994 congressional elections, the Republicans did particularly well in the House. Newt Gingrich of Georgia became speaker. He was a strong conservative voice and an outspoken partisan of Israel.

Chapter 12

1. For the text of the Hebron Agreement, see www.brookings.edu/press/appendix/peace_process.htm.

2. For the text of the Ross letter, see www.brookings.edu/press/appendix/peace_process.htm.

3. See www.brookings.edu/press/appendix/peace_process.htm for the text of Christopher's letter to Netanyahu.

4. See Steven Erlanger, "The Mideast Impasse," *New York Times*, August 7, 1997, p. A1.

5. Steven Erlanger, "Albright Expresses Irritation after Talks with Netanyahu," *New York Times*, November 15, 1997, p. A6.

6. David Gardner and Andrew Gowers, "FT Interviews Madeleine Albright," *Financial Times* (London), May 7, 1998, p. 18.

7. Barton Gellman, "U.S. Tones Down Stance on Israel," *Washington Post*, May 19, 1998, p. A1.

8. For accounts of the Wye talks, see David Makovsky, "A Wye Diary," *Haaretz* (English), October 25, 1998; Serge Schmemann and Steven Erlanger, "Mideast Marathon," *New York Times*, October 25, 1998. Clinton spent more than eighty hours in the talks, an unprecedented degree of personal engagement on his part in Arab-Israeli peace diplomacy.

9. On Clinton's use of ambiguity to get the Wye deal, see John F. Harris, "Clinton's Ambiguity Proves a Strength in Summit Role," *Washington Post*, October 25, 1998, p. A1.

10. See "Remarks by the President to the Members of the Palestine National Council and Other Palestinian Organizations," Gaza, Office of the White House Press Secretary, December 14, 1998. Most noteworthy was Clinton's statement to the Palestinian people: "Behind you a history of dispossession and dispersal, before you the opportunity to shape a new Palestinian future on your own land." He also said, "Israel must recognize the right of the Palestinians to aspire to live free today, tomorrow and forever."

11. For a detailed analysis of how American policy evolved, see Barton Gellman, "How Atrocity Transformed Policy," *Washington Post*, April 18, 1999, pp. A1, A30–31.

12. Henry A. Kissinger, "New World Disorder," *Newsweek*, May 31, 1999, pp. 41–43.

13. For the text of Clinton's April 26, 1999, letter to Arafat, see www.brookings.edu/press/appendix/peace_process.htm. Clinton noted: "The United States knows how destructive settlement activities, land confiscations, and house demolitions are to the pursuit of Palestinian-Israeli peace."

14. Patrick Seale's interviews with Asad and Barak can be found in *Mideast Mirror*, June 23, 1999.

15. See Aluf Benn, "More Strategy, Less Tactics," *Haaretz* (English), July 16, 1999.

16. William A. Orme Jr., "Israel Will Buy 50 F-16s in Its Biggest Arms Deal Ever," *New York Times*, July 19, 1999, p. A6.

17. Helena Cobban, *The Israeli-Syrian Peace Talks: 1991–96 and Beyond* (Washington D.C.: United States Institute of Peace Press, 1999), especially pp. 175–96.

18. During Netanyahu's prime ministry, contacts with Syria had been maintained through the Omanis; through the European Union representative, Miguel Moratinos; and through a wealthy American named Ron Lauder. Netanyahu was

unwilling to agree to withdraw Israeli troops from all of the Golan, and therefore no agreement was reached. He did claim, however, that some progress was made in discussions of security, specifically that Israeli personnel would be allowed to stay on Mt. Hermon, under American auspices, to monitor the security arrangements. Interview with senior intelligence advisor to Netanyahu, June 28, 1999. See also Ze'ev Schiff, "Syria Agreed to Foreign Troops on Hermon," *Haaretz* (English), May 28, 1999.

19. According to John F. Harris, "Going for Broke, Coming Up Short," *Washington Post*, July 26, 2000, p. A22, Clinton once said, "He viewed striving for Middle East peace as part of his 'personal journey of atonement' for his misdeeds in the Monica S. Lewinsky scandal."

20. Mrs. Clinton in 1998 had expressed her support for a Palestinian state, but once she became a candidate for the Senate she spoke instead of her belief that Jerusalem was the eternal and undivided capital of Israel and that the United States should move its embassy there, typical positions of candidates in New York, even though her husband's policy was at variance with these views.

21. For the text of the Sharm al-Sheikh agreement, see www.brookings.edu/press/appendix/peace_process.htm.

22. The text of the draft peace treaty was leaked to the Israeli press, much to the chagrin of the Syrians. See *Haaretz* (English), June 13, 2000.

23. Aluf Benn and others, "Barak: Past PMs Set Syria Talks on '67 Lines," *Haaretz* (English), February 28, 2000.

24. According to most accounts of the talks, Clinton conveyed the following Israeli position: Barak would not return the northeast quadrant of shoreline on the Sea of Galilee, an area that Syria had controlled before the June 1967 war. As an apparent quid pro quo, Barak was reportedly ready to return the Hama triangle to Syria. The problem was that Rabin had already implied that both of these areas would be returned to Syria, and therefore Asad saw the Israeli position as a retreat from Rabin's more far-reaching offer. Whatever the precise details, Clinton clearly had misjudged Asad when he arranged the summit. Nothing in Asad's previous negotiating would have led anyone to expect that he would readily accept the Barak proposal, and certainly he would not see it as "good news." James Baker, who had considerable experience dealing with Asad, later criticized Clinton for presenting Barak's position to Asad directly. He believed that it would have been better to formulate an American proposal based on full Israeli withdrawal in exchange for full peace and security from Syria. See James A. Baker III, "Peace, One Step at a Time," *New York Times*, July 27, 2000, p. A27.

25. Barak, who had invested heavily in this track of diplomacy while ignoring the Palestinians, now signaled that he was ready to turn his attention to a last-ditch effort to get agreement with Arafat by September 13, 2000, the seventh anniversary of Oslo and a new self-imposed deadline. Interview with American participant in the talks with Asad, April 24, 2000.

26. Elaine Sciolino, "This Is the Moment in the Mideast. (But for What?)," *New York Times*, Week in Review, June 11, 2000, p. 6.

27. See Akram Haniyah, "Camp David Diary," *Al-Ayyam* (Arabic), translated in FBIS-*Near East/South Asia*, part one, July 29, 200, pp. 1, 11.

28. John F. Harris, "Going for Broke, Coming Up Short," *Washington Post*, July 26, 2000, p. A22.

29. The full text can be found at www.brookings.edu/press/appendix/peace_process.htm.

30. A good summary of what happened at Camp David is provided by Jane Perlez and Elaine Sciolino, "Against Backdrop of History, High Drama and Hard Talks at Camp David," *New York Times*, July 29, 2000, p. A5. Also, see Lee Hockstader, "'Unique Opportunity' Lost at Camp David," *Washington Post*, July 30, 2000, p. A1. For Clinton's praise of Barak, see Jane Perlez, "Clinton Ends Deadlocked Peace Talks," *New York Times*, July 26, 2000, pp. A1, 10. The most authoritative account from the Palestinian perspective can be found in Akram Haniyah, "Camp David Diary," *Al-Ayyam* (Arabic), translated in FBIS-*Near East/South Asia*, seven installments, July 29, 31; August 1, 3, 6, 8, 10, 2000.

31. Interview with American official who participated in the Camp David II talks, July 28, 2000.

32. John Kifner, "Clinton Hints That He Is Ready to Move Embassy to Jerusalem," *New York Times*, July 29, 2000, pp. A1, 5.

33. An authoritative version of the Clinton proposals can be found at www.brookings.edu/press/appendix/peace_process.htm. The Palestinian response can be found in "Remarks and Questions from the Palestinian Negotiating Team Regarding the United States Proposal," Negotiating Affairs Department, Palestine Liberation Organization, www.nad-plo.org/eye/new15.html. On January 7, 2001, Clinton outlined his proposals in a public speech to the Israel Policy Forum. See the text at www.brookings.edu/press/appendix/peace_process.htm.

34. David Maraniss, *First in His Class: The Biography of Bill Clinton* (Simon & Schuster, 1995), pp. 450–64.

35. After Barak's election, Henry Kissinger called for American mediation to exploit "an unprecedented opportunity for a breakthrough toward Middle East peace." See his "U.S. Mediation Essential," *Washington Post*, July 19, 1999, p. A19.

Chapter 13

1. Trude B. Feldman, "On the First Anniversary of the Peace Talks in Madrid Bill Clinton Pledges to Maintain the Momentum," *Middle East Insight*, vol. 9 (November-December, 1992), pp. 10–15.

2. Karen L. Puschel, *U.S.-Israeli Strategic Cooperation in the Post–Cold War Era: An American Perspective* (Boulder, Colo.: Westview, 1992), pp. 153–54, correctly concludes: "Peace is the watershed issue that will determine whether strategic cooperation is significantly expanded in terms of aid and commitments. Certainly, when there has been demonstrable progress on the peace front, U.S. aid has followed in its wake. . . . In the absence of peace, particularly should Israel be perceived as an obstacle, it is hard to envision a U.S. decision to significantly expand U.S.-Israeli strategic cooperation."

Selected Bibliography

Albin, Cecilia, and Harold H. Saunders. "Sinai II: The Politics of International Mediation." FPI Case Study 17. Johns Hopkins University, School of Advanced International Studies, Foreign Policy Institute, Washington, D.C., 1991.

Arian, Asher. *The Second Republic: Politics in Israel*. Chatham, N.J.: Chatham House Publishers, Inc., 1998.

Ashrawi, Hanan. *This Side of Peace: A Personal Account*. Simon and Schuster, 1995.

Bailey, Sydney Dawson. *Four Arab-Israeli Wars and the Peace Process*. St. Martin's, 1990.

Baker, James A., III (with Thomas M. DeFrank). *The Politics of Diplomacy: Revolution, War and Peace, 1989–1992*. G. P. Putnam's Sons, 1995.

Bard, Mitchell Geoffrey. *The Water's Edge and Beyond: Defining the Limits to Domestic Influence on United States Middle East Policy*. New Brunswick, N.J.: Transaction Publishers, 1991.

Bar-Siman-Tov, Yaacov. *The Israeli-Egyptian War of Attrition, 1969–1970: A Case Study of a Limited War*. Columbia University Press, 1980.

Bar-Zohar, Michael. *Embassies in Crisis: Diplomats and Demagogues behind the Six-Day War*. Prentice-Hall, 1970.

Beling, Willard A., ed. *The Middle East: Quest for an American Policy*. State University of New York Press, 1973.

Black, Ian, and Benny Morris. *Israel's Secret Wars: A History of Israel's Intelligence Services*. New York: Grove Weidenfeld, 1991.

Blitzer, Wolf. *Territory of Lies: The Exclusive Story of Jonathan Jay Pollard. The American Who Spied on His Country for Israel and How He Was Betrayed*. Harper and Row, 1989.

Brandon, Henry. *The Retreat of American Power: The Inside Story of How Nixon and Kissinger Changed American Foreign Policy for Years to Come*. Doubleday and Co., 1973.

Brecher, Michael. *Decisions in Crisis: Israel, 1967 and 1973.* University of California Press, 1980.

———. *Decisions in Israel's Foreign Policy.* Yale University Press, 1975.

Brzezinski, Zbigniew. *Power and Principle: Memoirs of the National Security Adviser, 1977–1981.* Farrar, Straus and Giroux, 1983.

Bush, George, and Brent Scowcroft. *A World Transformed.* Alfred A. Knopf, 1998.

Cannon, Lou. *President Reagan: The Role of a Lifetime.* Simon and Schuster, 1991.

Carter, Jimmy. *The Blood of Abraham.* Houghton Mifflin Co., 1985.

———. *Keeping Faith: Memoirs of a President.* Bantam Books, 1982.

Christopher, Warren. *In the Stream of History: Shaping Foreign Policy for a New Era.* Stanford University Press, 1998.

Cobban, Helena. *The Israeli-Syrian Peace Talks: 1991–1996 and Beyond.* Washington, D.C.: U.S. Institute of Peace, 1999.

———. "The P.L.O. and the Intifada." *Middle East Journal*, vol. 44 (Spring 1990), pp. 207–33.

———. *The Superpowers and the Syrian-Israeli Conflict: Beyond Crisis Management?* Praeger, 1991.

Cockburn, Andrew, and Leslie Cockburn. *Dangerous Liaison: The Inside Story of the U.S.-Israeli Covert Relationship.* HarperCollins Publishers, 1991.

Cohen, Avner. *Israel and the Bomb.* Columbia University Press, 1998.

Cooley, John K. *Payback: America's Long War in the Middle East.* New York: Brassey's, 1991.

Corbin, Jane. *The Norway Channel: The Secret Talks That Led to the Middle East Peace Accord.* New York: Atlantic Monthly Press, 1994.

Dayan, Moshe. *Breakthrough: A Personal Account of the Egypt-Israel Peace Negotiations.* Alfred A. Knopf, 1981.

———. *Moshe Dayan: Story of My Life.* New York: William Morrow and Co., 1976.

Dobrynin, Anatoly. *In Confidence: Moscow's Ambassador to America's Six Cold War Presidents (1962–1986).* Random House, 1995.

Dowty, Alan. *Middle East Crisis: U.S. Decision-Making in 1958, 1970, and 1973.* University of California Press, 1984.

Eban, Abba. *An Autobiography.* Random House, 1977.

———. *Personal Witness: Israel through My Eyes.* G. P. Putnam's Sons, 1993.

Eilts, Hermann Frederick. "Improve the Framework." *Foreign Policy*, no. 41 (Winter 1980–81), pp. 3–20.

Eisenberg, Laura Zittrain, and Neil Caplan. *Negotiating Arab-Israeli Peace: Patterns, Problems, Possibilities.* Indiana University Press, 1998.

Ennes, James M., Jr. *Assault on the Liberty: The True Story of the Israeli Attack on an American Intelligence Ship.* Random House, 1979.

Fahmy, Ismail. *Negotiating for Peace in the Middle East.* Johns Hopkins University Press, 1983.

Ford, Gerald R. *A Time to Heal: The Autobiography of Gerald R. Ford.* Harper and Row, 1979.

Friedman, Thomas L. *From Beirut to Jerusalem.* Farrar, Straus and Giroux, 1989.

Garfinkle, Adam. *Israel and Jordan in the Shadow of War: Functional Ties and Futile Diplomacy in a Small Place.* St. Martin's, 1992.

———. "U.S. Decision Making in the Jordan Crisis: Correcting the Record." *Political Science Quarterly*, vol. 100 (Spring 1985), pp. 117–38.

Garthoff, Raymond L. *Détente and Confrontation: American-Soviet Relations from Nixon to Reagan*. Brookings, 1985.

Gerson, Allan. *The Kirkpatrick Mission: Diplomacy without Apology. America at the United Nations, 1981–1985*. Free Press, 1991.

Golan, Matti. *The Secret Conversations of Henry Kissinger: Step-by-Step Diplomacy in the Middle East*. Quadrangle, 1976.

Goodman, Hirsch, and Ze'ev Schiff. "The Attack on the Liberty." *Atlantic Monthly*, September 1984, pp. 78–84.

Green, Stephen. *Living by the Sword: America and Israel in the Middle East, 1968–87*. Brattleboro, Vt.: Amana Books, 1988.

———. *Taking Sides: America's Secret Relations with a Militant Israel*. William Morrow, 1984.

Haass, Richard. *Conflicts Unending: The United States and Regional Disputes*. Yale University Press, 1990.

Haig, Alexander M., Jr. *Caveat: Realism, Reagan, and Foreign Policy*. Macmillan, 1984.

Haig, Alexander M., Jr., with Charles McCarry. *Inner Circles: How America Changed the World. A Memoir*. New York: Warner Books, 1992.

Heikal, Mohamed. *Autumn of Fury: The Assassination of Sadat*. Random House, 1983.

———. *The Cairo Documents: The Inside Story of Nasser and His Relationship with World Leaders, Rebels, and Statesmen*. Doubleday, 1973.

———. *1967: Al-Infijar*. Cairo: Markaz al-Ahram, 1990.

———. *The Road to Ramadan*. Quadrangle Books, 1975.

Hersh, Seymour M. *The Price of Power: Kissinger in the Nixon White House*. New York: Summit Books, 1983.

———. *The Samson Option: Israel's Nuclear Arsenal and American Foreign Policy*. Random House, 1991.

Indyk, Martin. *"To the Ends of the Earth": Sadat's Jerusalem Initiative*. Cambridge, Mass.: Harvard University, Center for Middle Eastern Studies, 1984.

Insight Team of the London Sunday Times. *The Yom Kippur War*. Doubleday, 1974.

Isaacson, Walter. *Kissinger: A Biography*. Simon and Schuster, 1992.

Johnson, Lyndon Baines. *The Vantage Point: Perspectives of the Presidency, 1963–1969*. Holt, Rinehart and Winston, 1971.

Kalb, Marvin, and Bernard Kalb. *Kissinger*. Little, Brown and Co., 1974.

Kalman, Laura. *Abe Fortas: A Biography*. Yale University Press, 1990.

Kemp, Geoffrey. "Lessons of Lebanon: A Guideline for Future U.S. Policy." *Middle East Insight*, vol. 6 (Summer 1988), pp. 57–68.

Kimche, David. *The Last Option: After Nasser, Arafat, and Saddam Hussein. The Quest for Peace in the Middle East*. Charles Scribner's Sons, 1991.

Kissinger, Henry. *White House Years*. Little, Brown and Co., 1979.

———. *Years of Renewal*. Simon and Schuster, 1999.

———. *Years of Upheaval*. Little, Brown and Co., 1982.

Korn, David A. *Stalemate: The War of Attrition and Great Power Diplomacy in the Middle East, 1967–1970*. Boulder, Colo.: Westview Press, 1992.

Lebow, Richard Ned, and Janice Gross Stein. *We All Lost the Cold War.* Princeton University Press, 1994.

Lewis, Samuel W. "The United States and Israel: Evolution of an Unwritten Alliance." *Middle East Journal,* vol. 53, no. 3 (Summer 1999).

Linowitz, Sol. "The Prospects for the Camp David Peace Process." *SAIS Review,* no. 2 (Summer 1981), pp. 93–100.

Luttwak, Edward N., and Walter Laqueur. "Kissinger and the Yom Kippur War." *Commentary,* vol. 58 (September 1974), pp. 33–40.

Makovsky, David. *Making Peace with the PLO: The Rabin Government's Road to the Oslo Accord.* Boulder, Colo.: Westview Press, in cooperation with Washington Institute for Near East Policy, 1996.

Maraniss, David. *First in His Class: The Biography of Bill Clinton.* Simon and Schuster, 1995.

Martin, David C., and John Walcott. *Best Laid Plans: The Inside Story of America's War against Terrorism.* Harper and Row, 1988.

Meir, Golda. *My Life: The Autobiography of Golda Meir.* London: Futura, 1976.

Melman, Yossi, and Dan Raviv. *Behind the Uprising: Israelis, Jordanians, and Palestinians.* New York: Greenwood Press, 1989.

Miller, Merle. *Lyndon: An Oral Biography.* G. P. Putnam's Sons, 1980.

———. *Plain Speaking: An Oral Biography of Harry S. Truman.* New York: Berkley Publishing, 1973.

Neff, Donald. *Warriors against Israel.* Brattleboro, Vt.: Amana Books, 1988.

———. *Warriors for Jerusalem: The Six Days That Changed the Middle East.* Linden Press/Simon and Schuster, 1984.

Nixon, Richard M. *RN: The Memoirs of Richard Nixon.* Grosset and Dunlap, 1978.

———. *Seize the Moment: America's Challenge in a One-Superpower World.* Simon and Schuster, 1992.

Novik, Nimrod. *Encounter with Reality: Reagan and the Middle East (The First Term).* Boulder, Colo.: Westview Press for the Jaffee Center for Strategic Studies, 1985.

O'Brien, Conor Cruise. *The Siege: The Saga of Israel and Zionism.* Simon and Schuster, 1986.

Parker, Richard B., ed. *The Six-Day War: A Retrospective.* University Press of Florida, 1996.

———. "The June 1967 War: Some Mysteries Explored." *Middle East Journal,* vol. 46 (Spring 1992), pp. 177–97.

———. "USAF in the Sinai in the 1967 War: Fact or Fiction?" *Journal of Palestine Studies,* vol. 27, no. 1 (Autumn 1997), pp. 67–75.

Perry, Mark. *A Fire in Zion: The Israeli-Palestinian Peace.* William Morrow, 1994.

Powell, Jody. *The Other Side of the Story.* New York: William Morrow, 1984.

Puschel, Karen L. *U.S.-Israeli Strategic Cooperation in the Post–Cold War Era: An American Perspective.* Boulder, Colo.: Westview Press, 1992.

Quandt, William B. *Camp David: Peacemaking and Politics.* Brookings, 1986.

———. *Decade of Decisions: American Policy toward the Arab-Israeli Conflict, 1967–1976.* University of California Press, 1977.

———. "Kissinger and the Arab-Israeli Disengagement Negotiations." *Journal of International Affairs,* vol. 29 (Spring 1975), pp. 33–48.

————. "Reagan's Lebanon Policy: Trial and Error." *Middle East Journal*, vol. 38 (Spring 1984), pp. 237–54.

————. "The Urge for Democracy." *Foreign Affairs*, vol. 73, no. 4 (July/August 1994), pp. 2–7.

Rabie, Mohamed. "The U.S.-PLO Dialogue: The Swedish Connection." *Journal of Palestine Studies*, vol. 21 (Summer 1992), pp. 54–66.

————. *U.S.-PLO Dialogue: Secret Diplomacy and Conflict Resolution*. University Press of Florida, 1995.

Rabin, Yitzhak. *The Rabin Memoirs*. Little, Brown and Co., 1979.

Rabinovich, Itamar. *The Brink of Peace: The Israeli-Syrian Negotiations*. Princeton University Press, 1998.

————. *Waging Peace: Israel and the Arabs at the End of the Century*. Farrar, Straus and Giroux, 1999.

Rafael, Gideon. *Destination Peace: Three Decades of Israeli Foreign Policy. A Personal Memoir*. New York: Stein and Day, 1981.

Reagan, Ronald. *An American Life*. Simon and Schuster, 1990.

Riad, Mahmoud. *The Struggle for Peace in the Middle East*. New York: Quartet Books, 1981.

Rostow, Eugene V. *Peace in the Balance: The Future of American Foreign Policy*. Simon and Schuster, 1972.

Rostow, Walt. *The Diffusion of Power: An Essay in Recent History*. Macmillan, 1972.

Rusk, Dean. *As I Saw It*. W. W. Norton, 1990.

Safran, Nadav. *Israel: The Embattled Ally*. Belknap Press of Harvard University Press, 1978.

Savir, Uri. *The Process: 1,100 Days That Changed the Middle East*. Random House, 1998.

Schiff, Ze'ev, and Ehud Ya'ari. *Intifada: The Palestinian Uprising. Israel's Third Front*. Simon and Schuster, 1989.

————. *Israel's Lebanon War*. Simon and Schuster, 1984.

Sheehan, Edward R. F. *The Arabs, Israelis, and Kissinger: A Secret History of American Diplomacy in the Middle East*. New York: Reader's Digest Press, 1976.

Shikaki, Khalil. "Peace Now or Hamas Later." *Foreign Affairs*, vol 77, no. 4 (July/August 1998), pp. 29–43.

Shlaim, Avi. *The Iron Wall: Israel and the Arab World*. W. W. Norton, 1999.

Shultz, George. *Turmoil and Triumph: My Years as Secretary of State*. Charles Scribner's Sons, 1993.

Sicherman, Harvey. *Palestinian Self-Government (Autonomy): Its Past and Its Future*. Washington, D.C.: Washington Institute for Near East Policy, 1991.

Sick, Gary. *All Fall Down: America's Tragic Encounter with Iran*. Random House, 1985.

Spiegel, Steven L. *The Other Arab-Israeli Conflict: Making America's Middle East Policy from Truman to Reagan*. University of Chicago Press, 1985.

Tanter, Raymond. *Who's at the Helm? Lessons of Lebanon*. Boulder, Colo.: Westview Press, 1990.

Telhami, Shibley. *Power and Leadership in International Bargaining: The Path to the Camp David Accords*. Columbia University Press, 1990.

Vance, Cyrus. *Hard Choices: Critical Years in America's Foreign Policy*. Simon and Schuster, 1983.

Wallach, Janet, and John Wallach. *Arafat: In the Eyes of the Beholder*. New York: Carol Publishing Group, 1990.

Washington Institute for Near East Policy. "Special Policy Forum Report: The Past, Present and Future of the Oslo Process: View from the Labor Party, Yossi Beilin, MK." *Peacewatch*, no. 112 (December 11, 1996).

Washington Institute's Presidential Study Group. *Building for Peace: An American Strategy for the Middle East*. Washington, D.C.: Washington Institute for Near East Policy, 1988.

Weizman, Ezer. *The Battle for Peace*. Bantam Books, 1981.

Whetten, Lawrence L. *The Canal War: Four-Power Conflict in the Middle East*. MIT Press, 1974.

Woodward, Bob. *The Commanders*. Simon and Schuster, 1991.

———. *Veil: The Secret Wars of the CIA, 1981–1987*. Simon and Schuster, 1987.

Yergin, Daniel. *The Prize: The Epic Quest for Oil, Money, and Power*. Simon and Schuster, 1991.

Index